Passio discerpta. 106

Monumenta aperta

Dum moreris, Mea Vita, ipsi vixere sepulti,
    Proq; vno victo turba soluta fuit.
Tu tamen haud tibi tu moreris, quae vivis in illis,
    Asserit & vitam Mors animata tuam.
Scilicet è tumulis, Crucifixum quaerite, Vivit:
    Convincunt vnae multa sepulcra Crucem.
Sic, pro Maiestate, Deum, non perdere vitam
    Quam tribuit, verum multiplicare decet.

Terra-motus

Te fixo vel Terra movet: nam, cum Cruce, totam
    Circumferre potest; Sampson ut antè, fores.
Heu stolidi, primum fugientem figite Terram,
    Tunc Dominus clavis aggrediendus erit.

Herbert's autograph of *Passio Discerpta*, xviii (Dr. Williams's Library, MS. Jones B 62)

THE WORKS OF GEORGE HERBERT

THE WORKS OF GEORGE HERBERT

Edited with a Commentary by

F. E. HUTCHINSON
sometime
Fellow of All Souls College

CLARENDON PRESS · OXFORD

Oxford University Press, Walton Street, Oxford OX2 6DP

OXFORD LONDON GLASGOW
NEW YORK TORONTO MELBOURNE WELLINGTON
IBADAN NAIROBI DAR ES SALAAM CAPE TOWN
KUALA LUMPUR SINGAPORE JAKARTA HONG KONG TOKYO
DELHI BOMBAY CALCUTTA MADRAS KARACHI

ISBN 0 19 811812 0

First published 1941
Reprinted from corrected sheets of the first edition
1945, 1953, 1959, 1964, 1967, 1970, 1972, 1978

Printed in Great Britain
by Thomson Litho Ltd,
East Kilbride, Scotland

PREFACE

THE main object of this edition is to establish the text of *The Temple* by providing a more complete and more accurate collection of the evidence than has been hitherto available. The principles which I have adopted, after much trial and error, for determining the relative authority of the two manuscripts and the first edition are set out in section vii of the Introduction. *The Temple* was fortunate in having Thomas Buck, a scholar and a lover of literature, for its first printer. The five editions for which he was responsible all testify to his continued vigilance. After his retirement the degeneration of the text set in. I have, however, recorded the variants of all the seventeenth-century editions, since, although they have no authority, many of the errors which they introduced have had a long life and have been able to mislead critics as acute as Coleridge. I have also recorded the variants due to Walton, because the popularity of his *Lives* has given them wide currency. Mrs. Bernard Hall has generously placed at my disposal the notes on the text made by her late husband, a lifelong and devoted student of Herbert's poems. Although his theory about the manuscripts, communicated to *The Times Literary Supplement* of 26 October 1933, was in my judgement disproved by Mr. John Sparrow in a letter to the same journal on 14 December, some of the emendations suggested by him deserve to be recorded.

The authenticity of the occasional writings is discussed in the Commentary. There is new evidence (see pp. 570–2) for ascribing to Herbert the nucleus at least of *Outlandish Proverbs*. Professor H. G. Wright published in 1935 a transcript of seventy-two proverbs made by Sir Henry Herbert in 1637, three years before the appearance in print of *Outlandish Proverbs*. By the kindness of the Hon. Lady Langman I have had access to a collection of more than 200 of the proverbs, contained in a Little Gidding Story-Book, which she inherited from her Ferrar ancestors.

For the Latin texts I have had the help of Mr. Bruce

Goldie and Mr. Lionel James. As these texts reach us from widely differing sources—autographs and manuscript copies, some books printed in Herbert's lifetime and others thirty years after his death—they present a distracting variety of spelling and accentuation. I have throughout adopted the standard of spellings and accents which Herbert himself used, with occasional inconsistencies and oversights, in the autographs of his Latin poems. Although many of the youthful poems have little merit, it may be hoped that Mr. Edmund Blunden's verse-translations in *Essays and Studies by members of the English Association*, vol. xix, will revive interest in Herbert's elegies on his mother and in the vigorous poem, 'Triumphus Mortis', which has its prose counterpart in the third Oration.

There are some additions to the *corpus* of Herbert's writings: an English poem to Bacon (p. 209); a long gossiping letter to Sir Robert Harley, included by the kindness of the Duke of Portland (p. 367); extracts from two letters to Nicholas Ferrar (pp. 577–8); a paper of advice for Arthur Woodnoth, included by the kind permission of Magdalene College, Cambridge, and of the Cambridge University Press and with the cordial assent of its discoverer, Dr. Bernard Blackstone (p. 380); and a Latin speech on the occasion of James I leaving Cambridge in 1622/3 (p. 443).

'No poet except Donne is in such need of a commentator as Herbert.' Ten years after Dean Beeching wrote these words in 1895, the late Professor George Herbert Palmer's edition of *The English Works of George Herbert* appeared and put every student of Herbert in his debt; but he leaves some of Herbert's many obscurities unexplained, and not all his explanations are acceptable. Even the plainness of Herbert's diction is sometimes deceptive, because words still in familiar use are used by him in senses which are now obsolete. I have had the advantage, denied to previous editors, of using the *Oxford English Dictionary*. Whoever read *The Temple* for the purposes of this dictionary must have read it with exemplary care. For the interpretation of specially difficult passages I have had much help from Mrs. H. S. Bennett, Mr. H. F. B. Brett-Smith, Miss K. M. Lea, and Mr. John

Sparrow. As might be expected, Bacon's and, still more, Donne's writings supply many striking parallels to Herbert's thoughts and expressions. He was also evidently familiar with Sidney's and Southwell's poems. He owes little to any other literary source except the Bible, from which he sought to 'suck ev'ry letter, and a hony gain'. The Authorized Version appeared when he was in his nineteenth year, and I have therefore in quoting from it retained the spelling of the text of 1611.

The late Mr. A. Edward Newton brought from America and placed in the Bodleian Library for my use his specially fine copy of the first edition of *The Temple*, and he completed his kindness by allowing photographs of two pages to be taken for illustration of this volume. For permission to make and use other photographs I have to thank the authorities of the Bodleian Library and of Dr. Williams's Library, Gordon Square, London.

In dealing with the proofs I have received valuable help and suggestions from my former tutor, the Rev. Dr. H. E. D. Blakiston (for the Introduction), and from Miss K. M. Lea and Mr. John Butt (for the Commentary). The long list of those who have helped me with their special knowledge is a happy illustration of the generosity of scholars. It is a pleasure to acknowledge my indebtedness to the Rev. M. F. Alderson (of Bemerton), Mr. Norman Ault, Miss K. I. Barratt, Dr. Bernard Blackstone, Mr. G. Brimley Bowes, the Rev. Dr. S. W. Carruthers, Dr. R. W. Chapman, Professor G. N. Clark, the late Rev. Dr. G. A. Cooke, Mr. H. R. Creswick, the Rev. M. C. D'Arcy, S.J., the Rev. R. Trevor Davies, Professor W. J. Entwistle, the Rev. A. M. Farrer, the Rev. Canon W. H. Ferguson (of Salisbury), Professor C. Foligno, Mr. A. D. Franklin, Mr. Strickland Gibson of the Bodleian Library, the late Dr. R. W. T. Gunther, Sir Arthur Hill, Mr. J. Isaacs, Mr. J. D. K. Lloyd (of Montgomery), the Rev. Dr. W. F. Lofthouse, Professor L. C. Martin, Mr. Francis Meynell (for the loan of photostats), Mr. Francis Needham, Professor D. Nichol Smith, Dr. C. T. Onions, Mr. G. S. H. Pearson (of Baynton), Professor E. Allison Peers, Mr. H. L. Pink of the Cambridge

University Library, the Earl of Powis, Mr. S. C. Roberts of the Cambridge University Press, Professor G. Rudler, Professor C. J. Sisson, the Rev. Dr. J. H. Srawley (of Lincoln), Mr. W. Force Stead, the Rev. Dr. Darwell Stone, Mr. Geoffrey Tillotson, the late Rev. W. H. Tozer (of Dauntsey), Dr. C. C. J. Webb, and Professor H. G. Wright.

I have also to thank the Registrary of the University of Cambridge for access to the Orator's Book, and the Librarians of Clare, Pembroke, St. John's, Magdalene and Trinity Colleges, Cambridge, the Bodleian Library, the Cambridge University Library, the University of St. Andrews Library, the British Museum, Dr. Williams's Library, Harvard College Library, the Henry E. Huntington Library and other libraries, both public and private, in this country and in the United States.

I am most grateful to the Delegates of the Clarendon Press for going forward with this book in spite of the War, and to the staff of the Press for their unremitting care and skill. Such technical excellence is appropriately bestowed on the work of a poet who had a peculiar delight in 'neatness' and form.

F. E. H.

19 January 1941

NOTE

I TAKE the opportunity of a reprint to add a fact of biographical importance. There seems good reason to identify the poet with the George Herbert who was elected M.P. for Montgomery in 1624 and again in Charles I's first parliament which met on 18 May 1625 and was dissolved on 12 August (W. R. Williams, *Parl. Hist. of Wales*, 1895, pp. 147–8). By 1626 the poet was in deacon's orders and in that year his brother Sir Henry was elected for Montgomery. I should also like to draw attention to Professor F. P. Wilson's 'A Note on George Herbert's "The Quidditie"' (*Review of English Studies*, Oct. 1943), and to Professor E. de Selincourt's 'George Herbert' (*Hibbert Journal*, July 1941). A few mistakes are now corrected.

1945 F. E. H.

CONTENTS

ILLUSTRATIONS

ABBREVIATIONS

USED IN FOOTNOTES AND COMMENTARY

B = MS. Tanner 307 in the Bodleian Library (see p. l).

W = MS. Jones B 62 in Dr. Williams's Library (see p. lii).

A.V. = *The Holy Bible: an exact reprint in roman type of the Authorized Version of 1611.* Oxford, 1911.

B.C.P. = *The Book of Common Prayer.* R. Barker, London, 1611.

B.M. = The British Museum.

Bodl. = The Bodleian Library, Oxford.

D.N.B. = *The Dictionary of National Biography.*

Gibson = *The Temple*, ed. E. C. S. Gibson. 2nd edn. 1905.

Grosart = *The Complete Works of George Herbert*, ed. A. B. Grosart. 3 vols. 1874.

Hall = 'The Text of George Herbert', by Bernard G. Hall, in *The Times Literary Supplement*, 26 Oct. 1933.

O.E.D. = *The Oxford English Dictionary.* 1933.

Onions = *A Shakespeare Glossary*, by C. T. Onions. 1911.

Palmer = *The English Works of George Herbert*, ed. G. H. Palmer. 3 vols. 3rd edn. 1915.

Pickering = *The Works of George Herbert.* Vol. i, Remains, 1836; vol. ii, Poems, 1835.

Walton = 'Life of Herbert' in *Lives*, 1670.

Willmott = *The Works of George Herbert*, ed. R. A. Willmott. 1854.

conj. = conjectural emendation.

corr. to = corrected in the MS. by the original copyist.

corr. by 2nd hand to = corrected in the MS. by a hand other than that of the original copyist.

om. = omitted.

The editions of *The Temple* from 1633 to 1809 are cited by the year of publication, the 2nd edition, issued in the same year as the 1st, being cited as *1633*[2], and the 'seventh Edition' without imprint as *undated 7th edn.* The edition of 1695, using the sheets of 1674 without alteration, is ignored. Such a description as *1638–* is used to imply that a reading first adopted in 1638 was retained in subsequent editions of the seventeenth century, and *1638–60* implies that a reading first adopted in 1638 kept its place in all editions up to and including that of 1660.

For works other than *The Temple* the MS. or printed book used as the basis of the text is named first in the footnotes, and all deviations from it are noted. Other MSS. and printed books containing the text are separately named in the appropriate footnotes.

INTRODUCTION

1. *Biography*

GEORGE HERBERT, the fifth son of Richard and Magdalen Herbert, was born on 3 April 1593. As Walton candidly admits that Herbert, in his earlier years at Cambridge, 'put too great a value on his parts and parentage', something must be said of his ancestry. The Herberts, a family of Norman descent, had by 1210 taken root in Wales and by the beginning of the fifteenth century, through intermarriage with leading Welsh families and by favour of the Crown, had become the most conspicuous Border family. George's eldest brother Edward describes their great-grandfather, Sir Richard, a nephew of the first Herbert to become earl of Pembroke, as 'steward, in the time of King Henry the Eighth, of the lordships and marches of North Wales, East Wales, and Cardiganshire'.[1] He states that Sir Richard and their grandfather Edward, who died a few weeks after George was born, 'lived in Montgomery Castle', an ancient Border fortress of which the Herberts were hereditary governors, but that 'my grandfather erected in his age' another house, Blackhall, 'a low building, but of great capacity',[2] which is believed to have been in the north-east part of the town. Oley and Walton state that George Herbert was born in the Castle, and certainly it continued to be habitable until its demolition by the Parliamentarians in 1649, and was intermittently the residence of George's brother Edward from the age of 18,[3] but the more commodious Elizabethan house may have been the birthplace of George; it is significant that a marginal note printed in Donne's sermon commemorating Herbert's mother describes her husband as 'Rich. Herbert *of* Blachehall *in* Montgomery, *Esqu.*'

The painted effigies of Herbert's parents are on the splendid Renaissance tomb in Montgomery Church.

[1] Lord Herbert of Cherbury, *Autobiography*, ed. Sidney Lee, 1906, p. 5.
[2] Ibid. p. 4.
[3] Ibid. p. 23.

Richard Herbert is described by his son Edward,[1] who was himself later known as 'the black Lord Herbert', as 'black-haired and bearded, as all my ancestors of his side are said to have been', handsome but of 'somewhat stern look', a terror to evil-doers, yet one to whom even his enemies could appeal successfully for justice; though a man of affairs, he had a good knowledge of Latin and history. But, as he was buried on 15 October 1596, when his son George was aged only three years and a half, the influence of home upon his younger children belongs almost wholly to his gifted wife.

Magdalen, daughter of Sir Richard Newport of High Ercall and Eyton, reputed to be the largest landowner in Shropshire, was left a widow with seven sons (including William, born posthumously) and three daughters, '*Iobs* number and *Iobs* distribution (as shee her selfe would very often remember)'.[2] Donne knew her well for over twenty years, and probably as early as 1604[3] addressed a verse-letter to her. On St. Mary Magdalen's Day 1607 he sent her his 'La Corona' sonnets, together with a sonnet addressed to herself and a covering letter.[4] Sir Herbert Grierson suggests[5] that it was perhaps shortly before her second marriage at about the age of 40 to Sir John Danvers in the early spring of 1608/9 that Donne daringly began 'The Autumnall' with the lines:

No *Spring*, nor *Summer* Beauty hath such grace,
As I have seen in one *Autumnall* face.

Besides such complimentary verse, there are two full-length descriptions of Magdalen Herbert's character and manner of life, in Donne's sermon at her 'month's mind' and in the long Latin poem which stands second in George Herbert's collection of elegies appended to the sermon. Even when allowance is made for the occasion and for heightened feeling, the two accounts corroborate one another closely and record authentic traits. Donne describes

[1] Lord Herbert of Cherbury, op. cit. pp. 2–3.

[2] J. Donne, *A Sermon of Commemoration of the Lady Dāuers* (1627), p. 139.

[3] *The Poems of John Donne*, ed. H. J. C. Grierson, ii. 132.

[4] Ibid. ii. 228–9.

[5] Ibid. ii. 62–3.

her high intelligence and 'sharpness of wit', as well as her devotion to the Scriptures and the services of the Church: 'the wit of our time is profaneness; *nevertheless*, she that loved that hated this'; 'her house was a court in the conversation of the best'. He mentions also her unremitting care of the household and her lavish charity, especially during 'the late heavy visitation' of the plague in 1625, when Donne himself found refuge in her house at Chelsea. George Herbert describes the orderliness of her life, in which everything had its place and its due attention—the family and household, the garden, her neighbours, her care for the needy and the sick, the offices of religion. He tells too of her love of music, her embroidery, her exquisite penmanship (for which he was himself distinguished), her pleasant and witty talk, her correspondence with men of letters. He calls her 'severa parens',[1] but he says that to her he owes his love of good letters,[2] and as well his second birth:[3]

Per te nascor in hunc globum,
Exemploque tuo nascor in alterum:
Bis tu mater eras mihi.

There is much evidence to support Donne's assertion that, on the death of her husband, Mrs. Herbert 'proposed to herself, as her principal care, the education of her children'. Edward had already matriculated at Oxford as a gentleman-commoner of University College in May 1596 and in February 1598/9 he married at Eyton a cousin, Mary Herbert. Magdalen Herbert, after living for a while with her widowed mother, Lady Newport, at Eyton, took a house at Oxford for herself and the younger children and the married pair.[4] The next move was to London, where Mrs. Herbert again 'took a house'. The young children had a tutor until George was 'about the age of twelve years' when or 'not long after' (Walton) he was sent to Westminster School. The school records give no date of his admission, but, if Walton is right about his age at the time, it would be in 1605. Many writers have been tempted to

[1] *Memoriae Matris Sacrum*, xiii. 2.
[2] Ibid. ii. 61–5.
[3] Ibid. iv. 13–15.
[4] Lord Herbert of Cherbury, op. cit. p. 23.

infer that this year began Herbert's acquaintance with Lancelot Andrewes, who, as dean of Westminster, took much interest in the more promising boys. Bishop John Hacket gratefully records that Andrewes 'was the first that planted me in my tender Studies'; but, as he was seven months older than Herbert, he may have entered the school earlier. In Walton's account, Mrs. Herbert committed her son to the care of Dr. Neile, who was installed as dean on 5 November 1605 (the day of the discovery of the Gunpowder Plot), Andrewes having vacated the deanery on becoming bishop of Chichester.

It is probable that for his first school year George Herbert continued to live at home, especially as Mrs. Herbert's house was 'near Charing Cross' when her son Edward visited her in 1605. After one year in the school he was eligible for nomination as a King's Scholar, which involved residence in the school. The reputation of Westminster at the universities for classical scholarship stood higher than that of other schools, and Herbert had the best opportunities of laying the foundation of his knowledge of Latin and Greek. He would also have practice in writing such Latin epigrams on sacred themes as he was afterwards to write at Cambridge, since it was in 1630 and probably earlier a regular employment of King's Scholars on Sunday afternoons to write 'verses upon the preacher's sermon or the epistle and gospell',[1] just as Crashaw had similar practice a few years later at Charterhouse. It may even be that Herbert began at school his answers to Andrew Melville's *Anti-Tami-Cami-Categoria*, which, according to Walton, was 'brought into *Westminster-School*, where Mr. *George Herbert* then, and often after, made such answers',[2] but this reference to Westminster is absent from Walton's first edition (1670). At the election of Westminster Scholars to Christ Church, Oxford, and Trinity College, Cambridge, in 1608, Henry King was among those elected to Christ Church, and Hacket and Herbert among those elected to Trinity. Richard Ireland, who had succeeded William

[1] *Lusus Alteri Westmonasterienses* (1863), p. 331.
[2] *Lives* (1675), p. 275.

Camden as headmaster in 1598, said, at parting, to Hacket and Herbert that

> he expected to have credit by *them two* at the *University*, or would never hope for it afterwards by any while he lived: and added withal, that he need give them no counsel to follow their Books, but rather to study moderately, and use exercise; their parts being so good, that if they were careful not to impair their health with too much study, they would not fail to arrive at the top of learning in any *Art* or *Science*.[1]

'Georgius Harbert' (a spelling often found, and probably corresponding to the contemporary pronunciation) was matriculated, first of the pensioners of Trinity College, on 18 December 1609. Another who entered Trinity from Westminster in that academic year was Charles Chauncy, the future second President of Harvard College. For the ensuing New Year's Day Herbert sent his mother two sonnets avowing his dedication to sacred poetry. From this early resolve he was never to retreat, although at times he drew back from the project of taking holy orders, which his discerning mother had early implanted in his mind. Apart from some complimentary verses to Bacon and other public personages, he wrote on religious themes only, whether in Latin or English, and Gosse has no warrant for asserting[2] that Herbert destroyed his 'amatory verse' when at last he entered the ministry. The sonnets have the inevitable faults of immaturity; he was not yet seventeen. They are clearly imitative of Sir Philip Sidney; but, both in theme and manner, they already suggest the later Herbert, especially in the effective close of the second sonnet. In the fragment, which alone remains of the accompanying letter, there is an allusion to 'my late Ague', the first of many references in his letters and poems to the ill health which dogged him throughout his short life, and of which his headmaster had warned him. His first appearance in print was shortly before taking the B.A. degree, when he contributed two Latin poems to the Cambridge volume of 1612 commemorating the death of Prince Henry, Herbert's exact

[1] J. Hacket, *A Century of Sermons* (1675): Life by T. Plume, p. v.
[2] *Life and Letters of Donne*, ii. 346.

contemporary. In the *Ordo Senioritatis* of 1612/13 his name stood second, but the high position was in those days often accorded as much for aristocratic connexion as for intellectual distinction.[1] He was elected a minor fellow of Trinity on 3 October 1614 and major fellow on 15 March 1615/16, and in 1616 proceeded to the master's degree. Among the fellows of Trinity with whom he was intimate were Herbert Thorndyke ('Thorndick nostrum'[2]), Robert Creighton, also of Westminster School, who succeeded Herbert as Orator, and Henry Fairfax, son of the first Lord Fairfax, who was 'familiarly acquainted' with him; 'their dispositions were much alike, and both were exemplary for learning and piety'.[3] Thomas Nevile, who built the New Court of Trinity, was Master till his death in 1615, and was followed for ten years by John Richardson.

For the first few years after taking his first degree Herbert was free, so far as his health allowed, to pursue his studies in classics and divinity, except for such small amount of teaching as was involved in his holding a minor college office, that of Sublector quartae classis, from 2 October 1617. He was free also to exercise his gift for Latin and English verse. We cannot safely assign any English verse to these Cambridge years, though it is likely enough that he began 'The Church-porch' and wrote early drafts of poems which eventually found a place in *The Temple*. There have survived no less than nine letters at dates from shortly before his 25th birthday till he was approaching the age of 27. Six of them are to his stepfather, Sir John Danvers, who seems always to have treated him generously, and one each to his favourite brother Henry, his first cousin Sir Robert Harley and a sick sister, Elizabeth, Lady Johnes. He writes to Sir John on 18 March 1617/18: 'I want Books extremely: You know, Sir, how I am now setting foot into Divinity, to lay the platform of my future life.'[4] He alludes to his having been 'sick last Vacation', and hardly yet recovered; his ill health adds to his expenses, as he must

[1] J. A. Venn, *Alumni Cantabrigienses*, I. vii.

[2] *Epistola* XVII.

[3] *The Fairfax Correspondence*, ed. G. W. Johnson (1848), i. 64.

[4] *Letter* III.

supplement the Lenten fare in the college hall and ride to Newmarket 'and there lie a day or two for fresh Air', rather than that he should incur greater expense by falling 'absolutely sick'. His brother Henry, who spent the year 1618 in Paris, sent him a parcel of books, 'which were not to be got in *England*', and, partly to pay for similar needs, George asks Sir John if his annuity may be doubled until he shall have 'enter'd into a Benefice'.[1] What Walton calls 'his gentile humour for Cloaths' must also have added to his expenses. His principal recreation was music; according to Aubrey, 'he had a very good hand on the lute, and sett his own lyricks or sacred poems'.[2]

On St. Barnabas' Day or its eve in 1618 Herbert was appointed to his first university office as Praelector or Reader in Rhetoric on the foundation of Sir Robert Rede. The 'Barnaby' lecturers (there were four of them—in mathematics, philosophy, rhetoric, and logic) were required to lecture four or five mornings a week. The lecturer in Rhetoric was to expound in English, for the special benefit of first-year students, such authors as Cicero or Quintilian. The only lectures at which Sir Symonds D'Ewes expressly mentions his attendance as an undergraduate were 'Mr. Downes his publike Greeke lectures & Mr. Harberts publike rhetoricke lectures in the Uniuersitie'.[3] Hacket comments severely on his schoolfellow's choice of a subject:

> Mr. *George Herbert* being Praelector in the Rhetorique School in *Cambridge anno* 1618 Pass'd by those fluent Orators, that Domineered in the Pulpits of *Athens* and *Rome*, and insisted to Read upon an Oration of King *James*, which he Analysed, shew'd the concinnity of the Parts, the propriety of the Phrase, the height and Power of it to move Affections, the Style utterly unknown to the Ancients, who could not conceive what Kingly Eloquence was, in respect of which, those noted Demagogi were but Hirelings, and Triobulary Rhetoricians.[4]

It was, indeed, a presage of what Herbert might do as Public Orator of the university, an office to which he was

[1] *Letter* V.
[2] J. Aubrey, *Brief Lives*, ed. A. Clark, i. 310.
[3] *Autobiography*, ed. J. O. Halliwell (1845), i. 121, anno 1618.
[4] *Scrinia Reserata* (1693), i. 175.

aspiring before his year's duty as Praelector was ended. He had already acted at least once for the Orator when he wrote a Latin letter of congratulation in the name of the university to Buckingham on his being created marquis on 1 January 1617/18. Writing to Sir John Danvers in September 1618, he announces that soon after Michaelmas he is 'to make an Oration to the whole University of an hour long in *Latin*';[1] and, as no doubt he was expecting, a Grace was passed by the Senate on 21 October giving the Orator, Sir Francis Nethersole, leave of absence on the king's business abroad and appointing 'Georgius Harbert Trinitatis' his deputy. Nethersole, like his predecessor Sir Robert Naunton, found the Oratorship, with its opportunities of approach to the king and other influential persons, a stepping-stone to a career as a secretary of state. There can be little doubt that Herbert also for a while cherished the same ambition. Already, in September 1618, he guessed, or perhaps knew for certain, that Nethersole intended soon to relinquish the office altogether, and he began at once to make interest for the succession. He does not, it is true, hint to Danvers that he may one day seek a secular career; he urges only that the Orator's is 'the finest place in the University', for he 'writes all the University Letters, makes all the Orations, be it to King, Prince, or whatever comes to the University', sits above the Proctors and enjoys 'such like Gaynesses, which will please a young man well'.[2] And when he hears Nethersole's comment that 'this place being civil may divert me too much from Divinity, at which, not without cause, he thinks, I aim', he makes the too facile reply that he sees 'no such earthiness' in this dignity 'but it may very well be joined with Heaven'.[3] It is true, also, that Herbert's successor as Orator, Dr. Robert Creighton, a sober divine, had no political ambitions and ended his exemplary life as bishop of Bath and Wells. Yet for the time being ambition had the better of Herbert and he used every influence to secure the post of vantage. It rested with the heads of colleges to nominate two persons between whom the Senate must make its choice. Herbert was eager to 'work

[1] *Letter* VII. [2] Ibid. [3] *Letter* VIII.

the heads' to his purpose, while his stepfather was securing the support of other Cambridge men of influence. On Friday 21 January 1619/20 he was duly elected in the Senate House, put on the Orator's habit, received the Orator's book and lamp, and took his place next to the Doctors.[1]

When, a little over seven years later, Herbert was about to relinquish the office, he gave admirable counsel to his successor on the art of writing and speaking in the name of the university and on subordinating his personal opinions,[2] and he may fairly be said to have carried out his precepts. He was well fitted, as he knew, to 'trade in courtesies and wit'; and, if some of the compliments which he paid to distinguished men were extravagant, it was the interest of the university to please them. It was not the Orator's business to select the men whom the university was to honour, but to honour those whom it selected. In the first year of his appointment Herbert showed himself very active, there being no less than thirteen letters written by him between May 1620 and the following February. As it happened, the first letter[3] which he wrote as Orator was to King James, thanking him for the gift of a copy of his *Opera Latina*;[4] other kings, he writes, have given books, but none before had given his own book. Appended to the letter is an epigram asserting that, if visitors to Cambridge look in vain for a library like the Vatican or the Bodleian, Cambridge can answer that the king's book is a library in itself; this was too insincere to take in even the vain king himself, but it would amuse him. Wholly sincere, as is clear from much other evidence, was Herbert's praise of James's pacific policy. In the year 1623 he delivered three orations, the first and third of which were printed at the time; the second is printed here for the first time.

After a letter dated 8 October 1621 there are no further entries in the Orator's Book until after Herbert had resigned in 1627/8. It is at least doubtful if he was much or at all in

[1] H. Gunning, *Ceremonies observed in the Senate House*, pp. 239–41.

[2] *Epistola* XVII.

[3] *Epistola* III.

[4] Not the *Basilikon Doron* only, as Walton and others have stated.

Cambridge after the summer of 1624. According to Walton, he was sitting loose to Cambridge and fastening his hopes on the Court and the public service. On 11 June 1624 he obtained a Grace giving him six months' leave of absence 'on account of many businesses away'; probably such leave was extended, as there is no record of his taking any further part in Cambridge business. In the university commemoration of James I's death in 1625 'Mr. Thorndike then Deputy Orator did make an Oration'; Herbert contributed no verses to the official collections on James's death and Charles's marriage. There is, however, something chivalrous in the prominent part taken by Herbert in the volume of Cambridge verses commemorating his old friend Bacon upon his death in 1626. The university was perhaps shy of paying honour to the disgraced statesman; the book was printed in London and without any contribution from the Vice-Chancellor or other dignitaries except the Orator and the Provost of King's, but it included verses from ten members of Trinity, seven of whom had been at Westminster School; it looks as if Herbert had helped to collect this team of writers, although Bacon's chaplain, Rawley, was the editor. Herbert's last appearance as Orator, so far as is now known, was at the installation of the duke of Buckingham as Chancellor of Cambridge at York House on 13 July 1626, when 'the orator'[1] made a Latin speech, which, however, is no longer extant. According to Walton, Herbert retained the Oratorship as long as he did at the wish of his mother, and certainly it was only a few months after her death in June 1627 that he resigned. By that time, as the following facts will show, he had dismissed his thoughts of a secular career.

It was Walton's view that 'all Mr. *Herbert's* Court-hopes' died with the death in rapid succession during the years 1624 and 1625 of his patrons, the duke of Richmond, the marquis of Hamilton, and King James; the lack of their support may well have served to check his plans and to make him reconsider his future, though it is difficult to

[1] Mede's account, printed in J. B. Mullinger, *The University of Cambridge*, iii. 672–3.

suppose that all such chances were gone for a man of suitable gifts and personality who still had influential friends and kinsmen. For a while after the king's death on 27 March 1625, he lived a retired life with an unidentified 'Friend in Kent', and upon his return to London announced 'his resolution to enter into *Sacred Orders*'.[1] In the latter months of that year Donne was sheltering from the plague in Sir John Danvers's house at Chelsea, and, in a letter to Sir Henry Goodyer dated 21 December 1625, he writes, 'Mr. *George Herbert* is here'.[2] We may assume that Donne, as well as Lady Danvers, confirmed Herbert in his resolution. The date and place of his ordination as deacon have not been discovered, but the Lincoln Chapter Acts describe him as deacon when he was instituted by proxy at Lincoln on 5 July 1626 into 'the canonry and prebend of Leighton Ecclesia founded in the said cathedral church'.[3] This appointment did not, indeed, commit him to parochial life. What Oley calls 'the corps of the Prebend', that is, the landed property which endowed it, was at Leighton Bromswold in Huntingdonshire, but the prebendary had no obligation of residence or cure of souls, as that parish had its own vicar.[4] The prebend was a sinecure except for the duty of preaching once a year in the cathedral church, and even this could be discharged by a paid deputy. A preaching list for 1629, in the hand of a later dean, Michael Honywood, has survived with the entry: 'Dom. Pentecost. Leighton Ecclesia. Georgius Herbert.'[5] John Williams, bishop of Lincoln, who appointed Herbert to the Lincoln prebend, had already eighteen months before procured him another small sinecure, a portion of the church of Llandinam, Montgomeryshire.[6] Herbert was a comportioner, that is, one of two holding the rectory of Llandinam, from 6

1 Walton, *Lives* (1670), 'Life of Herbert', p. 31.

2 Gosse, *Life and Letters of Donne*, ii. 227.

3 Lincoln Chapter Acts, A. iii. 9. The document of institution is printed in J. J. Daniell, *Life of George Herbert* (1902), p. 103.

4 *The Ferrar Papers*, ed. B. Blackstone (1938), p. 58.

5 Lincoln Cathedral Muniments, D. vi. 28.

6 A. I. Pryce, *The Diocese of Bangor in the Sixteenth Century* (1923), pp. 41, 86, and letter of H. Ince Anderton to *The Times Literary Supplement* of 9 March 1933.

December 1624 until his death. He may in 1625 or 1626 have been ordained on this title, as his immediate predecessor was,[1] although the sinecure had sometimes been held by a layman. Walton states that James I gave Herbert a sinecure 'which fell into His Majesties disposal, I think, by the death of the Bishop of St. *Asaph*. It was the same, that Queen *Elizabeth* had formerly given to her Favourite Sir *Philip Sidney*.'[2] Grosart[3] identified this with the sinecure rectory of Whitford, Flintshire, which Sidney held for a few months, but there seems to be no room for Herbert in the list of its rectors. Archdeacon D. R. Thomas in the first edition (1874) of his *History of the Diocese of St. Asaph* gave a complete list of rectors without Herbert; but in his second edition (1908–13) he inserted Herbert's name against the year 1629, though apparently without any warrant except Grosart's inference from Walton's hesitating statement ('I think'), which did not mention Whitford.[4]

Though Herbert's ordination in or before 1626 did not commit him to parochial life, it debarred him from civil employment. He had counted the cost; Barnabas Oley said that he had 'heard sober men censure him as a man that did not manage his brave parts to his best advantage and preferment, but lost himself *in an humble way*; That was the phrase, I well remember it'.[5] If Herbert hung back from the further step, it was now less from ambition than from a sense of unworthiness, as he reveals in 'Aaron' and 'The Priesthood', and also from his continued ill health. One reason for his leaving the fenny district of Cambridge, according to Walton, was that 'he had a body apt to a *Consumption*, and to *Fevers*, and other infirmities which he

[1] A. I. Pryce, op. cit. p. 72.

[2] *Lives*, p. 28.

[3] *Works of Herbert* (1874), i, p. li.

[4] Grosart is wrong in stating that Herbert succeeded Bishop Parry of St. Asaph at his death on 26 Sept. 1623; Parry was never rector of Whitford, and the rectory was not vacant till 1624, when Dr. Robert King was appointed. Thomas could apparently find room for Herbert only by supposing that King resigned just before the see next became vacant by the death of Bishop Hanmer on 23 June 1629, and that *sede vacante* Charles I then appointed Herbert: Hanmer's successor in the see, John Owen, on 15 Sept. 1629, five days before his consecration, obtained a grant from the Crown to hold Whitford and other benefices *in commendam*.

[5] *Herbert's Remains*, sig. a 11v.

judg'd were increas'd by his Studies'; 'About the year 1629 and the 34th of his Age, Mr. *Herbert* was seized with a sharp *Quotidian Ague*, and thought to remove it by the change of Air.'[1] He entered his 34th year in April 1626, and we may accept Mr. Leishman's suggestion that the fourth figure of '1629' is an inverted 6. He went, therefore, in 1626 to live with his brother Sir Henry at Woodford, Essex, for about a twelvemonth, and there 'cur'd himself of his Ague' by a strict diet, which, however, induced 'a disposition to Rheums, and other weaknesses, and a supposed Consumption'.[2] His movements in the next two years are difficult to trace. From the seventh poem in memory of his mother, written in the summer of 1627, he appears to be living in a country cottage (*domuncula*) with a luxuriant flower-garden. He has chosen a humble lot (*parvam piamque semitam*),[3] but still finds difficulty in reconciling himself to it. He is also conscious of living an ineffective life, as he confesses sadly in the two poems called 'Employment'. To this period, no doubt, belong many of the poems in the Williams MS. which reflect his indecision and discontent. We next find him living with his stepfather's elder brother, Henry Danvers, earl of Danby, at Dauntsey, near Chippenham in Wiltshire; Walton places this before his marriage, but John Aubrey says: 'When he was maried he lived a yeare or better at Dantesey house.'[4] He had sufficiently recovered health to contemplate marriage and admission to the priesthood, as his mother had always desired. We need not take too seriously Walton's story of Danby's cousin, Jane Danvers, that from mere hearsay she 'became so much of a Platonick, as to fall in love with Mr. *Herbert* unseen', but, at any rate, after a very brief courtship, they were married on 5 March 1628/9 in the noble parish church of Edington,[5] built by William

[1] *Lives*, pp. 28, 35.
[2] Ibid. pp. 35–6.
[3] *Memoriae Matris Sacrum*, viii. 1.
[4] Aubrey, op. cit. i. 310.
[5] The Edington register is lost, but the transcript of it in Salisbury Diocesan Registry includes among 'all Weddings . . . from the 25the of March 1628 unto the 25the of March 1629, at Edington in Wilts' this entry, following entries for Oct. and Nov. 1628: 'Mr. George Herbert and Miss Jane Danvers were maryed by a licence procured from Sarum the 5the of March 1628.'

of Edington, the immediate predecessor of William of Wykeham in the see of Winchester. Aubrey, a Wiltshire man, who had a Danvers for grandmother, remarks: 'My kinswoman was a handsome *bona roba* and ingeniose.'[1] Jane's father, Charles Danvers, had died in 1626, but his widow and family continued to live at Baynton House in the parish of Edington; and here Arthur Woodnoth found George Herbert and his wife when he visited them a year after their marriage. The offer of Bemerton had just come, and Walton tells of Herbert and Woodnoth going to Wilton House, where or at Salisbury the combined persuasions of King Charles, the earl of Pembroke, and Bishop Laud overcame Herbert's hesitation. Some of the facts which are ascertainable do not bear out Walton's account. The rectory had become vacant by the resignation of the non-resident Dr. Walter Curll on his translation from the see of Rochester to that of Bath and Wells. Although Bemerton was in the gift of the earl of Pembroke, it fell for this turn to the Crown, because the king had promoted the outgoing rector. It would, however, be customary for the Crown to consider the patron's wish; and we may accept Walton's statement that Pembroke 'requested the King to bestow it upon his Kinsman *George Herbert*'. It is unlikely that the Court was at Wilton or Salisbury, as Walton alleges. William, the third earl, died suddenly at his London house on 10 April 1630; the Court had not gone to Wiltshire in April for his burial, as has sometimes been suggested, since William was not buried in the family vault in Salisbury Cathedral until 7 May. Moreover, there was good cause for friction between Laud and Philip, earl of Montgomery, lord chamberlain, who now succeeded his brother as fourth earl of Pembroke. On 12 April Laud had been elected Chancellor of Oxford by a majority of only nine votes over Pembroke; 'too hard for my lord chamberlain', as Joseph Mede wrote on 17 April to his cousin, Sir Martin Stutevile.[2] The deed of presentation of the rectory to Herbert is

[1] Aubrey, op. cit. i. 310, and editor's comment on Aubrey's hostility to the Herberts, preface v–vi.

[2] T. Birch, *Court and Times of Charles I*, ii. 74.

dated from Westminster, 16 April 1630.[1] He was instituted at Salisbury on 26 April by Bishop Davenant, who had been resident at Cambridge during most of the years that Herbert spent there, and he was inducted the same day at Bemerton Church, a little more than a mile from Salisbury, into the rectory of Fulston or Fuggleston St. Peter with Bemerton St. Andrew. He describes himself as deacon in both of the two extant documents which he signed that day in Salisbury. On Sunday 19 September he was ordained priest by Davenant, and among the priests who joined in the laying on of hands was Humphrey Henchman, prebendary of Salisbury and later bishop of London. Walton had this latter fact from the bishop of London himself, who 'tells me, *He laid his hand on Mr.* Herberts *Head, and (alas!) within less than three Years, lent his Shoulder to carry his dear Friend to his Grave*'.[2]

There can have been few external attractions to bring Herbert to Bemerton. The two churches, though old, are small and undistinguished: the parish church of Fulston is just outside the entrance to Wilton Park, and Bemerton, 'a pitifull little chappell of ease', as Aubrey calls it, is across the road from the rectory. Both churches needed considerable repair and the greater part of the rectory had to be rebuilt. Herbert describes himself, in a letter to his brother Henry, as 'being more beggarly now than I have been these many years, as having spent two hundred pounds in building; which to me that have nothing yett, is very much'.[3] He maintained a curate, Nathaniel Bostock, and when his sickness increased, a second curate of the name of Hays; both of them are remembered in his will. He had no children, but, in spite of his having far less means than his surviving brothers, Edward and Henry, he made a home for two orphaned daughters of his sister Margaret Vaughan, and when there was a difficulty about providing for the third daughter, she too was brought to Bemerton. Nothing can exceed the delicacy and good sense with which he

[1] Rymer, *Foedera*, xix. 258.

[2] *Lives*, p. 48.

[3] *Letter* XII. The value of the living is given in the *Valor Ecclesiasticus* of 1536 as £24, but it would have considerably appreciated by 1630.

discusses with Henry the provision to be made for their nieces.[1] Aubrey states that Herbert was also chaplain to Lord Pembroke. His relations with that ill-conditioned nobleman cannot have been easy, but it was otherwise with the remarkable woman whom Pembroke took for his second wife six weeks after Herbert's institution, the Lady Anne Clifford, widow of the third earl of Dorset. She was ill treated by Pembroke and found her chief solace in books, until, on succeeding to the great estates of the earls of Cumberland, she had the opportunity of revealing her qualities as a builder and administrator. The good understanding between the countess and her chaplain is shown in the graceful letter which he sent to her at Court with 'a Priests blessing, though it be none of the Court-stile'.[2]

Herbert's complete devotion to his calling, once he had accepted it, and his fitness for it, are evident, not only from the stories which Walton collected from his own acquaintance round Salisbury, but from earlier and more trustworthy testimony. 'Holy Mr. Herbert' is no invention of Izaak Walton, writing thirty-seven years after his death and without first-hand knowledge ('I have only seen him'), but it is a contemporary estimate. Lord Herbert of Cherbury says of his brother: 'His life was most holy and exemplary; insomuch, that about Salisbury, where he lived, beneficed for many years, he was little less than sainted.'[3] Nicholas Ferrar, within a few months of Herbert's death, described his character and manner of life in the preface which he wrote for *The Temple*. Contemporary letters of Arthur Woodnoth exhibit the same veneration for Herbert's saintliness. The letters which Herbert wrote from Bemerton show how far he had travelled since his Cambridge days; they manifest an achieved character of humility, tenderness, moral sensitiveness, and personal consecration, which he was very far from having attained or even envisaged when he was dazzled by the attractions of the great world. Above all, *The Temple*, in which he laid bare the long story of his inner life with all its faults and its ardours, and *A Priest to the*

[1] *Letter* XII. [2] *Letter* XIII. See further, on Lady Anne Clifford, p. 583.
[3] *Autobiography*, p. 11.

Temple, which he wrote at Bemerton that he might have 'a Mark to aim at', reveal the man, both as he had been and as he had become. In the lyrics he is not directly addressing the reader, but either God or himself. They are colloquies of the soul with God or self-communings which seek to bring harmony into that complex personality of his which he analyses so unsparingly. These intimate poems exactly correspond to the description which he gave of them in his last message to Ferrar, that he would find there 'a picture of the many spiritual Conflicts that have past betwixt God and my Soul, before I could subject mine to the will of Jesus my Master, in whose service I have now found perfect freedom'. The inward conflict which had lent such poignancy to the poems written in the period of indecision and inaction was quieted when Herbert went to Bemerton, and there are only occasional echoes of it. Many of the later poems breathe a spirit of content, like 'The Odour', or even of exaltation, like the first 'Antiphon', the second 'Praise', and 'The Call'. 'The Flower' is a happy example of his power of recovery from depression, though it, too, reveals the intensity of the struggle he has endured:

O my onely light,
It cannot be
That I am he
On whom thy tempests fell all night.

If the note of conflict is still heard in the Bemerton poems, it is for reasons that differ from his earlier struggle with ambition. He does not now question the rightness of his decision but its utility, since his health failed so rapidly. In 'The Crosse' he exclaims:

And then when after much delay,
Much wrastling, many a combate, this deare end,
So much desir'd, is giv'n, to take away
My power to serve thee.

There are also poems of even sadder and more poignant tone, like 'Home' and 'Longing', when the sense of frustration and fruitless suffering would overpower him, were it not for his ardent loyalty to the Divine will. Even in 'The Collar', which comes nearest to rebellion, the passionate lines, with their gathering pace and momentum, are arrested at their height by a sudden and complete submission. Palmer has wisely observed that in poetry Herbert 'probably found one of his few defences against pain': to make music of his suffering and disappointment was to gain relief and to fortify his faith.

No one could have written of the pastoral life as Herbert did in *A Priest to the Temple* without having experienced much of its happiness. In this little book he unconsciously portrays himself and reveals his good sense and large charity. In what he has to say about the conduct of the church services we may recognize Herbert's own practice: 'The Countrey Parson being to administer the Sacraments, is at a stand with himself, how or what behaviour to assume for so holy things'; and 'The Countrey Parson preacheth constantly, the pulpit is his joy and his throne.' Twice every day, Ferrar relates, Herbert said the offices in his humble little church and never failed to have others to keep him company. Outside the church this once proud man, distant with his social inferiors, became accessible to the humblest, made up differences between his parishioners, encouraged them in the habit of reading, and befriended the needy. He summarizes his ideal of the Country Parson: 'Now love is his business and aime.' This ministry of three brief years was rightly presented by Oley to the clergy of the Restoration as the model for the English parish priest.

The Bemerton years were also a time of much literary activity; besides revising many of the earlier poems and writing perhaps the larger half of *The Temple* and the whole of *A Priest to the Temple*, he translated Cornaro's treatise on Temperance and annotated Valdesso's *Considerations*. According to Walton, there were other writings which his widow 'intended to make publick', but they were destroyed at the burning of her second husband's house at Highnam, near Gloucester, in the Civil War.[1]

Herbert's life did not end in sadness and disillusion, as Palmer's grouping of the sadder poems at the end in his

[1] Cf. Aubrey's allusion, quoted below, p. 586, to a folio which Herbert wrote in Latin.

edition might suggest. The testimony about his serenity is singularly trustworthy. Ferrar had the account from his cousin Woodnoth, who was with Herbert throughout the last weeks of his illness, and from Edmund Duncon, who visited the dying man twice at the instance of his friends at Little Gidding. In describing one of the last scenes, Walton expressly names his authority—'*This Mr.* Duncon *tells me*', and he reports Duncon as assuring him about Herbert's discourse and demeanour 'that after almost forty years, they remain still fresh in his memory'.[1]

The exact day of Herbert's death can now at last be put beyond a doubt. From a memorandum of Nicholas Ferrar, quoted by his brother, we could already infer that Herbert died on a Friday, and from the Bemerton register it was known that he was buried on 3 March 1632 (i.e. 1632/3), which was a Sunday. A letter from Woodnoth to Ferrar,[2] written within a few days of Herbert's death and printed for the first time in 1938, shows that this Friday was the one preceding the day of burial, namely, 1 March. It was on Quinquagesima Sunday, a day singularly appropriate for one whose feeling quickens at every mention in his poems of the Divine love, that Herbert was buried. Aubrey, whose uncle Thomas Danvers was at the funeral, reports that he 'was buryed (according to his owne desire) with the singing service for the buriall of the dead, by the singing men of Sarum. . . . He lyes in the chancell, under no large, nor yet very good, marble grave-stone, without any inscription'.[3]

II. *Contemporary and Later Reputation*

No writings of George Herbert were printed in his lifetime except 'Memoriae Matris Sacrum', occasional Latin verses, and two Latin orations. His English poems must, however, have been circulated in manuscript, as he enjoyed some reputation as a poet many years before his death. There was public recognition of this fact in Bacon's dedication of

[1] *Lives*, p. 67.

[2] *The Ferrar Papers*, p. 276; and see p. 79 for N. Ferrar's memorandum.

[3] *Brief Lives*, i. 309–10.

his *Translation of Certaine Psalmes into English Verse* (1625) to 'his very good frend, Mr. George Herbert':

The paines, that it pleased you to take, about some of my Writings, I cannot forget: which did put mee in minde, to dedicate to you, this poore Exercise of my sicknesse. Besides, it being my manner for Dedications, to choose those that I hold most fit for the Argument, I thought, that in respect of Diuinitie, and Poesie, met (whereof the one is the Matter, the other the Stile of this little Writing) I could not make better choice. So, with signification of my Loue and Acknowledgment, I euer rest

Your affectionate Frend,
FR: St. ALBAN.[1]

Lord Herbert of Cherbury in his *Autobiography* testifies not only to his brother's excellent scholarship 'in the Greek and Latin tongue, and all divine and human literature', but also mentions his 'English works'; although he does not expressly mention English poems, it is probable that they are intended in this reference, as, at the time of Lord Herbert's death in 1648, *A Priest to the Temple* was not yet published, and no English work of George Herbert was in print except *The Temple*, if the translation of Cornaro's little tract and the notes to Valdesso's *Considerations* be disregarded. Edward's esteem for his brother may also be inferred from the fact that a draft of his *De Veritate*[2] in the British Museum (MS. Sloane A 3957) has, in the author's hand, a dedication, dated 15 December 1622, to his brother George and his friend William Boswell, on the understanding that they expunge anything they find therein that is contrary to good morals or to the true Catholic faith. George Herbert was at the time approaching the age of 30, and was his brother's junior by about ten years. There can be little question that Donne, the friend and admirer of Magdalen Herbert, encouraged her son to cultivate his

[1] The reference in the first line of Bacon's dedication is to Herbert's share in translating *The Advancement of Learning* into Latin for incorporation in *De Augmentis Scientiae* (1623), which itself 'may serve in lieu of the *First Part of the Instauration*' (letter of Bacon to Andrewes). Tenison, in his introduction to *Baconiana* (1679), says that Bacon caused what he had written in English 'to be translated into the *Latine* Tongue by Mr. *Herbert*, and some others, who were esteemed Masters in the *Roman* Eloquence'.

[2] First printed in Paris in 1624.

poetic talent. A Latin poem accompanied the seal which he gave shortly before his death to George Herbert.

After the publication of *The Temple* and its immediate success, with four editions in three years, recognition became more general, not least among poets. Richard Crashaw modestly gave to his first volume of English sacred verse the title *Steps to the Temple* (1646) and included in it a further tribute to Herbert in his poem 'On Mr. G. Herberts booke sent to a Gentlewoman', beginning:

Know you faire, on what you looke;
Divinest love lyes in this booke:
Expecting fire from your eyes,
To kindle this his sacrifice.

The anonymous writer of the preface introduces the book: 'Here 's *Herbert's* second, but equall', just as Winstanley styles Crashaw 'the second *Herbert* of our late Times',[1] and David Lloyd calls him 'the other *Herbert* of our Church',[2] while he says of Herbert that 'all are ravished with his Poems'. But, though Crashaw doubtless shared with his friends at Little Gidding, where he was a constant visitor in his Cambridge years, their admiration for Herbert as man and poet, his own poems seldom recall the manner of the older poet; there is only an occasional borrowing or reminiscence of him, as, for example, when he calls prayer 'loves great Artillery'. It is otherwise with Henry Vaughan, whose debt to Herbert was generously acknowledged many times. Already in *The Mount of Olives* (1652) Vaughan called Herbert 'a most glorious true Saint, and a Seer', mentioning especially 'his incomparable prophetick Poems, and particularly these, *Church-musick*, *Church-rents and schisms*, *The Church militant*', and quoting *Life* in full. In the preface to the enlarged edition of *Silex Scintillans* (1655) he attributes his conversion to sacred poetry to 'the blessed man, Mr. *George Herbert*, whose holy *life* and *verse* gained many pious *Converts*, (of whom I am the least)'. He follows only too closely Herbert's subjects and titles, and incorporates into his verse a number, past reckoning, of quotations, conscious and unconscious, from the *Temple*

[1] *England's Worthies* (1660), p. 294.

[2] *Memoires* (1668), p. 619.

poems. Mr. Lewis Bettany, Professor L. C. Martin, and others have recorded scores of these borrowings, but no list yet compiled is anywhere near complete; a reader who knows well both *The Temple* and *Silex Scintillans* never comes to the end of the verbal parallels. There is no example in English literature of one poet adopting another poet's words so extensively. This is not to say that Vaughan does not often add lustre to the words he borrows or give them a new and happy turn, but even when he is most himself, and in his greatest poems like 'They are all gone into the world of light' and 'The World' there are still echoes of Herbert.

Joseph Beaumont paid a glowing and graceful tribute to his college friend, Crashaw, in *Psyche* (1648), but the stanza on Herbert did not appear till the second and posthumous edition of 1702: after the praise of Pindar and Horace as lyric poets, which had appeared in the first edition, he adds:

> Yet neither of their Empires was so vast
> But they left *Herbert* too full room to reign,
> Who Lyric's pure and precious Metal cast
> In holier moulds, and nobly durst maintain
> *Devotion in Verse*, whilst by the spheres
> He tunes his Lute, and plays to heav'nly ears.[1]

There are echoes of Herbert in the lesser poetry of the time, for example, in 'The Petition' in Thomas Beedome's *Poems Divine and Humane* (1641) and in most of the poems of Ralph Knevet (1600–71), who gives to a group of them the heading 'A Gallery to the Temple'.[2] Christopher Harvey published anonymously in 1640 *The Synagogue, or, The Shadow of the Temple . . . In imitation of M*r. *George Herbert.* The second (1647) and later editions of *The Synagogue* were commonly bound up with *The Temple* until the nineteenth century, a destiny to which its intrinsic merit did not entitle it. There are tributes to Herbert in the poems of Clement Barksdale (*Nympha Libethris*, 1651), James Duport (*Musae Subsecivae*, 1676), and Thomas Flatman, who wrote of 'noble *Herbert*'s Flame'. Charles Cotton contributed to the 1675 edition of Walton's *Lives*

[1] *Psyche*, iv, stanza 102.

[2] L. Birkett Marshall, *Rare Poems of the Seventeenth Century* (1936), p. 126.

a poem 'To my Old, and most Worthy Friend, Mr. Izaak Walton', which includes these verses:

> And *Herbert*: he, whose education,
> Manners, and parts, by high applauses blown,
> Was deeply tainted with Ambition:
>
> And fitted for a Court, made that his aim:
> At last, without regard to Birth or Name,
> For a poor Country-Cure, does all disclaim.
>
> Where, with a soul compos'd of Harmonies,
> Like a sweet *Swan*, he warbles, as he dies
> His makers praise, and his own obsequies.

Some of the best musicians of the day set Herbert's poems to music; *Harmonia Sacra* (1688) included Purcell's setting of 'Longing' and Dr. John Blow's setting of 'And art thou grieved?'[1]

There is abundant evidence of *The Temple* being read throughout the seventeenth century by men of widely different churchmanship and political attachments. Sir Thomas Herbert, in his *Memoirs of the Two last Years of the Reign of Charles I*, says that 'Herbert's divine Poems' was among the few books in which the king 'read often' during his captivity. Lady Anne Clifford, countess of Pembroke, once Herbert's neighbour at Wilton, was a lifelong admirer of his poetry.[2] In *The Standard of Eqvalitie* (1647) by Philo-Dicaeus the dedication to Sir John Danvers refers to 'the Poems of Mr. *George Herbert*, lately deceased (whose pious Life and Death have converted me to a full beliefe that there is a *St. George*)'. The anonymous author of *The Mirrour of Complements* added to the fourth edition (1650) a supplement of twelve 'Divine Poems', all but two of which are from *The Temple*. Still more significant is the marked devotion of leading Puritans to Herbert's poetry. Richard Baxter gave at the end of *The Saint's Everlasting Rest* (1650) Herbert's long poem 'Home' in full: and in the preface to his *Poetical Fragments* (1681), after naming Cowley, who 'for strength of Wit bears the Bell', Quarles, Sylvester,

[1] See below, p. 554, for John Playford's regard for Herbert's poetry.
[2] See below, p. 583.

Fulke Grevile, Davies, and other poets of the century, concludes:

But I must confess, after all that next the Scripture Poems, there are none so savoury to me, as Mr. *George Herbert*'s and Mr. *George Sandys*'s. I know that *Cooly* and others far excel *Herbert* in Wit and accurate composure. But (as *Seneca* takes with me above all his Contemporaries, because he speaketh *Things* by *words*, *feelingly* and *seriously*, like a man that is past jest, so) *Herbert* speaks *to God* like one that *really believeth a God*, and whose business in the world is most *with God*. *Heart-work* and *Heaven-work* make up his Book.

Similar reasons may have weighed with other Puritans. Thomas Hall (1610–65), an unbending Presbyterian, included *The Temple* with only four other poetical works in his extensive library. *The Temple* was a favourite book of Archbishop Robert Leighton (1611–84), who often quoted from it, and it seems to have been the only book of poetry owned by his saintly pupil, Henry Scougal (1650–78), author of one of the earliest Scottish religious classics. Peter Sterry, Cromwell's chaplain, in an undated letter[1] to his son at Eton, counsels him 'to reade the Scriptures, Mr. Bolton & Mr. Herbert'; his own mystical and poetic prose has phrases reminiscent of Herbert. John Bryan's *Dwelling with God. Opened in Eight Sermons* (1670), one of the few books owned by Bunyan, quotes three poems of 'the Divine Poet' in full and selections from seven others. The Nonconformist divines, Philip Henry (1631–96) and his son Matthew (1662–1714), the expositor of Scripture, both spoke of Herbert 'with reverence and affection' and often quoted his words.[2]

Until well past the turn of the century Herbert's poems were still widely popular and often quoted, sometimes, no doubt, as much for their piety as for their poetry. Winstanley in 1687 speaks of the 'so generally known and approved Poems' of Herbert,

Whose Vocal notes tun'd to a heavenly Lyre,
Both learned and unlearned all admire.[3]

[1] Communicated to me by Professor V. de S. Pinto.

[2] *Diaries of Philip Henry*, ed. M. H. Lee (1882), vi. 209, 345.

[3] *The Lives of the most famous English Poets*, p. 161.

As late as 1720 Giles Jacob in his *Poetical Register*[1] can describe Herbert's poetry as 'very much admired', but already for some time past the tide of critical opinion had been turning against the religious poets of the first half of the seventeenth century. As early as 1650 one fashion, to which Herbert had occasionally yielded, had come under censure. Sir William D'Avenant's *A Discourse upon Gondibert* (Paris, 1650) contains 'The Answer to it by Mr. Hobbs', which possibly reflects on Herbert. After commending the ten-syllable measure as 'proper for an Heroick', Hobbes continues:

> In an Epigramme or a Sonnet, a man may vary his measures, and seek glory from a needlesse difficulty, as he that contrived verses into the forms of an Organ, a Hatchet, an Egg, an Altar, and a pair of Wings; but in so great and noble a work as is an Epick Poeme, for a man to obstruct his own way with unprofitable difficulties, is great imprudence.

Herbert is not named by Hobbes and he was guiltless of any but the two last examples, for which there were many precedents, both classical and contemporary. The reference to Herbert is, however, certain in Dryden's satirical advice to his rival Shadwell:

> Thy Genius calls thee not to purchase fame
> In keen Iambicks, but mild Anagram:
> Leave writing Plays, and chuse for thy command
> Some peacefull Province in Acrostick Land.
> There thou maist wings display, and Altars raise,
> And torture one poor word Ten thousand ways;
> Or, if thou would'st thy diff'rent talents suit,
> Set thy own Songs, and sing them to thy lute.[2]

Addison, in *The Spectator* of 7 May 1711, mentions Herbert as a special offender in 'this Fashion of false Wit', which 'was revived by several Poets of the last Age'. In the same year appeared *An Essay on Criticism*, in which Pope makes the distinction of true and false wit and is severe on conceits and 'glitt'ring thoughts'. Spence attributes

[1] I owe the reference to Jacob to A. H. Nethercot's article 'The Reputation of the Metaphysical Poets during the Age of Pope' in the *Philological Quarterly*, April 1925.

[2] Dryden, *MacFlecknoe* (1682), ll. 203–10.

to him a remark that 'Herbert is lower than Crashaw, Sir John Beaumont higher, and Donne, a good deal so'. In a long letter to H. Cromwell, dated 17 December 1710,[1] Pope gave full attention to Crashaw, who, he thinks, 'may just deserve reading'; much of his adverse criticism would be applicable to Herbert also, though he does not name him. According to Warton, Pope 'very judiciously collected gold from the dregs of Crashaw, of Carew, of Herbert, and others (for it is well-known he was a great reader of all those poets)'.[2] Though it is difficult to detect more than a very few actual borrowings from Herbert in Pope's verse, the gnomic style of 'The Church-porch' and of such poems as 'Man' may have affected the writing of *An Essay on Man*; and Herbert's habit of drawing illustrations from the homely objects of indoor life and finding significance in them is carried farther by the later poet.

For the most part the religious poets of the seventeenth century suffer an eclipse in the following century and Herbert shares this general neglect. There are only a few individual writers and anthologists who keep him in remembrance. Thomas Hayward's *The British Muse* (1738), which owed much to the advice of William Oldys, quotes extensively from 'The Church-porch' and from three other of the *Temple* poems. An anonymous collection, mostly of songs without authors' names, *The Charmer* (Edinburgh, 1749, 2nd edition, 1752), includes a much altered version of 'Vertue', which is also found in its original form in many commonplace books of the seventeenth and eighteenth centuries. John Wheeldon produced in 1768 *Sacred Prolusions: or Sacred Pieces from Bishop Taylor and Mr. Herbert*, which included the whole of 'The Church-porch', 'The Sacrifice', and 'Dotage'. The most remarkable devotion to Herbert in the eighteenth century is John Wesley's. He included no less than forty-seven poems from *The Temple* in his various collections of hymns and sacred poems. It is regrettable that he cut down Herbert's intricate metrical patterns to the Procrustean bed of Common, Long, and

[1] Pope, *Works*, ed. J. Warton, 1797, vii. 142–3.

[2] J. Warton, *An Essay on the Genius of Pope* (1756), i. 87–8.

Short Measure, all of them iambic, to fit them for singing to familiar tunes. He also ruthlessly pruned the conceits and gave the poems an almost eighteenth-century dress, but in his rewriting of them he generally interpreted the meaning correctly and, at times, even skilfully. However unsatisfactory these adaptations were, they made Herbert's poems known to an ever-widening circle of new readers in that age. In his seventieth year Wesley rendered better service to Herbert by printing in their original form *Select Parts of Mr. Herbert's Sacred Poems* (1773), which consisted of twenty-two poems and the greater part of 'The Church-porch'; it is the most considerable printing of Herbert's poems between the editions of *The Temple* in 1709 and 1799.[1] Herbert's memory was also preserved by *The Country Parson*, which was often quoted and praised in the eighteenth century, and by Walton's *Lives*. Dr. Johnson at one time contemplated preparing an edition of the *Lives*, which, according to Boswell, was 'one of his most favourite books', and, when there appeared to be a chance that either Lord Hailes or Bishop George Horne would edit the book, he urged that the works of those whose lives Walton wrote 'must be carefully read by the editor'.[2] Horne himself rewrote Herbert's 'Vertue'.[3]

William Cowper tells of the relief he found in *The Temple* when he was first 'overtaken with a dejection of spirits' at the age of 21:

> At length I met with Herbert's Poems; and gothic and uncouth as they were, I yet found in them a strain of piety which I could not but admire. This was the only author I had any delight in reading. I pored over him all day long; and though I found not here what I might have found—a cure for my malady, yet it never seemed so much alleviated as while I was reading him.[4]

Eighteen years later Cowper writes to Mrs. Unwin that he has been reading Herbert to his brother.[5] Such testimony to

[1] I have fully explored John Wesley's concern with Herbert in an article, 'John Wesley and George Herbert', in *The London Quarterly*, Aug. 1936.

[2] Boswell, *Life of Johnson*, ed. Powell (1934), ii. 280.

[3] *Works* (1814), i. 236.

[4] *Memoirs of the early life of William Cowper, written by himself* (1816), pp. 26–7.

[5] *Correspondence of William Cowper*, ed. Wright, i. 115.

Herbert from a man of letters was rare in the eighteenth century, and the critical notices of his poetry towards the end of the century were increasingly depreciatory. Henry Headley, in his *Select Beauties of Ancient English Poetry* (1787), dismisses Herbert contemptuously:

> A writer of the same class, though infinitely inferior to both Quarles and Crashaw. His poetry is a compound of enthusiasm without sublimity, and conceit without either ingenuity or imagination. The piece I have selected ('Church-monuments') is perhaps the best in his book. When a name is once reduced to the impartial test of time, when partiality, friendship, fashion, and party, have withdrawn their influence, our surprise is frequently excited by past subjects of admiration that now cease to strike. He who now takes up the poems of Herbert would little suspect that he had been public orator of an University, and a favourite of his Sovereign; that he had received flattery and praise from Donne and from Bacon; and that the biographers of the day had enrolled his name amongst the first names of his country.[1]

George Ellis, who included one poem only of Herbert's, 'Life', in his *Specimens of Early English Poets* (1790), reckons that Crashaw 'possessed more fancy and genius' than Herbert, and William Hayley speaks of Herbert as 'that very religious and once popular Bard'.[2] The standard collections of the English poets by Anderson, Chalmers, and others generally ignore Herbert, while Crashaw is more fortunate, perhaps because of Pope's mild commendation. The writer of an article on Herbert in *The Retrospective Review* in 1821, believing that his poems 'would present such a mass of uninviting and even repulsive matter to modern readers of poetry', picks out 'a few flowers, which are almost lost amid weeds'. '*Vertue*', he says, 'though defaced by a vulgar expression or two', is 'on the whole, both beautiful and polished.' 'The quaintness and oddity of *The Pulley* are compensated for by some excellent lines.'

When Herbert's poetic credit stood lowest, the first notable critic to rediscover his quality was Coleridge. There

[1] Headley, op. cit. I. lvi.

[2] The reference to Hayley I owe to A. H. Nethercot's article 'The Reputation of the Metaphysical Poets during the Age of Johnson' in *Studies in Philology*, Jan. 1925. See ibid. July 1934 for 'The Reputation of Crashaw in the XVII and XVIII Centuries' by Austin Warren.

are references to his poetry in *The Friend* (1809–10) and considerable discussion of it in *Biographia Literaria* (1817). Pickering, in his edition of Herbert's collected *Works* (vol. II, 1835), printed many notes from a copy of *The Temple* and *The Synagogue*, which Coleridge had annotated. In *The Friend* Coleridge says of Herbert:

> The quaintness of some of his thoughts, not of his diction, than which nothing can be more pure, manly, and unaffected, has blinded modern readers to the great general merit of his poems, which are for the most part exquisite in their kind.

The tide had turned by the second quarter of the nineteenth century, and in the next hundred years there have been many editions, both scholarly and popular, of *The Temple*. After Coleridge's cordial appreciation it became respectable for critics to value Herbert's poetry, though it continued to be usual to apologize for his 'quaintness' and his conceits. Among those in the later nineteenth century with truer insight were Edward Dowden, H. C. Beeching, Alice Meynell, and George Herbert Palmer.

In the present age, with the revival of interest in Donne and his successors, there is a clearer perception of the aims and methods of the metaphysical poets. Conceits, which pleased in the seventeenth century, gave offence in the eighteenth, and elicited a half-hearted defence in the nineteenth, are again seen to be no idle exercise of ingenuity but an effective way of expressing that blend of thought and passion which characterized such poetry. Herbert's conceits are less recondite than Donne's, and are oftener drawn from the familiar and homely facts of common life; they are seldom merely ingenious, though they do not always explain themselves at first reading. Sometimes, in spite of his own protests against such lack of directness in 'Jordan', we can only 'catch the sense at two removes'.

Certain excellences of Herbert as a poet are generally recognized to-day. His craftsmanship is conspicuous. Almost any poem of his has its object well defined; its leading idea is followed through with economy and brought to an effective conclusion, the imagery which runs through it commonly helping to knit it together. He takes much care to select a verse-form to match the content, and he constantly varies the incidence of the rhymes and the length of the lines. Examples of perfect adaptation of form to content are 'Aaron', 'Sinnes Round', the fourth 'Affliction', 'Deniall', and 'The Collar'. The purity of his diction is another claim to distinction. Few English poets have been able to use the plain words of ordinary speech with a greater effect of simple dignity than Herbert. From Donne he had learnt the use of the conversational tone, which establishes an intimacy between poet and reader; and when his poems are read aloud, the emphasis falls easily on the natural order of the speaking idiom. He does not always succeed: sometimes he uses a conceit or a hyperbole which offends sober taste; sometimes he leaves his verse crabbed and obscure, but it is seldom flat. There is passion behind the subtle workings of his mind and imagination; and what Mr. T. S. Eliot calls 'the spiritual stamina of his work' saves it from descending to the commonplace. The short religious lyric was eminently fitted to portray the succession of moods, varying from poignancy to serenity, of a peculiarly sensitive personality. And if to-day there is a less general sympathy with Herbert's religion, the beauty and sincerity of its expression are appreciated by those who do not share it. There is as much readiness in this generation as in any since *The Temple* appeared to admit the justice of Coleridge's dictum that Herbert was 'a true poet'.

III. *Manuscripts of 'The Temple' Poems*

I. MS. Tanner 307 in the Bodleian Library. (Hereafter designated *B*.) Folio. $12\frac{1}{4}$ by $7\frac{5}{8}$ inches. 152 leaves.

In the right-hand top corner is the signature of a former owner, 'W. Sancroft', and below it, in the same hand, are the words: 'The Original of Mr George Herbert's Temple; as it was at first Licenced for the presse.' The form 'W. Sancroft' suggests that it was inscribed before the owner became 'W. Cantuar.' on 27 January 1677/8. William Sancroft (1617–93) entered Emmanuel College, of which his uncle with the same names was Master 1628–37, in

1633, was a resident fellow 1642–51, and was himself Master for three years from 1662. From early years he kept commonplace books of Greek and Latin and English poetry and amassed a large collection of manuscripts; during his many years' residence in Cambridge he would have had an opportunity of acquiring this manuscript of *The Temple*. Nearly 300 of his manuscripts were acquired by Thomas Tanner (1674–1735), bishop of St. Asaph, an Oxford man, who bequeathed them, by his will dated 22 November 1733, to the Bodleian Library.

In the lower part of the title-page are the autograph signatures of the licensers: 'B: Lany Procan:, Tho: Bainbrigg, M. Wren, William Beale, Tho: ffreman.' Benjamin Lany, Vice-Chancellor from Michaelmas 1632 to the following Michaelmas, was Master of Pembroke, and to him Crashaw dedicated his first book in the next year. Bainbrigg was Master of Christ's, Matthew Wren, uncle of Sir Christopher, was Master of Peterhouse, and William Beale, formerly of Westminster School, was Master of Jesus. The charter granted by Henry VIII in 1534, confirmed by a charter of Charles I on 6 February 1627/8, authorized the university to print such books as were approved by the Chancellor or his vice-gerent and three doctors. As the terms of the charter were satisfied by the first four signatures, it is probable that Thomas Freeman was a secretary or minor official; a man of that name graduated M.A. from Clare Hall in 1628. A book so licensed by the university authorities was not entered at Stationers' Hall.

On the title-page are the title 'The Temple' (without the further description 'Sacred Poems and Private Ejaculations', and without the author's name), the quotation from Psalm xxix. 8, and 'The Dedication'. The verso is blank, and then follow the poems in the same order as in the *editio princeps*, except that the two-line 'Anagram' is placed earlier, between 'Church-Musique' and 'Church-lock & key'. As in the printed text, the title does not occur again, the successive headlines being 'The Church-porch', 'The Church', and 'The Church Militant'. At the end is a table of the poems in the order of their appearance, not alphabetically arranged as in 1633. The date of this copy and the nature of the few corrections made in it are discussed below, pp. lxxii–iv.

II. MS. Jones B 62 in Dr. Williams's Library, Gordon Square, London. (Hereafter designated *W.*) $5\frac{3}{4}$ by $3\frac{3}{4}$ inches. 120 leaves (numbered 130, as by error 89 is followed by 100, 101, &c.) This includes 14 blank leaves.

On the fly-leaf is a note in the hand of John Jones: 'Doñ. J[ni] Jones, Cler. e Museo V.Cl.D.H.M. Venantoduñ. qui ob. 1730', and on the next leaf, in the same hand, is a roughly pencilled note: 'This Book came originally from the Family of Little Gidding, & was probably bound there. Q. Whether this be not the Manuscript Copy that was sent by Mr Herbert a little before his death to Mr Nic. Ferrar. See M[r] Herbert's Life.'

John Jones (1700–70) was serving a Huntingdonshire curacy when he first became interested in the annals of Little Gidding and was given this small volume 'from the library of the famous and learned H.M. of Huntingdon'. This donor can be safely identified as Hugh Mapletoft, formerly fellow of Trinity College, Cambridge, and rector of All Saints, Huntingdon, who died there on 26 August 1731. If, as is likely enough, Jones made the entry in the fly-leaf some years after he received the book, he might have been one year out in recording the date of Mapletoft's death. Palmer is mistaken in stating (*English Works of Herbert*, I. 178) that the name Henry Mapletoft occurs in MS. Jones B 87, and he admits that no Henry is to be found in the Mapletoft family. Hugh's parents were Solomon Mapletoft and Judith, daughter of John Collett and Susanna, Nicholas Ferrar's sister; with this ancestry it was natural that some of the Gidding papers should have become his property. John Jones, although he published little, was throughout life an indefatigable annalist and commentator. At his death his manuscript collections were acquired by Thomas Dawson, M.D. (1725?–82), who gave up the ministry of a Presbyterian church at Hackney to practise medicine. At Dawson's death the Jones manuscripts went to Dr. Williams's Library.

The book is in a dull red leather binding, with one gold line round the front and back and gold bands on the spine. It may be, as Jones's note suggests, that the book was bound at Gidding, or perhaps rebound, as a book that was in Herbert's use for some years is likely to have had some binding from the first.

There is no title-page and no author's name, and the title 'The Temple' is nowhere found in the volume, the headlines being as in *B* and 1633. The contents begin with 'The Dedication' on a page to itself with the verso blank. The same three divisions are found as in *B* and 1633, 'The Church Militant' being separated by five blank pages from 'The Church'. The handwriting of all the English poems is that of an amanuensis, who has made some corrections of his own, especially of obvious slips, but there are as well very many corrections in the author's unmistakable hand; in particular, the poem 'Perfection' is very freely recast and is given a new name, 'The Elixir'. It is generally possible to distinguish the corrections made by a second hand from those made by the copyist, and they are so recorded in the footnotes. I take most of these emendations to be in Herbert's own hand.

After the English poems there are three blank pages and then a pencilled note: 'The following supposed to be Mr Herbert's own Writing. See the Records in the Custody of the University Orator at Cambridge' (an allusion to Herbert's letters in the Orator's Book). The Latin poems which follow, in two groups entitled 'Passio Discerpta' and 'Lucus', are unquestionably in Herbert's beautiful hand (see an example reproduced as frontispiece).

Of the 164 poems in *The Temple*, as commonly reckoned (the two parts of 'Superliminare', 'Good Friday', 'Easter', 'Love (I, II)' and 'The H. Scriptures' being counted as one poem), 69 are found in *W*, which has the first part only of 'Christmas' and the second part only of 'The H. Communion'. As the order also differs in *W*, it is well to set it out fully for comparison. Those poems which were to be considerably altered before they reappeared in *B* are asterisked, and the six *W* poems which found no place in

B and 1633 are italicized. The figures in brackets indicate the position occupied by the poems in the text of 1633, which follows the order of *B* with the single exception of 'Anagram'.

The Dedication
*The Church-porch (1)
Perirranterium (2: = stanza 1 of Superliminare)
Superliminare (2: = stanza 2 of Superliminare)
The Altar (3)
*The Sacrifice (4)
*The Thanks-giving (5)
The Second Thanks-giving (6: = The Reprisall)
*The Passion (9: = part 2 of Good Friday)
The Passion (10: = Redemption)
Good Friday (9: = part 1 of Good Friday)
The Sinner (8)
Easter (12: = part 1 of Easter)
*Easter (12: = part 2 of Easter)
Easter-wings (13)
*H. Baptisme (14)
H. Baptisme (15)
Love 1 and 2 (24)
The H. Communion
*Church-Musick (38)
The Christian Temper (25: = The Temper [I])
The Christian Temper (26: = The Temper [II])
Prayer (21: = Prayer [I])
*Prayer (22: = part 2 of The H. Communion)
*Prayer (39: = Church-lock and key)
Imploiment (28: = Employment [I])
*Whitsunday (30)
The H. Scriptures 1 and 2 (29)
Love
Sinn (35: = Sinne [II])
Trinity Sunday (42)
Trinity Sunday
*Repentance (19)
*Praise (32: = Praise [I])
Nature (16)
*Grace (31)
Mattens (34)
Euen-song

Christmas-Day (56: = part 1 of Christmas)
Church-Monuments (37)
Frailty (46)
Content (43)
Poetry (44: = The Quidditie)
*Affliction (18: = Affliction [I])
Humility (45)
*Sunday (50)
Jordan (27: = Jordan [I])
Deniall (55)
Ungratfulnes (57)
*Imploiment (54: = Employment [II])
A Wreath (157)
To All Angels and Saints (53)
*The Pearle (64)
Tentation (65: = Affliction [IV])
The World (59)
Coloss. 3. 3. (60)
*Faith (20)
Lent (62)
*Man (66)
Ode (67: = Antiphon [II])
Affliction (73: = Affliction [V])
Sinn (17: = Sinne [I])
*Charmes and Knots (72)
Unkindnes (68)
Mortification (74)
*The Publican (76: = Miserie)
Prayer (78: = Prayer [II])
Obedience (79)
*Invention (77: = Jordan [II])
*Perfection (156: = The Elixir)
The Knell
Perseverance
Death (158)
Dooms-day (159)
Iudgment (160)
Heaven (161)
Love (162: = Love [III])
*The Church Militant (163)
L'Envoy (164)

It will be seen from the above list that the first sixteen

poems in *W* are in nearly the same order as in *B*, but that after them there are only nine instances of two poems in the same consecutive order in *W* and *B*, until the group of nine *W* poems at the end of *B*. There are no *W* poems in *B* between No. 79 'Obedience' and the final group beginning with No. 156 'The Elixir'.

Other Manuscript Versions of 'The Temple' Poems.

Several of *The Temple* poems are found in commonplace books of the seventeenth century, but in no case have I seen any reason to suppose that they were not transcribed from one or other of the printed editions, even when that fact is not explicitly stated. These manuscript versions have, therefore, no independent value and are negligible so far as the text is concerned.

There is in the Bodleian Library 'M[r] Herbert's Temple Explained and Improved' by George Ryley, 1714/15 (MS. Rawlinson D 199): it has no authority for the text, which, where it is cited, evidently follows a late edition; and the comments lack originality.

IV. *Early Editions of 'The Temple'*

The title, sub-title, author's name and (from No. 1*b*) description, and the text from Psalm xxix continue unchanged, except for insignificant typographical differences, from 1633 to 1709, and are therefore not recorded after No. 1*b*. All editions are 12mo, and the collation of Nos. 1–7 is identical.[1]

1*a*. THE | TEMPLE. | SACRED POEMS | AND | PRIVATE EJA-|CULATIONS. | [*rule*] | By M[r]. GEORGE HERBERT. | [*rule*] | PSAL. 29. | *In his Temple doth every* | *man speak of his honour.* | [*ornament between rules*] | CAMBRIDGE: | Printed by *Thom. Buck*, | and

[1] The late Professor Palmer printed privately in 1911 at Cambridge, Mass., *A Herbert Bibliography*, 'being a catalogue of a collection of books relating to George Herbert gathered by George Herbert Palmer.' Mr. Geoffrey Keynes contributed to the Nonesuch edition of *The Temple* (1927) a 'Bibliographical Note'. Both these valuable bibliographies require a few additions and amendments, which are here recorded.

Roger Daniel, printers | to the Universitie. | 1633. [See below, p. 1, a reproduction of this title-page.]

Collation: 12mo: ¶^{4}, A–H^{12}, I^{2}; pp. [8]+192+[4].

Contents: [¶^{1}] title (verso blank), ¶$^{2-3}$, The Printers to the Reader; [¶^{4}], The Dedication (verso blank); A–H^{12}, pp. 1–192, text; I$^{1-2}$, [pp. 193–5], The titles of the severall poems, [p. 196] blank.

1*b*. As 1*a*, except for title-page entirely reset thus: THE | TEMPLE. | SACRED POEMS | AND | PRIVATE EJA- | CULATIONS. | [*rule*] | By M^{r}. GEORGE HERBERT, | late Oratour of the Universitie | of *Cambridge.* | [*rule*] | PSAL. 29. | *In his Temple doth every* | *man speak of his honour.* | [*ornament between rules*] | CAMBRIDGE: | Printed by *Thomas Buck* | and *Roger Daniel:* | ¶And are to be sold by *Francis* | *Green*, stationer in | *Cambridge.*

This title-page is a cancel-leaf; the chain-lines run vertically, not horizontally as in the rest of the book, and the stub or cancellatum, to which the leaf is gummed, is visible. The description of the author as 'late Oratour' kept its place in all subsequent editions. Francis Green, a Cambridge stationer in business from 1628 to 1635, had an interest in having his name on at least so many copies as he was likely to sell in Cambridge, though it had no relevance for the larger number needed for the London market. The second edition of Giles Fletcher's *Christs Victorie*, though printed by the university printers, has for its imprint these words only, 'Cambridge Printed for Francis Green. 1632'. One effect of introducing his name and description in a limited number of copies of the first edition of *The Temple* was to extend the imprint from five to six lines, and, probably for no other reason than to avoid crowding and lack of symmetry, the date was omitted. This does not, however, constitute a distinct issue, as, apart from the title-page, the copies with a dated and an undated title-page are indistinguishable. There were, indeed, a few insignificant changes, made while the book was still printing (e.g. *power* for *pow'r* in 'The Altar', l. 8; *pitie* for *pittie* in 'The Sacrifice', l..143; *pursue*, for *pursu* in 'Peace', l. 41;

and a missing mark of interrogation supplied in 'Love unknown', l. 36), but these variants are distributed promiscuously in dated and undated copies. The sheets in their first or in their corrected state were placed indifferently behind a dated or an undated title-page. By personal examination or from the particulars kindly supplied to me by owners and librarians I have ascertained these facts about fourteen dated and four undated copies of the first edition. Grosart had no warrant for assigning the undated copies to 1632.[1]

2*a*. The second Edition. Printed by *T. Buck*, and *R. Daniel*, printers to the Universitie of *Cambridge*, 1633.

2*b*. Identical with 2*a*, except for an addition to the imprint of a single line: ¶ And are to be sold by *Fr. Green*.

This title-page, like that of 1*b*, is a cancel, but, whereas the copies of the first edition with Green's name are in the proportion of less than one to four (so far as copies can now be traced), the copies of the second edition with his name are far commoner than those without. Palmer and Keynes have not recorded 2*a*.

The only important textual difference introduced in the second edition is the change of *Abstain wholly* to *Wholly abstain* in 'The Church-porch', l. 13, but the type is entirely reset and the printer has taken occasion to effect a large number of minor typographical corrections in spacing, punctuation, and spelling.

3. The third Edition. Printed by *T. Buck*, and *R. Daniel*, printers to the Universitie of *Cambridge*, 1634. And are to be sold by *Fr. Green*.

I have found no copies without Green's name, and there is no indication of the title-page with his name being a cancel.

Again the printer has exercised care over the typographical minutiae. There are two verbal changes: *I'm* for *am* in 'The Sacrifice', l. 234, and *who for me* for *who from*

[1] For fuller proof of these statements see F. E. Hutchinson, 'The First Edition of Herbert's *Temple*', in *Proceedings of the Oxford Bibliographical Society*, v. iii. 1938.

me in 'The H. Communion', l. 3; the latter change agrees with the reading of *B*, but it might have been guessed from the same phrase occurring twice elsewhere in *The Temple*.

4. The fourth Edition. Printed by *T. Buck*, and *R. Daniel* . . . Cambridge, 1635.

The line about Green is absent; he went out of business this year.

5. The fifth Edition. Printed by *T. Buck*, and *R. Daniel* . . . Cambridge, 1638.

This, the last edition for which Buck was responsible, is remarkable for several textual alterations, which can only be explained by resort being again had to the manuscript (see below, p. lxxvi).

6. The sixth Edition. Printed by *Roger Daniel* . . . Cambridge. 1641.

Some copies are bound with the anonymous work of Christopher Harvey (1597–1663), *The Synagogue, or, The Shadow of the Temple . . . In imitation of Mr. George Herbert* (London, Printed by J. L. for Philemon Stephens. 1640).

7. The seventh Edition. (Without imprint or date.)

This is recorded in the British Museum catalogue as '? Cambridge ? 1656', but there are good reasons for dating it earlier and ascribing its printing to London. Although it follows the Cambridge lay-out, the printing is much below the university printers' standard; also, there are printers' ornaments, notably the uncouth Gorgon's head on p. 16, which are not found in any Cambridge book of the period. The ornament below 'The Altar' on p. 18 is found on the title-page of the second edition of *The Synagogue* (Printed by J. L. for Philemon Stephens, at the gilded Lion in Pauls Churchyard. 1647), which is often bound with this edition of *The Temple*. Stephens had already a connexion with Herbert as the publisher of Donne's sermon commemorating Lady Danvers (1627), to which Herbert's Latin elegies were appended. He was also the publisher of the first edition of

The Synagogue in 1640, and was to publish 'The seventh Edition' of *The Temple* with his imprint and the date 1656 (see No. 8). Moreover, in John Trapp's *A Commentary upon the XII Minor Prophets*, printed by R. N. for Philemon Stephens in 1654, there is a list of books to be sold by Stephens, which includes Donne's sermon, *The Temple*, and *The Synagogue*. E. Arber (*Bibliographica*, vol. iii, part ix, pp. 181–2) states that Stephens was 'the first English publisher who put a list of his Publications at the end of his books', but he fails to notice that some of the books on Stephens's lists had other publishers; he was not only a publisher, but a bookseller with a special interest in theological and devotional books. The last Cambridge edition of *The Temple* (1641) may have been exhausted by 1647. Perhaps Stephens reckoned that the new edition of *The Synagogue* would go off better if it were bound up with *The Temple*, and he may have found difficulty in inducing the Cambridge printers to reprint owing to the Civil War and risked getting it printed in London without authorization, and therefore without imprint. If this edition without imprint was issued in or about 1647, it would bridge the unaccountably wide gap in the reproduction of so popular a book between the Cambridge edition of 1641 and the dated London edition of 1656.

8. The seventh Edition, with an Alphabeticall Table for ready finding out chief places. London, Printed by *T. R.* for *Philemon Stephens*. 1656.

Collation: [*]^{6}, A–I^{12}, K^{6}; pp. [12]+192+[36]. 'The Titles of the several Poems' [*$^{5-6}$] precede the text of the poems instead of following, as hitherto. The text has the same signatures and pagination as in the Cambridge editions. The signatures of the text continue unaltered from 1633 to 1703, when a slight alteration is made; the pagination of the text is unaltered from 1633 to 1709 inclusive. The Alphabetical Table is included in all subsequent editions to 1709, and some edition of *The Synagogue*, with its own separate title-page, signatures, and pagination, is generally bound with *The Temple*.

9. The Eighth Edition. London, Printed by *R. N.* for *Philemon Stephens*, 1660.

Collation as No. 8.

10. The Ninth Edition. London, Printed by *J. M.* for *Philemon Stephens*, and are to be Sold at the *Kings Arms* in *Chancery*-Lane, 1667.

Some copies add 'and *J. Stephens*' after '*Philemon Stephens*'.

Collation as No. 8.

11. The Tenth Edition. Together with his Life. With several Additions. London, Printed by *W. Godbid*, for *R. S.* and are to be Sold by *John Williams* Junior . . . 1674.

Collation: [a]^{6}, A–B^{12}, C^{6}, *^{6} [*^{1} cancelled, probably a discarded title-page], A–I^{12}, K^{6}. In some copies the same matter is differently distributed, * following [a], and the Life (A–B^{12}, C^{6}) either preceding the poems and Table (A–I^{12}, K^{6}) or following. In the arrangement first described Keynes detects that 'probably all the preliminary matter on the leaves [a]^{1}–C^{6}, including the portrait and Walton's *Life*, were added as an afterthought and substituted for the original title'.

An important edition for its new matter—the portrait by R. White, engraved first for Walton's *Lives* (1670), and here after slight retouching used as frontispiece; eight lines of verse headed 'These Lines should have been under his Picture', placed on the first leaf after the title-page; the Life, reproduced with small changes from Walton's *Lives*; and three commendatory poems, 'A Memorial to the Honorable George Herbert' (anonymous), 'An Epitaph upon the Honorable George Herbert' by 'P.D. *Esq*;', and 'The Church Militant', a new poem in heroic couplets, subscribed '*Adversus Impia*, Anno 1670'. 'Superliminare' (p. 16) and 'The Altar' (p. 17) appear in engraved settings, which are reproduced or imitated in subsequent editions. The portrait and the Life also keep their place till 1709 inclusive.

12*a*. The Eleventh Edition. Together with his Life. (The words 'With several Additions' are absent.) London,

Printed by *S. Roycroft*, for *R.S.* and are to be Sold by *John Williams* Junior . . . 1678.

Collation: A¹², A–B¹², C⁶, A–I¹², K⁶. In some copies the Life (A–B¹², C⁶) comes last.

12*b*. Identical with 12*a*, except that the date is 167.9 [*sic*] or in some copies 1679. This title-page is not a cancel.

13. The Eleventh Edition. Together with his Life. With several Additions. London, Printed for *R. S.* and are to be Sold by *Richard Willington* . . . 1695.

Collation as No. 11, except for the preliminaries (a), which are reset; an extra blank page is secured before the frontispiece by transferring the Lines on the Picture, which in 1674 were on (a)3 with verso blank, to the verso of (a)6. The rest of the book consists of unused sheets of 1674, with even the most obvious misprints uncorrected; this reissue is, therefore, negligible, so far as the text of the poems is concerned. Perhaps Willington did not know of No. 12, and therefore called this edition the Eleventh. Details from a copy in the editor's possession.

14. The Twelfth Edition Corrected. London, Printed by *J. Barber*, for Jeffery Wale . . . 1703.

Collation: A–K¹², A–E¹², F⁶. The first sheet of 12 leaves contains the preliminaries and up to p. 10 of 'The Church-porch', so that, for the first time, the signature of the text of the poems begins from A⁸ instead of A¹, as in all previous editions. The paging of the text runs, as before, from 1 to 192. The Life follows *The Synagogue* and carries on its signatures. White's engraving is redone by Sturt, and the Lines on the Picture, for the first time, appear under the portrait, as originally intended.

15. The Thirteenth Edition Corrected. London: Printed for *John Wyat* and *Eben. Tracy.* 1709.

Collation as No. 14.

There is no further edition of *The Temple* till the Bristol edition of 1799 (see below, p. lxv).

v. '*A Priest to the Temple*' and Other *Writings*

1. *HERBERT'S* | Remains. | [*rule*] | *Or*, | SUNDRY | PIECES | *Of* that sweet SINGER | of the TEMPLE, | *Mr George Herbert*, | Sometime | Orator of the University of | CAMBRIDG. | [*rule*] | *Now exposed to publick light.* | [*rule*] | LONDON, | Printed for *Timothy Garthwait*, | at the little North door of Saint | *Paul's*. 1652.

Collation: 12mo: A^6, a–b^{12}, c^6, B–H^{12}, A–D^{12}; pp. [lxxii], 1–168, [2], 1–70, 171–94.

Contents: title, separate title [A^2] A PRIEST | To the | TEMPLE, | [*rule*] | OR, | The Countrey PARSON | HIS | CHARACTER, | AND | Rule of Holy Life. | [*rule*] | The AUTHOUR, | Mr *G. H.* | [*ornament between rules*] | LONDON, | Printed by *T. Maxey* for *T. Garthwait*, at the | little North door of St *Paul's*. 1652. A^{3-4} The Authour to the Reader (dated 1632), [A^{5-6}] A Table of Contents to the Country Parson; [A^6], Errata; [A^{6v}], half-title, A Prefatory View of the Life of Mr. Geo. Herbert; a–b^{12}, c^6 (unpaged) text of A Prefatory View (acknowledged as his by Barnabas Oley in the 2nd edn.); B–H^{12}, pp. 1–168, text of A Priest to the Temple; separate title [A^1], JACULA | PRUDENTUM. | [*rule*] | OR | *Outlandish* | PROVERBS, | SENTENCES, *&c.* | [*rule*] | SELECTED | By Mr *George Herbert*, | Late | Orator of the Universitie of | CAMBRIDG. | [*ornament between rules*] | LONDON, | Printed by *T. Maxey* for *T. Garthwait*, at the | little North door of St *Paul's*. 1651. A^2–C^{12}, pp. 1–70, text of proverbs; D^{1-3}, pp. 171–5 The Authour's Prayers, D^{3v-5}, pp. 176–9 letter to N.F., D^{5v-6}, pp. 180–2 three Latin poems to Bacon and Donne, [D^{7-12}], pp. 183–94 An Addition of Apothegmes by Severall Authours. In some copies an Imprimatur (June 30. 1651) is on p. 194.

Palmer's copy (*A Herbert Bibliography*, No. 19) has the preliminary leaves A^{1-4} duplicated.

The miscellaneous pieces at the end (pp. 171–94) exactly fill sheet D. Some of the 'Apothegmes by Severall Authours' can be traced to Bacon, and there is no reason to assign any of them to Herbert; they were probably added to complete the sheet in what was in any case a small book. The paging of this last section picks up from the paging of 'A Priest to the Temple', though it begins with p. 171, not p. 169 (now represented by the separate title-page of 'Jacula Prudentum', with verso blank). The erratic pagination suggests that the inclusion of 'Jacula Prudentum', which, as thus printed, probably had an independent existence in 1651, was an afterthought; the proverbs are not mentioned in the title-page of 1652 or in 'A Prefatory View'. The bibliography of *Outlandish Proverbs* and of its enlarged form, *Jacula Prudentum*, is so complicated that it is treated in a separate excursus (below, p. 568), where also the question of Herbert's responsibility for the proverbs is discussed.

2. A | PRIEST | TO THE | Temple. | OR THE | Country Parson | HIS | CHARACTER, | AND | Rule of Holy Life. | [*rule*] | *By Mr.* Geo. Herbert, *Orator of the* | *University of Cambridge.* | [*rule*] | The second Edition; With a new | Praeface, by *B.O.* | [*rule*] | *LONDON,* | Printed by *T. Roycroft,* for *Benj. Tooke,* at | the *Ship* in St. *Paul's* Church-yard. | 1671.

Collation: 8vo: A^{8}, a^{8}, B–O^{8}; pp. (xxxii)+139+[69].

Contents: [A^{1v}] Imprimatur. *Ex Æd. Lambethanis* Maii 24, 1671. Tho. Tomkyns; [A^{2}], title; A$^{3-4}$, Author to Reader; [A$^{5-8}$]–a$^{1-7}$, Publisher to the Christian Reader, signed Barnabas Oley; [a^{8}], Contents; B–I^{8}, K^{6}, text; [K^{7}], An Advertisement to Reader; K^{8}–O^{6}, A Prefatory View; [O^{7}], list of books to be sold by Benjamin Took.

'A Prefatory View' is displaced by Oley's new preface, but it is included in the book at the end. The Author's Prayers are not included.

3. A PRIEST TO THE TEMPLE (*&c., as in No.* 2). The Third Impression. London, Printed by *T. R.* for *Benj. Tooke*, at the *Ship* in St. *Paul's* Church-yard. 1675.

Collation: 12mo: A^{12}, a^{8}, B–L^{12}, M^{4}; pp. [xl]+166+[72]. M$^{1-4}$ absent from some copies.

Contents: as in No. 2. M$^{1-4}$, a longer list of books for sale.

4. A PRIEST To The Temple (*&c. as in No.* 3). The Fourth Edition. London: Printed for *Benj. Tooke*, at the *Middle-Temple-Gate* in *Fleetstreet*. 1701.

Collation: 12mo: A^{12}, a^4, B–H^{12} [sheet H is misprinted G], I^8; pp. [xxxii]+141+[43].

Contents: as in No. 3, including both of Oley's prefaces. Some copies are without preface of 1671 (A^{3-12}, a^4).

The other manuscripts and printed books containing the occasional writings of Herbert are named in the footnotes to the pages where these writings occur in the text, and questions of authenticity are discussed in the Commentary.

VI. *Modern Editions of Herbert's Works*

After a gap of ninety years *The Temple* began to appear again with growing frequency from 1799, when it was printed at Bristol 'by and for R. Edwards; and sold by T. Hurst, Pater-Noster-Row, London', together with Walton's *Life* (abridged) and *The Synagogue*. In 1806 Edwards, who is now described as of Crane Court, Fleet Street, printed *The Temple* and *The Country Parson* for a group of London publishers, and another edition of the same, with Walton's *Life* added, was published in 1809 by the same group, with Edwards still as printer. The text of the last Cambridge edition (1641) was followed. The same three works were published in one volume by Edward Suter of Cheapside in 1835; the unnamed editor states that 'each work has been collated with the first edition', though he also made intelligent use of some corrections in the later Cambridge editions; it was in many ways a more scholarly text of *The Temple* than Pickering's which appeared in the same year. From now on there were very many editions of *The Temple* throughout the century, and it is sufficient to name those only which added to knowledge.

The first collected *Works of George Herbert* was edited and published by William Pickering, vol. ii 'Poems' appearing in 1835, and vol. i 'Life and Remains' in 1836. The 1835 volume included, besides *The Temple* and *The Synagogue*, most of the Latin poems, and also Coleridge's notes made in a copy of *The Temple*. Before the 1836 volume was out, Pickering had found 'Memoriae Matris Sacrum'; he printed it, *faute de mieux*, at the end of the prose volume, and as well, from a manuscript in his possession, 'Inventa Bellica' (a version of the poem 'Triumphus Mortis', which is among the Latin poems in the Williams MS., with which Pickering was not acquainted). The prose volume, besides giving Oley's and Walton's lives, included *A Priest to the Temple*, the notes on Valdesso, the translation of Cornaro, *Jacula Prudentum*, the oration on Charles's return from Spain, the Latin letters from the Orator's Book and eight English letters —a notable gathering. In the many editions which followed in Pickering's lifetime, he was able to add a few more items, viz. the oration before the ambassadors, four more English letters (from Rebecca Warner's *Epistolary Curiosities*, 1818) and a few poems ascribed to Herbert. A useful one-volume edition of the Works, with notes, was edited in 1854 by R. A. Willmott. James Yeowell, sub-editor of *Notes and Queries*, added notes to a reissue of Pickering's collected edition for Bell and Daldy in 1859. So far, little work had been done on the text of *The Temple*.

Grosart's *Complete Works in verse and prose of George Herbert* (1874, 3 vols.) was the first to make use of the Williams MS. From it he printed the six discarded English poems and the two collections of Latin verse. Unfortunately his reading of this MS. and of the Bodleian MS. was careless, and there was nothing he did which does not need to be done again. In compiling his text of *The Temple* he pleased his fancy in adopting many readings from *W*, although he should have borne in mind that it represented an earlier stage of Herbert's work. It is the more unfortunate that Grosart's faulty and eclectic text, with little alteration, has been used for many popular editions. Grosart as well compiled a large body of miscellaneous information and comment.

Of the later popular editions two only deserve mention. R. Seeley carefully edited the text of *The Temple* in 1894 from the first edition, and illustrated it with much felicity and taste by engravings of Dürer, Holbein, and English artists of the Elizabethan age. E. C. S. Gibson's edition of *The Temple* (1899; revised 1905) reproduced the text of the *editio princeps* with very few slips and gave also most of the variant readings of the manuscripts.

In 1876 appeared two type-facsimile reproductions of the first edition of *The Temple*; one, edited by Grosart, was made from the undated copy then belonging to Mr. Henry Huth; the other, published by Wells Gardner without editor's name, from the dated copy in the British Museum. Both were several times reprinted, and to the third (1882) and subsequent editions of the latter (published, or taken over, by Fisher Unwin) an essay by J. H. Shorthouse was prefixed. Grosart's facsimile was the more accurate of the two but both have many mistakes. An edition of *The Temple*, 'Printed from the Manuscript in the *Bodleian* Library by the *Nonesuch* Press', appeared in 1927. It is a book of much typographical beauty and gives the reader a fair idea of the text before editor and printer revised it for the *editio princeps*, although there are some misprints and misreadings of the manuscript; here and there the defective punctuation of the manuscript is silently corrected.

All previous studies of Herbert, except for his Latin writings, were surpassed by the monumental edition, *The English Works of George Herbert* (3 vols., 1905; revised, 1907; reissued, 1915), by George Herbert Palmer of Harvard. The introductory essays and the very full commentary, the devoted work of a lifetime, have done much to interpret the many obscurities and allusions in Herbert's poetry. The treatment of the text is less satisfactory; Palmer did not himself collate the manuscripts and some forty readings are inaccurately recorded. Palmer attributed most importance, after the commentary, to the fact that his was the first attempt to arrange the poems in chronological order. He was the first to discern that no poems in *W* refer to the author having reached the priesthood, and on that ground he inferred that the collection was completed before Herbert went to Bemerton in 1630; sometimes he dated its completion 'about 1629' (ibid. i. 187), sometimes 'about 1628' (iii. 3). On the strength of this inference he proceeded to divide the poems into three sections; the first he called 'Cambridge Poems', although the description is not entirely satisfactory, as Herbert ceased to reside regularly at Cambridge as early as 1624; the third he called 'Bemerton Poems'. With these two divisions there can be no quarrel, although the reader of the poems in Palmer's first section will do well to remember that he is reading them in their final form, which often differs considerably from their unrevised form in *W*. Between these two main sections of Cambridge and Bemerton poems, Palmer places a group, consisting of eight *W* poems and ten from the later collection, and entitles them 'The Crisis', as he detects in them references to Herbert's hesitation about entering the priesthood. Palmer calls 1627–9 the years of crisis, but he might well have begun the period earlier—with the death of Herbert's powerful friends in 1624 and 1625, and with his serious illness which belongs probably to 1626 (see above, p. xxxiii). Also, a secular career was ruled out when, in or before 1626, he was ordained deacon. At no period of his life did Herbert wholly escape the tension arising from his self-confessed habit of procrastination—'My soul doth love thee, yet it loves delay'—or from his recurring attacks of illness. Palmer was right to stress this note of conflict and divided aims, which, indeed, saves the poems from tameness, the bane of religious verse; and this note is heard in many poems before and after 'the crisis'. It is possible that Palmer over-emphasizes the conflict of mind about the priesthood, and that Herbert's spiritual struggle was over the more general issue of his submission to the Divine will.

More serious risks are taken when Palmer makes five subdivisions within each of the main sections, 'Cambridge Poems' and 'Bemerton Poems'. This inner grouping is useful if it is regarded as what he expressly calls it, 'a classification according to the subject-matter of the poems', 'a topical order'. Thus, for example, the 'Bemerton Poems' are grouped under the titles, 'The Happy Priest','Bemerton Study', 'Restlessness', 'Suffering', 'Death'. When, however, he goes on to speak of it as 'a classification which is also largely chronological' (i. 190), great caution is needed before accepting a view which must seriously affect the interpretation of Herbert's character and poetic development. In Palmer's arrangement of the 'Bemerton Poems' almost all the happier poems come at the beginning, and are followed by poems of *malaise*, which lead on to poems of gloom. Nothing can be less like the contemporary evidence of Herbert's character and disposition at the end of life. As the two poems named 'The Temper' show, he was a man of moods, which succeed one another quickly. Mr. Aldous Huxley has exactly described Herbert's temperament when he says (*Texts and Pretexts*, p. 12): 'The climate of the mind is positively English in its variableness and instability. Frost, sunshine, hopeless drought and refreshing rains succeed one another with bewildering rapidity. Herbert is the poet of this inner weather.' He is resilient and passes quickly from fits of depression to reassurance; the saddest poems either end with harmony restored or are followed in the original order by a poem in which he recovers peace of mind. Palmer holds that there is 'probably nothing expressive of Herbert's mind or wish' in the order of poems in *B*; but, though it may sometimes be accidental, there are many instances of purpose, and on the whole more is lost than is gained by dispersing the poems in groups on such slender internal evidence. Something of Herbert's orderly mind is lost when Palmer separates 'The Thanksgiving' from 'The Sacrifice', 'Redemption' from 'Good Friday', 'Church-musick' from 'Church-lock and key', and 'Man' from 'Antiphon'. The Bemerton poems suffer most by this dispersion: for instance, in the traditional order 'Longing', with its plaintive cry at the close, 'My love, my sweetnesse, heare!', is immediately followed by 'The Bag', which begins: 'Away despair! my gracious Lord doth heare.' To separate these poems by 122 pages, as Palmer does, is a grave disadvantage to the study of Herbert's mind. There are such far-reaching results from taking Palmer's topical arrangement as chronological that this *caveat* must be entered. The indebtedness of every student of Herbert to Palmer is so great that this note of dissent on one important feature of his edition may be allowed.

The Country Parson was admirably edited, with an introduction and notes, by H. C. Beeching in 1898. There are also comments of his on Herbert's poems in essays and anthologies which show such insight and subtlety as to make us believe that he would have been an ideal editor of *The Temple.* Beeching had also an advantage, which Palmer lacked, of an intimate knowledge of England and its church-life in the seventeenth century.

VII. *The Text of 'The Temple'*

The manuscript authority for determining the text of *The Temple* is less decisive than in the case of many famous books; it would have been otherwise if the 'little book' had survived which Herbert on his death-bed put into Edmund Duncon's hands to convey to Ferrar. Walton derived his account of this transaction and of Herbert's words on the occasion from Duncon himself, who was still alive when the *Life of Herbert* first appeared in 1670.[1] There are good reasons why the 'little book' cannot be identified with the Bodleian manuscript (*B*). It is not merely that *B* is a particularly large folio, which Duncon would not be likely to forget if he had been the bearer of it to Little Gidding. Walton, preferring edification to accuracy, may be using 'little' to emphasize Herbert's modesty: 'Thus meanly did this humble man think of this excellent Book.' The only surviving manuscript book of his poems, which Herbert certainly handled, namely, the one in Dr. Williams's Library (*W*), is a very small book, and he may well have affected a book of similar size for his later collection. More decisive is the style of the handwriting of *B*. So much has survived of Gidding writing that its characteristics can be recognized with some assurance. There are not only the tall flourished letters with their loops filled in, but also the unusual accenting of the indefinite article (á), which is not found in any autograph of Herbert or in the earlier manuscript. Evidently *B* is a fair copy of the 'little book', made for the licensers, not necessarily by Ferrar

[1] *Lives*, pp. 66–7, and see above, p. xxxix.

himself but quite as probably by one of the Gidding community under his supervision. There are very few corrections in *B*, compared with the many found in *W*; most of them appear to be made by the copyist, especially of words misspelt or misread, but a few are added by another hand and in an ink which now looks yellower than the first writing; there is no correction which at all suggests the author's hand. It may be presumed that all the corrections in *B* were made before *The Temple* was printed, as they would have no point afterwards. The making of the fair copy was a labour of love, and no pains were spared in executing it on handsome paper in elaborate and carefully formed letters, all within a frame of lines ruled in red. It was, no doubt, the copyist's intention to reproduce exactly the contents of the 'little book', even if he or she sometimes copied mechanically with more attention to the calligraphy than to the sense, or made slips from tiredness—as many as three or four on a page now and then. Except for such slips, for which allowance must be made, *B* brings us nearer the author's text than anything else that survives, and therefore its readings have the first claim on our respect.

We have next to consider what degree of authority belongs to the other extant manuscript. The English poems in *W*, like those in *B*, are in the hand of an amanuensis, but *W* has one advantage over the later manuscript in its having been overseen and corrected by the author; all the differences in *W* from *B* and 1633 deserve, therefore, to be recorded in the footnotes, but, since they do not represent the author's final judgement, an editor is not free, as Grosart held himself to be, to adopt its readings at pleasure, but only for specially cogent reasons. I have resisted the temptation to adopt any words from *W* except in three instances; I think that the amanuensis of *B* misread 'cause' for 'case' in 'The Sacrifice', l. 115, and 'house of death' for 'houre of death' in 'Mortification', l. 18, and the argument of 'Man' seems to require the reading of *W*, 'He is a tree, yet bears more fruit.'[1] The chief value of *W* is to corroborate the readings of *B* where they differ from 1633,

[1] See further, p. 508.

or to support 1633 where it has corrected a slip of *B*; it is also useful for checking the rather capricious and defective punctuation of *B*.

The relation of the *editio princeps* to *B* must next be considered. Was the type set up from this manuscript, the primary purpose of which was to procure the university licence for printing? Dr. Percy Simpson doubts whether the printer had the use of the licensers' copy because it is 'spotless'.[1] His authority carries great weight, but I think it not inconceivable that, if this fine copy were put in the compositor's hand with an injunction to treat it with special care, it might escape injury. It was not unusual for a licenser's copy to be used by the printer; Miss Helen Darbishire maintains that the manuscript of Book I of *Paradise Lost*, now in the Pierpont Morgan Library, which bears the licensers' Imprimatur, 'was used by the printer for setting up his type for the first edition'.[2] I dismiss the possibility that the 'little book' was used by the printer, since, if it at all resembled the other small manuscript (*W*) in the number and small writing of its corrections, it would have been less fit for printer's copy than *B*. I am also a little unwilling to suppose that the Gidding community prepared a special copy for the printer as well as the one for the licensers, even if the licensers might not take exception to the printer using a text other than the one which they had licensed. I am more concerned by the time it would involve. Duncon received the 'little book' from Herbert 'about three Weeks before his death',[3] which took place on 1 March 1632/3. Within that year there have to be crowded many events, each of which would occupy considerable time: the making of a fair copy, or even of two, the negotiations with the licensers, when the Vice-Chancellor, only 'after some time',[4] withdrew his objection to the lines about religion passing 'to the *American* strand', the negotiations with the printer, the setting up of the type and the proof-reading, which was done with exemplary care, and—still

[1] *Proof Reading in the Sixteenth and Seventeenth Centuries*, pp. 37–8.

[2] *The Manuscript of Milton's Paradise Lost, Book I*, p. ix.

[3] Walton, *Lives*, p. 76.

[4] Ibid. p. 75.

within that year—the production of the second edition with the type reset throughout.

An objection to the view that the printer used *B* is the large number of differences between it and the printed text. The innumerable differences in spelling and punctuation need not greatly affect the question, as the practice of the age would allow this to be the province of the printer, who would follow his own standards. The verbal differences, for the most part consisting of such minor variants as *my*, *dost*, *farther*, for *mine*, *doth*, *further*, amount to less than a hundred: even if such corrections were not made until the proof stage, it would mean only one correction in every other page. There is no need on that score to suppose that the printer was using some copy other than *B*. If, however, a second fair copy was made for the printer, we must suppose it to have been made, like *B*, from the 'little book', and to have been copied not less exactly. In the absence of the 'little book' and of any other copy of it except *B*, we must regard *B* as our highest authority for the author's words and superior to the *editio princeps*, which may include amendments of editor and printer. I have, therefore, scrupulously weighed every difference between *B* and 1633, and have adopted the readings of *B*, unless they are evident slips. I have found as many as twenty-eight such slips, and in all the instances of the kind where an error is suspected and *W* contains the passage, the earlier manuscript is free from the error. Thus in 'Humilitie', l. 29, the word in *B* 'banding' makes the line a syllable too short, and the 'bandying' of 1633 is confirmed by that word being found in *W*. In 'Ungratefulnesse', l. 23, 'Bone' in *B* is corrected to 'box' in 1633, and the latter word is found in *W*. In 'Obedience', l. 2, 'waies' fails to rhyme with 'may', but both *W* and 1633 have 'way' without any loss in meaning; it cannot have been the author's intention to lose the rhyme. Such failures in scansion or rhyme are due, not to the author, but to the copyist. Where the poem or the particular line is not in *W*, the requirements of metre or rhyme will often indicate that *B* is in error; for example, the reading of *B* in 'Self-condemnation', l. 4, 'thine owne state', makes the line a syllable short, and 'thine own estate' in 1633 is clearly right. In 'The Jews', l. 2, 'sinnes' in *B* not only yields no sense but it mars the scansion; probably the copyist failed to recognize the unfamilar word 'cyens', which the editor of 1633 got right. Many of the differences between *B* and 1633 are in themselves unimportant (e.g. 'does' for 'doth'), but I have preferred *B* as being more likely to reproduce the text of Herbert's 'little book'. In no case does the difference go beyond a single word or the use of a different part of the same word (e.g. 'give' for 'gave'), but perhaps in a dozen cases the word found in *B* is more characteristic of Herbert and improves the text (e.g. 'pink' for 'prick' in 'Affliction' IV, l. 12).

While, therefore, the present text follows *B* verbally, except where there is good reason to suspect a mere copyist's error, it remains to justify the following of 1633 in the presentation of the text, so far as the minor details are concerned—spelling, punctuation, use of capitals, and italics. The justification lies both in the deficiencies of *B* and the unusual excellence of 1633. There would be no advantage to the reader in a reproduction of the copyist's spelling vagaries: e.g. *slite*, *the Diety*, *woe* (= woo), *cold* (= could), *on* (= one), *felst* (= feel'st); the more eccentric of such spellings are not found in Herbert's autograph writings and do not represent his own practice. The printer of 1633 adopts the useful distinction between *of* and *off*, *clothes* and *cloths*, and, though less uniformly, between *loose* and *lose*. Initial capitals were freely used by Herbert, but in *B* they are more plentiful than in *W*, and they are there often affixed to unimportant words without any discoverable significance: there can be no real reason for distinguishing 'day and Night', as is done several times in *B*, and capitals have lost any distinction when there are as many as six in a line, e.g. 'Is Clothing, Meat & Trencher, Drink & Can'. When, however, capitals are used in *B* for a title or institution, like 'Lord of Hosts' and 'Court of Rolls', I have restored them. In both manuscripts words intended to be italicized in print are 'distinguished' (to use Professor L. C. Martin's useful term) by being written in larger letters, though it is not always certain that distinction is intended. Distinguishing is used, not only for specially emphatic words, but for spoken sentences and Scriptural quotations, but 1633 is more consistent than the manuscripts in the following of this practice. The punctuation of *B* is often defective: stops necessary to the sense are omitted, and the mark of interrogation is sometimes missing; the vigilant care of the Cambridge printer has made good such omissions, and the punctuation of 1633 is throughout more logical, clear, and consistent. A comparison of *B* with *W* will show that the capricious punctuation of *B* does not represent the author's habit or intention, and, indeed, *W* is often right where *B* is plainly wrong. It should, however, be stated that there are a few important examples of 1633 having missed the sense by departing from the punctuation of *B*; the fifth edition (1638) recovered the true punctuation of 'The Collar', ll. 20–1 ('leave thy cold dispute Of what is fit, and not. Forsake thy cage'), and of 'The Thanksgiving', l. 11, ('skipping thy dolefull storie'). Wherever the punctuation of *B* could be supposed to affect the meaning, it is recorded in the footnotes, but if all the immaterial differences were to be recorded, they would average two to every line of the text. The punctuation of both manuscripts and of 1633 is heavier than the modern practice, but the usage of Herbert's time is admirably exemplified in the Cambridge early editions of *The Temple*. The text of the present edition retains the seventeenth-century practice in spelling and punctuation and in the use of capitals and italics. Herbert clearly attached importance to the intricate metrical patterns of his verse, as may be seen already in *W*, and the printer of 1633 followed his model closely; his mistakes in arranging 'The British Church' in triplets, instead of six-line stanzas, and in printing 'Evensong' in stanzas of four instead of eight lines, are here corrected. In setting out the sonnets I have returned to the general practice of *B* of giving them solid without line-spaces between the quatrains.

The unusually good craftsmanship shown by the Cambridge printer in presenting Herbert's poems to the reader is too valuable to be sacrificed. It was good fortune for *The Temple* to be first printed by Thomas Buck, the best printer that Cambridge had yet had. The lay-out was so obviously right that for the next fourteen editions, that is for seventy-six years, it was unchanged. Buck was a scholar and a lover of good letters. Elected fellow of St. Catherine's in the same year that Herbert became a fellow of Trinity, Buck was appointed printer to the university in 1625. It is true that his partner Leonard Greene, with perhaps forty years' experience of printing and bookselling, mostly in London, spoke of 'Mr. Buck being unexperienced, having lead a student's life', but Buck's influence upon Cambridge printing was at once evident. Whereas in the six years preceding his appointment the Cambridge printers had produced an average of less than two books a year, in the six years following the average rose to seven, and in the years which covered the first four editions of *The Temple* the numbers were 12, 11, and 20. There was also a marked attention to literature; instead of confining themselves to theology, textbooks, and almanacks, they printed in 1632 Thomas Heywood's *England's Elizabeth*, the second edition of Giles Fletcher's *Christs Victorie* and Randolph's *The Iealous Louers*, and next year Phineas Fletcher's *The Purple Island* with a delectable title-page, as well as the first two editions of *The Temple*. Sir Herbert Grierson has described *The Temple* as one of the best edited books of its time;[1] writers have not given Buck his full due for the care which he took, not only with the first edition, but with the next four editions which appeared in his time. These Cambridge editions do not show, as the London editions from 1656 do, a steady deterioration, but a vigilant correction of any remaining defects in punctuation, spacing, and italicizing.[2] In the last edition (the fifth, 1638) for which Buck was responsible the corrections extend beyond typographical details and introduce eight verbal changes, some of which can only be accounted for by the manuscript having been re-examined (e.g. 'where' for 'neare' in 'Affliction' I, l. 47,

[1] *The Year's Work in English Studies*, 1927, viii. 205–7.

[2] For further instances of the printer's vigilance, see the General Note, p. 475.

and 'my great stable' in 'The Quidditie', l. 8). It is possible that this fresh consultation of the manuscript was a last instance of Ferrar's exemplary care shortly before his death, which occurred in the preceding December.

The London editions from 1656, except for an occasional improvement in punctuation, have nothing to teach, and they originate errors which established themselves in subsequent editions and have even affected modern reprints. Walton also, quoting from late editions or from memory, has put into wide circulation departures from the true text; since such errors have passed into common use, it is worth while to record them in the footnotes that their origin and their prevalence may be recognized. It is not, I trust, ungracious to note also the very few oversights in Palmer's text, as scholars will long continue to resort to his admirable commentary. The errors of Grosart are too many to record: I have noted those only which are most misleading, since they continue to circulate in many popular editions.

An editor's business is to present the text as near to the author's intention as he has the means of judging; but this is not identical, in the case of *The Temple*, with a mere reproduction of a copy which the author never saw (*B*), or of the first edition, however much care was bestowed upon it by the original editor and by a scholarly printer. To have lived in close familiarity with the two manuscripts and the first five editions of *The Temple* for now ten years may encourage the present editor to hope that the text, as it is here presented, is nearer to what Herbert intended than what has hitherto appeared. Where his judgements may be at fault, he has at any rate provided in the full collation of the manuscripts and early editions the material for other scholars, and he will be the last to grudge any better use they can make of that material.

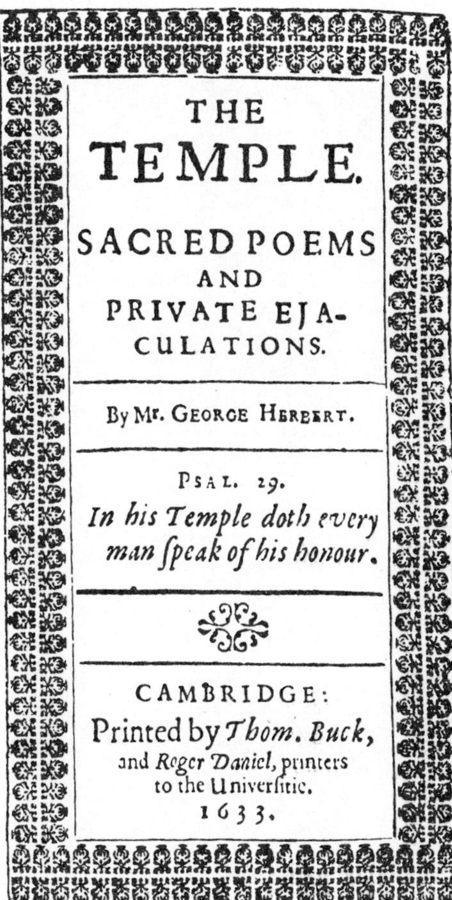

THE

TEMPLE.

SACRED POEMS
AND
PRIVATE EJA-
CULATIONS.

By Mr. George Herbert.

Psal. 29.
In his Temple doth every man ſpeak of his honour.

CAMBRIDGE:
Printed by *Thom. Buck*,
and *Roger Daniel*, printers
to the Univerſitie.
1633.

The Printers to the Reader.

THe dedication of this work having been made by the Authour to the *Divine Majestie* onely, how should we now presume to interest any mortall man in the patronage of it? Much lesse think we it meet to seek the recommendation of the Muses, for that which himself was confident to have been inspired by a diviner breath then flows from *Helicon*. The world therefore shall receive it in that naked simplicitie, with which he left it, without any addition either of support or ornament, more then is included in it self. We leave it free and unforestalled to every mans judgement, and to the benefit that he shall finde by perusall. Onely for the clearing of some passages, we have thought it not unfit to make the common Reader privie to some few particularities of the condition and disposition of the Person;

Being nobly born, and as eminently endued with gifts of the minde, and having by industrie and happy education perfected them to that great height of excellencie, whereof his fellowship of Trinitie Colledge in Cambridge, and his Orator-ship in the Universitie, together with that knowledge which the Kings Court had taken of him, could make relation farre above ordinarie. Quitting both his deserts and all the opportunities that he had for worldly preferment, he betook himself to the Sanctuarie and Temple of God, choosing rather to serve at Gods Altar, then to seek the honour of State-employments. As for those inward enforcements to this course (for outward there was none) which many of these ensuing verses bear witnesse of, they detract not from the freedome, but adde to the honour of this resolution in him. As God had enabled him, so he accounted him meet not onely to be called, but to be compelled to this service: Wherein his faithfull discharge was such, as may make him justly a companion to the primitive Saints, and a pattern or more for the age he lived in.

This preface, not in MSS., is in all printed editions 1633–95   Printers] altered to Printer in 1641 when Daniel's name alone is on title-page.

To testifie his independencie upon all others, and to quicken his diligence in this kinde, he used in his ordinarie speech, when he made mention of the blessed name of our Lord and Saviour Jesus Christ, to adde, *My Master*.

Next God, he loved that which God himself hath magnified above all things, that is, his Word: so as he hath been heard to make solemne protestation, that he would not part with one leaf thereof for the whole world, if it were offered him in exchange.

His obedience and conformitie to the Church and the discipline thereof was singularly remarkable. Though he abounded in private devotions, yet went he every morning and evening with his familie to the Church; and by his example, exhortations, and encouragements drew the greater part of his parishioners to accompanie him dayly in the publick celebration of Divine Service.

As for worldly matters, his love and esteem to them was so little, as no man can more ambitiously seek, then he did earnestly endeavour the resignation of an Ecclesiasticall dignitie, which he was possessour of. But God permitted not the accomplishment of this desire, having ordained him his instrument for reedifying of the Church belonging thereunto, that had layen ruinated almost twenty yeares. The reparation whereof, having been uneffectually attempted by publick collections, was in the end by his own and some few others private free-will-offerings succesfully effected. With the remembrance whereof, as of an especiall good work, when a friend went about to comfort him on his deathbed, he made answer, *It is a good work, if it be sprinkled with the bloud of Christ:* otherwise then in this respect he could finde nothing to glorie or comfort himself with, neither in this, nor in any other thing.

And these are but a few of many that might be said, which we have chosen to premise as a glance to some parts of the ensuing book, and for an example to the Reader. We conclude all with his own Motto, with which he used to

20 possessour] *misprinted* professor *1674–95*, *Pickering 1835* (*but corrected in 2nd edn 1838*) 33 a few] *misprinted* few *1674–95*, *Pickering 1835* (*but corrected in 2nd edn 1838*)

conclude all things that might seem to tend any way to his own honour;

Lesse then the least of Gods mercies.

The Dedication.

LOrd, my first fruits present themselves to thee;
Yet not mine neither: for from thee they came,
And must return. Accept of them and me,
And make us strive, who shall sing best thy name.
Turn their eyes hither, who shall make a gain:
Theirs, who shall hurt themselves or me, refrain.

The Dedication. *On title-page of B; in W, which has no title-page, it stands alone on the first written page; in 1633 it stands alone, with opposite page blank, after* The Printers to the Reader.

The Church-porch.

Perirrhanteriuм

1

THou, whose sweet youth and early hopes inhance
Thy rate and price, and mark thee for a treasure;
Hearken unto a Verser, who may chance
Ryme thee to good, and make a bait of pleasure.
  A verse may finde him, who a sermon flies,
  And turn delight into a sacrifice.

2

Beware of lust: it doth pollute and foul
Whom God in Baptisme washt with his own blood.
It blots thy lesson written in thy soul;
The holy lines cannot be understood.
  How dare those eyes upon a Bible look,
  Much lesse towards God, whose lust is all their book?

The Church-porch. *Used not only as title of poem but as page-heading in B W 1633– to the end of the poem* Perirrhanterium] *letter* h *added with caret in B*: Perirranterium *is found in W, not here, but as title of the 1st quatrain of* Superliminare (*p.* 25) *Numbering of stanzas from B: not in W 1633–* 2 Thy rate and price] The price of thee *W* 7–24 *For earlier version of these 3 stanzas in W see below* 9 thy lesson] the lesson *1638–1809, Pickering* *See note*

7–24

Beware of Lust (startle not) o beware
It makes thy soule a blott: it is a rodd
Whose twigs are pleasures, & they whip thee bare,
It spoils an Angel: robs thee of thy God.
  How dare those eyes vpon a bible looke
  Much lesse towards God, whose Lust is all their book?

Abstaine or wedd: if thou canst not abstaine
Yet wedding marrs thy fortune, fast & pray:
If this seeme Monkish; think wch brings most paine
Need or Incontinency: the first way
  If thou chuse brauely & rely on God
  Hee'le make thy wife a blessing not a rodd.

Let not each fansy make thee to detest
A Virgin-bed, wch hath a speciall Crowne
If it concurr wth vertue: doe thy best
And God will show thee how to take the towne,
  And winne thy selfe: Compare the ioyes & so
  If rottennes haue more, lett Heauen goe. *W*

(l. 19 fansy *substituted by 2nd hand for* motion)

3

Abstain wholly, or wed. Thy bounteous Lord
Allows thee choise of paths: take no by-wayes;
But gladly welcome what he doth afford;
Not grudging, that thy lust hath bounds and staies.
  Continence hath his joy: weigh both; and so
  If rottennesse have more, let Heaven go.

4

If God had laid all common, certainly
Man would have been th' incloser: but since now
God hath impal'd us, on the contrarie
Man breaks the fence, and every ground will plough.
  O what were man, might he himself misplace!
  Sure to be crosse he would shift feet and face.

5

Drink not the third glasse, which thou canst not tame,
When once it is within thee; but before
Mayst rule it, as thou list; and poure the shame,
Which it would poure on thee, upon the floore.
  It is most just to throw that on the ground,
  Which would throw me there, if I keep the round.

6

He that is drunken, may his mother kill
Bigge with his sister: he hath lost the reins,
Is outlawd by himself: all kinde of ill
Did with his liquour slide into his veins.
  The drunkard forfets Man, and doth devest
  All worldly right, save what he hath by beast.

13 Abstain wholly] Wholly abstain *1633^{2}–1809, Pickering, Grosart* 29–30 *W has here the lines which are in B and 1633– at ll. 35–6* 32 the reins] his rains *corr. by 2nd hand to* the rains *W* 33 kinde] kinds *W* 35 devest] divest *1809 Pickering*

35–6 Hee that has all ill, & can haue no good
Because no knowledg, is not earth but mudd. *W*

7

Shall I, to please anothers wine-sprung minde,
Lose all mine own? God hath giv'n me a measure
Short of his canne and bodie; must I finde
A pain in that, wherein he findes a pleasure?
  Stay at the third glasse: if thou lose thy hold,
  Then thou art modest, and the wine grows bold.

8

If reason move not Gallants, quit the room,
(All in a shipwrack shift their severall way)
Let not a common ruine thee intombe:
Be not a beast in courtesie; but stay,
  Stay at the third cup, or forgo the place.
  Wine above all things doth Gods stamp deface.

9

Yet, if thou sinne in wine or wantonnesse,
Boast not thereof; nor make thy shame thy glorie.
Frailtie gets pardon by submissivenesse;
But he that boasts, shuts that out of his storie.
  He makes flat warre with God, and doth defie
  With his poore clod of earth the spacious sky.

10

Take not his name, who made thy mouth, in vain:
It gets thee nothing, and hath no excuse.
Lust and wine plead a pleasure, avarice gain:
But the cheap swearer through his open sluce
  Lets his soul runne for nought, as little fearing.
  Were I an *Epicure*, I could bate swearing.

38 Lose] Loose *B W* (*as generally, e.g. ll. 41, 174, 194, 201, 202, but at l. 143* Loose *is corrected to* Lose *in B*)   39 canne (cann) *W 1635–* : canne, *B 1633–4*   40 in] of *corr. to* in *W*   44 shipwreck *1799–1809, Pickering*   56 hath] has *W*   57 avarice] cheating, *W*

11

When thou dost tell anothers jest, therein
Omit the oathes, which true wit cannot need:
Pick out of tales the mirth, but not the sinne.
He pares his apple, that will cleanly feed.
Play not away the vertue of that name,
Which is thy best stake, when griefs make thee tame.

12

The cheapest sinnes most dearely punisht are;
Because to shun them also is so cheap:
For we have wit to mark them, and to spare.
O crumble not away thy souls fair heap.
If thou wilt die, the gates of hell are broad:
Pride and full sinnes have made the way a road.

13

Lie not; but let thy heart be true to God,
Thy mouth to it, thy actions to them both:
Cowards tell lies, and those that fear the rod;
The stormie working soul spits lies and froth.
Dare to be true. Nothing can need a ly:
A fault, which needs it most, grows two thereby.

14

Flie idlenesse, which yet thou canst not flie
By dressing, mistressing, and complement.
If those take up thy day, the sunne will crie
Against thee: for his light was onely lent.
God gave thy soul brave wings; put not those feathers
Into a bed, to sleep out all ill weathers.

61 dost] doest *B* 64 apple] *Palmer misreads B as* apples 66 thy] the *1667–1799, Willmott, Grosart* 81 take up] bee all *W*

15

Art thou a Magistrate? then be severe:
If studious, copie fair, what time hath blurr'd;
Redeem truth from his jawes: if souldier,
Chase brave employments with a naked sword
  Throughout the world. Fool not: for all may have,
  If they dare try, a glorious life, or grave.

16

O England! full of sinne, but most of sloth;
Spit out thy flegme, and fill thy brest with glorie:
Thy Gentrie bleats, as if thy native cloth
Transfus'd a sheepishnesse into thy storie:
  Not that they all are so; but that the most
  Are gone to grasse, and in the pasture lost.

17

This losse springs chiefly from our education.
Some till their ground, but let weeds choke their sonne:
Some mark a partridge, never their childes fashion:
Some ship them over, and the thing is done.
  Studie this art, make it thy great designe;
  And if Gods image move thee not, let thine.

18

Some great estates provide, but doe not breed
A mast'ring minde; so both are lost thereby:
Or els they breed them tender, make them need
All that they leave: this is flat povertie.
  For he, that needs five thousand pound to live,
  Is full as poore as he, that needs but five.

86 studious, *B 1633*[2]–: studious; *W 1633* 87 jawes] chawes *corr. to* Iawes *B*: chawes W (*cf.* Providence, *l. 139*, *and* Ezek. xxix. 4 *in* A.V., 1611) 88 employments] employment *W* 91 *Between stanzas* 15 *and* 16, *as above*, *W has this stanza*:

If thou art nothing, think what thou wouldst bee
Hee that desires is more then halfe y[e] way.
But if thou coole, then take some shame to thee
Desire and shame, will make thy labour, play:
  This is Earth's language, for if Heauen come in,
  Thou hast run all thy race, ere thou beginn.

91 O England, full of all sinn, most of sloth, *W* 95 all are] are all *W* 106 they leave] is left *W*

19

The way to make thy sonne rich is to fill
His minde with rest, before his trunk with riches:
For wealth without contentment climbes a hill
To feel those tempests, which fly over ditches.
But if thy sonne can make ten pound his measure,
Then all thou addest may be call'd his treasure.

20

When thou dost purpose ought within thy power,
Be sure to doe it, though it be but small:
Constancie knits the bones, and makes us stowre,
When wanton pleasures becken us to thrall.
Who breaks his own bond, forfeiteth himself:
What nature made a ship, he makes a shelf.

21

Doe all things like a man, not sneakingly:
Think the king sees thee still; for his King does.
Simpring is but a lay-hypocrisie:
Give it a corner, and the clue undoes.
Who fears to do ill, sets himself to task:
Who fears to do well, sure should wear a mask.

22

Look to thy mouth; diseases enter there.
Thou hast two sconses, if thy stomack call;
Carve, or discourse; do not a famine fear.
Who carves, is kind to two; who talks, to all.
Look on meat, think it dirt, then eat a bit;
And say withall, Earth to earth I commit.

109 rich *B*: rich, *W 1633–* 110 trunk] trunks *W* 111 contentment *B W*: contentment, *1633–* 115 dost] doest *B* ought within thy power, *B W* (powre *without comma in W*) *1641–60*: ought, (within thy power) *1633–8* 117 stowre] sowre *B W*: tower *1674–1809* *See note* 120 And though hee bee a ship, is his owne shelf. *W* 125 fears] *Palmer misreads W as* fearest 128 Tast all, but feed not. If thy stomach call *W* 132 And] But *W*

23

Slight those who say amidst their sickly healths,
Thou liv'st by rule. What doth not so, but man?
Houses are built by rule, and common-wealths.
Entice the trusty sunne, if that thou can,
  From his Ecliptick line: becken the skie.
  Who lives by rule then, keeps good companie.

24

Who keeps no guard upon himself, is slack,
And rots to nothing at the next great thaw.
Man is a shop of rules, a well truss'd pack,
Whose every parcell under-writes a law.
  Lose not thy self, nor give thy humours way:
  God gave them to thee under lock and key.

25

By all means use sometimes to be alone.
Salute thy self: see what thy soul doth wear.
Dare to look in thy chest, for 'tis thine own:
And tumble up and down what thou find'st there.
  Who cannot rest till hee good-fellows finde,
  He breaks up house, turns out of doores his minde.

26

Be thriftie, but not covetous: therefore give
Thy need, thine honour, and thy friend his due.
Never was scraper brave man. Get to live;
Then live, and use it: els, it is not true
  That thou hast gotten. Surely use alone
  Makes money not a contemptible stone.

134 doth] does *W* 136 thou *W*: you *B 1633–* 143 Lose] Loose *corr. to* Lose *B*: Loose *W* 147 chest, *B W*: chest; *1633–* 149 good-fellows *B*: *no hyphen* *W 1633–* 151 cou'etous *W* 154 not] most *corr. to* not *B*

27

Never exceed thy income. Youth may make
Ev'n with the yeare: but age, if it will hit,
Shoots a bow short, and lessens still his stake,
As the day lessens, and his life with it.
  Thy children, kindred, friends upon thee call;
  Before thy journey fairly part with all.

28

Yet in thy thriving still misdoubt some evil;
Lest gaining gain on thee, and make thee dimme
To all things els. Wealth is the conjurers devil;
Whom when he thinks he hath, the devil hath him.
  Gold thou mayst safely touch; but if it stick
  Unto thy hands, it woundeth to the quick.

29

What skills it, if a bag of stones or gold
About thy neck do drown thee? raise thy head;
Take starres for money; starres not to be told
By any art, yet to be purchased.
  None is so wastefull as the scraping dame.
  She loseth three for one; her soul, rest, fame.

30

By no means runne in debt: take thine own measure.
Who cannot live on twentie pound a yeare,
Cannot on fourtie: he's a man of pleasure,
A kinde of thing that's for it self too deere.
  The curious unthrift makes his clothes too wide,
  And spares himself, but would his taylor chide.

163–8
Yett in thy pursing still thy self distrust
Least gaining gaine on thee, & fill thy hart
Wch if it cleaue to coine, one common rust
Will canker both, yett thou alone shallt smart:
  One common waight will press downe both, yet so
  As that thy self alone to hell shalt goe. *W*

(*l.* 168 shall *corr. to* shalt)

164 Lest] Least *B W* (*so generally in the MSS. for the conjunction* lest: *later instances are not recorded*) 178 it] its *B* 179 clothes *W 1638–, Pickering*: cloth *corr. to* cloths (*the* s *written above the line, for want of space before* too) *B*: cloth *1633–5, Willmott, Grosart, Palmer*

31

Spend not on hopes. They that by pleading clothes
Do fortunes seek, when worth and service fail,
Would have their tale beleeved for their oathes,
And are like empty vessels under sail.
  Old courtiers know this; therefore set out so,
  As all the day thou mayst hold out to go.

32

In clothes, cheap handsomnesse doth bear the bell.
Wisedome's a trimmer thing then shop e're gave.
Say not then, This with that lace will do well;
But, This with my discretion will be brave.
  Much curiousnesse is a perpetuall wooing,
  Nothing with labour, folly long a-doing.

33

Play not for gain, but sport Who playes for more
Then he can lose with pleasure, stakes his heart;
Perhaps his wives too, and whom she hath bore:
Servants and churches also play their part.
  Onely a herauld, who that way doth passe,
  Findes his crackt name at length in the church-glasse.

34

If yet thou love game at so deere a rate,
Learn this, that hath old gamesters deerely cost:
Dost lose? rise up: dost winne? rise in that state.
Who strive to sit out losing hands, are lost.
  Game is a civil gunpowder, in peace
  Blowing up houses with their whole increase.

181 clothes] cloths *B W* (*often for* clothes: *cf. ll.* 187, 372) 186 As] That *W* 188 thing *W 1638*–: thing, *B 1633–5* 191 wooing, *B 1674*–: wooing: *W*: wooing *1633–67* 192 labour, *B* 1633^{2}–: labour: *W*: labour; *1633* a-doing *B*: *no hyphen W 1633*– 193 more *W* 1633^{2}–: more, *B 1633* 195 wives] Wifes (*or* Wife's) *1678*– 200 that] it *corr. by 2nd hand to* that *W* 201 Dost . . . dost] Doest . . . doest *W*

35

In conversation boldnesse now bears sway.
But know, that nothing can so foolish be,
As empty boldnesse: therefore first assay
To stuffe thy minde with solid braverie;
Then march on gallant: get substantiall worth.
Boldnesse guilds finely, and will set it forth.

36

Be sweet to all. Is thy complexion sowre?
Then keep such companie; make them thy allay:
Get a sharp wife, a servant that will lowre.
A stumbler stumbles least in rugged way.
Command thy self in chief. He lifes warre knows,
Whom all his passions follow, as he goes.

37

Catch not at quarrels. He that dares not speak
Plainly and home, is coward of the two.
Think not thy fame at ev'ry twitch will break:
By great deeds shew, that thou canst little do;
And do them not: that shall thy wisdome be;
And change thy temperance into braverie.

38

If that thy fame with ev'ry toy be pos'd,
'Tis a thinne webbe, which poysonous fancies make:
But the great souldiers honour was compos'd
Of thicker stuffe, which would endure a shake.
Wisdome picks friends; civilitie playes the rest.
A toy shunn'd cleanly passeth with the best.

39

Laugh not too much: the wittie man laughs least:
For wit is newes onely to ignorance.
Lesse at thine own things laugh; lest in the jest
Thy person share, and the conceit advance.
Make not thy sport, abuses: for the fly
That feeds on dung, is coloured thereby.

225 compos'd] composed *corr. to* compos'd *B* 228 passeth with the best] is fames interest *W* 232 the conceit advance] thou thy mirth inhanse *W*

40

Pick out of mirth, like stones out of thy ground,
Profanenesse, filthinesse, abusivenesse.
These are the scumme, with which course wits abound:
The fine may spare these well, yet not go lesse.
  All things are bigge with jest: nothing that's plain,
  But may be wittie, if thou hast the vein.

41

Wit's an unruly engine, wildly striking
Sometimes a friend, sometimes the engineer.
Hast thou the knack? pamper it not with liking:
But if thou want it, buy it not too deere.
  Many, affecting wit beyond their power,
  Have got to be a deare fool for an houre.

42

A sad wise valour is the brave complexion,
That leads the van, and swallows up the cities.
The gigler is a milk-maid, whom infection
Or a fir'd beacon frighteth from his ditties.
  Then he's the sport: the mirth then in him rests,
  And the sad man is cock of all his jests.

43

Towards great persons use respective boldnesse:
That temper gives them theirs, and yet doth take
Nothing from thine: in service, care or coldnesse
Doth ratably thy fortunes marre or make.
  Feed no man in his sinnes: for adulation
  Doth make thee parcell-devil in damnation.

44

Envie not greatnesse: for thou mak'st thereby
Thy self the worse, and so the distance greater.
Be not thine own worm: yet such jealousie,
As hurts not others, but may make thee better,
  Is a good spurre. Correct thy passions spite;
  Then may the beasts draw thee to happy light.

245 Many, *B*: Many *1633–*   249 infection *no comma W 1634–*: *comma B 1633* 1633^{2} 253 respective] respectfull *W*   255 care *no comma W 1634–*: *comma B 1633* 1633^{2}

45

When basenesse is exalted, do not bate
The place its honour, for the persons sake.
The shrine is that which thou dost venerate,
And not the beast, that bears it on his back.
  I care not though the cloth of state should be
  Not of rich arras, but mean tapestrie.

46

Thy friend put in thy bosome: wear his eies
Still in thy heart, that he may see what's there.
If cause require, thou art his sacrifice;
Thy drops of bloud must pay down all his fear:
  But love is lost, the way of friendship 's gone,
  Though *David* had his *Jonathan*, *Christ* his *John*.

47

Yet be not surety, if thou be a father.
Love is a personall debt. I cannot give
My childrens right, nor ought he take it: rather
Both friends should die, then hinder them to live.
  Fathers first enter bonds to natures ends;
  And are her sureties, ere they are a friends.

48

If thou be single, all thy goods and ground
Submit to love; but yet not more then all.
Give one estate, as one life. None is bound
To work for two, who brought himself to thrall.
  God made me one man; love makes me no more,
  Till labour come, and make my weaknesse score.

265 basenesse is] base men are *W*   266 its] it's *W*   267 venerate, *B*: venerate *W*: venerate; *1633–*   275 lost, *B W 1634–* : lost; *1633 1633*[2] way] art *W*   286 who] that *W*

49

In thy discourse, if thou desire to please,
All such is courteous, usefull, new, or wittie.
Usefulnesse comes by labour, wit by ease;
Courtesie grows in court; news in the citie.
  Get a good stock of these, then draw the card
  That suites him best, of whom thy speech is heard.

50

Entice all neatly to what they know best;
For so thou dost thy self and him a pleasure:
(But a proud ignorance will lose his rest,
Rather then shew his cards.) Steal from his treasure
  What to ask further. Doubts well rais'd do lock
  The speaker to thee, and preserve thy stock.

51

If thou be Master-gunner, spend not all
That thou canst speak, at once; but husband it,
And give men turns of speech: do not forestall
By lavishnesse thine own, and others wit,
  As if thou mad'st thy will. A civil guest
  Will no more talk all, then eat all the feast.

52

Be calm in arguing: for fiercenesse makes
Errour a fault, and truth discourtesie.
Why should I feel another mans mistakes
More then his sicknesses or povertie?
  In love I should: but anger is not love,
  Nor wisdome neither: therefore gently move.

289 please, *1634–* : please *W*: please: *B 1633 1633*^{2} 292 in court] at Court *W* 293 card *W*: Card, *B*: card; *1633* 298 cards.) Steal *Ed*: cards) steale *B W*: cards) steal *1633–* 299 further] farther *W* (*cf.* The Sacrifice, *l. 245*) 308 truth discourtesie] truth a discourtesy *B* 310 More *W 1634–* : More, *B 1633 1633*^{2}

53

Calmnesse is great advantage: he that lets
Another chafe, may warm him at his fire,
Mark all his wandrings, and enjoy his frets;
As cunning fencers suffer heat to tire.
  Truth dwels not in the clouds: the bow that's there
  Doth often aim at, never hit the sphere.

54

Mark what another sayes: for many are
Full of themselves, and answer their own notion.
Take all into thee; then with equall care
Ballance each dramme of reason, like a potion.
  If truth be with thy friend, be with them both:
  Share in the conquest, and confesse a troth.

55

Be usefull where thou livest, that they may
Both want and wish thy pleasing presence still.
Kindnesse, good parts, great places are the way
To compasse this. Finde out mens wants and will,
  And meet them there. All worldly joyes go lesse
  To the one joy of doing kindnesses.

56

Pitch thy behaviour low, thy projects high;
So shalt thou humble and magnanimous be:
Sink not in spirit: who aimeth at the sky,
Shoots higher much then he that means a tree.
  A grain of glorie mixt with humblenesse
  Cures both a fever and lethargicknesse.

314 fire, *B W* 1633^2–: fire : *1633* 317 there *B 1638*–: there, *1633–5*
317–18 the bow . . . sphere.] that Bow doth hitt
No more then passion when shee talkes of it. *W*
326 want 1633^2– : want, *B 1633* Need & bee glad, & wish thy presence still : *W* 329 worldly] wordly *W* 330 the] that *W* 336 lethargicknesse] a drowsines *W*

57

Let thy minde still be bent, still plotting where,
And when, and how the businesse may be done.
Slacknesse breeds worms; but the sure traveller,
Though he alight sometimes, still goeth on.
  Active and stirring spirits live alone.
  Write on the others, Here lies such a one.

58

Slight not the smallest losse, whether it be
In love or honour: take account of all;
Shine like the sunne in every corner: see
Whether thy stock of credit swell, or fall.
  Who say, I care not, those I give for lost;
  And to instruct them, will not quit the cost.

59

Scorn no mans love, though of a mean degree;
Love is a present for a mightie king.
Much lesse make any one thy enemie.
As gunnes destroy, so may a little sling.
  The cunning workman never doth refuse
  The meanest tool, that he may chance to use.

60

All forrain wisdome doth amount to this,
To take all that is given; whether wealth,
Or love, or language; nothing comes amisse:
A good digestion turneth all to health:
  And then as farre as fair behaviour may,
  Strike off all scores; none are so cleare as they.

337 thy] thine *corr. to* thy *B* (*cf. l. 361*)   343 whether] whither *W* (*cf. ll. 346, 356, &c.: later instances are not recorded*)   347 those I give] I give those *corr. by 2nd hand to* those I give *W*   lost] gone *W*   348 will *B 1638–67 1809*: 'twill *1633–5 1674–1799*   They dye in holes where glory never shone. *W*   350 *bracketed 1633–, but not in B W*   a mightie king] ye greatest king *W*   351 thy *B W*: thine *1633–*   352 As swords cause death, so may a little sting. *W*   360 off] of *B W* (*later instances are not recorded unless there is a possible ambiguity: see General Note, p.* 475)

61

Keep all thy native good, and naturalize
All forrain of that name; but scorn their ill:
Embrace their activenesse, not vanities.
Who follows all things, forfeiteth his will.
  If thou observest strangers in each fit,
  In time they'l runne thee out of all thy wit.

62

Affect in things about thee cleanlinesse,
That all may gladly board thee, as a flowre.
Slovens take up their stock of noisomnesse
Beforehand, and anticipate their last houre.
  Let thy mindes sweetnesse have his operation
  Upon thy body, clothes, and habitation.

63

In Almes regard thy means, and others merit.
Think heav'n a better bargain, then to give
Onely thy single market-money for it.
Joyn hands with God to make a man to live.
  Give to all something; to a good poore man,
  Till thou change names, and be where he began.

64

Man is Gods image; but a poore man is
Christs stamp to boot: both images regard.
God reckons for him, counts the favour his:
Write, So much giv'n to God; thou shalt be heard.
  Let thy almes go before, and keep heav'ns gate
  Open for thee; or both may come too late.

361 thy] thine *corr. to* thy *B*

367–70 Leave not thine owne deere-cuntry-cleanlines
ffor this ffrench sluttery wch so currant goes:
As if none could bee brave, but who profess
ffirst to bee Slovens, & forsake their nose. *W*

(*A rough cross is inserted at the top of this stanza in W, perhaps indicating that the author intended to revise it*)

384 both] they *W*

65

Restore to God his due in tithe and time:
A tithe purloin'd cankers the whole estate.
Sundaies observe: think when the bells do chime,
'Tis angels musick; therefore come not late.
  God then deals blessings: If a king did so,
  Who would not haste, nay give, to see the show?

66

Twice on the day his due is understood;
For all the week thy food so oft he gave thee.
Thy cheere is mended; bate not of the food,
Because 'tis better, and perhaps may save thee.
  Thwart not the Mighty God: O be not crosse.
  Fast when thou wilt but then, 'tis gain not losse.

67

Though private prayer be a brave designe,
Yet publick hath more promises, more love:
And love's a weight to hearts, to eies a signe.
We all are but cold suitours; let us move
  Where it is warmest. Leave thy six and seven;
  Pray with the most: for where most pray, is heaven.

68

When once thy foot enters the church, be bare.
God is more there, then thou: for thou art there
Onely by his permission. Then beware,
And make thy self all reverence and fear.
  Kneeling ne're spoil'd silk stocking: quit thy state.
  All equall are within the churches gate.

391 the] that *W*   395 ye Mighty *B* : ye mighty *W* : th'Almighty *1633–* *See note*   396 ffast when thou wilt but then, tis gain not loss. *W* : Fast when thou wilt, but then 'tis gaine, not losse. *B* : Fast when thou wilt; but then 'tis gain, not losse. *1633–8* : wilt, but *then; 1641* *See note*   398 hath] has *W*   407 silk stocking] silk-stockings *W* (*for the hyphen cf.* The Pearl *l. 38*, silk-twist *W*)

69

Resort to sermons, but to prayers most:
Praying 's the end of preaching. O be drest;
Stay not for th' other pin: why, thou hast lost
A joy for it worth worlds. Thus hell doth jest
  Away thy blessings, and extreamly flout thee,
  Thy clothes being fast, but thy soul loose about thee.

70

In time of service seal up both thine eies,
And send them to thine heart; that spying sinne,
They may weep out the stains by them did rise:
Those doores being shut, all by the eare comes in.
  Who marks in church-time others symmetrie,
  Makes all their beautie his deformitie.

71

Let vain or busie thoughts have there no part:
Bring not thy plough, thy plots, thy pleasures thither.
Christ purg'd his temple; so must thou thy heart.
All worldly thoughts are but theeves met together
  To couzin thee. Look to thy actions well:
  For churches are either our heav'n or hell.

72

Judge not the preacher; for he is thy Judge:
If thou mislike him, thou conceiv'st him not.
God calleth preaching folly. Do not grudge
To pick out treasures from an earthen pot.
  The worst speak something good: if all want sense,
  God takes a text, and preacheth patience.

411 why, *1633*[2]– : why *B W 1633* 413 Away thy blessings] Our blessings from vs *W* 416 thine] thy *W 1674–1809, Pickering, Grosart* 419 symmetrie] comlines *W* 420 Turns all their beauty to his vglines. *W* 421 or] & *W* : and *Grosart* 426 are either] either are *W 1678–1809, Pickering, Willmott*

73

He that gets patience, and the blessing which
Preachers conclude with, hath not lost his pains.
He that by being at church escapes the ditch,
Which he might fall in by companions, gains.
  He that loves Gods abode, and to combine
  With saints on earth, shall one day with them shine.

74

Jest not at preachers language, or expression:
How know'st thou, but thy sinnes made him miscarrie?
Then turn thy faults and his into confession:
God sent him, whatsoe're he be: O tarry,
  And love him for his Master: his condition,
  Though it be ill, makes him no ill Physician.

75

None shall in hell such bitter pangs endure,
As those, who mock at Gods way of salvation.
Whom oil and balsames kill, what salve can cure?
They drink with greedinesse a full damnation.
  The Jews refused thunder; and we, folly.
  Though God do hedge us in, yet who is holy?

76

Summe up at night, what thou hast done by day;
And in the morning, what thou hast to do.
Dresse and undresse thy soul: mark the decay
And growth of it: if with thy watch, that too
  Be down, then winde up both; since we shall be
  Most surely judg'd, make thy accounts agree.

77

In brief, acquit thee bravely; play the man.
Look not on pleasures as they come, but go.
Deferre not the least vertue: lifes poore span
Make not an ell, by trifling in thy wo.
  If thou do ill; the joy fades, not the pains:
  If well; the pain doth fade, the joy remains.

441 faults] fault *W*   447 balsames] mercies *W*   451 by day] y^{t} day *W*

THou, whom the former precepts have
Sprinkled and taught, how to behave
Thy self in church; approach, and taste
The churches mysticall repast.

AVoid, Profanenesse; come not here:
Nothing but holy, pure, and cleare,
Or that which groneth to be so,
May at his perill further go.

Superliminare. *W gives the first quatrain on a page to itself with title* Perirranterium, *and the second on the opposite page with title* Superliminare ; *neither page has a page-heading. B has both quatrains, with a double line dividing them, on the same page, with* Superliminare *for page-heading and no titles to the quatrains. 1633 has both quatrains, with a line dividing them, on the same page, with title* Superliminare *above the first, and no page-heading. For the engravings in editions from 1674 see note; 1799 omits engravings and both quatrains* 5 Avoid, *Grosart, Palmer*: Avoid *B W 1633– See note* Profanenesse *cap. from B W*

The Altar.

A broken A L T A R, Lord, thy servant reares,
Made of a heart, and cemented with teares:
Whose parts are as thy hand did frame;
No workmans tool hath touch'd the same.
A H E A R T alone
Is such a stone,
As nothing but
Thy pow'r doth cut.
Wherefore each part
Of my hard heart
Meets in this frame,
To praise thy Name:
That, if I chance to hold my peace,
These stones to praise thee may not cease.
O let thy blessed S A C R I F I C E be mine,
And sanctifie this A L T A R to be thine.

The Sacrifice.

O*H all ye*, *who passe by*, whose eyes and minde
To worldly things are sharp, but to me blinde;
To me, who took eyes that I might you finde:
Was ever grief like mine?

The Princes of my people make a head
Against their Maker: they do wish me dead,
Who cannot wish, except I give them bread:
Was ever grief like mine?

From here to the page preceding The Church Militant *the page-heading in both MSS. and* 1633 *is* The Church. The Altar. *1799 omits this poem. For the frames or engravings in editions from 1634 see note* 8 pow'r] *both dated and undated copies of the first edition vary between* pow'r *and* power : power *B* : powre *W* 12 Name. *B* : name *W* : name. *1633* : name: *1633*^{2}– 13 That, *B 1634*– : That *W 1633 1633*^{2} 15 blessed] onely *corr. by 2nd hand to* blessed *W*

The Sacrifice. 1 '*who passe by*' *italicized 1633*^{2}– (*as l. 201 in 1633*): *roman 1633*: *no words in this line are distinguished in B W* 4, 8 &c. *The refrain is italicized 1633*^{2}– , *but it is not distinguished in B W*

The Altar.

A broken ALTAR, Lord, thy servant reares,
Made of a heart, and cemented with teares:
Whose parts are as thy hand did frame;
No workmans tool hath touch'd the same.
A HEART alone
Is such a stone,
As nothing but
Thy pow'r doth cut.
Wherefore each part
Of my hard heart
Meets in this frame,
To praise thy name.
That if I chance to hold my peace,
These stones to praise thee may not cease.
O let thy blessed SACRIFICE be mine,
And sanctifie this ALTAR to be thine.

The

'The Altar' from p. 18 of the dated first edition of *The Temple* (Mr. A. E. Newton's copy)

Without me each one, who doth now me brave,
Had to this day been an Egyptian slave.
They use that power against me, which I gave:
Was ever grief like mine?

Mine own Apostle, who the bag did beare,
Though he had all I had, did not forbeare
To sell me also, and to put me there:
Was ever grief, &c.

For thirtie pence he did my death devise,
Who at three hundred did the ointment prize,
Not half so sweet as my sweet sacrifice:
Was ever grief, &c.

Therefore my soul melts, and my hearts deare treasure
Drops bloud (the onely beads) my words to measure:
O let this cup passe, if it be thy pleasure:
Was ever grief, &c.

These drops being temper'd with a sinners tears
A Balsome are for both the Hemispheres:
Curing all wounds, but mine; all, but my fears:
Was ever grief, &c.

Yet my Disciples sleep: I cannot gain
One houre of watching; but their drowsie brain
Comforts not me, and doth my doctrine stain:
Was ever grief, &c.

Arise, arise, they come. Look how they runne!
Alas! what haste they make to be undone!
How with their lanterns do they seek the sunne!
Was ever grief, &c.

With clubs and staves they seek me, as a thief,
Who am the Way and Truth, the true relief;
Most true to those, who are my greatest grief:
Was ever grief, &c.

25 teares *B W*: tears, *1633–* 33 runne! *1634–* : runne? *B* (*which often has question-mark for exclamation*): runn. *W*: runne. *1633* 1633^2 38 Way and Truth *Ed*: way & Truth *B W* (*cf. l. 179*): way of truth *1633–67*: way of Truth *1674–1809* *See note*

Judas, dost thou betray me with a kisse?
Canst thou finde hell about my lips? and misse
Of life, just at the gates of life and blisse?
Was ever grief like mine?

See, they lay hold on me, not with the hands
Of faith, but furie: yet at their commands
I suffer binding, who have loos'd their bands:
Was ever grief, &c.

All my Disciples flie; fear puts a barre
Betwixt my friends and me. They leave the starre,
That brought the wise men of the East from farre.
Was ever grief, &c.

Then from one ruler to another bound
They leade me; urging, that it was not sound
What I taught: Comments would the text confound.
Was ever grief, &c.

The Priest and rulers all false witnesse seek
'Gainst him, who seeks not life, but is the meek
And readie Paschal Lambe of this great week:
Was ever grief, &c.

Then they accuse me of great blasphemie,
That I did thrust into the Deitie,
Who never thought that any robberie:
Was ever grief, &c.

Some said, that I the Temple to the floore
In three dayes raz'd, and raised as before.
Why, he that built the world can do much more:
Was ever grief, &c.

Then they condemne me all with that same breath,
Which I do give them daily, unto death.
Thus *Adam* my first breathing rendereth:
Was ever grief, &c.

46 Commande *B* (*a slip*) 49 flie] flee *1634–* , *Pickering* 50 the] y^{t} *W* 54 that] that *inserted by 2nd hand with caret in W* 57 Priest] Priests *W 1674–1809*, *Pickering*, *Willmott* *See note* 69–70 with that . . . daily] *bracketed W*

They binde, and leade me unto *Herod:* he
Sends me to *Pilate*. This makes them agree;
But yet their friendship is my enmitie:
Was ever grief like mine?

Herod and all his bands do set me light,
Who teach all hands to warre, fingers to fight,
And onely am the Lord of Hosts and might:
Was ever grief, &c.

Herod in judgement sits, while I do stand;
Examines me with a censorious hand:
I him obey, who all things else command:
Was ever grief, &c.

The *Jews* accuse me with despitefulnesse;
And vying malice with my gentlenesse,
Pick quarrels with their onely happinesse:
Was ever grief, &c.

I answer nothing, but with patience prove
If stonie hearts will melt with gentle love.
But who does hawk at eagles with a dove?
Was ever grief, &c.

My silence rather doth augment their crie;
My dove doth back into my bosome flie,
Because the raging waters still are high:
Was ever grief, &c.

Heark how they crie aloud still, *Crucifie:*
It is not fit he live a day, they crie,
Who cannot live lesse then eternally:
Was ever grief, &c.

Pilate, a stranger, holdeth off; but they,
Mine owne deare people, cry, *Away*, *away*,
With noises confused frighting the day:
Was ever grief, &c.

79 To whose powre Thunder is but weake and slight *struck through and corr. by 2nd hand to line as above W* Hosts *B W* (*distinguished in B but not in W*): hosts *1633–* 101 *Pilate,* a stranger, *commas 1634– : no commas B W 1633 1633*[2]
103 frighting] *Palmer misreads B as* fighting

Yet still they shout, and crie, and stop their eares,
Putting my life among their sinnes and fears,
And therefore wish *my bloud on them and theirs:*
Was ever grief like mine?

See how spite cankers things. These words aright
Used, and wished, are the whole worlds light:
But hony is their gall, brightnesse their night:
Was ever grief, &c.

They choose a murderer, and all agree
In him to do themselves a courtesie:
For it was their own case who killed me:
Was ever grief, &c.

And a seditious murderer he was:
But I the Prince of peace; peace that doth passe
All understanding, more then heav'n doth glasse:
Was ever grief, &c.

Why, Cæsar is their onely King, not I:
He clave the stonie rock, when they were drie;
But surely not their hearts, as I well trie:
Was ever grief, &c.

Ah! how they scourge me! yet my tendernesse
Doubles each lash: and yet their bitternesse
Windes up my grief to a mysteriousnesse:
Was ever grief, &c.

They buffet him, and box him as they list,
Who grasps the earth and heaven with his fist,
And never yet, whom he would punish, miss'd:
Was ever grief, &c.

107 wish] with *Grosart, Gibson, Palmer See note* 110 wished] *misprinted* wish'd *Pickering* 115 case *W* : cause *B 1633– See note* 119 more, then Heaven, glass *W* 121 Cæsar *B 1674–1799* : Cesar *W 1633–67* 123 But not their harts, as I by proofe doe try. *W* well] will *corr. to* well *B* 129 him (*bis*) *B W* : me *1633– See note* 130 grasps *B* : graspes *W* : grasp *1633–* with] in *corr. by 2nd hand with caret to* wth *W* his *B W* : my *1633–* 131 he *B W* : I *1633–*

Behold, they spit on me in scornfull wise,
Who by my spittle gave the blinde man eies,
Leaving his blindnesse to my enemies:
Was ever grief like mine?

My face they cover, though it be divine.
As *Moses* face was vailed, so is mine,
Lest on their double-dark souls either shine:
Was ever grief, &c.

Servants and abjects flout me; they are wittie:
Now prophesie who strikes thee, is their dittie.
So they in me denie themselves all pitie:
Was ever grief, &c.

And now I am deliver'd unto death,
Which each one calls for so with utmost breath,
That he before me well nigh suffereth:
Was ever grief, &c.

Weep not, deare friends, since I for both have wept
When all my tears were bloud, the while you slept:
Your tears for your own fortunes should be kept:
Was ever grief, &c.

The souldiers lead me to the Common Hall;
There they deride me, they abuse me all:
Yet for twelve heav'nly legions I could call:
Was ever grief, &c.

Then with a scarlet robe they me aray;
Which shews my bloud to be the onely way
And cordiall left to repair mans decay:
Was ever grief, &c.

Then on my head a crown of thorns I wear:
For these are all the grapes *Sion* doth bear,
Though I my vine planted and watred there:
Was ever grief, &c.

134 the] y^{t} *corr. to* y^{e} *W* 135 my *B W* : mine *1633–* 137 they] thy *B* (*a slip*) 138 is] was *corr. to* is *W* 143 pitie] *both dated and undated copies of the first edition vary between* pitie *and* pittie : pitty *B W* 146 calls *B W* *1633*^{2}*–* : cals *1633* 153 Common Hall *B W* : common hall *1633–* 158 way *W* : way, *B 1633–* 163 watred] watered *B*

So sits the earths great curse in *Adams* fall
Upon my head: so I remove it all
From th' earth unto my brows, and bear the thrall:
Was ever grief like mine?

Then with the reed they gave to me before,
They strike my head, the rock from whence all store
Of heav'nly blessings issue evermore:
Was ever grief, &c.

They bow their knees to me, and cry, *Hail king:*
What ever scoffes & scornfulnesse can bring,
I am the floore, the sink, where they it fling:
Was ever grief, &c.

Yet since mans scepters are as frail as reeds,
And thorny all their crowns, bloudie their weeds;
I, who am Truth, turn into truth their deeds:
Was ever grief, &c.

The souldiers also spit upon that face,
Which Angels did desire to have the grace,
And Prophets, once to see, but found no place:
Was ever grief, &c.

Thus trimmed, forth they bring me to the rout,
Who *Crucifie him*, crie with one strong shout.
God holds his peace at man, and man cries out:
Was ever grief, &c.

They leade me in once more, and putting then
Mine own clothes on, they leade me out agen.
Whom devils flie, thus is he toss'd of men:
Was ever grief, &c.

169 they gave mee heertofore *W* 171 evermore] to the poore *W* 173 knees] heads *1656 1660* 174 & *B W*: or *1633–*

177–8 Yet since in frailty, cruelty, shrowd turns,
All Scepters, Reeds: Cloths, Scarlet: Crowns are Thorns: *W*

179 deeds] scorns *W* 181–2 that face, Which] my Face, Whom *W* 183 Prophets, *Ed: no comma B W 1633–* 185 trimmed, *B*: trimmed *W 1633–* 187 Wth stronger blows strike mee as I come out *W* (*with comma at end of l. 186*)

And now wearie of sport, glad to ingrosse
All spite in one, counting my life their losse,
They carrie me to my most bitter crosse:
Was ever grief like mine?

My crosse I bear my self, untill I faint:
Then Simon bears it for me by constraint,
The decreed burden of each mortall Saint:
Was ever grief, &c.

O all ye who passe by, behold and see;
Man stole the fruit, but I must climbe the tree;
The tree of life to all, but onely me:
Was ever grief, &c.

Lo, here I hang, charg'd with a world of sinne,
The greater world o' th' two; for that came in
By words, but this by sorrow I must win:
Was ever grief, &c.

Such sorrow as, if sinfull man could feel,
Or feel his part, he would not cease to kneel,
Till all were melted, though he were all steel:
Was ever grief, &c.

But, *O my God, my God!* why leav'st thou me,
The sonne, in whom thou dost delight to be?
My God, my God——
Never was grief like mine.

Shame tears my soul, my bodie many a wound;
Sharp nails pierce this, but sharper that confound;
Reproches, which are free, while I am bound.
Was ever grief, &c.

199 The gladsome burden (*corr. from* burthen) of a mortal saint. *W* 206 came] comes *corr. to* came *W* 209 Such sorrow as, if *Palmer*: Such sorrow, as if *B W 1633–* 210 part] share *W* 214 dost delight] art well pleas'd *W* 216 Never was] *misprinted* Was ever *1674–1799, Pickering* 217 My soule is full of shame, my flesh of wound: *W*

Now heal thy self, Physician; now come down.
Alas! I did so, when I left my crown
And fathers smile for you, to feel his frown:
Was ever grief like mine?

In healing not my self, there doth consist
All that salvation, which ye now resist;
Your safetie in my sicknesse doth subsist:
Was ever grief, &c.

Betwixt two theeves I spend my utmost breath,
As he that for some robberie suffereth.
Alas! what have I stollen from you? Death.
Was ever grief, &c.

A king my title is, prefixt on high;
Yet by my subjects am condemn'd to die
A servile death in servile companie:
Was ever grief, &c.

They give me vineger mingled with gall,
But more with malice: yet, when they did call,
With Manna, Angels food, I fed them all:
Was ever grief, &c.

They part my garments, and by lot dispose
My coat, the type of love, which once cur'd those
Who sought for help, never malicious foes:
Was ever grief, &c.

Nay, after death their spite shall further go;
For they will pierce my side, I full well know;
That as sinne came, so Sacraments might flow:
Was ever grief, &c.

But now I die; now all is finished.
My wo, mans weal: and now I bow my head.
Onely let others say, when I am dead,
Never was grief like mine.

221 *ital. Palmer* : *roman 1633–* : *not distinguished B W* 222 left] lost *corr. to* left *W* 223 for you, to feel] to feele for you *W*, *Grosart* 226 ye] you *W* 231 Death. *B W* : death : *1633–* 234 am] I'm *1634–* , *Pickering* *See note* 237 give *B W*: gave *1633–* 245 further] farther *W*

The Thanksgiving.

OH King of grief! (a title strange, yet true,
To thee of all kings onely due)
Oh King of wounds! how shall I grieve for thee,
Who in all grief preventest me?
Shall I weep bloud? why, thou hast wept such store
That all thy body was one doore.
Shall I be scourged, flouted, boxed, sold?
'Tis but to tell the tale is told.
My God, my God, why dost thou part from me?
Was such a grief as cannot be.
Shall I then sing, skipping thy dolefull storie,
And side with thy triumphant glorie?
Shall thy strokes be my stroking? thorns, my flower?
Thy rod, my posie? crosse, my bower?
But how then shall I imitate thee, and
Copie thy fair, though bloudie hand?
Surely I will revenge me on thy love,
And trie who shall victorious prove.
If thou dost give me wealth, I will restore
All back unto thee by the poore.
If thou dost give me honour, men shall see,
The honour doth belong to thee.
I will not marry; or, if she be mine,
She and her children shall be thine.
My bosome friend, if he blaspheme thy Name,
I will tear thence his love and fame.
One half of me being gone, the rest I give
Unto some Chappell, die or live.
As for thy passion—But of that anon,
When with the other I have done.

The Thanksgiving. 1 Oh King of grief!] King of all Grief *W* 3 Oh King of wounds!] King of all wounds, *W* 5 why, *1633^2–60* : why *B W 1633 1667–* 6 doore] gore *1678–1809* : sore *conj. Hall See note* 11 sing, skipping thy dolefull *B 1638–* , *Pickering* : sing, skipping, thy dolefull *1633–5*, *Willmott* : sing, neglecting thy sad *W See note* 17 revenge *B W 1633^2–* : reuenge *1633* 19 wealth, *B 1633^2–* : wealth ; *W 1633* 20 by] in *W* 21 honour, *B 1633^2–* : honour ; *W 1633* 22 The] That *W* 25 Name *B* : name *corr. to* Name *W* : name *1633–* 26 tear thence] ripp out *corr. by 2nd hand to* teare out *W* 27 I give] I'le give *W* 29 thy] my *1674–1799* (*cf. l.* 49)

For thy predestination I'le contrive,
    That three yeares hence, if I survive,
I'le build a spittle, or mend common wayes,
    But mend mine own without delayes.
Then I will use the works of thy creation,
    As if I us'd them but for fashion.
The world and I will quarrell; and the yeare
    Shall not perceive, that I am here.
My musick shall finde thee, and ev'ry string
    Shall have his attribute to sing;
That all together may accord in thee,
    And prove one God, one harmonie.
If thou shalt give me wit, it shall appeare,
    If thou hast giv'n it me, 'tis here.
Nay, I will reade thy book, and never move
    Till I have found therein thy love,
Thy art of love, which I'le turn back on thee:
    O my deare Saviour, Victorie!
Then for thy passion—I will do for that—
    Alas, my God, I know not what.

The Reprisall.

I Have consider'd it, and finde
    There is no dealing with thy mighty passion:
For though I die for thee, I am behinde;
    My sinnes deserve the condemnation.

    O make me innocent, that I
May give a disentangled state and free:
And yet thy wounds still my attempts defie,
    For by thy death I die for thee.

34 mine] my *W 1678–1809, Pickering* 35 I will] will I *W* 36 fashion] *misprinted* a fashion *Willmott* 39–40 *cited in Walton's* Lives, *arranged in 3 lines* 41 all together] *misprinted* altogether *1641–1799* (*except undated 7th edn. and 1667*), *Pickering* 45–6 never move . . . love] never linn Till I have found thy love therin *W* 46 love, *1809, Grosart, Palmer*: Loue. *B*: love; *1633–* 47 thee: *W*: thee, *B 1633–* 49 thy] my *1678–1799* (*cf. l. 29, though 1674 has* my *in l. 29 only*)

The Reprisall. *Title in W*: The Second Thanks-giving (*cf.* The Thanksgiving, *ll. 29–30*) *Arranged in verses in W and 1633– , as above, but undivided in B* 2 dealing] medling *W*

Ah! was it not enough that thou
By thy eternall glorie didst outgo me?
Couldst thou not griefs sad conquests me allow,
But in all vict'ries overthrow me?

Yet by confession will I come
Into thy conquest: though I can do nought
Against thee, in thee I will overcome
The man, who once against thee fought.

The Agonie.

PHilosophers have measur'd mountains,
Fathom'd the depths of seas, of states, and kings,
Walk'd with a staffe to heav'n, and traced fountains:
But there are two vast, spacious things,
The which to measure it doth more behove:
Yet few there are that sound them; Sinne and Love.

Who would know Sinne, let him repair
Unto Mount Olivet; there shall he see
A man so wrung with pains, that all his hair,
His skinne, his garments bloudie be.
Sinne is that presse and vice, which forceth pain
To hunt his cruell food through ev'ry vein.

Who knows not Love, let him assay
And taste that juice, which on the crosse a pike
Did set again abroach; then let him say
If ever he did taste the like.
Love is that liquour sweet and most divine,
Which my God feels as bloud; but I, as wine.

11 conquests] conquest *1634–1809* (*except 1660*) 14 thy *B W* : the *1633–* *See note* conquest *colon B* : *comma W* : *full stop 1633–*

The Agonie. *Not in W* 2 Fathom'd] Fadom'd *B* 6 sound] found *Gibson* 8 Mount *B 1667–1709* : mount *1633–60* 15 again] *om. 1667–1809, Pickering*

The Sinner.

LOrd, how I am all ague, when I seek
What I have treasur'd in my memorie!
Since, if my soul make even with the week,
Each seventh note by right is due to thee.
I finde there quarries of pil'd vanities,
But shreds of holinesse, that dare not venture
To shew their face, since crosse to thy decrees:
There the circumference earth is, heav'n the centre.
In so much dregs the quintessence is small:
The spirit and good extract of my heart
Comes to about the many hundred part.
Yet Lord restore thine image, heare my call:
And though my hard heart scarce to thee can grone,
Remember that thou once didst write in stone.

Good Friday.

O My chief good,
How shall I measure out thy bloud?
How shall I count what thee befell,
And each grief tell?

Shall I thy woes
Number according to thy foes?
Or, since one starre show'd thy first breath,
Shall all thy death?

Or shall each leaf,
Which falls in Autumne, score a grief?
Or can not leaves, but fruit, be signe
Of the true vine?

The Sinner. *Without line-spaces after ll. 4, 8, 12 in B W 1633– See note*
8 centre] centure *W* (*cf.* Content, *l. 18, where it rhymes with* adventure)
11 hundred *B W* : hundredth *1633–*

Good Friday. 11 can not *W* : cannot *B 1633–*

Then let each houre
Of my whole life one grief devoure;
That thy distresse through all may runne,
And be my sunne.

Or rather let
My severall sinnes their sorrows get;
That as each beast his cure doth know,
Each sinne may so.

SInce bloud is fittest, Lord, to write
Thy sorrows in, and bloudie fight;
My heart hath store, write there, where in
One box doth lie both ink and sinne:

That when sinne spies so many foes,
Thy whips, thy nails, thy wounds, thy woes,
All come to lodge there, sinne may say,
No room for me, and flie away.

Sinne being gone, oh fill the place,
And keep possession with thy grace;
Lest sinne take courage and return,
And all the writings blot or burn.

21–32 *A version of these lines appears in W as a separate poem entitled* The Passion, *following* The Second Thanks-giving (i.e. The Reprisall). *These lines begin a new page in B, but have no title. From 1638* Since (*l. 21*) *is printed with a large initial capital, indicating a new poem or section of a poem*

21–2 Since nothing Lord can bee so good
To write thy sorrows in, as blood *W*

22 fight] *Palmer misreads B as* sight : flight *1667–1799* 27 sinne] he *W*

29–32 Sinn being gone o doe thou fill
The Place, & keep possession still.
ffor by the writings all may see
Thou hast an ancient claime to mee. *W*

Redemption.

HAving been tenant long to a rich Lord,
Not thriving, I resolved to be bold,
And make a suit unto him, to afford
A new small-rented lease, and cancell th' old.
In heaven at his manour I him sought:
They told me there, that he was lately gone
About some land, which he had dearly bought
Long since on earth, to take possession.
I straight return'd, and knowing his great birth,
Sought him accordingly in great resorts;
In cities, theatres, gardens, parks, and courts:
At length I heard a ragged noise and mirth
Of theeves and murderers: there I him espied,
Who straight, *Your suit is granted*, said, & died.

Sepulchre.

O Blessed bodie! Whither art thou thrown?
No lodging for thee, but a cold hard stone?
So many hearts on earth, and yet not one
Receive thee?
Sure there is room within our hearts good store;
For they can lodge transgressions by the score:
Thousands of toyes dwell there, yet out of doore
They leave thee.

Redemption. *Title in W*: The Passion (*as also of the preceding poem in W, i.e. ll. 21–32 of* Good Friday)

10–11 Sought him in Citties, Theaters, resorts
In grottos, gardens, Palaces & Courts *W* (*corr. by 2nd hand to the words found in B and 1633, as above*)

Sepulchre. *Not in W Arranged in 8-line stanzas, because l. 4 rhymes with l. 8, 12 with 16 &c. Ed*: *no line-spaces in B*: *4-line stanzas, with line-spaces 1633–*

But that which shews them large, shews them unfit.
What ever sinne did this pure rock commit,
Which holds thee now? Who hath indited it
Of murder?
Where our hard hearts have took up stones to brain thee,
And missing this, most falsly did arraigne thee;
Onely these stones in quiet entertain thee,
And order.

And as of old the Law by heav'nly art
Was writ in stone; so thou, which also art
The letter of the word, find'st no fit heart
To hold thee.
Yet do we still persist as we began,
And so should perish, but that nothing can,
Though it be cold, hard, foul, from loving man
Withhold thee.

Easter.

RIse heart; thy Lord is risen. Sing his praise
Without delayes,
Who takes thee by the hand, that thou likewise
With him mayst rise:
That, as his death calcined thee to dust,
His life may make thee gold, and much more, just.

Awake, my lute, and struggle for thy part
With all thy art.
The crosse taught all wood to resound his name,
Who bore the same.
His stretched sinews taught all strings, what key
Is best to celebrate this most high day.

17 old *B 1633*^{2}– : old, *1633* Law *B 1633*^{2}– : law *1633* 24 withhold *B 1633*^{2}– : withold *1633*

Easter. 6 more, *W 1638–67 1809* : more *B 1633–5 1674–1799* 11 stretched *B W 1633*^{2}– : streched *1633*

Consort both heart and lute, and twist a song
Pleasant and long:
Or, since all musick is but three parts vied
And multiplied,
O let thy blessed Spirit bear a part,
And make up our defects with his sweet art.

I Got me flowers to straw thy way;
I got me boughs off many a tree:
But thou wast up by break of day,
And brought'st thy sweets along with thee.

The Sunne arising in the East,
Though he give light, & th' East perfume;
If they should offer to contest
With thy arising, they presume.

Can there be any day but this,
Though many sunnes to shine endeavour?
We count three hundred, but we misse:
There is but one, and that one ever.

15 Or, *1633*[2]–: Or *B W 1633* 16 multiplied, *Grosart*: *no stop B W*: *semicolon 1633–* 19–30 *W has an earlier version as a separate poem entitled* Easter: *see below* 19 I Got *1638–* (*marking a separate section*): I got *1633–5* straw] strew *1703–1809, Pickering* 20 off] of *B* (*which never uses the form* off)

Easter.

I had prepared many a flowre
To strow thy way and Victorie,
But thou wa'st vp before myne houre
Bringinge thy sweets along wth thee.

The Sunn arising in the East
Though hee bring light & th'other sents:
Can not make vp so braue a feast
As thy discouerie presents.

Yet though my flours be lost, they say
A hart can never come too late.
Teach it to sing thy praise, this day,
And then this day, my life shall date. *W*

(*l.* 4 Bringinge *substituted by 2nd hand for* And brought)

Easter-wings.

LOrd, who createdst man in wealth and store,
Though foolishly he lost the same,
Decaying more and more,
Till he became
Most poore:
With thee
O let me rise
As larks, harmoniously,
And sing this day thy victories:
Then shall the fall further the flight in me.

My tender age in sorrow did beginne:
And still with sicknesses and shame
Thou didst so punish sinne,
That I became
Most thinne.
With thee
Let me combine
And feel this day thy victorie:
For, if I imp my wing on thine,
Affliction shall advance the flight in me.

H. Baptisme (I).

AS he that sees a dark and shadie grove,
Stayes not, but looks beyond it on the skie;
So when I view my sinnes, mine eyes remove
More backward still, and to that water flie,

Easter-wings. *Title*: *hyphen B W 1633*[2]*–* *and in* 'The titles of the severall poems' *1633: no hyphen in title 1633. The lines are written horizontally in B and W, as printed above: all early editions print them vertically. From 1634 line-spaces after ll. 5 and 15* 8 harmoniously] doe by degree *corr. by 2nd hand to* harmoniouslie *W* 9 victories] sacrifice *corr. by 2nd hand* to victories *W* 10 the fall] my fall *W* 12 And still] Yet thou *corr. by 2nd hand to* And still *W* 13 Thou didst so] Dayly didst *corr. by 2nd hand to* Thou didst so *W* 14 That] Till *corr. by 2nd hand to* That *W* 18 this day] *absent from W* (this day, *found in B and 1633–* , *assists the parallelism to l. 9, but makes l. 18 a foot longer than the corresponding l. 8*)

H. Baptisme (I). *Numbering Ed. Considerably rewritten since its earlier form in W* 1–9 When backward on my sins I turne mine eyes
And then beyond them all my Baptisme view [*continued overleaf*

Which is above the heav'ns, whose spring and vent
Is in my deare Redeemers pierced side.
O blessed streams! either ye do prevent
And stop our sinnes from growing thick and wide,
Or else give tears to drown them, as they grow.
In you Redemption measures all my time,
And spreads the plaister equall to the crime.
You taught the Book of Life my name, that so
What ever future sinnes should me miscall,
Your first acquaintance might discredit all.

H. Baptisme (II).

SInce, Lord, to thee
A narrow way and little gate
Is all the passage, on my infancie
Thou didst lay hold, and antedate
My faith in me.

O let me still
Write thee great God, and me a childe:
Let me be soft and supple to thy will,
Small to my self, to others milde,
Behither ill.

Although by stealth
My flesh get on, yet let her sister
My soul bid nothing, but preserve her wealth:
The growth of flesh is but a blister;
Childhood is health.

As he y^{t} Heaven beyond much thicket spyes
I pass ye shades, & fixe vpon the true
Waters aboue ye Heavens. O sweet streams
Yo^{u} doe prevent most sins & for ye rest
You give vs teares to wash them: lett those beams
W^{ch} then ioin'd wth you still meet in my brest
And mend as rising starres & rivers doe. *W*

5 vent *B 1638–1809, Pickering*: rent *1633–5, Willmott, Grosart, Palmer* 10 you] *misprinted* your *1703–99* 11 And spreads the] Spredding y^{e} *W* crime. *B 1633^{2}–8*: crime: *1633*: cryme *W* 12 Book of Life *initial capitals from B*

H. Baptisme (II). *Numbering Ed* 11 Although] Though y^{t} *W* 12 get] got *1667–1799* on, *Ed*: on: *B*: on; *W 1633–* 13 preserve her] keep hir first *W*

Nature.

FUll of rebellion, I would die,
Or fight, or travell, or denie
That thou hast ought to do with me.
O tame my heart;
It is thy highest art
To captivate strong holds to thee.

If thou shalt let this venome lurk,
And in suggestions fume and work,
My soul will turn to bubbles straight,
And thence by kinde
Vanish into a winde,
Making thy workmanship deceit.

O smooth my rugged heart, and there
Engrave thy rev'rend Law and fear;
Or make a new one, since the old
Is saplesse grown,
And a much fitter stone
To hide my dust, then thee to hold.

Sinne (I).

LOrd, with what care hast thou begirt us round!
Parents first season us: then schoolmasters
Deliver us to laws; they send us bound
To rules of reason, holy messengers,
Pulpits and Sundayes, sorrow dogging sinne,
Afflictions sorted, anguish of all sizes,
Fine nets and stratagems to catch us in,
Bibles laid open, millions of surprises,

Nature. 9 turn to bubbles] bee all bubble *corr. by 2nd hand to* turne to bubbles *W* 14 Law *B W 1633*[2]– : law *1633*

Sinne (I). *Numbering Ed* 5 Sundayes *cap. from B W* 7 stratagems] casualties *W*

Blessings beforehand, tyes of gratefulnesse,
The sound of glorie ringing in our eares:
Without, our shame; within, our consciences;
Angels and grace, eternall hopes and fears.
Yet all these fences and their whole aray
One cunning bosome-sinne blows quite away.

Affliction (I).

WHen first thou didst entice to thee my heart,
I thought the service brave:
So many joyes I writ down for my part,
Besides what I might have
Out of my stock of naturall delights,
Augmented with thy gracious benefits.

I looked on thy furniture so fine,
And made it fine to me:
Thy glorious houshold-stuffe did me entwine,
And 'tice me unto thee.
Such starres I counted mine: both heav'n and earth
Payd me my wages in a world of mirth.

What pleasures could I want, whose King I served,
Where joyes my fellows were?
Thus argu'd into hopes, my thoughts reserved
No place for grief or fear.
Therefore my sudden soul caught at the place,
And made her youth and fiercenesse seek thy face.

13–14 Yet all these fences wth one bosome sinn
Are blowne away, as if they nere had bin. *W*

Affliction (I). *Numbering Ed* 37–66 *quoted in Walton's* Lives 6 gracious benefits] graces perquisites *W* 7 *and* 8 fine] rich *W* 9–10 entwine, . . . unto thee.] bewitch Into thy familie. *W* 13–14 served, . . . were? *1633*[2]–: served? . . . were: *B*: served? . . . were? *W*: served? . . . were. *1633* 15–16 my thoughts . . . fear.] I was preserved Before y[t] I could feare. *W*

At first thou gav'st me milk and sweetnesses;
I had my wish and way:
My dayes were straw'd with flow'rs and happinesse;
There was no moneth but May.
But with my yeares sorrow did twist and grow,
And made a partie unawares for wo.

My flesh began unto my soul in pain,
Sicknesses cleave my bones;
Consuming agues dwell in ev'ry vein,
And tune my breath to grones.
Sorrow was all my soul; I scarce beleeved,
Till grief did tell me roundly, that I lived.

When I got health, thou took'st away my life,
And more; for my friends die:
My mirth and edge was lost; a blunted knife
Was of more use then I.
Thus thinne and lean without a fence or friend,
I was blown through with ev'ry storm and winde.

Whereas my birth and spirit rather took
The way that takes the town;
Thou didst betray me to a lingring book,
And wrap me in a gown.
I was entangled in the world of strife,
Before I had the power to change my life.

Yet, for I threatned oft the siege to raise,
Not simpring all mine age,
Thou often didst with Academick praise
Melt and dissolve my rage.
I took thy sweetned pill, till I came where
I could not go away, nor persevere.

21 straw'd] strowd *W*: strew'd *1703–1809, Pickering* happinesse] happinesses *Willmott, Grosart* (*though they both preserve* unhappinesse *at l. 50, where there is a similar rhyme*) 23 sorrow] sorrows *W* 25 began] begun *Grosart* 26 cleave] clave *1678–1799, Pickering* 29–30 I scarce . . . I lived.]

I did not know
That I did live, but by a pang of woe. *W*

36 through] tho'rough *W* 41 the] a *Walton* 44 mine] my *corr. by 2nd hand to* mine *W* 47 where *W 1638–67, Walton, 1809*: where (*without comma*) *is written by a different hand above* neere (*with comma*), *which is underlined but not crossed out B*: neare; *1633–5 1674–1799 See note*

Yet lest perchance I should too happie be
In my unhappinesse,
Turning my purge to food, thou throwest me
Into more sicknesses.
Thus doth thy power crosse-bias me, not making
Thine own gift good, yet me from my wayes taking.

Now I am here, what thou wilt do with me
None of my books will show:
I reade, and sigh, and wish I were a tree;
For sure then I should grow
To fruit or shade: at least some bird would trust
Her houshold to me, and I should be just.

Yet, though thou troublest me, I must be meek;
In weaknesse must be stout.
Well, I will change the service, and go seek
Some other master out.
Ah my deare God! though I am clean forgot,
Let me not love thee, if I love thee not.

Repentance.

LOrd, I confesse my sinne is great;
Great is my sinne. Oh! gently treat
With thy quick flow'r, thy momentarie bloom;
Whose life still pressing
Is one undressing,
A steadie aiming at a tombe.

Mans age is two houres work, or three:
Each day doth round about us see.
Thus are we to delights: but we are all
To sorrows old,
If life be told
From what life feeleth, Adams fall.

51 throwest] throwst *corr. to* throwest *W*: throwst *Walton in collected* Lives (1670), *but* throwest *in his* Life of Herbert (1670) 54 gift] gifts *Walton* 58 sure then] then sure *Walton* should] *Palmer misreads B as* could 60 to] with *Walton* should] would *Walton* 63 the] my *Walton* 65 God] King *W*

Repentance. 3 momentarie *B*: momentary *W 1709–1809*: momentanie *1633–1703* 9–10 Looking on this side, & beyond vs all:
Wee are born old. *W* (*with no stop in l. 8*)

O let thy height of mercie then
Compassionate short-breathed men.
Cut me not off for my most foul transgression:
I do confesse
My foolishnesse;
My God, accept of my confession.

Sweeten at length this bitter bowl,
Which thou hast pour'd into my soul;
Thy wormwood turn to health, windes to fair weather:
For if thou stay,
I and this day,
As we did rise, we die together.

When thou for sinne rebukest man,
Forthwith he waxeth wo and wan:
Bitternesse fills our bowels; all our hearts
Pine, and decay,
And drop away,
And carrie with them th' other parts.

But thou wilt sinne and grief destroy;
That so the broken bones may joy,
And tune together in a well-set song,
Full of his praises,
Who dead men raises.
Fractures well cur'd make us more strong.

Faith.

LOrd, how couldst thou so much appease
Thy wrath for sinne as, when mans sight was dimme,
And could see little, to regard his ease,
And bring by Faith all things to him?

28–30 Melt & consume
To smoke & fume
ffretting to death our other parts. *W* (smoke & fume *written by 2nd hand cancelling* a salt rhume)
29 drop] drope *B* *See note*
Faith. 2 sinne as, when *Ed*: sinne, as when *B W 1633–*

Hungrie I was, and had no meat:
I did conceit a most delicious feast;
I had it straight, and did as truly eat,
As ever did a welcome guest.

There is a rare outlandish root,
Which when I could not get, I thought it here:
That apprehension cur'd so well my foot,
That I can walk to heav'n well neare.

I owed thousands and much more:
I did beleeve that I did nothing owe,
And liv'd accordingly; my creditor
Beleeves so too, and lets me go.

Faith makes me any thing, or all
That I beleeve is in the sacred storie:
And where sinne placeth me in Adams fall,
Faith sets me higher in his glorie.

If I go lower in the book,
What can be lower then the common manger?
Faith puts me there with him, who sweetly took
Our flesh and frailtie, death and danger.

If blisse had lien in art or strength,
None but the wise or strong had gained it:
Where now by Faith all arms are of a length;
One size doth all conditions fit.

A peasant may beleeve as much
As a great Clerk, and reach the highest stature.
Thus dost thou make proud knowledge bend & crouch,
While grace fills up uneven nature.

15–16 And livd accordingly wth no new score,
My Creditour beleeu'd so too. *W*

19 where] when *1674–1799, Pickering* placeth] places *W* 24 My nature on him, wth the danger. *W* 26 gained] *misprinted* gain'd *1799–1809, Pickering* 31 bend] bow *W* crouch *comma B* : *no comma W 1633–*

When creatures had no reall light
Inherent in them, thou didst make the sunne
Impute a lustre, and allow them bright;
And in this shew, what Christ hath done.

That which before was darkned clean
With bushie groves, pricking the lookers eie,
Vanisht away, when Faith did change the scene:
And then appear'd a glorious skie.

What though my bodie runne to dust?
Faith cleaves unto it, counting evr'y grain
With an exact and most particular trust,
Reserving all for flesh again.

Prayer (I).

PRayer the Churches banquet, Angels age,
Gods breath in man returning to his birth,
The soul in paraphrase, heart in pilgrimage,
The Christian plummet sounding heav'n and earth;
Engine against th' Almightie, sinners towre,
Reversed thunder, Christ-side-piercing spear,
The six-daies world transposing in an houre,
A kinde of tune, which all things heare and fear;
Softnesse, and peace, and joy, and love, and blisse,
Exalted Manna, gladnesse of the best,
Heaven in ordinarie, man well drest,
The milkie way, the bird of Paradise,
Church-bels beyond the starres heard, the souls bloud,
The land of spices; something understood.

34 sunne *no comma W 1635–* : *comma B 1633–4* 35 Impute] Impart *corr. by 2nd hand to* Impute *W* 36 This shadowes out what Christ hath done. *W*
Prayer (I). *Numbering Ed* 5 towre] fort *W* 7 world transposing *B*: world-transposing *1633–* Transposer of ye world, wonders ressort, *W*

The H. Communion.

NOt in rich furniture, or fine aray,
Nor in a wedge of gold,
Thou, who for me wast sold,
To me dost now thy self convey;
For so thou should'st without me still have been,
Leaving within me sinne:

But by the way of nourishment and strength
Thou creep'st into my breast;
Making thy way my rest,
And thy small quantities my length;
Which spread their forces into every part,
Meeting sinnes force and art.

Yet can these not get over to my soul,
Leaping the wall that parts
Our souls and fleshy hearts;
But as th' outworks, they may controll
My rebel-flesh, and carrying thy name,
Affright both sinne and shame.

Onely thy grace, which with these elements comes,
Knoweth the ready way,
And hath the privie key,
Op'ning the souls most subtile rooms;
While those to spirits refin'd, at doore attend
Dispatches from their friend.

GIve me my captive soul, or take
My bodie also thither.
Another lift like this will make
Them both to be together.

The H. Communion. *W has the second part only (ll. 25–40) with the title* Prayer. *W has another poem entitled* The H. Communion, *not included in B and 1633; see below, p. 200* 3 for *B 1634–67 1809*: from *1633 1633*[2] *1674–1799 See note* 7 strength *B 1633*[2]*–* : strengh *1633* 15 fleshy *B, Grosart*: fleshly *1633– See note* 25–40 *A separate poem in W entitled* Prayer. *In B a 4-line space separates this poem from the preceding; it may have been intended to insert a title in this space, but the rewording of l. 38 (contrast W) perhaps suggested the inclusion of the poem under the same title as the preceding poem* 27 lift] *Palmer misreads B as* life

Before that sinne turn'd flesh to stone,
    And all our lump to leaven;
A fervent sigh might well have blown
    Our innocent earth to heaven.

For sure when Adam did not know
    To sinne, or sinne to smother;
He might to heav'n from Paradise go,
    As from one room t'another.

Thou hast restor'd us to this ease
    By this thy heav'nly bloud;
Which I can go to, when I please,
    And leave th' earth to their food.

Antiphon (1).

Cho. LEt all the world in ev'ry corner sing,
    My God and King.

Vers. The heav'ns are not too high,
His praise may thither flie:
The earth is not too low,
His praises there may grow.

Cho. Let all the world in ev'ry corner sing,
    My God and King.

Vers. The church with psalms must shout,
No doore can keep them out:
But above all, the heart
Must bear the longest part.

Cho. Let all the world in ev'ry corner sing,
    My God and King.

37–40 But wee are strangers grown, o Lord,
    Lett Prayer help our losses,
Since thou hast taught vs by thy word,
    That wee may gaine by crosses. *W*

Antiphon (I). *Not in W* *Numbering Ed* *Quoted in full in preface of J. Playford's* Psalms & Hymns in solemn musick (1671) 9 shout, *B* 1633^2– : *the comma has failed to be printed in some copies of 1633* 12 longest] chiefest *Playford*

Love I.

IMmortall Love, authour of this great frame,
Sprung from that beautie which can never fade;
How hath man parcel'd out thy glorious name,
And thrown it on that dust which thou hast made,
While mortall love doth all the title gain!
Which siding with invention, they together
Bear all the sway, possessing heart and brain,
(Thy workmanship) and give thee share in neither.
Wit fancies beautie, beautie raiseth wit:
The world is theirs; they two play out the game,
Thou standing by: and though thy glorious name
Wrought our deliverance from th' infernall pit,
Who sings thy praise? onely a skarf or glove
Doth warm our hands, and make them write of love.

II.

IMmortall Heat, O let thy greater flame
Attract the lesser to it: let those fires,
Which shall consume the world, first make it tame;
And kindle in our hearts such true desires,
As may consume our lusts, and make thee way.
Then shall our hearts pant thee; then shall our brain
All her invention on thine Altar lay,
And there in hymnes send back thy fire again:
Our eies shall see thee, which before saw dust;
Dust blown by wit, till that they both were blinde:
Thou shalt recover all thy goods in kinde,
Who wert disseized by usurping lust:
All knees shall bow to thee; all wits shall rise,
And praise him who did make and mend our eies.

Love I. 2 that] y[e] *W* 4 on] in *W*, *Grosart* 5 doth] does *W*
Love II. 5 thee] the *corr. to* thee *B* : yee *W* 11 goods] *Palmer misreads B as* good : *misprinted* gods *Willmott* 13 wits] *misprinted* wit *Gibson*, *Palmer*

The Temper (I).

HOw should I praise thee, Lord! how should my rymes
Gladly engrave thy love in steel,
If what my soul doth feel sometimes,
My soul might ever feel!

Although there were some fourtie heav'ns, or more,
Sometimes I peere above them all;
Sometimes I hardly reach a score,
Sometimes to hell I fall.

O rack me not to such a vast extent;
Those distances belong to thee:
The world's too little for thy tent,
A grave too big for me.

Wilt thou meet arms with man, that thou dost stretch
A crumme of dust from heav'n to hell?
Will great God measure with a wretch?
Shall he thy stature spell?

O let me, when thy roof my soul hath hid,
O let me roost and nestle there:
Then of a sinner thou art rid,
And I of hope and fear.

Yet take thy way; for sure thy way is best:
Stretch or contract me, thy poore debter:
This is but tuning of my breast,
To make the musick better.

Whether I flie with angels, fall with dust,
Thy hands made both, and I am there:
Thy power and love, my love and trust
Make one place ev'ry where.

The Temper (I). *Numbering Ed Title in W*: The Christian Temper. *Palmer, without assigning reason, reverses the order, found in B W 1633– , of this and the succeeding poem* 5 some fourtie] a hundred *W* 22 mee, *B W*: me *1633–* 25 Whether I Angell it, or fall to dust *W*

The Temper (II).

IT cannot be. Where is that mightie joy,
  Which just now took up all my heart?
  Lord, if thou must needs use thy dart,
Save that, and me; or sin for both destroy.

The grosser world stands to thy word and art;
  But thy diviner world of grace
  Thou suddenly dost raise and race,
And ev'ry day a new Creatour art.

O fix thy chair of grace, that all my powers
  May also fix their reverence:
  For when thou dost depart from hence,
They grow unruly, and sit in thy bowers.

Scatter, or binde them all to bend to thee:
  Though elements change, and heaven move,
  Let not thy higher Court remove,
But keep a standing Majestie in me.

Jordan (I).

WHo sayes that fictions onely and false hair
Become a verse? Is there in truth no beautie?
Is all good structure in a winding stair?
May no lines passe, except they do their dutie
  Not to a true, but painted chair?

Is it no verse, except enchanted groves
And sudden arbours shadow course-spunne lines?
Must purling streams refresh a lovers loves?
Must all be vail'd, while he that reades, divines,
  Catching the sense at two removes?

The Temper (II). *Numbering Ed* *Title in W*: The Christian Temper. 7 race] rase *1635–1703* : raze *1709–1809*, *Pickering*

Jordan (I). *Numbering Ed* 1 onely] only *inserted by 2nd hand with caret in W* 6 no] not *1674–1809*, *Pickering*, *Willmott*, *Grosart*

Shepherds are honest people; let them sing:
Riddle who list, for me, and pull for Prime:
I envie no mans nightingale or spring;
Nor let them punish me with losse of rime,
Who plainly say, *My God, My King.*

Employment (1).

IF as a flowre doth spread and die,
Thou wouldst extend me to some good,
Before I were by frosts extremitie
Nipt in the bud;

The sweetnesse and the praise were thine;
But the extension and the room,
Which in thy garland I should fill, were mine
At thy great doom.

For as thou dost impart thy grace,
The greater shall our glorie be.
The measure of our joyes is in this place,
The stuffe with thee.

Let me not languish then, and spend
A life as barren to thy praise,
As is the dust, to which that life doth tend,
But with delaies.

All things are busie; onely I
Neither bring hony with the bees,
Nor flowres to make that, nor the husbandrie
To water these.

I am no link of thy great chain,
But all my companie is a weed.
Lord place me in thy consort; give one strain
To my poore reed.

14 rime *W*: time *corr. to* rime *B* : ryme *1633–*
Employment (I). *Numbering Ed* 23 consort] comfort *undated 7th edn, Gibson* : concert *1799–1809*

23–4 Lord that I may the Sunns perfection gaine
Give mee his speed. *W*

The H. Scriptures. I.

OH Book! infinite sweetnesse! let my heart
Suck ev'ry letter, and a hony gain,
Precious for any grief in any part;
To cleare the breast, to mollifie all pain.
Thou art all health, health thriving till it make
A full eternitie: thou art a masse
Of strange delights, where we may wish & take.
Ladies, look here; this is the thankfull glasse,
That mends the lookers eyes: this is the well
That washes what it shows. Who can indeare
Thy praise too much? thou art heav'ns Lidger here,
Working against the states of death and hell.
Thou art joyes handsell: heav'n lies flat in thee,
Subject to ev'ry mounters bended knee.

II.

OH that I knew how all thy lights combine,
And the configurations of their glorie!
Seeing not onely how each verse doth shine,
But all the constellations of the storie.
This verse marks that, and both do make a motion
Unto a third, that ten leaves off doth lie:
Then as dispersed herbs do watch a potion,
These three make up some Christians destinie:
Such are thy secrets, which my life makes good,
And comments on thee: for in ev'ry thing
Thy words do finde me out, & parallels bring,
And in another make me understood.
Starres are poore books, & oftentimes do misse:
This book of starres lights to eternall blisse.

The H. Scriptures I. 'The titles of the severall poems' *in 1633– has* H. Scripture, *but the similar table in B has* H. Scriptures 4 mollifie all pain] suple outward paine *W* 5 all Health, health thriving till *W*: all health health, thriuing till *B*: all health, health thriving, till *1633–* 11 too much] enough *W* Lidger *B W 1633* : Lieger *1633*[2] : Leiger *1634–*

The H. Scriptures II. 4 the storie] *Palmer misreads B as* thy story 5 *and* 7 do] to *1656* 7 watch] *See note for modern conjectural readings* 10 And comments on thee] And more then fancy *W* 13 poore] *Palmer misreads B as* poores 14 lights to] can spell *W*

Whitsunday.

LIsten sweet Dove unto my song,
And spread thy golden wings in me;
Hatching my tender heart so long,
Till it get wing, and flie away with thee.

Where is that fire which once descended
On thy Apostles? thou didst then
Keep open house, richly attended,
Feasting all comers by twelve chosen men.

Such glorious gifts thou didst bestow,
That th' earth did like a heav'n appeare;
The starres were coming down to know
If they might mend their wages, and serve here.

The sunne, which once did shine alone,
Hung down his head, and wisht for night,
When he beheld twelve sunnes for one
Going about the world, and giving light.

But since those pipes of gold, which brought
That cordiall water to our ground,
Were cut and martyr'd by the fault
Of those, who did themselves through their side wound,

Whitsunday. *The earlier form of this poem in W is considerably rewritten in B, and the last 3 verses of W are discarded for 4 new verses in B* 1 Come blessed Doue charm'd wth my song *W* 2 And spread] Display *W* 4 Till I gett wing to fly away wth thee. *W* 8 W^th^ livery-graces furnishing thy men. *W* 20 wound, *B* : *no stop 1633–41* (*perhaps because the printed line reaches the margin*)

13–28 *In place of these 4 verses W has the following:*

But wee are falne from Heaven to Earth,
And if wee can stay there, it 's well.
He y^t^ first fell from his great birth
W^th^out thy help, leads vs his way to Hell.

Lord once more shake ye Heaven & earth
Least want of Graces seeme thy thrift:
ffor sinn would faine remoue ye dearth
And lay it on thy husbandry, for shift.

Show y^t^ thy brests can not be dry,
But y^t^ from them ioyes purle for ever
Melt into blessings all the sky,
So wee may cease to suck: to praise thee, never.

Thou shutt'st the doore, and keep'st within;
Scarce a good joy creeps through the chink:
And if the braves of conqu'ring sinne
Did not excite thee, we should wholly sink.

Lord, though we change, thou art the same;
The same sweet God of love and light:
Restore this day, for thy great name,
Unto his ancient and miraculous right.

Grace.

MY stock lies dead, and no increase
Doth my dull husbandrie improve:
O let thy graces without cease
Drop from above!

If still the sunne should hide his face,
Thy house would but a dungeon prove,
Thy works nights captives: O let grace
Drop from above!

The dew doth ev'ry morning fall;
And shall the dew out-strip thy Dove?
The dew, for which grasse cannot call,
Drop from above.

Death is still working like a mole,
And digs my grave at each remove:
Let grace work too, and on my soul
Drop from above.

Sinne is still hammering my heart
Unto a hardnesse, void of love:
Let suppling grace, to crosse his art,
Drop from above.

Grace. 5 If the Sunn still *W* 6 Thy great house would a dungeon proue *W* 10 Dove *W 1634–* : dove *B 1633 1633*[2] 13–16 *Wanting in W* 19 Let suppling] O lett thy *corr. by 2nd hand to* Lett suppling *W*

O come! for thou dost know the way:
Or if to me thou wilt not move,
Remove me, where I need not say,
Drop from above.

Praise (I).

TO write a verse or two is all the praise,
That I can raise:
Mend my estate in any wayes,
Thou shalt have more.

I go to Church; help me to wings, and I
Will thither flie;
Or, if I mount unto the skie,
I will do more.

Man is all weaknesse; there is no such thing
As Prince or King:
His arm is short; yet with a sling
He may do more.

An herb destill'd, and drunk, may dwell next doore,
On the same floore,
To a brave soul: exalt the poore,
They can do more.

O raise me then! Poore bees, that work all day,
Sting my delay,
Who have a work, as well as they,
And much, much more.

21 way : *B W* : way. *1633–*
21 *Between verses 5 and 6, as above, W has the following verse, later cancelled by lines drawn across it:*

What if I say thou seek'st delayes;
Wilt thou not then my fault reproue?
Prevent my Sinn to thine owne praise,
Drop from aboue.

Praise (I). *Numbering Ed* 1 two *B W*: two, *1633–* 5 I goe to Church; make me an Angel, I *W* 7 mount unto] steale vp to *W* 9–16 *W has verses 3 and 4 in reverse order* 14 *bracketed in W* 15 exalt *1634–* : Exalt *B 1633 1633*^{2} 15–16 exalt . . . more.] for to a poore It may doe more. *W*
17 Poore *B 1633*^{2}*–* : poore *1633*
17–20 O raise me then : for if a Spider may
Spin all ye day:
Not flyes, but I shall bee his prey
Who doe no more. *W*

Affliction (II).

KIll me not ev'ry day,
Thou Lord of life; since thy one death for me
Is more then all my deaths can be,
Though I in broken pay
Die over each houre of Methusalems stay.

If all mens tears were let
Into one common sewer, sea, and brine;
What were they all, compar'd to thine?
Wherein if they were set,
They would discolour thy most bloudy sweat.

Thou art my grief alone,
Thou Lord conceal it not: and as thou art
All my delight, so all my smart:
Thy crosse took up in one,
By way of imprest, all my future mone.

Mattens.

I Cannot ope mine eyes,
But thou art ready there to catch
My morning-soul and sacrifice:
Then we must needs for that day make a match.

My God, what is a heart?
Silver, or gold, or precious stone,
Or starre, or rainbow, or a part
Of all these things, or all of them in one?

My God, what is a heart,
That thou shouldst it so eye, and wooe,
Powring upon it all thy art,
As if that thou hadst nothing els to do?

Affliction (II). *Numbering Ed This poem is not in W* 5 over] once *conj. Hall*
13–14 All my delight; so all my smart
Thy crosse tooke vp in one *B*

Mattens. 12 that] *om. Grosart*: *Palmer states incorrectly that W om.* that

Indeed mans whole estate
Amounts (and richly) to serve thee:
He did not heav'n and earth create,
Yet studies them, not him by whom they be.

Teach me thy love to know;
That this new light, which now I see,
May both the work and workman show:
Then by a sunne-beam I will climbe to thee.

Sinne (II).

O That I could a sinne once see!
We paint the devil foul, yet he
Hath some good in him, all agree.
Sinne is flat opposite to th' Almighty, seeing
It wants the good of *vertue*, and of *being*.

But God more care of us hath had:
If apparitions make us sad,
By sight of sinne we should grow mad.
Yet as in sleep we see foul death, and live:
So devils are our sinnes in perspective.

Even-song.

BLest be the God of love,
Who gave me eyes, and light, and power this day,
Both to be busie, and to play.
But much more blest be God above,
Who gave me sight alone,
Which to himself he did denie:
For when he sees my waies, I dy:
But I have got his sonne, and he hath none.

Sinne (II). *Numbering Ed* 10 perspective] prospective *1674–1799, Pickering, Willmott*

Even-song. *This poem in B replaces a wholly different poem with same title in W* (*see below, p. 203*). *In W the earlier* Euen-song *follows* Mattens; *it is not clear why in B and 1633* Sinne *comes between* Mattens *and the new poem* Even-song. *The arrangement of B in 8-line stanzas, balancing the two long 2nd and 8th lines, is exchanged in 1633 for 4-line stanzas*

What have I brought thee home
For this thy love? have I discharg'd the debt,
Which this dayes favour did beget?
I ranne; but all I brought, was fome.
Thy diet, care, and cost
Do end in bubbles, balls of winde;
Of winde to thee whom I have crost,
But balls of wilde-fire to my troubled minde.

Yet still thou goest on,
And now with darknesse closest wearie eyes,
Saying to man, *It doth suffice:*
Henceforth repose; your work is done.
Thus in thy ebony box
Thou dost inclose us, till the day
Put our amendment in our way,
And give new wheels to our disorder'd clocks.

I muse, which shows more love,
The day or night: that is the gale, this th' harbour;
That is the walk, and this the arbour;
Or that the garden, this the grove.
My God, thou art all love.
Not one poore minute scapes thy breast,
But brings a favour from above;
And in this love, more then in bed, I rest.

Church-monuments.

WHile that my soul repairs to her devotion,
Here I intombe my flesh, that it betimes
May take acquaintance of this heap of dust;
To which the blast of deaths incessant motion,
Fed with the exhalation of our crimes,
Drives all at last. Therefore I gladly trust

21 ebony *B*: Ebony *1633–* box] bone *corr. to* boxe *B* (*cf. a similar correction in* Ungratefulnesse, *l. 29*)

Church-monuments. *B and W do not divide the poem into stanzas See note*

My bodie to this school, that it may learn
To spell his elements, and finde his birth
Written in dustie heraldrie and lines;
Which dissolution sure doth best discern,
Comparing dust with dust, and earth with earth.
These laugh at Jeat and Marble put for signes,

To sever the good fellowship of dust,
And spoil the meeting. What shall point out them,
When they shall bow, and kneel, and fall down flat
To kisse those heaps, which now they have in trust?
Deare flesh, while I do pray, learn here thy stemme
And true descent; that when thou shalt grow fat,

And wanton in thy cravings, thou mayst know,
That flesh is but the glasse, which holds the dust
That measures all our time; which also shall
Be crumbled into dust. Mark here below
How tame these ashes are, how free from lust,
That thou mayst fit thy self against thy fall.

Church-musick.

SWeetest of sweets, I thank you: when displeasure
Did through my bodie wound my minde,
You took me thence, and in your house of pleasure
A daintie lodging me assign'd.

Now I in you without a bodie move,
Rising and falling with your wings:
We both together sweetly live and love,
Yet say sometimes, *God help poore Kings.*

7 this] the *1678–1799*, *Pickering* 12 Iett *W* : Iet, *B* : Ieat, *1633* : Jeat, *1633*[2]– 17 *indented in W, indicating a new paragraph : in B this line, not indented, begins a new page* 22 crumbled] broken *W*

Church-musick. 9 *Between verses 2 and 3, as above, W has this verse :*

O what a state is this, wch never knew
Sicknes, or shame, or sinn, or sorrow :
Where all my debts are payd, none can accrue
Wch knoweth not, what means, too Morrow.

Comfort, I'le die; for if you poste from me,
Sure I shall do so, and much more:
But if I travell in your companie,
You know the way to heavens doore.

Church-lock and key.

I Know it is my sinne, which locks thine eares,
And bindes thy hands,
Out-crying my requests, drowning my tears;
Or else the chilnesse of my faint demands.

But as cold hands are angrie with the fire,
And mend it still;
So I do lay the want of my desire,
Not on my sinnes, or coldnesse, but thy will.

Yet heare, O God, onely for his bloods sake
Which pleads for me:
For though sinnes plead too, yet like stones they make
His bloods sweet current much more loud to be.

The Church-floore.

MArk you the floore? that square & speckled stone,
Which looks so firm and strong,
Is *Patience*:

9 I'le *B W 1634–* : 'Ile *1633* *1633*^{2} poste] part *W*
Church-lock and key. *Title in W*: Prayer 1 locks] stops *W* 5 *Between verses 1 and 2, as above, W has this verse:*

If either Innocence or ffervencie
did play their part
Armies of blessings would contend & vye
Wch of them soonest should attaine my hart.

5 But] Yet *W* 6 And mend] Mending *W* 9 heare] here 1678–1709.
9–12 O make mee wholy guiltles, or at least
Guiltles so farr;
That zele and purenes circling my request
May guard it safe beyond ye highest starr. *W*
The Church-floore. *Not in W*

And th' other black and grave, wherewith each one
Is checker'd all along,
Humilitie:

The gentle rising, which on either hand
Leads to the Quire above,
Is *Confidence*:

But the sweet cement, which in one sure band
Ties the whole frame, is *Love*
And *Charitie*.

Hither sometimes Sinne steals, and stains
The marbles neat and curious veins:
But all is cleansed when the marble weeps.
Sometimes Death, puffing at the doore,
Blows all the dust about the floore:
But while he thinks to spoil the room, he sweeps.
Blest be the *Architect*, whose art
Could build so strong in a weak heart.

The Windows.

LOrd, how can man preach thy eternall word?
He is a brittle crazie glasse:
Yet in thy temple thou dost him afford
This glorious and transcendent place,
To be a window, through thy grace.

But when thou dost anneal in glasse thy storie,
Making thy life to shine within
The holy Preachers; then the light and glorie
More rev'rend grows, & more doth win:
Which else shows watrish, bleak, & thin.

The Windows. 'The titles of the severall poems' *in 1633– has* Church-windows, *but the similar table in B has* The Windowes *This poem is not in W*

Doctrine and life, colours and light, in one
When they combine and mingle, bring
A strong regard and aw: but speech alone
Doth vanish like a flaring thing,
And in the eare, not conscience ring.

Trinitie Sunday.

LOrd, who hast form'd me out of mud,
And hast redeem'd me through thy bloud,
And sanctifi'd me to do good;

Purge all my sinnes done heretofore:
For I confesse my heavie score,
And I will strive to sinne no more.

Enrich my heart, mouth, hands in me,
With faith, with hope, with charitie;
That I may runne, rise, rest with thee.

Content.

PEace mutt'ring thoughts, and do not grudge to keep
Within the walls of your own breast:
Who cannot on his own bed sweetly sleep,
Can on anothers hardly rest.

Gad not abroad at ev'ry quest and call
Of an untrained hope or passion.
To court each place or fortune that doth fall,
Is wantonnesse in contemplation.

Mark how the fire in flints doth quiet lie,
Content and warm t' it self alone:
But when it would appeare to others eye,
Without a knock it never shone.

14 flaring] flaming *corr. to* flaring *B*

Trinitie Sunday. *A second poem with the same title follows this poem in W; it is not included in B or 1633: see p. 202* 1 form'd me out of mud] made me living mudd *corr. by 2nd hand to* rais'd me from the mudd *W* 9 with] in *W*

Content. 2 the] *added by 2nd hand with caret in W* 6 or] & *corr. to* or *B* : and *W* 7 doth] does *W* 9 flints] flint *corr. to* Flint *W* 10 t' it] to it *B* : to'it *W*

Give me the pliant minde, whose gentle measure
    Complies and suits with all estates;
Which can let loose to a crown, and yet with pleasure
    Take up within a cloisters gates.

This soul doth span the world, and hang content
    From either pole unto the centre:
Where in each room of the well-furnisht tent
    He lies warm, and without adventure.

The brags of life are but a nine dayes wonder;
    And after death the fumes that spring
From private bodies make as big a thunder,
    As those which rise from a huge King.

Onely thy Chronicle is lost; and yet
    Better by worms be all once spent,
Then to have hellish moths still gnaw and fret
    Thy name in books, which may not rent:

When all thy deeds, whose brunt thou feel'st alone,
    Are chaw'd by others pens and tongue;
And as their wit is, their digestion,
    Thy nourisht fame is weak or strong.

Then cease discoursing soul, till thine own ground,
    Do not thy self or friends importune.
He that by seeking hath himself once found,
    Hath ever found a happie fortune.

The Quidditie.

MY God, a verse is not a crown,
    No point of honour, or gay suit,
No hawk, or banquet, or renown,
    Nor a good sword, nor yet a lute:

15 to a] to'a *W* 17 hang] range *conj. Hall* 18 centre] centure *W* (*cf.* The Sinner, *l. 8*) 19 the] y[t] *W* 23 bodies *W* : bodies, *B 1633–* 28 rent] vent *W 1638–67 1809* 30 pens] pen *W* 33 cease, *B* : cease *W 1633–* 36 ever *W 1633*[2] : euer *B 1633*

The Quidditie. *Title in W*: Poetry 3 Nor hawke, nor banquet, nor renowne *W* 4 nor yet] not yet *W*

It cannot vault, or dance, or play;
It never was in *France* or *Spain*;
Nor can it entertain the day
With my great stable or demain:

It is no office, art, or news,
Nor the Exchange, or busie Hall;
But it is that which while I use
I am with thee, and *most take all.*

Humilitie.

I Saw the Vertues sitting hand in hand
In sev'rall ranks upon an azure throne,
Where all the beasts and fowl by their command
Presented tokens of submission.
Humilitie, who sat the lowest there
To execute their call,
When by the beasts the presents tendred were,
Gave them about to all.

The angrie Lion did present his paw,
Which by consent was giv'n to Mansuetude.
The fearfull Hare her eares, which by their law
Humilitie did reach to Fortitude.
The jealous Turkie brought his corall-chain;
That went to Temperance.
On Justice was bestow'd the Foxes brain,
Kill'd in the way by chance.

At length the Crow bringing the Peacocks plume,
(For he would not) as they beheld the grace
Of that brave gift, each one began to fume,
And challenge it, as proper to his place,
Till they fell out: which when the beasts espied,
They leapt upon the throne;
And if the Fox had liv'd to rule their side,
They had depos'd each one.

8 my *B W 1638–56 1667 1809*: a *1633–5 1660 1674–1799 and all modern edns.*
12 *ital. 1633– : distinguished in W, but not in B* *Most 1633–: no cap. B W*
Humilitie. 3 Foule *B W*: fowls *1633– See note* 11 their] y^e *corr. to* their *B*

Humilitie, who held the plume, at this
Did weep so fast, that the tears trickling down
Spoil'd all the train: then saying, *Here it is*
For which ye wrangle, made them turn their frown
Against the beasts: so joyntly bandying,
They drive them soon away;
And then amerc'd them, double gifts to bring
At the next Session-day.

Frailtie.

LOrd, in my silence how do I despise
What upon trust
Is styled *honour*, *riches*, or *fair eyes*;
But is *fair dust!*
I surname them *guilded clay*,
Deare earth, *fine grasse* or *hay*;
In all, I think my foot doth ever tread
Upon their head.

But when I view abroad both Regiments;
The worlds, and thine:
Thine clad with simplenesse, and sad events;
The other fine,
Full of glorie and gay weeds,
Brave language, braver deeds:
That which was dust before, doth quickly rise,
And prick mine eyes.

O brook not this, lest if what even now
My foot did tread,
Affront those joyes, wherewith thou didst endow
And long since wed

29 bandying *W 1633–* : banding *B* *See note*
Frailtie. 6–7 Misuse them all the day:
And ever as I walk my foot doth tredd *W*
7 In all, I think] In all I think, *B* 16 And prick] Troubling *corr. by 2nd hand to* And prick *W* 17 what even now] y^t, wch iust now *W* 19 endow *W 1634–* : endow, *B 1633 1633*²

My poore soul, ev'n sick of love:
It may a Babel prove
Commodious to conquer heav'n and thee
Planted in me.

Constancie.

WHo is the honest man?
He that doth still and strongly good pursue,
To God, his neighbour, and himself most true:
Whom neither force nor fawning can
Unpinne, or wrench from giving all their due.

Whose honestie is not
So loose or easie, that a ruffling winde
Can blow away, or glittering look it blinde:
Who rides his sure and even trot,
While the world now rides by, now lags behinde.

Who, when great trials come,
Nor seeks, nor shunnes them; but doth calmly stay,
Till he the thing and the example weigh:
All being brought into a summe,
What place or person calls for, he doth pay.

Whom none can work or wooe
To use in any thing a trick or sleight;
For above all things he abhorres deceit:
His words and works and fashion too
All of a piece, and all are cleare and straight.

Who never melts or thaws
At close tentations: when the day is done,
His goodnesse sets not, but in dark can runne:
The sunne to others writeth laws,
And is their vertue; Vertue is his Sunne.

Constancie. *Not in W* 18 deceit] deceits *B* (*a slip*) 22 tentations] temptations *1634–* , *Pickering*

24–5 The Sunne to others writeth Laws;
And is their vertue, vertue is his Sonne. *B*

Who, when he is to treat
With sick folks, women, those whom passions sway,
Allows for that, and keeps his constant way:
Whom others faults do not defeat;
But though men fail him, yet his part doth play.

Whom nothing can procure,
When the wide world runnes bias from his will,
To writhe his limbes, and share, not mend the ill.
This is the Mark-man, safe and sure,
Who still is right, and prayes to be so still.

Affliction (III).

MY heart did heave, and there came forth, *O God!*
By that I knew that thou wast in the grief,
To guide and govern it to my relief,
Making a scepter of the rod:
Hadst thou not had thy part,
Sure the unruly sigh had broke my heart.

But since thy breath gave me both life and shape,
Thou knowst my tallies; and when there's assign'd
So much breath to a sigh, what's then behinde?
Or if some yeares with it escape,
The sigh then onely is
A gale to bring me sooner to my blisse.

Thy life on earth was grief, and thou art still
Constant unto it, making it to be
A point of honour, now to grieve in me,
And in thy members suffer ill.
They who lament one crosse,
Thou dying dayly, praise thee to thy losse.

32 Bias *B*: bias, *1633–* will, *1638–56*: will *B 1633–5* 33 share] thare *B* (*possibly altered to* share, *as* feltt *is altered to* felst *in* Content, *l. 29; not* there, *as in Nonesuch edn.*) 34 Mark-man] marksman *Pickering*

Affliction (III). *Numbering Ed* *This poem is not in W*

The Starre.

BRight spark, shot from a brighter place,
Where beams surround my Saviours face,
Canst thou be any where
So well as there?

Yet, if thou wilt from thence depart,
Take a bad lodging in my heart;
For thou canst make a debter,
And make it better.

First with thy fire-work burn to dust
Folly, and worse then folly, lust:
Then with thy light refine,
And make it shine:

So disengag'd from sinne and sicknesse,
Touch it with thy celestiall quicknesse,
That it may hang and move
After thy love.

Then with our trinitie of light,
Motion, and heat, let's take our flight
Unto the place where thou
Before didst bow.

Get me a standing there, and place
Among the beams, which crown the face
Of him, who dy'd to part
Sinne and my heart:

That so among the rest I may
Glitter, and curle, and winde as they:
That winding is their fashion
Of adoration.

Sure thou wilt joy, by gaining me
To flie home like a laden bee
Unto that hive of beams
And garland-streams.

The Starre. *Not in W*

Sunday.

O Day most calm, most bright,
The fruit of this, the next worlds bud,
Th' indorsement of supreme delight,
Writ by a friend, and with his bloud;
The couch of time; cares balm and bay:
The week were dark, but for thy light:
Thy torch doth show the way.

The other dayes and thou
Make up one man; whose face thou art,
Knocking at heaven with thy brow:
The worky-daies are the back-part;
The burden of the week lies there,
Making the whole to stoup and bow,
Till thy release appeare.

Man had straight forward gone
To endlesse death: but thou dost pull
And turn us round to look on one,
Whom, if we were not very dull,
We could not choose but look on still;
Since there is no place so alone,
The which he doth not fill.

Sundaies the pillars are,
On which heav'ns palace arched lies:
The other dayes fill up the spare
And hollow room with vanities.
They are the fruitfull beds and borders
In Gods rich garden: that is bare,
Which parts their ranks and orders.

Sunday. 1–7

O Day so calme, so bright:
The Couch of Tyme, ye balme of tears,
Th'Indorsment of supreme delight,
The parter of my wrangling feares
Setting in order what they tumble:
The week were dark, but y^{t} thy light
Teaches it not to stumble. *W*

(*In l. 2* teares *corr. to* tears *and in l. 4* partner *corr. to* parter)

11 worky-daies] working days *Pickering* 23 On wch heav'ens kingdome arch'd doth stand *W* 25 with vanities] on either hand *W*

26–8 They are ye rowes of fruitfull trees
Parted wth alleys or wth grass
In Gods rich Paradice. *W*

The Sundaies of mans life,
Thredded together on times string,
Make bracelets to adorn the wife
Of the eternall glorious King.
On Sunday heavens gate stands ope;
Blessings are plentifull and rife,
More plentifull then hope.

This day my Saviour rose,
And did inclose this light for his:
That, as each beast his manger knows,
Man might not of his fodder misse.
Christ hath took in this piece of ground,
And made a garden there for those
Who want herbs for their wound.

The rest of our Creation
Our great Redeemer did remove
With the same shake, which at his passion
Did th' earth and all things with it move.
As Sampson bore the doores away,
Christs hands, though nail'd, wrought our salvation,
And did unhinge that day.

The brightnesse of that day
We sullied by our foul offence:
Wherefore that robe we cast away,
Having a new at his expence,
Whose drops of bloud paid the full price,
That was requir'd to make us gay,
And fit for Paradise.

Thou art a day of mirth:
And where the week-dayes trail on ground,
Thy flight is higher, as thy birth.
O let me take thee at the bound,

29–35 *Quoted in Walton's* Lives
31–2 Make bracelets for ye spouse & wife
Of the Im̄ortall onely King. *W*
33 gate] dore *Walton* 35 then] and *corr. by 2nd hand to* then *W*
47 Sampson *B W 1709–99* : Samson *1633–1703 1809 See note*

Leaping with thee from sev'n to sev'n,
Till that we both, being toss'd from earth,
Flie hand in hand to heav'n!

Avarice.

MOney, thou bane of blisse, & sourse of wo,
Whence com'st thou, that thou art so fresh and fine?
I know thy parentage is base and low:
Man found thee poore and dirtie in a mine.
Surely thou didst so little contribute
To this great kingdome, which thou now hast got,
That he was fain, when thou wert destitute,
To digge thee out of thy dark cave and grot:
Then forcing thee by fire he made thee bright:
Nay, thou hast got the face of man; for we
Have with our stamp and seal transferr'd our right:
Thou art the man, and man but drosse to thee.
Man calleth thee his wealth, who made thee rich;
And while he digs out thee, falls in the ditch.

Ana- { MARY / ARMY } *gram.*

HOw well her name an *Army* doth present,
In whom the *Lord of Hosts* did pitch his tent!

To all Angels and Saints.

OH glorious spirits, who after all your bands
See the smooth face of God without a frown
Or strict commands;
Where ev'ry one is king, and hath his crown,
If not upon his head, yet in his hands:

Avarice. *Not in W* 7 wert] wast *1678–1799, Pickering* 9 forcing thee by fire *B* (*cf.* The Pearl, *l.* 6 'forc'd by fire') : forcing thee, by fire *1633–*
Anagram. *Not in W In B it comes between* Church-Musique *and* Church-lock & key, *the only difference in the order of poems in B from that adopted in 1633*
2 *Hosts B* : *hosts 1633–* tent!] *exclamation-mark not discernible in some copies of 1633*
To all Angels &c. 2 God *B* : God, *W 1633–*

Not out of envie or maliciousnesse
Do I forbear to crave your speciall aid:
I would addresse
My vows to thee most gladly, Blessed Maid,
And Mother of my God, in my distresse.

Thou art the holy mine, whence came the gold,
The great restorative for all decay
In young and old;
Thou art the cabinet where the jewell lay:
Chiefly to thee would I my soul unfold:

But now, alas, I dare not; for our King,
Whom we do all joyntly adore and praise,
Bids no such thing:
And where his pleasure no injunction layes,
('Tis your own case) ye never move a wing.

All worship is prerogative, and a flower
Of his rich crown, from whom lyes no appeal
At the last houre:
Therefore we dare not from his garland steal,
To make a posie for inferiour power.

Although then others court you, if ye know
What 's done on earth, we shall not fare the worse,
Who do not so;
Since we are ever ready to disburse,
If any one our Masters hand can show.

Employment (II).

HE that is weary, let him sit.
My soul would stirre
And trade in courtesies and wit,
Quitting the furre
To cold complexions needing it.

9 Blessed *B W*: blessed *1633–* 11 holy] sacred *W* 16 now, alas, *B*: now alas *W*: now (alas!) *1633–* our] my *W* 20 *no brackets but comma after* case *B W* a] your *W* 22 rich] great *W* 25 posie] garland *corr. by 2nd hand to* posye *W* 27 fare] feare *corr. to* fare *B* 29 disburse] discourse *corr. to* disburse *B*

Employment (II). *Numbering Ed*

Man is no starre, but a quick coal
Of mortall fire:
Who blows it not, nor doth controll
A faint desire,
Lets his own ashes choke his soul.

When th' elements did for place contest
With him, whose will
Ordain'd the highest to be best;
The earth sat still,
And by the others is opprest.

Life is a businesse, not good cheer;
Ever in warres.
The sunne still shineth there or here,
Whereas the starres
Watch an advantage to appeare.

Oh that I were an Orenge-tree,
That busie plant!
Then should I ever laden be,
And never want
Some fruit for him that dressed me.

But we are still too young or old;
The Man is gone,
Before we do our wares unfold:
So we freeze on,
Untill the grave increase our cold.

Deniall.

WHen my devotions could not pierce
Thy silent eares;
Then was my heart broken, as was my verse:
My breast was full of fears
And disorder:

21–5 O that I had the wing and thigh
Of laden Bees;
Then would I mount vp instantly
And by degrees
On men dropp blessings as I fly. *W*

25 dressed] dresseth *1674–1799*, *Pickering* 26 still too] ever *W* 27 Man *B W*: man *1633–* 29 Thus wee creep on *W*

My bent thoughts, like a brittle bow,
Did flie asunder:
Each took his way; some would to pleasures go,
Some to the warres and thunder
Of alarms.

As good go any where, they say,
As to benumme
Both knees and heart, in crying night and day,
Come, come, my God, O come,
But no hearing.

O that thou shouldst give dust a tongue
To crie to thee,
And then not heare it crying! all day long
My heart was in my knee,
But no hearing.

Therefore my soul lay out of sight,
Untun'd, unstrung:
My feeble spirit, unable to look right,
Like a nipt blossome, hung
Discontented.

O cheer and tune my heartlesse breast,
Deferre no time;
That so thy favours granting my request,
They and my minde may chime,
And mend my ryme.

Christmas.

ALl after pleasures as I rid one day,
My horse and I, both tir'd, bodie and minde,
With full crie of affections, quite astray,
I took up in the next inne I could finde.

Deniall. 8 pleasures] pleasure *1674–1809, Pickering* 13 knees and heart] hart & knees *W* 16 O that thou] *misprinted* O thou that *1674–1709, Pickering, Willmott* 20 But] Yet *W* 29 minde] hart *corr. by 2nd hand to* soule *W* 30 mend] meet *W*

Christmas. *Title in W* : Christmas-Day. *The second part* (*ll. 15–34*) *is not in W* 1 as I rid one day] riding on a Day *W* 3 astray, *B W* : astray ; *1633–*

There when I came, whom found I but my deare,
My dearest Lord, expecting till the grief
Of pleasures brought me to him, readie there
To be all passengers most sweet relief?
O Thou, whose glorious, yet contracted light,
Wrapt in nights mantle, stole into a manger;
Since my dark soul and brutish is thy right,
To Man of all beasts be not thou a stranger:
Furnish & deck my soul, that thou mayst have
A better lodging then a rack or grave.

THe shepherds sing; and shall I silent be?
My God, no hymne for thee?
My soul 's a shepherd too; a flock it feeds
Of thoughts, and words, and deeds.
The pasture is thy word: the streams, thy grace
Enriching all the place.
Shepherd and flock shall sing, and all my powers
Out-sing the day-light houres.
Then we will chide the sunne for letting night
Take up his place and right:
We sing one common Lord; wherefore he should
Himself the candle hold.
I will go searching, till I finde a sunne
Shall stay, till we have done;
A willing shiner, that shall shine as gladly,
As frost-nipt sunnes look sadly.
Then we will sing, and shine all our own day,
And one another pay:
His beams shall cheer my breast, and both so twine,
Till ev'n his beams sing, and my musick shine.

13–14 ffurnish my soule to thee, yt being drest
Of better lodging thou maist be possest. *W*

14 lodging then a rack *1633*[2]– : lodging, then a rack, *B 1633* 15–34 *om. W*

Ungratefulnesse.

LOrd, with what bountie and rare clemencie
Hast thou redeem'd us from the grave!
If thou hadst let us runne,
Gladly had man ador'd the sunne,
And thought his god most brave;
Where now we shall be better gods then he.

Thou hast but two rare cabinets full of treasure,
The *Trinitie*, and *Incarnation*:
Thou hast unlockt them both,
And made them jewels to betroth
The work of thy creation
Unto thy self in everlasting pleasure.

The statelier cabinet is the *Trinitie*,
Whose sparkling light accesse denies:
Therefore thou dost not show
This fully to us, till death blow
The dust into our eyes:
For by that powder thou wilt make us see.

But all thy sweets are packt up in the other;
Thy mercies thither flock and flow:
That as the first affrights,
This may allure us with delights;
Because this box we know;
For we have all of us just such another.

But man is close, reserv'd, and dark to thee:
When thou demandest but a heart,
He cavils instantly.
In his poore cabinet of bone
Sinnes have their box apart,
Defrauding thee, who gavest two for one.

Ungratefulnesse. 7 Thou hadst but two rich Cabinets of treasure, *W* 9 unlockt them] layd open *W* 16 fully to us] to vs fully *W* 18 that] this *W* 22 allure] allures *B* (*a slip*) 23 box] Boxe *W*: Bone *B* (*cf. l. 29*) 29 box] bone *corr. to* boxe *B*

Sighs and Grones.

O Do not use me
After my sinnes! look not on my desert,
But on thy glorie! then thou wilt reform
And not refuse me: for thou onely art
The mightie God, but I a sillie worm;
O do not bruise me!

O do not urge me!
For what account can thy ill steward make?
I have abus'd thy stock, destroy'd thy woods,
Suckt all thy magazens: my head did ake,
Till it found out how to consume thy goods:
O do not scourge me!

O do not blinde me!
I have deserv'd that an Egyptian night
Should thicken all my powers; because my lust
Hath still sow'd fig-leaves to exclude thy light:
But I am frailtie, and already dust;
O do not grinde me!

O do not fill me
With the turn'd viall of thy bitter wrath!
For thou hast other vessels full of bloud,
A part whereof my Saviour empti'd hath,
Ev'n unto death: since he di'd for my good,
O do not kill me!

But O reprieve me!
For thou hast life and death at thy command;
Thou art both *Judge* and *Saviour*, *feast* and *rod*,
Cordiall and *Corrosive*: put not thy hand
Into the bitter box; but O my God,
My God, relieve me!

Sighs and Grones. *Not in W*
in B, as the words in ll. 27–8 are

26 *life* and *death* 1633– : *not distinguished*

The World.

LOve built a stately house; where *Fortune* came,
And spinning phansies, she was heard to say,
That her fine cobwebs did support the frame,
Whereas they were supported by the same:
But *Wisdome* quickly swept them all away.

Then *Pleasure* came, who, liking not the fashion,
Began to make *Balcones*, *Terraces*,
Till she had weakned all by alteration:
But rev'rend *laws*, and many a *proclamation*
Reformed all at length with menaces.

Then enter'd *Sinne*, and with that Sycomore,
Whose leaves first sheltred man from drought & dew,
Working and winding slily evermore,
The inward walls and sommers cleft and tore:
But *Grace* shor'd these, and cut that as it grew.

Then *Sinne* combin'd with *Death* in a firm band
To raze the building to the very floore:
Which they effected, none could them withstand.
But *Love* and *Grace* took *Glorie* by the hand,
And built a braver Palace then before.

Coloss. 3. 3.

Our life is hid with Christ in God.

MY words & thoughts do both expresse this notion,
That *Life* hath with the sun a double motion.
The first *Is* straight, and our diurnall friend,
The other *Hid* and doth obliquely bend.
One life is wrapt *In* flesh, and tends to earth:
The other winds towards *Him*, whose happie birth

The World. 6 who, *B 1634–* : who *W 1633 1633²* 10 Reformed all at length] Quickly reformed all *W* 12 sheltred] shelterd *B* 14 inward] *Palmer misreads W as* inner sommers *Ed*: Sommers *B W 1633–*: summers *Pickering* 17 raze *B W 1633² 1634*: rase *1633 1635–* 19 But Love took Grace & Glory by the hand *W*

Our life is hid &c. 5 earth: *B 1638–* : earth. *W 1633* : earth; *1633²–5*

Taught me to live here so, *That* still one eye
Should aim and shoot at that which *Is* on high:
Quitting with daily labour all *My* pleasure,
To gain at harvest an eternall *Treasure.*

Vanitie (I).

THe fleet Astronomer can bore,
And thred the spheres with his quick-piercing minde:
He views their stations, walks from doore to doore,
Surveys, as if he had design'd
To make a purchase there: he sees their dances,
And knoweth long before
Both their full-ey'd aspects, and secret glances.

The nimble Diver with his side
Cuts through the working waves, that he may fetch
His dearely-earned pearl, which God did hide
On purpose from the ventrous wretch;
That he might save his life, and also hers,
Who with excessive pride
Her own destruction and his danger wears.

The subtil Chymick can devest
And strip the creature naked, till he finde
The callow principles within their nest:
There he imparts to them his minde,
Admitted to their bed-chamber, before
They appeare trim and drest
To ordinarie suitours at the doore.

What hath not man sought out and found,
But his deare God? who yet his glorious law
Embosomes in us, mellowing the ground
With showres and frosts, with love & aw,

Vanitie (I). *Numbering Ed This poem is not in W* 6 before *1633²–* : before, *B 1633* 14 Her] His *written over* Her *in B See note* 15 devest] divest *1709–1809, Pickering* 22 sought] wrought *B See note*

So that we need not say, Where 's this command?
Poore man, thou searchest round
To finde out *death*, but missest *life* at hand.

Lent.

WElcome deare feast of Lent: who loves not thee,
He loves not Temperance, or Authoritie,
But is compos'd of passion.
The Scriptures bid us *fast*; the Church sayes, *now*:
Give to thy Mother, what thou wouldst allow
To ev'ry Corporation.

The humble soul compos'd of love and fear
Begins at home, and layes the burden there,
When doctrines disagree.
He sayes, in things which use hath justly got,
I am a scandall to the Church, and not
The Church is so to me.

True Christians should be glad of an occasion
To use their temperance, seeking no evasion,
When good is seasonable;
Unlesse Authoritie, which should increase
The obligation in us, make it lesse,
And Power it self disable.

Besides the cleannesse of sweet abstinence,
Quick thoughts and motions at a small expense,
A face not fearing light:
Whereas in fulnesse there are sluttish fumes,
Sowre exhalations, and dishonest rheumes,
Revenging the delight.

Then those same pendant profits, which the spring
And Easter intimate, enlarge the thing,
And goodnesse of the deed.
Neither ought other mens abuse of Lent
Spoil the good use; lest by that argument
We forfeit all our Creed.

Lent. 3 compos'd of] a child of *W* 25 pendant profits] *hyphened in W* 29 the] our *W*

It 's true, we cannot reach Christs forti'th day;
Yet to go part of that religious way,
Is better then to rest:
We cannot reach our Saviours puritie;
Yet are we bid, *Be holy ev'n as he.*
In both let 's do our best.

Who goeth in the way which Christ hath gone,
Is much more sure to meet with him, then one
That travelleth by-wayes:
Perhaps my God, though he be farre before,
May turn, and take me by the hand, and more
May strengthen my decayes.

Yet Lord instruct us to improve our fast
By starving sinne and taking such repast
As may our faults controll:
That ev'ry man may revell at his doore,
Not in his parlour; banquetting the poore,
And among those his soul.

Vertue.

SWeet day, so cool, so calm, so bright,
The bridall of the earth and skie:
The dew shall weep thy fall to night;
For thou must die.

Sweet rose, whose hue angrie and brave
Bids the rash gazer wipe his eye:
Thy root is ever in its grave,
And thou must die.

37 in the way which] in that way, wch *B*: in ye way that *W* 39 by-wayes] crosswayes *corr. by 2nd hand to* by-wayes *W* 44 repast *W* 1633^{2}– : repast, *B* *1633* 45 our faults] all vice *W*

Vertue. *Not in W Quoted in full in Walton's* The Compleat Angler (1653), Part I, ch. v 3 The dew] Sweet dews *Walton* 7 its] his *B* *See note*

Sweet spring, full of sweet dayes and roses,
A box where sweets compacted lie;
My musick shows ye have your closes,
And all must die.

Onely a sweet and vertuous soul,
Like season'd timber, never gives;
But though the whole world turn to coal,
Then chiefly lives.

The Pearl. Matth. 13. 45.

I Know the wayes of Learning; both the head
And pipes that feed the presse, and make it runne;
What reason hath from nature borrowed,
Or of it self, like a good huswife, spunne
In laws and policie; what the starres conspire,
What willing nature speaks, what forc'd by fire;
Both th' old discoveries, and the new-found seas,
The stock and surplus, cause and historie:
All these stand open, or I have the keyes:
Yet I love thee.

I know the wayes of Honour, what maintains
The quick returns of courtesie and wit:
In vies of favours whether partie gains,
When glorie swells the heart, and moldeth it
To all expressions both of hand and eye,
Which on the world a true-love-knot may tie,
And bear the bundle, wheresoe're it goes:
How many drammes of spirit there must be
To sell my life unto my friends or foes:
Yet I love thee.

11 ye] you *Walton* 15 though . . . turn] when the whole world turns *Walton* coal] a Coal *1703–99*

The Pearl. *Matth.* 13. 45 (45 *added from W*) 1 Learning *B W* 1633^{2}– : learning *1633* (*cf. ll. 11, 21*) 3 borrowed] purchased *W* 11 Honour *B W* 1633^{2}– : honour *1633*

I know the wayes of Pleasure, the sweet strains,
The lullings and the relishes of it;
The propositions of hot bloud and brains;
What mirth and musick mean; what love and wit
Have done these twentie hundred yeares, and more:
I know the projects of unbridled store:
My stuffe is flesh, not brasse; my senses live,
And grumble oft, that they have more in me
Then he that curbs them, being but one to five:
Yet I love thee.

I know all these, and have them in my hand:
Therefore not sealed, but with open eyes
I flie to thee, and fully understand
Both the main sale, and the commodities;
And at what rate and price I have thy love;
With all the circumstances that may move:
Yet through these labyrinths, not my groveling wit,
But thy silk twist let down from heav'n to me,
Did both conduct and teach me, how by it
To climbe to thee.

Affliction (IV).

BRoken in pieces all asunder,
Lord, hunt me not,
A thing forgot,
Once a poore creature, now a wonder,

21 Pleasure *B W* 1633^{2}– : pleasure *1633* 22 lullings] gustos *corr. by 2nd hand to* lullings *W* 25 twentie] twenty *corr. by 2nd hand to* many *W* (*yet* twenty *is in B*) 26 unbridled] unbundled *B* (*cf. l. 17* bundle)
26–30 Where both their baskets are wth all their store,
The smacks of dainties and their exaltation :
What both ye stops and pegs of pleasure bee :
The ioyes of Company or Contemplation
Yet I love Thee. *W*
(*ll. 26–8 are cancelled in W by lines drawn across, but no alternative lines replace them ; ll. 29–30 are left standing*) 32 sealed] seeled *W* *See note* 37–40 *cited in Walton's* Lives 37 Yet through] That, through *Walton* these *B W 1638–67, Walton, 1809* : the *1633–5 1674–1799 and all modern edns* 38 silk twist] silk-twist *W 1638–1809, Walton* 40 thee] Thee *B* (*which has* thee *in ll. 10, 20, 30 : W has* Thee *throughout*)
Affliction (IV). *Numbering Ed* *Title in W* : Tentation

A wonder tortur'd in the space
Betwixt this world and that of grace.

My thoughts are all a case of knives,
Wounding my heart
With scatter'd smart,
As watring pots give flowers their lives.
Nothing their furie can controll,
While they do wound and pink my soul.

All my attendants are at strife,
Quitting their place
Unto my face:
Nothing performs the task of life:
The elements are let loose to fight,
And while I live, trie out their right.

Oh help, my God! let not their plot
Kill them and me,
And also thee,
Who art my life: dissolve the knot,
As the sunne scatters by his light
All the rebellions of the night.

Then shall those powers, which work for grief,
Enter thy pay,
And day by day
Labour thy praise, and my relief;
With care and courage building me,
Till I reach heav'n, and much more, thee.

Man.

MY God, I heard this day,
That none doth build a stately habitation,
But he that means to dwell therein.
What house more stately hath there been,
Or can be, then is Man? to whose creation
All things are in decay.

12 pink *B* : pinke *W* : prick *1633–* *See note* 30 more, *B W* : more *1633–* thee] Thee *B W*

Man. 2 none doth build] no man builds *W*

For Man is ev'ry thing,
And more: He is a tree, yet bears more fruit;
A beast, yet is, or should be more:
Reason and speech we onely bring.
Parrats may thank us, if they are not mute,
They go upon the score.

Man is all symmetrie,
Full of proportions, one limbe to another,
And all to all the world besides:
Each part may call the furthest, brother:
For head with foot hath private amitie,
And both with moons and tides.

Nothing hath got so farre,
But Man hath caught and kept it, as his prey.
His eyes dismount the highest starre:
He is in little all the sphere.
Herbs gladly cure our flesh; because that they
Finde their acquaintance there.

For us the windes do blow,
The earth doth rest, heav'n move, and fountains flow.
Nothing we see, but means our good,
As our delight, or as our treasure:
The whole is, either our cupboard of food,
Or cabinet of pleasure.

The starres have us to bed;
Night draws the curtain, which the sunne withdraws;
Musick and light attend our head.
All things unto our flesh are kinde
In their descent and being; to our minde
In their ascent and cause.

8 more fruit *W*: no fruit *B 1633–*: mo fruit *Grosart See note* 16 furthest *B*: farthest *W 1633–* 20 hath] has *W* 26 Earth resteth, Heaven moueth, fountains flow *W* (*Grosart adopts*) 28–30, 34–6 *The words* delight, treasure, food, pleasure (28–30), flesh, descent, being, minde, ascent, cause (34–6), *are italicized 1633–, but they are not distinguished in B and W*

Each thing is full of dutie:
Waters united are our navigation;
Distinguished, our habitation;
Below, our drink; above, our meat;
Both are our cleanlinesse. Hath one such beautie?
Then how are all things neat?

More servants wait on Man,
Then he'l take notice of: in ev'ry path
He treads down that which doth befriend him,
When sicknesse makes him pale and wan.
Oh mightie love! Man is one world, and hath
Another to attend him.

Since then, my God, thou hast
So brave a Palace built; O dwell in it,
That it may dwell with thee at last!
Till then, afford us so much wit;
That, as the world serves us, we may serve thee,
And both thy servants be.

Antiphon (II).

Chor. PRaised be the God of love,
Men. Here below,
Angels. And here above:
Cho. Who hath dealt his mercies so,
Ang. To his friend,
Men. And to his foe;

Cho. That both grace and glorie tend
Ang. Us of old,
Men. And us in th'end.
Cho. The great shepherd of the fold
Ang. Us did make,
Men. For us was sold.

41 cleanlines : if one have beauty, *W* 53 as the world serue vs *B*
53–4 That as ye world to vs is kind and free
So we may bee to Thee. *W*
Antiphon (II). *Numbering Ed* *Title in W* : Ode

Cho. He our foes in pieces brake;
Ang. Him we touch;
Men. And him we take.
Cho. Wherefore since that he is such,
Ang. We adore,
Men. And we do crouch.

Cho. Lord, thy praises should be more.
Men. We have none,
Ang. And we no store.
Cho. Praised be the God alone,
Who hath made of two folds one.

Unkindnesse.

LOrd, make me coy and tender to offend:
In friendship, first I think, if that agree,
Which I intend,
Unto my friends intent and end.
I would not use a friend, as I use Thee.

If any touch my friend, or his good name,
It is my honour and my love to free
His blasted fame
From the least spot or thought of blame.
I could not use a friend, as I use Thee.

My friend may spit upon my curious floore:
Would he have gold? I lend it instantly;
But let the poore,
And thou within them, starve at doore.
I cannot use a friend, as I use Thee.

19 should] shall *1667–1799, Pickering*
19–21 Cho. Lord thou dost deserve much more
Ang. Wee have none,
Men. Wee haue no store. *W*
23 *line indented 1633– , but not in B and W* Who] Wch *W*
Unkindnesse. 6 name, *B 1633²–* : name ; *W 1633* 8 blasted] darkned *W*
14 them, *W* : them *B 1633–*

When that my friend pretendeth to a place,
I quit my interest, and leave it free:
But when thy grace
Sues for my heart, I thee displace,
Nor would I use a friend, as I use Thee.

Yet can a friend what thou hast done fulfill?
O write in brasse, *My God upon a tree*
His bloud did spill
Onely to purchase my good-will.
Yet use I not my foes, as I use Thee.

Life.

I Made a posie, while the day ran by:
Here will I smell my remnant out, and tie
My life within this band.
But Time did becken to the flowers, and they
By noon most cunningly did steal away,
And wither'd in my hand.

My hand was next to them, and then my heart:
I took, without more thinking, in good part
Times gentle admonition:
Who did so sweetly deaths sad taste convey,
Making my minde to smell my fatall day;
Yet sugring the suspicion.

Farewell deare flowers, sweetly your time ye spent,
Fit, while ye liv'd, for smell or ornament,
And after death for cures.
I follow straight without complaints or grief,
Since if my sent be good, I care not if
It be as short as yours.

24 *good-will*] *full stop B W*: *colon 1633–* 25 *italicized 1633–* , *but not distinguished, as ll. 22–4 are, in B and W* Thee *B W* : *Thee 1634–* : *thee 1633 1633*[2]
Life. *Not in W* *Quoted in full in Vaughan's* The Mount of Olives (1652)
4 Time *B 1634–* : time *1633 1633*[2] 16 complaints] complaint *Vaughan*
17 not *1633*[2]*–* : not, *B 1633*

Submission.

BUt that thou art my wisdome, Lord,
And both mine eyes are thine,
My minde would be extreamly stirr'd
For missing my designe.

Were it not better to bestow
Some place and power on me?
Then should thy praises with me grow,
And share in my degree.

But when I thus dispute and grieve,
I do resume my sight,
And pilfring what I once did give,
Disseize thee of thy right.

How know I, if thou shouldst me raise,
That I should then raise thee?
Perhaps great places and thy praise
Do not so well agree.

Wherefore unto my gift I stand;
I will no more advise:
Onely do thou lend me a hand,
Since thou hast both mine eyes.

Justice (I).

I Cannot skill of these thy wayes.
Lord, thou didst make me, yet thou woundest me;
Lord, thou dost wound me, yet thou dost relieve me:
Lord, thou relievest, yet I die by thee:
Lord, thou dost kill me, yet thou dost reprieve me.

Submission. *Not in W* 10 sight] fight *Grosart* (*misreading* ſight)
Justice (I). *Numbering Ed* *Not in W* 1 thy] *Palmer incorrectly states that B has* my

But when I mark my life and praise,
Thy justice me most fitly payes:
For, *I do praise thee, yet I praise thee not:*
My prayers mean thee, yet my prayers stray:
I would do well, yet sinne the hand hath got:
My soul doth love thee, yet it loves delay.
I cannot skill of these my wayes.

Charms and Knots.

WHo reade a chapter when they rise,
Shall ne're be troubled with ill eyes.

A poore mans rod, when thou dost ride,
Is both a weapon and a guide.

Who shuts his hand, hath lost his gold:
Who opens it, hath it twice told.

Who goes to bed and does not pray,
Maketh two nights to ev'ry day.

Who by aspersions throw a stone
At th' head of others, hit their own.

Who looks on ground with humble eyes,
Findes himself there, and seeks to rise.

When th' hair is sweet through pride or lust,
The powder doth forget the dust.

Take one from ten, and what remains?
Ten still, if sermons go for gains.

Charms and Knots. 2 ill] sore *W*

3–4 A poore mans rod if thou wilt hire
Thy horse shal never fall or tire. *W*

7 does *B W*: doth *1633–* 8 Doubles the night, & trips by day. *W* 10 th' head] th' hart *W* 11–14 *W has 6th and 7th couplets in reverse order, and then this verse, which is not in B:*

Who turnes a trencher, setteth free
A prisoner crusht wth gluttonie.

14 doth] does *W* 16 Ten, if a Sermon goe for gains. *W*

In shallow waters heav'n doth show;
But who drinks on, to hell may go.

Affliction (v).

MY God, I read this day,
That planted Paradise was not so firm,
As was and is thy floting Ark; whose stay
And anchor thou art onely, to confirm
And strengthen it in ev'ry age,
When waves do rise, and tempests rage.

At first we liv'd in pleasure;
Thine own delights thou didst to us impart:
When we grew wanton, thou didst use displeasure
To make us thine: yet that we might not part,
As we at first did board with thee,
Now thou wouldst taste our miserie.

There is but joy and grief;
If either will convert us, we are thine:
Some Angels us'd the first; if our relief
Take up the second, then thy double line
And sev'rall baits in either kinde
Furnish thy table to thy minde.

Affliction then is ours;
We are the trees, whom shaking fastens more,
While blustring windes destroy the wanton bowres,
And ruffle all their curious knots and store.
My God, so temper joy and wo,
That thy bright beams may tame thy bow.

Charms and Knots. 17–18 *W ends with the following 3 couplets, the last being an earlier draft of the one which stands last in B and 1633– :*

The world thinks all things bigg and tall
Grace turnes ye Optick, then they fall.

A falling starr has lost his place:
The Courtier getts it, that has grace.

In small draughts Heau'en does shine & dwell:
Who dives on further may find Hell.

Affliction (V). *Numbering Ed*

Mortification.

HOw soon doth man decay!
When clothes are taken from a chest of sweets
To swaddle infants, whose young breath
Scarce knows the way;
Those clouts are little winding sheets,
Which do consigne and send them unto death.

When boyes go first to bed,
They step into their voluntarie graves,
Sleep bindes them fast; onely their breath
Makes them not dead:
Successive nights, like rolling waves,
Convey them quickly, who are bound for death.

When youth is frank and free,
And calls for musick, while his veins do swell,
All day exchanging mirth and breath
In companie;
That musick summons to the knell,
Which shall befriend him at the houre of death.

When man grows staid and wise,
Getting a house and home, where he may move
Within the circle of his breath,
Schooling his eyes;
That dumbe inclosure maketh love
Unto the coffin, that attends his death.

When age grows low and weak,
Marking his grave, and thawing ev'ry yeare,
Till all do melt, and drown his breath
When he would speak;
A chair or litter shows the biere,
Which shall convey him to the house of death.

Mortification. 1 doth] does *W* 2 clothes] cloths *B* 18 houre *W*: house *B 1633–* *See note* 30 house] place *W*

Man, ere he is aware,
Hath put together a solemnitie,
And drest his herse, while he has breath
As yet to spare:
Yet Lord, instruct us so to die,
That all these dyings may be life in death.

Decay.

SWeet were the dayes, when thou didst lodge with Lot,
Struggle with Jacob, sit with Gideon,
Advise with Abraham, when thy power could not
Encounter Moses strong complaints and mone:
Thy words were then, *Let me alone.*

One might have sought and found thee presently
At some fair oak, or bush, or cave, or well:
Is my God this way? No, they would reply:
He is to Sinai gone, as we heard tell:
List, ye may heare great Aarons bell.

But now thou dost thy self immure and close
In some one corner of a feeble heart:
Where yet both Sinne and Satan, thy old foes,
Do pinch and straiten thee, and use much art
To gain thy thirds and little part.

I see the world grows old, when as the heat
Of thy great love, once spread, as in an urn
Doth closet up it self, and still retreat,
Cold Sinne still forcing it, till it return,
And calling *Justice*, all things burn.

Decay. *Not in W* 17 love, *1656–60* : *no comma B 1633–41* 19 Sinne *B* : sinne *1633* (*though it has* Sinne *in l. 13*) 20 Justice *distinguished in B* : Justice *1633–*

Miserie.

LOrd, let the Angels praise thy name.
Man is a foolish thing, a foolish thing,
Folly and Sinne play all his game.
His house still burns, and yet he still doth sing,
Man is but grasse,
He knows it, fill the glasse.

How canst thou brook his foolishnesse?
Why, he'l not lose a cup of drink for thee:
Bid him but temper his excesse;
Not he: he knows where he can better be,
As he will swear,
Then to serve thee in fear.

What strange pollutions doth he wed,
And make his own? as if none knew but he.
No man shall beat into his head,
That thou within his curtains drawn canst see:
They are of cloth,
Where never yet came moth.

The best of men, turn but thy hand
For one poore minute, stumble at a pinne:
They would not have their actions scann'd,
Nor any sorrow tell them that they sinne,
Though it be small,
And measure not their fall.

They quarrell thee, and would give over
The bargain made to serve thee: but thy love
Holds them unto it, and doth cover
Their follies with the wing of thy milde Dove,
Not suff'ring those
Who would, to be thy foes.

Miserie. *Title in W*: The Publican 3 play all] play out *W* 8 Why, 1633^2– : Why *B W 1633* 10 knows 1633^2– : *comma B W 1633* 14 knew *W* 1633^2– : *comma B 1633* 21 scann'd] *Palmer misreads* scand *in W as* stand 28 wing] wings *W*

My God, Man cannot praise thy name:
Thou art all brightnesse, perfect puritie;
The sunne holds down his head for shame,
Dead with eclipses, when we speak of thee:
How shall infection
Presume on thy perfection?

As dirtie hands foul all they touch,
And those things most, which are most pure and fine:
So our clay hearts, ev'n when we crouch
To sing thy praises, make them lesse divine.
Yet either this,
Or none, thy portion is.

Man cannot serve thee; let him go,
And serve the swine: there, there is his delight:
He doth not like this vertue, no;
Give him his dirt to wallow in all night:
These Preachers make
His head to shoot and ake.

Oh foolish man! where are thine eyes?
How hast thou lost them in a croud of cares?
Thou pull'st the rug, and wilt not rise,
No, not to purchase the whole pack of starres:
There let them shine,
Thou must go sleep, or dine.

The bird that sees a daintie bowre
Made in the tree, where she was wont to sit,
Wonders and sings, but not his power
Who made the arbour: this exceeds her wit.
But Man doth know
The spring, whence all things flow:

39 So our] *Palmer misreads B as* Some 42 none, *B W*: none *1633–*
43–8 Man can not serue thee : lett him goe
And feed the swine, wth all his mind & might :
ffor this he wondrous well doth know
They will be kind, and all his pains requite,
Making him free
Of that good companie. *W*
46–7 wallow in, all night These preachers make *B* 48 ake] shake *corr. to* Ake *B* 51 pull'st the rug] lyest warme *W* 52 No, *B W* *1633^2–* : No *1633*

And yet, as though he knew it not,
His knowledge winks, and lets his humours reigne;
They make his life a constant blot,
And all the bloud of God to run in vain.
Ah wretch! what verse
Can thy strange wayes rehearse?

Indeed at first Man was a treasure,
A box of jewels, shop of rarities,
A ring, whose posie was, *My pleasure:*
He was a garden in a Paradise:
Glorie and grace
Did crown his heart and face.

But sinne hath fool'd him. Now he is
A lump of flesh, without a foot or wing
To raise him to a glimpse of blisse:
A sick toss'd vessel, dashing on each thing;
Nay, his own shelf:
My God, I mean my self.

Jordan (II).

WHen first my lines of heav'nly joyes made mention,
Such was their lustre, they did so excell,
That I sought out quaint words, and trim invention;
My thoughts began to burnish, sprout, and swell,
Curling with metaphors a plain intention,
Decking the sense, as if it were to sell.

Thousands of notions in my brain did runne,
Off'ring their service, if I were not sped:
I often blotted what I had begunne;
This was not quick enough, and that was dead.
Nothing could seem too rich to clothe the sunne,
Much lesse those joyes which trample on his head.

61 yet, *1634–* : yet *B W 1633* 1633^2
65–6 Ah wretched man
Who may thy follies span? *W*
75 *indented in B W* 1633^2*–* *, but not, by oversight, in 1633* a glimpse *B W 1638–67 1809, Grosart*: the glimpse *1633–5 1674–1799, Pickering, Willmott, Palmer*
Jordan (II). *Numbering Ed* *Title in W*: Invention (*cf. l.* 3) 1 lines] verse *W*
4 sprout] spredd *W* 6 Decking] Praising *W*

As flames do work and winde, when they ascend,
So did I weave my self into the sense.
But while I bustled, I might heare a friend
Whisper, *How wide is all this long pretence!*
There is in love a sweetnesse readie penn'd:
Copie out onely that, and save expense.

Prayer (II).

OF what an easie quick accesse,
My blessed Lord, art thou! how suddenly
May our requests thine eare invade!
To shew that state dislikes not easinesse,
If I but lift mine eyes, my suit is made:
Thou canst no more not heare, then thou canst die.

Of what supreme almightie power
Is thy great arm, which spans the east and west,
And tacks the centre to the sphere!
By it do all things live their measur'd houre:
We cannot ask the thing, which is not there,
Blaming the shallownesse of our request.

Of what unmeasurable love
Art thou possest, who, when thou couldst not die,
Wert fain to take our flesh and curse,
And for our sakes in person sinne reprove,
That by destroying that which ty'd thy purse,
Thou mightst make way for liberalitie!

Since then these three wait on thy throne,
Ease, *Power*, and *Love*; I value prayer so,
That were I to leave all but one,
Wealth, fame, endowments, vertues, all should go;
I and deare prayer would together dwell,
And quickly gain, for each inch lost, an ell.

14 So I bespoke me much insinuation: *W* 16 *long pretence*] preparation *W*
18 Coppy out that : there needs no alteration. *W*

Prayer (II). *Numbering Ed* 1–2 accesse, . . . thou!] access Art thou, my blessed King? *W* 3 eare] eares *W* 4 easinesse, *Willmott, Grosart, Palmer* : *full stop B W 1633–* 8 arm, *1634–* : Arme, *B W*: arm *1633 1633*[2]
10 measur'd] silly *W*

Obedience.

MY God, if writings may
Convey a Lordship any way
Whither the buyer and the seller please;
Let it not thee displease,
If this poore paper do as much as they.

On it my heart doth bleed
As many lines, as there doth need
To passe it self and all it hath to thee.
To which I do agree,
And here present it as my speciall Deed.

If that hereafter Pleasure
Cavill, and claim her part and measure,
As if this passed with a reservation,
Or some such words in fashion;
I here exclude the wrangler from thy treasure.

O let thy sacred will
All thy delight in me fulfill!
Let me not think an action mine own way,
But as thy love shall sway,
Resigning up the rudder to thy skill.

Lord, what is man to thee,
That thou shouldst minde a rotten tree?
Yet since thou canst not choose but see my actions;
So great are thy perfections,
Thou mayst as well my actions guide, as see.

Besides, thy death and bloud
Show'd a strange love to all our good:
Thy sorrows were in earnest; no faint proffer,
Or superficiall offer
Of what we might not take, or be withstood.

Obedience. 2 way] waies *B*: was *corr. to* way *W* 7 as there doth] as it does *W* 8 hath] has *W* 10 Deed *B W*: deed *1633–* (*cf. ll. 33, 38*) 15 exclude] shutt out *W* 22 *indented B W 1641– , but not, by oversight, 1633–8*

Wherefore I all forgo:
To one word onely I say, No:
Where in the Deed there was an intimation
Of a gift or donation,
Lord, let it now by way of purchase go.

He that will passe his land,
As I have mine, may set his hand
And heart unto this Deed, when he hath read;
And make the purchase spread
To both our goods, if he to it will stand.

How happie were my part,
If some kinde man would thrust his heart
Into these lines; till in heav'ns Court of Rolls
They were by winged souls
Entred for both, farre above their desert!

Conscience.

PEace pratler, do not lowre:
Not a fair look, but thou dost call it foul:
Not a sweet dish, but thou dost call it sowre:
Musick to thee doth howl.
By listning to thy chatting fears
I have both lost mine eyes and eares.

Pratler, no more, I say:
My thoughts must work, but like a noiselesse sphere;
Harmonious peace must rock them all the day:
No room for pratlers there.
If thou persistest, I will tell thee,
That I have physick to expell thee.

33 Deed *B W*: deed *1633–* 34 Of gift or a donation *conj. Palmer* (*to improve the scansion*) 34–5 *The words* gift, donation, purchase, *italicized in 1633, are not distinguished in B W* 38 Deed *W*: deed *B 1633–* hath read;] doth read *W* 43 Court of Rolls *capitals from B W, not in 1633–* 45 Entred] Enterd *B*

Conscience. *The poems which follow from here to the group beginning with* The Elixir, *p. 184, are absent from W* 8 sphere ;] sphere *B* : sphere. *1634– See note*

And the receit shall be
My Saviours bloud: when ever at his board
I do but taste it, straight it cleanseth me,
And leaves thee not a word;
No, not a tooth or nail to scratch,
And at my actions carp, or catch.

Yet if thou talkest still,
Besides my physick, know there's some for thee:
Some wood and nails to make a staffe or bill
For those that trouble me:
The bloudie crosse of my deare Lord
Is both my physick and my sword.

Sion.

LOrd, with what glorie wast thou serv'd of old,
When Solomons temple stood and flourished!
Where most things were of purest gold;
The wood was all embellished
With flowers and carvings, mysticall and rare:
All show'd the builders, crav'd the seeers care.

Yet all this glorie, all this pomp and state
Did not affect thee much, was not thy aim;
Something there was, that sow'd debate:
Wherefore thou quitt'st thy ancient claim:
And now thy Architecture meets with sinne;
For all thy frame and fabrick is within.

There thou art struggling with a peevish heart,
Which sometimes crosseth thee, thou sometimes it:
The fight is hard on either part.
Great God doth fight, he doth submit.
All Solomons sea of brasse and world of stone
Is not so deare to thee as one good grone.

Sion. *Not in W* 6 seeers *B*: seers *1633–* *See note*

And truly brasse and stones are heavie things,
Tombes for the dead, not temples fit for thee:
But grones are quick, and full of wings,
And all their motions upward be;
And ever as they mount, like larks they sing;
The note is sad, yet musick for a King.

Home.

COme Lord, my head doth burn, my heart is sick,
While thou dost ever, ever stay:
Thy long deferrings wound me to the quick,
My spirit gaspeth night and day.
O show thy self to me,
Or take me up to thee!

How canst thou stay, considering the pace
The bloud did make, which thou didst waste?
When I behold it trickling down thy face,
I never saw thing make such haste.
O show thy, &c.

When man was lost, thy pitie lookt about
To see what help in th' earth or skie:
But there was none; at least no help without:
The help did in thy bosome lie.
O show thy, &c.

There lay thy sonne: and must he leave that nest,
That hive of sweetnesse, to remove
Thraldome from those, who would not at a feast
Leave one poore apple for thy love?
O show thy, &c.

23 And euer as they mount like larks, they sing, *B* 24 King *B*: king *1633–*
Home. *Not in W* 5 show *1633*[2]– : *this spelling is used in B in all stanzas except 1, 2, and 7, and in 1633 in all stanzas except 1, where* shew *is used*
9 behold] beheld *1678–1809, Pickering* 22 love?] loue. *B*

He did, he came: O my Redeemer deare,
After all this canst thou be strange?
So many yeares baptiz'd, and not appeare?
As if thy love could fail or change.
O show thy self to me,
Or take me up to thee!

Yet if thou stayest still, why must I stay?
My God, what is this world to me,
This world of wo? hence all ye clouds, away,
Away; I must get up and see.
O show thy, &c.

What is this weary world; this meat and drink,
That chains us by the teeth so fast?
What is this woman-kinde, which I can wink
Into a blacknesse and distaste?
O show thy, &c.

With one small sigh thou gav'st me th' other day
I blasted all the joyes about me:
And scouling on them as they pin'd away,
Now come again, said I, and flout me.
O show thy, &c.

Nothing but drought and dearth, but bush and brake,
Which way so-e're I look, I see.
Some may dream merrily, but when they wake,
They dresse themselves and come to thee.
O show thy, &c.

We talk of harvests; there are no such things,
But when we leave our corn and hay:
There is no fruitfull yeare, but that which brings
The last and lov'd, though dreadfull day.
O show thy, &c.

32 me, *1809*, *Palmer* : mee? *B* : me? *1633–1799*

Oh loose this frame, this knot of man untie!
    That my free soul may use her wing,
Which now is pinion'd with mortalitie,
    As an intangled, hamper'd thing.
        O show thy, &c.

What have I left, that I should stay and grone?
    The most of me to heav'n is fled:
My thoughts and joyes are all packt up and gone,
    And for their old acquaintance plead.
        O show thy, &c.

Come dearest Lord, passe not this holy season,
    My flesh and bones and joynts do pray:
And ev'n my verse, when by the ryme and reason
    The word is, *Stay*, sayes ever, *Come*.
        O show thy, &c.

The British Church.

I Joy, deare Mother, when I view
Thy perfect lineaments and hue
        Both sweet and bright.
Beautie in thee takes up her place,
And dates her letters from thy face,
        When she doth write.

A fine aspect in fit aray,
Neither too mean, nor yet too gay,
        Shows who is best.
Outlandish looks may not compare:
For all they either painted are,
        Or else undrest.

The British Church. *Not in W Arranged in B in verses of 6 lines, the 3rd and 6th rhyming; all printed editions before Pickering have verses of 3 lines* 2 lineaments *B*: lineaments, *1633–* 4 her] the *B*

She on the hills, which wantonly
Allureth all in hope to be
By her preferr'd,
Hath kiss'd so long her painted shrines,
That ev'n her face by kissing shines,
For her reward.

She in the valley is so shie
Of dressing, that her hair doth lie
About her eares:
While she avoids her neighbours pride,
She wholly goes on th' other side,
And nothing wears.

But, dearest Mother, what those misse,
The mean, thy praise and glorie is,
And long may be.
Blessed be God, whose love it was
To double-moat thee with his grace,
And none but thee.

The Quip.

THe merrie world did on a day
With his train-bands and mates agree
To meet together, where I lay,
And all in sport to geere at me.

First, Beautie crept into a rose,
Which when I pluckt not, Sir, said she,
Tell me, I pray, Whose hands are those?
But thou shalt answer, Lord, for me.

Then Money came, and chinking still,
What tune is this, poore man? said he:
I heard in Musick you had skill.
But thou shalt answer, Lord, for me.

25 But, *1635–67* : But *B 1633–4 1674–* 25–6 what those misse, The meane, *B* : (what those misse) The mean *1633–*

The Quip. *Not in W The refrain* (*ll. 8, 12, 16, 20*), *from* Ps. xxxviii. 15 (B.C.P.), *italicized 1633*^{2}*–* : *roman 1633*

Then came brave Glorie puffing by
In silks that whistled, who but he?
He scarce allow'd me half an eie.
But thou shalt answer, Lord, for me.

Then came quick Wit and Conversation,
And he would needs a comfort be,
And, to be short, make an Oration.
But thou shalt answer, Lord, for me.

Yet when the houre of thy designe
To answer these fine things shall come;
Speak not at large; say, I am thine:
And then they have their answer home.

Vanitie (II).

POore silly soul, whose hope and head lies low;
Whose flat delights on earth do creep and grow;
To whom the starres shine not so fair, as eyes;
Nor solid work, as false embroyderies;
Heark and beware, lest what you now do measure
And write for sweet, prove a most sowre displeasure.

O heare betimes, lest thy relenting
May come too late!
To purchase heaven for repenting
Is no hard rate.
If souls be made of earthly mold,
Let them love gold;
If born on high,
Let them unto their kindred flie:
For they can never be at rest,
Till they regain their ancient nest.
Then silly soul take heed; for earthly joy
Is but a bubble, and makes thee a boy.

19 Oration *B*: oration *1633–* *See note* 23 large; *B*: large, *1633–*
Vanitie (II). *Not in W* *Numbering Ed* 9 repenting *B*: repenting, *1633–*

The Dawning.

AWake sad heart, whom sorrow ever drowns;
  Take up thine eyes, which feed on earth;
Unfold thy forehead gather'd into frowns:
  Thy Saviour comes, and with him mirth:
          Awake, awake;
And with a thankfull heart his comforts take.
  But thou dost still lament, and pine, and crie;
  And feel his death, but not his victorie.

Arise sad heart; if thou doe not withstand,
  Christs resurrection thine may be:
Do not by hanging down break from the hand,
  Which as it riseth, raiseth thee:
          Arise, arise;
And with his buriall-linen drie thine eyes:
  Christ left his grave-clothes, that we might, when grief
  Draws tears, or bloud, not want a handkerchief.

JESU.

JESU is in my heart, his sacred name
Is deeply carved there: but th'other week
A great affliction broke the little frame,
Ev'n all to pieces: which I went to seek:
And first I found the corner, where was *J*,
After, where *E S*, and next where *U* was graved.
When I had got these parcels, instantly
I sat me down to spell them, and perceived
That to my broken heart he was *I ease you*,
        And to my whole is *JESU*.

The Dawning. *Not in W*   3 gather'd] gathered *B*   9 doe *B*: dost *1633–* *See note*   witstand *B*   15 graue-cloths, *B*   16 a *B* : an *1633–*
JESU. *Not in W*   *The writing of consonantal* J *and the vowel* I *is identical in B, but the modern distinction is observed in 1633* *See note*

Businesse.

CAnst be idle? canst thou play,
Foolish soul who sinn'd to day?

Rivers run, and springs each one
Know their home, and get them gone:
Hast thou tears, or hast thou none?

If, poore soul, thou hast no tears,
Would thou hadst no faults or fears!
Who hath these, those ill forbears.

Windes still work: it is their plot,
Be the season cold, or hot:
Hast thou sighs, or hast thou not?

If thou hast no sighs or grones,
Would thou hadst no flesh and bones!
Lesser pains scape greater ones.

But if yet thou idle be,
Foolish soul, Who di'd for thee?

Who did leave his Fathers throne,
To assume thy flesh and bone;
Had he life, or had he none?

If he had not liv'd for thee,
Thou hadst di'd most wretchedly;
And two deaths had been thy fee.

He so farre thy good did plot,
That his own self he forgot.
Did he die, or did he not?

If he had not di'd for thee,
Thou hadst liv'd in miserie.
Two lives worse then ten deaths be.

Businesse. *Not in W* 1 play,] play? *B* 6 teares, *B* : tears, *1633*[2]– : tears ; *1633* 8 ill] *misprinted* ills *1667–1799*, *Pickering*

And hath any space of breath
'Twixt his sinnes and Saviours death?

He that loseth gold, though drosse,
Tells to all he meets, his crosse:
He that sinnes, hath he no losse?

He that findes a silver vein,
Thinks on it, and thinks again:
Brings thy Saviours death no gain?

Who in heart not ever kneels,
Neither sinne nor Saviour feels.

Dialogue.

SWeetest Saviour, if my soul
Were but worth the having,
Quickly should I then controll
Any thought of waving.
But when all my care and pains
Cannot give the name of gains
To thy wretch so full of stains,
What delight or hope remains?

What, Child, is the ballance thine,
Thine the poise and measure?
If I say, Thou shalt be mine;
Finger not my treasure.
What the gains in having thee
Do amount to, onely he,
Who for man was sold, can see;
That transferr'd th' accounts to me.

29 space] spare *B* (*probably a slip*) 32 Tells to all, he meets his Crosse, *B*
34 silver vein] siluer-vaine *B*

Dialogue. *Not in W* 7 staines, *B* : stains ; *1633–* 9 *What, Child, Ed* : What *Child B* : *What* (*childe*) *1633–*

But as I can see no merit,
Leading to this favour:
So the way to fit me for it
Is beyond my savour.
As the reason then is thine;
So the way is none of mine:
I disclaim the whole designe:
Sinne disclaims and I resigne.

That is all, if that I could
Get without repining;
And my clay, my creature, would
Follow my resigning:
That as I did freely part
With my glorie and desert,
Left all joyes to feel all smart—— —
Ah! no more: thou break'st my heart.

Dulnesse.

WHy do I languish thus, drooping and dull,
As if I were all earth?
O give me quicknesse, that I may with mirth
Praise thee brim-full!

The wanton lover in a curious strain
Can praise his fairest fair;
And with quaint metaphors her curled hair
Curl o're again.

Thou art my lovelinesse, my life, my light,
Beautie alone to me:
Thy bloudy death and undeserv'd, makes thee
Pure red and white.

When all perfections as but one appeare,
That those thy form doth show,
The very dust, where thou dost tread and go,
Makes beauties here.

19 it *B* : it, *1633–* 27 *clay, B 1634–* : *clay 1633* 1633^{2} *creature*, *Ed* : *creature B 1633–* 28 *resigning* : *1634–* : *resigning. B 1633* 1633^{2}
Dulnesse. *Not in W* 16 heere. *B* : here. 1633^{2}– : here ; *1633*

Where are my lines then? my approaches? views?
Where are my window-songs?
Lovers are still pretending, & ev'n wrongs
Sharpen their Muse:

But I am lost in flesh, whose sugred lyes
Still mock me, and grow bold:
Sure thou didst put a minde there, if I could
Finde where it lies.

Lord, cleare thy gift, that with a constant wit
I may but look towards thee:
Look onely; for to *love* thee, who can be,
What angel fit?

Love-joy.

AS on a window late I cast mine eye,
I saw a vine drop grapes with *J* and *C*
Anneal'd on every bunch. One standing by
Ask'd what it meant. I, who am never loth
To spend my judgement, said, It seem'd to me
To be the bodie and the letters both
Of *Joy* and *Charitie*. Sir, you have not miss'd,
The man reply'd; It figures *JESUS CHRIST*.

Providence.

O Sacred Providence, who from end to end
Strongly and sweetly movest, shall I write,
And not of thee, through whom my fingers bend
To hold my quill? shall they not do thee right?

Love-joy. *Not in W* 4–5 I, who . . . judgement, *commas in B replaced by brackets 1633–* 5 judgement *1633^{2}–* : iudgement *B 1633*
Providence. *Not in W* 2 movest, *B* : movest! *1633–*

Of all the creatures both in sea and land
Onely to Man thou hast made known thy wayes,
And put the penne alone into his hand,
And made him Secretarie of thy praise.

Beasts fain would sing; birds dittie to their notes;
Trees would be tuning on their native lute
To thy renown: but all their hands and throats
Are brought to Man, while they are lame and mute.

Man is the worlds high Priest: he doth present
The sacrifice for all; while they below
Unto the service mutter an assent,
Such as springs use that fall, and windes that blow.

He that to praise and laud thee doth refrain,
Doth not refrain unto himself alone,
But robs a thousand who would praise thee fain,
And doth commit a world of sinne in one.

The beasts say, Eat me: but, if beasts must teach,
The tongue is yours to eat, but mine to praise.
The trees say, Pull me: but the hand you stretch,
Is mine to write, as it is yours to raise.

Wherefore, most sacred Spirit, I here present
For me and all my fellows praise to thee:
And just it is that I should pay the rent,
Because the benefit accrues to me.

We all acknowledge both thy power and love
To be exact, transcendent, and divine;
Who dost so strongly and so sweetly move,
While all things have their will, yet none but thine.

For either thy command or thy permission
Lay hands on all: they are thy right and left.
The first puts on with speed and expedition;
The other curbs sinnes stealing pace and theft.

13 high-preist. *B.* 33 command *no comma B 1634– : comma 1633 1633*[2]
33–4 *The words* command, permission, right, left, *italicized 1633– , but not distinguished in B*

Nothing escapes them both; all must appeare,
And be dispos'd, and dress'd, and tun'd by thee,
Who sweetly temper'st all. If we could heare
Thy skill and art, what musick would it be!

Thou art in small things great, not small in any:
Thy even praise can neither rise, nor fall.
Thou art in all things one, in each thing many:
For thou art infinite in one and all.

Tempests are calm to thee; they know thy hand,
And hold it fast, as children do their fathers,
Which crie and follow. Thou hast made poore sand
Check the proud sea, ev'n when it swells and gathers.

Thy cupboard serves the world: the meat is set,
Where all may reach: no beast but knows his feed.
Birds teach us hawking; fishes have their net:
The great prey on the lesse, they on some weed.

Nothing ingendred doth prevent his meat:
Flies have their table spread, ere they appeare.
Some creatures have in winter what to eat;
Others do sleep, and envie not their cheer.

How finely dost thou times and seasons spin,
And make a twist checker'd with night and day!
Which as it lengthens windes, and windes us in,
As bouls go on, but turning all the way.

Each creature hath a wisdome for his good.
The pigeons feed their tender off-spring, crying,
When they are callow; but withdraw their food
When they are fledge, that need may teach them flying.

Bees work for man; and yet they never bruise
Their masters flower, but leave it, having done,
As fair as ever, and as fit to use;
So both the flower doth stay, and hony run.

39 temper'st] temperest *B*   49 cupboard] cubbord *B* (*which has* cupbord *in* Grief, *l. 11*)   56 Others] Other *B*   64 fledge] fledged *Willmott, Grosart*   them *1634–78* : thē *1633* 1633^{2} (*to avoid turning the line*): 'em *1703–99*

Sheep eat the grasse, and dung the ground for more:
Trees after bearing drop their leaves for soil:
Springs vent their streams, and by expense get store:
Clouds cool by heat, and baths by cooling boil.

Who hath the vertue to expresse the rare
And curious vertues both of herbs and stones?
Is there an herb for that? O that thy care
Would show a root, that gives expressions!

And if an herb hath power, what have the starres?
A rose, besides his beautie, is a cure.
Doubtlesse our plagues and plentie, peace and warres
Are there much surer then our art is sure.

Thou hast hid metals: man may take them thence;
But at his perill: when he digs the place,
He makes a grave; as if the thing had sense,
And threatned man, that he should fill the space.

Ev'n poysons praise thee. Should a thing be lost?
Should creatures want for want of heed their due?
Since where are poysons, antidotes are most:
The help stands close, and keeps the fear in view.

The sea, which seems to stop the traveller,
Is by a ship the speedier passage made.
The windes, who think they rule the mariner,
Are rul'd by him, and taught to serve his trade.

And as thy house is full, so I adore
Thy curious art in marshalling thy goods.
The hills with health abound; the vales with store;
The South with marble; North with furres & woods.

Hard things are glorious; easie things good cheap.
The common all men have; that which is rare
Men therefore seek to have, and care to keep.
The healthy frosts with summer-fruits compare.

84 threatned] threaten'd *1809, Pickering, Grosart*: threatened *Willmott* 87 antidotes *B 1635 1641–* : antidots *1633–4 1638* 98 rare *B* : rare, *1633–*

Light without winde is glasse: warm without weight
Is wooll and furre: cool without closenesse, shade:
Speed without pains, a horse: tall without height,
A servile hawk: low without losse, a spade.

All countreys have enough to serve their need:
If they seek fine things, thou dost make them run
For their offence; and then dost turn their speed
To be commerce and trade from sunne to sunne.

Nothing wears clothes, but Man; nothing doth need
But he to wear them. Nothing useth fire,
But Man alone, to show his heav'nly breed:
And onely he hath fuell in desire.

When th' earth was dry, thou mad'st a sea of wet:
When that lay gather'd, thou didst broach the mountains:
When yet some places could no moisture get,
The windes grew gard'ners, and the clouds good fountains.

Rain, do not hurt my flowers; but gently spend
Your hony drops: presse not to smell them here:
When they are ripe, their odour will ascend,
And at your lodging with their thanks appeare.

How harsh are thorns to pears! and yet they make
A better hedge, and need lesse reparation.
How smooth are silks compared with a stake,
Or with a stone! yet make no good foundation.

Sometimes thou dost divide thy gifts to man,
Sometimes unite. The Indian nut alone
Is clothing, meat and trencher, drink and can,
Boat, cable, sail and needle, all in one.

Most herbs that grow in brooks, are hot and dry.
Cold fruits warm kernells help against the winde.
The lemmons juice and rinde cure mutually.
The whey of milk doth loose, the milk doth binde.

102 furre *B* : furres *1633–* 114 When *B* : Whē *1633–74* mountaines *B* : moũtains *1633–5* 127 Can *B* : canne *1638–* : kan *1633–5* 130 fruits] fruits, *B* : fruit's *1678*, *Pickering* : fruits' *Grosart*, *Palmer* *See note*

Thy creatures leap not, but expresse a feast,
Where all the guests sit close, and nothing wants.
Frogs marry fish and flesh; bats, bird and beast;
Sponges, non-sense and sense; mines, th' earth & plants.

To show thou art not bound, as if thy lot
Were worse then ours, sometimes thou shiftest hands.
Most things move th' under-jaw; the Crocodile not.
Most things sleep lying; th' Elephant leans or stands.

But who hath praise enough? nay, who hath any?
None can expresse thy works, but he that knows them:
And none can know thy works, which are so many,
And so complete, but onely he that owes them.

All things that are, though they have sev'rall wayes,
Yet in their being joyn with one advise
To honour thee: and so I give thee praise
In all my other hymnes, but in this twice.

Each thing that is, although in use and name
It go for one, hath many wayes in store
To honour thee; and so each hymne thy fame
Extolleth many wayes, yet this one more.

Hope.

I Gave to Hope a watch of mine: but he
An anchor gave to me.
Then an old prayer-book I did present:
And he an optick sent.
With that I gave a viall full of tears:
But he a few green eares.
Ah Loyterer! I'le no more, no more I'le bring:
I did expect a ring.

138 ours, *1633*^{2}– : ours ; *B 1633* 139 th' under-jaw] th' vnderchaw *B* 140 leans or stands] leane or stand *B* (*with marks of erasure at the end of the first word*) 141 nay, *1633*^{2}–: nay *B 1633* 146 advise] advice *1634*– , *Pickering, Willmott* 149–52 *perhaps an alternative to 145–8 See note*
Hope. *Not in W* 6 eares. *B 1634*– : eares : *1633 1633*^{2}

Sinnes round.

SOrrie I am, my God, sorrie I am,
That my offences course it in a ring.
My thoughts are working like a busie flame,
Untill their cockatrice they hatch and bring:
And when they once have perfected their draughts,
My words take fire from my inflamed thoughts.

My words take fire from my inflamed thoughts,
Which spit it forth like the Sicilian Hill.
They vent the wares, and passe them with their faults,
And by their breathing ventilate the ill.
But words suffice not, where are lewd intentions:
My hands do joyn to finish the inventions.

My hands do joyn to finish the inventions:
And so my sinnes ascend three stories high,
As Babel grew, before there were dissensions.
Yet ill deeds loyter not: for they supplie
New thoughts of sinning: wherefore, to my shame,
Sorrie I am, my God, sorrie I am.

Time.

MEeting with Time, Slack thing, said I,
Thy sithe is dull; whet it for shame.
No marvell Sir, he did replie,
If it at length deserve some blame:
But where one man would have me grinde it,
Twentie for one too sharp do finde it.

Perhaps some such of old did passe,
Who above all things lov'd this life;
To whom thy sithe a hatchet was,
Which now is but a pruning-knife.
Christs coming hath made man thy debter,
Since by thy cutting he grows better.

Sinnes round. *Not in W* 8 Hill *B*: hill *1633–* 9 faults] fauts *B* (*cf.* Marie Magdalene, *l.* 9, *where the same rhyme occurs*) 15 dissensions *B 1641–* : dissentions *1633–8*

Time. *Not in W* 1 Slack *B 1633²–* : slack *1633*

And in his blessing thou art blest:
For where thou onely wert before
An executioner at best;
Thou art a gard'ner now, and more,
  An usher to convey our souls
  Beyond the utmost starres and poles.

And this is that makes life so long,
While it detains us from our God.
Ev'n pleasures here increase the wrong,
And length of dayes lengthen the rod.
  Who wants the place, where God doth dwell,
  Partakes already half of hell.

Of what strange length must that needs be,
Which ev'n eternitie excludes!
Thus farre Time heard me patiently:
Then chafing said, This man deludes:
  What do I here before his doore?
  He doth not crave lesse time, but more.

Gratefulnesse.

THou that hast giv'n so much to me,
  Give one thing more, a gratefull heart.
See how thy beggar works on thee
          By art.

He makes thy gifts occasion more,
And sayes, If he in this be crost,
All thou hast giv'n him heretofore
          Is lost.

But thou didst reckon, when at first
Thy word our hearts and hands did crave,
What it would come to at the worst
          To save.

19 long *misprinted* !ong *1633*   22 lengthen] lengthens *Willmott, Grosart*   29 here] heere *B* (*which invariably spells the adverb* here *or* heere, *and the verb* heare): hear *Palmer*

Gratefulnesse. *Not in W*   1 Thou] O thou *Willmott*   7 giv'n him heretofore] giuen heretofore *B*

Perpetuall knockings at thy doore,
Tears sullying thy transparent rooms,
Gift upon gift, much would have more,
And comes.

This notwithstanding, thou wentst on,
And didst allow us all our noise:
Nay, thou hast made a sigh and grone
Thy joyes.

Not that thou hast not still above
Much better tunes, then grones can make;
But that these countrey-aires thy love
Did take.

Wherefore I crie, and crie again;
And in no quiet canst thou be,
Till I a thankfull heart obtain
Of thee:

Not thankfull, when it pleaseth me;
As if thy blessings had spare dayes:
But such a heart, whose pulse may be
Thy praise.

Peace.

SWeet Peace, where dost thou dwell? I humbly crave,
Let me once know.
I sought thee in a secret cave,
And ask'd, if Peace were there.
A hollow winde did seem to answer, No:
Go seek elsewhere.

I did; and going did a rainbow note:
Surely, thought I,
This is the lace of Peaces coat:
I will search out the matter.
But while I lookt, the clouds immediately
Did break and scatter.

17 notwithstanding *B 1638–* : not withstanding *1633–5* 19 Nay, *1633*[2]*–* : Nay *B 1633*

Peace. *Not in W Indentation of 4th line in B not adopted for first 4 stanzas till 1674*

Then went I to a garden, and did spy
A gallant flower,
The Crown Imperiall: Sure, said I,
Peace at the root must dwell.
But when I digg'd, I saw a worm devoure
What show'd so well.

At length I met a rev'rend good old man,
Whom when for Peace
I did demand, he thus began:
There was a Prince of old
At Salem dwelt, who liv'd with good increase
Of flock and fold.

He sweetly liv'd; yet sweetnesse did not save
His life from foes.
But after death out of his grave
There sprang twelve stalks of wheat:
Which many wondring at, got some of those
To plant and set.

It prosper'd strangely, and did soon disperse
Through all the earth:
For they that taste it do rehearse,
That vertue lies therein,
A secret vertue bringing peace and mirth
By flight of sinne.

Take of this grain, which in my garden grows,
And grows for you;
Make bread of it: and that repose
And peace, which ev'ry where
With so much earnestnesse you do pursue,
Is onely there.

15 Crowne *B*: Crown *1703–* : crown *1633–78* 21 demand, *1633*[2]*–* : demand ; *B 1633* 34 vertue lies] vertues lie *1678–1799* 40 peace, *B 1634–* : peace *1633 1633*[2] 41 pursue, *B, some dated and undated copies of 1633, 1633*[2] : *imperfectly printed as* pursu (*without comma*) *in some dated and undated copies of 1633*

Confession.

O What a cunning guest
Is this same grief! within my heart I made
Closets; and in them many a chest;
And, like a master in my trade,
In those chests, boxes; in each box, a till:
Yet grief knows all, and enters when he will.

No scrue, no piercer can
Into a piece of timber work and winde,
As Gods afflictions into man,
When he a torture hath design'd.
They are too subtill for the subt'llest hearts;
And fall, like rheumes, upon the tendrest parts.

We are the earth; and they,
Like moles within us, heave, and cast about:
And till they foot and clutch their prey,
They never cool, much lesse give out.
No smith can make such locks but they have keyes:
Closets are halls to them; and hearts, high-wayes.

Onely an open breast
Doth shut them out, so that they cannot enter;
Or, if they enter, cannot rest,
But quickly seek some new adventure.
Smooth open hearts no fastning have; but fiction
Doth give a hold and handle to affliction.

Wherefore my faults and sinnes,
Lord, I acknowledge; take thy plagues away:
For since confession pardon winnes,
I challenge here the brightest day,
The clearest diamond: let them do their best,
They shall be thick and cloudie to my breast.

Confession. *Not in W* 4 And, *B 1634–* : And *1633 1633*[2] 17 locks *1633*[2]*–* : locks, *B 1633*

Giddinesse.

OH, what a thing is man! how farre from power,
From setled peace and rest!
He is some twentie sev'rall men at least
Each sev'rall houre.

One while he counts of heav'n, as of his treasure:
But then a thought creeps in,
And calls him coward, who for fear of sinne
Will lose a pleasure.

Now he will fight it out, and to the warres;
Now eat his bread in peace,
And snudge in quiet: now he scorns increase;
Now all day spares.

He builds a house, which quickly down must go,
As if a whirlwinde blew
And crusht the building: and it's partly true,
His minde is so.

O what a sight were Man, if his attires
Did alter with his minde;
And like a Dolphins skinne, his clothes combin'd
With his desires!

Surely if each one saw anothers heart,
There would be no commerce,
No sale or bargain passe: all would disperse,
And live apart.

Lord, mend or rather make us: one creation
Will not suffice our turn:
Except thou make us dayly, we shall spurn
Our own salvation.

Giddinesse. *Not in W* 13 a] an *1634–67* 15 it 's] 'tis *Pickering*

The Bunch of Grapes.

JOy, I did lock thee up: but some bad man
Hath let thee out again:
And now, me thinks, I am where I began
Sev'n yeares ago: one vogue and vein,
One aire of thoughts usurps my brain.
I did towards Canaan draw; but now I am
Brought back to the Red sea, the sea of shame.

For as the Jews of old by Gods command
Travell'd, and saw no town;
So now each Christian hath his journeys spann'd:
Their storie pennes and sets us down.
A single deed is small renown.
Gods works are wide, and let in future times;
His ancient justice overflows our crimes.

Then have we too our guardian fires and clouds;
Our Scripture-dew drops fast:
We have our sands and serpents, tents and shrowds;
Alas! our murmurings come not last.
But where's the cluster? where's the taste
Of mine inheritance? Lord, if I must borrow,
Let me as well take up their joy, as sorrow.

But can he want the grape, who hath the wine?
I have their fruit and more.
Blessed be God, who prosper'd *Noahs* vine,
And made it bring forth grapes good store.
But much more him I must adore,
Who of the Laws sowre juice sweet wine did make,
Ev'n God himself being pressed for my sake.

The Bunch of Grapes. *Not in W* *Title*: *initial capitals in B and in* 'The titles of the severall poems' *in 1633, but not in the heading of the poem in 1633* 6 towards *B 1641–1799* (*except 1667*): toward *1633–8* (*a form not found elsewhere in 1633, and not at all in B*) 9 town; *1633²–* : *colon B 1633* 13 works] words *conj. Hall* 15 too] to *B* 18 not last] not at last *B* (*a slip*) 22 wine] vine *B* (*probably a slip*: *cf. l. 24*) 27 Laws *B 1633²–* : laws *1633* 28 himselfe *B* : himself, *1633–*

Love unknown.

DEare Friend, sit down, the tale is long and sad:
And in my faintings I presume your love
Will more complie then help. A Lord I had,
And have, of whom some grounds, which may improve,
I hold for two lives, and both lives in me.
To him I brought a dish of fruit one day,
And in the middle plac'd my heart. But he
(I sigh to say)
Lookt on a servant, who did know his eye
Better then you know me, or (which is one)
Then I my self. The servant instantly
Quitting the fruit, seiz'd on my heart alone,
And threw it in a font, wherein did fall
A stream of bloud, which issu'd from the side
Of a great rock: I well remember all,
And have good cause: there it was dipt and dy'd,
And washt, and wrung: the very wringing yet
Enforceth tears. *Your heart was foul, I fear.*
Indeed 'tis true. I did and do commit
Many a fault more then my lease will bear;
Yet still askt pardon, and was not deni'd.
But you shall heare. After my heart was well,
And clean and fair, as I one even-tide
(I sigh to tell)
Walkt by my self abroad, I saw a large
And spacious fornace flaming, and thereon
A boyling caldron, round about whose verge
Was in great letters set *AFFLICTION*.
The greatnesse shew'd the owner. So I went
To fetch a sacrifice out of my fold,
Thinking with that, which I did thus present,
To warm his love, which I did fear grew cold.
But as my heart did tender it, the man,

Love unknown. *Not in W* 2 love *1633²–* : loue *B 1633* 3 complie *1634–* : *comma B 1633 1633²* 4 grounds, *B*: grounds *1633–* 5 and *misprinted* aud *1633* 9 servant *B 1633²–* : seruant *1633* (*but* servant *l. 11*) 10 know] knew *1674–1799* 16 dy'd *1674–1799*: dyed *B*: di'd *1633–67* 26 fornace *B 1633*: furnace *1633²–* 33 man, *B*: man *1633–*

Who was to take it from me, slipt his hand,
And threw my heart into the scalding pan;
My heart, that brought it (do you understand?)
The offerers heart. *Your heart was hard, I fear.*
Indeed it's true. I found a callous matter
Began to spread and to expatiate there:
But with a richer drug then scalding water
I bath'd it often, ev'n with holy bloud,
Which at a board, while many drunk bare wine,
A friend did steal into my cup for good,
Ev'n taken inwardly, and most divine
To supple hardnesses. But at the length
Out of the caldron getting, soon I fled
Unto my house, where to repair the strength
Which I had lost, I hasted to my bed.
But when I thought to sleep out all these faults
(I sigh to speak)
I found that some had stuff'd the bed with thoughts,
I would say *thorns*. Deare, could my heart not break,
When with my pleasures ev'n my rest was gone?
Full well I understood, who had been there:
For I had giv'n the key to none, but one:
It must be he. *Your heart was dull, I fear.*
Indeed a slack and sleepie state of minde
Did oft possesse me, so that when I pray'd,
Though my lips went, my heart did stay behinde.
But all my scores were by another paid,
Who took the debt upon him. *Truly, Friend,*
For ought I heare, your Master shows to you
More favour then you wot of. Mark the end.
The Font did onely, what was old, renew:
The Caldron suppled, what was grown too hard:
The Thorns did quicken, what was grown too dull:
All did but strive to mend, what you had marr'd.
Wherefore be cheer'd, and praise him to the full

36 understand?] *question-mark absent from B and from the Bodleian copy of the undated 1633, but found in other dated and undated copies of 1633* 38 it's *B*: 'tis *1633*– (*cf. l. 19*) 40 drug *1633*^{2}: drug, *B 1633* water *1634*: water, *B 1633 1633*^{2} 42 drunk] drank *1809, Pickering, Willmott, Grosart* 65 *too*] to *B* (*but* too *in next line*)

Each day, each houre, each moment of the week,
Who fain would have you be new, tender, quick.

Mans medley.

HEark, how the birds do sing,
And woods do ring.
All creatures have their joy: and man hath his.
Yet if we rightly measure,
Mans joy and pleasure
Rather hereafter, then in present, is.

To this life things of sense
Make their pretence:
In th' other Angels have a right by birth:
Man ties them both alone,
And makes them one,
With th' one hand touching heav'n, with th' other earth.

In soul he mounts and flies,
In flesh he dies.
He wears a stuffe whose thread is course and round,
But trimm'd with curious lace,
And should take place
After the trimming, not the stuffe and ground.

Not that he may not here
Taste of the cheer,
But as birds drink, and straight lift up their head,
So he must sip and think
Of better drink
He may attain to, after he is dead.

But as his joyes are double;
So is his trouble.
He hath two winters, other things but one:
Both frosts and thoughts do nip,
And bite his lip;
And he of all things fears two deaths alone.

70 *be 1633*^{2}*–* : be, *B*: *be, 1633*
Mans medley. *Not in W* 19 Not that *1641–* : Not, that *B 1633–8*
22 he must *B* : must he *1633–*

Yet ev'n the greatest griefs
May be reliefs,
Could he but take them right, and in their wayes.
Happie is he, whose heart
Hath found the art
To turn his double pains to double praise.

The Storm.

IF as the windes and waters here below
Do flie and flow,
My sighs and tears as busie were above;
Sure they would move
And much affect thee, as tempestuous times
Amaze poore mortals, and object their crimes.

Starres have their storms, ev'n in a high degree,
As well as we.
A throbbing conscience spurred by remorse
Hath a strange force:
It quits the earth, and mounting more and more
Dares to assault thee, and besiege thy doore.

There it stands knocking, to thy musicks wrong,
And drowns the song.
Glorie and honour are set by, till it
An answer get.
Poets have wrong'd poore storms: such dayes are best;
They purge the aire without, within the breast.

Paradise.

I Blesse thee, Lord, because I GROW
Among thy trees, which in a ROW
To thee both fruit and order OW.

The Storm. *Not in W* 6 Amaze] Amuse *B* *See note* 11 & more *B*: and more, *1633–* 15 by, *B*: by *1633–*
Paradise. *Not in W*

What open force, or hidden CHARM
Can blast my fruit, or bring me HARM,
While the inclosure is thine ARM?

Inclose me still for fear I START.
Be to me rather sharp and TART,
Then let me want thy hand & ART.

When thou dost greater judgements SPARE,
And with thy knife but prune and PARE,
Ev'n fruitfull trees more fruitfull ARE.

Such sharpnes shows the sweetest FREND:
Such cuttings rather heal then REND:
And such beginnings touch their END.

The Method.

POore heart, lament.
For since thy God refuseth still,
There is some rub, some discontent,
Which cools his will.

Thy Father could
Quickly effect, what thou dost move;
For he is *Power*: and sure he would;
For he is *Love*.

Go search this thing,
Tumble thy breast, and turn thy book.
If thou hadst lost a glove or ring,
Wouldst thou not look?

What do I see
Written above there? *Yesterday*
I did behave me carelesly,
When I did pray.

13 FREND] Freind *corr. to* Frend *B* (*probably to secure symmetry*)
The Method. *Not in W* 5–8 *B distinguishes* (*i.e. for italicizing*) Powre *and* Loue, *but not* could *and* would, *which are italicized 1633–*

And should Gods eare
To such indifferents chained be,
Who do not their own motions heare?
Is God lesse free?

But stay! what's there?
Late when I would have something done,
I had a motion to forbear,
Yet I went on.

And should Gods eare,
Which needs not man, be ty'd to those
Who heare not him, but quickly heare
His utter foes?

Then once more pray:
Down with thy knees, up with thy voice.
Seek pardon first, and God will say,
Glad heart rejoyce.

Divinitie.

As men, for fear the starres should sleep and nod,
And trip at night, have spheres suppli'd;
As if a starre were duller then a clod,
Which knows his way without a guide:

Just so the other heav'n they also serve,
Divinities transcendent skie:
Which with the edge of wit they cut and carve.
Reason triumphs, and faith lies by.

Could not that Wisdome, which first broacht the wine,
Have thicken'd it with definitions?
And jagg'd his seamlesse coat, had that been fine,
With curious questions and divisions?

Divinitie. *Not in W* 9 Wisdome *cap. from B*

But all the doctrine, which he taught and gave,
Was cleare as heav'n, from whence it came.
At least those beams of truth, which onely save,
Surpasse in brightnesse any flame.

Love God, and love your neighbour. Watch and pray.
Do as ye would be done unto.
O dark instructions; ev'n as dark as day!
Who can these Gordian knots undo?

But he doth bid us take his bloud for wine.
Bid what he please; yet I am sure,
To take and taste what he doth there designe,
Is all that saves, and not obscure.

Then burn thy Epicycles, foolish man;
Break all thy spheres, and save thy head.
Faith needs no staffe of flesh, but stoutly can
To heav'n alone both go, and leade.

Ephes. 4. 30.

Grieve not the Holy Spirit, &c.

AND art thou grieved, sweet and sacred Dove,
When I am sowre,
And crosse thy love?
Grieved for me? the God of strength and power
Griev'd for a worm, which when I tread,
I passe away and leave it dead?

Then weep mine eyes, the God of love doth grieve:
Weep foolish heart,
And weeping live:
For death is drie as dust. Yet if ye part,
End as the night, whose sable hue
Your sinnes expresse; melt into dew.

19 ev'n as] *Grosart omits* as
Grieve not &c. This poem is not in W 5 Griev'd] *misprinted* Grieved *Pickering*
6 dead?] dead. *B*

When sawcie mirth shall knock or call at doore,
Cry out, Get hence,
Or cry no more.
Almightie God doth grieve, he puts on sense:
I sinne not to my grief alone,
But to my Gods too; he doth grone.

Oh take thy lute, and tune it to a strain,
Which may with thee
All day complain.
There can no discord but in ceasing be.
Marbles can weep; and surely strings
More bowels have, then such hard things.

Lord, I adjudge my self to tears and grief,
Ev'n endlesse tears
Without relief.
If a cleare spring for me no time forbears,
But runnes, although I be not drie;
I am no Crystall, what shall I?

Yet if I wail not still, since still to wail
Nature denies;
And flesh would fail,
If my deserts were masters of mine eyes:
Lord, pardon, for thy Sonne makes good
My want of tears with store of bloud.

The Familie.

WHat doth this noise of thoughts within my heart,
As if they had a part?
What do these loud complaints and puling fears,
As if there were no rule or eares?

But, Lord, the house and familie are thine,
Though some of them repine.
Turn out these wranglers, which defile thy seat:
For where thou dwellest all is neat.

35 Sonne *B 1634–* : sonne *1633* 1633^2
The Familie. *Not in W* 1 heart, *1635–* : *no comma B 1633–4* 3 pulling *corr. by erasure to* puling *B*: pulling *1633–* *See note*

First Peace and Silence all disputes controll,
Then Order plaies the soul;
And giving all things their set forms and houres,
Makes of wilde woods sweet walks and bowres.

Humble Obedience neare the doore doth stand,
Expecting a command:
Then whom in waiting nothing seems more slow,
Nothing more quick when she doth go.

Joyes oft are there, and griefs as oft as joyes;
But griefs without a noise:
Yet speak they louder then distemper'd fears.
What is so shrill as silent tears?

This is thy house, with these it doth abound:
And where these are not found,
Perhaps thou com'st sometimes, and for a day;
But not to make a constant stay.

The Size.

COntent thee, greedie heart.
Modest and moderate joyes to those, that have
Title to more hereafter when they part,
Are passing brave.
Let th' upper springs into the low
Descend and fall, and thou dost flow.

What though some have a fraught
Of cloves and nutmegs, and in cinamon sail;
If thou hast wherewithall to spice a draught,
When griefs prevail;
And for the future time art heir
To th' Isle of spices, is 't not fair?

19 louder *1633*[2]– : *comma B 1633*
The Size. *Not in W* 5 springs] *Palmer misreads B as* strings 12 spices, is't *1633*[2]– : spices. Is't *B* : spices? Is't *1633*

To be in both worlds full
Is more then God was, who was hungrie here.
Wouldst thou his laws of fasting disanull?
Enact good cheer?
Lay out thy joy, yet hope to save it?
Wouldst thou both eat thy cake, and have it?

Great joyes are all at once;
But little do reserve themselves for more:
Those have their hopes; these what they have renounce,
And live on score:
Those are at home; these journey still,
And meet the rest on Sions hill.

Thy Saviour sentenc'd joy,
And in the flesh condemn'd it as unfit,
At least in lump: for such doth oft destroy;
Whereas a bit
Doth tice us on to hopes of more,
And for the present health restore.

A Christians state and case
Is not a corpulent, but a thinne and spare,
Yet active strength: whose long and bonie face
Content and care
Do seem to equally divide,
Like a pretender, not a bride.

Wherefore sit down, good heart;
Grasp not at much, for fear thou losest all.
If comforts fell according to desert,
They would great frosts and snows destroy:
For we should count, Since the last joy.

Then close again the seam,
Which thou hast open'd: do not spread thy robe
In hope of great things. Call to minde thy dream,
An earthly globe,
On whose meridian was engraven,
These seas are tears, and heav'n the haven.

16 Enact] Exact *B* *See note* 39 *The metre requires another line, of two feet, but there is no indication of a gap in B*: At all times fall *conj. Grosart*: Did always fall *conj. E. Rhys* : As waters fall *conj. Hall*

Artillerie.

As I one ev'ning sat before my cell,
Me thoughts a starre did shoot into my lap.
I rose, and shook my clothes, as knowing well,
That from small fires comes oft no small mishap.
When suddenly I heard one say,
Do as thou usest, disobey,
Expell good motions from thy breast,
Which have the face of fire, but end in rest.

I, who had heard of musick in the spheres,
But not of speech in starres, began to muse:
But turning to my God, whose ministers
The starres and all things are; If I refuse,
Dread Lord, said I, so oft my good;
Then I refuse not ev'n with bloud
To wash away my stubborn thought:
For I will do or suffer what I ought.

But I have also starres and shooters too,
Born where thy servants both artilleries use.
My tears and prayers night and day do wooe,
And work up to thee; yet thou dost refuse.
Not but I am (I must say still)
Much more oblig'd to do thy will,
Then thou to grant mine: but because
Thy promise now hath ev'n set thee thy laws.

Then we are shooters both, and thou dost deigne
To enter combate with us, and contest
With thine own clay. But I would parley fain:
Shunne not my arrows, and behold my breast.
Yet if thou shunnest, I am thine:
I must be so, if I am mine.
There is no articling with thee:
I am but finite, yet thine infinitely.

Artillerie. *Not in W* 2 Me thoughts] Methought (*or* Me thought) *1799* *1809*, *Pickering*, *Willmott*, *Grosart* (*cf.* The Collar, *l.* 35) 16 doe *B*: do, *1633*– 21 Not *1634*– : Not, *B* *1633* *1633*[2]

Church-rents and schismes.

BRave rose, (alas!) where art thou? in the chair
Where thou didst lately so triumph and shine
A worm doth sit, whose many feet and hair
Are the more foul, the more thou wert divine.
This, this hath done it, this did bite the root
And bottome of the leaves: which when the winde
Did once perceive, it blew them under foot,
Where rude unhallow'd steps do crush and grinde
Their beauteous glories. Onely shreds of thee,
And those all bitten, in thy chair I see.

Why doth my Mother blush? is she the rose,
And shows it so? Indeed Christs precious bloud
Gave you a colour once; which when your foes
Thought to let out, the bleeding did you good,
And made you look much fresher then before.
But when debates and fretting jealousies
Did worm and work within you more and more,
Your colour vaded, and calamities
Turned your ruddie into pale and bleak:
Your health and beautie both began to break.

Then did your sev'rall parts unloose and start:
Which when your neighbours saw, like a north-winde
They rushed in, and cast them in the dirt
Where Pagans tread. O Mother deare and kinde,
Where shall I get me eyes enough to weep,
As many eyes as starres? since it is night,
And much of Asia and Europe fast asleep,
And ev'n all Africk; would at least I might
With these two poore ones lick up all the dew,
Which falls by night, and poure it out for you!

Church-rents and schismes. *Not in W* *Title in B*: Church-rents or schismes (*similarly in the table of contents in B*) 1 chair] place *B* *See note* 2 shine *B*: shine, *1633–* 7 them] thee *B* 9 glories. Onely] glories onely *B* 10 bitten, in] sitten in *B* *See note* 18 vaded *B*: faded *1633–* *See note* 22 north-winde *no comma B 1634–* : *comma 1633 1633*[2]

Justice (II).

O Dreadfull Justice, what a fright and terrour
Wast thou of old,
When sinne and errour
Did show and shape thy looks to me,
And through their glasse discolour thee!
He that did but look up, was proud and bold.

The dishes of thy ballance seem'd to gape,
Like two great pits;
The beam and scape
Did like some torturing engine show;
Thy hand above did burn and glow,
Danting the stoutest hearts, the proudest wits.

But now that Christs pure vail presents the sight,
I see no fears:
Thy hand is white,
Thy scales like buckets, which attend
And interchangeably descend,
Lifting to heaven from this well of tears.

For where before thou still didst call on me,
Now I still touch
And harp on thee.
Gods promises have made thee mine;
Why should I justice now decline?
Against me there is none, but for me much.

The Pilgrimage.

I Travell'd on, seeing the hill, where lay
My expectation.
A long it was and weary way.
The gloomy cave of Desperation

Justice (II). *Not in W Numbering Ed* 10 torturing *B*: tort'ring *1633–41 1667–1809* (*except 1799*): tottering (tot'tring, tott'ring) *1656 1660 1799, Pickering, Willmott* 13 presents the sight] prevents that sight *conj. Hall* 16 attend] ascend *conj. Hall See note* 22 have] *misprinted* hath *Willmott, Grosart*

The Pilgrimage. *Not in W*

I left on th' one, and on the other side
The rock of Pride.

And so I came to Fancies medow strow'd
With many a flower:
Fain would I here have made abode,
But I was quicken'd by my houre.
So to Cares cops I came, and there got through
With much ado.

That led me to the wilde of Passion, which
Some call the wold;
A wasted place, but sometimes rich.
Here I was robb'd of all my gold,
Save one good Angell, which a friend had ti'd
Close to my side.

At length I got unto the gladsome hill,
Where lay my hope,
Where lay my heart; and climbing still,
When I had gain'd the brow and top,
A lake of brackish waters on the ground
Was all I found.

With that abash'd and struck with many a sting
Of swarming fears,
I fell, and cry'd, Alas my King!
Can both the way and end be tears?
Yet taking heart I rose, and then perceiv'd
I was deceiv'd:

My hill was further: so I flung away,
Yet heard a crie
Just as I went, *None goes that way*
And lives: If that be all, said I,
After so foul a journey death is fair,
And but a chair.

7 Fancies *B*: phansies *1633–4*: Phansies *1635–* 11 Cares *B 1635–* : cares *1633–4* 13 Passion *B 1635–* : passion *1633–4* 14 wold] would *B*: world *1656 1678–1799* 27 King! *1633*[2]*–* : King, *B*: King; *1633*

The Holdfast.

I Threatned to observe the strict decree
Of my deare God with all my power & might.
But I was told by one, it could not be;
Yet I might trust in God to be my light.
Then will I trust, said I, in him alone.
Nay, ev'n to trust in him, was also his:
We must confesse that nothing is our own.
Then I confesse that he my succour is:
But to have nought is ours, not to confesse
That we have nought. I stood amaz'd at this,
Much troubled, till I heard a friend expresse,
That all things were more ours by being his.
What Adam had, and forfeited for all,
Christ keepeth now, who cannot fail or fall.

Complaining.

DO not beguile my heart,
Because thou art
My power and wisdome. Put me not to shame,
Because I am
Thy clay that weeps, thy dust that calls.

Thou art the Lord of glorie;
The deed and storie
Are both thy due: but I a silly flie,
That live or die
According as the weather falls.

Art thou all justice, Lord?
Shows not thy word
More attributes? Am I all throat or eye,
To weep or crie?
Have I no parts but those of grief?

The Holdfast. *Not in W* 1 Threatned] threaten'd *1809*, *Pickering*: threatened *Willmott*, *Grosart* strict] sweet *1678–1799* 7 confesse *1633^{2}–* : confesse, *B 1633*

Complaining. *Not in W*

Let not thy wrathfull power
Afflict my houre,
My inch of life: or let thy gracious power
Contract my houre,
That I may climbe and finde relief.

The Discharge.

BUsie enquiring heart, what wouldst thou know?
Why dost thou prie,
And turn, and leer, and with a licorous eye
Look high and low;
And in thy lookings stretch and grow?

Hast thou not made thy counts, and summ'd up all?
Did not thy heart
Give up the whole, and with the whole depart?
Let what will fall:
That which is past who can recall?

Thy life is Gods, thy time to come is gone,
And is his right.
He is thy night at noon: he is at night
Thy noon alone.
The crop is his, for he hath sown.

And well it was for thee, when this befell,
That God did make
Thy businesse his, and in thy life partake:
For thou canst tell,
If it be his once, all is well.

Onely the present is thy part and fee.
And happy thou,
If, though thou didst not beat thy future brow,
Thou couldst well see
What present things requir'd of thee.

The Discharge. *Not in W*

They ask enough; why shouldst thou further go?
Raise not the mudde
Of future depths, but drink the cleare and good.
Dig not for wo
In times to come; for it will grow.

Man and the present fit: if he provide,
He breaks the square.
This houre is mine: if for the next I care,
I grow too wide,
And do encroach upon deaths side.

For death each houre environs and surrounds.
He that would know
And care for future chances, cannot go
Unto those grounds,
But through a Church-yard which them bounds.

Things present shrink and die: but they that spend
Their thoughts and sense
On future grief, do not remove it thence,
But it extend,
And draw the bottome out an end.

God chains the dog till night: wilt loose the chain,
And wake thy sorrow?
Wilt thou forestall it, and now grieve to morrow,
And then again
Grieve over freshly all thy pain?

Either grief will not come: or if it must,
Do not forecast.
And while it cometh, it is almost past.
Away distrust:
My God hath promis'd; he is just.

40 them bounds *1634–* : thē boūds *1633* : thē bounds *1633*^{2} 46 till] all *conj. Hall* 50 Grieve *1633*^{2} : Greive *B 1633* (*which has* grieve *l. 48*) 53 And while] While *Willmott, Grosart* 55 promis'd; *1633*^{2}*–* : *full stop B* : *comma 1633*

Praise (II).

KIng of Glorie, King of Peace,
I will love thee:
And that love may never cease,
I will move thee.

Thou hast granted my request,
Thou hast heard me:
Thou didst note my working breast,
Thou hast spar'd me.

Wherefore with my utmost art
I will sing thee,
And the cream of all my heart
I will bring thee.

Though my sinnes against me cried,
Thou didst cleare me;
And alone, when they replied,
Thou didst heare me.

Sev'n whole dayes, not one in seven,
I will praise thee.
In my heart, though not in heaven,
I can raise thee.

Thou grew'st soft and moist with tears,
Thou relentedst:
And when Justice call'd for fears,
Thou dissentedst.

Small it is, in this poore sort
To enroll thee:
Ev'n eternitie is too short
To extoll thee.

Praise (II). *Not in W Numbering Ed*

An Offering.

COme, bring thy gift. If blessings were as slow
 As mens returns, what would become of fools?
What hast thou there? a heart? but is it pure?
Search well and see; for hearts have many holes.
Yet one pure heart is nothing to bestow:
In Christ two natures met to be thy cure.

O that within us hearts had propagation,
Since many gifts do challenge many hearts!
Yet one, if good, may title to a number;
And single things grow fruitfull by deserts.
In publick judgements one may be a nation,
And fence a plague, while others sleep and slumber.

But all I fear is lest thy heart displease,
As neither good, nor one: so oft divisions
Thy lusts have made, and not thy lusts alone;
Thy passions also have their set partitions.
These parcell out thy heart: recover these,
And thou mayst offer many gifts in one.

There is a balsome, or indeed a bloud,
Dropping from heav'n, which doth both cleanse and close
All sorts of wounds; of such strange force it is.
Seek out this All-heal, and seek no repose,
Untill thou finde and use it to thy good:
Then bring thy gift, and let thy hymne be this;

SInce my sadnesse
 Into gladnesse
Lord thou dost convert,
 O accept
 What thou hast kept,
As thy due desert.

An Offering. *Not in W* 12 while] whiles *B* 24 gift *comma B 1633*[2]*–* : *semicolon 1633* 25 SInce *1641–* (*to mark the beginning of* thy hymne, *l. 24*): Since *1633–8*

Had I many,
Had I any,
(For this heart is none)
All were thine
And none of mine:
Surely thine alone.

Yet thy favour
May give savour
To this poore oblation;
And it raise
To be thy praise,
And be my salvation.

Longing.

With sick and famisht eyes,
With doubling knees and weary bones,
To thee my cries,
To thee my grones,
To thee my sighs, my tears ascend:
No end?

My throat, my soul is hoarse;
My heart is wither'd like a ground
Which thou dost curse.
My thoughts turn round,
And make me giddie; Lord, I fall,
Yet call.

From thee all pitie flows.
Mothers are kinde, because thou art,
And dost dispose
To them a part:
Their infants, them; and they suck thee
More free.

Longing. *Not in W*   17 suck] seek *1678–1799*

Bowels of pitie, heare!
Lord of my soul, love of my minde,
Bow down thine eare!
Let not the winde
Scatter my words, and in the same
Thy name!

Look on my sorrows round!
Mark well my furnace! O what flames,
What heats abound!
What griefs, what shames!
Consider, Lord; Lord, bow thine eare,
And heare!

Lord Jesu, thou didst bow
Thy dying head upon the tree:
O be not now
More dead to me!
Lord heare! *Shall he that made the eare,*
Not heare?

Behold, thy dust doth stirre,
It moves, it creeps, it aims at thee:
Wilt thou deferre
To succour me,
Thy pile of dust, wherein each crumme
Sayes, Come?

To thee help appertains.
Hast thou left all things to their course,
And laid the reins
Upon the horse?
Is all lockt? hath a sinners plea
No key?

Indeed the world's thy book,
Where all things have their leafe assign'd:
Yet a meek look
Hath interlin'd.
Thy board is full, yet humble guests
Finde nests.

26 furnace] fornace *B* (*cf.* Love unknown, *l.* 26) 50 leafe] lease *Willmott*, *Palmer*

Thou tarriest, while I die,
And fall to nothing: thou dost reigne,
And rule on high,
While I remain
In bitter grief: yet am I stil'd
Thy childe.

Lord, didst thou leave thy throne,
Not to relieve? how can it be,
That thou art grown
Thus hard to me?
Were sinne alive, good cause there were
To bear.

But now both sinne is dead,
And all thy promises live and bide.
That wants his head;
These speak and chide,
And in thy bosome poure my tears,
As theirs.

Lord JESU, heare my heart,
Which hath been broken now so long,
That ev'ry part
Hath got a tongue!
Thy beggars grow; rid them away
To day.

My love, my sweetnesse, heare!
By these thy feet, at which my heart
Lies all the yeare,
Pluck out thy dart,
And heal my troubled breast which cryes,
Which dyes.

66 bear] fear *conj. Hall.* 83 which] w^th^ *B* (*probably by mistake for* w^ch^, *as in next line*)

The Bag.

AWay despair! my gracious Lord doth heare.
Though windes and waves assault my keel,
He doth preserve it: he doth steer,
Ev'n when the boat seems most to reel.
Storms are the triumph of his art:
Well may he close his eyes, but not his heart.

Hast thou not heard, that my Lord JESUS di'd?
Then let me tell thee a strange storie.
The God of power, as he did ride
In his majestick robes of glorie,
Resolv'd to light; and so one day
He did descend, undressing all the way.

The starres his tire of light and rings obtain'd,
The cloud his bow, the fire his spear,
The sky his azure mantle gain'd.
And when they ask'd, what he would wear;
He smil'd and said as he did go,
He had new clothes a making here below.

When he was come, as travellers are wont,
He did repair unto an inne.
Both then, and after, many a brunt
He did endure to cancell sinne:
And having giv'n the rest before,
Here he gave up his life to pay our score.

But as he was returning, there came one
That ran upon him with a spear.
He, who came hither all alone,
Bringing nor man, nor arms, nor fear,
Receiv'd the blow upon his side,
And straight he turn'd, and to his brethren cry'd,

The Bag. *Not in W* 1 despaire! *B* : despair; *1633–*

If ye have any thing to send or write,
I have no bag, but here is room:
Unto my Fathers hands and sight,
Beleeve me, it shall safely come.
That I shall minde, what you impart,
Look, you may put it very neare my heart.

Or if hereafter any of my friends
Will use me in this kinde, the doore
Shall still be open; what he sends
I will present, and somewhat more,
Not to his hurt. Sighs will convey
Any thing to me. Harke, Despair away.

The Jews.

POore nation, whose sweet sap and juice
Our cyens have purloin'd, and left you drie:
Whose streams we got by the Apostles sluce,
And use in baptisme, while ye pine and die:
Who by not keeping once, became a debter;
And now by keeping lose the letter:

Oh that my prayers! mine, alas!
Oh that some Angel might a trumpet sound;
At which the Church falling upon her face
Should crie so loud, untill the trump were drown'd,
And by that crie of her deare Lord obtain,
That your sweet sap might come again!

32–5 *punctuation from B; that of 1633 is recorded* 32 *bracketed, and no colon 1633–* 33 Fathers *B* : fathers *1633–* 33–4 sight (Beleeve me) *1633–* 35 impart, *B* : impart; *1633–* 42 Harke, Despaire away. *B* (*cf. l. 1*): Heark despair, away. *1633–*

The Jews. *Not in W* 1 sappe *B* : sap *1633*[2]*–* : sap, *1633* 2 cyens] sinnes *B* *See note*

The Collar.

I Struck the board, and cry'd, No more.
I will abroad.
What? shall I ever sigh and pine?
My lines and life are free; free as the rode,
Loose as the winde, as large as store.
Shall I be still in suit?
Have I no harvest but a thorn
To let me bloud, and not restore
What I have lost with cordiall fruit?
Sure there was wine
Before my sighs did drie it: there was corn
Before my tears did drown it.
Is the yeare onely lost to me?
Have I no bayes to crown it?
No flowers, no garlands gay? all blasted?
All wasted?
Not so, my heart: but there is fruit,
And thou hast hands.
Recover all thy sigh-blown age
On double pleasures: leave thy cold dispute
Of what is fit, and not. Forsake thy cage,
Thy rope of sands,
Which pettie thoughts have made, and made to thee
Good cable, to enforce and draw,
And be thy law,
While thou didst wink and wouldst not see.
Away; take heed:
I will abroad.
Call in thy deaths head there: tie up thy fears.
He that forbears
To suit and serve his need,
Deserves his load.
But as I rav'd and grew more fierce and wilde
At every word,

The Collar. *Not in W* 21 not. Forsake *B* : not : forsake *1638–67* (*semicolon 1656*): not forsake *1633–5 1674–1799, Pickering, Willmott. Many editions from 1641 italicize* 'fit, and not:'

Me thoughts I heard one calling, *Child!*
And I reply'd, *My Lord.*

The Glimpse.

WHither away delight?
Thou cam'st but now; wilt thou so soon depart,
And give me up to night?
For many weeks of lingring pain and smart
But one half houre of comfort to my heart?

Me thinks delight should have
More skill in musick, and keep better time.
Wert thou a winde or wave,
They quickly go and come with lesser crime:
Flowers look about, and die not in their prime.

Thy short abode and stay
Feeds not, but addes to the desire of meat.
Lime begg'd of old, they say,
A neighbour spring to cool his inward heat;
Which by the springs accesse grew much more great.

In hope of thee my heart
Pickt here and there a crumme, and would not die;
But constant to his part,
When as my fears foretold this, did replie,
A slender thread a gentle guest will tie.

Yet if the heart that wept
Must let thee go, return when it doth knock.
Although thy heap be kept
For future times, the droppings of the stock
May oft break forth, and never break the lock.

35 Me thoughts] Methought *1799 1809, Pickering, Willmott, Grosart* 35 *Child! B* : *Childe : 1633–*

The Glimpse. *Not in W* 5 to *B* : for *1633–* : from *undated 7th edn See note*
9 crime:] crime? *B* (*probably the copyist was misled by l. 8 looking like a question*)
13 of old, they say, *B* : of old (they say) *1633–* 18 part, *1633*^{2}*–* : part *B 1633*

If I have more to spinne,
The wheel shall go, so that thy stay be short.
Thou knowst how grief and sinne
Disturb the work. O make me not their sport,
Who by thy coming may be made a court!

Assurance.

O Spitefull bitter thought!
Bitterly spitefull thought! Couldst thou invent
So high a torture? Is such poyson bought?
Doubtlesse, but in the way of punishment.
When wit contrives to meet with thee,
No such rank poyson can there be.

Thou said'st but even now,
That all was not so fair, as I conceiv'd,
Betwixt my God and me; that I allow
And coin large hopes, but that I was deceiv'd:
Either the league was broke, or neare it;
And, that I had great cause to fear it.

And what to this? what more
Could poyson, if it had a tongue, expresse?
What is thy aim? wouldst thou unlock the doore
To cold despairs, and gnawing pensivenesse?
Wouldst thou raise devils? I see, I know,
I writ thy purpose long ago.

But I will to my Father,
Who heard thee say it. O most gracious Lord,
If all the hope and comfort that I gather,
Were from my self, I had not half a word,
Not half a letter to oppose
What is objected by my foes.

Assurance. *Not in W* 4 punishment. *B*: punishment, *1633–* 10 hopes, but *B*: hopes; but, *1633–*

But thou art my desert:
And in this league, which now my foes invade,
Thou art not onely to perform thy part,
But also mine; as when the league was made
Thou didst at once thy self indite,
And hold my hand, while I did write.

Wherefore if thou canst fail,
Then can thy truth and I: but while rocks stand,
And rivers stirre, thou canst not shrink or quail:
Yea, when both rocks and all things shall disband,
Then shalt thou be my rock and tower,
And make their ruine praise thy power.

Now foolish thought go on,
Spin out thy thread, and make thereof a coat
To hide thy shame: for thou hast cast a bone
Which bounds on thee, and will not down thy throat:
What for it self love once began,
Now love and truth will end in man.

The Call.

COme, my Way, my Truth, my Life:
Such a Way, as gives us breath:
Such a Truth, as ends all strife:
Such a Life, as killeth death.

Come, my Light, my Feast, my Strength:
Such a Light, as shows a feast:
Such a Feast, as mends in length:
Such a Strength, as makes his guest.

Come, my Joy, my Love, my Heart:
Such a Joy, as none can move:
Such a Love, as none can part:
Such a Heart, as joyes in love.

The Call. *Not in W* 4 Such *B 1638–1809*: And such *1633–5*

Clasping of hands.

LOrd, thou art mine, and I am thine,
If mine I am: and thine much more,
Then I or ought, or can be mine.
Yet to be thine, doth me restore;
So that again I now am mine,
And with advantage mine the more,
Since this being mine, brings with it thine,
And thou with me dost thee restore.
If I without thee would be mine,
I neither should be mine nor thine.

Lord, I am thine, and thou art mine:
So mine thou art, that something more
I may presume thee mine, then thine.
For thou didst suffer to restore
Not thee, but me, and to be mine,
And with advantage mine the more,
Since thou in death wast none of thine,
Yet then as mine didst me restore.
O be mine still! still make me thine!
Or rather make no Thine and Mine!

Praise (III).

LOrd, I will mean and speak thy praise,
Thy praise alone.
My busie heart shall spin it all my dayes:
And when it stops for want of store,
Then will I wring it with a sigh or grone,
That thou mayst yet have more.

Clasping of hands. *Not in W* 6 more, *Ed* (*to match l. 16*): more *B*: more. *1633*: more: *1633*[2]– 15 mine, *Ed* (*to match l. 5*): mine: *B 1633*–
Praise (III). *Not in W* *Numbering Ed*

When thou dost favour any action,
It runnes, it flies:
All things concurre to give it a perfection.
That which had but two legs before,
When thou dost blesse, hath twelve: one wheel doth rise
To twentie then, or more.

But when thou dost on businesse blow,
It hangs, it clogs:
Not all the teams of Albion in a row
Can hale or draw it out of doore.
Legs are but stumps, and Pharaohs wheels but logs,
And struggling hinders more.

Thousands of things do thee employ
In ruling all
This spacious globe: Angels must have their joy,
Devils their rod, the sea his shore,
The windes their stint: and yet when I did call,
Thou heardst my call, and more.

I have not lost one single tear:
But when mine eyes
Did weep to heav'n, they found a bottle there
(As we have boxes for the poore)
Readie to take them in; yet of a size
That would contain much more.

But after thou hadst slipt a drop
From thy right eye,
(Which there did hang like streamers neare the top
Of some fair church, to show the sore
And bloudie battell which thou once didst trie)
The glasse was full and more.

25 one] on *B* 34 church, *1633*[2]– : church *B 1633*

Wherefore I sing. Yet since my heart,
Though press'd, runnes thin;
O that I might some other hearts convert,
And so take up at use good store:
That to thy chest there might be coming in
Both all my praise, and more!

Josephs coat.

WOunded I sing, tormented I indite,
Thrown down I fall into a bed, and rest:
Sorrow hath chang'd its note: such is his will,
Who changeth all things, as him pleaseth best.
For well he knows, if but one grief and smart
Among my many had his full career,
Sure it would carrie with it ev'n my heart,
And both would runne untill they found a biere
To fetch the bodie; both being due to grief.
But he hath spoil'd the race; and giv'n to anguish
One of Joyes coats, ticing it with relief
To linger in me, and together languish.
I live to shew his power, who once did bring
My *joyes* to *weep*, and now my *griefs* to *sing*.

The Pulley.

WHen God at first made man,
Having a glasse of blessings standing by;
Let us (said he) poure on him all we can:
Let the worlds riches, which dispersed lie,
Contract into a span.

41 chest *B*: chests *1633*–
Josephs coat. *Not in W* 3 will] right *conj. Palmer* (*for the rhyme*)
The Pulley. *Not in W*

So strength first made a way;
Then beautie flow'd, then wisdome, honour, pleasure:
When almost all was out, God made a stay,
Perceiving that alone of all his treasure
Rest in the bottome lay.

For if I should (said he)
Bestow this jewell also on my creature,
He would adore my gifts in stead of me,
And rest in Nature, not the God of Nature:
So both should losers be.

Yet let him keep the rest,
But keep them with repining restlesnesse:
Let him be rich and wearie, that at least,
If goodnesse leade him not, yet wearinesse
May tosse him to my breast.

The Priesthood.

BLest Order, which in power dost so excell,
That with th' one hand thou liftest to the sky,
And with the other throwest down to hell
In thy just censures; fain would I draw nigh,
Fain put thee on, exchanging my lay-sword
For that of th' holy Word.

But thou art fire, sacred and hallow'd fire;
And I but earth and clay: should I presume
To wear thy habit, the severe attire
My slender compositions might consume.
I am both foul and brittle; much unfit
To deal in holy Writ.

The Priesthood. *Not in W* 1 dost] doth *corr. to* dost *B* 6 Word *1633*[2] (*cf.* Writ, *l. 12*): word *B 1633*

Yet have I often seen, by cunning hand
And force of fire, what curious things are made
Of wretched earth. Where once I scorn'd to stand,
That earth is fitted by the fire and trade
Of skilfull artists, for the boards of those
Who make the bravest shows.

But since those great ones, be they ne're so great,
Come from the earth, from whence those vessels come;
So that at once both feeder, dish, and meat
Have one beginning and one finall summe:
I do not greatly wonder at the sight,
If earth in earth delight.

But th' holy men of God such vessels are,
As serve him up, who all the world commands:
When God vouchsafeth to become our fare,
Their hands convey him, who conveys their hands.
O what pure things, most pure must those things be,
Who bring my God to me!

Wherefore I dare not, I, put forth my hand
To hold the Ark, although it seem to shake
Through th' old sinnes and new doctrines of our land.
Onely, since God doth often vessels make
Of lowly matter for high uses meet,
I throw me at his feet.

There will I lie, untill my Maker seek
For some mean stuffe whereon to show his skill:
Then is my time. The distance of the meek
Doth flatter power. Lest good come short of ill
In praising might, the poore do by submission
What pride by opposition.

28 convey *B 1633*[2]– : conuey *1633* (*which has* conveys *in the same line*) 29–30 *cited in H. Vaughan's* The Mount of Olives (1652) 29 those things] those hands *Vaughan* 30 Who] which *Vaughan*

The Search.

WHither, O, whither art thou fled,
My Lord, my Love?
My searches are my daily bread;
Yet never prove.

My knees pierce th' earth, mine eies the skie;
And yet the sphere
And centre both to me denie
That thou art there.

Yet can I mark how herbs below
Grow green and gay,
As if to meet thee they did know,
While I decay.

Yet can I mark how starres above
Simper and shine,
As having keyes unto thy love,
While poore I pine.

I sent a sigh to seek thee out,
Deep drawn in pain,
Wing'd like an arrow: but my scout
Returns in vain.

I tun'd another (having store)
Into a grone;
Because the search was dumbe before:
But all was one.

Lord, dost thou some new fabrick mould,
Which favour winnes,
And keeps thee present, leaving th' old
Unto their sinnes?

The Search. *Not in W* 21 tun'd] turn'd *1656 1678–1799, Pickering* 25 mould, *B*: mold *1633–*

Where is my God? what hidden place
Conceals thee still?
What covert dare eclipse thy face?
Is it thy will?

O let not that of any thing;
Let rather brasse,
Or steel, or mountains be thy ring,
And I will passe.

Thy will such an intrenching is,
As passeth thought:
To it all strength, all subtilties
Are things of nought.

Thy will such a strange distance is,
As that to it
East and West touch, the poles do kisse,
And parallels meet.

Since then my grief must be as large,
As is thy space,
Thy distance from me; see my charge,
Lord, see my case.

O take these barres, these lengths away;
Turn, and restore me:
Be not Almightie, let me say,
Against, but for me.

When thou dost turn, and wilt be neare;
What edge so keen,
What point so piercing can appeare
To come between?

For as thy absence doth excell
All distance known:
So doth thy nearenesse bear the bell,
Making two one.

Grief.

O Who will give me tears? Come all ye springs,
Dwell in my head & eyes: come clouds, & rain:
My grief hath need of all the watry things,
That nature hath produc'd. Let ev'ry vein
Suck up a river to supply mine eyes,
My weary weeping eyes, too drie for me,
Unlesse they get new conduits, new supplies
To bear them out, and with my state agree.
What are two shallow foords, two little spouts
Of a lesse world? the greater is but small,
A narrow cupboard for my griefs and doubts,
Which want provision in the midst of all.
Verses, ye are too fine a thing, too wise
For my rough sorrows: cease, be dumbe and mute,
Give up your feet and running to mine eyes,
And keep your measures for some lovers lute,
Whose grief allows him musick and a ryme:
For mine excludes both measure, tune, and time.
Alas, my God!

The Crosse.

WHat is this strange and uncouth thing?
To make me sigh, and seek, and faint, and die,
Untill I had some place, where I might sing,
And serve thee; and not onely I,
But all my wealth and familie might combine
To set thy honour up, as our designe.

And then when after much delay,
Much wrastling, many a combate, this deare end,
So much desir'd, is giv'n, to take away
My power to serve thee; to unbend
All my abilities, my designes confound,
And lay my threatnings bleeding on the ground.

Grief. *Not in W* 6 eyes *comma from B, not in 1633*
The Crosse. *Not in W* 5 wealth *B 1633*^{2}– : wealth, *1633* 8 wrastling] wrestling *1656–60 1678–1809, Pickering, Willmott, Grosart*

One ague dwelleth in my bones,
Another in my soul (the memorie
What I would do for thee, if once my grones
Could be allow'd for harmonie):
I am in all a weak disabled thing,
Save in the sight thereof, where strength doth sting.

Besides, things sort not to my will,
Ev'n when my will doth studie thy renown:
Thou turnest th' edge of all things on me still,
Taking me up to throw me down:
So that, ev'n when my hopes seem to be sped,
I am to grief alive, to them as dead.

To have my aim, and yet to be
Further from it then when I bent my bow;
To make my hopes my torture, and the fee
Of all my woes another wo,
Is in the midst of delicates to need,
And ev'n in Paradise to be a weed.

Ah my deare Father, ease my smart!
These contrarieties crush me: these crosse actions
Doe winde a rope about, and cut my heart:
And yet since these thy contradictions
Are properly a crosse felt by thy Sonne,
With but foure words, my words, *Thy will be done.*

The Flower.

HOw fresh, O Lord, how sweet and clean
Are thy returns! ev'n as the flowers in spring;
To which, besides their own demean,
The late-past frosts tributes of pleasure bring.
Grief melts away
Like snow in May,
As if there were no such cold thing.

16 harmonie)] *colon added by Ed* 26 Further *B*: Farther *1633–* 35 Sonne *B 1634–* : sonne *1633 1633*[2]
The Flower. *Not in W* 4 pleasure] pleasures *corr. to* pleasure *B*

Who would have thought my shrivel'd heart
Could have recover'd greennesse? It was gone
Quite under ground; as flowers depart
To see their mother-root, when they have blown;
Where they together
All the hard weather,
Dead to the world, keep house unknown.

These are thy wonders, Lord of power,
Killing and quickning, bringing down to hell
And up to heaven in an houre;
Making a chiming of a passing-bell.
We say amisse,
This or that is:
Thy word is all, if we could spell.

O that I once past changing were,
Fast in thy Paradise, where no flower can wither!
Many a spring I shoot up fair,
Offring at heav'n, growing and groning thither:
Nor doth my flower
Want a spring-showre,
My sinnes and I joining together.

But while I grow in a straight line,
Still upwards bent, as if heav'n were mine own,
Thy anger comes, and I decline:
What frost to that? what pole is not the zone,
Where all things burn,
When thou dost turn,
And the least frown of thine is shown?

And now in age I bud again,
After so many deaths I live and write;
I once more smell the dew and rain,
And relish versing: O my onely light,
It cannot be
That I am he
On whom thy tempests fell all night.

28 together. *B 1633²–* : *colon 1633*

These are thy wonders, Lord of love,
To make us see we are but flowers that glide:
Which when we once can finde and prove,
Thou hast a garden for us, where to bide.
Who would be more,
Swelling through store,
Forfeit their Paradise by their pride.

Dotage.

FAlse glozing pleasures, casks of happinesse,
Foolish night-fires, womens and childrens wishes,
Chases in Arras, guilded emptinesse,
Shadows well mounted, dreams in a career,
Embroider'd lyes, nothing between two dishes;
These are the pleasures here.

True earnest sorrows, rooted miseries,
Anguish in grain, vexations ripe and blown,
Sure-footed griefs, solid calamities,
Plain demonstrations, evident and cleare,
Fetching their proofs ev'n from the very bone;
These are the sorrows here.

But oh the folly of distracted men,
Who griefs in earnest, joyes in jest pursue;
Preferring, like brute beasts, a lothsome den
Before a court, ev'n that above so cleare,
Where are no sorrows, but delights more true
Then miseries are here!

The Sonne.

LEt forrain nations of their language boast,
What fine varietie each tongue affords:
I like our language, as our men and coast:
Who cannot dresse it well, want wit, not words.

Dotage. *Not in W* 17 true *1634–* : true, *B 1633 1633*[2]
The Sonne. *Not in W*

How neatly doe we give one onely name
To parents issue and the sunnes bright starre!
A sonne is light and fruit; a fruitfull flame
Chasing the fathers dimnesse, carri'd farre
From the first man in th' East, to fresh and new
Western discov'ries of posteritie.
So in one word our Lords humilitie
We turn upon him in a sense most true:
For what Christ once in humblenesse began,
We him in glorie call, *The Sonne of Man.*

A true Hymne.

MY joy, my life, my crown!
My heart was meaning all the day,
Somewhat it fain would say:
And still it runneth mutt'ring up and down
With onely this, *My joy, my life, my crown.*

Yet slight not these few words:
If truly said, they may take part
Among the best in art.
The finenesse which a hymne or psalme affords,
Is, when the soul unto the lines accords.

He who craves all the minde,
And all the soul, and strength, and time,
If the words onely ryme,
Justly complains, that somewhat is behinde
To make his verse, or write a hymne in kinde.

Whereas if th' heart be moved,
Although the verse be somewhat scant,
God doth supplie the want.
As when th' heart sayes (sighing to be approved)
O, could I love! and stops: God writeth, *Loved.*

6 sunnes] sonnes *B*

A true Hymne. *Not in W* 17 the] *B omits (a slip, as the metre requires another syllable)*

The Answer.

MY comforts drop and melt away like snow:
I shake my head, and all the thoughts and ends,
Which my fierce youth did bandie, fall and flow
Like leaves about me: or like summer friends,
Flyes of estates and sunne-shine. But to all,
Who think me eager, hot, and undertaking,
But in my prosecutions slack and small;
As a young exhalation, newly waking,
Scorns his first bed of dirt, and means the sky;
But cooling by the way, grows pursie and slow,
And setling to a cloud, doth live and die
In that dark state of tears: to all, that so
Show me, and set me, I have one reply,
Which they that know the rest, know more then I.

A Dialogue-Antheme.

Christian. Death.

Chr. ALas, poore Death, where is thy glorie?
Where is thy famous force, thy ancient sting?
Dea. *Alas poore mortall, void of storie,*
Go spell and reade how I have kill'd thy King.
Chr. Poore Death! and who was hurt thereby?
Thy curse being laid on him, makes thee accurst.
Dea. *Let losers talk: yet thou shalt die;*
These arms shall crush thee.
Chr. Spare not, do thy worst.
I shall be one day better then before:
Thou so much worse, that thou shalt be no more.

The Answer. *Not in W* 14 *indented in B, but not in 1633 (probably to avoid turning the line)*

A Dialogue-Antheme. *Not in W* 5 Death *cap. in B (cf. l. 1)*: death *1633–*

The Water-course.

THou who dost dwell and linger here below,
Since the condition of this world is frail,
Where of all plants afflictions soonest grow;
If troubles overtake thee, do not wail:
For who can look for lesse, that loveth {Life? Strife?}

But rather turn the pipe and waters course
To serve thy sinnes, and furnish thee with store
Of sov'raigne tears, springing from true remorse:
That so in purenesse thou mayst him adore,
Who gives to man, as he sees fit, {Salvation. Damnation.}

Self-condemnation.

THou who condemnest Jewish hate,
For choosing Barrabas a murderer
Before the Lord of glorie;
Look back upon thine own estate,
Call home thine eye (that busie wanderer):
That choice may be thy storie.

He that doth love, and love amisse,
This worlds delights before true Christian joy,
Hath made a Jewish choice:
The world an ancient murderer is;
Thousands of souls it hath and doth destroy
With her enchanting voice.

The Water-course. *Not in W* 5 *marks of interrogation* 1633^2– : *full stops B 1633* 6 pipe *1635–* : *comma B 1633–4* 10 fit, 1633^2– : *no comma B 1633*

Self-condemnation. *Not in W* 2 Barrabas *B*: Barabbas *1633–* *See note* 4 own estate] owne state *B* (*a slip, as the metre requires another syllable*) 5 *colon Ed*: *no stop B 1633–* 7 amisse, *1667–* : amisse *B 1633–60* 11 hath] hath, *B*

He that hath made a sorrie wedding
Between his soul and gold, and hath preferr'd
False gain before the true,
Hath done what he condemnes in reading:
For he hath sold for money his deare Lord,
And is a Judas-Jew.

Thus we prevent the last great day,
And judge our selves. That light, which sin & passion
Did before dimme and choke,
When once those snuffes are ta'ne away,
Shines bright and cleare, ev'n unto condemnation,
Without excuse or cloke.

Bitter-sweet.

AH my deare angrie Lord,
Since thou dost love, yet strike;
Cast down, yet help afford;
Sure I will do the like.

I will complain, yet praise;
I will bewail, approve:
And all my sowre-sweet dayes
I will lament, and love.

The Glance.

WHen first thy sweet and gracious eye
Vouchsaf'd ev'n in the midst of youth and night
To look upon me, who before did lie
Weltring in sinne;
I felt a sugred strange delight,
Passing all cordials made by any art,
Bedew, embalme, and overrunne my heart,
And take it in.

22 ta'ne] taken *B*: ta'n *1638–1799*: ta'en *1809, Pickering, Willmott*
Bitter-sweet. *Not in W*
The Glance. *Not in W*

Since that time many a bitter storm
My soul hath felt, ev'n able to destroy,
Had the malicious and ill-meaning harm
His swing and sway:
But still thy sweet originall joy,
Sprung from thine eye, did work within my soul,
And surging griefs, when they grew bold, controll,
And got the day.

If thy first glance so powerfull be,
A mirth but open'd and seal'd up again;
What wonders shall we feel, when we shall see
Thy full-ey'd love!
When thou shalt look us out of pain,
And one aspect of thine spend in delight
More then a thousand sunnes disburse in light,
In heav'n above.

The 23d Psalme.

THe God of love my shepherd is,
And he that doth me feed:
While he is mine, and I am his,
What can I want or need?

He leads me to the tender grasse,
Where I both feed and rest;
Then to the streams that gently passe:
In both I have the best.

Or if I stray, he doth convert
And bring my minde in frame:
And all this not for my desert,
But for his holy name.

13 joy, *1678–* : *no comma B 1633–74*
The 23d Psalme. *Not in W* *Title* : 23[d] *B* : 23 *1633–*

Yea, in deaths shadie black abode
Well may I walk, not fear:
For thou art with me; and thy rod
To guide, thy staffe to bear.

Nay, thou dost make me sit and dine,
Ev'n in my enemies sight:
My head with oyl, my cup with wine
Runnes over day and night.

Surely thy sweet and wondrous love
Shall measure all my dayes;
And as it never shall remove,
So neither shall my praise.

Marie Magdalene.

WHen blessed Marie wip'd her Saviours feet,
(Whose precepts she had trampled on before)
And wore them for a jewell on her head,
Shewing his steps should be the street,
Wherein she thenceforth evermore
With pensive humblenesse would live and tread:

She being stain'd her self, why did she strive
To make him clean, who could not be defil'd?
Why kept she not her tears for her own faults,
And not his feet? Though we could dive
In tears like seas, our sinnes are pil'd
Deeper then they, in words, and works, and thoughts.

Deare soul, she knew who did vouchsafe and deigne
To bear her filth; and that her sinnes did dash
Ev'n God himself: wherefore she was not loth,
As she had brought wherewith to stain,
So to bring in wherewith to wash:
And yet in washing one, she washed both.

18 my] mine *B* 24 my] thy *B* *See note*
Marie Magdalene. *Not in W* *Title in* 'The titles of the severall poems' *1633–* : S. Marie Magdalene 9 faults] fauts *B*

Aaron.

HOlinesse on the head,
Light and perfections on the breast,
Harmonious bells below, raising the dead
To leade them unto life and rest:
Thus are true Aarons drest.

Profanenesse in my head,
Defects and darknesse in my breast,
A noise of passions ringing me for dead
Unto a place where is no rest:
Poore priest thus am I drest.

Onely another head
I have, another heart and breast,
Another musick, making live not dead,
Without whom I could have no rest:
In him I am well drest.

Christ is my onely head,
My alone onely heart and breast,
My onely musick, striking me ev'n dead;
That to the old man I may rest,
And be in him new drest.

So holy in my head,
Perfect and light in my deare breast,
My doctrine tun'd by Christ, (who is not dead,
But lives in me while I do rest)
Come people; Aaron's drest.

The Odour. 2. Cor. 2. 15.

HOw sweetly doth *My Master* sound! *My Master!*
As Amber-greese leaves a rich sent
Unto the taster:
So do these words a sweet content,
An orientall fragrancie, *My Master.*

Aaron. *Not in W* 4 *and* 9 rest: *1633*[2] (*to correspond with l. 14*): rest, *B*: rest. *1633* 22 deare] cleare *conj. Hall*
The Odour. *Not in W* *Title*: 15 *added by Ed*

With these all day I do perfume my minde,
My minde ev'n thrust into them both:
That I might finde
What cordials make this curious broth,
This broth of smells, that feeds and fats my minde.

My Master, shall I speak? O that to thee
My servant were a little so,
As flesh may be;
That these two words might creep & grow
To some degree of spicinesse to thee!

Then should the Pomander, which was before
A speaking sweet, mend by reflection,
And tell me more:
For pardon of my imperfection
Would warm and work it sweeter then before.

For when *My Master*, which alone is sweet,
And ev'n in my unworthinesse pleasing,
Shall call and meet,
My servant, as thee not displeasing,
That call is but the breathing of the sweet.

This breathing would with gains by sweetning me
(As sweet things traffick when they meet)
Return to thee.
And so this new commerce and sweet
Should all my life employ and busie me.

The Foil.

IF we could see below
The sphere of vertue, and each shining grace
As plainly as that above doth show;
This were the better skie, the brighter place.

30 employ *1634–* : imploy *B* : employ, *1633 1633*[2]
The Foil. *Not in W*

God hath made starres the foil
To set off vertues; griefs to set off sinning:
Yet in this wretched world we toil,
As if grief were not foul, nor vertue winning.

The Forerunners.

THe harbingers are come. See, see their mark;
White is their colour, and behold my head.
But must they have my brain? must they dispark
Those sparkling notions, which therein were bred?
Must dulnesse turn me to a clod?
Yet have they left me, *Thou art still my God.*

Good men ye be, to leave me my best room,
Ev'n all my heart, and what is lodged there:
I passe not, I, what of the rest become,
So *Thou art still my God*, be out of fear.
He will be pleased with that dittie;
And if I please him, I write fine and wittie.

Farewell sweet phrases, lovely metaphors.
But will ye leave me thus? when ye before
Of stews and brothels onely knew the doores,
Then did I wash you with my tears, and more,
Brought you to Church well drest and clad:
My God must have my best, ev'n all I had.

Lovely enchanting language, sugar-cane,
Hony of roses, whither wilt thou flie?
Hath some fond lover tic'd thee to thy bane?
And wilt thou leave the Church, and love a stie?
Fie, thou wilt soil thy broider'd coat,
And hurt thy self, and him that sings the note.

8 grief] sin *conj. Palmer See note*
The Forerunners. *Not in W* 10 So (Thou art still my *God*) be out of feare. *B* (*cf. l. 32*) 19 Lovely *1633*[2]– : Louely *B 1633* (*which has* lovely *in l. 13*)

Let foolish lovers, if they will love dung,
With canvas, not with arras, clothe their shame:
Let follie speak in her own native tongue.
True beautie dwells on high: ours is a flame
    But borrow'd thence to light us thither.
Beautie and beauteous words should go together.

Yet if you go, I passe not; take your way:
For, *Thou art still my God*, is all that ye
Perhaps with more embellishment can say.
Go birds of spring: let winter have his fee;
    Let a bleak palenesse chalk the doore,
So all within be livelier then before.

The Rose.

PResse me not to take more pleasure
    In this world of sugred lies,
And to use a larger measure
    Then my strict, yet welcome size.

First, there is no pleasure here:
    Colour'd griefs indeed there are,
Blushing woes, that look as cleare
    As if they could beautie spare.

Or if such deceits there be,
    Such delights I meant to say;
There are no such things to me,
    Who have pass'd my right away.

But I will not much oppose
    Unto what you now advise:
Onely take this gentle rose,
    And therein my answer lies.

26 arras, *1635–* : Arras *B*: arras *1633–4*   32 For (Thou art still my *God*) is all, y^{t} yee *B*   33 say. *B* *1633*^{2}*–* : say, *1633*   34 fee ; *1633*^{2}*–* : fee : *B* : fee, *1633*

The Rose. *Not in W*

What is fairer then a rose?
What is sweeter? yet it purgeth.
Purgings enmitie disclose,
Enmitie forbearance urgeth.

If then all that worldlings prize
Be contracted to a rose;
Sweetly there indeed it lies,
But it biteth in the close.

So this flower doth judge and sentence
Worldly joyes to be a scourge:
For they all produce repentance,
And repentance is a purge.

But I health, not physick choose:
Onely though I you oppose,
Say that fairly I refuse,
For my answer is a rose.

Discipline.

THrow away thy rod,
Throw away thy wrath:
O my God,
Take the gentle path.

For my hearts desire
Unto thine is bent:
I aspire
To a full consent.

Not a word or look
I affect to own,
But by book,
And thy book alone.

Discipline. *Not in W*

Though I fail, I weep:
Though I halt in pace,
Yet I creep
To the throne of grace.

Then let wrath remove;
Love will do the deed:
For with love
Stonie hearts will bleed.

Love is swift of foot;
Love 's a man of warre,
And can shoot,
And can hit from farre.

Who can scape his bow?
That which wrought on thee,
Brought thee low,
Needs must work on me.

Throw away thy rod;
Though man frailties hath,
Thou art God:
Throw away thy wrath.

The Invitation.

COme ye hither All, whose taste
Is your waste;
Save your cost, and mend your fare.
God is here prepar'd and drest,
And the feast,
God, in whom all dainties are.

The Invitation. *Not in W* 1 All *B* (*also in ll.* 7, 13, 19, 25, 36, *but* all *in l.* 31): all *1633–* (*throughout the poem*)

Come ye hither All, whom wine
Doth define,
Naming you not to your good:
Weep what ye have drunk amisse,
And drink this,
Which before ye drink is bloud.

Come ye hither All, whom pain
Doth arraigne,
Bringing all your sinnes to sight:
Taste and fear not: God is here
In this cheer,
And on sinne doth cast the fright.

Come ye hither All, whom joy
Doth destroy,
While ye graze without your bounds:
Here is joy that drowneth quite
Your delight,
As a floud the lower grounds.

Come ye hither All, whose love
Is your dove,
And exalts you to the skie:
Here is love, which having breath
Ev'n in death,
After death can never die.

Lord I have invited all,
And I shall
Still invite, still call to thee:
For it seems but just and right
In my sight,
Where is All, there All should be.

The Banquet.

WElcome sweet and sacred cheer,
Welcome deare;
With me, in me, live and dwell:
For thy neatnesse passeth sight,
Thy delight
Passeth tongue to taste or tell.

O what sweetnesse from the bowl
Fills my soul,
Such as is, and makes divine!
Is some starre (fled from the sphere)
Melted there,
As we sugar melt in wine?

Or hath sweetnesse in the bread
Made a head
To subdue the smell of sinne;
Flowers, and gummes, and powders giving
All their living,
Lest the Enemy should winne?

Doubtlesse, neither starre nor flower
Hath the power
Such a sweetnesse to impart:
Onely God, who gives perfumes,
Flesh assumes,
And with it perfumes my heart.

But as Pomanders and wood
Still are good,
Yet being bruis'd are better sented:
God, to show how farre his love
Could improve,
Here, as broken, is presented.

The Banquet. *Not in W* 7 from] to *corr. to* from *B* 18 Enemy *B*: enemie *1633–* 27 are] *misprinted* or *Gibson*

When I had forgot my birth,
And on earth
In delights of earth was drown'd;
God took bloud, and needs would be
Spilt with me,
And so found me on the ground.

Having rais'd me to look up,
In a cup
Sweetly he doth meet my taste.
But I still being low and short,
Farre from court,
Wine becomes a wing at last.

For with it alone I flie
To the skie:
Where I wipe mine eyes, and see
What I seek, for what I sue;
Him I view,
Who hath done so much for me.

Let the wonder of his pitie
Be my dittie,
And take up my lines and life:
Hearken under pain of death,
Hands and breath;
Strive in this, and love the strife.

The Posie.

LEt wits contest,
And with their words and posies windows fill:
Lesse then the least
Of all thy mercies, is my posie still.

46 What I seek for, what I sue; *Willmott, Grosart* *See note* 49 his *B*: this *1633–*
The Posie. *Not in W*

This on my ring,
This by my picture, in my book I write:
Whether I sing,
Or say, or dictate, this is my delight.

Invention rest,
Comparisons go play, wit use thy will:
Lesse then the least
Of all Gods mercies, is my posie still.

A Parodie.

SOuls joy, when thou art gone,
And I alone,
Which cannot be,
Because thou dost abide with me,
And I depend on thee;

Yet when thou dost suppresse
The cheerfulnesse
Of thy abode,
And in my powers not stirre abroad,
But leave me to my load:

O what a damp and shade
Doth me invade!
No stormie night
Can so afflict or so affright,
As thy eclipsed light.

Ah Lord! do not withdraw,
Lest want of aw
Make Sinne appeare;
And when thou dost but shine lesse cleare,
Say, that thou art not here.

And then what life I have,
While Sinne doth rave,
And falsly boast,
That I may seek, but thou art lost;
Thou and alone thou know'st.

A Parodie. *Not in W*

O what a deadly cold
Doth me infold!
I half beleeve,
That Sinne sayes true: but while I grieve,
Thou com'st and dost relieve.

The Elixir.

TEach me, my God and King,
In all things thee to see,
And what I do in any thing,
To do it as for thee:

Not rudely, as a beast,
To runne into an action;
But still to make thee prepossest,
And give it his perfection.

A man that looks on glasse,
On it may stay his eye;
Or if he pleaseth, through it passe,
And then the heav'n espie.

All may of thee partake:
Nothing can be so mean,
Which with his tincture (for thy sake)
Will not grow bright and clean.

The Elixir. *This and the remaining six poems are found in W as well as in B* *Title*: *the amanuensis of W headed the poem* Perfection; *Herbert added* The Elixir *without crossing out* Perfection; *the new title was, no doubt, chosen after he had added the new last verse* (*ll. 21–4, as above*): *B has* The Elixer *corr. to* The Elixir, *which is also the spelling in the table of contents of B and of 1638–* : *at head of poem* The Elixer *1633–8*: The Elixir *1641–* *The many alterations of this poem in W are in Herbert's hand*

1–4
Lord teach mee to referr
All things I doe to thee
That I not onely may not erre
But allso pleasing bee. *W*

5–8 *absent from W* 12–13 *Between these two verses W has the following, which is cancelled by four sloping lines*:

He that does ought for thee,
Marketh y[t] deed for thine:
And when the Divel shakes y[e] tree,
Thou saist, this fruit is mine.

14 mean] low *corr. by Herbert to* meane *W* 15 his] this *1656–74* 16 grow bright and clean] to Heauen grow *corr. by Herbert to* grow bright & cleane *W*

A servant with this clause
Makes drudgerie divine:
Who sweeps a room, as for thy laws,
Makes that and th' action fine.

This is the famous stone
That turneth all to gold:
For that which God doth touch and own
Cannot for lesse be told.

A Wreath.

A Wreathed garland of deserved praise,
Of praise deserved, unto thee I give,
I give to thee, who knowest all my wayes,
My crooked winding wayes, wherein I live,
Wherein I die, not live: for life is straight,
Straight as a line, and ever tends to thee,
To thee, who art more farre above deceit,
Then deceit seems above simplicitie.
Give me simplicitie, that I may live,
So live and like, that I may know, thy wayes,
Know them and practise them: then shall I give
For this poore wreath, give thee a crown of praise.

Death.

DEath, thou wast once an uncouth hideous thing,
Nothing but bones,
The sad effect of sadder grones:
Thy mouth was open, but thou couldst not sing.

19 room, as] chamber, *corr. by Herbert to* roome, as *W* 21–4 *W at first has the following, with a flourish at the end indicating the close of the poem:*

But these are high perfections:
Happy are they that dare
Lett in the Light to all their actions
And show them as they are.

Herbert has struck through these lines and substituted the verse as it reappears in B and 1633 (ll. 21–4)

A Wreath. *In W this poem precedes* To all Angels and Saints 10 know, *1809, Palmer*: know *B W 1633–*

For we consider'd thee as at some six
Or ten yeares hence,
After the losse of life and sense,
Flesh being turn'd to dust, and bones to sticks.

We lookt on this side of thee, shooting short;
Where we did finde
The shells of fledge souls left behinde,
Dry dust, which sheds no tears, but may extort.

But since our Saviours death did put some bloud
Into thy face;
Thou art grown fair and full of grace,
Much in request, much sought for as a good.

For we do now behold thee gay and glad,
As at dooms-day;
When souls shall wear their new aray,
And all thy bones with beautie shall be clad.

Therefore we can go die as sleep, and trust
Half that we have
Unto an honest faithfull grave;
Making our pillows either down, or dust.

Dooms-day.

COme away,
Make no delay.
Summon all the dust to rise,
Till it stirre, and rubbe the eyes;
While this member jogs the other,
Each one whispring, *Live you brother?*

Come away,
Make this the day.
Dust, alas, no musick feels,
But thy trumpet: then it kneels,
As peculiar notes and strains
Cure Tarantulas raging pains.

Death. 16 sought for *B 1635–* : sought for, *1633–4* : long'd for *W*
Dooms-day. 6 *you*] *ye 1635–56* *brother?*] *Brother. B* 12 Tarantulas *W* : Tarantulaes *B 1633–*

Come away,
O make no stay!
Let the graves make their confession,
Lest at length they plead possession:
Fleshes stubbornnesse may have
Read that lesson to the grave.

Come away,
Thy flock doth stray.
Some to windes their bodie lend,
And in them may drown a friend:
Some in noisome vapours grow
To a plague and publick wo.

Come away,
Help our decay.
Man is out of order hurl'd,
Parcel'd out to all the world.
Lord, thy broken consort raise,
And the musick shall be praise.

Judgement.

ALmightie Judge, how shall poore wretches brook
Thy dreadfull look,
Able a heart of iron to appall,
When thou shalt call
For ev'ry mans peculiar book?

What others mean to do, I know not well;
Yet I heare tell,
That some will turn thee to some leaves therein
So void of sinne,
That they in merit shall excell.

21 windes] *misprinted* the windes *Willmott*: wines *conj. Hall* *See note* bodie] bodies *W*, *Grosart*: body *B*

Judgement. 7 heare] *misprinted* here *1660–1799*, *Pickering* *See note*

But I resolve, when thou shalt call for mine,
That to decline,
And thrust a Testament into thy hand:
Let that be scann'd.
There thou shalt finde my faults are thine.

Heaven.

O Who will show me those delights on high?
Echo. I.
Thou Echo, thou art mortall, all men know.
Echo. No.
Wert thou not born among the trees and leaves?
Echo. Leaves.
And are there any leaves, that still abide?
Echo. Bide.
What leaves are they? impart the matter wholly.
Echo. Holy.
Are holy leaves the Echo then of blisse?
Echo. Yes.
Then tell me, what is that supreme delight?
Echo. Light.
Light to the minde: what shall the will enjoy?
Echo. Joy.
But are there cares and businesse with the pleasure?
Echo. Leisure.
Light, joy, and leisure; but shall they persever?
Echo. Ever.

Love (III).

LOve bade me welcome: yet my soul drew back,
Guiltie of dust and sinne.
But quick-ey'd Love, observing me grow slack
From my first entrance in,
Drew nearer to me, sweetly questioning,
If I lack'd any thing.

Heaven. *The answers of Echo, italicized 1633– , are not distinguished in B and W*
5 trees] woods *W* 7 that] wch *W* 9 wholly.] wholly ? *B* 17 there] their *B*
Love (III). *Numbering Ed*

A guest, I answer'd, worthy to be here:
Love said, You shall be he.
I the unkinde, ungratefull? Ah my deare,
I cannot look on thee.
Love took my hand, and smiling did reply,
Who made the eyes but I?

Truth Lord, but I have marr'd them: let my shame
Go where it doth deserve.
And know you not, sayes Love, who bore the blame?
My deare, then I will serve.
You must sit down, sayes Love, and taste my meat:
So I did sit and eat.

FINIS.

Glory be to God *on high*
And on earth peace
Good will towards men.

8 You *1633*^{2}– : you *B W 1633* 14 doth] does *W*

Glory be &c. Printed here as written in B; arranged in two lines 1633– Not in W Vaughan ends The Mount of Olives (1652) *with these words, followed by the couplet which follows Herbert's* L'Envoy (*p. 199*)

THE CHURCH MILITANT

ALmightie Lord, who from thy glorious throne
Seest and rulest all things ev'n as one:
The smallest ant or atome knows thy power,
Known also to each minute of an houre:
Much more do Common-weals acknowledge thee,
And wrap their policies in thy decree,
Complying with thy counsels, doing nought
Which doth not meet with an eternall thought.
But above all, thy Church and Spouse doth prove
Not the decrees of power, but bands of love.
Early didst thou arise to plant this vine,
Which might the more indeare it to be thine.
Spices come from the East; so did thy Spouse,
Trimme as the light, sweet as the laden boughs
Of *Noahs* shadie vine, chaste as the dove;
Prepar'd and fitted to receive thy love.
The course was westward, that the sunne might light
As well our understanding as our sight.
Where th' Ark did rest, there *Abraham* began
To bring the other Ark from *Canaan*.
Moses pursu'd this: but King *Solomon*
Finish'd and fixt the old religion.
When it grew loose, the Jews did hope in vain
By nailing Christ to fasten it again.
But to the Gentiles he bore crosse and all,
Rending with earthquakes the partition-wall:
Onely whereas the Ark in glorie shone,
Now with the crosse, as with a staffe, alone,
Religion, like a pilgrime, westward bent,
Knocking at all doores, ever as she went.
Yet as the sunne, though forward be his flight,

The Church Militant. *A new section of the 1633 volume, as also of both MSS., is marked by the use of* The Church Militant *as the page-heading for all that follows, as well as by* FINIS *after the preceding poem. In B there is a blank page between the sections, and in W five blank pages.* 8 doth] does *W* 11 Thou didst rise early for to plant this vine *W* 16 All, Emblems, wch thy Darling doth improue. *W* 20 from] to *W* *See note*

Listens behinde him, and allows some light,
Till all depart: so went the Church her way,
Letting, while one foot stept, the other stay
Among the eastern nations for a time,
Till both removed to the western clime.
To *Egypt* first she came, where they did prove
Wonders of anger once, but now of love.
The ten Commandments there did flourish more
Then the ten bitter plagues had done before.
Holy *Macarius* and great *Anthonie*
Made *Pharaoh Moses*, changing th' historie.
Goshen was darknesse, *Egypt* full of lights,
Nilus for monsters brought forth Israelites.
Such power hath mightie Baptisme to produce
For things misshapen, things of highest use.
How deare to me, O God, thy counsels are!
Who may with thee compare?
Religion thence fled into *Greece*, where arts
Gave her the highest place in all mens hearts.
Learning was pos'd, Philosophie was set,
Sophisters taken in a fishers net.
Plato and *Aristotle* were at a losse,
And wheel'd about again to spell *Christ-Crosse*.
Prayers chas'd syllogismes into their den,
And *Ergo* was transform'd into *Amen*.
Though *Greece* took horse as soon as *Egypt* did,
And *Rome* as both; yet *Egypt* faster rid,
And spent her period and prefixed time
Before the other. *Greece* being past her prime,
Religion went to *Rome*, subduing those,
Who, that they might subdue, made all their foes.
The Warrier his deere skarres no more resounds,
But seems to yeeld Christ hath the greater wounds,

32–3 allows . . . depart:] giues them some light Till all be gone. *W* 49 Thence into Greece she fled, where curious Arts *W* 52 a fishers net] a ffisher-nett *W* 54 *Christ-Crosse*] *Christs-Crosse 1641–1809* (*except 1674*), *Pickering* 59 And spent] Spending *W*
60–2 Before y[e] other two were in their prime.
From Greece to Rome she went, subduing those
Who had subdued all the world for foes. *W*
64 hath] had *W*

Wounds willingly endur'd to work his blisse,
Who by an ambush lost his Paradise.
The great heart stoops, and taketh from the dust
A sad repentance, not the spoils of lust:
Quitting his spear, lest it should pierce again
Him in his members, who for him was slain.
The Shepherds hook grew to a scepter here,
Giving new names and numbers to the yeare.
But th' Empire dwelt in *Greece*, to comfort them
Who were cut short in *Alexanders* stemme.
In both of these Prowesse and Arts did tame
And tune mens hearts against the Gospel came:
Which using, and not fearing skill in th' one,
Or strength in th' other, did erect her throne.
Many a rent and struggling th' Empire knew,
(As dying things are wont) untill it flew
At length to *Germanie*, still westward bending,
And there the Churches festivall attending:
That as before Empire and Arts made way,
(For no lesse Harbingers would serve then they)
So they might still, and point us out the place
Where first the Church should raise her down-cast face.
Strength levels grounds, Art makes a garden there;
Then showres Religion, and makes all to bear.
Spain in the Empire shar'd with *Germanie*,
But *England* in the higher victorie:
Giving the Church a crown to keep her state,
And not go lesse then she had done of late.
Constantines British line meant this of old,
And did this mysterie wrap up and fold
Within a sheet of paper, which was rent
From times great Chronicle, and hither sent.
Thus both the Church and Sunne together ran
Unto the farthest old meridian.
How deare to me, O God, thy counsels are!
Who may with thee compare?
Much about one and the same time and place,
Both where and when the Church began her race,

76 tune] clense *W* 78 did erect her throne] took possession *W*

Sinne did set out of Eastern *Babylon*,
And travell'd westward also: journeying on
He chid the Church away, where e're he came,
Breaking her peace, and tainting her good name.
At first he got to *Egypt*, and did sow
Gardens of gods, which ev'ry yeare did grow
Fresh and fine deities. They were at great cost,
Who for a god clearely a sallet lost.
Ah, what a thing is man devoid of grace,
Adoring garlick with an humble face,
Begging his food of that which he may eat,
Starving the while he worshippeth his meat!
Who makes a root his god, how low is he,
If God and man be sever'd infinitely!
What wretchednesse can give him any room,
Whose house is foul, while he adores his broom?
None will beleeve this now, though money be
In us the same transplanted foolerie.
Thus Sinne in *Egypt* sneaked for a while;
His highest was an ox or crocodile,
And such poore game. Thence he to *Greece* doth passe,
And being craftier much then Goodnesse was,
He left behinde him garrisons of sinnes
To make good that which ev'ry day he winnes.
Here Sinne took heart, and for a garden-bed
Rich shrines and oracles he purchased:
He grew a gallant, and would needs foretell
As well what should befall, as what befell.
Nay, he became a poet, and would serve
His pills of sublimate in that conserve.
The world came in with hands and purses full
To this great lotterie, and all would pull.
But all was glorious cheating, brave deceit,
Where some poore truths were shuffled for a bait
To credit him, and to discredit those

104 westward also: journeying on] west-ward also iourneying on, *B*: Westward allso, coasting on, *W* 108 grow *W*: grow, *B 1633–* 123 poore] small *W* 133 came in with *W*: came with *B*: came both with *1633–* (*perhaps B inadvertently omitted* in, *and the editor of 1633, finding a syllable short, and not having W before him, supplied* both) 137 to discredit] so discreditt *W*

Who after him should braver truths disclose.
From *Greece* he went to *Rome*: and as before
He was a God, now he's an Emperour.
Nero and others lodg'd him bravely there,
Put him in trust to rule the Roman sphere.
Glorie was his chief instrument of old:
Pleasure succeeded straight, when that grew cold.
Which soon was blown to such a mightie flame,
That though our Saviour did destroy the game,
Disparking oracles, and all their treasure,
Setting affliction to encounter pleasure;
Yet did a rogue with hope of carnall joy
Cheat the most subtill nations. Who so coy,
So trimme, as *Greece* and *Egypt?* yet their hearts
Are given over, for their curious arts,
To such Mahometan stupidities,
As the old heathen would deem prodigies.
How deare to me, O God, thy counsels are!
                    Who may with thee compare?
Onely the West and *Rome* do keep them free
From this contagious infidelitie.
And this is all the Rock, whereof they boast,
As *Rome* will one day finde unto her cost.
Sinne being not able to extirpate quite
The Churches here, bravely resolv'd one night
To be a Church-man too, and wear a Mitre:
The old debauched ruffian would turn writer.
I saw him in his studie, where he sate
Busie in controversies sprung of late.
A gown and pen became him wondrous well:
His grave aspect had more of heav'n then hell:
Onely there was a handsome picture by,

142 Roman *B W 1656–* : Romane *1633–41 and undated 7th edn* 148 affliction] afflictions *W* 151 trimme] spruse *W* 157 Onely the West] Europe alone *corr. by 2nd hand to* Only the west *W* 159–60 boast, As *Rome* . . . cost.]

boast :
Traditions are accounts wthout our host.
They who rely on them must reckon twice
When written Truths shall censure mans devise. *W* (*having one couplet more than B and 1633*) 168 had more of] was liker *W*

To which he lent a corner of his eye.
As Sinne in *Greece* a Prophet was before,
And in old *Rome* a mightie Emperour;
So now being Priest he plainly did professe
To make a jest of Christs three offices:
The rather since his scatter'd jugglings were
United now in one both time and sphere.
From *Egypt* he took pettie deities,
From *Greece* oracular infallibilities,
And from old *Rome* the libertie of pleasure
By free dispensings of the Churches treasure.
Then in memoriall of his ancient throne
He did surname his palace, *Babylon*.
Yet that he might the better gain all nations,
And make that name good by their transmigrations,
From all these places, but at divers times,
He took fine vizards to conceal his crimes:
From *Egypt* Anchorisme and retirednesse,
Learning from *Greece*, from old *Rome* statelinesse:
And blending these he carri'd all mens eyes,
While Truth sat by, counting his victories:
Whereby he grew apace and scorn'd to use
Such force as once did captivate the Jews;
But did bewitch, and finely work each nation
Into a voluntarie transmigration.
All poste to *Rome:* Princes submit their necks
Either t' his publick foot or private tricks.
It did not fit his gravitie to stirre,
Nor his long journey, nor his gout and furre.
Therefore he sent out able ministers,
Statesmen within, without doores cloisterers:
Who without spear, or sword, or other drumme

179 pleasure *B W* pleasure, *1633–* 180 free dispensings] dispensations *W* 184 transmigrations *W*: transmigrations, *B*: transmigrations; *1633–* 190 his] *Palmer states wrongly that B omits* 193 finely] finally *Pickering, Willmott, Grosart* But did bewitch both kings & many a nation *W* 194 Into] Vnto *W* 196 t' his] to'his *B W* 198 and] or *W*

201–4 Who brought his doctrins & his deeds from Rome
But when they were vnto ye Sorbon come,
The waight was such they left ye doctrins there
Shipping ye vices onely for our sphere. *W*

Then what was in their tongue, did overcome;
And having conquer'd, did so strangely rule,
That the whole world did seem but the Popes mule.
As new and old *Rome* did one Empire twist;
So both together are one Antichrist,
Yet with two faces, as their *Janus* was,
Being in this their old crackt looking-glasse.
How deare to me, O God, thy counsels are!
Who may with thee compare?
Thus Sinne triumphs in Western *Babylon;*
Yet not as Sinne, but as Religion.
Of his two thrones he made the latter best,
And to defray his journey from the east.
Old and new *Babylon* are to hell and night,
As is the moon and sunne to heav'n and light.
When th' one did set, the other did take place,
Confronting equally the Law and Grace.
They are hells land-marks, Satans double crest:
They are Sinnes nipples, feeding th' east and west.
But as in vice the copie still exceeds
The pattern, but not so in vertuous deeds;
So though Sinne made his latter seat the better,
The latter Church is to the first a debter.
The second Temple could not reach the first:
And the late reformation never durst
Compare with ancient times and purer yeares;
But in the Jews and us deserveth tears.
Nay, it shall ev'ry yeare decrease and fade;
Till such a darknesse do the world invade
At Christs last coming, as his first did finde:
Yet must there such proportion be assign'd
To these diminishings, as is between
The spacious world and *Jurie* to be seen.
Religion stands on tip-toe in our land,
Readie to passe to the *American* strand.

207 was, *B*: was *W*: was; *1633–* 218 *capitals from B W, not in 1633* 223 *and* 224 latter] later *W* (*but* latter *in l. 213*) 232 proportion *W*: proportions *B 1633–* 235–59 *quoted by Oley in* Herbert's Remains, *with no variation except in punctuation and use of capitals* 235–6 *quoted in Walton's* Lives 235 on tip-toe] a Tip-toe *Walton*

When height of malice, and prodigious lusts,
Impudent sinning, witchcrafts, and distrusts
(The marks of future bane) shall fill our cup
Unto the brimme, and make our measure up;
When *Sein* shall swallow *Tiber*, and the *Thames*
By letting in them both pollutes her streams:
When *Italie* of us shall have her will,
And all her calender of sinnes fulfill;
Whereby one may foretell, what sinnes next yeare
Shall both in *France* and *England* domineer:
Then shall Religion to *America* flee:
They have their times of Gospel, ev'n as we.
My God, thou dost prepare for them a way
By carrying first their gold from them away:
For gold and grace did never yet agree:
Religion alwaies sides with povertie.
We think we rob them, but we think amisse:
We are more poore, and they more rich by this.
Thou wilt revenge their quarrell, making grace
To pay our debts, and leave her ancient place
To go to them, while that which now their nation
But lends to us, shall be our desolation.
Yet as the Church shall thither westward flie,
So Sinne shall trace and dog her instantly:
They have their period also and set times
Both for their vertuous actions and their crimes.
And where of old the Empire and the Arts
Usher'd the Gospel ever in mens hearts,
Spain hath done one; when Arts perform the other,
The Church shall come, & Sinne the Church shall smother:
That when they have accomplished their round,
And met in th' east their first and ancient sound,
Judgement may meet them both & search them round.
Thus do both lights, as well in Church as Sunne,

242 both *B W 1634–* : both, *1633 1633*[2] pollutes] pollute *W* 245 foretell *B W 1633*[2]*–* : fortell *1633* 248 times] time *W* 252 alwaies] alway *W* 256 her ancient *B W* : our ancient *1633– See note* 258 But lends to us] Lendeth to vs *W* 267 have *W 1633*[2]*–* : haue *B 1633* their *B W* : the *1633–* 267–9 *W has an external bracket to the left of this triplet* 269 them round] ye round *B*

Light one another, and together runne.
Thus also Sinne and Darknesse follow still
The Church and Sunne with all their power and skill.
But as the Sunne still goes both west and east;
So also did the Church by going west
Still eastward go; because it drew more neare
To time and place, where judgement shall appeare.
How deare to me, O God, thy counsels are!
Who may with thee compare?

271–3 Like Comick Lovers euer one way runn:
Thus also sinn and darknes constantly
ffollow ye Church & sunn where ere they fly. *W*

L'Envoy.

K*Ing of Glorie, King of Peace,*
With the one make warre to cease;
With the other blesse thy sheep,
Thee to love, in thee to sleep.
Let not Sinne devoure thy fold,
Bragging that thy bloud is cold,
That thy death is also dead,
While his conquests dayly spread;
That thy flesh hath lost his food,
And thy Crosse is common wood.
Choke him, let him say no more,
But reserve his breath in store,
Till thy conquests and his fall
Make his sighs to use it all,
And then bargain with the winde
To discharge what is behinde.

Blessed be God *alone,*
Thrice blessed Three in One.

FINIS.

L'Envoy. *Both MSS. continue the page-heading* The Church Militant; *no page-heading in 1633–* *In W the title* L'envoy *is in a different hand from the copyist's, perhaps the author's* 1 *Glorie . . . Peace*] *initial capitals from B W*: *cf. the same opening line in* Praise (II) 2 warre] warrs *W*: wars *1678–1809* *See note* 11 say] speak *W* 12 But] Or *corr. by 2nd hand to* But *W* 13 conquests] conquest *1674–1809, Pickering, Willmott, Grosart* (*cf. l.* 8)

Blessed be God &c. *Not in W* *These words in B are separated from the poem by double lines* 1 God *distinguished in B*: *in same italic as the rest 1633–*

FINIS. Not in B and W

ENGLISH POEMS IN THE WILLIAMS MS. NOT INCLUDED IN *THE TEMPLE*

I. *The H. Communion.*

O Gratious Lord, how shall I know
Whether in these gifts thou bee so
As thou art evry-where;
Or rather so, as thou alone
Tak'st all the Lodging, leaving none
ffor thy poore creature there?

ffirst I am sure, whether bread stay
Or whether Bread doe fly away
Concerneth bread, not mee.
But that both thou and all thy traine
Bee there, to thy truth, & my gaine,
Concerneth mee & Thee.

And if in comming to thy foes
Thou dost come first to them, that showes
The hast of thy good will.
Or if that thou two stations makest
In Bread & mee, the way thou takest
Is more, but for mee still.

Then of this also I am sure
That thou didst all those pains endure
To' abolish Sinn, not Wheat.
Creatures are good, & have their place;
Sinn onely, which did all deface,
Thou drivest from his seat.

I–VI *from* MS. Jones B 62 *in Dr. Williams's Library* (*here cited as W*): *the MS. abbreviations* ye y^t wch w^{th} *are here printed in full. First printed by Grosart in* 1874. *The readings at foot are from W unless otherwise described.* I. 1 Lord   6 there   9 bread   10 thou,   11 gaine   20 those] these *Grosart*   22 place   23 deface

I could beleeue an Impanation
At the rate of an Incarnation,
If thou hadst dyde for Bread.
But that which made my soule to dye,
My flesh, & fleshly villany,
That allso made thee dead.

That fflesh is there, mine eyes deny:
And what shold flesh but flesh discry,
The noblest sence of five?
If glorious bodies pass the sight,
Shall they be food & strength & might
Euen there, where they deceiue?

Into my soule this cannot pass;
fflesh (though exalted) keeps his grass
And cannot turn to soule.
Bodyes & Minds are different Spheres,
Nor can they change their bounds & meres,
But keep a constant Pole.

This gift of all gifts is the best,
Thy flesh the least that I request.
Thou took'st that pledg from mee:
Give me not that I had before,
Or give mee that, so I have more;
My God, give mee all Thee.

II. *Love.*

THou art too hard for me in Love:
There is no dealing with thee in that Art:
That is thy Master-peece I see.
When I contrive & plott to prove
Something that may be conquest on my part,
Thou still, O Lord, outstrippest mee.

26 Incarnation 28 dye 29 fleshly] fleshy *Grosart* 33 five. 34 sight 35 strength, 37 pass 40 Spheres 47 more
II. 3 see 5 part

Sometimes, when as I wash, I say,
And shrodely, as I think, Lord wash my soule
More spotted then my flesh can bee.
But then there comes into my way
Thy ancient baptism, which when I was foule
And knew it not, yet cleansed mee.

I took a time when thou didst sleep,
Great waves of trouble combating my brest:
I thought it braue to praise thee then,
Yet then I found, that thou didst creep
Into my hart with ioye, giving more rest
Then flesh did lend thee back agen.

Let mee but once the conquest have
Vpon the matter, 'twill thy conquest prove:
If thou subdue mortalitie,
Thou do'st no more then doth the graue:
Whereas if I orecome thee & thy Love,
Hell, Death & Divel come short of mee.

III. *Trinity Sunday.*

HE that is one,
Is none.
Two reacheth thee
In some degree.
Nature & Grace
With Glory may attaine thy Face.
Steele & a flint strike fire,
Witt & desire
Never to thee aspire,
Except life catch & hold those fast.
That which beleefe
Did not confess in the first Theefe
His fall can tell,
ffrom Heaven, through Earth, to Hell.

7 say 8 think. 11 baptism 13 sleep 18 thee, back agen, 20 matter 21 mortalitie 22 more, 23 Love

Lett two of those alone
To them that fall,
Who God & Saints and Angels loose at last.
Hee that has one,
Has all.

IV. *Euen-song.*

THe Day is spent, & hath his will on mee:
I and the Sunn haue runn our races,
I went the slower, yet more paces,
ffor I decay, not hee.

Lord make my Losses vp, & sett mee free:
That I who cannot now by day
Look on his daring brightnes, may
Shine then more bright then hee.

If thou deferr this light, then shadow mee:
Least that the Night, earths gloomy shade,
ffouling her nest, my earth invade,
As if shades knew not Thee.

But thou art Light & darknes both togeather:
If that bee dark we can not see,
The sunn is darker then a Tree,
And thou more dark then either.

Yet Thou art not so dark, since I know this,
But that my darknes may touch thine,
And hope, that may teach it to shine,
Since Light thy Darknes is.

O lett my Soule, whose keyes I must deliver
Into the hands of senceles Dreames
Which know not thee, suck in thy beames
And wake with thee for ever.

IV. 4 decay 5 Losses] Loss *Grosart* 10 shade 14 see: 15 then] than *Palmer* 18 thine: 23 thee;

v. *The Knell.*

THe Bell doth tolle:
Lord help thy servant whose perplexed Soule
Doth wishly look
On either hand
And sometimes offers, sometimes makes a stand,
Strugling on th' hook.

Now is the season,
Now the great combat of our flesh & reason:
O help, my God!
See, they breake in,
Disbanded humours, sorrows, troops of Sinn,
Each with his rodd.

Lord make thy Blood
Convert & colour all the other flood
And streams of grief,
That they may bee
Julips & Cordials when wee call on thee
ffor some relief.

vi. *Perseverance.*

MY God, the poore expressions of my Love
Which warme these lines & serve them vp to thee
Are so, as for the present I did moue,
Or rather as thou mouedst mee.

But what shall issue, whither these my words
Shal help another, but my iudgment bee,
As a burst fouling-peece doth saue the birds
But kill the man, is seald with thee.

V. 1 tolle 5 stand 7 season 8 reason 9 help 10 in 11 sorrows Sinn 15 grief
VI. 2 lines, 3 present, moue 6 bee;

ffor who can tell, though thou hast dyde to winn
And wedd my soule in glorious paradise,
Whither my many crymes and vse of sinn
  May yet forbid the banes and bliss?

Onely my soule hangs on thy promisses
With face and hands clinging vnto thy brest,
Clinging and crying, crying without cease,
  Thou art my rock, thou art my rest.

10 paradise; 12 banes] banns *Palmer* bliss. 15 cease

POEMS FROM WALTON'S *LIVES*

Sonnets.

MY God, where is that ancient heat towards thee,
Wherewith whole showls of *Martyrs* once did burn,
Besides their other flames? Doth Poetry
Wear *Venus* Livery? only serve her turn?
Why are not *Sonnets* made of thee? and layes
Upon thine Altar burnt? Cannot thy love
Heighten a spirit to sound out thy praise
As well as any she? Cannot thy *Dove*
Out-strip their *Cupid* easily in flight?
Or, since thy wayes are deep, and still the same,
Will not a verse run smooth that bears thy name?
Why doth that fire, which by thy power and might
Each breast does feel, no braver fuel choose
Than that, which one day Worms may chance refuse?

SUre, Lord, there is enough in thee to dry
Oceans of *Ink*; for, as the Deluge did
Cover the Earth, so doth thy Majesty:
Each Cloud distills thy praise, and doth forbid
Poets to turn it to another use.
Roses and *Lillies* speak thee; and to make
A pair of Cheeks of them, is thy abuse.
Why should I *Womens eyes* for Chrystal take?
Such poor invention burns in their low mind
Whose fire is wild, and doth not upward go
To praise, and on thee, Lord, some *Ink* bestow.
Open the bones, and you shall nothing find
In the best *face* but *filth*, when, Lord, in thee
The *beauty* lies in the *discovery*.

Sonnets. *From Walton's* Lives (1670). *Also in* Life of Herbert (1670), *in the Life in* The Temple (1674) *and in* Lives (1675). *Printed in italic, with certain words in roman, here italicized. A line-space separates the sonnets, except in* 1675

I. 3 flames? *1674 1675*: flames. *1670* (*both edns*) 11 name? *Ed*: name! *Walton* 14 day Worms *Ed*: day, Worms, *Walton*

II. 1 Sure *comma supplied by Ed* 9 mind] mind, *1670* (*Life*) 11 thee, *Ed*: thee *Walton* 13 when, *Ed*: when *Walton* 14 lies *Ed*: lies, *Walton*

To my Successor.

IF thou chance for to find
A new House to thy mind,
And built without thy Cost:
Be good to the Poor,
As God gives thee store,
And then, my Labour 's not lost.

Another version.

IF thou dost find an house built to thy mind
Without thy cost,
Serve thou the more God and the poore;
My labour is not lost.

To my Successor. *From Walton (editions as in the preceding footnote)*
Another version. *From T. Fuller,* The Holy State (1642). *See note*
For Walton's version of the lines 'On Dr. Donne's Seal' *see below,* p. 439.

DOUBTFUL POEMS

On Sir John Danvers.

PAsse not by,
Search and you may
Find a treasure
Worth your stay.
What makes a Danvers
Would you find?
In a fayre bodie
A fayre mind.

S[r] John Danvers' earthly part
Here is copied out by art;
But his heavenly and divine,
In his progenie doth shine.
Had he only brought them forth,
Know that much had been his worth;
Ther's no monument to a sonne,
Reade him there, and I have done.

On Henry Danvers earl of Danby.

EPITAPH

SAcred Marble, safely keepe
His dvst who vnder thee must sleepe
Vntill the graues againe restore
Theire dead, and Time shalbe no more:
Meane while, if hee (w[ch] all thinges weares)
Doe ruine thee; or if the teares

On Sir John Danvers. *From John Aubrey's* Wiltshire Collections, ed. J. E. Jackson. Devizes, 1862. *Less correctly printed in Aubrey's* Collections for Wilts., Part I. London, 1821.

On Henry Danvers. *From Danby's tomb in Dauntsey Church, Wilts.: engraved throughout in capitals, with larger initial capitals. Printed in Zouch's edition of Walton's* Lives, 1796 (*Z*). *Also in Aubrey's* Collections for Wilts., 1821 *and* Wiltshire Collections, 1862 (*A*), *and in Pickering's* Works of George Herbert, 1836, vol. i (*Pk*)
3 graues] years *Z Pk*   6 Doe] Does *Z A Pk*   the] thy *Z A Pk*

Are shed for him, dissolve thy frame,
Thov art reqvited; for his Fame,
His Vertves, and his Worth shalbee
Another Monvment for Thee.

G: HERBER^T:

To the Right Hon. the L. Chancellor (Bacon).

MY Lord. A diamond to mee you sent,
And I to you a Blackamore present.
Gifts speake their Giuers. For as those Refractions,
Shining and sharp, point out your rare Perfections;
So by the Other, you may read in mee
(Whom Schollers Habitt & Obscurity
Hath soild with Black) the colour of my state,
Till your bright gift my darknesse did abate.
Onely, most noble Lord, shutt not the doore
Against this meane & humble Blackamore.
Perhaps some other subiect I had tryed
But that my Inke was factious for this side.

A Paradox.

That the Sicke are in better State then the Whole.

YOu whoe admire yourselues because
You neither groane nor weepe
And thinke it contrary to Natures Lawes
To want one ownce of sleepe,
Your stronge beilefe
Acquitts yourselues and giues the sicke all greife.

9 Vertves] virtue *Z Pk* 10 for] to *Z A Pk*

To the L. Chancellor. *From* B.M. Add. MS. 22602. *Also in* Bodl. MS. Rawl. Poet. 246. *First printed* 'from a small quarto volume of MS. Latin poetry' *in J. Fry's* Bibliographical Memoranda. Bristol, 1816. *Title*: Bacon *om. Rawl, Fry* 3 their Giuers] the giver *Rawl*: the giuers *Fry* 7 Hath] Haue *Rawl* 8 darknesse] blacknes *Rawl* 9 most] my *Fry* 10 this] the *Rawl* 12 for] on *Rawl* this] that *Fry* *For accompanying Latin poem see p. 437*

A Paradox. *From* B.M. Add. MS. 25303. *Also in* B.M. MS. Harl. 3910 *and* Bodl. MS. Rawl. Poet. 147. *First printed by Pickering* (1835). *Pickering, Grosart, and Palmer used Rawl only. Title*: better State] a better case *Rawl*

Your state, to ours, is contrary;
That makes you thinke us poore:
So Blackamoores repute us fowle, and wee
Are quit with them and more.
Nothinge can see
And iudge of things but Mediocritie.

The sicke are in themselues a State
Wheare health hath nought to doe;
How know you that our teares proceed from woe
And not from better ffate,
Since that mirth hath
Hir waters alsoe and desired Bathe.

How know you that the sighes we send
From wante of breath proceede,
Not from excesse, and therefore doe we spende
That which wee doe not neede:
So tremblinge may
As well show inward warblinge as decay.

Cease then to iudge calamityes
By outward forme and showe,
But veywe yourselues, & inward turn your eyes;
Then you shall fully knowe
That your estate
Is of the two the far more desperate.

You allwayes feare to feele those smarts
Which wee but somtymes proue:
Each little comforte much affects our hartes,
None but gross ioyes you moue:
Why then confesse
Your feares in number more, your ioyes are lesse.

9 Blackamoores repute] Black-Moores thinke *Rawl* 14 Wheare] Wch *Rawl* *See note* 21 doe we] we do *Rawl* 24 warblinge] warblings *Rawl* 25 calamityes *Rawl*: calamitie *25303*: calamity *Harl* 32 somtymes] sometime *Harl*

Then for yourselues not us embrace
Playntes to bad fortunes dew:
For though you vysit us, & wayle our case,
Wee doubt much whether you
Come to our bed
To comforte us, or to bee comforted.

To the Queene of Bohemia.

BRight soule, of whome if any countrey knowne
Worthy had bin, thou hadst not lost thine owne:
No Earth can bee thy Jointure. For the sunne
And starres alone vnto the pitch doe runne
And pace of thy swift vertues; onely they
Are thy dominion. Those that rule in clay
Stick fast therein, but thy transcendent soule
Doth for two clods of earth ten spheres controule,
And though starres shott from heauen loose their light,
Yet thy braue beames excluded from their right
Maintaine there Lustre still, & shining cleere
Turne watrish Holland to a chrystalline sphere.
Mee thinkes, in that Dutch optick I doe see
Thy curious vertues much more visibly:
There is thy best Throne. For afflictions are
A foile to sett of worth, & make it rare.
Through that black tiffany thy vertues shine
Fairer & richer. Now wee know, what 's thine,
And what is fortunes. Thou hast singled out
Sorrowes & griefs, to fight with them a bout
At there owne weapons, without pomp or state
To second thee against there cunning hate.

38 fortunes] fortune *Rawl* 39 wayle] plaint *Rawl* *See note* our] or *Pickering* (*a misreading of* o^r *in Rawl*)

To the Queene of Bohemia *and* L'Envoy. *From* B.M. MS. Harl. 3910. *First printed, from an undescribed MS., in H. Huth's* Inedited Poetical Miscellanies (1870). *Both MSS. ascribe to* 'G.H.' *Printed from Harl by Grosart* (1874). 2 Had worthy been *Huth* 3 Jointure 4 alone, the] thy *Huth* 5 vertues 6 dominion] dominions *Huth* 7 therein 8 earth, 9 heauen, light 12 chrystalline] crystal *Huth* sphere 18 richer] rich *Huth* 20 a bout *Huth*: a-bout *Harl* (*perhaps* a bout *written first, and the hyphen added in error later*): about *Grosart, Palmer* 22 hate

O what a poore thing 'tis to bee a Queene
When scepters, state, Attendants are the screen
Betwixt us & the people: when as glory
Lyes round about us to helpe out the story,
When all things pull & hale, that they may bring
A slow behauiour to the style of king,
When sense is made by Comments. But that face
Whose natiue beauty needs not dresse or lace
To serue it forth, & being stript of all
Is selfe-sufficient to bee the thrall
Of thousand harts: that face doth figure thee
And show thy vndiuided Maiestye
Which misery cannot vntwist but rather
Addes to the vnion, as lights doe gather
Splendour from darknes. So close sits the crowne
About thy temples that the furious frowne
Of opposition cannot place thee, where
Thou shalt not bee a Queene and conquer there.
 Yet hast thou more dominions: God doth giue
Children for kingdomes to thee; they shall liue
To conquere new ones, & shall share the frame
Of th' vniuerse, like as the windes, & name
The world anew: the sunne shall neuer rise
But it shall spy some of there victories.
There hands shall clipp the Eagles winges, & chase
Those rauening Harpyes, which peck at thy face,
At once to Hell, without a baiting while
At Purgatory, there inchanted Ile,
And Paris garden. Then let there perfume
And Spanish sents, wisely layd vp, presume
To deale with brimstone, that vntamed stench
Whose fier, like there malice, nought can quench.
 But ioyes are stord for thee: thou shalt returne
Laden with comforts thence, where now to morne
Is thy chief gouernment, to manage woe,

26 story 28 king 29 Comments 31 serue] set *Huth* 32 thrall] self-thrall *Huth* 40 shalt] should'st *Huth* there 42 thee 46 there] thy *Huth* 47 winges] *Huth MS. has* winds *which Huth as editor corrects to* wings 48 thy] their *Huth* face 53 vntamed] untimed *Huth* 54 quench 57 gouerment, woe

To curbe some Rebell teares, which faine would flow,
Making a Head & spring against thy Reason.
This is thy empire yet: till better season
Call thee from out of that surrounded land,
That habitable sea, & brinish strand,
Thy teares not needing. For that hand Divine
Which mingles water with thy Rhenish wine
Will pour full ioyes to thee, but dregs to those,
And meet theire tast, who are thy bitter foes.

L'Envoy.

SHine on, Maiestick soule, abide
Like Dauid's tree, planted beside
The Flemmish riuers: in the end
Thy fruite shall with there drops contend;
Great God will surely dry those teares,
Which now that moist land to thee beares.
Then shall thy Glory, fresh as flowers
In water kept, maugre the powers
Of Diuell, Jessuitt & Spaine,
From Holland saile into the Maine:
Thence wheeling on, it compass shall
This oure great Sublunary Ball,
And with that Ring thy fame shall wedd
Eternity into one Bedd.

The Convert.

AN ODE

IF ever Tears did flow from *Eyes*,
If ever *Voice* was hoarse with Cries,
If ever *Heart* was sore with Sighs;
Let now my *Eyes*, my *Voice*, my *Heart*,
Strive each to play their Part.

58 flow 59 spring, 61 land 62 strand 65 pour *Huth*: power *Harl* thee, *Huth*: thee; *Harl* those, *Huth*: those *Harl* 66 foes

L'Envoy. 1 on 4 contend 5 Great] Our *Huth* 9 Spaine 12 Ball

The Convert. *From* Miscellanea Sacra: or, Poems on Divine & Moral Subjects. Collected by N. Tate. 1696. (*No important variations in 2nd edn,* 1698)

My *Eyes*, from whence these Tears did spring,
Where treach'rous Syrens us'd to sing,
Shall flow no more—until they bring
  A Deluge on my sensual Flame,
    And wash away my Shame.

My *Voice*, that oft with foolish Lays,
With Vows and Rants, and sensless Praise,
Frail Beauty's Charms to Heav'n did raise,
  Henceforth shall only pierce the Skies,
    In Penitential Cryes.

My *Heart*, that gave fond Thoughts their Food,
(Till now averse to all that 's Good)
The Temple where an *Idol* stood,
  Henceforth in Sacred Flames shall Burn,
    And be that *Idol's* URN.

PSALMS

Psalm I.

BLest is the man that never would
  in councels of th' ungodly share,
Nor hath in way of sinners stood,
  nor sitten in the scorners chair.

But in God's Law sets his delight,
  and makes that law alone to be
His meditation day and night:
  he shall be like an happy tree,

Which, planted by the waters, shall
  with timely fruit still laden stand:
His leaf shall never fade, and all
  shall prosper that he takes in hand.

Psalms. *From* Psalms & Hymns in Solemn Musick of Foure Parts. By John Playford. 1671. *See note for his hesitating attribution of these Psalms to Herbert. The readings at foot are from Playford, unless marked G (Grosart), P (Palmer), or Farr.*

Ps. I. *Omitted by Palmer* 3 stood: 9 Which 10 laden] loden *G*

The wicked are not so, but they
are like the chaff, which from the face
Of earth is driven by winds away,
and finds no sure abiding place.

Therefore shall not the wicked be
able to stand the Judges doom:
Nor in the safe society
of good men shall the wicked come.

For God himself vouchsafes to know
the way that right'ous men have gone:
And those wayes which the wicked go
shall utterly be overthrown.

Psalm II.

WHy are the *Heathen* swell'd with rage,
the people vain exploits devise?
The Kings and Potentates of earth
combin'd in one great faction rise.

And taking councels 'gainst the Lord,
and 'gainst his *Christ*, presume to say,
Let us in sunder break their bonds,
and from us cast their cords away.

But He, that sits in Heaven, shall laugh,
the Lord himself shall them deride:
Then shall He speak to them in wrath,
and in sore anger vex their pride.

But I by God am seated King,
on *Sion* His most Holy hill,
I will declare the Lords decree,
nor can I hide his sacred will.

23 wayes,
Ps. II. 1 rage 2 devise: 3 earth, 13 by God and *Playford*: am God, and *conj. Grosart*: by God am *conj. Ed. See note*

He said to me, Thou art my Son,
 this day have I begotten thee:
Make thy request, and I will grant
 the *Heathen* shall thy portion be.

Thou shalt possess earth's farthest bounds
 and there an awful Scepter sway:
Whose pow'r shall dash and break them all
 like vessels made of brittle clay.

Now therefore, O ye Kings, be wise,
 be learned, ye that judge the earth:
Serve our great God in fear, rejoyce,
 but tremble in your highest mirth.

O kiss the Son, lest he be wrath,
 and straight ye perish from the way:
When once his anger burns, thrice blest
 are all that make the Son their stay.

Psalm III.

HOw are my foes increased, Lord?
 many are they that rise
Against me, saying, For my soul
 no help in God there is.
But thou, O Lord, art still the shield
 of my deliverance:
Thou art my glory, Lord, and he
 that doth my head advance.

I cry'd unto the Lord, he heard
 me from his holy hill:
I laid me down and slept, I wak'd;
 for God sustain'd me still.
Aided by him, I will not fear
 ten thousand enemies:
Nor all the people round about,
 that can against me rise.

17 thou 26 learned 28 but] And *P* 29 wrath] wroth *G P* *See note*
Ps. III. 3 for 5 ar't 11 wak'd] wak't *G P*

Arise, O Lord, and rescue me;
save me, my God, from thrall:
For thou upon the cheek-bone smit'st
mine adversaries all.
And thou hast brok th' *ungodly's* teeth:
Salvation unto thee
Belongs, O Lord, thy blessing shall
upon thy people be.

Psalm IV.

LOrd hear me when I call on Thee,
Lord of my righteousness:
O thou that hast enlarged me
when I was in distress.

Have mercy on me Lord, and hear
the Prayer that I frame:
How long will ye, vain men, convert
my glory into shame?

How long will ye seek after lies,
and vanity approve?
But know the Lord himself doth chuse
the righteous man to love.

The Lord will harken unto me
when I his grace implore:
O learn to stand in awe of him,
and sin not any more.

Within your chamber try your hearts,
offer to God on high
The sacrifice of righteousness,
and on his grace rely.

Many there are that say, O who
will shew us good? But, Lord,
Thy countenances cheering light
do thou to us afford.

19 For thou] 'Tis Thou *G P*
Ps. IV. 22 But

For that, O Lord, with perfect joy
  shall more replenish me,
Then worldlings joy'd with all their store
  of corn and wine can be.

Therefore will I lie down in peace,
  and take my restful sleep:
For thy protection, Lord, alone
  shall me in safety keep.

Psalm V.

LOrd to my words encline thine ear,
  my meditation weigh:
My King, my God, vouchsafe to hear
  my cry to thee, I pray.

Thou in the morn shalt have my mone,
  for in the morn will I
Direct my prayers to thy Throne,
  and thither lift mine eye.

Thou art a God whose puritie
  cannot in sins delight:
No evil, Lord, shall dwell with thee,
  nor fools stand in thy sight.

Thou hat'st those that unjustly do:
  thou slay'st the men that lye:
The bloody man, the false one too,
  shall be abhorr'd by thee.

But in th' abundance of thy Grace
  will I to thee draw near:
And toward thy most Holy place
  will worship thee in fear.

27 Then] Than *P*

Ps. V. *Printed also in* Select Poetry chiefly sacred of the Reign of King James I., collected by Edward Farr, 1847, *and there attributed to Herbert. Omitted by Palmer.* 1 ear 4 my cry, to thee I pray. 5 have] hear *Farr*, *G* 11 No evil Lord 14 men *Farr*, *G*: man *Playford* (*probably a misprint*) 17 Grace,

Lord lead me in thy righteousness,
because of all my foes:
And to my dym and sinful eyes
thy perfect way disclose.

For wickedness their insides are,
their mouths no truth retain.
Their throat an open Sepulcher,
their flattering tongues do fain.

Destroy them, Lord, and by their own
bad councels let them fall:
In hight of their transgression,
ô Lord, reject them all,

Because against thy Majesty
they vainly have rebell'd:
But let all those that trust in thee
with perfect joy be fill'd.

Yea, shout for joy for evermore,
protected still by thee:
Let them that do thy name adore
in that still joyful bee.

For God doth righteous men esteem,
and them for ever bless.
His favour shall encompass them,
a shield in their distress.

Psalm VI.

REbuke me not in wrath, O Lord,
nor in thine anger chasten me:
O pity me! for I (O Lord)
am nothing but Infirmitie.

23 eyes, 27 Sepulcher 32 all. 33 Majesty, 37 evermore

O heal me, for my bones are vex'd,
  my Soul is troubled very sore;
But, Lord, how long so much perplex'd
  shall I in vain thy Grace implore?

Return, O God! and rescue me,
  my Soul for thy great mercy save;
For who in death remember Thee?
  or who shall praise Thee in the grave?

With groaning I am wearied,
  all night I make my Couch to swim;
And water with salt tears my Bed,
  my sight with sorrow waxeth dim.

My beauty wears and doth decay
  because of all mine Enemies;
But now from me depart away,
  all ye that work Iniquities.

For God himself hath heard my cry;
  the Lord vouchsafes to weigh my tears;
Yea, he my prayer from on high
  and humble supplication hears.

And now my foes the Lord will blame
  that er'st so sorely vexed me,
And put them all to utter shame,
  and to confusion suddainly.

Psalm VII.

SAve me, my Lord, my God, because
  I put my trust in Thee:
From all that persecute my life,
  O Lord deliver mee!

Ps. VI. 9 me 12 grave. 19 away 22 the, Lord, tears 23 Yea high, *For the doxology appended in Playford, see note*

Lest like a Lion swollen with rage
  he do devour my soul:
And peace-meal rent it, while there's none
  his mallice to controul.

If I have done this thing, O Lord,
  if I so guilty be:
If I have ill rewarded him
  that was at peace with me:

Yea, have not oft deliver'd him
  that was my causeless foe:
Then let mine enemie prevail
  unto mine overthrow.

Let him pursue and take my soul,
  yea, let him to the Clay
Tread down my life, and in the dust
  my slaughter'd honour lay.

Arise in wrath, O Lord, advance
  against my foes disdain:
Wake and confirm that judgment now,
  which Thou did'st preordain.

So shall the people round about
  resort to give Thee praise;
For their sakes, Lord, return on high,
  and high thy Glory raise.

The Lord shall judge the people all:
  O God consider me
According to my righteousness,
  and mine integritie!

The wicked's malice, Lord, confound,
  but just men ever guide:
Thou art that righteous God by whom
  the hearts and reins are try'd.

Ps. VII. 12 me. 13 delivered 21 wrath 24 preordain] fore-ordain *G P* 25 about, 26 praise, 29 all, 34 men] me *G. P* 35 God *G P*: Good *Playford*

God is my shield, who doth preserve
 those that in heart are right:
He judgeth both the good, and those
 that do his justice slight.

Unless the wicked turn again,
 the Lord will whet his Sword:
His bow is bent, his quiver is
 with shafts of vengeance stor'd.

The fatal instruments of death
 in that prepared be:
His arrows are ordain'd 'gainst him
 that persecuteth me.

Behold, the wicked travelleth
 with his iniquitie:
Exploits of mischief he conceives,
 but shall bring forth a lye.

The wicked digged, and a pit
 for others ruine wrought:
But in the pit which he hath made
 shall he himself be caught.

To his own head his wickedness
 shall be returned home:
And on his own accursed pate
 his cruelty shall come.

But I for all his righteousness
 the Lord will magnifie:
And ever praise the Glorious name
 of him that is on high.

46 be] lie *G P* 49 Behold 55 pit,

A PRIEST
To the
TEMPLE,

OR,
The Countrey PARSON
HIS
CHARACTER,
AND
Rule of Holy Life.

The AUTHOUR,
M[r] *G.H.*

LONDON,
Printed by *T. Maxey* for *T. Garthwait*, at the
little North door of S[t] *Paul's*. 1652.

The Authour to the Reader.

BEing desirous (thorow the Mercy of God) to please Him, for whom I am, and live, and who giveth mee my Desires and Performances; and considering with my self, That the way to please him, is to feed my Flocke diligently and faithfully, since our Saviour hath made that the argument of a Pastour's love, I have resolved to set down the Form and Character of a true Pastour, that I may have a Mark to aim at: which also I will set as high as I can, since hee shoots higher that threatens the Moon, then hee that aims at a Tree. Not that I think, if a man do not all which is here expressed, hee presently sinns, and displeases God, but that it is a good strife to go as farre as wee can in pleasing of him, who hath done so much for us. The Lord prosper the intention to my selfe, and others, who may not despise my poor labours, but add to those points, which I have observed, untill the Book grow to a compleat Pastorall.

1632.

Geo. Herbert.

A PRIEST TO THE TEMPLE

OR,

THE COUNTRY PARSON HIS CHARACTER, &c.

Chap. I.

Of a Pastor.

A Pastor is the Deputy of Christ for the reducing of Man to the Obedience of God. This definition is evident, and containes the direct steps of Pastorall Duty and Auctority. For first, Man fell from God by disobedience. Secondly, Christ is the glorious instrument of God for the revoking of Man. Thirdly, Christ being not to continue on earth, but after hee had fulfilled the work of Reconciliation, to be received up into heaven, he constituted Deputies in his place, and these are Priests. And therefore St. *Paul* in the beginning of his Epistles, professeth this: and in the first to the *Colossians* plainly avoucheth, that he *fils up that which is behinde of the afflictions of Christ in his flesh, for his Bodie's sake, which is the Church.* Wherein is contained the complete definition of a Minister. Out of this Chartre of the Priesthood may be plainly gathered both the Dignity thereof, and the Duty: The Dignity, in that a Priest may do that which Christ did, and by his auctority, and as his Vicegerent. The Duty, in that a Priest is to do that which Christ did, and after his manner, both for Doctrine and Life.

Chap. II.

Their Diversities.

Of Pastors (intending mine own Nation only, and also therein setting aside the Reverend Prelates of the Church, to whom this discourse ariseth not) some live in the

From Herbert's Remains, 1652 (*cited as 52*). A Priest to the Temple *printed separately as* 'The second Edition', 1671 (*71*). 'The Third Impression', 1675 (*75*). *Where 75 agrees with 71, it is not recorded in the notes below.*

21 the Reverend] 75 *inserts* R. (*i.e.* Right) *before* Reverend

Universities, some in Noble houses, some in Parishes residing on their Cures. Of those that live in the Universities, some live there in office, whose rule is that of the Apostle; *Rom.* 12.6. *Having gifts differing, according to the grace that is given to us, whether prophecy, let us prophecy according to the proportion of faith; or ministry, let us wait on our ministring; or he that teacheth, on teaching,* &c. *he that ruleth, let him do it with diligence,* &c. Some in a preparatory way, whose aim and labour must be not only to get knowledg, but to subdue and mortifie all lusts and affections: and not to think, that when they have read the Fathers, or Schoolmen, a Minister is made, and the thing done. The greatest and hardest preparation is within: For, *Unto the ungodly, saith God, Why dost thou preach my Laws, and takest my Covenant in thy mouth? Psal.* 50.16. Those that live in Noble Houses are called Chaplains, whose duty and obligation being the same to the Houses they live in, as a Parsons to his Parish, in describing the one (which is indeed the bent of my Discourse) the other will be manifest. Let not Chaplains think themselves so free, as *many of them do*, and because they have different Names, think their Office different. Doubtlesse they are Parsons of the families they live in, and are entertained to that end, either by an open, or implicite Covenant. Before they are in Orders, they may be received for Companions, or discoursers; but after a man is once Minister, he cannot agree to come into any house, where he shall not exercise what he is, unlesse he forsake his plough, and look back. Wherfore they are not to be over-submissive, and base, but to keep up with the Lord and Lady of the house, and to preserve a boldness with them and all, even so farre as reproofe to their very face, when occasion cals, but seasonably and discreetly. They who do not thus, while they remember their earthly Lord, do much forget their heavenly; they wrong the Priesthood, neglect their duty, and shall be so farre from that which they seek with their over-submissivenesse, and cringings, that they shall ever be despised. They who for the hope of promotion neglect any necessary admonition, or reproofe, sell (with *Judas*) their Lord and Master.

35 cringings] cringing *71*

Chap. III.

The Parsons Life.

THe Countrey Parson is exceeding exact in his Life, being holy, just, prudent, temperate, bold, grave in all his wayes. And because the two highest points of Life, wherein a Christian is most seen, are Patience, and Mortification; Patience in regard of afflictions, Mortification in regard of lusts and affections, and the stupifying and deading of all the clamorous powers of the soul, therefore he hath throughly studied these, that he may be an absolute Master and commander of himself, for all the purposes which God hath ordained him. Yet in these points he labours most in those things which are most apt to scandalize his Parish. And first, because Countrey people live hardly, and therefore as feeling their own sweat, and consequently knowing the price of mony, are offended much with any, who by hard usage increase their travell, the Countrey Parson is very circumspect in avoiding all coveteousnesse, neither being greedy to get, nor nigardly to keep, nor troubled to lose any worldly wealth; but in all his words and actions slighting, and disesteeming it, even to a wondring, that the world should so much value wealth, which in the day of wrath hath not one dramme of comfort for us. Secondly, because Luxury is a very visible sinne, the Parson is very carefull to avoid all the kinds thereof, but especially that of drinking, because it is the most popular vice; into which if he come, *he prostitutes himself* both to shame, and sin, and by having *fellowship, with the unfruitfull works of darknesse*, he disableth himself of authority *to reprove them*: For sins make all equall, whom they finde together; and then they are worst, who ought to be best. Neither is it for the servant of Christ to haunt Innes, or Tavernes, or Ale-houses, *to the dishonour of his person and office.* The Parson doth not so, but orders his Life in such a fashion, that when death takes him, as the Jewes and *Judas* did Christ, he may say as He did, *I sate*

7 clamorous *71*: clamarous *52* 21 Secondly, *71*: Secondly *52*

daily with you teaching in the Temple. Thirdly, because Countrey people (as indeed all honest men) do much esteem their word, it being the Life of buying, and selling, and dealing in the world; therfore the Parson is very strict in keeping his word, though it be to his own hinderance, as knowing, that if he be not so, he wil quickly be discovered, and disregarded: neither will they beleeve him in the pulpit, whom they cannot trust in his Conversation. As for oaths, and apparell, the disorders thereof are also very manifest. The Parsons yea is yea, and nay nay; and his apparrell plaine, but reverend, and clean, without spots, or dust, or smell; the purity of his mind breaking out, and dilating it selfe even to his body, cloaths, and habitation.

Chap. IIII.

The Parsons Knowledg.

THe Countrey Parson is full of all knowledg. They say, it is an ill Mason that refuseth any stone: and there is no knowledg, but, in a skilfull hand, serves either positively as it is, or else to illustrate some other knowledge. He condescends even to the knowledge of tillage, and pastorage, and makes great use of them in teaching, because people by what they understand, are best led to what they understand not. But the chief and top of his knowledge consists in the book of books, the storehouse and magazene of life and comfort, the holy Scriptures. There he sucks, and lives. In the Scriptures hee findes four things; Precepts for life, Doctrines for knowledge, Examples for illustration, and Promises for comfort: These he hath digested severally. But for the understanding of these; the means he useth are first, a holy Life, remembring what his Master saith, that *if any do Gods will, he shall know of the Doctrine*, *John* 7. and assuring himself, that wicked men, however learned, do not know the Scriptures, because they feel them not, and because they are not understood but with the same Spirit that writ them. The second means is prayer, which if it be necessary even in temporall things, how much more in things of another world, where the well is deep, and we have nothing of our selves to draw with? Wherefore he ever begins the reading of the Scripture with some short inward ejaculation, as, *Lord, open mine eyes, that I may see the wondrous things of thy Law.* &c. The third means is a diligent Collation of Scripture with Scripture. For all Truth being consonant to it self, and all being penn'd by one and the self-same Spirit, it cannot be, but that an industrious, and judicious comparing of place with place must be a singular help for the right understanding of the Scriptures. To this may be added the consideration of any text with the coherence thereof, touching what goes before, and what follows after, as also the scope of the Holy Ghost. When the Apostles would have called down fire from Heaven, they were reproved, as ignorant of what spirit they were. For the Law required one thing, and the Gospel another: yet as diverse, not as repugnant: therefore the spirit of both is to be considered, and weighed. The fourth means are Commenters and Fathers, who have handled the places controverted, which the Parson by no means refuseth. As he doth not so study others, as to neglect the grace of God in himself, and what the Holy Spirit teacheth him; so doth he assure himself, that God in all ages hath had his servants, to whom he hath revealed his Truth, as well as to him; and that as one Countrey doth not bear all things, that there may be a Commerce; so neither hath God opened, or will open all to one, that there may be a traffick in knowledg between the servants of God, for the planting both of love, and humility. Wherfore he hath one Comment at least upon every book of Scripture, and ploughing with this, and his own meditations, he enters into the secrets of God treasured in the holy Scripture.

CHAP. V.

The Parsons Accessary Knowledges.

THe Countrey Parson hath read the Fathers also, and the Schoolmen, and the later Writers, or a good proportion of all, out of all which he hath compiled a book, and

17 Fathers *71* : fathers *52*　　33 compiled *Errata 52* : complied *text 52*

body of Divinity, which is the storehouse of his Sermons, and which he preacheth all his Life; but diversly clothed, illustrated, and inlarged. For though the world is full of such composures, yet every mans own is fittest, readyest, and most savory to him. Besides, this being to be done in his younger and preparatory times, it is an honest joy ever after to looke upon his well spent houres. This Body he made by way of expounding the Church Catechisme, to which all divinity may easily be reduced. For it being indifferent in it selfe to choose any Method, that is best to be chosen, of which there is likelyest to be most use. Now Catechizing being a work of singular, and admirable benefit to the Church of God, and a thing required under Canonicall obedience, the expounding of our Catechisme must needs be the most usefull forme. Yet hath the Parson, besides this laborious work, a slighter forme of Catechizing, fitter for country people; according as his audience is, so he useth one, or other; or somtimes both, if his audience be intermixed. He greatly esteemes also of cases of conscience, wherein he is much versed. And indeed, herein is the greatest ability of a Parson to lead his people exactly in the wayes of Truth, so that they neither decline to the right hand, nor to the left. Neither let any think this a slight thing. For every one hath not digested, when it is a sin to take something for mony lent, or when not; when it is a fault to discover anothers fault, or when not; *when the affections of the soul in desiring and procuring increase of means*, *or honour*, *be a sin of covetousnes or ambition*, *and when not*; *when the appetites of the body in eating*, *drinking*, *sleep*, *and the pleasure that comes with sleep*, *be sins of gluttony*, *drunkenness*, *sloath*, *lust*, *and when not*, and so in many circumstances of actions. Now if a shepherd know not which grass will bane, or which not, how is he fit to be a shepherd? Wherefore the Parson hath throughly canvassed al the particulars of humane actions, at least all those which he observeth are most incident to his Parish.

CHAP. VI.

The Parson praying.

THe Countrey Parson, when he is to read divine services, composeth himselfe to all possible reverence; lifting up his heart and hands, and eyes, and using all other gestures which may expresse a hearty, and unfeyned devotion. This he doth, first, as being truly touched and amazed with the Majesty of God, before whom he then presents himself; yet not as himself alone, but as presenting with himself the whole Congregation, whose sins he then beares, and brings with his own to the heavenly altar to be bathed, and washed in the sacred Laver of Christs blood. Secondly, as this is the true reason of his inward feare, so he is content to expresse this outwardly to the utmost of his power; that being first affected himself, hee may affect also his people, knowing that no Sermon moves them so much to a reverence, which they forget againe, when they come to pray, as a devout behaviour in the very act of praying. Accordingly his voyce is humble, his words treatable, and slow; yet not so slow neither, as to let the fervency of the supplicant hang and dy between speaking, but with a grave livelinesse, between fear and zeal, pausing yet pressing, he performes his duty. Besides his example, he having often instructed his people how to carry themselves in divine service, exacts of them all possible reverence, by no means enduring either talking, or sleeping, or gazing, or leaning, or halfe-kneeling, or any undutifull behaviour in them, but causing them, when they sit, or stand, or kneel, to do all in a strait, and steady posture, as attending to what is done in the Church, and every one, man, and child, answering aloud both Amen, and all other answers, which are on the Clerks and peoples part to answer; which answers also are to be done not in a hudling, or slubbering fashion, gaping, or scratching the head, or spitting even in the midst of their answer, but gently and pausably, thinking what they say; so that while they answer, *As it was in the beginning*, &c. they meditate as they speak, that God hath ever had his people, that have glorified him as wel as now, and that he shall have so for ever. And the like in other answers. This is that which the Apostle cals a reasonable service, *Rom.* 12. when we speak not as Parrats, without reason, or offer up such sacrifices as they did of old, which was of beasts devoyd of reason; but when we use our reason, and apply our powers to the service of him, that gives them. If there be any of the gentry or nobility of the Parish, who somtimes make it a piece of state not to come at the beginning of service with their poor neighbours, but at mid-prayers, both to their own loss, and of theirs also who gaze upon them when they come in, and neglect the present service of God, he by no means suffers it, but after divers gentle admonitions, if they persevere, he causes them to be presented: or if the poor Church-wardens be affrighted with their greatness, notwithstanding his instruction that they ought not to be so, but even to let the world sinke, so they do their duty; he presents them himself, only protesting to them, that not any ill will draws him to it, but the debt and obligation of his calling, being to obey God rather then men.

CHAP. VII.

The Parson preaching.

THe Countrey Parson preacheth constantly, the pulpit is his joy and his throne: if he at any time intermit, it is either for want of health, or against some great Festivall, that he may the better celebrate it, or for the variety of the hearers, that he may be heard at his returne more attentively. When he intermits, he is ever very well supplyed by some able man who treads in his steps, and will not throw down what he hath built; whom also he intreats to press some point, that he himself hath often urged with no great success, that so in the mouth of two or three witnesses the truth may be more established. When he preacheth, he procures attention by all possible art, both by earnestnesse of speech, it being naturall to men to think, that where is much earnestness, there is somewhat worth hearing; and by a diligent,

18 ill will draws] ill withdraws *71*: *ill-will* draws *75*   22 great] *om.* *71*

and busy cast of his eye on his auditors, with letting them know, that he observes who marks, and who not; and with particularizing of his speech now to the younger sort, then to the elder, now to the poor, and now to the rich. This is for you, and This is for you; for particulars ever touch, and awake more then generalls. Herein also he serves himselfe of the judgements of God, as of those of antient times, so especially of the late ones; and those most, which are nearest to his Parish; for people are very attentive at such discourses, and think it behoves them to be so, when God is so neer them, and even over their heads. Sometimes he tells them stories, and sayings of others, according as his text invites him; for them also men heed, and remember better then exhortations; which though earnest, yet often dy with the Sermon, especially with Countrey people; which are thick, and heavy, and hard to raise to a poynt of Zeal, and fervency, and need a mountaine of fire to kindle them; but stories and sayings they will well remember. He often tels them, that Sermons are dangerous things, that none goes out of Church as he came in, but either better, or worse; that none is careless before his Judg, and that the word of God shal judge us. By these and other means the Parson procures attention; but the character of his Sermon is Holiness; he is not witty, or learned, or eloquent, but Holy. A Character, that *Hermogenes* never dream'd of, and therefore he could give no precepts thereof. But it is gained, first, by choosing texts of Devotion, not Controversie, moving and ravishing texts, whereof the Scriptures are full. Secondly, by dipping, and seasoning all our words and sentences in our hearts, before they come into our mouths, truly affecting, and cordially expressing all that we say; so that the auditors may plainly perceive that every word is hart-deep. Thirdly, by turning often, and making many Apostrophes to God, as, Oh Lord blesse my people, and teach them this point; or, Oh my Master, on whose errand I come, let me hold my peace, and doe thou speak thy selfe; for thou art Love, and when thou teachest, all are Scholers. Some such irradiations scatteringly

18 well] *om. 71*   21 judge us *71*: Judge us *52*   26 precepts] precept *71*
26 gained, *75*: gained *52 71*   32 Thridly *52*

in the Sermon, carry great holiness in them. The Prophets are admirable in this. So *Isa*. 64. *Oh that thou would'st rent the Heavens, that thou wouldst come down*, &c. And *Jeremy*, Chapt. 10. after he had complained of the desolation of *Israel*, turnes to God suddenly, *Oh Lord, I know that the way of man is not in himself*, &c. Fourthly, by frequent wishes of the peoples good, and joying therein, though he himself were with Saint *Paul* even sacrificed upon the service of their faith. For there is no greater sign of holinesse, then the procuring, and rejoycing in anothers good. And herein St *Paul* excelled in all his Epistles. How did he put the *Romans* in all his prayers? *Rom*. 1.9. And ceased not to give thanks for the *Ephesians*, *Eph*. 1.16. And for the *Corinthians*, *chap*. 1.4. And for the *Philippians* made request with joy, *ch*. 1.4. And is in contention for them whither to live, or dy; be with them, or Christ, *verse* 23. which, setting aside his care of his Flock, were a madnesse to doubt of. What an admirable Epistle is the second to the *Corinthians?* how full of affections? he joyes, and he is sorry, he grieves, and he gloryes, never was there such care of a flock expressed, save in the great shepherd of the fold, who first shed teares over *Jerusalem*, and afterwards blood. Therefore this care may be learn'd there, and then woven into Sermons, which will make them appear exceeding reverend, and holy. Lastly, by an often urging of the presence, and majesty of God, by these, or such like speeches. Oh let us all take heed what we do, God sees us, he sees whether I speak as I ought, or you hear as you ought, he sees hearts, as we see faces: he is among us; for if we be here, hee must be here, since we are here by him, and without him could not be here. Then turning the discourse to his Majesty, And he is a great God, and terrible, as great in mercy, so great in judgement: There are but two devouring elements, fire, and water, he hath both in him; *His voyce is as the sound of many waters*, *Revelations* 1. And he himselfe *is a consuming fire*, *Hebrews* 12. Such discourses shew very Holy. The Parsons Method in

14 joy, *71* : joy *52* 15 whither] whether *75* 26 all] *om. 71* 34 His voyce . . . waters *rom. 52 71* : *ital. 75* 35 is a consuming fire *rom. 52 71* : *ital. 75*

handling of a text consists of two parts; first, a plain and evident declaration of the meaning of the text; and secondly, some choyce Observations drawn out of the whole text, as it lyes entire, and unbroken in the Scripture it self. This he thinks naturall, and sweet, and grave. Whereas the other way of crumbling a text into small parts, as, the Person speaking, or spoken to, the subject, and object, and the like, hath neither in it sweetnesse, nor gravity, nor variety, since the words apart are not Scripture, but a dictionary, and may be considered alike in all the Scripture. The Parson exceeds not an hour in preaching, because all ages have thought that a competency, and he that profits not in that time, will lesse afterwards, the same affection which made him not profit before, making him then weary, and so he grows from not relishing, to loathing.

Chap. VIII.

The Parson on Sundays.

THe Country Parson, as soon as he awakes on Sunday morning, presently falls to work, and seems to himselfe so as a Market-man is, when the Market day comes, or a shopkeeper, when customers use to come in. His thoughts are full of making the best of the day, and contriving it to his best gaines. To this end, besides his ordinary prayers, he makes a peculiar one for a blessing on the exercises of the day, That nothing befall him unworthy of that Majesty before which he is to present himself, but that all may be done with reverence to his glory, and with edification to his flock, humbly beseeching his Master, that how or whenever he punish him, it be not in his Ministry: then he turnes to request for his people, that the Lord would be pleased to sanctifie them all, that they may come with holy hearts, and awfull mindes into the Congregation, and that the good God would pardon all those, who come with lesse prepared hearts then they ought. This done, he sets himself to the Consideration of the duties of the day, and if there be any extraordinary addition to the customary exercises, either from the time of the year, or from the State, or from God by a child born, or dead, or any other accident, he contrives how and in what manner to induce it to the best advantage. Afterwards when the hour calls, with his family attending him, he goes to Church, at his first entrance *humbly adoring*, *and worshipping the invisible majesty*, *and presence of Almighty God*, and blessing the people either openly, or to himselfe. Then having read divine Service twice fully, and preached in the morning, and catechized in the afternoone, he thinks he hath in some measure, according to poor, and fraile man, discharged the publick duties of the Congregation. The rest of the day he spends either in reconciling neighbours that are at variance, or in visiting the sick, or in exhortations to some of his flock by themselves, whom his Sermons cannot, or doe not reach. And every one is more awaked, when we come, and say, *Thou art the man*. This way he findes exceeding usefull, and winning; and these exhortations he cals his privy purse, even as Princes have theirs, besides their publick disbursments. At night he thinks it a very fit time, both sutable to the joy of the day, and without hinderance to publick duties, either to entertaine some of his neighbours, or to be entertained of them, where he takes occasion to discourse *of such things as are both profitable*, *and pleasant*, *and to raise up their mindes to apprehend Gods good blessing to our Church*, *and State*; *that order is kept in the one*, *and peace in the other*, *without disturbance*, *or interruption of publick divine offices*. As he opened the day with prayer, so he closeth it, humbly beseeching the Almighty to pardon and accept our poor services, and to improve them, that we may grow therein, and that our feet may be like hindes feet ever climbing up higher, and higher unto him.

CHAP. IX.

The Parson's state of Life.

THe Country Parson considering that virginity is a higher state then Matrimony, and that the Ministry requires the best and highest things, is rather unmarryed, then

15 Thou art the man. *rom. 52 71*: *ital. 75* usefnll *52* 17 their *71*: ther *52* 25 *dvinie 52*

marryed. But yet as the temper of his body may be, or as the temper of his Parish may be, where he may have occasion to converse with women, and that among suspicious men, *and other like circumstances considered*, he is rather married then unmarried. Let him communicate the thing often by prayer unto God, and as his grace shall direct him, so let him proceed. If he be unmarried, and keepe house, he hath not a woman in his house, but findes opportunities of having his meat dress'd and other services done by men-servants at home, and his linnen washed abroad. If he be unmarryed, and sojourne, he never talkes with any woman alone, but in the audience of others, and that seldom, and then also in a serious manner, never jestingly or sportfully. *He is very circumspect in all companyes, both of his behaviour, speech, and very looks, knowing himself to be both suspected, and envyed. If he stand steadfast in his heart, having no necessity, but hath power over his own will, and hath so decreed in his heart, that he will keep himself a virgin, he spends his dayes in fasting and prayer, and blesseth God for the gift of continency, knowing that it can no way be preserved, but only by those means, by which at first it was obtained. He therefore thinkes it not enough for him to observe the fasting dayes of the Church, and the dayly prayers enjoyned him by auctority, which he observeth out of humble conformity, and obedience; but adds to them, out of choyce and devotion, some other dayes for fasting, and hours for prayers; and by these hee keeps his body tame, serviceable, and healthfull; and his soul fervent, active, young, and lusty as an eagle. He often readeth the Lives of the Primitive Monks, Hermits, and Virgins, and wondreth not so much at their patient suffering, and cheerfull dying under persecuting Emperours, (though that indeed be very admirable) as at their daily temperance, abstinence, watchings, and constant prayers, and mortifications in the times of peace and prosperity. To put on the profound humility, and the exact temperance of our Lord Jesus, with other exemplary vertues of that sort, and to keep them on in the sunshine, and noone of prosperity, he findeth to be as necessary, and as difficult at least, as to be cloathed with perfect patience, and Christian fortitude in the cold midnight stormes of persecution and adversity. He keepeth*

28 *Primi;tive* 52 29 *Virgins* 71 : *virgins* 52

his watch and ward, night and day against the proper and peculiar temptations of his state of Life, which are principally these two, Spirituall pride, and Impurity of heart: against these ghostly enemies he girdeth up his loynes, keepes the imagination from roving, puts on the whole Armour of God, and by the vertue of the shield of faith, he is not afraid of the pestilence that walketh in darkenesse, [carnall impurity,] nor of the sicknesse that destroyeth at noone day, [Ghostly pride and self-conceite.] Other temptations he hath, which, like mortall enemies, may sometimes disquiet him likewise; for the humane soule being bounded, and kept in, in her sensitive faculty, will runne out more or lesse in her intellectuall. Originall concupisence is such an active thing, by reason of continuall inward, or outward temptations, that it is ever attempting, or doing one mischief or other. Ambition, or untimely desire of promotion to an higher state, or place, under colour of accommodation, or necessary provision, is a common temptation to men of any eminency, especially being single men. Curiosity in prying into high speculative and unprofitable questions, is another great stumbling block to the holinesse of Scholars. These and many other spirituall wickednesses in high places doth the Parson fear, or experiment, or both; and that much more being single, then if he were marryed; for then commonly the stream of temptations is turned another way, into Covetousnesse, Love of pleasure, or ease, or the like. If the Parson be unmarryed, and means to continue so, he doth at least, as much as hath been said. If he be marryed, the choyce of his wife was made rather by his eare, then by his eye; his judgement, not his affection found out a fit wife for him, whose humble, and liberall disposition he preferred before beauty, riches, or honour. *He knew that (the good instrument of God to bring women to heaven) a wise and loving husband could out of humility, produce any speciall grace of faith, patience, meeknesse, love, obedience,* &c. *and out of liberality, make her fruitfull in all good works.* As hee is just in all things, so is he to his wife also, counting nothing so much his owne, as that he may be unjust unto it. Therefore he gives her respect both afore her servants, and others, and halfe at least of the government of the house, reserving so much of the affaires, as serve for a diversion for

11 *in, in* 75 : *in in* 52 71 13 *inward, or*] *inward, and* 71 36 sevants 52

him; yet never so giving over the raines, but that he sometimes looks how things go, demanding an account, but not by the way of an account. And this must bee done the oftner, or the seldomer, according as hee is satisfied of his Wifes discretion.

CHAP. X.

The Parson in his house.

THe Parson is very exact in the governing of his house, making it a copy and modell for his Parish. He knows the temper, and pulse of every person in his house, and accordingly either meets with their vices, or advanceth their vertues. His wife is either religious, or night and day he is winning her to it. In stead of the qualities of the world, he requires onely three of her; first, a trayning up of her children and mayds in the fear of God, with prayers, and catechizing, and all religious duties. Secondly, a curing, and healing of all wounds and sores with her owne hands; which skill either she brought with her, or he takes care she shall learn it of some religious neighbour. Thirdly, a providing for her family in such sort, as that neither they want a competent sustentation, nor her husband be brought in debt. His children he first makes Christians, and then Commonwealths-men; the one he owes to his heavenly Countrey, the other to his earthly, having no title to either, except he do good to both. Therefore having seasoned them with all Piety, not only of words in praying, and reading; but in actions, in visiting other sick children, and tending their wounds, and sending his charity by them to the poor, and somtimes giving them a little mony to do it of themselves, that they get a delight in it, and enter favour with God, who weighs even childrens actions, 1 *King.* 14. 12, 13. He afterwards turnes his care to fit all their dispositions with some calling, not sparing the eldest, but giving him the prerogative of his Fathers profession, which happily for his other children he is not able to do. Yet in binding them prentices (in case he think fit to do so) he takes care not to put them into

29 actions, *71*: actions. *52* 33 prentices] Apprentices *71*

vain trades, and unbefitting the reverence of their Fathers calling, such as are tavernes for men, and lace-making for women; because those trades, for the most part, serve but the vices and vanities of the world, which he is to deny, and not augment. However, he resolves with himself never to omit any present good deed of charity, in consideration of providing a stock for his children; but assures himselfe, that mony thus lent to God, is placed surer for his childrens advantage, then if it were given to the Chamber of *London*. Good deeds, and good breeding, are his two great stocks for his children; if God give any thing above those, and not spent in them, he blesseth God, and lays it out as he sees cause. His servants are all religious, and were it not his duty to have them so, it were his profit, for none are so well served, as by religious servants, both because they do best, and because what they do, is blessed, and prospers. After religion, he teacheth them, that three things make a compleate servant, Truth, and Diligence, and Neatnesse, or Cleanlinesse. Those that can read, are allowed times for it, and those that cannot, are taught; for all in his house are either teachers or learners, or both, so that his family is a Schoole of Religion, and they all account, that to teach the ignorant is the greatest almes. Even the wals are not idle, but something is written, or painted there, which may excite the reader to a thought of piety; especially the 101 *Psalm*, which is expressed in a fayre table, as being the rule of a family. And when they go abroad, his wife among her neighbours is the beginner of good discourses, his children among children, his servants among other servants; so that as in the house of those that are skill'd in Musick, all are Musicians; so in the house of a Preacher, all are preachers. He suffers not a ly or equivocation by any means in his house, but counts it the art, and secret of governing to preserve a directnesse, and open plainnesse in all things; so that all his house knowes, that there is no help for a fault done, but confession. He *himselfe*, or his *Wife*, takes account of Sermons, and how every one profits, comparing this yeer with the last: and besides the common prayers of the

34 directinesse, *52*

family, he straitly requires of all to pray by themselves before they sleep at night, and stir out in the morning, and knows what prayers they say, and till they have learned them, makes them kneel by him; esteeming that this private praying is a more voluntary act in them, then when they are called to others prayers, and that, which when they leave the family, they carry with them. He keeps his servants between love, and fear, according as hee findes them; but generally he distributes it thus, To his Children he shewes more love then terrour, to his servants more terrour then love; but an old good servant boards a child. The furniture of his house is very plain, but clean, whole, and sweet, as sweet as his garden can make; for he hath no mony for such things, charity being his only perfume, which deserves cost when he can spare it. His fare is plain, and common, but wholsome, what hee hath, is little, but very good; it consisteth most of mutton, beefe, and veal, if he addes any thing for a great day, or a stranger, his garden or orchard supplyes it, or his barne, and back-side: he goes no further for any entertainment, lest he goe into the world, esteeming it absurd, that he should exceed, who teacheth others temperance. But those which his home produceth, he refuseth not, as coming cheap, and easie, and arising from the improvement of things, which otherwise would be lost. Wherein he admires and imitates the wonderfull providence and thrift of the great householder of the world: for there being two things, which as they are, are unuseful to man, the one for smalnesse, as crums, and scattered corn, and the like; the other for the foulnesse, as wash, and durt, and things thereinto fallen; God hath provided Creatures for both; for the first, Poultry; for the second, swine. These save man the labour, and doing that which either he could not do, or was not fit for him to do, by taking both sorts of food into them, do as it were dresse and prepare both for man in themselves, by growing them selves fit for his table. The Parson in his house observes fasting dayes; and particularly, as Sunday is his day of joy, so Friday his day of Humiliation, which he celebrates not only with abstinence of diet, but also of company, recreation, and all outward contentments; and besides, with confession of sins, and all acts of Mortification. Now fasting dayes containe a treble obligation; first, of eating lesse that day, then on other dayes; secondly, of eating no pleasing, or over-nourishing things, as the Israelites did eate sowre herbs: Thirdly, of eating no flesh, which is but the determination of the second rule by Authority to this particular. The two former obligations are much more essentiall to a true fast, then the third and last; and fasting dayes were fully performed by keeping of the two former, had not Authority interposed: so that to eat little, and that unpleasant, is the naturall rule of fasting, although it be flesh. For since fasting in Scripture language is an afflicting of our souls, if a peece of dry flesh at my table be more unpleasant to me, then some fish there, certainly to eat the flesh, and not the fish, is to keep the fasting day naturally. And it is observable, that the prohibiting of flesh came from hot Countreys, where both flesh alone, and much more with wine, is apt to nourish more then in cold regions, and where flesh may be much better spared, and with more safety then elsewhere, where both the people and the drink being cold and flegmatick, the eating of flesh is an antidote to both. For it is certaine, that a weak stomack being prepossessed with flesh, shall much better brooke and bear a draught of beer, then if it had taken before either fish, or rootes, or such things; which will discover it selfe by spitting, and rheume, or flegme. To conclude, the Parson, if he be in full health, keeps the three obligations, eating fish, or roots, and that for quantity little, for quality unpleasant. If his body be weak and obstructed, as most Students are, he cannot keep the last obligation, nor suffer others in his house that are so, to keep it; but only the two former, which also in diseases of exinanition (as consumptions) must be broken: For meat was made for man, not man for meat. To all this may be added, not for emboldening the unruly, but for the comfort of the weak, that not onely sicknesse breaks these obligations of fasting, but sicklinesse also. For it is as unnatural to do any thing, that leads me to a sicknesse, to which I am inclined, as not to get out of that sicknesse, when I am in it, by any diet. One thing is evident,

23 daught *52*   31 exinanition *52 75* : examination *71*

that an English body, and a Students body, are two great obstructed vessels, and there is nothing that is food, and not phisick, which doth lesse obstruct, then flesh moderately taken; as being immoderately taken, it is exceeding obstructive. And obstructions are the cause of most diseases.

CHAP. XI.

The Parson's Courtesie.

THe Countrey Parson owing a debt of Charity to the poor, and of Courtesie to his other parishioners, he so distinguisheth, that he keeps his money for the poor, and his table for those that are above Alms. Not but that the poor are welcome also to his table, whom he sometimes purposely takes home with him, setting them close by him, and carving for them, both for his own humility, and their comfort, who are much cheered with such friendliness. But since both is to be done, the better sort invited, and meaner relieved, he chooseth rather to give the poor money, which they can better employ to their own advantage, and sutably to their needs, then so much given in meat at dinner. Having then invited some of his Parish, hee taketh his times to do the like to the rest; so that in the compasse of the year, hee hath them all with him, because countrey people are very observant of such things, and will not be perswaded, but being not invited, they are hated. Which perswasion the Parson by all means avoyds, knowing that where there are such conceits, there is no room for his doctrine to enter. Yet doth hee oftenest invite those, whom hee sees take best courses, that so both they may be encouraged to persevere, and others spurred to do well, that they may enjoy the like courtesie. For though he desire, that all should live well, and vertuously, not for any reward of his, but for vertues sake; yet that will not be so: and therefore as God, although we should love him onely for his own sake, yet out of his infinite pity hath set forth heaven for a reward to draw men to Piety, and is content, if

13 friendliness *71* : friendlineses *52* 16 needs, then *Errata 52* : needs, and then *text 52*

at least so, they will become good: So the Countrey Parson, who is a diligent observer, and tracker of Gods wayes, sets up as many encouragements to goodnesse as he can, both in honour, and profit, and fame; that he may, if not the best way, yet any way, make his Parish good.

Chap. XII.

The Parson's Charity.

THe Countrey Parson is full of Charity; it is his predominant element. For many and wonderfull things are spoken of thee, thou great Vertue. To Charity is given the covering of sins, 1 *Pet.* 4. 8. and the forgivenesse of sins, *Matthew* 6. 14. *Luke* 7. 47. The fulfilling of the Law, *Romans* 13. 10. The life of faith, *James* 2. 26. The blessings of this life, *Proverbs* 22. 9. *Psalm* 41. 2. And the reward of the next, *Matth.* 25. 35. In brief, it is the body of Religion, *John* 13. 35. And the top of Christian vertues, 1 *Corin.* 13. Wherefore all his works rellish of Charity. When he riseth in the morning, he bethinketh himselfe what good deeds he can do that day, and presently doth them; counting that day lost, wherein he hath not exercised his Charity. He first considers his own Parish, and takes care, that there be not a begger, or idle person in his Parish, but that all bee in a competent way of getting their living. This he effects either by bounty, or perswasion, or by authority, making use of that excellent statute, which bindes all Parishes to maintaine their own. If his Parish be rich, he exacts this of them; if poor, and he able, he easeth them therein. But he gives no set pension to any; for this in time will lose the name and effect of Charity with the poor people, though not with God: for then they will reckon upon it, as on a debt; and if it be taken away, though justly, they will murmur, and repine as much, as he that is disseized of his own inheritance. But the Parson having a double aime, and making a hook of his Charity, causeth them still to depend on him; and so by continuall,

1 good: So *75*: good. So *52 71* 10 The fulfilling *Ed*: the fulfilling *52*
21 effects *71*: affects *52* 25 therein *71*: therin *52*

and fresh bounties, unexpected to them, but resolved to himself, hee wins them to praise God more, to live more religiously, and to take more paines in their vocation, as not knowing when they shal be relieved; which otherwise they would reckon upon, and turn to idlenesse. Besides this generall provision, he hath other times of opening his hand; as at great Festivals, and Communions; not suffering any that day that hee receives, to want a good meal suting to the joy of the occasion. But specially, at hard times, and dearths, he even parts his Living, and life among them, giving some corn outright, and selling other at under rates; and when his own stock serves not, working those that are able to the same charity, still pressing it in the pulpit, and out of the pulpit, and never leaving them, till he obtaine his desire. Yet in all his Charity, he distinguisheth, giving them most, who live best, and take most paines, and are most charged: So is his charity in effect a Sermon. After the consideration of his own Parish, he inlargeth himself, if he be able, to the neighbour-hood; for that also is some kind of obligation; so doth he also to those at his door, whom God puts in his way, and makes his neighbours. But these he helps not without some testimony, except the evidence of the misery bring testimony with it. For though these testimonies also may be falsifyed, yet considering that the Law allows these in case they be true, but allows by no means to give without testimony, as he obeys Authority in the one, so that being once satisfied, he allows his Charity some blindnesse in the other; especially, since of the two commands, we are more injoyned to be charitable, then wise. But evident miseries have a naturall priviledge, and exemption from all law. When-ever hee gives any thing, and sees them labour in thanking of him, he exacts of them to let him alone, and say rather, God be praised, God be glorified; that so the thanks may go the right way, and thither onely, where they are onely due. So doth hee also before giving make them say their Prayers first, or the Creed, and ten Commandments, and as he finds them perfect, rewards them the more. For other givings are lay, and secular, but this is to give like a Priest.

Chap. XIII.

The Parson's Church.

THe Countrey Parson hath a speciall care of his Church, that all things there be decent, and befitting his Name by which it is called. Therefore first he takes order, that all things be in good repair; as walls plaistered, windows glazed, floore paved, seats whole, firm, and uniform, especially that the Pulpit, and Desk, and Communion Table, and Font be as they ought, for those great duties that are performed in them. Secondly, that the Church be swept, and kept cleane without dust, or Cobwebs, and at great festivalls strawed, and stuck with boughs, and perfumed with incense. Thirdly, That there be fit, and proper texts of Scripture every where painted, and that all the painting be grave, and reverend, not with light colours, or foolish anticks. Fourthly, That all the books appointed by Authority be there, and those not torne, or fouled, but whole and clean, and well bound; and that there be a fitting, and sightly Communion Cloth *of fine linnen, with an handsome, and seemly Carpet of good and costly Stuffe, or Cloth, and all kept sweet and clean, in a strong and decent chest, with a Chalice, and Cover, and a Stoop, or Flagon; and a Bason for Almes and offerings; besides which, he hath a Poor-mans Box conveniently seated, to receive the charity of well minded people, and to lay up treasure for the sick and needy.* And all this he doth, not as out of necessity, or as putting a holiness in the things, but as desiring to keep the middle way between superstition, and slovenlinesse, and as following the Apostles two great and admirable Rules in things of this nature: The first whereof is, *Let all things be done decently, and in order*: The second, *Let all things be done to edification*, 1 *Cor.* 14. For these two rules comprize and include the double object of our duty, God, and our neighbour; the first being for the honour of God; the second for the benefit of our neighbor. So that they excellently score out the way, and fully, and exactly contain, even in externall and indifferent things,

6 Desk *Errata 52* : Deck *text 52*   15 whole and clean *71* : whole ; and clean *52*
16–22 of fine linnen . . . sick and needy. *rom. within inverted commas 52* (*cf. pp.* 247, 249) : *ital. 71*

what course is to be taken; and put them to great shame, who deny the Scripture to be perfect.

Chap. XIV.

The Parson in Circuit.

THe Countrey Parson upon the afternoons in the week-days, takes occasion sometimes to visite in person, now one quarter of his Parish, now another. For there he shall find his flock most naturally as they are, wallowing in the midst of their affairs: whereas on Sundays it is easie for them to compose themselves to order, which they put on as their holy-day cloathes, and come to Church in frame, but commonly the next day put off both. When he comes to any house, first he blesseth it, and then as hee finds the persons of the house imployed, so he formes his discourse. Those that he findes religiously imployed, hee both commends them much, and furthers them when hee is gone, in their imployment; as if hee findes them reading, hee furnisheth them with good books; if curing poor people, hee supplies them with Receipts, and instructs them further in that skill, shewing them how acceptable such works are to God, and wishing them ever to do the Cures with their own hands, and not to put them over to servants. Those that he finds busie in the works of their calling, he commendeth them also: for it is a good and just thing for every one to do their own busines. But then he admonisheth them of two things; first, that they dive not too deep into worldly affairs, plunging themselves over head and eares into carking, and caring; but that they so labour, as neither to labour anxiously, nor distrustfully, nor profanely. Then they labour anxiously, when they overdo it, to the loss of their quiet, and health: then distrustfully, when they doubt Gods providence, thinking that their own labour is the cause of their thriving, as if it were in their own hands to thrive, or not to thrive. *Then they labour profanely, when they set themselves to work like brute*

7 Sundays] Sunday *71* 31 not to thrixe. *52* 31–248. 5 Then they labour . . . Harvest. *rom. within inverted commas 52 : ital. 71*

beasts, never raising their thoughts to God, nor sanctifying their labour with daily prayer; when on the Lords day they do unnecessary servile work, or in time of divine service on other holy days, except in the cases of extreme poverty, and in the seasons of Seed-time, and Harvest. Secondly, he adviseth them so to labour for wealth and maintenance, as that they make not that the end of their labour, but that they may have wherewithall to serve God the better, and to do good deeds. After these discourses, if they be poor and needy, whom he thus finds labouring, he gives them somewhat; and opens not only his mouth, but his purse to their relief, that so they go on more cheerfully in their vocation, and himself be ever the more welcome to them. Those that the Parson findes idle, or ill imployed, he chides not at first, for that were neither civill, nor profitable; but always in the close, before he departs from them: yet in this he distinguisheth; for if he be a plaine countryman, he reproves him plainly; for they are not sensible of finenesse: if they be of higher quality, they commonly are quick, and sensible, and very tender of reproof: and therefore he lays his discourse so, that he comes to the point very leasurely, and oftentimes, as *Nathan* did, in the person of another, making them to reprove themselves. However, one way or other, he ever reproves them, that he may keep himself pure, and not be intangled in others sinnes. Neither in this doth he forbear, though there be company by: for as when the offence is particular, and against mee, I am to follow our Saviours rule, and to take my brother aside, and reprove him; so when the offence is publicke, and against God, I am then to follow the Apostles rule, 1 *Timothy* 5. 20. and to *rebuke openly* that which is done openly. Besides these occasionall discourses, the Parson questions what order is kept in the house, as about prayers morning and evening on their knees, reading of Scripture, catechizing, singing of Psalms at their work, and on holy days; who can read, who not; and sometimes he hears the children read himselfe, and blesseth them, encouraging also the servants to learn to read, and offering to have them taught on holy-dayes by his servants. If the Parson were ashamed of particularizing in

32 morning *71* : morning, *52*   36 blesseth them *75* : blesseth *52 71*

these things, hee were not fit to be a Parson: but he holds the Rule, that Nothing is little in Gods service: If it once have the honour of that Name, it grows great instantly. Wherfore neither disdaineth he to enter into the poorest Cottage, though he even creep into it, and though it smell never so lothsomly. For both God is there also, and those for whom God dyed: and so much the rather doth he so, as his accesse to the poor is more comfortable, then to the rich; and in regard of himselfe, it is more humiliation. These are the Parsons generall aims in his Circuit; but with these he mingles other discourses for conversation sake, and to make his higher purposes slip the more easily.

CHAP. XV.

The Parson Comforting.

THe Countrey Parson, when any of his cure is sick, or afflicted with losse of friend, or estate, or any ways distressed, fails not to afford his best comforts, and rather goes to them, then sends for the afflicted, though they can, and otherwise ought to come to him. To this end he hath throughly digested all the points of consolation, as having continuall use of them, such as are from Gods generall providence extended even to lillyes; from his particular, to his Church; from his promises, from the examples of all Saints, that ever were; from Christ himself, perfecting our Redemption no other way, then by sorrow; from the Benefit of affliction, which softens, and works the stubborn heart of man; from the certainty both of deliverance, and reward, if we faint not; from the miserable comparison of the moment of griefs here with the weight of joyes hereafter. *Besides this, in his visiting the sick, or otherwise afflicted, he followeth the Churches counsell, namely, in perswading them to particular confession, labouring to make them understand the great good use of this antient and pious ordinance, and how necessary it is in some cases: he also urgeth them to do some pious charitable works, as a necessary evidence and fruit of their faith, at that time especi-*

27–250. 6 Besides this, . . . his perswasion. *rom. within inverted commas 52 : ital. 71*
33–250. 5 75 *emends the wording and punctuation thus:* fruit of their faith; at that

ally: the participation of the holy Sacrament, how comfortable, and Soveraigne a Medicine it is to all sin-sick souls; what strength, and joy, and peace it administers against all temptations, even to death it selfe, he plainly, and generally intimateth to the dis-affected, or sick person, that so the hunger and thirst after it may come rather from themselves, then from his perswasion.

Chap. XVI.

The Parson a Father.

THe Countrey Parson is not only a father to his flock, but also professeth himselfe throughly of the opinion, carrying it about with him as fully, as if he had begot his whole Parish. And of this he makes great use. For by this means, when any sinns, he hateth him not as an officer, but pityes him as a Father: and even in those wrongs which either in tithing, or otherwise are done to his owne person, hee considers the offender as a child, and forgives, so hee may have any signe of amendment; so also when after many admonitions, any continue to be refractory, yet hee gives him not over, but is long before hee proceede to disinherit-ing, or perhaps never goes so far; knowing, that some are called at the eleventh houre, and therefore hee still expects, and waits, least hee should determine Gods houre of coming; which as hee cannot, touching the last day, so neither touch-ing the intermediate days of Conversion.

Chap. XVII.

The Parson in Journey.

THe Countrey Parson, when a just occasion calleth him out of his Parish (which he diligently, and strictly weigheth, his Parish being all his joy, and thought) leaveth

time especially, to the participation of the Holy Sacrament; shewing them how comfortable, . . . to all sin-sick souls; what strength, . . . against all temptations, even in death it self. He plainly, and generally intimateth all this to the disaffected, . . .
2 *sin-sick souls*; *75* : sinsick souls, *52* : *sin sick souls*, *71*   16 continue] continues *75*   23 Countrey *71* : countrey *52*

not his Ministry behind him; but is himselfe where ever he is. Therefore those he meets on the way he blesseth audibly, and with those he overtakes or that overtake him, hee begins good discourses, such as may edify, interposing sometimes some short, and honest refreshments, which may make his other discourses more welcome, and lesse tedious. And when he comes to his Inn, he refuseth not to joyne, that he may enlarge the glory of God, to the company he is in, by a due blessing of God for their safe arrival, and saying grace at meat, and at going to bed by giving the Host notice, that he will have prayers in the hall, wishing him to informe his guests thereof, that if any be willing to partake, they may resort thither. The like he doth in the morning, using pleasantly the outlandish proverb, that *Prayers and Provender never hinder journey*. When he comes to any other house, where *his kindred, or other relations give him any authority over the Family*, if hee be to stay for a time, hee considers diligently the state thereof to Godward, and that in two points: First, what disorders there are either in Apparell, or Diet, or too open a Buttery, or reading vain books, or swearing, or breeding up children to no Calling, but in idleness, or the like. Secondly, what means of Piety, whether daily prayers be used, Grace, reading of Scriptures, and other good books, how *Sundayes, holy-days, and fasting days* are kept. And accordingly, as he finds any defect in these, hee first considers with himselfe, what kind of remedy fits the temper of the house best, and then hee faithfully, and boldly applyeth it; yet seasonably, and discreetly, by taking aside the Lord or Lady, or *Master* and *Mistres* of the house, and shewing them cleerly, that they respect them most, who wish them best, and that not a desire to meddle with others affairs, but the earnestnesse to do all the good he can, moves him to say thus and thus.

8 God, *Ed*: God *52 71*: *75 brackets* (that he may enlarge the Glorie of God)
28 Lord or Lady, *Ed*: Lord, or Lady; *52*

CHAP. XVIII.

The Parson in Sentinell.

THe Countrey Parson, where ever he is, keeps Gods watch; that is, there is nothing spoken, or done in the Company where he is, but comes under his Test and censure: If it be well spoken, or done, he takes occasion to commend, and enlarge it; if ill, he presently lays hold of it, least the poyson steal into some young and unwary spirits, and possesse them even before they themselves heed it. But this he doth discretely, with mollifying, and suppling words; This was not so well said, as it might have been forborn; We cannot allow this: or else if the thing will admit interpretation; Your meaning is not thus, but thus; or, So farr indeed what you say is true, and well said; but this will not stand. This is called keeping Gods watch, when the baits which the enemy lays in company, are discovered and avoyded: This is to be on Gods side, and be true to his party. Besides, if he perceive in company any discourse tending to ill, either by the wickedness or quarrelsomnesse thereof, he either prevents it judiciously, or breaks it off seasonably by some diversion. Wherein a pleasantness of disposition is of great use, men being willing to sell the interest, and ingagement of their discourses for no price sooner, then that of mirth; whither the nature of man, loving refreshment, gladly betakes it selfe, even to the losse of honour.

CHAP. XIX.

The Parson in reference.

THe Countrey Parson is sincere and upright in all his relations. And first, he is just to his Countrey; as when he is set at an armour, or horse, he borrowes them not to serve the turne, nor provides slight, and unusefull, but such as are every way fitting to do his Countrey true and laudable service, when occasion requires. To do otherwise, is deceit;

8 suppling] supplying *71* 24 and *Errata 52* : nnd *text 52*

and therefore not for him, who is hearty, and true in all his wayes, as being the servant of him, in whom there was no guile. Likewise in any other Countrey-duty, he considers what is the end of any Command, and then he suits things faithfully according to that end. Secondly, he carryes himself very respectively, as to all the Fathers of the Church, so especially to his Diocesan, honouring him both in word, and behaviour, and resorting unto him in any difficulty, either in his studies or in his Parish. He observes Visitations, and being there, makes due use of them, as of Clergy councels, for the benefit of the Diocese. And therefore before he comes, having observed some defects in the Ministry, he then either in Sermon, if he preach, or at some other time of the day, propounds among his Brethren what were fitting to be done. Thirdly, he keeps good Correspondence with all the neighbouring Pastours round about him, performing for them any Ministeriall office, which is not to the prejudice of his own Parish. Likewise he welcomes to his house any Minister, how poor or mean soever, with as joyfull a countenance, as if he were to entertain some great Lord. Fourthly, he fulfills the duty, and debt of neighbourhood to all the Parishes which are neer him. For the Apostles rule *Philip.* 4. being admirable, and large, that *we should do whatsoever things are honest*, or *just*, or *pure*, or *lovely*, or *of good report*, *if there be any vertue*, or *any praise*; and Neighbourhood being ever reputed, even among the Heathen, as an obligation to do good, rather then to those that are further, where things are otherwise equall, therefore he satisfies this duty also. Especially, if God have sent any calamity either by fire, or famine, to any neighbouring Parish, then he expects no Briefe; but taking his Parish together *the next Sunday*, or *holy-day*, and exposing to them the uncertainty of humane affairs, none knowing whose turne may be next, and then when he hath affrighted them with this, exposing the obligation of Charity, and Neighbour-hood, he first gives himself liberally, and then incites them to give; making together a summe either to be sent, or, which were more comfortable, all together choosing some fitt day to carry it themselves, and cheere the

25 *praise*; And 75 : *praise.* And 52 71

Afflicted. So, if any neighbouring village be overburdened with poore, and his owne lesse charged, hee findes some way of releeving it, and reducing the Manna, and bread of Charity to some equality, representing to his people, that the Blessing of God to them ought to make them the more charitable, and not the lesse, lest he cast their neighbours poverty on them also.

Chap. XX.

The Parson in Gods stead.

THe Countrey Parson is in Gods stead to his Parish, and dischargeth God what he can of his promises. Wherefore there is nothing done either wel or ill, whereof he is not the rewarder, or punisher. If he chance to finde any reading in anothers Bible, he provides him one of his own. If he finde another giving a poor man a penny, he gives him a tester for it, if the giver be fit to receive it; or if he be of a condition above such gifts, he sends him a good book, or easeth him in his Tithes, telling him when he hath forgotten it, This I do, because at such, and such a time you were charitable. This is in some sort a discharging of God; as concerning this life, who hath promised, that Godlinesse shall be gainfull: but in the other God is his own immediate paymaster, rewarding all good deeds to their full proportion. *The Parsons punishing of sin and vice, is rather by withdrawing his bounty and courtesie from the parties offending, or by private, or publick reproof, as the case requires, then by causing them to be presented, or otherwise complained of. And yet as the malice of the person, or hainousness of the crime may be, he is carefull to see condign punishment inflicted, and with truly godly zeal, without hatred to the person, hungreth and thirsteth after righteous punishment of unrighteousnesse. Thus both in rewarding vertue, and in punishing vice, the Parson endeavoureth to be in Gods stead, knowing that Countrey people are drawne, or led by sense, more then by faith, by present rewards, or punishments, more then by future.*

17 This *Ed*: this 52 71   22–33 The Parsons . . . future. *rom. within inverted commas* 52 71 : *ital. Ed*

CHAP. XXI.

The Parson Catechizing.

THe Countrey Parson values Catechizing highly: for there being three points of his duty, the one, to infuse a competent knowledge of salvation in every one of his Flock; the other, to multiply, and build up this knowledge to a spirituall Temple; the third, to inflame this knowledge, to presse, and drive it to practice, turning it to reformation of life, by pithy and lively exhortations; Catechizing is the first point, and but by Catechizing, the other cannot be attained. Besides, whereas in Sermons there is a kinde of state, in Catechizing there is an humblenesse very sutable to Christian regeneration, which exceedingly delights him as by way of exercise upon himself, and by way of preaching to himself, for the advancing of his own mortification; for in preaching to others, he forgets not himself, but is first a Sermon to himself, and then to others; growing with the growth of his Parish. He useth, and preferreth the ordinary Church-Catechism, partly for obedience to Authority, partly for uniformity sake, that the same common truths may be every where professed, especially since many remove from Parish to Parish, who like Christian Souldiers are to give the word, and to satisfie the Congregation by their Catholick answers. He exacts of all the Doctrine of the Catechisme; of the younger sort, the very words; of the elder, the substance. Those he Catechizeth publickly, these privately, giving age honour, according to the Apostles rule, 1 *Tim.* 5. 1. He requires all to be present at Catechizing: First, for the authority of the work; Secondly, that Parents, and Masters, as they hear the answers prove, may when they come home, either commend or reprove, either reward or punish. Thirdly, that those of the elder sort, who are not well grounded, may then by an honourable way take occasion to be better instructed. Fourthly, that those who are well grown in the knowledg of Religion, may examine their grounds, renew their vowes, and by occasion of both, inlarge their meditations. When

13 mortification, For *52* 26 *First 75* : first *52 71*

once all have learned the words of the Catechisme, he thinks it the most usefull way that a Pastor can take, to go over the same, but in other words: for many say the Catechisme by rote, as parrats, without ever piercing into the sense of it. In this course the order of the Catechisme would be kept, but the rest varyed: as thus, in the Creed: How came this world to be as it is? Was it made, or came it by chance? Who made it? Did you see God make it? Then are there some things to be beleeved that are not seen? Is this the nature of beliefe? Is not Christianity full of such things, as are not to be seen, but beleeved? You said, God made the world; Who is God? And so forward, requiring answers to all these, and helping and cherishing the Answerer, by making the Question very plaine with comparisons, and making much even of a word of truth from him. This order being used to one, would be a little varyed to another. And this is an admirable way of teaching, wherein the Catechized will at length finde delight, and by which the Catechizer, if he once get the skill of it, will draw out of ignorant and silly souls, even the dark and deep points of Religion. *Socrates* did thus in Philosophy, who held that the seeds of all truths lay in every body, and accordingly by questions well ordered he found Philosophy in silly Trades-men. That position will not hold in Christianity, because it contains things above nature: but after that the Catechisme is once learn'd, that which nature is towards Philosophy, the Catechism is towards Divinity. To this purpose, some dialogues in *Plato* were worth the reading, where the singular dexterity of *Socrates* in this kind may be observed, and imitated. Yet the skill consists but in these three points: First, an aim and mark of the whole discourse, whither to drive the Answerer, which the Questionist must have in his mind before any question be propounded, upon which and to which the questions are to be chained. Secondly, a most plain and easie framing the question, even containing in vertue the answer also, especially to the more ignorant. Thirdly, when the answerer sticks, an illustrating the thing by something else, which he knows, making what hee knows to serve him in

20 Religion. *71*: Religion, *52* 37 answerer *52 75*: *misprinted* answer *71*

that which he knows not: As, when the Parson once demanded after other questions about mans misery; since man is so miserable, what is to be done? And the answerer could not tell; He asked him again, what he would do, if he were in a ditch? This familiar illustration made the answer so plaine, that he was even ashamed of his ignorance; for he could not but say, he would hast out of it as fast as he could. Then he proceeded to ask, whether he could get out of the ditch alone, or whether he needed a helper, and who was that helper. This is the skill, and doubtlesse the Holy Scripture intends thus much, when it condescends to the naming of a plough, a hatchet, a bushell, leaven, boyes piping and dancing; shewing that things of ordinary use are not only to serve in the way of drudgery, but to be washed, and cleansed, and serve for lights even of Heavenly Truths. This is the Practice which the Parson so much commends to all his fellow-labourers; the secret of whose good consists in this, that at Sermons, and Prayers, men may sleep or wander; but when one is asked a question, he must discover what he is. This practice exceeds even Sermons in teaching: but there being two things in Sermons, the one Informing, the other Inflaming; as Sermons come short of questions in the one, so they farre exceed them in the other. For questions cannot inflame or ravish, that must be done by a set, and laboured, and continued speech.

CHAP. XXII.

The Parson in Sacraments.

THE Countrey Parson being to administer the Sacraments, is at a stand with himself, how or what behaviour to assume for so holy things. Especially at Communion times he is in a great confusion, as being not only to receive God, but to break, and administer him. Neither findes he any issue in this, but to throw himself down at the throne of grace, saying, Lord, thou knowest what thou didst, when thou appointedst it to be done thus; therefore doe thou fulfill what thou didst appoint; for thou art not only

7 as fast as he *71* : as fast he *52*

the feast, but the way to it. At Baptisme, being himselfe in white, he requires the presence of all, and Baptizeth not willingly, but on Sundayes, or great dayes. Hee admits no vaine or idle names, but such as are usuall and accustomed. Hee says that prayer with great devotion, where God is thanked for calling us to the knowledg of his grace, Baptisme being a blessing, that the world hath not the like. He willingly and cheerfully crosseth the child, and thinketh the Ceremony not onely innocent, but reverend. He instructeth the God-fathers, and God-mothers, that it is no complementall or light thing to sustain that place, but a great honour, and no less burden, as being done both in the presence of God, and his Saints, and by way of undertaking for a Christian soul. He adviseth all to call to minde their Baptism often; for if wise men have thought it the best way of preserving a state to reduce it to its principles by which it grew great; certainly, it is the safest course for Christians also to meditate on their Baptisme often (being the first step into their great and glorious calling) and upon what termes, and with what vowes they were Baptized. At the times of the Holy Communion, he first takes order with the Church-Wardens, that the elements be of the best, not cheape, or course, much lesse ill-tasted, or unwholsome. Secondly, hee considers and looks into the ignorance, or carelesness of his flock, and accordingly applies himselfe with Catechizings, and lively exhortations, not on the Sunday of the Communion only (for then it is too late) but the Sunday, or Sundayes before the Communion, or on the Eves of all those dayes. If there be any, who having not received yet, are to enter into this great work, he takes the more pains with them, that hee may lay the foundation of future Blessings. The time of every ones first receiving is not so much by yeers, as by understanding: particularly, the rule may be this: When any one can distinguish the Sacramentall from common bread, knowing the Institution, and the difference, hee ought to receive, of what age soever. Children and youths are usually deferred too long, under pretence of devotion to the Sacrament, but it is for want of Instruction;

27 late *71* : late ; *52*   29 are *75* : is *52 71*

their understandings being ripe enough for ill things, and why not then for better? But Parents, and Masters should make hast in this, as to a great purchase for their children, and servants; which while they deferr, both sides suffer; the one, in wanting many excitings of grace; the other, in being worse served and obeyed. The saying of the Catechism is necessary, but not enough; because to answer in form may still admit ignorance: but the Questions must be propounded loosely and wildely, and then the Answerer will discover what hee is. Thirdly, For the manner of receiving, as the Parson useth all reverence himself, so he administers to none but to the reverent. The Feast indeed requires sitting, because it is a Feast; but man's unpreparednesse asks kneeling. Hee that comes to the Sacrament, hath the confidence of a Guest, and hee that kneels, confesseth himself an unworthy one, and therefore differs from other Feasters: but hee that sits, or lies, puts up to an Apostle: Contentiousnesse in a feast of Charity is more scandall then any posture. Fourthly, touching the frequency of the Communion, the Parson celebrates it, if not duly once a month, yet at least five or six times in the year; as, at Easter, Christmasse, Whitsuntide, afore and after Harvest, and the beginning of Lent. And this hee doth, not onely for the benefit of the work, but also for the discharge of the Church-wardens, who being to present all that receive not thrice a year; if there be but three Communions, neither can all the people so order their affairs as to receive just at those times, nor the Church-Wardens so well take notice who receive thrice, and who not.

Chap. XXIII.

The Parson's Completenesse.

THe Countrey Parson desires to be all to his Parish, and not onely a Pastour, but a Lawyer also, and a Phisician. Therefore hee endures not that any of his Flock should go to Law; but in any Controversie, that they should resort to him as their Judge. To this end, he hath gotten to himself some insight in things ordinarily incident and controverted, by experience, and by reading some initiatory treatises in the Law, with *Daltons* Justice of Peace, and the Abridgements of the Statutes, as also by discourse with men of that profession, whom he hath ever some cases to ask, when he meets with them; holding that rule, that to put men to discourse of that, wherin they are most eminent, is the most gainfull way of Conversation. Yet when ever any controversie is brought to him, he never decides it alone, but sends for three or four of the ablest of the Parish to hear the cause with him, whom he makes to deliver their opinion first; out of which he gathers, in case he be ignorant himself, what to hold; and so the thing passeth with more authority, and lesse envy. In judging, he followes that, which is altogether right; so that if the poorest man of the Parish detain but a pin unjustly from the richest, he absolutely restores it as a Judge; but when he hath so done, then he assumes the Parson, and exhorts to Charity. Neverthelesse, there may happen somtimes some cases, wherein he chooseth to permit his Parishioners rather to make use of the Law, then himself: As in cases of an obscure and dark nature, not easily determinable by Lawyers themselves; or in cases of high consequence, as establishing of inheritances: or Lastly, when the persons in difference are of a contentious disposition, and cannot be gained, but that they still fall from all compromises that have been made. But then he shews them how to go to Law, even as Brethren, and not as enemies, neither avoyding therfore one anothers company, much lesse defaming one another. Now as the Parson is in Law, so is he in sicknesse also: if there be any of his flock sick, hee is their Physician, or at least his Wife, of whom in stead of the qualities of the world, he asks no other, but to have the skill of healing a wound, or helping the sick. But if neither himselfe, nor his wife have the skil, and his means serve, hee keepes some young practicioner in his house for the benefit of his Parish, whom yet he ever exhorts not to exceed his bounds, but in tickle cases to call in help. If all fail, then he keeps good correspondence with some neighbour Phisician,

13 envy, In Judging, *52* 22 establtshing *52* 25–8 But then . . . one another. *ital. 71* 36 tickle] ticklish *71*

and entertaines him for the Cure of his Parish. Yet is it easie for any Scholer to attaine to such a measure of Phisick, as may be of much use to him both for himself, and others. This is done by seeing one Anatomy, reading one Book of Phisick, having one Herball by him. And let *Fernelius* be the Phisick Authour, for he writes briefly, neatly, and judiciously; especially let his Method of Phisick be diligently perused, as being the practicall part, and of most use. Now both the reading of him, and the knowing of herbs may be done at such times, as they may be an help, and a recreation to more divine studies, Nature serving Grace both in comfort of diversion, and the benefit of application when need requires; as also by way of illustration, even as our Saviour made plants and seeds to teach the people: for he was the true householder, who bringeth out of his treasure things new and old; the old things of Philosophy, and the new of Grace; and maketh the one serve the other. And I conceive, our Saviour did this for three reasons: first, that by familiar things hee might make his Doctrine slip the more easily into the hearts even of the meanest. Secondly, that labouring people (whom he chiefly considered) might have every where monuments of his Doctrine, remembring in gardens, his mustard-seed, and lillyes; in the field, his seed-corn, and tares; and so not be drowned altogether in the works of their vocation, but sometimes lift up their minds to better things, even in the midst of their pains. Thirdly, that he might set a Copy for Parsons. In the knowledge of simples, wherein the manifold wisedome of God is wonderfully to be seen, one thing would be carefully observed; which is, to know what herbs may be used in stead of drugs of the same nature, and to make the garden the shop: For home-bred medicines are both more easie for the Parsons purse, and more familiar for all mens bodyes. So, where the Apothecary useth either for loosing, Rubarb, or for binding, Bolearmena, the Parson useth damask or white Roses for the one, and plantaine, shepherds purse, knot-grasse for the other, and that with better successe. As for spices, he doth not onely prefer home-bred things before them, but condemns them for vanities, and so shuts them out of his family,

1 is it] it is *71*   10 an help] a help *71*   21 of of *52*

esteeming that there is no spice comparable, for herbs, to rosemary, time, savoury, mints; and for seeds, to Fennell, and Carroway seeds. Accordingly, for salves, his wife seeks not the city, but preferrs her garden and fields before all outlandish gums. And surely hyssope, valerian, mercury, adders tongue, yerrow, melilot, and Saint *Johns* wort made into a salve; And Elder, camomill, mallowes, comphrey and smallage made into a Poultis, have done great and rare cures. In curing of any, the Parson and his Family use to premise prayers, for this is to cure like a Parson, and this raiseth the action from the Shop, to the Church. But though the Parson sets forward all Charitable deeds, yet he looks not in this point of Curing beyond his own Parish, except the person bee so poor, that he is not able to reward the Phisician: for as hee is Charitable, so he is just also. Now it is a justice and debt to the Common-wealth he lives in, not to incroach on others Professions, but to live on his own. And justice is the ground of Charity.

CHAP. XXIV.

The Parson arguing.

THe Countrey Parson, if there be any of his parish that hold strange Doctrins, useth all possible diligence to reduce them to the common Faith. The first means he useth is Prayer, beseeching the Father of lights to open their eyes, and to give him power so to fit his discourse to them, that it may effectually pierce their hearts, and convert them. The second means is a very loving, and sweet usage of them, both in going to, and sending for them often, and in finding out Courtesies to place on them; as in their tithes, or otherwise. The third means is the observation what is the main foundation, and pillar of their cause, whereon they rely; as if he be a Papist, the Church is the hinge he turnes on; if a Schismatick, scandall. Wherefore the Parson hath diligently examined these two with himselfe, as what the Church is,

16 Gommon-wealth *52* 29 whereon *71* : wherein *52* 31 Schismatick *71* : Scismatick *52* 32–263. 7 What the Church is . . . an exercise. *ital.* *75*

how it began, how it proceeded, whether it be a rule to it selfe, whether it hath a rule, whether having a rule, it ought not to be guided by it; whether any rule in the world be obscure, and how then should the best be so, at least in fundamentall things, the obscurity in some points being the exercise of the Church, the light in the foundations being the guide; The Church needing both an evidence, and an exercise. So for Scandall: what scandall is, when given or taken; whether, there being two precepts, one of obeying Authority, the other of not giving scandall, that ought not to be preferred, especially since in disobeying there is scandall also: whether things once indifferent, being made by the precept of Authority more then indifferent, it be in our power to omit or refuse them. These and the like points hee hath accurately digested, having ever besides two great helps and powerfull perswaders on his side; the one, a strict religious life; the other an humble, and ingenuous search of truth; being unmoved in arguing, and voyd of all contentiousnesse: which are two great lights able to dazle the eyes of the mis-led, while they consider, that God cannot be wanting to them in Doctrine, to whom he is so gracious in Life.

Chap. XXV.

The Parson punishing.

WHensoever the Countrey Parson proceeds so farre as to call in Authority, and to do such things of legall opposition either in the presenting, or punishing of any, as the vulgar ever consters for signes of ill will; he forbears not in any wise to use the delinquent as before, in his behaviour and carriage towards him, not avoyding his company, or doing any thing of aversenesse, save in the very act of punishment: neither doth he esteem him for an enemy, but as a brother still, except some small and temporary estranging may corroborate the punishment to a better subduing, and humbling of the delinquent; which if it happily take effect, he then comes on the faster, and makes so much the more of him, as before he alienated himselfe; doubling his regards, and shewing by all means, that the delinquents returne is to his advantage.

CHAP. XXVI.

The Parson's eye.

THe Countrey Parson at spare times from action, standing on a hill, and considering his Flock, discovers two sorts of vices, and two sorts of vicious persons. There are some vices, whose natures are alwayes cleer, and evident, as Adultery, Murder, Hatred, Lying, &c. There are other vices, whose natures, at least in the beginning, are dark and obscure: as Covetousnesse, and Gluttony. So likewise there are some persons, who abstain not even from known sins; there are others, who when they know a sin evidently, they commit it not. It is true indeed, they are long a knowing it, being partiall to themselves, and witty to others who shall reprove them from it. A man may be both Covetous, and Intemperate, and yet hear Sermons against both, and himselfe condemn both in good earnest: and the reason hereof is, because the natures of these vices being not evidently discussed, or known commonly, the beginnings of them are not easily observable: and the beginnings of them are not observed, because of the suddain passing from that which was just now lawfull, to that which is presently unlawfull, even in one continued action. So a man dining, eats at first lawfully; but proceeding on, comes to do unlawfully, even before he is aware; not knowing the bounds of the action, nor when his eating begins to be unlawfull. So a man storing up mony for his necessary provisions, both in present for his family, and in future for his children, hardly perceives when his storing becomes unlawfull: yet is there a period for his storing, and a point, or center, when his storing, which was even now good, passeth from good to bad. Wherefore the Parson being true to his businesse, hath exactly sifted the definitions of all vertues, and vices; especially canvasing those, whose natures are most stealing, and beginnings

19 observable *71*: observabled *52*

uncertaine. Particularly, concerning these two vices, not because they are all that are of this dark, and creeping disposition, but for example sake, and because they are most common, he thus thinks: first, for covetousnes, he lays this ground: Whosoever when a just occasion cals, either spends not at all, or not in some proportion to Gods blessing upon him, is covetous. The reason of the ground is manifest, because wealth is given to that end to supply our occasions. Now, if I do not give every thing its end, I abuse the Creature, I am false to my reason which should guide me, I offend the supreme Judg, in perverting that order which he hath set both to things, and to reason. The application of the ground would be infinite; but in brief, a poor man is an occasion, my countrey is an occasion, my friend is an occasion, my Table is an occasion, my apparell is an occasion: if in all these, and those more which concerne me, I either do nothing, or pinch, and scrape, and squeeze blood undecently to the station wherein God hath placed me, I am Covetous. More particularly, and to give one instance for all, if God have given me servants, and I either provide too little for them, or that which is unwholsome, being sometimes baned meat, sometimes too salt, and so not competent nourishment, I am Covetous. I bring this example, because men usually think, that servants for their mony are as other things that they buy, even as a piece of wood, which they may cut, or hack, or throw into the fire, and so they pay them their wages, all is well. Nay, to descend yet more particularly, if a man hath wherewithall to buy a spade, and yet hee chuseth rather to use his neighbours, and wear out that, he is covetous. Nevertheless, few bring covetousness thus low, or consider it so narrowly, which yet ought to be done, since there is a Justice in the least things, and for the least there shall be a judgment. Country people are full of these petty injustices, being cunning to make use of another, and spare themselves: And Scholers ought to be diligent in the observation of these, and driving of their generall Schoole

5 ground: *71*: ground, *52* 12 application *75*: application, *52 71* 14 countrey is an occasion, *71*: *no comma 52* 20 have] hath *71* 33 judgment. Country *Errata 52*: judgment Countrey. *text 52*

rules ever to the smallest actions of Life; which while they dwell in their bookes, they will never finde; but being seated in the Countrey, and doing their duty faithfully, they will soon discover: especially if they carry their eyes ever open, and fix them on their charge, and not on their preferment. Secondly, for Gluttony, The Parson lays this ground: He that either for quantity eats more then his health or imployments will bear, or for quality is licorous after dainties, is a glutton; as he that eats more then his estate will bear, is a Prodigall; and hee that eats offensively to the Company, either in his order, or length of eating, is scandalous and uncharitable. These three rules generally comprehend the faults of eating, and the truth of them needs no proofe: so that men must eat neither to the disturbance of their health, nor of their affairs, (which being overburdened, or studying dainties too much, they cannot wel dispatch) nor of their estate, nor of their brethren. One act in these things is bad, but it is the custome and habit that names a glutton. Many think they are at more liberty then they are, as if they were Masters of their health, and so they will stand to the pain, all is well. But to eat to ones hurt, comprehends, besides the hurt, an act against reason, because it is unnaturall to hurt ones self; and this they are not masters of. Yet of hurtfull things, I am more bound to abstain from those, which by mine own experience I have found hurtfull, then from those which by a Common tradition, and vulgar knowledge are reputed to be so. That which is said of hurtfull meats, extends to hurtfull drinks also. As for the quantity, touching our imployments, none must eat so as to disable themselves from a fit discharging either of Divine duties, or duties of their calling. So that if after dinner they are not fit (or un-weeldy) either to pray, or work, they are gluttons. Not that all must presently work after dinner; (For they rather must not work, especially Students, and those that are weakly,) but that they must rise so, as that it is not meate or drinke that hinders them from working. To guide them in this, there are three rules: first, the custome, and knowledg of their

6 ground: *Ed*: ground, *52 71* 8 dainties *71*: danties *52* (*but* dainties *in l.* 15) 15–16 much, they *Errata 52*: mucht; hey *text 52*

own body, and what it can well disgest: The second, the feeling of themselves in time of eating, which because it is deceitfull; (for one thinks in eating, that he can eat more, then afterwards he finds true:) The third is the observation with what appetite they sit down. This last rule joyned with the first, never fails. For knowing what one usually can well disgest, and feeling when I go to meat in what disposition I am, either hungry or not, according as I feele my self, either I take my wonted proportion, or diminish of it. Yet Phisicians bid those that would live in health, not keep an uniform diet, but to feed variously, now more, now lesse: And *Gerson*, a spirituall man, wisheth all to incline rather to too much, then to too little; his reason is, because diseases of exinanition are more dangerous, then diseases of repletion. But the Parson distinguisheth according to his double aime, either of Abstinence a morall vertue, or Mortification a divine. When he deals with any that is heavy, and carnall; he gives him those freer rules: but when he meets with a refined, and heavenly disposition, he carryes them higher, even somtimes to a forgetting of themselves, knowing that there is one, who when they forget, remembers for them; As when the people hungred and thirsted after our Saviours Doctrine, and tarryed so long at it, that they would have fainted, had they returned empty, He suffered it not; but rather made food miraculously, then suffered so good desires to miscarry.

CHAP. XXVII.

The Parson in mirth.

THE Countrey Parson is generally sad, because hee knows nothing but the Crosse of Christ, his minde being defixed on it with those nailes wherewith his Master was: or if he have any leisure to look off from thence, he meets continually with two most sad spectacles, Sin, and Misery; God dishonoured every day, and man afflicted. Neverthelesse, he somtimes refresheth himselfe, as knowing that nature will not bear everlasting droopings, and that

29 on it with *75* : on, and with *52 71* *See note*

pleasantnesse of disposition is a great key to do good; not onely because all men shun the company of perpetuall severity, but also for that when they are in company, instructions seasoned with pleasantnesse, both enter sooner, and roote deeper. Wherefore he condescends to humane frailties both in himselfe and others; and intermingles some mirth in his discourses occasionally, according to the pulse of the hearer.

Chap. XXVIII.

The Parson in Contempt.

THe Countrey Parson knows well, that both for the generall ignominy which is cast upon the profession, and much more for those rules, which out of his choysest judgment hee hath resolved to observe, and which are described in this Book, he must be despised; because this hath been the portion of God his Master, and of Gods Saints his Brethren, and this is foretold, that it shall be so still, until things be no more. Neverthelesse, according to the Apostles rule, he endeavours that none shall despise him; especially in his own Parish he suffers it not to his utmost power; for that, where contempt is, there is no room for instruction. This he procures, first by his holy and unblameable life; which carries a reverence with it, even above contempt. Secondly, by a courteous carriage, & winning behaviour: he that wil be respected, must respect; doing kindnesses, but receiving none; at least of those, who are apt to despise: for this argues a height and eminency of mind, which is not easily despised, except it degenerate to pride. Thirdly, by a bold and impartial reproof, even of the best in the Parish, when occasion requires: for this may produce hatred in those that are reproved, but never contempt either in them, or others. Lastly, if the contempt shall proceed so far as to do any thing punishable by law, as contempt is apt to do, if it be not thwarted, *the Parson having a due respect both to the person, and to the cause, referreth the whole matter to the examination,*

33–269. 1 the Parson . . . Authority *rom. within inverted commas 52 : ital. 71*

and punishment of those which are in Authority; that so the sentence lighting upon one, the example may reach to all. But if the Contempt be not punishable by Law, or being so, the Parson think it in his discretion either unfit, or bootelesse to contend, then when any despises him, he takes it either in an humble way, saying nothing at all; or else in a slighting way, shewing that reproaches touch him no more, then a stone thrown against heaven, where he is, and lives; or in a sad way, greived at his own, and others sins, which continually breake Gods Laws, and dishonour him with those mouths, which he continually fils, and feeds: or else in a doctrinall way, saying to the contemner, Alas, why do you thus? you hurt your selfe, not me; he that throws a stone at another, hits himselfe; and so between gentle reasoning, and pitying, he overcomes the evill: or lastly, in a Triumphant way, being glad, and joyfull, that hee is made conformable to his Master; and being in the world as he was, hath this undoubted pledge of his salvation. These are the five shields, wherewith the Godly receive the darts of the wicked; leaving anger, and retorting, and revenge to the children of the world, whom anothers ill mastereth, and leadeth captive without any resistance, even in resistance, to the same destruction. For while they resist the person that reviles, they resist not the evill which takes hold of them, and is farr the worse enemy.

CHAP. XXIX.

The Parson with his Church-Wardens.

THe Countrey Parson doth often, both publickly, and privately instruct his Church-Wardens, what a great Charge lyes upon them, and that indeed the whole order and discipline of the Parish is put into their hands. If himselfe reforme any thing, it is out of the overflowing of his Conscience, whereas they are to do it by Command, and by Oath. Neither hath the place its dignity from the Ecclesiasticall Laws only, since even by the Common Statute-Law they are

4 descretion *52* 30–1 Conscienee *52*

taken for a kinde of Corporation, as being persons enabled by that Name to take moveable goods, or chattels, and to sue, and to be sued at the Law concerning such goods for the use and profit of their Parish: and by the same Law they are to levy penalties for negligence in resorting to church, or for disorderly carriage in time of divine service. Wherefore the Parson suffers not the place to be vilified or debased, by being cast on the lower ranke of people; but invites and urges the best unto it, shewing that they do not loose, or go lesse, but gaine by it; it being the greatest honor of this world, to do God and his chosen service; or as *David* says, to be even a door-keeper in the house of God. Now the Canons being the Church-wardens rule, the Parson adviseth them to read, or hear them read often, as also the visitation Articles, which are grounded upon the Canons, that so they may know their duty, and keep their oath the better; in which regard, considering the great Consequence of their place, and more of their oath, he wisheth them by no means to spare any, though never so great; but if after gentle, and neighbourly admonitions they still persist in ill, to present them; yea though they be tenants, or otherwise ingaged to the delinquent: for their obligation to God, and their own soul, is above any temporall tye. Do well, and right, and let the world sinke.

CHAP. XXX.

The Parson's Consideration of Providence.

THe Countrey Parson considering the great aptnesse Countrey people have to think that all things come by a kind of naturall course; and that if they sow and soyle their grounds, they must have corn; if they keep and fodder well their cattel, they must have milk, and Calves; labours to reduce them to see Gods hand in all things, and to beleeve, that things are not set in such an inevitable order, but that God often changeth it according as he sees fit, either for reward or punishment. To this end he represents to his flock, that God hath and exerciseth a threefold power in

9 loose] lose *75* 23 well, and right *Errata 52*: well, right, and right *text 52*

every thing which concernes man. The first is a sustaining power; the second a governing power; the third a spirituall power. By his sustaining power he preserves and actuates every thing in his being; so that corne doth not grow by any other vertue, then by that which he continually supplyes, as the corn needs it; without which supply the corne would instantly dry up, as a river would if the fountain were stopped. And it is observable, that if anything could presume of an inevitable course, and constancy in its operations, certainly it should be either the sun in heaven, or the fire on earth, by reason of their fierce, strong, and violent natures: yet when God pleased, the sun stood stil, the fire burned not. By Gods governing power he preserves and orders the references of things one to the other, so that though the corn do grow, and be preserved in that act by his sustaining power, yet if he suite not other things to the growth, as seasons, and weather, and other accidents by his governing power, the fairest harvests come to nothing. And it is observeable, that God delights to have men feel, and acknowledg, and reverence his power, and therefore he often overturnes things, when they are thought past danger; that is his time of interposing: As when a Merchant hath a ship come home after many a storme, which it hath escaped, he destroyes it sometimes in the very Haven; or if the goods be housed, a fire hath broken forth, and suddenly consumed them. Now this he doth, that men should perpetuate, and not break off their acts of dependance, how faire soever the opportunities present themselves. So that if a farmer should depend upon God all the yeer, and being ready to put hand to sickle, shall then secure himself, and think all cock-sure; then God sends such weather, as lays the corn, and destroys it: or if he depend on God further, even till he imbarn his corn, and then think all sure; God sends a fire, and consumes all that he hath: For that he ought not to break off, but to continue his dependance on God, not onely before the corne is inned, but after also; and indeed, to depend, and fear continually. The third power is spirituall, by which God turnes all outward blessings to inward advantages. So that if a Farmer hath both a faire

9 its *75*: their *52 71* 11 stong *52*

harvest, and that also well inned, and imbarned, and continuing safe there; yet if God give him not the Grace to use, and utter this well, all his advantages are to his losse. Better were his corne burnt, then not spiritually improved. And it is observable in this, how Gods goodnesse strives with mans refractorinesse; Man would sit down at this world, God bids him sell it, and purchase a better: Just as a Father, who hath in his hand an apple, and a piece of Gold under it; the Child comes, and with pulling, gets the apple out of his Fathers hand: his Father bids him throw it away, and he will give him the gold for it, which the Child utterly refusing, eats it, and is troubled with wormes: So is the carnall and wilfull man with the worm of the grave in this world, and the worm of Conscience in the next.

Chap. XXXI.

The Parson in Liberty.

THe Countrey Parson observing the manifold wiles of Satan (who playes his part sometimes in drawing Gods Servants from him, sometimes in perplexing them in the service of God) stands fast in the Liberty wherewith Christ hath made us free. This Liberty hc compasseth by one distinction, and that is, of what is Necessary, and what is Additionary. As for example: It is necessary, that all Christians should pray twice a day, every day of the week, and four times on Sunday, if they be well. This is so necessary, and essentiall to a Christian, that he cannot without this maintain himself in a Christian state. Besides this, the Godly have ever added some houres of prayer, as at nine, or at three, or at midnight, or as they think fit, & see cause, or rather as Gods spirit leads them. But these prayers are not necessary, but additionary. Now it so happens, that the godly petitioner upon some emergent interruption in the day, or by oversleeping himself at night, omits his additionary prayer. Upon this his mind begins to be perplexed, and troubled, and Satan, who knows the exigent, blows the fire, endeavouring to disorder the Christian, and put him out of his station, and to inlarge the perplexity, untill it spread, and taint his other duties of piety, which none can perform so wel in trouble, as in calmness. Here the Parson interposeth with his distinction, and shews the perplexed Christian, that this prayer being additionary, not necessary; taken in, not commanded, the omission thereof upon just occasion ought by no means to trouble him. God knows the occasion as wel as he, and He is as a gracious Father, who more accepts a common course of devotion, then dislikes an occasionall interruption. And of this he is so to assure himself, as to admit no scruple, but to go on as cheerfully, as if he had not been interrupted. By this it is evident, that the distinction is of singular use and comfort, especially to pious minds, which are ever tender, and delicate. But here there are two Cautions to be added. First, that this interruption proceed not out of slacknes, or coldness, which will appear if the Pious soul foresee and prevent such interruptions, what he may, before they come, and when for all that they do come, he be a little affected therewith, but not afflicted, or troubled; if he resent it to a mislike, but not a griefe. Secondly, that this interruption proceede not out of shame. As for example: A godly man, not out of superstition, but of reverence to Gods house, resolves whenever he enters into a Church, to kneel down, and pray, either blessing God, that he will be pleased to dwell among men; or beseeching him, that whenever he repaires to his house, he may behave himself so as befits so great a presence; and this briefly. But it happens, that neer the place where he is to pray, he spyes some scoffing ruffian, who is likely to deride him for his paines: if he now, shall either for fear or shame, break his custome, he shall do passing ill: so much the rather ought he to proceed, as that by this he may take into his Prayer humiliation also. On the other side, if I am to visit the sick in haste, and my neerest way ly through the Church, I will not doubt to go without staying to pray there (but onely, as I passe, in my heart) because this kinde of Prayer is additionary, not necessary, and the other duty overweighs it: So that if any scruple arise, I will throw it away, and be most confident, that God

7 to trouble *71* : trouble *52*   19 trouled *52*

is not displeased. This distinction may runne through all Christian duties, and it is a great stay and setling to religious souls.

Chap. XXXII.

The Parson's Surveys.

THe Countrey Parson hath not onely taken a particular Survey of the faults of his own Parish, but a generall also of the diseases of the time, that so, when his occasions carry him abroad, or bring strangers to him, he may be the better armed to encounter them. The great and nationall sin of this Land he esteems to be Idlenesse; great in it selfe, and great in Consequence: For when men have nothing to do, then they fall to drink, to steal, to whore, to scoffe, to revile, to all sorts of gamings. Come, say they, we have nothing to do, lets go to the Tavern, or to the stews, or what not. Wherefore the Parson strongly opposeth this sin, whersoever he goes. And because Idleness is twofold, the one in having no calling, the other in walking carelesly in our calling, he first represents to every body the necessity of a vocation. The reason of this assertion is taken from the nature of man, wherein God hath placed two great Instruments, Reason in the soul, and a hand in the Body, as ingagements of working: So that even in Paradise man had a calling, and how much more out of Paradise, when the evills which he is now subject unto, may be prevented, or diverted by reasonable imployment. Besides, every gift or ability is a talent to be accounted for, and to be improved to our Masters Advantage. Yet is it also a debt to our Countrey to have a Calling, and it concernes the Common-wealth, that none should be idle, but all busied. Lastly, riches are the blessing of God, and the great Instrument of doing admirable good; therfore all are to procure them honestly, and seasonably, when they are not better imployed. Now this reason crosseth not our Saviours precept of selling what we have, because when we have sold all, and given it to the poor, we must not

5 Survey *Errata 52* : Servey *text 52*   6 so, *71* : so *52*   13–14 what not.] what not? *71*   26 is it] it is *71* : *75 italicizes* it is also . . . a Calling

be idle, but labour to get more, that we may give more, according to St. *Pauls* rule, *Ephes.* 4. 28. 1 *Thes.* 4. 11, 12. So that our Saviours selling is so far from crossing Saint *Pauls* working, that it rather establisheth it, since they that have nothing, are fittest to work. Now because the onely opposer to this Doctrine is the Gallant, who is witty enough to abuse both others, and himself, and who is ready to ask, if he shall mend shoos, or what he shall do? Therfore the Parson unmoved, sheweth, that *ingenuous and fit* imployment is never wanting to those that seek it. But if it should be, the Assertion stands thus: All are either to have a Calling, or prepare for it: He that hath or can have yet no imployment, if he truly, and seriously prepare for it, he is safe and within bounds. Wherefore all are either presently to enter into a Calling, if they be fit for it, and it for them; or else to examine with care, and advice, what they are fittest for, and to prepare for that with all diligence. But it will not be amisse in this exceeding usefull point to descend to particulars: for exactnesse lyes in particulars. Men are either single, or marryed: The marryed and house-keeper hath his hands full, if he do what he ought to do. For there are two branches of his affaires; first, the improvement of his family, by bringing them up in the fear and nurture of the Lord; and secondly, the improvement of his grounds, by drowning, or draining, or stocking, or fencing, and ordering his land to the best advantage both of himself, and his neighbours. The *Italian* says, None fouls his hands in his own businesse: and it is an honest, and just care, so it exceed not bounds, for every one to imploy himselfe to the advancement of his affairs, that hee may have wherewithall to do good. But his family is his best care, to labour Christian soules, and raise them to their height, even to heaven; to dresse and prune them, and take as much joy in a straight-growing childe, or servant, as a Gardiner doth in a choice tree. Could men finde out this delight, they would seldome be from home; whereas now, of any place, they are least there. But if after all this care well dispatched, the house-keepers Family be so small, and his

3 So *catchword 52* : so *text 52*   4 establisheth] stablisheth *71*   11 eitheir *52*
25 or stocking *71* : stocking *52*   and ordering] or ordering *71*

dexterity so great, that he have leisure to look out, the Village or Parish which either he lives in, or is neer unto it, is his imployment. Hee considers every one there, and either helps them in particular, or hath generall Propositions to the whole Towne or Hamlet, of advancing the publick Stock, and managing Commons, or Woods, according as the place suggests. But if hee may bee of the Commission of Peace, there is nothing to that: No Common-wealth in the world hath a braver Institution then that of Justices of the Peace: For it is both a security to the King, who hath so many dispersed Officers at his beck throughout the Kingdome, accountable for the publick good; and also an honourable Imployment of a Gentle, or Noble-man in the Country he lives in, inabling him with power to do good, and to restrain all those, who else might both trouble him and the whole State. Wherefore it behoves all, who are come to the gravitie, and ripenesse of judgement for so excellent a Place, not to refuse, but rather to procure it. And whereas there are usually three Objections made against the Place; the one, the abuse of it, by taking petty Countrey bribes; the other, the casting of it on mean persons, especially in some Shires: and lastly, the trouble of it: These are so far from deterring any good man from the place, that they kindle them rather to redeem the Dignity either from true faults, or unjust aspersions. Now, for single men, they are either Heirs, or younger Brothers: The Heirs are to prepare in all the fore-mentioned points against the time of their practice. Therefore they are to mark their Fathers discretion in ordering his House and Affairs; and also elsewhere, when they see any remarkable point of Education or good husbandry, and to transplant it in time to his own home, with the same care as others, when they meet with good fruit, get a graffe of the tree, inriching their Orchard, and neglecting their House. Besides, they are to read Books of Law, and Justice; especially, the Statutes at large. As for better Books of Divinity, they are not in this Consideration, because we are about a Calling, and a preparation thereunto. But chiefly, and above all

9 braver] better *71* 20 petty Countrey bribes *71* : petty-Countrey-bribes *52* 32 graffe] graft *75*

things, they are to frequent Sessions and Sizes; for it is both an honor which they owe to the Reverend Judges and Magistrates, to attend them, at least in their Shire; and it is a great advantage to know the practice of the Land; for our Law is Practice. Sometimes he may go to Court, as the eminent place both of good and ill. At other times he is to travell over the King's Dominions, cutting out the Kingdome into Portions, which every yeer he surveys peece-meal. When there is a Parliament, he is to endeavour by all means to be a Knight or Burgess there; for there is no School to a Parliament. And when he is there, he must not only be a morning man, but at Committees also; for there the particulars are exactly discussed, which are brought from thence to the House but in generall. When none of these occasions call him abroad, every morning that hee is at home hee must either ride the Great Horse, or exercise some of his Military gestures. For all Gentlemen, that are now weakned, and disarmed with sedentary lives, are to know the use of their Arms: and as the Husbandman labours for them, so must they fight for, and defend them, when occasion calls. This is the duty of each to other, which they ought to fulfill: And the Parson is a lover of and exciter to justice in all things, even as *John the Baptist* squared out to every one (even to Souldiers) what to do. As for younger Brothers, those whom the Parson finds loose, and not ingaged into some Profession by their Parents, whose neglect in this point is intolerable, and a shamefull wrong both to the Common-wealth, and their own House: To them, after he hath shew'd the unlawfulness of spending the day in dressing, Complementing, visiting, and sporting, he first commends the study of the Civill Law, as a brave, and wise knowledg, the Professours whereof were much imployed by Queen *Elizabeth*, because it is the key of Commerce, and discovers the Rules of forraine Nations. Secondly, he commends the Mathematicks, as the only wonder-working knowledg, and therefore requiring the best spirits. After the severall knowledg of these, he adviseth to

1 Sizes] Assizes *75* 17 gestures] Postures *75* 17 now *71* : *now 75* : not *52 See note* 22 lover of *75* : lover *52 71* 28 shew'd *71* : shewd *52* 32 Qneen *52* 35 wonder-working *71* : wonder working *52*

insist and dwell chiefly on the two noble branches therof, of Fortification, and Navigation; The one being usefull to all Countreys, and the other especially to Ilands. But if the young Gallant think these Courses dull, and phlegmatick, where can he busie himself better, then in those new Plantations, and discoveryes, which are not only a noble, but also as they may be handled, a religious imployment? Or let him travel into *Germany*, and *France*, and observing the Artifices, and Manufactures there, transplant them hither, as divers have done lately, to our Countrey's advantage.

Chap. XXXIII.

The Parson's Library.

THe Countrey Parson's Library is a holy Life: for besides the blessing that that brings upon it, there being a promise, that if the Kingdome of God be first sought, all other things shall be added, even it selfe is a Sermon. For the temptations with which a good man is beset, and the ways which he used to overcome them, being told to another, whether in private conference, or in the Church, are a Sermon. Hee that hath considered how to carry himself at table about his appetite, if he tell this to another, preacheth; and much more feelingly, and judiciously, then he writes his rules of temperance out of bookes. So that the Parson having studied, and mastered all his lusts and affections within, and the whole Army of Temptations without, hath ever so many sermons ready penn'd, as he hath victories. And it fares in this as it doth in Physick: He that hath been sick of a Consumption, and knows what recovered him, is a Physitian so far as he meetes with the same disease, and temper; and can much better, and particularly do it, then he that is generally learned, and was never sick. And if the same person had been sick of all diseases, and were recovered of all by things that he knew; there were no such Physician as he, both for skill and tendernesse. Just so it is in Divinity, and that not without manifest reason: for though the temptations may be diverse in divers Christians, yet the victory is alike in all, being by the self-same Spirit. Neither is this true onely in the military state of a Christian life, but even in the peaceable also; when the servant of God, freed for a while from temptation, in a quiet sweetnesse seeks how to please his God. Thus the Parson considering that repentance is the great vertue of the Gospel, and one of the first steps of pleasing God, having for his owne use examined the nature of it, is able to explaine it after to others. And particularly, having doubted sometimes, whether his repentance were true, or at least in that degree it ought to be, since he found himselfe sometimes to weepe more for the losse of some temporall things, then for offending God, he came at length to this resolution, that repentance is an act of the mind, not of the Body, even as the Originall signifies; and that the chiefe thing, which God in Scriptures requires, is the heart, and the spirit, and to worship him in truth, and spirit. Wherefore in case a Christian endeavour to weep, and cannot, since we are not Masters of our bodies, this sufficeth. And consequently he found, that the essence of repentance, that it may be alike in all Gods children (which as concerning weeping it cannot be, some being of a more melting temper then others) consisteth in a true detestation of the soul, abhorring, and renouncing sin, and turning unto God in truth of heart, and newnesse of life: Which acts of repentance are and must be found in all Gods servants: Not that weeping is not usefull, where it can be, that so the body may joyn in the grief, as it did in the sin; but that, so the other acts be, that is not necessary: so that he as truly repents, who performes the other acts of repentance, when he cannot more, as he that weeps a floud of tears. This Instruction and comfort the Parson getting for himself, when he tels it to others, becomes a Sermon. The like he doth in other Christian vertues, as of Faith, and Love, and the Cases of Conscience belonging thereto, wherein (as Saint *Paul* implyes that he ought, *Romans* 2.) hee first preacheth to himselfe, and then to others.

5 from *52 75*: for *71* 34 Faith *71*: faith *52*

Chap. XXXIV.

The Parson's Dexterity in applying of Remedies.

THe Countrey Parson knows, that there is a double state of a Christian even in this Life, the one military, the other peaceable. The military is, when we are assaulted with temptations either from within or from without. The Peaceable is, when the Divell for a time leaves us, as he did our Saviour, and the Angels minister to us their owne food, even joy, and peace; and comfort in the holy Ghost. These two states were in our Saviour, not only in the beginning of his preaching, but afterwards also, as *Mat.* 22. 35. He was tempted: And *Luke* 10. 21. He rejoyced in Spirit: And they must be likewise in all that are his. Now the Parson having a Spirituall Judgement, according as he discovers any of his Flock to be in one or the other state, so he applies himselfe to them. Those that he findes in the peaceable state, he adviseth to be very vigilant, and not to let go the raines as soon as the horse goes easie. Particularly, he counselleth them to two things: First, to take heed, lest their quiet betray them (as it is apt to do) to a coldnesse, and carelesnesse in their devotions, but to labour still to be as fervent in Christian Duties, as they remember themselves were, when affliction did blow the Coals. Secondly, not to take the full compasse, and liberty of their Peace: not to eate of all those dishes at table, which even their present health otherwise admits; nor to store their house with all those furnitures which even their present plenty of wealth otherwise admits; nor when they are among them that are merry, to extend themselves to all that mirth, which the present occasion of wit and company otherwise admits; but to put bounds, and hoopes to their joyes: so will they last the longer, and when they depart, returne the sooner. If we would judg ourselves, we should not be judged; and if we would bound our selves, we should not be bounded. But if they shall fear, that at such, or such a time their peace and mirth have carryed them further then this moderation, then to take *Jobs* admir-

11 that are] that is *71* : that be *75* 13 or] and *71* 28 wit *71* : wit, *52*

able Course, who sacrificed lest his Children should have transgressed in their mirth: So let them go, and find some poore afflicted soul, and there be bountifull, and liberall; for with such sacrifices God is well pleased. Those that the Parson findes in the military state, he fortifyes, and strengthens with his utmost skill. Now in those that are tempted, whatsoever is unruly, falls upon two heads; either they think, that there is none that can or will look after things, but all goes by chance, or wit: Or else, though there be a great Governour of all things, yet to them he is lost, as if they said, God doth forsake and persecute them, and there is none to deliver them. If the Parson suspect the first, and find sparkes of such thoughts now and then to break forth, then without opposing directly (for disputation is no Cure for Atheisme) he scatters in his discourse three sorts of arguments; the first taken from Nature, the second from the Law, the third from Grace.

For Nature, he sees not how a house could be either built without a builder, or kept in repaire without a house-keeper. He conceives not possibly, how the windes should blow so much as they can, and the sea rage so much as it can, and all things do what they can, and all, not only without dissolution of the whole, but also of any part, by taking away so much as the usuall seasons of summer and winter, earing and harvest. Let the weather be what it will, still we have bread, though sometimes more, somtimes lesse; wherewith also a carefull *Joseph* might meet. He conceives not possibly, how he that would beleeve a Divinity, if he had been at the Creation of all things, should lesse beleeve it, seeing the Preservation of all things; For Preservation is a Creation; and more, it is a continued Creation, and a creation every moment.

Secondly, for the Law, there may be so evident, though unused a proof of Divinity taken from thence, that the Atheist, or Epicurian can have nothing to contradict. The Jewes yet live, and are known: they have their Law and Language bearing witnesse to them, and they to it: they are

11–12 God doth . . . deliver them. *ital. 75* 18 For Nature *new par. Ed*: *75 begins new par. at l. 16* The first 21 rage so *71* : rage as *52* 32 Secondly *new par. 75*

Circumcised to this day, and expect the promises of the Scripture; their Countrey also is known, the places, and rivers travelled unto, and frequented by others, but to them an unpenetrable rock, an unaccessible desert. Wherefore if the Jewes live, all the great wonders of old live in them, and then who can deny the stretched out arme of a mighty God? especially since it may be a just doubt, whether, considering the stubbornnesse of the Nation, their living then in their Countrey under so many miracles were a stranger thing, then their present exile, and disability to live in their Countrey. And it is observable, that this very thing was intended by God, that the Jewes should be his proof, and witnesses, as he calls them, *Isaiah* 43. 12. And their very dispersion in all Lands, was intended not only for a punishment to them; but for an exciting of others by their sight, to the acknowledging of God, and his power, *Psalm* 59. 11. And therefore this kind of Punishment was chosen rather then any other.

Thirdly, for Grace. Besides the continuall succession (since the Gospell) of holy men, who have born witness to the truth, (there being no reason, why any should distrust Saint *Luke*, or *Tertullian*, or *Chrysostome*, more then *Tully*, *Virgill*, or *Livy*;) There are two Prophesies in the Gospel, which evidently argue Christs Divinity by their success: the one concerning the woman that spent the oyntment on our Saviour, for which he told, that it should never be forgotten, but with the Gospel it selfe be preached to all ages, *Matth.* 26. 13. The other concerning the destruction of *Jerusalem*; of which our Saviour said, that that generation should not passe, till all were fulfilled, *Luke* 21. 32. Which *Josephus's* History confirmeth, and the continuance of which verdict is yet evident. To these might be added the Preaching of the Gospel in all Nations, *Matthew* 24. 14. which we see even miraculously effected in these new discoveryes, God turning mens Covetousnesse, and Ambitions to the effecting of his word. Now a prophesie is a wonder sent to Posterity, least they complaine of want of wonders. It is a letter sealed, and sent, which to the bearer is but paper, but to the receiver, and opener, is full of power. Hee that saw Christ open a

18 Thirdly *new par. 75*   29–30 *Josephus*'s Historie *75* : *Josephus* his story *52 71*

blind mans eyes, saw not more Divinity, then he that reads the womans oyntment in the Gospell, or sees *Jerusalem* destroyed. With some of these heads enlarged, and woven into his discourse, at severall times and occasions, the Parson setleth wavering minds. But if he sees them neerer desperation, then Atheisme; not so much doubting a God, as that he is theirs; then he dives unto the boundlesse Ocean of Gods Love, and the unspeakeable riches of his loving kindnesse. He hath one argument unanswerable. If God hate them, either he doth it as they are Creatures, dust and ashes; or as they are sinfull. As Creatures, he must needs love them; for no perfect Artist ever yet hated his owne worke. As sinfull, he must much more love them; because notwithstanding his infinite hate of sinne, his Love overcame that hate; and with an exceeding great victory, which in the Creation needed not, gave them love for love, even the son of his love out of his bosome of love. So that man, which way soever he turnes, hath two pledges of Gods Love, that in the mouth of two or three witnesses every word may be established; the one in his being, the other in his sinfull being: and this as the more faulty in him, so the more glorious in God. And all may certainly conclude, that God loves them, till either they despise that Love, or despaire of his Mercy: not any sin else, but is within his Love; but the despising of Love must needs be without it. The thrusting away of his arme makes us onely not embraced.

CHAP. XXXV.

The Parson's Condescending.

THe Countrey Parson is a Lover of old Customes, if they be good, and harmlesse; and the rather, because Countrey people are much addicted to them, so that to favour them therein is to win their hearts, and to oppose them therin is to deject them. If there be any ill in the custome, that may be severed from the good, he pares the

5–6 desperation, then Atheism; *71*: desperation; then Atheisme, *52*   15 and with] & that with *75*   victory, *Ed*: victory; *52*

apple, and gives them the clean to feed on. Particularly, he loves Procession, and maintains it, because there are contained therein 4 manifest advantages. First, a blessing of God for the fruits of the field: Secondly, justice in the Preservation of bounds: Thirdly, Charity in loving walking, and neighbourly accompanying one another, with reconciling of differences at that time, if there be any: Fourthly, Mercy in releeving the poor by a liberall distribution and largesse, which at that time is, or ought to be used. Wherefore he exacts of all to bee present at the perambulation, and those that withdraw, and sever themselves from it, he mislikes, and reproves as uncharitable, and unneighbourly; and if they will not reforme, presents them. Nay, he is so farre from condemning such assemblies, that he rather procures them to be often, as knowing that absence breedes strangeness, but presence love. Now Love is his business, and aime; wherefore he likes well, that his Parish at good times invite one another to their houses, and he urgeth them to it: and somtimes, where he knowes there hath been or is a little difference, hee takes one of the parties, and goes with him to the other, and all dine or sup together. There is much preaching in this friendliness. Another old Custome there is of saying, when light is brought in, God send us the light of heaven; And the Parson likes this very well; neither is he affraid of praising, or praying to God at all times, but is rather glad of catching opportunities to do them. Light is a great Blessing, and as great as food, for which we give thanks: and those that thinke this superstitious, neither know superstition, nor themselves. As for those that are ashamed to use this forme, as being old, and obsolete, and not the fashion, he reformes, and teaches them, that at Baptisme they professed not to be ashamed of Christs Cross, or for any shame to leave that which is good. He that is ashamed in small things, will extend his pusillanimity to greater. Rather should a Christian Souldier take such occasions to harden himselfe, and to further his exercises of Mortification.

Chap. XXXVI.

The Parson Blessing.

THe Countrey Parson wonders, that Blessing the people is in so little use with his brethren: whereas he thinks it not onely a grave, and reverend thing, but a beneficial also. Those who use it not, do so either out of niceness, because they like the salutations, and complements, and formes of worldly language better; which conformity and fashionableness is so exceeding unbefitting a Minister, that it deserves reproof, not refutation: Or else, because they think it empty and superfluous. But that which the Apostles used so diligently in their writings, nay, which our Saviour himselfe used, *Marke* 10. 16, cannot bee vain and superfluous. But this was not proper to Christ, or the Apostles only, no more then to be a spirituall Father was appropriated to them. And if temporall Fathers blesse their children, how much more may, and ought Spirituall Fathers? Besides, the Priests of the Old Testament were commanded to Blesse the people, and the forme thereof is prescribed, *Numb.* 6. Now as the Apostle argues in another case; if the Ministration of condemnation did bless, how shall not the ministration of the spirit exceed in blessing? The fruit of this blessing good *Hannah* found, and received with great joy, 1 *Sam.* 1. 18. though it came from a man disallowed by God: for it was not the person, but Priesthood, that blessed; so that even ill Priests may blesse. Neither have the Ministers power of Blessing only, but also of cursing. So in the Old Testament *Elisha* cursed the children, 2 *Kin.* 2. 24. which though our Saviour reproved as unfitting for his particular, who was to shew all humility before his Passion, yet he allows in his Apostles. And therfore St. *Peter* used that fearfull imprecation to *Simon Magus*, *Act.* 8. *Thy mony perish with thee*: and the event confirmed it. So did St. *Paul*, 2 *Tim.* 4.14. and 1 *Tim.* 1. 20. Speaking of *Alexander* the Coppersmith, who had withstood his preaching, *The Lord* (saith he) *reward him according to his works.* And again, of *Hymeneus* and

16 *and* 25 Old 75: old 52 71 28 allows in] allows it in 71

Alexander, he saith, he had *delivered them to Satan*, *that they might learn not to Blaspheme*. The formes both of Blessing, & cursing are expounded in the Common-Prayer-book: the one in, The Grace of our Lord Jesus Christ, &c. and: The Peace of God, &c. The other in generall, in the Commination. Now blessing differs from prayer, in assurance, because it is not performed by way of request, but of confidence, and power, effectually applying Gods favour to the blessed, by the interesting of that dignity wherewith God hath invested the Priest, and ingaging of Gods own power and institution for a blessing. The neglect of this duty in Ministers themselves, hath made the people also neglect it; so that they are so far from craving this benefit from their ghostly Father, that they oftentimes goe out of church, before he hath blessed them. In the time of Popery, the Priests *Benedicite*, and his holy water were over highly valued; and now we are fallen to the clean contrary, even from superstition to coldnes, and Atheism. But the Parson first values the gift in himself, and then teacheth his parish to value it. And it is observable, that if a Minister talke with a great man in the ordinary course of complementing language, he shall be esteemed as ordinary complementers; but if he often interpose a Blessing, when the other gives him just opportunity, by speaking any good, this unusuall form begets a reverence, and makes him esteemed according to his Profession. The same is to be observed in writing Letters also. To conclude, if all men are to blesse upon occasion, as appears *Rom.* 12. 14. how much more those, who are spiritual Fathers?

CHAP. XXXVII.

Concerning detraction.

THE Countrey Parson perceiving, that most, when they are at leasure, make others faults their entertainment and discourse, and that even some good men think, so they speak truth, they may disclose anothers fault, finds it somwhat difficult how to proceed in this point. For if he absolutely shut up mens mouths, and forbid all disclosing of faults, many an evill may not only be, but also spread in his Parish, without any remedy (which cannot be applyed without notice) to the dishonor of God, and the infection of his flock, and the discomfort, discredit, & hinderance of the Pastor. On the other side, if it be unlawful to open faults, no benefit or advantage can make it lawfull: for we must not do evill, that good may come of it. Now the Parson taking this point to task, which is so exceeding useful, and hath taken so deep roote, that it seems the very life and substance of Conversation, hath proceeded thus far in the discussing of it. Faults are either notorious, or private. Again notorious faults are either such as are made known by common fame (and of these, those that know them, may talk, so they do it not with sport, but commiseration;) or else such as have passed judgment, & been corrected either by whipping, or imprisoning, or the like. Of these also men may talk, and more, they may discover them to those that know them not: because infamy is a part of the sentence against malefactours, which the Law intends, as is evident by those, which are branded for rogues, that they may be known; or put into the stocks, that they may be looked upon. But some may say, though the Law allow this, the Gospel doth not, which hath so much advanced Charity, and ranked backbiters among the generation of the wicked, *Rom.* 1. 30. But this is easily answered: As the executioner is not uncharitable, that takes away the life of the condemned, except besides his office, he add a tincture of private malice in the joy, and hast of acting his part; so neither is he that defames him, whom the Law would have defamed, except he also do it out of rancour. For in infamy, all are executioners, and the Law gives a malefactour to all to be defamed. And as malefactors may lose & forfeit their goods, or life; so may they their good name, and the possession thereof, which before their offence and Judgment they had in all mens brests: for all are honest, till the contrary be proved. Besides, it concerns the Common-Wealth, that Rogues should be known, and Charity to the publick hath the precedence of private charity. So that it is so far from being a fault to discover such offenders, that

4 dicredit *52*   33 offence, *52*   36 known, and *71*: kn ownand *52*

it is a duty rather, which may do much good, and save much harme. Neverthelesse, if the punished delinquent shall be much troubled for his sins, and turne quite another man, doubtlesse then also mens affections and words must turne, and forbear to speak of that, which even God himself hath forgotten.

The Authour's Prayer before Sermon.

O Almighty and ever-living Lord God! Majesty, and Power, and Brightnesse, and Glory! How shall we dare to appear before thy face, who are contrary to thee, in all we call thee? for we are darknesse, and weaknesse, and filthinesse, and shame. Misery and sin fill our days: yet art thou our Creatour, and we thy work: Thy hands both made us, and also made us Lords of all thy creatures; giving us one world in our selves, and another to serve us: then did'st thou place us in Paradise, and wert proceeding still on in thy Favours, untill we interrupted thy Counsels, disappointed thy Purposes, and sold our God, our glorious, our gracious God for an apple. O write it! O brand it in our foreheads for ever: for an apple once we lost our God, and still lose him for no more; for money, for meat, for diet: But thou Lord, art patience, and pity, and sweetnesse, and love; therefore we sons of men are not consumed. Thou hast exalted thy mercy above all things; and hast made our salvation, not our punishment, thy glory: so that then where sin abounded, not death, but grace superabounded; accordingly, when we had sinned beyond any help in heaven or earth, then thou saidest, Lo, I come! then did the Lord of life, unable of himselfe to die, contrive to do it. He took flesh, he wept, he died; for his enemies he died; even for those that derided him then, and still despise him. Blessed Saviour! many waters could not quench thy love! nor no pit overwhelme it. But though the streams of thy bloud were currant through darknesse, grave, and hell; yet by these thy conflicts, and

Prayers. *From* Herbert's Remains (1652). *There printed in italic, with the following words in roman*—wert (16), seemingly (2. 289), Our Father (36. 289), reach (11. 290) *See note* Prayers *not included in* 71 75

seemingly hazards, didst thou arise triumphant, and therein mad'st us victorious.

Neither doth thy love yet stay here! for, this word of thy rich peace, and reconciliation, thou hast committed, not to Thunder, or Angels, but to silly and sinfull men: even to me, pardoning my sins, and bidding me go feed the people of thy love.

Blessed be the God of Heaven and Earth! who onely doth wondrous things. Awake therefore, my Lute, and my Viol! awake all my powers to glorifie thee! We praise thee! we blesse thee! we magnifie thee for ever! And now, O Lord! in the power of thy Victories, and in the wayes of thy Ordinances, and in the truth of thy Love, Lo, we stand here, beseeching thee to blesse thy word, wher-ever spoken this day throughout the universall Church. O make it a word of power and peace, to convert those who are not yet thine, and to confirme those that are: particularly, blesse it in this thy own Kingdom, which thou hast made a Land of light, a store-house of thy treasures and mercies: O let not our foolish and unworthy hearts rob us of the continuance of this thy sweet love: but pardon our sins, and perfect what thou hast begun. Ride on Lord, because of the word of truth, and meeknesse, and righteousnesse; and thy right hand shall teach thee terrible things. Especially, blesse this portion here assembled together, with thy unworthy Servant speaking unto them: Lord Jesu! teach thou me, that I may teach them: Sanctifie, and inable all my powers, that in their full strength they may deliver thy message reverently, readily, faithfully, & fruitfully. O make thy word a swift word, passing from the ear to the heart, from the heart to the life and conversation: that as the rain returns not empty, so neither may thy word, but accomplish that for which it is given. O Lord hear, O Lord forgive! O Lord, hearken, and do so for thy blessed Son's sake, in whose sweet and pleasing words, we say, *Our Father*, &c.

A Prayer after Sermon.

BLessed be God! and the Father of all mercy! who continueth to pour his benefits upon us. Thou hast elected us, thou hast called us, thou hast justified us, sanctified, and glorified us: Thou wast born for us, and thou livedst and diedst for us: Thou hast given us the blessings of this life, and of a better. O Lord! thy blessings hang in clusters, they come trooping upon us! they break forth like mighty waters on every side. And now Lord, thou hast fed us with the bread of life: so man did eat Angels food: O Lord, blesse it: O Lord, make it health and strength unto us; still striving & prospering so long within us, untill our obedience reach the measure of thy love, who hast done for us as much as may be. Grant this dear Father, for thy Son's sake, our only Saviour: To whom with thee, and the Holy Ghost, three Persons, but one most glorious, incomprehensible God, be ascribed all Honour, and Glory, and Praise, ever. Amen.

9 Angel's *52* : Angels *Ed* (*plural*: *cf.* 'The Sacrifice', *l.* 239, *and* Ps. lxxviii. 25) besse 11–12 thy measure

A TREATISE OF TEMPERANCE AND SOBRIETIE:

Written by *Lud. Cornarus*,

Translated into English by Mr. *George Herbert.*

HAving observed in my time many of my friends, of excellent wit and noble disposition, overthrown and undone by Intemperance; who, if they had lived, would have been an ornament to the world, and a comfort to their friends: I thought fit to discover in a short Treatise, that Intemperance was not such an evil, but it might easily be remedied; which I undertake the more willingly, because divers worthy young men have obliged me unto it. For when they saw their parents and kindred snatcht away in the midst of their dayes, and me contrariwise, at the age of eightie and one, strong and lustie; they had a great desire to know the way of my life, and how I came to be so. Wherefore, that I may satisfie their honest desire, and withall help many others, who will take this into consideration, I will declare the causes which moved me to forsake Intemperance, and live a sober life, expressing also the means which I have used therein. I say therefore, that the infirmities, which did not onely begin, but had already gone farre in me, first caused me to leave Intemperance, to which I was much addicted: For by it, and my ill constitution, (having a most cold & moist stomack) I fell into divers diseases, to wit, into the pain of the stomack, and often of the side, and the beginning of the Gout, with almost a continuall fever and thirst.

From this ill temper there remained little else to be expected of me, then that after many troubles and griefs I should quickly come to an end; whereas my life seemed as farre from it by Nature, as it was neare it by Intemperance.

From Hygiasticon : Or, The right course of preserving Life and Health unto extream old Age. Written in Latine by Leonard Lessius, And now done into English. Cambridge, Printed by R. Daniel. 1634. (*Bodleian copy*, Douce L 2) (*cited as 34*): 2nd edn 1634 (*34^2*): 3rd, 1636 (*36*). *Reprinted as* 'The Temperate Man', 1678 (*78*) (*copy in Pemb. Coll. Cam. Library*). 7 remedied; *34^2*: remedied: *34*

When therefore I was thus affected from the thirtie fifth yeare of my age to the fortieth, having tried all remedies fruitlesly, the Physicians told me that yet there was one help for me, if I could constantly pursue it, to wit, *A sober and orderly life*: for this had every way great force for the recovering and preserving of Health, as a disorderly life to the overthrowing of it; as I too wel by experience found. For Temperance preserves even old men and sickly men sound: But Intemperance destroyes most healthy and flourishing constitutions: For contrarie causes have contrarie effects, and the faults of Nature are often amended by Art, as barren grounds are made fruitfull by good husbandry. They added withall, that unlesse I speedily used that remedy, within a few moneths I should be driven to that exigent, that there would be no help for me, but Death, shortly to be expected.

Upon this, weighing their reasons with my self, and abhorring from so sudden an end, and finding my self continually oppressed with pain and sicknesse, I grew fully perswaded, that all my griefs arose out of Intemperance: and therefore out of an hope of avoiding death and pain, I resolved to live a temperate life.

Whereupon, being directed by them in the way I ought to hold, I understood, that the food I was to use, was such as belonged to sickly constitutions, and that in a small quantitie. This they had told me before: But I, then not liking that kinde of Diet, followed my Appetite, and did eat meats pleasing to my taste; and, when I felt inward heats, drank delightfull wines, and that in great quantitie, telling my Physicians nothing thereof, as is the custome of sick people. But after I had resolved to follow Temperance and Reason, and saw that it was no hard thing to do so, but the proper duty of man; I so addicted my self to this course of life, that I never went a foot out of the way. Upon this, I found within a few dayes, that I was exceedingly helped, and by continuance thereof, within lesse then one yeare (although it may seem to some incredible) I was perfectly cured of all my infirmities.

1 affected] afflicted *Palmer*

Being now sound and well, I began to consider the force of Temperance, and to think thus with my self: If *Temperance* had so much power as to bring me health; how much more to preserve it! Wherefore I began to search out most diligently what meats were agreeable unto me, and what disagreeable: And I purposed to try, whether those that pleased my taste brought me commoditie or discommoditie; and whether that Proverb, wherewith Gluttons use to defend themselves, to wit, *That which savours, is good and nourisheth*, be consonant to truth. This upon triall I found most false: for strong and very cool wines pleased my taste best, as also melons, and other fruit; in like manner, raw lettice, fish, pork, sausages, pulse, and cake, and py-crust, and the like: and yet all these I found hurtfull.

Therefore trusting on experience, I forsook all these kinde of meats and drinks, and chose that wine that fitted my stomack, and in such measure, as easily might be digested: Above all, taking care never to rise with a full stomack, but so as I might well both eat and drink more. By this means, within lesse then a yeare I was not onely freed from all those evils which had so long beset me, and were almost become incurable; but also afterwards I fell not into that yearely disease, whereinto I was wont, when I pleased my Sense & Appetite. Which benefits also still continue, because from the time that I was made whole, I never since departed from my setled course of *Sobrietie*, whose admirable power causeth that the meat and drink that is taken in fit measure, gives true strength to the bodie, all superfluities passing away without difficultie, and no ill humours being ingendred in the body.

Yet with this diet I avoided other hurtfull things also, as too much heat and cold, wearinesse, watching, ill aire, overmuch use of the benefit of marriage. For although the power of health consists most in the proportion of meat and drink. yet these forenamed things have also their force. I preserved me also, asmuch as I could, from hatred and melancholie, and other perturbations of the minde, which have a great power over our constitutions. Yet could I not so avoid all these, but that now and then I fell into them; which gained

38 them; *34*[2]: them, *34*

me this experience, that I perceived, that they had no great power to hurt those bodies, which were kept in good order by a moderate Diet: So that I can truly say, That they who in these two things that enter in at the mouth, keep a fit proportion, shall receive little hurt from other excesses.

This *Galen* confirms, when he sayes, that immoderate heats and colds, and windes and labours did little hurt him, because in his meats and drinks he kept a due moderation; and therefore never was sick by any of these inconveniences, except it were for one onely day. But mine own experience confirmeth this more; as all that know me, can testifie: For having endured many heats & colds, and other like discommodities of the bodie, and troubles of the minde, all these did hurt me little, whereas they hurt them very much who live intemperately. For when my brother and others of my kindred saw some great powerfull men pick quarrels against me, fearing lest I should be overthrown, they were possessed with a deep Melancholie (a thing usuall to disorderly lives) which increased so much in them, that it brought them to a sudden end. But I, whom that matter ought to have affected most, received no inconvenience thereby, because that humour abounded not in me.

Nay, I began to perswade my self, that this suit and contention was raised by the Divine Providence, that I might know what great power a sober and temperate life hath over our bodies and mindes, and that at length I should be a conquerour, as also a little after it came to passe: For in the end I got the victorie, to my great honour, and no lesse profit: whereupon also I joyed exceedingly; which excesse of joy neither could do me any hurt. By which it is manifest, That neither melancholie, nor any other passion can hurt a temperate life.

Moreover I say, that even bruises and squats, and falls, which often kill others, can bring little grief or hurt to those that are temperate. This I found by experience, when I was seventie yeares old: for riding in a coach in great haste, it happened that the coach was overturned, and then was dragged for a good space by the furie of the horses, whereby my head and whole bodie was sore hurt, and also one of my arms and legges put out of joynt. Being carried home, when the Physicians saw in what case I was, they concluded that I would die within three dayes. Neverthelesse at a venture two remedies might be used, letting of bloud, and purging, that the store of humours, and inflammation, and fever (which was certainly expected) might be hindred.

But I, considering what an orderly life I had led for many yeares together, which must needs so temper the humours of the bodie, that they could not be much troubled, or make a great concourse, refused both remedies, and onely commanded that my arm and legge should be set, and my whole bodie anointed with oyl: and so without other remedie or inconvenience I recovered; which seemed as a miracle to the Physicians. Whence I conclude, That they that live a temperate life, can receive little hurt from other inconveniences.

But my experience taught me another thing also, to wit, That an orderly and regular life can hardly be altered without exceeding great danger.

About foure yeares since, I was led by the advice of Physicians, and the dayly importunitie of my friends, to adde something to my usuall stint and measure. Divers reasons they brought, as, that old age could not be sustained with so little meat and drink; which yet needs not onely to be sustained, but also to gather strength, which could not be but by meat & drink. On the other side I argued, that Nature was contented with a little, and that I had for many yeares continued in good health, with that little measure; that Custome was turned into Nature, and therefore it was agreeable to reason, that my yeares increasing, and strength decreasing, my stint of meat and drink should be diminished, rather then increased; that the patient might be proportionable to the agent, and especially since the power of my stomack every day decreased. To this agreed two Italian Proverbs, the one whereof was, *He that will eat much, let him eat little**; because by eating little he prolongs his life. The

10 concourse *34*^{2} : concurse *34* 19 advice *34*^{2} : advise *34* 35 eating little *34*^{2} : eating little, *34*

* Mangierà più chi manco mangia. Ed è contrario, Chi più mangia, manco mangia. Il senso è, Poco vive, chi troppo sparecchia.

other Proverb was, *The meat which remaineth, profits more then that which is eaten.** By which is intimated, that the hurt of too much meat is greater, then the commoditie of meat taken in a moderate proportion.

But all these things could not defend me against their importunities. Therefore, to avoid obstinacie, and gratifie my friends, at length I yeelded, and permitted the quantitie of meat to be increased, yet but two ounces onely. For whereas before the measure of my whole dayes meat, viz. of my bread, and egges, and flesh, and broth, was twelve ounces exactly weighed; I increased it to the quantitie of two ounces more; and the measure of my drink, which before was foureteen ounces, I made now sixteen.

This addition after ten dayes wrought so much upon me, that of a cheerfull and merrie man I became melancholie and cholerick; so that all things were troublesome to me: neither did I know well, what I did or said. On the twelfth day, a pain of the side took me, which held me two and twentie houres. Upon the neck of it came a terrible fever, which continued thirtie five dayes and nights; although after the fifteenth day it grew lesse and lesse. Besides all this, I could not sleep, no not a quarter of an houre: whereupon all gave me for dead.

Nevertheless, I by the grace of God cured my self, onely with returning to my former course of Diet, although I was now seventie eight yeares old, and my bodie spent with extream leannesse, and the season of the yeare was winter and most cold aire. And I am confident, that under God nothing holp me, but that exact rule which I had so long continued. In all which time I felt no grief, save now and then a little indisposition for a day or two.

For the Temperance of so many yeares spent all ill humours, and suffered not any new of that kinde to arise, neither the good humours to be corrupted, or contract any ill qualitie, as usually happens in old mens bodies, which live without rule. For there is no malignitie of old age in the humours of my bodie, which commonly kills men. And

* Fa più pro quel' che si lascia sul' tondo, che quel' che si mette nel ventre.

that new one, which I contracted by breaking my diet, although it was a sore evil, yet had no power to kill me.

By this it may clearely be perceived, how great is the power of order and disorder; whereof the one kept me well for many yeares; the other, though it was but a little excesse, in a few dayes had so soon overthrown me. If the world consist of order, if our corporall life depend on the harmonie of humours & elements, it is no wonder that order should preserve, and disorder destroy. Order makes arts easie, and armies victorious, and retains and confirms kingdomes, cities, and families in peace. Whence I conclude, That an orderly life is the most sure way & ground of health and long dayes, and the true and onely medicine of many diseases.

Neither can any man denie this, who will narrowly consider it. Hence it comes, that a Physician, when he cometh to visit his patient, prescribes this Physick first, That he use a moderate diet: and when he hath cured him, commends this also to him, if he will live in health. Neither is it to be doubted, but that he shall ever after live free from diseases, if he will keep such a course of life; because this will cut off all causes of diseases, so that he shall need neither Physick nor Physician: yea, if he will give his minde to those things which he should, he will prove himself a Physician, and that a very compleat one: For indeed no man can be a perfect Physician to another, but to himself onely. The reason whereof is this, Every one by long experience may know the qualities of his own nature, and what hidden properties it hath, what meat and drink agrees best with it: which things in others cannot be known without such observation, as is not easily to be made upon others; especially since there is a greater diversitie of tempers, then of faces. Who would beleeve that old wine should hurt my stomack, and new should help it; or that cinnamon should heat me more then pepper? What Physician could have discovered these hidden qualities to me, if I had not found them out by long experience? Wherefore one to another cannot be a perfect Physician. Whereupon I conclude, since none can have a

20 life; *34*[2]: life: *34*

better Physician then himself, nor better Physick then a Temperate Life, Temperance by all means is to be embraced.

Neverthelesse, I denie not but that Physicians are necessarie, and greatly to be esteemed for the knowing & curing of diseases, into which they often fall, who live disorderly: For if a friend who visits thee in thy sicknesse, and onely comforts and condoles, doth perform an acceptable thing to thee; how much more dearely should a Physician be esteemed, who not onely as a friend doth visit thee, but help thee!

But that a man may preserve himself in health, I advise, that in stead of a Physician a regular life is to be embraced, which, as is manifest by experience, is a naturall Physick most agreeable to us, and also doth preserve even ill tempers in good health, and procure that they prolong their life even to a hundred yeares and more, and that at length they shut up their dayes like a Lamp, onely by a pure consumption of the radicall moisture, without grief or perturbation of humours. Many have thought that this could be done by *Aurum potabile*, or the *Philosophers stone*, sought of many, and found of few. But surely there is no such matter, if Temperance be wanting.

But sensuall men (as most are) desiring to satisfie their Appetite, and pamper their belly, although they see themselves ill handled by their intemperance, yet shunne a sober life: because they say, It is better to please the Appetite (though they live ten yeares lesse then otherwise they should do) then alwayes to live under bit and bridle. But they consider not, of how great moment ten yeares are in mature age, wherein wisdome and all kinde of vertues is most vigorous; which, but in that age, can hardly be perfected. And that I may say nothing of other things, are not almost all the learned books that we have, written by their Authors in that age, and those ten yeares, which they set at naught in regard of their belly?

Besides, these Belly-gods say, that an orderly life is so hard a thing that it cannot be kept. To this I answer, that *Galen* kept it, and held it for the best *Physick*: so did *Plato* also, and *Isocrates*, and *Tullie*, and many others of the

Ancients; and in our age, *Paul the third*, and Cardinal *Bembo*, who therefore lived so long; and among our Dukes, *Landus*, and *Donatus*, and many others of inferiour condition, not onely in the citie, but also in villages and hamlets.

Wherefore since many have observed a regular life, both of old times and later yeares, it is no such thing which may not be performed; especially since in observing it, there needs not many and curious things, but onely that a man should begin and by little and little accustome himself unto it.

Neither doth it hinder, that *Plato* sayes, That they who are employed in the common wealth, cannot live regularly, because they must often endure heats, and colds, and windes, and showers, and divers labours, which suit not with an orderly life: For I answer, That those inconveniences are of no great moment (as I shewed before) if a man be temperate in meat and drink; which is both easie for common-wealsmen, and very convenient, both that they may preserve themselves from diseases, which hinder publick employment; as also that their minde, in all things wherein they deal, may be more lively and vigorous.

But some may say, He which lives a regular life, eating alwayes light meats, and in a little quantitie, what diet shall he use in diseases, which being in health he hath anticipated? I answer first; Nature, which endeavours to preserve a man as much as she can, teacheth us how to govern our selves in sicknesse: For suddenly it takes away our appetite, so that we can eat but a very little, wherewith she is very well contented: So that a sick man, whether he hath lived heretofore orderly or disorderly, when he is sick, ought not to eat, but such meats as are agreeable to his disease, and that in much smaller quantitie then when he was well. For if he should keep his former proportion, Nature, which is alreadie burdened with a disease, would be wholly oppressed. Secondly, I answer better, That he which lives a temperate life, cannot fall into diseases, and but very seldome into indispositions;

1 Ancients *Ed* (*plural, as in the original Italian and in Lessius*) : Ancient *34* 2 Landus *Ed* (*as in original and in Lessius*) : Laudus *34* *See note* 11 That they *36* : that they *34* *34*[2]

because Temperance takes away the cause of diseases: and the cause being taken away, there is no place for the effect.

Wherefore since an orderly life is so profitable, so vertuous, so decent, and so holy, it is worthy by all means to be embraced; especially since it is easie and most agreeable to the nature of Man. No man that followes it, is bound to eat and drink so little as I: No man is forbidden to eat fruit or fish, which I eat not: For I eat little, because a little sufficeth my weak stomack: and I abstain from fruit, and fish, and the like, because they hurt me. But they who finde benefit in these meats, may, yea ought to use them: yet all must take heed, lest they take a greater quantitie of any meat or drink (though most agreeable to them) then their stomack can easily digest: So that he which is offended with no kinde of meat and drink, hath the *quantitie*, and not the *qualitie* for his rule, which is very easie to be observed.

Let no man here object unto me, That there are many, who, though they live disorderly, yet continue in health to their lives end: Because since this is at the best but uncertain, dangerous, and very rare, the presuming upon it ought not to leade us to a disorderly life.

It is not the part of a wise man, to expose himself to so many dangers of diseases and death, onely upon a hope of an happie issue, which yet befalls verie few. An old man of an ill constitution, but living orderly, is more sure of life, then the most strong young man who lives disorderly.

But some, too much given to Appetite, object, That a long life is no such desirable thing, because that after one is once sixtie five yeares old, all the time we live after, is rather death then life. But these erre greatly, as I will shew by my self, recounting the delights and pleasures in this age of eighty three, which now I take, and which are such, as that men generally account me happie.

I am continually in health, and I am so nimble, that I can easily get on horseback without the advantage of the ground, and sometimes I go up high stairs and hills on foot. Then, I am ever cheerfull, merrie, and well-contented, free from all

1 cause *Ed* (*singular, as in original and in Lessius: cf.* cause *in next line*): causes *34*
4 means] *perhaps a misprint for* men *See note* 11 must take] must needs take *78*

troubles and troublesome thoughts; in whose place, joy and peace have taken up their standing in my heart. I am not wearie of life, which I passe with great delight. I conferre often with worthie men, excelling in wit, learning, behaviour, and other vertues. When I cannot have their companie, I give my self to the reading of some learned book, and afterwards to writing; making it my aim in all things, how I may help others to the furthest of my power.

All these things I do at my ease, and at fit seasons, and in mine own houses; which, besides that they are in the fairest place of this learned Citie of *Padua*, are verie beautifull and convenient above most in this age, being so built by me according to the rules of Architecture, that they are cool in summer, and warm in winter.

I enjoy also my gardens, and those divers, parted with rills of running water, which truely is very delightfull. Some times of the yeare I enjoy the pleasure of the *Euganean* hills, where also I have fountains and gardens, and a very convenient house. At other times, I repair to a village of mine, seated in the valley; which is therefore very pleasant, because many wayes thither are so ordered, that they all meet and end in a fair plot of ground; in the midst whereof is a Church suitable to the condition of the place. This place is washed with the river *Brenta*; on both sides whereof are great and fruitfull fields, well manured and adorned with many habitations. In former time it was not so, because the place was moorish and unhealthy, fitter for beasts then men. But I drained the ground, and made the aire good: Whereupon men flockt thither, and built houses with happy successe. By this means the place is come to that perfection we now see it is: So that I can truly say, That I have both given God a Temple, and men to worship him in it: The memorie whereof is exceeding delightfull to me.

Sometimes I ride to some of the neighbour-cities, that I may enjoy the sight & communication of my friends, as also of excellent Artificers in *Architecture*, *painting*, *stone-cutting*, *musick*, and *husbandrie*, whereof in this age there is

19 village] *perhaps a misprint for* villa *See note* 24 river] river of *Grosart, Palmer* 35 sight *Errata 34*: right *text of 34*

great plentie. I view their pieces, I compare them with those of Antiquitie; and ever I learn somewhat which is worthy of my knowledge: I survey *palaces*, *gardens*, and *antiquities*, publick *fabricks*, *temples*, and *fortifications*: neither omit I any thing that may either teach, or delight me. I am much pleased also in my travells, with the beauty of situation. Neither is this my pleasure made lesse by the decaying dulnesse of my senses, which are all in their perfect vigour, but especially my Taste; so that any simple fare is more savourie to me now, then heretofore, when I was given to disorder and all the delights that could be.

To change my bed, troubles me not; I sleep well and quietly any where, and my dreams are fair and pleasant. But this chiefly delights me, that my advice hath taken effect in the reducing of many rude and untoiled places in my countrey, to cultivation and good husbandrie. I was one of those that was deputed for the managing of that work, and abode in those fenny places two whole moneths in the heat of summer (which in *Italie* is very great) receiving not any hurt or inconvenience thereby: So great is the power and efficacie of that *Temperance* which ever accompanied me.

These are the delights and solaces of my old age, which is altogether to be preferred before others youth: Because that by *Temperance* and the *Grace of God* I feel not those perturbations of bodie and minde, wherewith infinite both young and old are afflicted.

Moreover, by this also, in what estate I am, may be discovered, because at these yeares (*viz.* 83) I have made a most pleasant comedie, full of honest wit and merriment: which kinde of Poems useth to be the childe of Youth, which it most suits withall for variety and pleasantnesse; as a Tragedie with old Age, by reason of the sad events which it contains. And if a *Greek Poet* of old was praised, that at the age of 73 yeares he writ a Tragedie; why should I be accounted lesse happie, or lesse my self, who being ten yeares older have made a Comedie?

Now lest there should be any delight wanting to my old

2 Antiquitie; and *34²*: Antiquitie: And *34* 8 senses, *34²*: senses; *34*
16 cultivation *Errata 34*: constivation *text of 34*

age, I daily behold a kinde of immortalitie in the succession of my posteritie. For when I come home, I finde eleven grand-children of mine, all the sonnes of one father and mother, all in perfect health; all, as farre as I can conjecture, very apt and well given both for learning and behaviour. I am delighted with their musick and fashion, and I my self also sing often; because I have now a clearer voice, then ever I had in my life.

By which it is evident, That the life which I live at this age, is not a dead, dumpish, and sowre life; but cheerfull, lively, and pleasant. Neither, if I had my wish, would I change age and constitution with them who follow their youthfull appetites, although they be of a most strong temper: Because such are daily exposed to a thousand dangers and deaths, as daily experience sheweth, and I also, when I was a young man, too well found. I know how inconsiderate that age is, and, though subject to death, yet continually afraid of it: For death to all young men is a terrible thing, as also to those that live in sinne, and follow their appetites: whereas I by the experience of so many yeares have learned to give way to Reason: whence it seems to me, not onely a shamefull thing to fear that which cannot be avoided; but also I hope, when I shall come to that point, I shall finde no little comfort in the favour of Jesus Christ. Yet I am sure, that my end is farre from me: for I know that (setting casualties aside) I shall not die but by a pure resolution: because that by the regularitie of my life I have shut out death all other wayes. And that is a fair and desirable death, which Nature brings by way of resolution.

Since therefore a temperate life is so happie and pleasant a thing; what remains, but that I should wish all who have the care of themselves, to embrace it with open arms?

Many things more might be said in commendation hereof: but lest in any thing I forsake that *Temperance* which I have found so good, I here make an end.

BRIEFE NOTES ON VALDESSO'S *CONSIDERATIONS*

A Copy of a letter written by MR GEORGE HERBERT *to his friend the Translator of this Book.*

MY deare and deserving Brother, your *Valdesso* I now returne with many thanks, and some notes, in which perhaps you will discover some care, which I forbare not in the midst of my griefes; First for your sake, because I would doe nothing negligently that you commit unto mee; Secondly for the Authors sake, whom I conceive to have been a true servant of God; and to such, and all that is theirs, I owe diligence; Thirdly for the Churches sake, to whom by Printing it I would have you consecrate it. You owe the Church a debt, and God hath put this into your hands (as he sent the fish with mony to S. *Peter*,) to discharge it: happily also with this (as his thoughts are fruitfull) intending the honour of his servant the Author, who being obscured in his own country he would have to flourish in this land of light, and region of the Gospell, among his chosen. It is true, there are some things which I like not in him, as my fragments will expresse, when you read them; neverthelesse I wish you by all meanes to publish it, for these three eminent things observable therein: First, that God in the midst of Popery should open the eyes of one to understand and expresse so clearely and excellently the intent of the Gospell in the acceptation of Christs righteousnesse (as he

From The Hundred and Ten Considerations of Signior Iohn Valdesso. Written in Spanish, Brought out of Italy by Vergerius, and first set forth in Italian at Basil by Coelius Secundus Curio, Anno 1550. And now translated out of the Italian Copy into English, with notes. Oxford, Printed by Leonard Lichfield, Printer to the Vniversity, 1638. *Anather edn entitled* Divine Considerations. Cambridge, 1646. *Herbert's* Letter, *but not his* Notes, *is printed in* Herbert's Remains, 1652, *and in Walton's* Lives, 1670 *and* 1675. *Heading of Letter in 1646*: Mr. *George Herbert* to *N.F.* the Translatour of this Book. 3 forbare] forbear *1652 1670 1675* 21 clearely, *1638* sheweth through all his Considerations) a thing strangely buried, and darkned by the Adversaries, and their great stumbling-block. Secondly, the great honour and reverence, which he every where beares towards our deare Master and Lord, concluding every Consideration almost with his holy Name, and setting his merit forth so piously, for which I doe so love him, that were there nothing else, I would Print it, that with it the honour of my Lord might be published. Thirdly, the many pious rules of ordering our life, about mortification, and observation of Gods Kingdome within us, and the working thereof, of which he was a very diligent observer. These three things are very eminent in the Author, and overweigh the defects (as I conceive) towards the publishing thereof, &c.

Bemmorton Sept. 29.

3 Secondly, *1646*: Secondly *1638* 4 deare] great *1652* 15 *Bemmorton Sept.* 29.] From his Parsonage of *Bemmorton* near *Salisbury*. Sept. 29. 1632. *1646*: *so, except for spelling* Bemerton, *1670 1675*: From Bemmerton near Salisbury, Septemb. 29. 1632. *1652*: Bemerton, Sep. 29, 1632 *Peckard* (*who possessed the original letter: see note*)

BRIEFE NOTES

relating to the dvbious and offensive places in the following CONSIDERATIONS.

To the 3 CONSID.

In what the Sonnes of God differ from the Sonnes of Adam.

Upon these words:

'These selfe same *sonnes of God* as they goe approaching to God, they goe becomming like unto them of *Samaria*, that said unto the woman, *Not for thy speech:* they also saying unto holy Scripture, *Not for thy speech:* Other law, and other Doctrine haue we, that maintaines and conserves us in holinesse, & justice. This is the Spirit of God which abides in us, which rules, and governes us in such manner, that no need haue we of other regiment, nor of other government, so long as we shall not sever ourselves from our heavenly Father.'

These words about the H. Scripture suite with what he writes elsewhere, especially Consid. 32. But I like none of it, for it slights the Scripture too much: holy Scriptures have not only an Elementary use, but a use of perfection, and are able to make the man of God perfect, 2 *Tim.* 3. And *David* (though *David*) studied all the day long in it: And *Ioshua* was to meditate therein Day and Night. *Iosh.* the 1.

Upon these words:

'The sonnes of God will make use of the Physitians, & of the physick to conserue the health of the body, as they also make use of the Scripture to conserve the health of their mindes: but they doe it without putting confidence either in this, or in that; for all their trust stands put in God.'

All the Saints of God may be said in some sence to have put confidence in Scripture, but not as a naked Word

6 Upon these words] *Here and throughout in this edition the passages of Valdesso specially commented on by Herbert are cited in full: in 1638 incomplete sentences are cited, which do not explain themselves without reference to the book. The Notes are printed together at the beginning of the edition of 1638: in 1646 they are printed marginally against the appropriate passage in the text of the book.* 15–21 *1646 omits this note* 19 2 *Tim.* 3. *Ed:* 1 *Tim.* 4 *1638* 22 these *Ed*: those *1638* 28–307. 4 *1646 omits this note*

severed from God, but as the Word of God: And in so doing they doe not sever their trust from God. But by trusting in the word of God they trust in God. Hee that trusts in the Kings word for any thing trusts in the King.

To the 5 Consid.

The difficulty that is to enter into the kingdome of God; how it is to be entred, and in what it consists.

Vpon these words:

'From whence I consider the perversity of man, and I also consider the goodnesse of God, in as much as he doth help, and favour them, who when they can doe no otherwise, remit themselves to his divine will; and for the rest he regards not how pious, or how impious we be, but only hath respect to this that he hath promised his help to them, that shall remit themselves to him, and that it belongs to him to maintain his promise.'

This place together with many other, as namely Consid. 71. upon *Our Father;* and Consid. 94. upon these words: *God doth not hold them for good, or for evill, for that they observe or not observe the Decorum of christian piety; but for the fidelity, or infidelity, with which they persevere, or sever themselves from the Gospell and from Christ,* though it were the Authors opinion, yet the truth of it would be examined. See the note upon Consid. 36.

To the 6 Consid.

Two depravations of Man, the one Naturall, the other Acquisite.

'The Depravation acquisite with the inflammation of the Naturall, I understand, that as it was got by habit, so it may be lost by habit: and to this serue, as I understand, the Laws, and Precepts, which humane wisdome hath found out; in such manner, that a man may of himselfe free him selfe from the acquisite depravation, and from the inflammation of the Naturall, as wee read, that many did free themselues; but he shall never be able to free himselfe by himself from the naturall depravation. For from this, as I haue said, The grace of our Lord Iesus Christ doth free us.'

2 there trust *1638*
Consid. 5. 16–23 *1646 omits this note* 19–21 *the Decorum . . . Christ* (*completion of Valdesso's sentence supplied by Ed: 1638 has* 'not observe &c.')

The Doctrine of the last passage must be warily understood. First, that it is not to be understood of actuall sinnes, but habituall, for I can no more free my selfe from actuall sinnes after Baptisme, then I could of Originall before, and without Baptisme. The exemption from both, is by the Grace of God. Secondly, among Habits, some oppose Theologicall vertues, as Vncharitablenesse opposes Charity; Infidelity, Faith; Distrust, Hope: Of these none can free themselves of themselves, but only by the Grace of God: Other Habits oppose morall vertues, as Prodigality opposes Moderation; and Pusillanimity, Magnanimity: Of these the heathen freed themselves, only by the generall Providence of God, as *Socrates* and *Aristides*, &c. Where he sayes the *Inflammation of the naturall*, he sayes aptly, so it be understood with the former distinction, for *Fomes* is not taken away, but *Accensio Fomitis*; the naturall concupiscence is not quite extinguished, but the heate of it asswaged.

To the 10 Consid.

In what regard the estate of the Christian person, that believes with difficulty, is better, then of that Person which believes with ease.

'When a person equally giues credit to all things that are said unto him, he is without the spirit of God, he believes by relation, humane perswasion, and by opinion, and not by revelation, nor inspiration. And it being true, that the blessednesse of a Christian man doth not consist in believing, but in believing by revelation, and not by relation, it is concluded, that it is not Christian faith that which is by relation, but onely that which is by revelation is the Christian.'

He often useth this manner of speech *Beleeving by Revelation, not by relation*, whereby I understand he meaneth only the effectuall operation or illumination of the holy spirit, testifying, and applying the revealed truth of the Gospell; and not any private Enthusiasmes, or Revelations: As if he should say: A generall apprehension, or assent to the

Consid. 6. 1–17 *1646 omits this note* 17 quite] *om. Palmer*
18 To the 11 Consid. *1638* (*by mistake for* 10: *corrected in 1646*) 30 *not by relation*] *om. 1646* meaneth, Only *1638* 34 say; a *1638*

promises of the Gospell by heare-say, or relation from others, is not that which filleth the heart with joy and peace in believing; but the spirits bearing witnesse with our spirit, revealing and applying the generall promises to every one in particular with such syncerity and efficacy, that it makes him godly, righteous, and sober all his life long; this I call *beleeving by Revelation, and not by Relation.*

To the 32 Consid.

In what consisteth the abuse, and in what consisteth the use of Images, and of Holy Scriptures.

'The unlearned man, that hath the spirit, serveth himselfe of *Images* as of an Alphabet of Christian Pietie; forasmuch as hee so much serves himselfe of the *Picture* of Christ Crucified, as much as serves to imprint in his mind that which Christ suffered. . . . In like manner a learned man, that hath the spirit, serveth himselfe of *holy Scriptures,* as of an Alphabet of Christian pietie, . . . untill such time, as it penetrate into his minde.'

I much mislike the Comparison of Images, and H. Scripture, as if they were both but Alphabets and after a time to be left. The H. Scriptures (as I wrote before) have not only an Elementary use, but a use of perfection, neither can they ever be exhausted, (as Pictures may be by a plenarie circumspection) but still even to the most learned and perfect in them, there is somewhat to be learned more: Therefore *David* desireth God in the 119 *Psalme,* to open his eyes that he might see the wondrous things of his Lawes, and that he would make them his study. Although by other words of the same *Psalme* it is evident, that he was not meanly conversant in them. Indeed he that shall so attend to the bark of the letter, as to neglect the Consideration of Gods Worke in his heart through the Word, doth amisse; both are to be done, the Scriptures still used, and Gods worke within us still

3 with *1646*: which *1638*

Consid. 32. 18 Images *1646*: the Images *1638* 20 Scriptures . . . before] *some copies of 1638 misprint* Scripture . . . befores (as I wrote before)] *om. 1646* (*which omits Herbert's first note*) 26 Lawes] law *1646* (*cf.* Psalm cxix. 18) 29 bark] back *Pickering* *See note* 31 done, *1646*: done *1638* 32 Scripture *1646*

observed, who workes by his Word, and ever in the reading of it. As for the Text, *They shall be all taught of God*, it being Scripture cannot be spoken to the disparagement of Scripture; but the meaning is this, That God in the dayes of the Gospell will not give an outward Law of Ceremonies as of old, but such a one as shall still have the assistance of the holy spirit applying it to our hearts, and ever outrunning the Teacher, as it did when *Peter* taught *Cornelius*: there the case is plaine, *Cornelius* had revelation, yet *Peter* was to be sent for, and those that have inspirations must still use *Peter*, Gods Word: if we make another sence of that Text, wee shall overthrow all means, save catechizing, and set up Enthusiasmes.

In the Scripture are { *Doctrines, these ever teach more and more.*
Promises, these ever comfort more and more. Rom. 15. 4.

To the 33 Consid.

In what manner through the patience, and through the Consolation of the Scriptures we maintain our selves in Hope.

'And the *consolation of Scriptures* consisteth in this, that reading in them the promises of God, we doe anew confirm, and fortify our selves in Hope; there betiding unto us that which betides to one, to whom a Lord promiseth by his Letters a thousand Duckets of In-comes, who maintains himselfe in the Hope to haue that revenew through patience, . . . comforting himselfe with the Letter of the Lord, in which reading the promise, he doth anew comfort himselfe in hope.'

The Doctrine of this Consideration cleareth that of the precedent. For as the servant leaves not the letter when he hath read it, but keepes it by him, and reads it againe and againe, and the more the promise is delayed, the more he reads it, and fortifies himselfe with it; so are wee to doe with the Scriptures and this is the use of the promises of the Scriptures. But the use of the Doctrinall part is more, in regard it presents us not with the same thing only when it is read as the promises doe, but enlightens us with new Considerations the more we read it.

2 the Text] that Text *1646* 6 a] an *1646* 11 that Text] the Text *1646*
14 *Scriptures 1646*
Consid. 33. 27 precedent] former *1646*

Much more might be said, but this sufficeth, he himselfe allowes it for a holy conversation and refreshment.

To the 36 Consid.

In what the Christian Liberty doth consist, how it is knowne, and how it is exercised.

On these words:

'They who by the holy spirit feele the *Christian liberty* . . . know, that *Christian liberty consisteth in this, that a Christian shall not bee chastized for his evill living, nor shall not be rewarded for his well living*; knowing, that chastizement is for the unbelievers, and the reward for the faithfull. . . . They doe well exercise the *Christian liberty*: For being governed by the holy spirit, on one side they finde, and know themselves to bee free, and exempted from the law, in so much that it seemes to them, that they may say with S. *Paul, All things are lawfull unto me*: Neither fearing to be chastized for transgression, nor hoping to bee rewarded for observation; in which they feele, and know the *Christian liberty*. And on the other side they finde, and know themselves obliged to be like unto Christ in their life, and manners, and therefore they say with S. *Paul, All things are not expedient*.'

All the discourse from this line till the end of this Chapter may seeme strange, but it is sutable to what the Author holds elsewhere, for he maintaines that it is Faith and Infidelity that shall judge us now since the Gospell, and that no other sin or vertue hath any thing to doe with us; if we believe, no sinne shall hurt us; if we believe not, no vertue shall helpe us. Therefore he saith here, we shall not be punished (which word I like here better then chastizement, because even the godly are chastized but not punished) for evill doing nor rewarded for weldoing or living, for all the point lies in believing or not believing. And with this exposition the Chapter is cleare enough, but the truth of the

2 refreshment.] refreshment, in the 32 Consideration, and amongst all divine and spirituall exercises and duties, he nameth the reading and meditation of holy Scriptures for the first and principall, as Consid. 47, and others; so that it is plain the Authour had a very reverend esteem of the holy Scripture, especially considering the time and place where he lived. *1646*

Consid. 36. 20 line till] place to *1646* (*the* line *or* place *refers to l. 16 in the above citation from Valdesso*)   26 here, *1646* : here *1638*   27–8 *1646 omits the bracketed clauses*

Doctrine would be examined, however it may passe for his opinion: in the Church of God there is one fundamentall, but else variety.

To the 46 CONSID.

That they, who walke through the Christian path without the inward light of the holy Spirit, are like unto them, that walke in the night without the light of the Sunne.

On these words:

'And if any person shall demand me, saying, How shall I doe to firme my selfe in this journey? I will answer him, Exercise not thy selfe in any thing *pretending Iustification* thereby nor Religion of any sort, nor of any quality; and pray God affectionately, that hee would send thee his Spirit, which may be unto thee as a *Sunne* in this journey.'

He meaneth (I suppose) that a man presume not to merit, that is, to oblige God, or justify himselfe before God, by any acts or exercises of Religion; but that he ought to pray God affectionately and fervently to send him the light of his spirit, which may be unto him as the sunne to a Travellour in his journey, hee in the meane while applying himselfe to the duties of true Piety, and syncere Religion, such as are Prayer, Fasting, Almes-deedes, &c. after the example of devout *Cornelius*.

To the 49 CONSID.

Whence it proceeds, that humane wisdome will not attribute all things to God: And in what manner they ought to bee attributed to him.

On these words:

'And albeit they haue their imperfections by Gods will, their desire

2 opinion: *Ed*: opinion, *1638* 3 *1646 adds* The Authors good meaning in this, will better appear by his 98 Consideration of faith and good works.

Consid. 37. *Here in 1638 follows a note (omitted in this edition), and in the margin is printed* 'This note is the French Translators.'

Consid. 46. 20 the unquestioned duties *1646* 22 *1646 adds*: Or thus; There are two sorts of acts in religion; acts of humiliation, and acts of confidence and joy; the person here described to be in the dark, ought to use the first, and to forbear the second; Of the first sort are repentance, prayers, fasting, almes, mortifications, &c.; of the second, receiving of the Communion, prayses, Psalmes, &c. These in diverse cases ought, and were of old forborn for a time.

is to become perfect. And although they hold the sufferings of their neighbour to bee the will of God, they hold likewise their motions to help, and favour them to be the will of God; And knowing in their own imperfections, and in the sufferings of their neighbours the will of God, which is with wrath, and knowing in their own desires of perfection, and in their motions to succour their neighbours the will of God, which is with mercy, loving the will which is with mercy, and flying from that which is with wrath, they doe attend unto perfection, and doe attend to succour their neighbours, remaining quiet, when they doe not perceive any motion, understanding it, that God would haue them to remain quiet.'

In indifferent things there is roome for motions and expecting of them; but in things good, as to relieve my Neighbour, God hath already revealed his Will about it. Therefore wee ought to proceed, except there be a restraining motion (as *S. Paul* had when hee would have preached in Asia), and I conceive that restraining motions are much more frequent to the godly, then inviting motions; because the Scripture invites enough, for it invites us to all good, according to that singular place, *Phil.* 4. 8. A man is to embrace all good, but because he cannot doe all, God often chuseth which he shall doe, and that by restraining him from what he would not have him doe.

Vpon these words:

'In God I consider two wills . . . one Mediate, in as much as it workes by these, which we call second Causes: And the other Immediate, in as much as it works by it selfe . . . I suppose, that in a mans flying those things, which by this Mediate will might doe him harme, and in applying himselfe to those things, which by the selfe same might doe him good, a mans freewill doth consist; all those things appertaining to good or ill being exteriour, & corporall to vertuous, or vitious living in the outward.'

He meanes a mans fre-will is only in outward, not in spirituall things.

On these words:

'Neither *Pharaoh*, nor *Iudas*, nor those who are *vessels of wrath*, could cease to be such.'

Consid. 49. 12 motions] notions *1646* 16–17 (as *S. Paul* had) when . . . Asia, *1638 1646* 17 that *1646*: the *1638* 33–4 *1646 omits this note*

This doctrine however true in substance, yet needeth discreet, and wary explaining.

To the 58 CONSID.

Eight differences between them, who pretend, and procure to mortifie themselves with their proper industry, and them, who are mortified by the holy Spirit.

Vpon the seventh difference:

'The *seaventh Difference* is, that they who *mortifie themselves* in the occasions of erring doe miserably loose themselves: For being deceived by humane wisdome they doe alwaies goe avoiding the occasions, which incite them to erre: And they who are *mortified*, in the occasions of erring, that offer themselues unto them, are refined as gold in the fire, for being helped by the holy spirit in the proper occasions they are mortified, not avoiding any of them; and therefore they are the same in the occasions, as out of the occasions.'

By *occasions* (I suppose) hee meaneth the ordinary, or necessary duties, and occasions of our calling and condition of life; and not those which are in themselves occasions of sinne; such as are all vain conversations: For as for these, pious persons ought alwaies to avoid them: but in those other occasions, Gods Spirit will mortify and try them as gold in the fire.

To the 59 CONSID.

That in the motions to pray the Spirit doth certifie a man, that he shall obtaine that which he demands.

Upon these words:

'The proper countersigne, whereby they may be able to judge between these motions, is the *Inward certainty, or uncertainty with which they shall finde themselves in prayer*. Finding themselves uncer-

1 howsoever it is true *1646* yet needeth] yet it requireth *1646*
Consid. 55. *1646 adds a marginal note*:
By renouncing the help of humane learning in the studying to understand holy Scripture, he meaneth that we should not use it as the onely, or as the principall means; because the anointing which we have received, and abideth in us, teacheth us, 1 John 2. 27.
Consid. 58. 16–22 *1646 omits this note*

tain that they should obtain of God that which they demand, they shall judge, that the motion is of *humane spirit*; And finding themselves certain to obtain it, they shall judge that the motion is of the *holy spirit*. . . . With this *assurance* I see, that Christ *prayed*, raising up *Lazarus*, and *praying* for the conservation of his Disciples. And with *doubtfulnesse* I see he prayed in the *Garden*; and because he felt, whence this motion did arise in praying, he remitted himselfe unto the will of God.'

To say our Saviour prayed with doubtfulnesse, is more then I can or dare say; But with condition, or conditionally he prayed as man, though as God he knew the event. Feare is given to Christ, but not doubt, and upon good ground.

To the 62 Consid.

That humane wisdome hath no more iurisdiction in the judgement of their workes, who are the sonnes of God, then in the iudgement of the proper works of God.

'That rashnesse of men is not lesse, which follow the iudgement of humane wisdome, when they sett themselves to iudge evill of *Moses* for the Hebrews whom he slew when they worshipped the Calfe; and when they sett themselves to judge evill of *Abraham*, because he commanded his wife *Sarah*, that she should lye, saying that she was his sister, and not his wife: And because S. *Paul* cursed *Ananias* standing at iudgement in his presence. And because hee excused his cursing, saying, he did not know him. . . . Humane wisdome hath no more iurisdiction in the iudgement of the works of pious men, then in the iudgement of the works of God. . . . Men should not haue had more reason to haue chastised *Abraham*, if he had killed his sonne *Isaac*, then to condemne God, because he slaies many men by suddain death.'

This Chapter is considerable. The intent of it, that the world *pierceth* not godly mens actions no more then Gods, is in some sort true because they are spiritually discerned, 1 *Cor*. 2. 14. So likewise are the godly in some sort exempt from Lawes, for *Lex iusto non est posita*: But when he enlargeth he goes too farre. For first concerning *Abraham* and

Consid. 59. 9–12 *1646 omits this note*

Consid. 62. 29 considerable, the *1638 1646* 33 *Lex . . . posita*] the law is not made for a righteous man *1646* (*substituting A.V. for the Vulgate rendering of* 1 Tim. 1. 9) 33–4 enlargeth *1646*: enlargeth them *1638*

Sara, I ever tooke that for a weaknesse in the great Patriark: And that the best of Gods Servants should have weaknesses is no way repugnant to the way of Gods Spirit in them, or to the Scriptures, or to themselves being still men, though godly men. Nay they are purposely recorded in holy Writ. Wherefore as *David's* Adultery cannot be excused, so need not *Abraham's* Equivocation, nor *Paul's* neither, when he professed himselfe a Pharisee, which strictly he was not, though in the point of Resurrection he agreed with them, and they with him. The reviling also of *Ananias* seemes, by his owne recalling, an oversight; yet I remember the Fathers forbid us to judge of the doubtfull actions of Saints in the Scriptures; which is a modest admonition. But it is one thing not to judge, another to defend them. Secondly, when he useth the word Iurisdiction, allowing no Iurisdiction over the godly, this cannot stand, and it is ill Doctrine in a common-wealth. The godly are punishable as others, when they doe amisse, and they are to be judged according to the outward fact, unlesse it be evident to others, as well as to themselves, that God moved them. For otherwise any Malefactor may pretend motions, which is unsufferable in a Common-wealth. Neither doe I doubt but if *Abraham* had lived in our Kingdome under government, and had killed his sonne *Isaac*, but he might have been justly put to death for it by the Magistrate, unlesse he could have made it appeare, that it was done by Gods immediate precept. He had done justly, and yet he had been punished justly, that is *in humano foro & secundum praesumptionem legalem*. So may a warre be just on both sides, and was just in the Canaanites and Israelites both. How the godly are exempt from Laws is a known point among Divines, but when he sayes they are equally exempt with God, that is dangerous and too farre.

The best salve for the whole Chapter, is to distinguish Iudgment: There is a judgment of authority (upon a fact)

5 recorded *1646*: accorded *1638* 10 seemes, *Ed*: seemes *1638* 13 in Scriptures *1646* 15 word *1646*: Word *1638* Iurisdiction] *comma from 1646* 20 themselves] *comma Ed* 21–2 insufferable *1646* (*cf. p. 318, l. 6*) 24–5 might justly have been *1646* 27 yet he had] yet had *1646* 29 *legalem*] *1646 adds* according to the common and legal proceedings among men.

and there is a judgment of the Learned; for as a Magistrate judgeth in his tribunall, so a Scholar judgeth in his study, and censureth this or that; whence come so many Books of severall mens opinions: perhaps he meant all of this later not of the former. Worldly learned men cannot judg spirituall mens actions, but the Magistrate may.

To the 63 Consid.

That the holy Scripture is like a Candle in a dark place, and that the holy spirit is like the Sunne. This shewed by seaven conformities.

'S. *Peter* well commends the study of holy Scripture; but whilst a man stands in the dark place of humane wisdome, and reason, and he wills that this study should continue so long, untill the light of the holy spirit shine into the mind of a man: understanding that this light being come, a man hath no more need to seek that of holy Scripture, which departs of it selfe, as the light of the candle departs, when the Sun-beames enter. . . . The man that enjoyes the light of the holy spirit, knowing certainly that it cannot fayle him, albeit he doe not cast away holy Scripture, but rather leaues it, that it may serue to another for that which it hath served for unto him; neverthelesse hee doth not serue himselfe of it, in that whereof hee did formerly serve himselfe.'

The Authour doth still discover too slight a regard of the Scripture, as if it were but childrens meat, whereas there is not onely milke there, *but strong meat also. Heb.* 5. 14. *Things hard to bee understood.* 2 *Pet.* 3. 1.6. *Things needing great Consideration. Mat.* 24. 15. Besides he opposeth the teaching of the spirit to the teaching of the scripture, which the holy spirit wrot. Although the holy spirit apply the scripture, yet what the scripture teacheth, the spirit teacheth, the holy spirit indeed sometime doubly teaching both in penning and in applying. I wonder how this opinion could befall so good a man as it seems *Valdesso* was, since the Saints of God in all ages have ever held in so pretious esteem the word of God, as their Ioy, and Crowne, and their Treasure on earth. Yet his owne practice seemes to confute his opinion, for the most

4 later] latter *1646* 6 may.] may, and surely this the Author meant by the word *Jurisdiction*, for so he useth the same word in Consideration 68 *ad finem. 1646*

Consid. 63. 23 Scripture *1646*: Scriptures *1638*

of his Considerations being grounded upon some text of scripture, shewes that he was continually conversant in it, and not used it for a time onely, and then cast it away, as he sayes strangely.

There is no more to be said of this Chapter but that his opinion of the scripture is unsufferable. As for the text of *S. Pet.* 2 *Ep.* 1. 19. which he makes the ground of his Consideration, building it all upon the word *untill the day starre arise*, it is nothing. How many places doe the Fathers bring about *Untill* against the Heretiques who disputed against the Virginity of the blessed Virgin out of that text *Mat.* 1.25. where it is said, *Joseph knew her not*, *untill shee had brought forth her first borne Sonne*, as if afterwards he had knowne her: and indeed in common sence, if I bid a man stay in a place untill I come, I doe not then bid him goe away but rather stay longer, that I may speak with him or doe some thing else when I doe come. So S. Peter bidding the dispersed Hebrews attend to the word till the day dawn, doth not bid them then cast away the word, or leave it off: but however he would have them attend to it till that time, and then afterward they will attend it of themselves without his exhortation. Nay it is observeable that in that very place he preferres the Word before the sight of the Transfiguration of Christ. So that the Word hath the precedence even of Revelations and Visions. And so his whole discourse and sevenfold observation falls to the ground.

To the 69 Consid.

That a man ought alwaies to acknowledge himselfe incredulous, and defectiue in faith: and that there is so much faith in a man, as much as there is knowledge of God, and Christ.

Upon these words:

'A man ought to judge himselfe incredulous, and defectiue in the

5 Chapter] Chapter, especially of the fifth thing in it, *1646* 5–6 his opinion] this his opinion *1646* 7 his] this *1646* 10 *Untill 1646*: Vntil *1638* 11 that] the *1646* 17 doe] *om. 1646* come. *1646* : come ; *1638* 21 of themselves attend it *1646* 25–6 And so . . . ground] *om. 1646*

Consid. 65. *Here in 1638 follows a note* (*omitted in this edition*), *and in the margin is printed* 'This note is the French Translators.'

Faith, as long as he hath not *so much faith as sufficeth therewith to remoue mountaines* from one place to another; & that judging himselfe such, he ought to demand of God, that he should giue him faith, not contenting himselfe to testifie in divine things by heare-say, and by relation, but by certain knowledge, and proper experience.'

Divines hold, that justifying faith, and the faith of miracles are divers guifts, and of a different nature, the one being *gratia gratis data*, the other *gratia gratum faciens*, this being given only to the godly, and the other sometimes to the wicked. Yet doubtlesse the best faith in us is defective, and arrives not to the point it should, which if it did, it would doe more, then it does. And miracle-working as it may be severed from justifying faith, so it may be a fruit of it, and an exaltation. 1 *Iohn* 5. 14.

To the 94 Consid.

Three sorts of Conscience: one by the Law naturall, and the other by the written Lawes: and the other by the Gospell.

'The men, that attend to *Hebrew piety* without having *christian piety*, are ordinarily superstitious, and are scrupulous; nay from hence arise all the scruples, and all the doubts in those that are called *cases of conscience*.'

By *Hebrew piety*, he meaneth not the very Ceremonies of

Consid. 71. *1646 adds the following marginal note against the words* 'If I should call him Father', *and repeats the same marginal note against the words* 'He doth not hold them for good nor for evill' *in* Consid. 94:

Though this were the Authors opinion, yet the truth of it would be examined. The 98. Consid. about being justified by faith, or by good works, or condemned for unbelief or evil works, make plain the Authors meaning.

Consid. 76 *ad init. 1646 adds a marginal note*:

By the Saints of the world he every where understands the cunning hypocrite who by the world is counted a very Saint, for his outward shew of holinesse: and we meet with two sorts of these Saints of the world; one, whose holinesse consists in a few ceremonious and superstitious observations; the others, in a zeal against these, and in a strict performance of a few cheap and easie duties of religion, with no lesse superstition; both of them having forms or vizars of godlinesse, but denying the power thereof.

Consid. 94. 21 *1646 adds this marginal note*:

This is true onley of the Popish *Cases of Conscience*, which depend almost wholly on their Canon law and Decretals, knots of their own tying and untying: But their are other *Cases of Conscience* grounded on Piety and Morality, and the difficulty of applying their generall rules to particular actions, which are a most noble study.

the Iewes, which no Christian observes now; but an analogat observation of Ecclesiasticall and Canonicall lawes, superinduced to the scriptures, like to that of the Iewes, which they added to their divine law. This being well weighed, will make the Consideration easy, and very observeable: For at least some of the Papists are come now, to what the Pharisees were come in our Saviours time.

3 the Jews *1646*: Iewes *1638* 6 least *1646*: least, *1638* 7 come] come to *1646*

OVTLANDISH

PROVERBS,

SELECTED

LONDON,

Printed by *T. P.* for *Humphrey Blunden*; at the *Castle in Corn-hill.* 1640.

Title-page of 'Ovtlandish Proverbs' in *Witts Recreations*, 1640 (the Bodleian copy, in which the words 'By Mr. *G. H.*' are obliterated by hand)

OUTLANDISH PROVERBS

1. MAN Proposeth, God disposeth.
2. Hee begins to die, that quits his desires.
3. A handfull of good life is better then a bushell of learning.
4. He that studies his content, wants it.
5. Every day brings his bread with it.
6. Humble Hearts have humble desires.
7. Hee that stumbles and falles not, mends his pace.

*8. The House shewes the owner.
*9. Hee that gets out of debt, growes rich.
*10. All is well with him, who is beloved of his neighbours.
*11. Building and marrying of Children are great wasters.
12. A good bargaine is a pick-purse.
*13. The scalded dog feares cold water.
14. Pleasing ware is halfe sould.
*15. Light burthens, long borne, growe heavie.
16. The Wolfe knowes, what the ill beast thinkes.
17. Who hath none to still him, may weepe out his eyes.
*18. When all sinnes grow old, coveteousnesse is young.
19. If yee would know a knave, give him a staffe.
*20. You cannot know wine by the barrell.
*21. A coole mouth, and warme feet, live long.
22. A Horse made, and a man to make.
*23. Looke not for muske in a dogges kennell.
*24. Not a long day, but a good heart rids worke.

From Outlandish Proverbs, selected by Mr. G. H. 1640 *(cited as OP: a few superfluous commas are omitted in the present text): reissued without change as 2nd part of the 1st edn only of* Witts Recreations. With A Thousand outLandish Proverbs. 1640. *Enlarged edn as* Jacula Prudentum. Or Outlandish Proverbs selected by Mr George Herbert. 1651 *(cited as JP): perhaps issued separately in 1651; included without change, with separate title-page of 1651, in* Herbert's Remains. 1652. MS. Story Books of Little Gidding, vol. II*a (cited as LG): contains a collection of the 204 proverbs here asterisked* (*). National Library of Wales MS. 5301 E *(cited as HH): contains* 'Outlandishe Prouerbs', *transcribed by Sir Henry Herbert on 6 Aug. 1637, corresponding, with two exceptions, to the first 72 proverbs in OP (1640)* 1 Proposeth] purposethe *HH* 5 his] Its *HH* 9 groweth *LG* 10 with] to *LG* that is loved of *HH LG* 13 dog] head *JP* 15 burdens *HH JP* growe] are *HH LG* 18 grow old *HH LG JP*: growes old *OP* is] grows *HH* 19 yee] you *HH* 22 An Horse *HH* 24 the worke *LG*

*25. Hee puls with a long rope, that waits for anothers death.
*26. Great strokes make not sweete musick.
*27. A Cake and an ill custome must be broken.
*28. A fat house-keeper makes leane Executors.
*29. Empty Chambers make foolish maides.
30. The gentle Hawke halfe mans her selfe.
31. The Devill is not alwaies at one doore.
*32. When a friend askes, there is no to morrow.
*33. God sends cold according to Cloathes.
34. One sound blow will serve to undo all.
*35. Hee looseth nothing, that looseth not God.
36. The Germans wit is in his fingers.
37. At dinner my man appeares.
*38. Who gives to all, denies all.
*39. Quick beleevers neede broad shoulders.
40. Who remove stones, bruise their fingers.
*41. All came from, and will goe to others.
*42. He that will take the bird, must not skare it.
*43. He lives unsafely, that lookes too neere on things.
*44. A gentle houswife marres the houshold.
45. A crooked log makes a strait fire.
*46. He hath great neede of a foole, that plaies the foole himselfe.
*47. A Marchant that gaines not, looseth.
*48. Let not him that feares feathers come among wild-foule.
49. Love and a Cough cannot be hid.
*50. A Dwarfe on a Gyants shoulder sees further of the two.
*51. Hee that sendes a foole, means to follow him.
*52. Brabling Curres never want torne eares.
*53. Better the feet slip then the tongue.

25 that] who *LG* waits *HH JP*: waights *OP*: looks *LG* 26 not] no *LG* 27 Cake *HH LG* (Fr. *gasteau*) : caske *OP JP* an ill] *LG om.* an must] must both of them *LG* 28 leane Executors] a leane Executor *LG HH* 34 vndoe all *HH*: undo us all *OP JP* 36 is] lies *HH* 38 denies to all *HH*: denies all *LG OP JP* 46 hath] had *LG* 47 looses *HH* 48 amongst *HH* 50 A Dwarfe on a Gyants shoulders sees farther then they two. *HH* 51 *Between* 51 *and* 52, *as above*, *HH and LG have* (*) The longest Day hath an Eueninge. 52 Brabling] Brawling *LG* torne *LG*: toren *HH* (Fr. *deschirées*) : sore *OP JP* 53 thy foote slip then thy *LG*

*54. For washing his hands, none sels his lands.
55. A Lyons skin is never cheape.
56. The goate must browse where she is tyed.
*57. Who hath a Wolfe for his mate, needes a Dog for his man.
*58. In a good house all is quickly ready.
59. A bad dog never sees the Wolfe.
60. God oft hath a great share in a little house.
61. Ill ware is never cheape.
*62. A cherefull looke makes a dish a feast.
*63. If all fooles had bables, wee should want fuell.
64. Vertue never growes old.
65. Evening words are not like to morning.
*66. Were there no fooles, badd ware would not passe.
67. Never had ill workeman good tooles.
68. Hee stands not surely, that never slips.
*69. Were there no hearers, there would be no backbiters.
*70. Every thing is of use to a houskeeper.
71. When prayers are done, my Lady is ready.
*72. At Length the Fox turnes Monk.
73. Flies are busiest about leane horses.
*74. Harken to reason or shee will bee heard.
75. The bird loves her nest.
*76. Every thing new is fine.
77. When a dog is a drowning, every one offers him drink.
78. Better a bare foote then none.
*79. Who is so deafe, as he that will not heare?
*80. He that is warme, thinkes all so.
*81. At length the Fox is brought to the Furrier.
*82. Hee that goes barefoot, must not plant thornes.
83. They that are booted are not alwaies ready.
*84. He that will learne to pray, let him goe to Sea.
85. In spending lies the advantage.
*86. Hee that lives well is learned enough.

54 sellethe *HH* 59 *absent from HH* 61 *Between* 61 *and* 62, *as above*, *HH has* Who eates the Kings Goose uoydes the feathers an hundred years after. 62 one dish *LG* 63 bawbles *Pickering* 68 slipte *HH* 72 *absent from HH* 79 that] who *LG* hear? *JP*: heare. *OP* 80 all are soe *LG* 84 that] who *LG* 85 *LG has here instead* (*) Better bend then break. 86 that] who *LG*

87. Ill vessells seldome miscarry.
88. A full belly neither fights nor flies well.
89. All truths are not to be told.
90. An old wise mans shaddow is better then a young buzzards sword.
91. Noble houskeepers neede no dores.
92. Every ill man hath his ill day.
93. Sleepe without supping, and wake without owing.
94. I gave the mouse a hole, and she is become my heire.
95. Assaile who will, the valiant attends.
96. Whether goest, griefe? where I am wont.
97. Praise day at night, and life at the end.
98. Whether shall the Oxe goe, where he shall not labour?
99. Where you thinke there is bacon, there is no Chimney.
100. Mend your cloathes, and you may hold out this yeare.
101. Dresse a stick, and it seemes a youth.
102. The tongue walkes where the teeth speede not.
103. A faire wife and a frontire Castle breede quarrels.
104. Leave jesting whiles it pleaseth, lest it turne to earnest.
105. Deceive not thy Physitian, Confessor, nor Lawyer.
106. Ill natures, the more you aske them, the more they stick.
107. Vertue and a Trade are the best portion for Children.
108. The Chicken is the Countries, but the Citie eates it.
109. He that gives thee a Capon, give him the leg and the wing.
110. Hee that lives ill, feare followes him.
111. Give a clowne your finger, and he will take your hand.
112. Good is to bee sought out, and evill attended.
113. A good pay-master starts not at assurances.
114. No Alchymy to saving.
115. To a gratefull man give mony when he askes.
116. Who would doe ill ne're wants occasion.
117. To fine folkes a little ill finely wrapt.
*118. A child correct behind and not before.

98 labour? *JP*: labour. *OP* 101 Dresse *Ed*: Presse *OP JP* *See note* 108 *Copies of OP vary between* eates *and* eateth: eats *JP* 115 gratefull *JP*: grate full *OP* 118 A horse and a child *LG* and not] not *LG*

119. To a fair day open the window, but make you ready as to a foule.
120. Keepe good men company, and you shall be of the number.
121. No love to a Fathers.
122. The Mill gets by going.
123. To a boyling pot flies come not.
124. Make hast to an ill way that you may get out of it.
125. A snow yeare, a rich yeare.
126. Better to be blinde, then to see ill.
127. Learne weeping, and thou shalt laugh gayning.
128. Who hath no more bread then neede, must not keepe a dog.
129. A garden must be lookt unto and drest as the body.
130. The Fox, when hee cannot reach the grapes, saies they are not ripe.
131. Water trotted is as good as oates.
132. Though the Mastiffe be gentle, yet bite him not by the lippe.
133. Though a lie be well drest, it is ever overcome.
*134. Though old and wise, yet still advise.
*135. Three helping one another, beare the burthen of sixe.
136. Old wine, and an old friend, are good provisions.
137. Happie is hee that chastens himselfe.
138. Well may hee smell fire, whose gowne burnes.
139. The wrongs of a Husband or Master are not reproached.
*140. Welcome evill, if thou commest alone.
*141. Love your neighbour, yet pull not downe your hedge.
142. The bit that one eates, no friend makes.
143. A drunkards purse is a bottle.
*144. Shee spins well that breedes her children.
145. Good is the *mora* that makes all sure.
*146. Play with a foole at home, and he will play with you in the market.
147. Every one stretcheth his legges according to his coverlet.

123 come] comes *JP* 132 gentle] gentile *JP* 141 yet] but *LG* 144 child *LG*

148. Autumnall Agues are long, or mortall.
149. Marry your sonne when you will; your daughter when you can.
150. Dally not with mony or women.
151. Men speake of the faire, as things went with them there.
152. The best remedy against an ill man is much ground betweene both.
153. The mill cannot grind with the water that's past.
154. Corne is cleaned with winde, and the soule with chastnings.
*155. Good words are worth much, and cost little.
*156. To buy deare is not bounty.
157. Jest not with the eye or with Religion.
158. The eye and Religion can beare no jesting.
*159. Without favour none will know you, and with it you will not know your selfe.
*160. Buy at a faire, but sell at home.
161. Cover your selfe with your shield, and care not for cryes.
162. A wicked mans gift hath a touch of his master.
*163. None is a foole alwaies, every one sometimes.
164. From a chollerick man withdraw a little; from him that saies nothing, for ever.
165. Debters are lyers.
166. Of all smells, bread: of all tasts, salt.
167. In a great River great fish are found, but take heede, lest you bee drowned.
168. Ever since we weare cloathes, we know not one another.
169. God heales, and the Physitian hath the thankes.
*170. Hell is full of good meanings and wishings.
171. Take heede of still waters, the quick passe away.
172. After the house is finisht, leave it.
*173. Our owne actions are our security, not others judgements.

153 *misnumbered* 143 *in OP* the water] *JP om.* the 159 not] hardly *LG* 163 alway *LG* 164 little; *JP*: little, *OP* 166 *Cf. No.* 741 170 *LG om.* and wishings 173 are our security] secure us *LG*

*178. Thinke of ease, but worke on.
179. Hee that lies long a bed, his estate feeles it.
180. Whether you boyle snow or pound it, you can have but water of it.
181. One stroke fells not an oke.
182. God complaines not, but doth what is fitting.
183. A diligent Scholler, and the Master 's paid.
184. Milke saies to wine, welcome friend.
185. They that know one another salute a farre off.
186. Where there is no honour, there is no griefe.
187. Where the drink goes in, there the wit goes out.
188. He that staies does the businesse.
189. Almes never make poore. *Or thus*,
190. Great almes-giving lessens no mans living.
191. Giving much to the poore, doth inrich a mans store.
192. It takes much from the account, to which his sin doth amount.
193. It adds to the glory both of soule and body.
194. Ill comes in by ells, and goes out by inches.
195. The Smith and his penny both are black.
196. Whose house is of glasse, must not throw stones at another.
197. If the old dog barke he gives counsell.
198. The tree that growes slowly, keepes it selfe for another.
*199. I wept when I was borne, and every day shewes why.
*200. Hee that lookes not before, finds himselfe behind.
201. He that plaies his mony ought not to value it.
202. He that riseth first, is first drest.
*203. Diseases of the eye are to bee cured with the elbow.
204. The hole calls the thiefe.
205. A gentlemans grayhound, and a salt-box; seeke them at the fire.
206. A childs service is little, yet hee is no little foole that despiseth it.
207. The river past, and God forgotten.

178 *The mistakes in OP in numbering here and after Nos.* 778, 831, *and* 947 *are retained for convenient reference* 183 *Copies of OP vary between* Shcoller *and* Scholler: Scholer *JP* 188 *Cf. No.* 852 189 Or thus, *JP*: *copies of OP vary between* others *and* orthus. *and* or thus: 190–3 *alternatives and explanations of No.* 189 203 eyes *LG*

208. Evils have their comfort, good none can support (to wit—with a moderate and contented heart).

*209. Who must account for himselfe and others, must know both.

210. Hee that eats the hard shall eate the ripe.

*211. The miserable man makes a peny of a farthing, and the liberall of a farthing sixe pence.

212. The honey is sweet, but the Bee stings.

213. Waight and measure take away strife.

214. The sonne full and tattered, the daughter empty and fine.

215. Every path hath a puddle.

216. In good yeares corne is hay, in ill yeares straw is corne.

217. Send a wise man on an errand, and say nothing unto him.

218. In life you lov'd me not, in death you bewaile me.

219. Into a mouth shut flies flie not.

220. The hearts letter is read in the eyes.

221. The ill that comes out of our mouth falles into our bosome.

222. In great pedigrees there are Governours and Chandlers.

223. In the house of a Fidler, all fiddle.

224. Sometimes the best gaine is to lose.

225. Working and making a fire doth discretion require.

226. One graine fills not a sacke, but helpes his fellowes.

227. It is a great victory that comes without blood.

228. In war, hunting, and love, men for one pleasure a thousand griefes prove.

229. Reckon right, and February hath one and thirty daies.

230. Honour without profit is a ring on the finger.

231. Estate in two parishes is bread in two wallets.

232. Honour and profit lie not in one sacke.

233. A naughty child is better sick then whole.

234. Truth and oyle are ever above.

208 with a . . . heart *not included in the brackets in OP JP* 209 Who] Who so *LG* 211 The miserable] A miserable *LG* but the Liberall makes of a farthing six pense. *LG*

235. He that riseth betimes hath some thing in his head.
*236. Advise none to marry or to goe to warre.
237. To steale the Hog, and give the feet for almes.
238. The thorne comes forth with his point forwards.
239. One hand washeth another, and both the face.
240. The fault of the horse is put on the saddle.
241. The corne hides it self in the snow, as an old man in furrs.
242. The Jewes spend at Easter, the Mores at marriages, the Christians in sutes.
243. Fine dressing is a foule house swept before the doores.
244. A woman and a glasse are ever in danger.
245. An ill wound is cured, not an ill name.
246. The wise hand doth not all that the foolish mouth speakes.
247. On painting and fighting looke aloofe.
248. Knowledge is folly, except grace guide it.
249. Punishment is lame, but it comes.
250. The more women looke in their glasse, the lesse they looke to their house.
*251. A long tongue is a signe of a short hand.
252. Marry a widdow before she leave mourning.
253. The worst of law is, that one suit breedes twenty.
*254. Providence is better then a rent.
255. What your glasse telles you, will not be told by Councell.
256. There are more men threatned then stricken.
257. A foole knowes more in his house, then a wise man in anothers.
258. I had rather ride on an asse that carries me, then a horse that throwes me.
259. The hard gives more then he that hath nothing.
260. The beast that goes alwaies never wants blowes.
261. Good cheape is deare.
262. It costs more to doe ill then to doe well.
*263. Good words quench more then a bucket of water.
264. An ill agreement is better then a good judgement.

236 or to goe] nor to goe *LG*: or goe *JP* 238 his] the *JP* 242 Mores] Moors *JP* 263 Soft words quench more then cold water. *LG*

265. There is more talke then trouble.
*266. Better spare to have of thine own, then aske of other men.
267. Better good afarre off, then evill at hand.
268. Feare keepes the garden better then the gardiner.
269. I had rather aske of my sire browne bread, then borrow of my neighbour white.
270. Your pot broken seemes better then my whole one.
271. Let an ill man lie in thy straw, and he lookes to be thy heire.
*272. By suppers more have beene killed then Galen ever cured.
273. While the discreet advise, the foole doth his busines.
274. A mountaine and a river are good neighbours.
275. Gossips are frogs, they drinke and talke.
276. Much spends the traveller, more then the abider.
*277. Prayers and provender hinder no journey.
278. A well-bred youth neither speakes of himselfe, nor being spoken to is silent.
279. A journying woman speakes much of all, and all of her.
280. The Fox knowes much, but more he that catcheth him.
*281. Many friends in generall, one in speciall.
282. The foole askes much, but hee is more foole that grants it.
*283. Many kisse the hand they wish cut off.
*284. Neither bribe nor loose thy right.
*285. In the world who knowes not to swimme, goes to the bottome.
286. Chuse not an house neere an Inne (viz. for noise) or in a corner (for filth).
287. Hee is a foole that thinks not that another thinks.
288. Neither eyes on letters, nor hands in coffers.
289. The Lyon is not so fierce as they paint him.

269 ſire *indistinctly printed here and in No.* 300 : fire *Grosart* 271 *Copies of OP vary between* looke *and* lookes : looks *JP* 272 have beene] are *LG* Galen *LG* : *Gallen OP JP* 273 advise, *JP* : advise *OP* 276 *om.* then *conj. Ed See note* 277 hinder no journey.] never hinder any. *LG* 285 knowes not to] can not *LG* goes] goe *LG*

290. Goe not for every griefe to the Physitian, nor for every quarrell to the Lawyer, nor for every thirst to the pot.
291. Good service is a great inchantment.
*292. There would bee no great ones if there were no little ones.
293. It 's no sure rule to fish with a cros-bow.
294. There were no ill language, if it were not ill taken.
295. The groundsell speakes not save what it heard at the hinges.
296. The best mirrour is an old friend.
297. Say no ill of the yeere, till it be past.
*298. A mans discontent is his worst evill.
299. Feare nothing but sinne.
300. The child saies nothing, but what it heard by the fire.
301. Call me not an olive, till thou see me gathered.
302. That is not good language which all understand not.
303. Hee that burnes his house warmes himselfe for once.
304. He will burne his house, to warme his hands.
305. Hee will spend a whole yeares rent at one meales meate.
306. All is not gold that glisters.
307. A blustering night, a faire day.
*308. Bee not idle and you shall not bee longing.
309. He is not poore that hath little, but he that desireth much.
*310. Let none say, I will not drinke water.
311. Hee wrongs not an old man that steales his supper from him.
312. The tongue talkes at the heads cost.
*313. Hee that strikes with his tongue, must ward with his head.
314. Keep not ill men company, lest you increase the number.
315. God strikes not with both hands, for to the sea he made havens, and to rivers foords.

292 little] mean *LG* 300 fire] (Fr. *foyer*: Span. *hogár*) : ſire *Pickering, 1859*
313 head] (Ital. *testa*) : hand *LG* 315 havens] heavens *JP*

316. A rugged stone growes smooth from hand to hand.
*317. No lock will hold against the power of gold.
*318. The absent partie is still faultie.
319. Peace, and Patience, and death with repentance.
320. If you loose your time, you cannot get mony nor gaine.
321. Bee not a Baker, if your head be of butter.
322. Aske much to have a little.
323. Litle stickes kindle the fire; great ones put it out.
*324. Anothers bread costs deare.
325. Although it raine, throw not away thy watering pot.
*326. Although the sun shine, leave not thy cloake at home.
327. A little with quiet is the onely dyet.
328. In vaine is the mill-clacke, if the Miller his hearing lack.
329. By the needle you shall draw the thread, and by that which is past, see how that which is to come will be drawne on.
330. Stay a little and news will find you.
*331. Stay till the lame messenger come, if you will know the truth of the thing.
332. When God will, no winde but brings raine.
333. Though you rise early, yet the day comes at his time, and not till then.
334. Pull downe your hatt on the winds side.
335. As the yeere is, your pot must seeth.
336. Since you know all, and I nothing, tell me what I dreamed last night.
*337. When the Foxe preacheth, beware your geese.
338. When you are an Anvill, hold you still; when you are a hammer, strike your fill.
*339. Poore and liberall, rich and coveteous.
340. He that makes his bed ill, lies there.
341. Hee that labours and thrives spins gold.
342. He that sowes trusts in God.
343. Hee that lies with the dogs, riseth with fleas.

317 No Lockes can hold against gold. *LG* 326 Although] Though *LG*
331 *LG om.* of the thing 337 your geese *LG* : geese *OP JP*

*344. Hee that repaires not a part, builds all.
*345. A discontented man knowes not where to sit easie.
346. Who spits against heaven, it falls in his face.
347. Hee that dines and leaves, layes the cloth twice.
*348. Who eates his cock alone must saddle his horse alone.
349. He that is not handsome at 20, nor strong at 30, nor rich at 40, nor wise at 50, will never bee handsome, strong, rich, or wise.
350. Hee that doth what hee will, doth not what he ought.
*351. Hee that will deceive the fox, must rise betimes.
352. He that lives well sees a farre off.
353. He that hath a mouth of his owne, must not say to another; Blow.
*354. He that will be served must bee patient.
355. Hee that gives thee a bone, would not have thee die.
356. He that chastens one, chastens 20.
357. He that hath lost his credit is dead to the world.
*358. He that hath no ill fortune is troubled with good.
359. Hee that demands misseth not, unlesse his demands be foolish.
*360. He that hath no hony in his pot, let him have it in his mouth.
361. He that takes not up a pin, slights his wife.
362. He that owes nothing, if he makes not mouthes at us, is courteous.
*363. Hee that looseth his due, gets no thankes.
364. He that beleeveth all, misseth; hee that beleeveth nothing, hitts not.
*365. Pardons and pleasantnesse are great revenges of slanders.
366. A married man turns his staffe into a stake.
*367. If you would know secrets, looke them in griefe or pleasure.
368. Serve a noble disposition, though poore, the time comes that hee will repay thee.
369. The fault is as great as hee that is faulty.

344 at length must build all. *LG* 348 cock] (Span. *gallo*): cake *LG* 351 will] would *LG* 363 no *LG*: not *OP JP* 364 misseth; *JP*: misseth, *OP* 365 the great Revengers *LG* 367 would] will *LG*

*370. If folly were griefe every house would weepe.
371. Hee that would bee well old, must bee old betimes.
372. Sit in your place and none can make you rise.
373. If you could runne, as you drinke, you might catch a hare.
*374. Would you know what mony is, Go borrow some.
375. The morning Sunne never lasts a day.
376. Thou hast death in thy house, and dost bewaile anothers.
*377. All griefes with bread are lesse.
378. All things require skill, but an appetite.
379. All things have their place, knew wee how to place them.
380. Little pitchers have wide eares.
381. We are fooles one to another.
382. This world is nothing except it tend to another.
*383. There are three waies, the Vniversities, the Sea, the Court.
384. God comes to see without a bell.
385. Life without a friend is death without a witnesse.
386. Cloath thee in war, arme thee in peace.
387. The horse thinkes one thing, and he that sadles him another.
388. Mills and wives ever want.
389. The dog that licks ashes, trust not with meale.
390. The buyer needes a hundred eyes, the seller not one.
391. He carries well, to whom it waighes not.
392. The comforters head never akes.
393. Step after step the ladder is ascended.
394. Who likes not the drinke, God deprives him of bread.
395. To a crazy ship all winds are contrary.
*396. Justice pleaseth few in their owne house.
397. In time comes he whom God sends.
398. Water a farre off quencheth not fire.
*399. In sports and journeys men are knowne.
400. An old friend, a new house.
*401. Love is not found in the market.

377 *LG adds* or Noe woe to want. 383 the Court, vniversities, & sea *LG* 397 time *JP* : times *OP* 400 friend, a *Ed* : friend is a *OP JP See note* 401 the] a *LG*

402. Dry feet, warme head, bring safe to bed.
403. Hee is rich enough that wants nothing.
*404. One father is enough to governe one hundred sons, but not a hundred sons one father.
405. Faire shooting never kild bird.
406. An upbraided morsell never choaked any.
407. Dearths foreseene come not.
408. An ill labourer quarrells with his tooles.
409. Hee that falles into the durt, the longer he stayes there, the fowler he is.
410. He that blames would buy.
411. He that sings on friday, will weepe on Sunday.
412. The charges of building and making of gardens are unknowne.
413. My house, my house, though thou art small, thou art to me the Escuriall.
*414. A hundred loade of thought will not pay one of debts.
*415. Hee that comes of a hen must scrape.
416. He that seekes trouble never misses.
*417. He that once deceives is ever suspected.
418. Being on sea saile, being on land settle.
419. Who doth his owne businesse, foules not his hands.
420. Hee that makes a good warre makes a good peace.
421. Hee that workes after his owne manner, his head akes not at the matter.
422. Who hath bitter in his mouth, spits not all sweet.
*423. He that hath children, all his morsels are not his owne.
*424. He that hath the spice, may season as he list.
425. He that hath a head of waxe must not walke in the sunne.
426. He that hath love in his brest, hath spurres in his sides.
*427. Hee that respects not, is not respected.
428. Hee that hath a Fox for his mate, hath neede of a net at his girdle.

404 but an 100 sons are not enough to gouerne one Father. *LG* 405 Faire *Ed* (Ital. *Bel colpo*): Farre *OP JP See note* 407 Dearths] (Ital. *Carestia*): Deaths *1859* 414 A] An *LG* 415 of a hen] after *LG* 417 He that] Who so *LG* 423 that] who *LG* 424 that] who *LG* list] pleaseth *LG*

429. Hee that hath right, feares; he that hath wrong, hopes.
430. Hee that hath patience hath fatt thrushes for a farthing.
431. Never was strumpet faire.
432. He that measures not himselfe, is measured.
*433. Hee that hath one hogge makes him fat, and hee that hath one son makes him a foole.
434. Who letts his wife goe to every feast, and his horse drinke at every water, shall neither have good wife nor good horse.
*435. He that speakes sowes, and he that holds his peace, gathers.
436. He that hath little is the lesse durtie.
437. He that lives most dies most.
438. He that hath one foot in the straw, hath another in the spittle.
*439. Hee that's fed at anothers hand may stay long ere he be full.
440. Hee that makes a thing too fine, breakes it.
441. Hee that bewailes himselfe hath the cure in his hands.
442. He that would be well, needs not goe from his owne house.
443. Councell breakes not the head.
*444. Fly the pleasure that bites to morrow.
445. Hee that knowes what may bee gained in a day never steales.
446. Mony refused looseth its brightnesse.
447. Health and mony goe farre.
*448. Where your will is ready, your feete are light.
449. A great ship askes deepe waters.
450. Woe to the house where there is no chiding.
*451. Take heede of the viniger of sweet wine.
452. Fooles bite one another, but wise-men agree together.
453. Trust not one nights ice.

433 Hee that] Hee who *LG* who hath but one sonne *LG* 435 holds his peace] hears *LG* 439 Who is fed by anothers hand stays long ere he be full. *LG* 441 *Copies of OP vary between* in hands *and* in his hands: in his hands *JP* 448 Where] When *LG* the feet are swift *LG*

454. Good is good, but better carries it.
455. To gaine teacheth how to spend.
456. Good finds good.
457. The dog gnawes the bone because he cannot swallow it.
458. The crow bewailes the sheepe, and then eates it.
*459. Building is a sweet impoverishing.
*460. The first degree of folly is to hold ones selfe wise, the second to professe it, the third to despise counsell.
461. The greatest step is that out of doores.
462. To weepe for joy is a kinde of Manna.
463. The first service a child doth his father is to make him foolish.
464. The resolved minde hath no eares.
465. In the kingdome of a cheater the wallet is carried before.
466. The eye will have his part.
467. The good mother sayes not, Will you? but gives.
468. A house and a woman sute excellently.
469. In the kingdome of blind men the one ey'd is king.
470. A little Kitchin makes a large house.
471. Warre makes theeves, and peace hangs them.
472. Poverty is the mother of health.
473. In the morning mountaines, in the evening fountaines.
474. The back-doore robs the house.
475. Wealth is like rheume, it falles on the weakest parts.
476. The gowne is his that weares it, and the world his that enjoyes it.
477. Hope is the poore mans bread.
*478. Vertue now is in herbs and stones and words onely.
479. Fine words dresse ill deedes.
*480. Labour as long liu'd, pray as ever dying.
*481. A poore beauty finds more lovers then husbands.
482. Discreet women have neither eyes nor eares.
483. Things well fitted abide.

460 dsepise *OP* is to think ourselves wise *LG* 464 eares *Ed* (Ital. *orecchio*): cares *OP JP* 478 in stones, herbs & words only. *LG* 480 even *indistinctly printed in OP, possibly* ever : even *JP*: alwayes *LG* (Ital. *all'hora*)

484. Prettinesse dies first.
485. Talking payes no toll.
486. The masters eye fattens the horse, and his foote the ground.
*487. Disgraces are like cherries, one drawes another.
488. Praise a hill, but keepe below.
489. Praise the Sea, but keepe on land.
*490. In chusing a wife, and buying a sword, we ought not to trust another.
491. The wearer knowes, where the shoe wrings.
*492. Faire is not faire, but that which pleaseth.
493. There is no jollitie but hath a smack of folly.
494. He that 's long a giving, knowes not how to give.
495. The filth under the white snow, the sunne discovers.
*496. Every one fastens where there is gaine.
497. All feete tread not in one shoe.
*498. Patience, time and money accommodate all things.
499. For want of a naile the shoe is lost, for want of a shoe the horse is lost, for want of a horse the rider is lost.
500. Weigh justly and sell dearely.
501. Little wealth, little care.
502. Little journeys and good cost bring safe home.
503. Gluttony kills more then the sword.
504. When children stand quiet, they have done some ill.
505. A little and good fills the trencher.
506. A penny spar'd is twice got.
507. When a knave is in a plumtree he hath neither friend nor kin.
508. Short boughs, long vintage.
*509. Health without money is halfe an ague.
*510. If the wise erred not, it would goe hard with fooles.
511. Beare with evill, and expect good.
*512. He that tells a secret is anothers servant.
513. If all fooles wore white Caps, wee should seeme a flock of geese.
514. Water, fire, and souldiers, quickly make roome.

487 drawes on *LG* 490 a sword, trust not another. *LG* 496 *LG om.* there 500 Weigh] Weight *JP* 510 If wise men *LG*

*515. Pension never inriched young man.
516. Vnder water, famine; under snow, bread.
517. The Lame goes as farre as your staggerer.
518. He that looseth is Marchant as well as he that gaines.
519. A jade eates as much as a good horse.
520. All things in their beeing are good for something.
521. One flower makes no garland.
*522. A faire death honours the whole life.
523. One enemy is too much.
524. Living well is the best revenge.
525. One foole makes a hundred.
*526. One paire of eares drawes dry a hundred tongues.
527. A foole may throw a stone into a well, which a hundred wise men cannot pull out.
528. One slumber finds another.
529. On a good bargaine thinke twice.
*530. To a good spender God is the Treasurer.
531. A curst Cow hath short hornes.
532. Musick helps not the tooth-ach.
*533. We cannot come to honour under a Coverlet.
534. Great paines quickly find ease.
535. To the counsell of fooles a woodden bell.
536. The cholerick man never wants woe.
*537. Helpe thy selfe, and God will helpe thee.
538. At the games end we shall see who gaines.
539. There are many waies to fame.
540. Love is the true price of love.
541. Love rules his kingdome without a sword.
542. Love makes all hard hearts gentle.
543. Love makes a good eye squint.
*544. Love askes faith, and faith firmenesse.
545. A scepter is one thing, and a ladle another.
546. Great trees are good for nothing but shade.
547. Hee commands enough that obeyes a wise man.
548. Faire words make mee looke to my purse.
549. Though the Fox run, the chicken hath wings.
550. He plaies well that winnes.

515 a young man *Pickering* 526 a hundred] an hundred *JP*: an hundreth *LG*
533 a *LG*: *om. OP JP* 548 make *Ed*: makes *OP JP* 550 *numbered* 750 *in OP*

551. You must strike in measure, when there are many to strike on one Anvile.

*552. The shortest answer is doing.

553. It's a poore stake that cannot stand one yeare in the ground.

554. He that commits a fault, thinkes every one speakes of it.

555. He that's foolish in the fault, let him be wise in the punishment.

556. The blind eate many a flie.

557. He that can make a fire well, can end a quarrell.

558. The tooth-ach is more ease then to deale with ill people.

*559. Hee that should have what hee hath not, should doe what he doth not.

560. He that hath no good trade, it is to his losse.

561. The offender never pardons.

562. He that lives not well one yeare, sorrowes seven after.

563. He that hopes not for good, feares not evill.

564. He that is angry at a feast is rude.

565. He that mockes a cripple, ought to be whole.

566. When the tree is fallen, all goe with their hatchet.

*567. He that hath hornes in his bosom, let him not put them on his head.

568. He that burnes most shines most.

*569. He that trusts in a lie, shall perish in truth.

570. Hee that blowes in the dust fills his eyes with it.

571. Bells call others, but themselves enter not into the Church.

572. Of faire things, the Autumne is faire.

*573. Giving is dead, restoring very sicke.

574. A gift much expected is paid, not given.

575. Two ill meales make the third a glutton.

*576. The Royall Crowne cures not the head-ach.

577. 'Tis hard to be wretched, but worse to be knowne so.

578. A feather in hand is better then a bird in the ayre.

*579. It's better to be the head of a Lyzard, then the tayle of a Lyon.

559 should have] would have *LG* should doe] must doe *LG* 567 on] in *LG*
569 by the truth *LG* 579 the head *LG*: head *OP JP* Lyzard] mouse *LG*

580. Good & quickly seldome meete.
581. Folly growes without watering.
*582. Happier are the hands compast with yron, then a heart with thoughts.
583. If the staffe be crooked, the shadow cannot be straight.
584. To take the nuts from the fire with the dogges foot.
585. He is a foole that makes a wedge of his fist.
586. Valour that parlies is neare yeelding.
587. Thursday come, and the week's gone.
588. A flatterers throat is an open Sepulcher.
*589. There is great force hidden in a sweet command.
590. The command of custome is great.
*591. To have money is a feare, not to have it a griefe.
592. The Catt sees not the mouse ever.
593. Little dogs start the Hare, the great get her.
594. Willowes are weak, yet they bind other wood.
595. A good payer is master of anothers purse.
596. The thread breakes, where it is weakest.
597. Old men, when they scorne young, make much of death.
598. God is at the end, when we thinke he is furthest off it.
599. A good Judge conceives quickly, judges slowly.
600. Rivers neede a spring.
601. He that contemplates hath a day without night.
602. Give loosers leave to talke.
603. Losse embraceth shame.
604. Gaming, women, and wine, while they laugh they make men pine.
605. The fatt man knoweth not, what the leane thinketh.
606. Wood halfe burnt is easily kindled.
607. The fish adores the bait.
608. He that goeth farre hath many encounters.
609. Every bees hony is sweet.
*610. The slothful is the servant of the counters.
611. Wisedome hath one foot on Land, and another on Sea.

582 Happier the hands fetter'd then the head distracted. *LG* 589 a great force in *LG* 591 not to have it] to want it is *LG* 595 payer *Pickering* (Ital. *pagadore*): prayer *OP JP* 597 young, *JP*: young *OP* 610 a seruant of the vertuous. *LG*

612. The thought hath good leggs, and the quill a good tongue.
613. A wise man needes not blush for changing his purpose.
614. The March sunne raises but dissolves not.
*615. Time is the Rider that breakes youth.
616. The wine in the bottell doth not quench thirst.
617. The sight of a man hath the force of a Lyon.
618. An examin'd enterprize goes on boldly.
619. In every Art it is good to have a master.
620. In every country dogges bite.
621. In every countrey the sun rises in the morning.
622. A noble plant suites not with a stubborne ground.
623. You may bring a horse to the river, but he will drinke when and what he pleaseth.
*624. Before you make a friend, eate a bushell of salt with him.
*625. Speake fitly, or be silent wisely.
626. Skill and confidence are an unconquered army.
627. I was taken by a morsell, saies the fish.
628. A disarmed peace is weake.
629. The ballance distinguisheth not betweene gold and lead.
630. The perswasion of the fortunate swaies the doubtfull.
631. To bee beloved is above all bargaines.
*632. To deceive ones selfe is very easie.
*633. The reasons of the poore weigh not.
634. Perversnes makes one squint ey'd.
635. The evening praises the day, and the morning a host.
636. The table robbes more then a thiefe.
637. When age is jocond it makes sport for death.
638. True praise rootes and spreedes.
639. Feares are divided in the midst.
*640. The soule needs few things, the body many.
641. Astrologie is true, but the Astrologers cannot finde it.
642. Ty it well, and let it goe.
643. Emptie vessels sound most.
*644. Send not a Catt for Lard.

635 host *Ed* (Ital. *l'hoste*): frost *OP JP* *See note* 640 few] some *LG*

645. Foolish tongues talke by the dozen.
646. Love makes one fitt for any work.
647. A pittifull mother makes a scald head.
648. An old Physitian, and a young Lawyer.
*649. Talke much and erre much, saies the Spanyard.
650. Some make a conscience of spitting in the Church, yet robbe the Altar.
651. An idle head is a boxe for the winde.
652. Shew me a lyer, and I'le shew thee a theefe.
653. A beane in liberty is better then a comfit in prison.
654. None is borne Master.
*655. Shew a good man his errour and he turnes it to a vertue, but an ill man doubles his fault.
656. None is offended but by himselfe.
657. None saies his Garner is full.
658. In the husband wisedome, in the wife gentlenesse.
659. Nothing dries sooner then a teare.
660. In a Leopard the spotts are not observed.
661. Nothing lasts but the Church.
662. A wise man cares not for what he cannot have.
663. It 's not good fishing before the net.
664. He cannot be vertuous that is not rigorous.
665. That which will not be spun, let it not come betweene the spindle and the distaffe.
666. When my house burnes, it 's not good playing at Chesse.
667. No barber shaves so close but another finds worke.
668. Ther 's no great banquet but some fares ill.
669. A holy habit clenseth not a foule soule.
670. Forbeare not sowing because of birds.
671. Mention not a halter in the house of him that was hanged.
672. Speake not of a dead man at the table.
673. A hatt is not made for one shower.
674. No sooner is a Temple built to God but the Devill builds a Chappell hard by.
*675. Every one puts his fault on the Times.

649 *LG om.* saies the Spanyard   652 I'le *JP*: ile *OP*   655 an ill man doubleth *LG* : an ill, it doubles *OP JP*   675 putt their faults *LG*

676. You cannot make a wind-mill goe with a paire of bellowes.
677. Pardon all but thy selfe.
*678. Every one is weary, the poore in seeking, the rich in keeping, the good in learning.
679. The escaped mouse ever feeles the taste of the bait.
680. A litle wind kindles; much puts out the fire.
*681. Dry bread at home is better then rost meate abroad.
682. More have repented speech then silence.
683. The coveteous spends more then the liberall.
684. Divine ashes are better then earthly meale.
685. Beauty drawes more then oxen.
686. One father is more then a hundred Schoolemasters.
687. One eye of the masters sees more, then ten of the servants.
688. When God will punish, hee will first take away the understanding.
689. A little labour, much health.
690. When it thunders, the theefe becomes honest.
691. The tree that God plants, no winde hurts it.
692. Knowledge is no burthen.
693. It's a bold mouse that nestles in the catts eare.
694. Long jesting was never good.
695. If a good man thrive, all thrive with him.
696. If the mother had not beene in the oven, shee had never sought her daughter there.
697. If great men would have care of little ones, both would last long.
698. Though you see a Church-man ill, yet continue in the Church still.
699. Old praise dies, unlesse you feede it.
*700. If things were to be done twice, all would be wise.
701. Had you the world on your Chesse-bord, you could not fit all to your mind.
*702. Suffer and expect.
703. If fooles should not foole it, they should loose their season.

678 in (3 *times*)] a *LG* 692 burden *JP* 700 If all things might be *LG*
701 fit] fill *JP* 702 *LG adds* sustine, abstine. 703 should loose] shall lose *JP*

*704. Love and businesse teach eloquence.
705. That which two will, takes effect.
*706. He complaines wrongfully of the sea that twice suffers shipwrack.
707. He is onely bright that shines by himselfe.
708. A valiant mans looke is more then a cowards sword.
709. The effect speakes, the tongue needes not.
710. Divine grace was never slow.
*711. Reason lies betweene the spurre and the bridle.
712. It's a proud horse that will not carry his owne provender.
713. Three women make a market.
714. Three can hold their peace, if two be away.
715. It's an ill councell that hath no escape.
716. All our pompe the earth covers.
717. To whirle the eyes too much shewes a Kites braine.
718. Comparisons are odious.
719. All keyes hang not on one girdle.
720. Great businesses turne on a little pinne.
721. The wind in ones face makes one wise.
722. All the Armes of England will not arme feare.
723. One sword keepes another in the sheath.
724. Be what thou wouldst seeme to be.
725. Let all live as they would die.
726. A gentle heart is tyed with an easie thread.
727. Sweet discourse makes short daies and nights.
728. God provides for him that trusteth.
729. He that will not have peace, God gives him warre.
730. To him that will, waies are not wanting.
731. To a great night, a great Lanthorne.
732. To a child all weather is cold.
733. Where there is peace, God is.
*734. None is so wise, but the foole overtakes him.
735. Fooles give to please all but their owne.
736. Prosperity lets goe the bridle.
*737. The Frier preached against stealing, and had a goose in his sleeve.

706 of *LG* (Ital. *del mare*): on *OP JP* that] who *LG* 711 lyeth *LG*
731 night] *misprinted* light *1859* 734 but that the foole *LG*

738. To be too busie gets contempt.
739. February makes a bridge and March breakes it.
740. A horse stumbles that hath foure legges.
741. The best smell is bread, the best savour, salt, the best love that of children.
742. That's the best gowne that goes up and downe the house.
743. The market is the best garden.
744. The first dish pleaseth all.
745. The higher the Ape goes, the more he shewes his taile.
746. Night is the mother of Councels.
747. Gods Mill grinds slow, but sure.
748. Every one thinkes his sacke heaviest.
749. Drought never brought dearth.
750. All complaine.
751. Gamsters and race-horses never last long.
752. It's a poore sport that's not worth the candle.
753. He that is fallen cannot helpe him that is downe.
754. Every one is witty for his owne purpose.
755. A little lett lets an ill workeman.
756. Good workemen are seldome rich.
757. By doing nothing we learne to do ill.
758. A great dowry is a bed full of brables.
759. No profit to honour, no honour to Religion.
760. Every sin brings it's punishment with it.
761. Of him that speakes ill, consider the life more then the words.
762. You cannot hide an eele in a sacke.
763. Give not S. *Peter* so much, to leave Saint *Paul* nothing.
764. You cannot flea a stone.
765. The chiefe disease that raignes this yeare is folly.
766. A sleepy master makes his servant a Lowt.
767. Better speake truth rudely, then lye covertly.
768. He that feares leaves, let him not goe into the wood.
769. One foote is better then two crutches.
770. Better suffer ill, then doe ill.

752 not *JP*: nor *OP* 758 brambles *Pickering, 1859* 761 words] word *JP*
762 an eele] a needle *conj. Ed* (Fr. *aiguilles*) *See note*

*771. Neither praise nor dispraise thy selfe, thy actions serve the turne.
772. Soft and faire goes farre.
773. The constancy of the benefits of the yeere in their seasons argues a Deity.
*774. Praise none too much, for all are fickle.
775. It's absurd to warme one in his armour.
776. Law sutes consume time, and mony, and rest, and friends.
777. Nature drawes more then ten teemes.
778. Hee that hath a wife and children wants not businesse.
780. A shippe and a woman are ever repairing.
781. He that feares death lives not.
782. He that pitties another, remembers himselfe.
783. He that doth what he should not, shall feele what he would not.
*784. Hee that marries for wealth sells his liberty.
785. He that once hitts, is ever bending.
786. He that serves, must serve.
787. He that lends, gives.
788. He that preacheth giveth almes.
789. He that cockers his child, provides for his enemie.
790. A pittifull looke askes enough.
791. Who will sell the Cow, must say the word.
792. Service is no Inheritance.
793. The faulty stands on his guard.
794. A kinsman, a friend, or whom you intreate, take not to serve you, if you will be served neately.
795. At Court, every one for himselfe.
796. To a crafty man, a crafty and an halfe.
797. Hee that is throwne would ever wrestle.
798. He that serves well needes not ask his wages.
799. Faire language grates not the tongue.
800. A good heart cannot lye.
801. Good swimmers at length are drowned.
802. Good land, evill way.
803. In doing we learne.

771 Prayse not thyself, thy actions serue the Turne. *LG* 773 benefits *Ed*: benefit *OP JP* 774 too *JP*: to *OP* 780 *numbered thus in OP*

804. It's good walking with a horse in ones hand.
805. God, and Parents, and our Master, can never be requited.
806. An ill deede cannot bring honour.
807. A small heart hath small desires.
*808. All are not merry that dance lightly.
809. Curtesie on one side only lasts not long.
810. Wine-Counsels seldome prosper.
811. Weening is not measure.
812. The best of the sport is to doe the deede, and say nothing.
*813. If thou thy selfe canst doe it, attend no others helpe or hand.
814. Of a little thing a little displeaseth.
815. He warmes too neere that burnes.
*816. God keepe me from foure houses, an Vsurers, a Taverne, a Spittle, and a Prison.
817. In an hundred elles of contention, there is not an inch of love.
*818. Doe what thou oughtest, and come what come can.
819. Hunger makes dinners, pastime suppers.
820. In a long journey straw waighs.
821. Women laugh when they can, and weepe when they will.
822. Warre is deaths feast.
823. Set good against evill.
824. Hee that brings good newes knockes hard.
825. Beate the dog before the Lyon.
826. Hast comes not alone.
*827. You must loose a flie to catch a trout.
828. Better a snotty child, then his nose wip'd off.
*829. No prison is faire, nor love foule.
830. Hee is not free that drawes his chaine.
831. Hee goes not out of his way, that goes to a good Inne.
833. There comes nought out of the sacke but what was there.

813 *LG om.* or hand (*absent also from Fr.*) 817 In an *JP*: In *OP* 818 come what can. *LG* 829 & no Loue fowl. *LG* 829 *omitted here in JP but included later* (*No.* 1122) 833 *numbered thus in OP* comes *Ed*: come *OP JP*

*834. A little given seasonably excuses a great gift.
835. Hee lookes not well to himselfe that lookes not ever.
836. He thinkes not well, that thinkes not againe.
837. Religion, Credit, and the Eye are not to be touched.
*838. The tongue is not steele, yet it cuts.
839. A white wall is the paper of a foole.
840. They talke of Christmas so long, that it comes.
841. That is gold which is worth gold.
842. It's good tying the sack before it be full.
843. Words are women, deedes are men.
844. Poverty is no sinne.
845. A stone in a well is not lost.
*846. He can give little to his servant, that lickes his knife.
847. Promising is the eve of giving.
848. Hee that keepes his owne makes warre.
849. The Wolfe must dye in his owne skinne.
850. Goods are theirs that enjoy them.
851. He that sends a foole expects one.
852. He that can stay obtaines.
*853. He that gaines well and spends well, needes no count booke.
854. He that endures is not overcome.
*855. He that gives all before hee dies provides to suffer.
*856. He that talkes much of his happinesse summons griefe.
857. Hee that loves the tree, loves the branch.
858. Who hastens a glutton choakes him.
859. Who praiseth Saint *Peter*, doth not blame Saint *Paul*.
*860. He that hath not the craft, let him shut up shop.
861. He that knowes nothing, doubts nothing.
862. Greene wood makes a hott fire.
*863. He that marries late, marries ill.
864. He that passeth a winters day escapes an enemy.
*865. The Rich knowes not who is his friend.
866. A morning sunne, and a wine-bred child, and a latin-bred woman, seldome end well.
867. To a close shorne sheepe, God gives wind by measure.

834 excuseth *LG* 853 count] account *Pickering* booke] books *LG* 855 before] ere *LG* 856 that] who *LG* 863 marries (*bis*)] marrieth *LG*

868. A pleasure long expected is deare enough sold.
869. A poore mans Cow dies, a rich mans child.
870. The Cow knowes not what her taile is worth, till she have lost it.
871. Chuse a horse made, and a wife to make.
872. It's an ill aire where wee gaine nothing.
873. Hee hath not liv'd, that lives not after death.
874. So many men in Court and so many strangers.
875. He quits his place well, that leaves his friend there.
876. That which sufficeth is not little.
877. Good newes may bee told at any time, but ill in the morning.
878. Hee that would be a Gentleman, let him goe to an assault.
879. Who paies the Physitian, does the cure.
*880. None knowes the weight of anothers burthen.
*881. Every one hath a foole in his sleeve.
882. One houres sleepe before midnight is worth three after.
883. In a retreat the lame are formost.
884. It's more paine to doe nothing then something.
885. Amongst good men two men suffice.
886. There needs a long time to know the worlds pulse.
887. The ofspring of those that are very young, or very old, lasts not.
888. A Tyrant is most tyrant to himselfe.
889. Too much taking heede is losse.
890. Craft against craft makes no living.
891. The Reverend are ever before.
892. *France* is a meddow that cuts thrice a yeere.
893. 'Tis easier to build two chimneys, then to maintaine one.
894. The Court hath no Almanack.
895. He that will enter into Paradise, must have a good key.
896. When you enter into a house, leave the anger ever at the doore.

869 dies, a *Ed*: dies a *JP*: dies *OP* 875 there] here *Pickering*, *Grosart*
880 *is followed in LG by* (*) Hee payes too deare for honey that licks it from thornes.

897. Hee hath no leisure who useth it not.
898. It's a wicked thing to make a dearth ones garner.
899. He that deales in the world needes foure seeves.
*900. Take heede of an oxe before, of an horse behind, of a monke on all sides.
901. The yeare doth nothing else but open and shut.
902. The ignorant hath an Eagles wings, and an Owles eyes.
903. There are more Physitians in health then drunkards.
904. The wife is the key of the house.
905. The Law is not the same at morning and at night.
906. Warre and Physicke are governed by the eye.
907. Halfe the world knowes not how the other halfe lives.
908. Death keepes no Calender.
909. Ships feare fire more then water.
*910. The least foolish is wise.
911. The chiefe boxe of health is time.
*912. Silkes and Satins put out the fire in the chimney.
913. The first blow is as much as two.
914. The life of man is a winter way.
915. The way is an ill neighbour.
916. An old mans staffe is the rapper of deaths doore.
917. Life is halfe spent before we know what it is.
918. The singing man keepes his shop in his throate.
919. The body is more drest then the soule.
920. The body is sooner drest then the soule.
921. The Physitian owes all to the patient, but the patient owes nothing to him but a little mony.
922. The little cannot bee great, unlesse he devoure many.
923. Time undermines us.
*924. The Chollerick drinkes, the Melancholick eates, the Flegmatick sleepes.
925. The Apothecaries morter spoiles the Luters musick.
*926. Conversation makes one what he is.
927. The deafe gaines the injury.
*928. Yeeres know more then bookes.
929. Wine is a turne-coate (first a friend, then an enemy).

900 sides] hands *LG* 907 lives *1859* (Fr. *vit*): lies *OP JP* 912 in] of *LG* 924 eats, *JP*: eates; *OP* 926 one what they are. *LG*

930. Wine ever paies for his lodging.
931. Wine makes all sorts of creatures at table.
932. Wine that cost nothing is digested before it be drunke.
933. Trees eate but once.
934. Armour is light at table.
935. Good horses make short miles.
936. Castles are Forrests of stones.
937. The dainties of the great are the teares of the poore.
938. Parsons are soules waggoners.
*939. Children when they are little make parents fooles, when they are great they make them mad.
940. The Mr absent, and the house dead.
941. Dogs are fine in the field.
942. Sinnes are not knowne till they bee acted.
943. Thornes whiten yet doe nothing.
944. All are presumed good, till they are found in a fault.
945. The great put the little on the hooke.
946. The great would have none great and the little all little.
947. The Italians are wise before the deede, the Germanes in the deede, the French after the deede.
949. Every mile is two in winter.
950. Spectacles are deaths Harquebuze.
951. Lawyers houses are built on the heads of fooles.
952. The house is a fine house, when good folke are within.
*953. The best bred have the best portion.
954. The first and last frosts are the worst.
955. Gifts enter every where without a wimble.
956. Princes have no way.
957. Knowledge makes one laugh, but wealth makes one dance.
958. The Citizen is at his businesse before he rise.
959. The eyes have one language every where.
960. It is better to have wings then hornes.
961. Better be a foole then a knave.
962. Count not fowre except you have them in a wallett.

939 their parents *LG* 949 *numbered thus in OP* 952 folke] folks *JP*
953 portions *LG*

963. To live peaceably with all breedes good blood.
964. You may be on land, yet not in a garden.
965. You cannot make the fire so low but it will get out.
966. Wee know not who lives or dies.
*967. An Oxe is taken by the horns, and a Man by the tongue.
968. Manie things are lost for want of asking.
969. No Church-yard is so handsom, that a man would desire straight to bee buried there.
970. Citties are taken by the eares.
971. Once a yeare a man may say: On his conscience.
972. Wee leave more to do when wee dye, then wee have done.
973. With customes wee live well, but Lawes undoe us.
974. To speake of an Vsurer at the table marres the wine.
975. Paines to get, care to keep, feare to lose.
976. For a morning raine leave not your journey.
977. One faire day in winter makes not birds merrie.
978. Hee that learnes a trade hath a purchase made.
979. When all men have what belongs to them, it cannot bee much.
980. Though God take the sunne out of the Heaven, yet we must have patience.
981. When a man sleepes, his head is in his stomach.
982. When one is on horsebacke hee knowes all things.
983. When God is made master of a family, he orders the disorderly.
984. When a Lackey comes to hells doore, the devills locke the gates.
985. He that is at ease seekes dainties.
986. Hee that hath charge of soules transports them not in bundles.
987. Hee that tells his wife newes is but newly married.
988. Hee that is in a towne in May loseth his spring.
989. Hee that is in a Taverne thinkes he is in a vine-garden.
990. He that praiseth himselfe spattereth himselfe.

967 Take an oxe by his hornes & a man by his tongue. *LG* 971 On *JP*: on *OP* 974 *numbered* 674 *in OP* 978 *numbered* 278 *in OP* 983 the master *JP* orders] disorders *JP*

991. Hee that is a master must serve (another).
992. He that is surprized with the first frost feeles it all the winter after.
993. Hee a beast doth die, that hath done no good to his country.
994. He that followes the Lord hopes to goe before.
995. He that dies without the company of good men puts not himselfe into a good way.
996. Who hath no head, needes no hatt.
997. Who hath no hast in his businesse, mountaines to him seeme valleys.
998. Speake not of my debts, unlesse you meane to pay them.
999. He that is not in the warres is not out of danger.
1000. He that gives me small gifts would have me live.
1001. He that is his owne Counsellor knowes nothing sure but what hee hath laid out.
1002. He that hath lands hath quarrells.
1003. Hee that goes to bed thirsty riseth healthy.
1004. Who will make a doore of gold must knock a naile every day.
1005. A trade is better then service.
1006. Hee that lives in hope danceth without musick.
1007. To review ones store is to mow twice.
1008. Saint *Luke* was a Saint and a Physitian, yet is dead.
1009. Without businesse debauchery.
1010. Without danger we cannot get beyond danger.
1011. Health and sicknesse surely are mens double enemies.
1012. If gold knew what gold is, gold would get gold I wis.
1013. Little losses amaze, great tame.
1014. Chuse none for thy servant who have served thy betters.
1015. Service without reward is punishment.
1016. If the husband be not at home, there is nobodie.
1017. An oath that is not to bee made is not to be kept.

996 hatt] heart *JP* 1010 *One of the B.M. copies* (C 63 c 6) *of* Witts Recreations *ends here*; *the last leaf is a cancel, having Nos.* 1003–10 *reset, followed by* Finis *and* Imprimatur; *in No.* 1010 *it has* before *instead of* beyond

1018. The eye is bigger then the belly.
1019. If you would bee at ease, all the world is not.
1020. Were it not for the bone in the legge, all the world would turne Carpenters (to make them crutches).
1021. If you must flie, flie well.
1022. All that shakes falles not.
1023. All beasts of prey are strong or treacherous.
1024. If the braine sowes not corne, it plants thistles.
1025. A man well mounted is ever Cholerick.
1026. Every one is a master and servant.
1027. A piece of a Churchyard fitts every body.
1028. One month doth nothing without another.
1029. A master of straw eates a servant of steele.
1030. An old cat sports not with her prey.
1031. A woman conceales what shee knowes not.
1032. Hee that wipes the childs nose, kisseth the mothers cheeke.

FINIS

1028 month *Grosart* (Fr. *mois*, Gn. *Monat*): mouth *OP JP*

JACULA PRUDENTUM

Or Outlandish Proverbs, Sentences, &c. Selected By M[r] George Herbert, Late Orator of the Universitie of Cambridg.

[*Includes all the proverbs in* Outlandish Proverbs (1640), *with the following additions.*]

(1*a*). Old men go to Death, Death comes to Young men. (*Before No.* 1.)

(40*a*). Benefits please like flowers while they are fresh. (*After No.* 40.)

(40*b*). Between the businesse of life and the day of death, a space ought to be interposed. (*After No.* 40*a*.)

(56*a*). Nothing is to be presumed on, or despaired of. (*After No.* 56.)

(71*a*). Cities seldome change Religion only. (*After No.* 71.)

(135*a*). Slander is a shipwrack by a dry Tempest. (*After No.* 135.)

[*The following come after No.* 1032.]

1033. Gentility is nothing but Ancient Riches.
1034. To go where the King goes afoot (i.e. to the stool).
1035. To go upon the Franciscans Hackney (i.e. on foot).
1036. *Amiens* was taken by the Fox, and retaken by the Lion.
1037. After Death the Doctor.
1038. Ready mony is a ready Medicine.
1039. It is the Philosophy of the Distaffe.
1040. It is a sheep of *Berry*, it is marked on the nose (applyed to those that have a blow).
1041. To build castles in Spain.
1042. An Idle youth, a needy Age.
1043. Silke doth quench the fire in the Kitchin.

From Herbert's Remains (1652) : *separate title-page to* Jacula Prudentum, *worded as above and dated* 1651. *No proverbs are numbered in that edition. Explanations of* Nos. 1034, 1035, 1040, &c., *there given without brackets, are here bracketed.*
1040 *Berry* (Fr. *Berry* or *Berri*): *Beery JP* 1043 *Cf. No.* 912

1044. The words ending in *Ique* do mocke the Physician (as Hectique, Paralitique, Apoplectique, Lethargique).
1045. He that trusts much Obliges much, says the Spaniard.
1046. He that thinks amiss, concludes worse.
1047. A man would live in Italy (a place of pleasure) but he would chuse to dy in Spain (where they say the Catholick Religion is professed with greatest strictness).
1048. Whatsoever was the father of a disease, an ill dyet was the mother.
1049. Frenzy, Heresie, and Jealovsie, seldome cured.
1050. There is no heat of affection but is joyned with some idlenesse of brain, says the Spaniard.
1051. The War is not don so long as my Enemy lives.
1052. Some evils are cured by contempt.
1053. Power seldome grows old at Court.
1054. Danger it selfe the best remedy for danger.
1055. Favour will as surely perish as life.
1056. Feare, the Bedle of the Law.
1057. Heresie is the school of pride.
1058. For the same man to be an heretick and a good subject, is incompossible.
1059. Heresie may be easier kept out, then shooke off.
1060. Infants manners are moulded more by the example of Parents, then by stars at their nativities.
1061. They favour learning whose actions are worthy of a learned pen.
1062. Modesty sets off one newly come to honour.
1063. No naked man is sought after to be rifled.
1064. There's no such conquering weapon as the necessity of conquering.
1065. Nothing secure unlesse suspected.
1066. No tye can oblige the perfidious.
1067. Spies are the ears and eyes of Princes.
1068. The life of spies is to know, not bee known.
1069. Religion a stalking horse to shoot other foul.
1070. It's a dangerous fire begins in the bed-straw.

1071. Covetousnesse breaks the bag.
1072. Fear keepes and looks to the vineyard, and not the owner.
1073. The noise is greater then the nuts.
1074. Two sparrows on one Ear of Corn make an ill agreement.
1075. The world is now adayes, God save the Conquerour.
1076. Unsound minds like unsound Bodies, if you feed, you poyson.
1077. Not only ought fortune to be pictured on a wheel, but every thing else in this world.
1078. All covet, all lose.
1079. Better is one *Accipe*, then twice to say, *Dabo tibi*.
1080. An Asse endures his burden, but not more then his burden.
1081. Threatned men eat bread, says the Spaniard.
1082. The beades in the Hand, and the Divell in Capuch (or cape of the cloak).
1083. He that will do thee a good turne, either he will be gon or dye.
1084. I escaped the Thunder, and fell into the Lightning.
1085. A man of a great memory without learning hath a rock and a spindle, and no staffe to spin.
1086. The death of wolves is the safety of the sheep.
1087. He that is once borne, once must dy.
1088. He that hath but one eye, must bee afraid to lose it.
1089. Hee that makes himself a sheep, shall be eat by the wolfe.
1090. He that steals an egge, will steal an oxe.
1091. He that will be surety, shall pay.
1092. He that is afraid of leaves, goes not to the wood.
1093. In the mouth of a bad dog fals often a good bone.
1094. Those that God loves, do not live long.
1095. Still fisheth he that catcheth one.
1096. All flesh is not venison.
1097. A City that parlies is half gotten.
1098. A dead Bee maketh no Hony.
1099. An old dog barks not in vain.

1092 *Cf. No.* 768 1097 *Cf. No.* 586

1100. They that hold the greatest farmes, pay the least rent (applyed to rich men that are unthankful to God).
1101. Old Camels carry young Camels skins to the Market.
1102. He that hath time and looks for better time, time comes that he repents himself of time.
1103. Words and feathers the wind carries away.
1104. Of a pigs taile you can never make a good shaft.
1105. The Bathe of the Blackamoor hath sworne not to whiten.
1106. To a greedy eating horse a short halter.
1107. The Divell divides the world between Atheisme and Superstition.
1108. Such a Saint, such an offering.
1109. We do it soon enough, if that we do be well.
1110. Cruelty is more cruell, if we defer the pain.
1111. What one day gives us, another takes away from us.
1112. To seek in a Sheep five feet when there is but four.
1113. A scab'd horse cannot abide the comb.
1114. God strikes with his finger, and not with all his arme.
1115. God gives his wrath by weight, and without weight his mercy.
1116. Of a new Prince, new bondage.
1117. New things are fair.
1118. Fortune to one is Mother, to another is Step-mother.
1119. There is no man, though never so little, but sometimes he can hurt.
1120. The horse that drawes after him his halter, is not altogether escaped.
1121. We must recoile a little, to the end we may leap the better.
1122. No love is foule, nor prison fair.
1123. No day so clear but hath dark clouds.
1124. No hair so small but hath his shadow.
1125. A wolfe will never make war against another wolfe.
1126. We must love, as looking one day to hate.
1127. It is good to have some friends both in heaven and hell.
1128. It is very hard to shave an egge.

1122 *already included in* Outlandish Proverbs, *No.* 829

1129. It is good to hold the asse by the bridle.
1130. The healthfull man can give counsell to the sick.
1131. The death of a young wolfe doth never come too soon.
1132. The rage of a wild boar is able to spoil more then one wood.
1133. Vertue flies from the heart of a Mercenary man.
1134. The wolfe eats oft of the sheep that have been warn'd.
1135. The mouse that hath but one hole is quickly taken.
1136. To play at Chesse when the house is on fire.
1137. The itch of disputing is the scab of the Church.
1138. Follow not truth too near the heels, lest it dash out thy teeth.
1139. Either wealth is much increased, or moderation is much decayed.
1140. Say to pleasure, Gentle *Eve*, I will none of your apple.
1141. When war begins, then hell openeth.
1142. There is a remedy for every thing, could men find it.
1143. There is an hour wherein a man might be happy all his life, could he find it.
1144. Great Fortune brings with it Great misfortune.
1145. A fair day in winter is the mother of a storme.
1146. Wo be to him that reads but one book.
1147. Tithe, and be rich.
1148. Take heed of the wrath of a mighty man, and the tumult of the people.
1149. Take heed of mad folks in a narrow place.
1150. Take heed of credit decaid, and people that have nothing.
1151. Take heed of a young wench, a prophetesse, and a Lattin bred woman.
1152. Take heed of a person marked, and a Widdow thrice married.
1153. Take heed of foul dirty wayes, and long sicknesse.
1154. Take heed of winde that comes in at a hole, and a reconciled Enemy.
1155. Take heed of a step-mother; the very name of her sufficeth.
1156. Princes are venison in Heaven.
1157. Criticks are like brushers of Noblemens cloaths.

1158. He is a great Necromancer, for he asks counsell of the Dead (i.e. books).
1159. A man is known to be mortal by two things, Sleep and Lust.
1160. Love without end, hath no end, says the Spaniard: (meaning, if it were not begun on particular ends, it would last).
1161. Stay a while, that we may make an end the sooner.
1162. Presents of love fear not to be ill taken of strangers.
1163. To seek these things is lost labour; Geese in an oyle pot, fat Hogs among Jews, and Wine in a fishing net.
1164. Some men plant an opinion they seem to erradicate.
1165. The Philosophy of Princes is to dive into the Secrets of men, leaving the secrets of nature to those that have spare time.
1166. States have their conversions and periods as well as naturall bodies.
1167. Great deservers grow Intolerable presumers.
1168. The love of money and the love of learning rarely meet.
1169. Trust no friend with that you need fear him if he were your enemy.
1170. Some had rather lose their friend then their Jest.
1171. Marry your daughters betimes, lest they marry themselves.
1172. Souldiers in peace are like chimneys in summer.
1173. Here is a talk of the Turk and the Pope, but my next neighbour doth me more harm then either of them both.
1174. Civill Wars of *France* made a million of Atheists, and 30000 Witches.
1175. We Batchelors laugh and shew our teeth, but you married men laugh till your hearts ake.
1176. The Divell never assailes a man, except he find him either void of knowledge, or of the fear of God.
1177. There is no body will go to hell for company.
1178. Much money makes a Countrey poor, for it sets a dearer price on every thing.

1179. The vertue of a coward is suspition.

1180. A man's destiny is alwayes dark.

1181. Every man's censure is first moulded in his own nature.

1182. Money wants no followers.

1183. Your thoughts close, and your countenance loose.

1184. Whatever is made by the hand of man, by the hand of man may be overturned.

FINIS

LETTERS

I. *Part of a letter to his Mother.*

['this following Letter and Sonnet . . . were in the first year of his going to *Cambridge* sent his dear Mother for a New-years gift.' Walton's *Lives* (1670).]

— But I fear the heat of my late *Ague* hath dryed up those springs, by which Scholars say, the Muses use to take up their habitations. However, I need not their help, to reprove the vanity of those many Love-poems, that are daily writ and consecrated to *Venus*; nor to bewail that so few are writ, that look towards *God* and *Heaven*. For my own part, my meaning (*dear Mother*) is in these Sonnets, to declare my resolution to be, that my poor Abilities in *Poetry*, shall be all, and ever consecrated to Gods glory. And —

[New-year, 1609/10]

II. *To Sir J[ohn] D[anvers].*

SIR,

Though I had the best wit in the World, yet it would easily tyre me, to find out variety of thanks for the diversity of your favours, if I sought to do so; but, I profess it not: And therefore let it be sufficient for me, that the same heart, which you have won long since, is still true to you, and hath nothing else to answer your infinite kindnesses, but a constancy of obedience; only hereafter I will take heed how I propose my desires unto you, since I find you so willing to yield to my requests; for, since your favours come a Horse-back, there is reason, that my desires should go a-foot; neither do I make any question, but that you have performed your

I. *From Walton's* Lives (1670). *Also in* Life of Herbert (1670). *Reprinted in the Life in* The Temple (1674) *and in* Lives (1675). *For the sonnets which accompanied this letter see above*, p. 206   12 glory. And —] glory; and I beg you to receive this as one testimony. *Added in* Lives (1675)

II. *This and Nos.* III, V, VII–X *from Walton's* Lives, 1670 (*here cited as* 70) *and in* Life of Herbert, 1670. *Reprinted in* Lives, 1675 (75). *They were not included in the Life in* The Temple, 1674

kindness to the full, and that the Horse is every way fit for me, and I will strive to imitate the compleatness of your love, with being in some proportion, and after my manner,

Your most obedient Servant,

[1617/18] GEORGE HERBERT.

III. *To the same.*

SIR,

I dare no longer be silent, least while I think I am modest, I wrong both my self, and also the confidence my Friends have in me; wherefore I will open my case unto you, which I think deserves the reading at the least; and it is this, I want Books extremely; You know Sir, how I am now setting foot into Divinity, to lay the platform of my future life, and shall I then be fain alwayes to borrow Books, and build on anothers foundation? What Trades-man is there who will set up without his Tools? Pardon my boldness Sir, it is a most serious Case, nor can I write coldly in that, wherein consisteth the making good of my former education, of obeying that Spirit which hath guided me hitherto, and of atchieving my (I dare say) holy ends. This also is aggravated, in that I apprehend what my Friends would have been forward to say, if I had taken ill courses, *Follow your Book, and you shall want nothing*: You know Sir, it is their ordinary speech, and now let them make it good; for, since, I hope, I have not deceived their expectation, let not them deceive mine: But perhaps they will say, you are sickly, you must not study too hard; it is true (God knows) I am weak, yet not so, but that every day, I may step one step towards my journies end; and I love my friends so well, as that if all things proved not well, I had rather the fault should lie on me, than on them; but they will object again, What becomes of your Annuity? Sir, if there be any truth in me, I find it little enough to keep me in health. You know I was sick last Vacation, neither am I yet recovered, so that I am fain ever and anon, to buy somewhat tending towards my health; for

III. *From Walton* (*edns as for* II)

infirmities are both painful and costly. Now this *Lent* I am forbid utterly to eat any Fish, so that I am fain to dyet in my Chamber at mine own cost; for in our publick Halls, you know, is nothing but Fish and Whit-meats: Out of *Lent* also, twice a Week, on *Fridayes* and *Saturdayes*, I must do so, which yet sometimes I fast. Sometimes also I ride to *New-market*, and there lie a day or two for fresh Air; all which tend to avoiding of costlier matters, if I should fall absolutely sick: I protest and vow, I even study Thrift, and yet I am scarce able with much ado to make one half years allowance, shake hands with the other: And yet if a Book of four or five Shillings come in my way, I buy it, though I fast for it; yea, sometimes of Ten Shillings: But, alas Sir, what is that to those infinite Volumes of Divinity, which yet every day swell, and grow bigger. Noble Sir, pardon my boldness, and consider but these three things. First, the Bulk of Divinity. Secondly, the time when I desire this (which is now, when I must lay the foundation of my whole life). Thirdly, what I desire, and to what end, not vain pleasures, nor to a vain end. If then, Sir, there be any course, either by engaging my future Annuity, or any other way, I desire you, Sir, to be my Mediator to them in my behalf.

Now I write to you, Sir, because to you I have ever opened my heart; and have reason, by the Patents of your perpetual favour to do so still, for I am sure you love

Your faithfullest Servant,

GEORGE HERBERT.

March 18. 1617. [i.e. 1617/18]
Trin: Coll.

IV. *To Mr. Henry Herbert.*

BROTHER,

The disease which I am troubled with now is the shortness of time, for it hath been my fortune of late to have such sudden warning, that I have not leazure to impart unto you

6–7 *New-Market* 75

IV. *From* Epistolary Curiosities. Unpublished Letters of the Seventeenth Century, Illustrative of the Herbert Family, ed. Rebecca Warner. 1st series. 1818

some of those observations which I have framed to myself in conversation; and whereof I would not have you ignorant. As I shal find occasion, you shal receive them by peeces; and if there be any such which you have found useful to yourself, communicate them to me. You live in a brave nation, where, except you wink, you cannot but see many brave examples. Bee covetous, then, of all good which you see in Frenchmen, whether it be in knowledge, or in fashion, or in words; for I would have you, even in speeches, to observe so much, as when you meet with a witty French speech, try to speak the like in English: so shall you play a good marchant, by transporting French commodities to your own country. Let there be no kind of excellency which it is possible for you to attain to, which you seek not; and have a good conceit of your wit, mark what I say, have a good conceit of your wit; that is, be proud, not with a foolish vanting of yourself when there is no caus, but by setting a just price of your qualities: and it is the part of a poor spirit to undervalue himself and blush. But I am out of my time: when I have more time, you shall hear more; and write you freely to mee in your letters, for I am

your ever loving brother,
G. HERBERT.

P.S. My brother is somewhat of the same temper, and perhaps a little more mild, but you will hardly perceive it.

To my dear brother,
Mr. Henry Herbert, at Paris. [1618]

v. *To the truly Noble Sir J. D.*

SIR,

I understand by a Letter from my Brother *Henry*, that he hath bought a parcel of Books for me, and that they are coming over. Now though they have hitherto travelled upon

4 be *Ed*: by *Warner* 27 *Warner gives the date 1618, which agrees with Henry Herbert's residence in Paris, but it is not clear whether she found the date in the autograph*

V. *From Walton* (*edns as for* II)

your charge, yet if my Sister were acquainted that they are ready, I dare say she would make good her promise of taking five or six pound upon her, which she hath hitherto deferred to do, not of her self, but upon the want of those Books which were not to be got in *England*; for that which surmounts, though your noble disposition is infinitely free, yet I had rather flie to my old ward, that if any course could be taken of doubling my Annuity now, upon condition that I should surcease from all title to it, after I enter'd into a Benefice, I should be most glad to entertain it, and both pay for the surplusage of these Books, and for ever after cease my clamorous and greedy bookish requests. It is high time now that I should be no more a burden to you, since I can never answer what I have already received; for your favours are so ancient, that they prevent my memory, and yet still grow upon

Your humblest Servant,
GEORGE HERBERT.

[1618]

I remember my most humble duty to my Mother. I have wrote to my dear sick Sister this week already, and therefore now I hope may be excused.

I pray Sir, pardon my boldness of inclosing my Brothers Letter in yours, for it was because I know your Lodging, but not his.

VI. *To Sir Robert Harley, at Brampton.*

S[r]

This letter runs to you with much eagernes, for I am enioined to write to you by S[r] John Dāvers, to w[ch] mine owne obligations were occasion inough, & therfore I am not over much beholding to those busnesses w[ch] iustly excuse him from writing at this time, because my recompenses of your favours consist in this only. Now his desire is to

VI. *From* Welbeck Abbey Harley Papers, vol. i, *by kind permission of the Duke of Portland. First printed in* Hist. MSS. Comm. 14th Report, Appendix, Part II. The Manuscripts of the Duke of Portland, vol. iii, p. 10. 1894

acquaint you with those passages of newes which this time affords; for though it is likely that the time after the Holydaye will bee fruitfuller of novelties, yet his loue expects them not but first certifies you that there are come agents hither from the low-Cuntries to treat of divers matters, as of certaine iniuries w[ch] they are thought to haue offerd to our Merchants at the Indies, wherein they haue satisfied the King reasonably. but yet he will heare of no other affaires, untill they haue satisfied him also concerning the fishing w[ch] the Hollanders use in our coasts, w[ch] the King would so appropriate to himselfe, as that either his subiects only should practise it, or at least that the Hollanders should pay him tribute out of their fishing. now to the answering of this demand of the Kings these Agents pretend they haue no comission, & therfore deferr it untill they heare farther from the States. My Lord of Buckingham was observed on Christmas day to bee so devout as to come to the Chappell an howre before prayers began, of w[ch] is doubted whether it have some further meaning. S[r] Charles Howard & his Lady are at much difference, & shee being at London sent for him (as shee sayes) to make peace with him, w[ch] he refusing to doe hath giuen her occasion to protest shee will never speake with him againe, & to threaten him that if he will not giue her halfe her estate to liue on by her selfe (for shee desires no more) shee will find friends to compell him to it. There is a Spanish Lawyer hath written a treatise concerning the lawfulnes of kings resuming the donation of spirituall livings into their owne hands, & taking it from the Popes: this passeth in Spaine freely with consent of King & counsell. There is a Frenchman who writt a poem heere in England & presented it to the King, who because of his importunities gaue him a reward, but not so great as he expected & therfore he grumblingly said that if he had giuen it to the pope he should haue had a greater reward. upon this he was forbid Court & kingdome, yet was seene lately neere the king, w[ch] some observing who heard the interdiction denounced to him, told the King & so he is committed to

7 at the Indies *MS*: of the Indies *1894* 14 Agent *MS* 15 heare *MS*: trace *1894* 27 donations *MS* 35 kingdome. *MS*

prison. These are the things I am to acquaint you with, of whose rude delivery my hast makes mee ashamed, only my comfort is that this is but an occasion for you to amplify your favour to mee in pardoning

Your most indebted kinsman
GEORGE HERBERT.

Decemb. 26. 1618.
Charing Cross.

VII. *To Sir John Danvers.*

SIR,

This Week hath loaded me with your Favours; I wish I could have come in person to thank you, but it is not possible; presently after *Michaelmas*, I am to make an Oration to the whole University of an hour long in *Latin*, and my *Lincoln* journey hath set me much behind hand: neither can I so much as go to *Bugden*, and deliver your Letter, yet have I sent it thither by a faithful Messenger this day: I beseech you all, you and my dear Mother and Sister to pardon me, for my *Cambridge* necessities are stronger to tye me here, than yours to *London*: If I could possibly have come, none should have done my message to Sir *Fr: Nethersole* for me; he and I are ancient acquaintance, and I have a strong opinion of him, that if he can do me a courtesie, he will of himself; yet your appearing in it, affects me strangely. I have sent you here inclosed a Letter from our Master in my behalf, which if you can send to Sir *Francis* before his departure, it will do well, for it expresseth the Universities inclination to me; yet if you cannot send it with much convenience, it is no matter, for the Gentleman needs no incitation to love me.

The Orators place (that you may understand what it is) is the finest place in the University, though not the gainfullest; yet that will be about 30 *l. per an.* but the commodiousness is beyond the Revenue; for the Orator writes all the University Letters, makes all the Orations, be it to King, Prince, or whatever comes to the University; to requite

VII. *From Walton* (*edns as for* II) 14 journey *Ed*: journey, *70 75* 16 have I] I have *Grosart, Palmer* 25 in] on *Pickering, Grosart, Palmer*

these pains, he takes place next the Doctors, is at all their Assemblies and Meetings, and sits above the Proctors, is Regent or Non-regent at his pleasure, and such like Gaynesses, which will please a young man well.

I long to hear from Sir *Francis*, I pray Sir send the Letter you receive from him to me as soon as you can, that I may work the heads to my purpose. I hope I shall get this place without all your *London* helps, of which I am very proud, not but that I joy in your favours, but that you may see, that if all fail, yet I am able to stand on mine own legs. Noble Sir, I thank you for your infinite favours, I fear only that I have omitted some fitting circumstance, yet you will pardon my haste, which is very great, though never so, but that I have both time and work to be

Your extreme Servant,
GEORGE HERBERT.

[Sept. 1619]

VIII. *To the same.*

SIR,

I understand by Sir *Francis Nethersols* Letter, that he fears I have not fully resolved of the matter, since this place being civil may divert me too much from Divinity, at which, not without cause, he thinks, I aim; but, I have wrote him back, that this dignity, hath no such earthiness in it, but it may very well be joined with Heaven; or if it had to others, yet to me it should not, for ought I yet knew; and therefore I desire him to send me a direct answer in his next Letter. I pray Sir therefore, cause this inclosed to be carried to his brothers house of his own name (as I think) at the sign of the *Pedler* and the *Pack* on *London-bridge*, for there he assigns me. I cannot yet find leisure to write to my Lord, or Sir *Benjamin Ruddyard*; but I hope I shall shortly, though for the reckoning of your favours, I shall never find time and paper enough, yet am I

Your readiest Servant,
GEORGE HERBERT.

Octob. 6. 1619.
Trin: Coll.

VIII. *From Walton* (*edns as for* II) 23 others, *Life of Herbert, 1670*: others; *Lives, 1670* 32 am I] I am 75

I remember my most humble duty to my Mother, who cannot think me lazy, since I rode 200 mile to see a Sister, in a way I knew not, in the midst of much business, and all in a Fortnight, not long since.

IX. *To the same.*

SIR,

I have received the things you sent me, safe; and now the only thing I long for, is to hear of my dear sick Sister; first, how her health fares, next, whether my peace be yet made with her concerning my unkind departure. Can I be so happy, as to hear of both these that they succeed well? Is it not too much for me? Good Sir, make it plain to her, that I loved her even in my departure, in looking to her Son, and my charge. I suppose she is not disposed to spend her eyesight on a piece of paper, or else I had wrote to her; when I shall understand that a Letter will be seasonable, my Pen is ready. Concerning the Orators place all goes well yet, the next *Friday* it is tryed, and accordingly you shall hear. I have forty businesses in my hands, your Courtesie will pardon the haste of

Your humblest Servant,
GEORGE HERBERT.

Jan. 19. 1619. [i.e. 1619/20]
Trin: Coll.

X. *For my dear sick Sister.*

MOST DEAR SISTER,

Think not my silence forgetfulness; or, that my love is as dumb as my papers; though businesses may stop my hand, yet my heart, a much better member, is alwayes with you: and which is more, with our good and gracious God, incessantly begging some ease of your pains, with that earnestness,

2 mile] miles *Pickering, Grosart, Palmer* 3 in the] and in the *Palmer*
IX. *From Walton* (*edns as for* II)
X. *From Walton* (*edns as for* II) 26 papers; *Life of Herbert, 1670*: papers, *Lives, 1670* 26 businesses] businesse *Grosart, Palmer*

that becomes your griefs, and my love. God who knows and sees this Writing, knows also that my solliciting him has been much, and my tears many for you; judge me then by those waters, and not by my ink, and then you shall justly value

Your most truly,
most heartily,
affectionate Brother,
and Servant,
GEORGE HERBERT.

Decem. 6. 1620.
Trin: Coll.

XI. *To his Mother, in her sickness.*

MADAM,

At my last parting from you, I was the better content because I was in hope I should my self carry all sickness out of your family: but, since I know I did not, and that your share continues, or rather increaseth, I wish earnestly that I were again with you: and, would quickly make good my wish but that my employment does fix me here, it being now but a month to our *Commencement*: wherein, my absence by how much it naturally augmenteth suspicion, by so much shall it make my prayers the more constant and the more earnest for you to the God of all Consolation.—In the mean time, I beseech you to be chearful, and comfort your self in the God of all Comfort, who is not willing to behold any sorrow but for sin.—What hath Affliction grievous in it more then for a moment? or why should our afflictions here, have so much power or boldness as to oppose the hope of our Joyes hereafter!—*Madam!* As the Earth is but a point in respect of the heavens, so are earthly Troubles compar'd to heavenly Joyes; therefore, if either Age or Sickness lead you to those Joyes? consider what advantage you have over *Youth* and *Health*, who are now so near those true Comforts. —Your last Letter gave me Earthly preferment, and kept

XI. *From Walton's Life of Herbert in* The Temple, 1674, *where it was first printed* (*here cited as* 74). *Reprinted in* Lives, 1675 (75) 19 here, it being 75: here being 74 34 Earthly] an earthly *Grosart, Palmer* and kept] and I hope kept 75

Heavenly for your self: but, wou'd you divide and choose too? our Colledge Customs allow not that, and I shou'd account my self most happy if I might change with you; for, I have alwaies observ'd the thred of Life to be like other threds or skenes of silk, full of snarles and incumbrances: Happy is he, whose bottom is wound up and laid ready for work in the New *Jerusalem.*—For my self, *dear Mother*, I alwaies fear'd sickness more then death, because sickness hath made me unable to perform those Offices for which I came into the world, and must yet be kept in it; but you are freed from that fear, who have already abundantly discharg'd that part, having both ordered your Family, and so brought up your Children that they have attain'd to the years of Discretion, and competent Maintenance.—So that now if they do not well the falt cannot be charg'd on you; whose Example and Care of them will justifie you both to the world and your own Conscience: insomuch, that whether you turn your thoughts on the life past, or on the Joyes that are to come, you have strong preservatives against all disquiet.—And, for temporal Afflictions! I beseech you consider all that can happen to you are either afflictions of Estate, or Body, or Mind.—For those of Estate? of what poor regard ought they to be, since if we had Riches we are commanded to give them away: so that the best use of them is, having, not to have them.—But perhaps being above the Common people, our Credit and estimation calls on us to live in a more splendid fashion?—but, Oh God! how easily is that answered, when we consider that the Blessings in the holy Scripture, are never given to the rich, but to the poor. I never find Blessed be the Rich; or, Blessed be the Noble; but, *Blessed be the Meek*, and *Blessed be the Poor*, and, *Blessed be the Mourners, for they shall be comforted.*—And yet, Oh God! most carry themselves so, as if they not only not desir'd, but, even fear'd to be blessed.—And for afflictions of the Body, *dear Madam*, remember the holy Martyrs of God, how they have been burnt by thousands, and have endur'd such other Tortures, as the very mention of them might

23 had] have *Grosart, Palmer* 32 *Mourners*] *comma from 75* 36 and 75 : and, *74*

beget amazement; but, their Fiery-tryals have had an end: and yours (which praised be God are less) are not like to continue long.—I beseech you let such thoughts as these, moderate your present fear and sorrow; and know, that if any of yours shou'd prove a *Goliah*-like trouble, yet you may say with *David*,—*That God who hath delivered me out of the paws of the Lyon and Bear, will also deliver me out of the hands of this uncircumcised* Philistin.—Lastly, for those Afflictions of the Soul, consider that God intends that to be as a *sacred Temple* for himself to dwell in, and will not allow any room there for such an in-mate as Grief; or, allow that any sadness shall be his Competitor.—And above all, If any care of future things molest you? remember those admirable words of the Psalmist: *Cast thy Care on the Lord and he shall nourish thee.* (*Psal.* 55.) To which joyn that of St. *Peter*, *Casting all your Care on the Lord, for he careth for you.* (1 *Pet.* 5. 7.)—What an admirable thing is this, that God puts his shoulder to our burthen; and, entertains our Care for us that we may the more quietly intend his service.—To Conclude, Let me commend only one place more to you (*Philip.* 4. 4.) St. *Paul* saith there: *Rejoyce in the Lord alwaies, and again I say rejoyce.* He doubles it to take away the scruple of those that might say, What shall we rejoyce in afflictions? yes, I say again rejoyce; so that it is not left to us to rejoyce or not rejoyce: but, whatsoever befals us we must alwaies, at all times rejoyce in the Lord, who taketh care for us: and, it follows in the next verse: *Let your moderation appear to all men, the Lord is at hand: be careful for nothing.* What can be said more comfortably? trouble not your selves, God is at hand to deliver us from all, or, in all.—*Dear Madam*, pardon my boldness, and, accept the good meaning of,

Your most obedient Son,

GEORGE HERBERT.

Trin. Col.
May 29.
1622.

6 hath] *om. Grosart, Palmer* 35 *May* 29] *May* 25 *in some modern reprints, perhaps from the defective printing of the second figure in the Bodleian copy of Walton's* Lives, 1675. *In other copies the date is clearly printed May* 29

XII. *To Sir Henry Herbert.*

Dear Bro;

That you did not only entertain my proposals, but advance them, was lovingly done, and like a good brother. Yet truly it was none of my meaning, when I wrote, to putt one of our neeces into your hands but barely what I wrote I meant, and no more; and am glad that although you offer more, yet you will doe, as you write, that alsoe. I was desirous to putt a good mind into the way of charity, and that was all I intended. For concerning your offer of receiving one, I will tell you what I wrote to our eldest brother, when he urged one upon me, and but one, and that at my choice. I wrote to him that I would have both or neither; and that upon this ground, because they were to come into an unknown country, tender in knowledge, sense, and age, and knew none but one who could be no company to them. Therefore I considered that if one only came, the comfort intended would prove a discomfort. Since that I have seen the fruit of my observation, for they have lived so lovingly, lying, eating, walking, praying, working, still together, that I take a comfort therein; and would not have to part them yet, till I take some opportunity to let them know your love, for which both they shall, and I doe, thank you. It is true there is a third sister, whom to receive were the greatest charitie of all, for she is youngest, and least looked unto; having none to doe it but her school-mistresse, and you know what those mercenary creatures are. Neither hath she any to repair unto at good times, as Christmas, &c. which, you know, is the encouragement of learning all the year after, except my cousin Bett take pitty of her, which yet at that distance is some difficulty. If you could think of taking her, as once you did, surely it were a great good deed, and I would have her conveyed to you. But I judge you not: doe that which God shall put into your hart, and the Lord bless all your purposes to his glory. Yet, truly if you take her not, I am thinking to do it, even beyond my strengthe; especially at this time, being more beggarly now than I have

XII. *From Warner*, op. cit.

been these many years, as having spent two hundred pounds in building; which to me that have nothing yett, is very much. But though I both consider this, and your observation, also, of the unthankfulness of kindred bredd up, (which generally is very true,) yet I care not; I forgett all thinges, so I may doe them good who want it. So I doe my part to them, lett them think of me what they will or can. I have another judge, to whom I stand or fall. Yf I should regard such things, it were in another's power to defeat my charity, and evill shold be stronger then good: but difficulties are so farr from cooling christians, that they whett them. Truly it grieves me to think of the child, how destitute she is, and that in this necessary time of education. For the time of breeding is the time of doing children good; and not as many who think they have done fairly, if they leave them a good portion after their decease. But take this rule, and it is an outlandish one, which I commend to you as being now a father, 'the best-bredd child hath the best portion'. Well; the good God bless you more and more; and all yours; and make your family, a housefull of God's servants. So prayes

Your ever loving brother,

G. Herbert.

My wife's and neeces' service.

To my very dear brother
Sir Henry Herbert, at Court.
[? Autumn, 1630]

XIII. *To the Right Honourable the Lady Anne, Countess of Pembr. and Montg. at Court.*

Madam,

What a trouble hath your Goodness brought on you, by admitting our poor services? now they creep in a Vessel of *Metheglin*, and still they will be presenting or wishing to see, if at length they may find out some thing not unworthy of

10 difficultie *Warner*
XIII. *First printed in Walton's* Lives, 1675

those hands at which they aim. In the mean time a Priests blessing, though it be none of the Court-stile, yet doubtless Madam, can do you no hurt: Wherefore the Lord make good the blessing of your Mother upon you, and cause all her wishes, diligence, prayers and tears, to bud, blow and bear fruit in your Soul, to his glory, your own good, and the great joy of

Madam,
Your most faithful Servant
in Christ Jesu,

GEORGE HERBERT.

Dec. 10. 1631.
Bemerton.

Madam, Your poor Colony of Servants present their humble duties.

XIV. *To Sir Henry Herbert.*

DEAR BRO;

I was glad of your Cambridge newes, but you joyed me exceedingly with your relation of my Lady Duchess's forwardnes in our church building. I am glad I used you in it, and you have no cause to be sorry, since it is GOD's business. If there fall out yet any rubb, you shall heare of me; and your offering of yourself to move my Lords of Manchester and Boollingbrook is very welcome to mee. To shew a forwardness in religious works is a good testimony of a good spirit. The LORD bless you, and make you abound in every good worke, to the joy of

your ever loving brother,

G. HERBERT.

March 21, Bemerton. [1631/2]
To my deere brother,
Sir Henry Herbert, at Court.

XIV. *From Warner*, op. cit.

XV. *To Mr. Nicholas Ferrar.*

My exceeding Dear Brother.

Although you have a much better Paymaster then my self, even him, whome we both serve: yet I shall ever put your care of Leighton, upon my accompt, & give you my self for it, to be yours for ever. God knowes, I have desired a long time, to doe the place good, & have endeavoured many wayes, to find out a man for it. And now My gratious Lord God, is pleased to give me you for the Man, I desired, for wch I humbly thank him, & am so far from giving you cause, to apology, about your counselling me herein: that I take it exceeding kindly of you. I refuse not advice from the meanest, that creeps upon Gods earth, no not tho' the advice step so far, as to be reproof: much less can I dis-esteem it from you, whome I esteem to be God's faithfull & diligent Servant, not considering you any other wayes, as neyther I my self desire to be considered. Particularly, I like all your Addresses, & for ought I see, they are ever to be liked. [*So he goes on in the discourse of the building the Church, in such & such a forme as N.F. advised, & letting N.F. know, all he had, & would doe, to gett moneys to proceed in it. And concludes thus.*] You write very lovingly that all your things are mine. If so, let this of Leighton Church the care, be amongst the chiefest also, so also have I required Mr W. for his part. Now God the Father of our Lord Jesus Christ bless you more & more, & so turn you all, in your severall wayes, one to the other, that ye may be a heavenly comfort, to his prayse, & the great Joy of

Your Brother & Servant in Christ Jesus

George Herbert.

Postscript.

As I had written thus much, I received a Letter, from My Brother, Sr Henry H: of the blessed Success, that God

XV. *From the transcript of John Ferrar's life of his brother in* Cam. Univ. Libr. Baker MSS. (Mm. I. 46, f. 410). *This and the following letter were first printed in Mayor's* Nicholas Ferrar, 1855   18–21 *The bracketed words suggest by their spelling that they are John Ferrar's summarizing, not Baker's*   22 mine, If   23 required] requested *Mayor, Grosart, Palmer*

had given us, by moving the Duches's heart, to an exceeding cheerfulness, in signing 100 *lib.* with her own hands (& promising to get her Son to doe as much) with some little Apology that she had done nothing in it (as my Brother writes) hitherto. She referred it also to My Brother, to name at first, what the summe should be, but he told her Grace, that he would by no meanes do so, urging, that Charity must be free. She liked our Book well, & has given order to ye Tenants, at Leighton, to make payment of it. God Almighty prosper the Work. Amen.

[March 1631/2]

XVI. *To the same.*

My Dear Brother

I thanke you heartily for Leighton, your care, your Counsell, your Cost. And as I am glad for the thing, so no less glad for the Heart, that God has given you & yours, to pious works. Blessed be My God & Dear Master, the Spring & Fountain of all Goodness. As for my assistance, doubt not, through Gods blessing, but it shall be to the full; & for my power, I have sent my Letters, to your Brother, investing him, in all that I have. [*And so he goes on in his advice, for the ordering of things, to that business.*]

XVII. *To Sir Henry Herbert.*

Dear Bro;

It is so long since I heard from you, that I long to heare both how you and your's doe: and also what becomes of you this sommer. It is the whole amount of this letter, and therefore entertaine it accordingly from

Your very affectionate bro;

G. Herbert.

7 *June*, Bemerton. [1631 or 1632]

My wife's and neeces' service to you.

4 Apology *bracketed by Baker, and perhaps supplied by him*
XVI. *From the* Baker MSS. (Mm. I. 46, f. 411) 20–21 *The bracketed words are presumably John Ferrar's summary of the remainder of the letter*
XVII. *From Warner,* op. cit.

XVIII. *To N.F. the Translatour of Valdesso.*

[*See above, p. 304, for this letter.*]

XIX. *Reasons for Arthur Woodnoth's living with Sir John Danvers.*

In ye name of God. Amen

1° Higher opportunities of doeing good are to be preferred before lower, euen where to continue in ye lower is no sinn. by ye Apostles rule. 1 Cor. 7, 21. & in ye whole chapter therfore your choice at first was good

2° yet are you now ingaged. It is a different thing to advize you now, & before you took Sr Johns affairs. you haue bin at charges: you haue stockd the grounds: you have layed out thoughts & prayers[:] you have sowed. therfore Expect a harvest.

3° To Change shewes not well & you are by ye Apostles rule (Philip 4, 8.) not only to pursue pure things, but things y^{t} are lovely, & of good report if there be any vertue or any praise. now Constancy is such & of great esteem wth all. As in things inwardly good to have an eye to ye world may be pharisaicall: so in things naturally visible & apparent, as ye course of our life & ye changes thereof, we are to regard others, & neither to scandalize them, nor wound our owne reputation.

4° When two things dislike you: the one for the nature thereof (as your trade) the other only for the success (as assistance of Sr John) doe as David did: putt your self into ye hands of God (whose the success of things is) & not into the hands of men or mens trades: especially no obligation lying upon you either for ye execution or benefitt of a trade, by ye way of supporting either it (in regard of ye citty) or your self or your kindred.

XIX. *From the autograph memorandum of Herbert in the Ferrar Papers at Magdalene College, Cambridge. The use of capitals and of marks of punctuation cannot always be determined. The paper is inscribed, in a Ferrar hand,* Mr Herberts reasons for Arth. Woodenoths Liuing wth Sr Jhon Daũers. *Printed in* The Ferrar Papers, ed. B. Blackstone, 1938.

5° Whereas you complaine of want of success consider how long God knocks at our harts, before he be heard, & yet desists not. to be without dores with him, is no ill company. yf God had done y^{t} (wch you are thinking to doe) to blessed Mary Magd. & Paul, heauen had wanted chief saints: therfore God is styled wth y^{t} glorious title, Long Suffering. 6° you doe not want all success. As God where he finds no roome for his Inclining grace, yet useth his Restraining grace, euen in ye most wicked: so though you incline not, happily you restraine. things may grow worse by your withdrawing wch grow not better by your presence. & if upon your withdrawing it shold doe so, it would trouble your conscience.

7 Though you want all success either in inclining or restraining, To desire good & endeavour it when we can doe no more, is to doe it. Complaine not of ye want of success, when you have the fruit of it. In Gods accepting you have done ye good you intended, & whom serve you? or whom would you please? David built the temple as much as Solomon because he desired it, & prepared for it. Doe this & be a man as David, after Gods hart.

For any scruple of leaving y^{r} trade, throw it away. When we exhort people to continue in their vocation, it is in opposition to idlenes. work rather then doe nothing. but to chuse a higher work, as God gives me higher thoughts, & to rise wth his favours, can not but be not only allowable but com̄endable. The case of ministers and magistrates is another thing, the one are Gods servants, ye other y^{e} com̄onwealths, & therfore not relinquishable without their masters consent. but a Trade having two things, the one imployment, the other profitt, the work I may change, the profitt, I am master of.

[October, 1631]

22–32 *A postscript added a few days later: see note* 25 me] *possibly for* mē (= men) 31 profitt. the work *MS*

THE WILL OF GEORGE HERBERT

I GEORGE HERBERT commending my soule and body to Almightie God that made them doe thus dispose of my goods. I giue all my goods both within doores and without doores both monneys and bookes and howshould stuffe whether in my possession or out of my possession that properly belonge to me vnto my deare wife excepting onely these legacies hereafter insuing. First there is seauen hvndred pounds in Mr Thomas Lawleys hands a Merchant of London which fell to me by the death of my deare Neece Mrs Dorothy Vaughan whereof two hvndred pounds belongs to my two Neeces that survive and the rest unto my selfe, this whole sum of fiue hvndred pounds I bequeath vnto my Neeces equally to be devided betweene them excepting some legacies of my deceased Neece which are to be payd out of it vnto some whose names shalbe annexed vnto this bill. Then I bequeath twenty pounds vnto the poore of this parish to be devided according to my deare wiues discretion. Then I bequeath to Mr Hays the Comment of Lucas Brugensis vppon the Scripture and his halfe yeares wages aforehand, then I bequeath to Mr. Bostocke St. Augustines workes and his halfe yeares wages aforehand, then I leave to my servant Elizabeth her dubble wages giuen her, three pound more besides that which is due to her, to Ann I leave thirty shillings: to Margeret twenty shillings: To William Twenty Nobles, To John twentie shillings, all these are over and aboue their wages, To Sara thirteene shillings foure pence, Alsoe my will and pleasure is that Mr Woodnoth should be mine Executor to whome I bequeath twenty pound whereof fifteene pound shalbe bestowed vppon Leighton Church, the other fiue pound I giue to himselfe. Lastlie I besech Sr John Danvers that he would be pleased to be Overseer of this Will.

George: Herbert

(testes Nathaniell Bostocke, Elizabeth: Burden)

The Will. From the Principal Registry of H.M.'s Court of Probate, Somerset House (Russell 33)

On the other side are the names of those to whome my deceased Neece left legacyes.

All those that are crost are discharged already the rest are to be payd.

To Mrss Magdalen Vaughan one hvndred pound, To Mrs Catharine Vaughan One hvndred pound, To Mr George Herbert one hvndred pound× To Mrs Beatrice Herbert forty pound×, To Mrs Jane Herbert tenn pound×, To Mrs Danvers five pound×, To Amy Danvers thirty shillings, To Mrs Anne Danvers twenty shillings, To Mrs Mary Danvers twenty shillings, To Mrs Michel twenty shillings, To Mrs. Elizabeth Danvers Mr Henry Danvers wife twenty shillings, to the poore of the parish twenty pound× To my Lord of Cherbury tenn pound, To Mr Bostocke forty shillings× To Elizabeth Burthen thirty shillings× To Mary Gifford tenn shillings× To Anne Hibbert tenn shillings× To William Scuce twenty shillings× To Mrs Judith Spencer five pound To Mary Owens forty shillings To Mrs Mary Lawly fifty shillings× To Mr Gardiner tenn pound MS. that the fiue pound due to Mrs Judeth Spenser is to be payd to Mrs Mary Lawly at Chelsey MS. that there are diuers moneys of mine in Mr Stephens hands Stationer of London, having lately receaved an hvndred and two pounds besides some Remainders of monyes wherof he is to giue as I know he will a Just account: if there be any body els that owe me any thing else of old debt I forgiue them.

GEORGII HERBERTI ANGLI

MUSAE RESPONSORIAE

AD ANDREAE MELVINI SCOTI
ANTI-TAMI-CAMI-CATEGORIAM

Augustissimo Potentissimóque Monarchae

IACOBO, D.G.

Magnae Britanniae, Franciae, & Hiberniae
Regi, Fidei Defensori &c.
Geo. Herbertus.

ECce recedentis foecundo in littore Nili
Sol generat populum luce fouente nouum.
Antè tui, *CAESAR*, quàm fulserat aura fauoris,
Nostrae etiam Musae vile fuere lutum:
Nunc adeò per te viuunt, vt repere possint,
Síntque ausae thalamum solis adire tui.

Illustriss. Celsissimóque

CAROLO,

Walliae, & Iuuentutis Principi.

QVam chartam tibi porrigo recentem,
Humanae decus atque apex iuuentae,
Obtutu placido benignus affles,
Namque aspectibus è tuis vel vnus

Musae Responsoriae. *From* Ecclesiastes Solomonis. Auctore Joan. Viviano. Canticum Solomonis : Nec non Epigrammata Sacra, Per Ja. Duportum. Accedunt Georgii Herberti Musae Responsoriae ad Andreae Melvini Anti-Tami-Cami-Categoriam. Cantabrigiae : Ex Officina Joannis Field, celeberrimae Academiae Typographi. Anno Domini, 1662. (*A copy in library of Trin. Coll. Cam.*) (*Here cited as D*) *For Melville's* Anti-Tami-Cami-Categoria, *see Appendix*, p. 609.

Carolo Principi. 1 recentem 2 decus, 4 Namque *Pickering's emendation* : Nam *D*

Mordaces tineas, nigrásque blattas,
Quas liuor mihi parturit, retundet,
Ceu, quas culta timet seges, pruinas
Nascentes radij fugant, vel acres
Tantùm dulcia leniunt catarrhos.
Sic o te (iuuenem, senémue) credat
Mors semper iuuenem, senem Britanni.

Reuerendissimo in Christo Patri ac Domino, EPISCOPO VINTONIENSI, *&c.*

SAncte Pater, coeli custos, quo doctius vno
  Terra nihil, nec quo sanctius astra vident;
Cùm mea futilibus numeris se verba viderent
  Claudi, penè tuas praeteriêre fores.
Sed properè dextréque reduxit euntia sensus,
  Ista docens soli scripta quadrare tibi.

PRO DISCIPLINA ECCLESIAE NOSTRAE EPIGRAMMATA APOLOGETICA

I. Ad Regem

Instituti Epigrammatici ratio.

CVm millena tuam pulsare negotia mentem
  Constet, & ex illâ pendeat orbis ope;
Ne te productis videar lassare Camoenis,
  Pro solido, CAESAR, carmine frusta dabo.
Cùm tu contundis *Catharos*, vultúque librísque,
  Grata mihi mensae sunt analecta tuae.

Episcopo Vintoniensi. 5 properè,
I. 5 contundis *Ed*: contundens *D*

II. Ad Melvinum

NOn mea fert aetas, vt te, veterane, lacessam;
Non vt te superem: res tamen ipsa feret.
Aetatis numerum supplebit causa minorem:
Sic tu nunc iuuenis factus, egóque senex.
Aspice, dum perstas, vt te tua deserat aetas,
Et mea sint canis scripta referta tuis.
Ecce tamen quàm suauis ero! cùm, fine duelli,
Clauserit extremas pugna peracta vices,
Tum tibi, si placeat, fugientia tempora reddam;
Sufficiet votis ista iuuenta meis.

III. Ad eundem

In Monstrum vocabuli Anti-Tami-Cami-Categoria.

O Quàm bellus homo es! lepido quàm nomine fingis
Istas *Anti-Tami-Cami-Categorias*!
Sic Catharis noua sola placent; res, verba nouantur:
Quae sapiunt aeuum, ceu cariosa iacent.
Quin liceat nobis aliquas procudere voces:
Non tibi fingendi sola taberna patet.
Cùm sacra perturbet vester furor omnia, scriptum
Hoc erit, *Anti-furi-Puri-Categoria.*
Pollubra vel cùm olim damnâris Regiâ in arâ,
Est *Anti-pelvi-Melvi-Categoria.*

IV. *Partitio* Anti-Tami-Cami-Categoriae.

TRes video partes, quò re distinctiùs vtar,
Anticategoriae, Scoto-Britanne, tuae:
Ritibus vna[1] Sacris opponitur; altera[2] Sanctos
Praedicat autores; tertia[3] plena Deo est.
Postremis ambabus idem sentimus vterque;
Ipse pios laudo; Numen & ipse colo.
Non nisi prima suas patiuntur praelia lites.
O bene quòd dubium possideamus agrum!

[1] *Ab initio ad vers.* 64
[2] *Inde ad vers.* 128
[3] *Inde* 177

IV. *The marginal references, taken from Duport, are to the lines* (versus) *of Melville's* Anti-Tami-Cami-Categoria (*see below*, p. 609); *a few references are corrected, and three are added*

V. *In metri genus.*

CVr, vbi tot ludat numeris antiqua poesis,
  Sola tibi Sappho, femináque vna placet?
Cur tibi tam facilè non arrisêre poetae
  Heroum grandi carmina fulta pede?
Cur non lugentes Elegi? non acer Iambus?
  Commotos animos rectiùs ista decent.
Scilicet hoc vobis proprium, qui puriùs itis,
  Et populi spurcas creditis esse vias:
Vos ducibus missis, missis doctoribus, omnes
  Femineum blandâ fallitis arte genus:
Nunc etiam teneras quò versus gratior aures
  Mulceat, imbelles complacuêre modi.

VI. *De Laruatâ Gorgone.**

* *In titulo*

GOrgona cur diram laruásque obtrudis inanes,
  Cùm propè sit nobis Musa, Medusa procul?
Si, quia felices olim dixêre poetae
  Pallada gorgoneam, sic tua verba placent.
Vel potiùs liceat distinguere. Túque tuíque
  Sumite *gorgoneam*, nostráque *Pallas* erit.

VII. *De Praesulum fastu.**

* *vers.* 21

PRaesulibus nostris fastus, *Melvine*, tumentes
  Saepiùs aspergis. Siste, pudore vacas.
An quod semotum populo laquearibus altis
  Eminet, id tumidum protinus esse feres?
Ergo etiam Solem dicas, ignaue, superbum,
  Qui tam sublimi conspicit orbe viam:
Ille tamen, quamuìs altus, tua crimina ridens
  Assiduo vilem lumine cingit humum.
Sic laudandus erit nactus sublimia Praesul,
  Qui dulci miseros irradiabit ope.

V. 11 aures,
VI. 1 diram,

VIII. *De geminâ Academiâ.**

* *In titulo*

QVis hìc superbit, oro? túne, an Praesules,
Quos dente nigro corripis?
Tu duplicem solus Camoenarum thronum
Virtute percellis tuâ;
Et vnus impar aestimatur viribus,
Vtrumque sternis calcitro:
Omnésque stulti audimus, aut hypocritae,
Te perspicaci atque integro.
An rectiùs nos, si vices vertas, probi,
Te contumaci & liuido?
Quisquis tuetur perspicillis Belgicis
Quâ parte tractari solent,
Res ampliantur, sin per aduersam videt,
Minora fiunt omnia:
Tu qui superbos caeteros existimas
(Superbius cùm te nihil)
Vertas specillum: nam, prout se res habent,
Vitro minùs rectè vteris.

IX. *De S. Baptismi Ritu.**

* *Vers.* 34

CVm tener ad sacros infans sistatur aquales,
Quòd puer ignorat, verba profana putas?
Annon sic mercamur agros? quibus ecce Redemptor
Comparat aeterni regna beata Dei.
Scilicet emptorem si res aut parcior aetas
Impediant, apices legis amicus obit.
Forsitan & prohibes infans portetur ad vndas,
Et per se Templi limen adire velis:
Sin, *Melvine*, pedes alienos postulet infans,
Cur sic displiceat vox aliena tibi?
Rectiùs innocuis lactentibus omnia praestes,
Quae ratio per se, si sit adulta, facit.
Quid vetat vt pueri vagitus suppleat alter,
Cùm nequeat claras ipse litare preces?

VIII. 1 Praesules? 8 perspicaci, 10 contumaci,

Saeuus es eripiens paruis vadimonia coeli:
Et tibi sit nemo praes, vbi poscis opem.

X. *De Signaculo Crucis.**

* *Vers.* 29

CVr tanta sufflas probra in innocuam Crucem?
Non plùs maligni daemones Christi cruce
Vnquam fugari, quàm tui socij solent.
Apostolorum culpa non leuis fuit
Vitâsse Christi spiritum efflantis crucem.
Et Christianus quisque piscis dicitur
Tertulliano, propter vndae pollubrum,
Quo tingimur parui. Ecquis autem brachijs
Natare sine clarissimâ potest cruce?
Sed non moramur: namque vestra crux erit,
Vobis fauentibúsue, vel negantibus.

XI. *De iuramento Ecclesiae.**

* *Vers.* 25

ARticulis sacris quidam subscribere iussus,
Ah! Cheiragra vetat, quò minùs, inquit, agam.
O verè dictum, & bellè! cùm torqueat omnes
Ordinis osores articulare malum.

XII. *De Purificatione post puerperium.**

* *Vers.* 44

ENixas pueros matres se sistere templis
Displicet, & laudis tura litare Deo.
Fortè quidem, cùm per vestras Ecclesia turbas
Fluctibus internis exagitata natet,
Vos sine maternis hymnis infantia vidit,
Vitáque neglectas est satìs vlta preces.
Sed nos, cùm nequeat paruorum lingua, parentem
Non laudare Deum, credimus esse nefas.
Quotidiana suas poscant si fercula grates,
Nostra caro sanctae nescia laudis erit?

XI. 1 iussus
XII. 7 lingua

Adde pijs animis quaeuis occasio lucro est,
Quâ possint humili fundere corde preces.
Sic vbi iam mulier decerpti conscia pomi
Ingemat ob partus, ceu maledicta, suos,
Appositè quem commotum subfugerat olim,
Nunc redit ad mitem, ceu benedicta, Deum.

XIII. *De Antichristi decore Pontificali.**

* *Vers.* 48

NOn quia Pontificum sunt olim afflata veneno,
Omnia sunt temere proijcienda foras.
Tollantur si cuncta malus quae polluit vsus,
Non remanent nobis corpora, non animae.

XIV. *De Superpelliceo.**

* *Vers.* 47

QVid sacrae tandem meruêre vestes,
Quas malus liuor iaculis lacessit
Polluens castum chlamydis colorem
Dentibus atris?

Quicquid ex vrnâ meliore ductum
Luce praelustri, vel honore pollet,
Mens sub insigni specie coloris
Concipit albi.

Scilicet talem liquet esse solem;
Angeli vultu radiante candent;
Incolae coeli melioris albâ
Veste triumphant.

E creaturis* sine mentis vsu
Conditis binas homini sequendas
Spiritus proponit, & est vtrique
Candor amicus.

* *Ovis, & Columba.* Columel. lib. 7 c. 2 & lib. 8 c. 8

Ergo ringantur pietatis hostes,
Filij noctis, populus malignus,
Dum suum nomen tenet, & triumphat
Albion albo.

12 Qua *Grosart*: Quae *D* 15 quem] quum *Grosart*
XIV. 1 vestes? 3 *misprinted* castam (*cf.* albi, *l.* 8)

XV. *De Pileo quadrato.**

* *Vers.* 45

QVae dicteria fuderat Britannus
Superpellicei tremendus hostis,
Isthaec pileus audijt propinquus,
Et partem capitis petit supremam;
Non sic effugit angulus vel vnus
Quò dictis minùs acribus notetur.
  Verùm heus! si reputes, tibi tuísque
Longè pileus anteit galerum,
Vt feruor cerebri refrigeretur,
Qui vestras edit intimè medullas.
Sed qui tam malè pileos habetis,
Quos Ecclesia comprobat, verendum
Ne tandem caput eius impetatis.

XVI. *In Catharum.*

CVr Latiam linguam reris nimis esse profanam,
  Quam praemissa probant secula, nostra probant?
Cur teretem Graecam damnas, atque Hellada totam,
  Quâ tamen occisi foedera scripta Dei?
Scilicet Hebraeam cantas, & perstrepis vnam:
  Haec facit ad nasum sola loquela tuum.

XVII. *De Episcopis.**

* *Vers.* 186

QVos charos habuit Christus Apostolos,
Testatósque suo tradiderat gregi;
Vt, cùm mors rabidis vnguibus imminens
Doctrinae fluuios clauderet aureae,
Mites acciperent Lampada Praesules,
Seruaréntque sacrum clauibus ordinem;
Hos nunc barbaries impia vellicat
Indulgens proprijs ambitionibus,
Et, quos ipsa nequit scandere vertices,
Hos ad se trahere et mergere gestiens.

XV. 7 reputes tibi,
XVI. 1 profanam? XVII. 9 Et vertices 10 trahere,

O caecum populum! si bona res siet
Praesul, cur renuis? sin mala, pauculos
Quàm cunctos fieri praestat Episcopos.

XVIII. Ad Melvinum

*De ijsdem.**

* *Vers.* 185

PRaesulibus dirum te Musa coarguit hostem,
An quia Textores Artificésque probas?

XIX. *De Textore Catharo.*

CVm piscatores Textor legit esse vocatos,
Vt sanctum Domini persequerentur opus;
Ille quoque inuadit Diuinam Flaminis artem,
Subtegmen reti dignius esse putans,
Et nunc perlongas Scripturae stamine telas*
Torquet, & in Textu Doctor vtroque cluet.

* *Vers.* 59

XX. *De Magicis rotatibus.**

* *Vers.* 30, 32

QVos tu rotatus, quale murmur auscultas
In ritibus nostris? Ego audio nullum.
Agè, prouocemus vsque ad Angelos ipsos,
Aurésque superas: arbitri ipsi sint litis,
Vtrum tenore sacra nostra sint nécne
Aequabili facta. Ecquid ergo te tanta
Calumniandi concitauit vrtica,
Vt, quae Papicolis propria, assuas nobis,
Falsúmque potiùs quàm crepes [verum] versu?
Tu perstrepis tamen; ýtque turgeat carmen
Tuum tibi, poeta belle, non mystes,
Magicos rotatus, & perhorridas Striges,*
Dicterijs mordacibus notans, clamas
Non conuenire precibus ista Diuinis.
O saeuus hostis! quàm ferociter pugnas!
Nihílne respondebimus tibi? Fatemur.

* *Vers.* 33

XVIII. 2 Textores,
XX. 9 verum *supplied by Ed See note* 10 turgeat] tingeat *Grosart*
13 clamas] clausus *Grosart*

XXI. *Ad fratres.*

O Sec'lum lepidum! circumstant vndique Fratres,
Papicolísque sui sunt, Catharísque sui.
Sic nunc plena boni sunt omnia Fratris, amore
Cùm nil fraterno rarius esse queat.

XXII. *De labe maculísque.**

* *Vers.* 23

LAbeculas maculásque nobis obijcis:
Quid? hoccine est mirum? Viatores sumus.
Quò sanguis est Christi, nisi vt maculas lauet,
Quas spargit animae corporis propius lutum?
Vos ergo puri! o nomen appositissimum
Quo vulgus ornat vos! At audias parum;
Astronomus olim (vt fama) dum maculas diu,
Quas Luna habet, tuetur, in foueam cadit,
Totúsque caenum Cynthiae ignoscit notis.
Ecclesia est mihi Luna; perge in Fabulâ.

XXIII. *De Musicâ Sacrâ.**

* *Vers.* 54

CVr efficaci, Deucalion, manu,
Post restitutos fluctibus obices,
Mutas in humanam figuram
Saxa superuacuásque cautes?

Quin redde formas, o bone, pristinas,
Et nos reducas ad lapides auos:
Nam saxa mirantur canentes,
Saxa lyras citharásque callent.

Rupes tenaces & silices ferunt
Potentiori carmine percitas
Saltus per incultos lacúsque
Orphea mellifluum secutas.

XXII. 1 Labeculas, obijcis,
XXIII. 4 cautes *Errata D* : caules *text D* : *cf. l.* 20 8 lyras, 9 tenaces, 11 incultos,

Et saxa diris hispida montibus
Amphionis testudine nobili
  Percussa dum currunt ad vrbem
    Moenia contribuêre Thebis.

Tantùm repertum est trux hominum genus,
Qui templa sacris expoliant choris,
  Non erubescentes vel ipsas
    Duritiâ superare cautes.

O plena centum Musica Gratijs,
Praeclariorum spirituum cibus,
  Quò me vocas tandem, tuúmque
    Vt celebrem decus insusurras?

Tu Diua miro pollice spiritum
Caeno profani corporis exuens
  Ter millies coelo reponis:
    Astra rogant, Nouus hic quis hospes?

Ardore Moses concitus entheo,
Mersis reuertens laetus ab hostibus
  Exuscitat plebem sacratos
    Ad Dominum properare cantus.

Quid hocce? Psalmos audión'? o dapes!
O succulenti balsama spiritûs!
  Ramenta coeli, guttulaéque
    Deciduae melioris orbis!

Quos David, ipsae deliciae Dei,
Ingens piorum gloria Principum,
  Sionis excelsas ad arces
    Cum citharis lituísque miscet.

Miratur aequor finitimum sonos,
Et ipse Iordan sistit aquas stupens;
  Prae quo Tibris vultum recondit,
    Eridanúsque pudore fusus.

14 testudine *Ed*: testitudine *D, Grosart*   15 vrbem,   40 citharis,

Tún' obdis aures, grex noue, barbaras,
Et nullus audis? cantibus obstrepens,
Vt, quò fatiges verberésque
Pulpita, plus spatij lucreris?

At cui videri prodigium potest
Mentes, quietis tympana publicae,
Discordijs plenas sonoris
Harmoniam tolerare nullam?

XXIV. *De eâdem.**

* *Vers.* 55

CAntus sacros, profane, mugitus vocas?
Mugire multò mauelim quàm rudere.

XXV. *De rituum vsu.**

* *Vers.* 21

CVm primùm ratibus suis
nostram Caesar ad insulam
olim appelleret, intuens
omnes indigenas loci
viuentes sine vestibus,
O victoria, clamitat,
certa, ac perfacilis mihi!
Non alio Cathari modo
dum sponsam Domini pijs
orbam ritibus expetunt,
atque ad barbariem patrum
vellent omnia regredi,
illam tegminis insciam
prorsus Daemoni & hostibus
exponunt superabilem.
Atqui vos secus, o boni,
sentire ac sapere addecet,
si vestros animos regant
Scripturae canones sacrae:
Namque haec, iure, cuipiam

XXV. 6 clamitat 14 Daemoni, 17 sentire, ac] *om. Grosart*

vestem non adimi suam,
sed nudis & egentibus
non suam tribui iubet.

XXVI. *De annulo coniugali.*

SEd nec coniugij signum, Melvine, probabis?
Nec vel tantillum pignus habebit amor?
Nulla tibi si signa placent, è nubibus arcum
Eripe coelesti qui moderatur aquae.
Illa quidem à nostro non multùm abludit imago,
Annulus & plenus tempore forsan erit.
Sin nebulis parcas, & nostro parcito signo,
Cui non absimilis sensus inesse solet.
Scilicet, vt quos ante suas cum coniuge tedas
Merserat in lustris perniciosa venus,
Annulus hos reuocet, sistátque libidinis vndas
Legitimi signum connubiale tori.

XXVII. *De Mundis & mundanis.*

EX praelio vndae ignísque (si Physicis fides)
Tranquillus aer nascitur:
Sic ex profano Cosmico & Catharo potest
Christianus extundi bonus.

XXVIII. *De oratione Dominicâ.**

* *Vers.* 31

QVam Christus immortalis innocuo gregi
voce suâ dederat,
quis crederet mortalibus
orationem reijci septemplicem,
quae miseris clypeo
Aiacis est praestantior?
Haec verba superos aduolaturus thronos
Christus, vt auxilij
nos haud inanes linqueret,

XXVI. 7 parcas XXVII. 3 Cosmico,

(cùm dignius nil posset aut melius dare)
pignora chara sui
fruenda nobis tradidit.
Quis sic amicum excipiet, vt Cathari Deum,
qui renouare sacri
audent amoris Symbolum?
Tu verò quisquis es, caue ne, dum neges,
improbe, verba Dei,
te deneget VERBVM Deus.

XXIX. *In Catharum quendam.*

CVm templis effare, madent sudaria, mappae,
Trux caper alarum, suppara, laena, sagum.
Quin populo, clemens, aliquid largire caloris:
Nunc sudas solus; caetera turba riget.

XXX. *De lupâ lustri Vaticani.**

* *Vers.* 61

CAlumniarum nec pudor quis nec modus?
Nec *Vaticanae* desines vnquam *Lupae*
Metus inanes? Nos pari praeteruehi
Illam Charybdim cautione nouimus
Vestrámque Scyllam, aequis parati spiculis
Britannicam in Vulpem, ínque Romanam Lupam.
Dicti fidem firmabimus Anagrammate.

XXXI. *De impositione manuum.**

* *Vers.* 37

NEc dextra te fugit, almi Amoris emblema?
Atqui manus imponere integras praestat,
Quàm (more vestro) imponere inscio vulgo.
Quantò Impositio melior est Imposturâ!

XXVIII. 10 nihil 16–17 caue, nè dum neges improbe
XXX. 2 *Lupae?* 7 Anagrammate. *Here follows in Duport the Anagram included in the Williams MS. poems (see below, p.* 416) XXXI. 1 fugit

XXXII. *Supplicum Ministrorum raptus κωμῳδούμενος.*

AMbitio Cathari quinque constat Actibus.
I. Primò, vnus aut alter parum ritus placet:
Iam repit impietas volatura illico.
II. Mox displicent omnes. Vbi hoc permanserit
III. Paulò, secretis mussitans in angulis
Quaerit recessus. Incalescit fabula:
IV. Erumpit inde, & contineri nescius
V. Syluas pererrat. Fibulis dein omnibus
Prae spiritu ruptis, quò eas resarciat
Amstellodamum corripit se. *Plaudite.*

XXXIII. *De Autorum enumeratione.**

* *Vers.* 65–128

QVò magìs inuidiam nobis & crimina confles,
Pertrahis in partes nomina magna tuas;
Martyra, *Calvinum*, *Bezam*, doctúmque *Bucerum*,
Qui tamen in nostros fortiter ire negant.
Whitaker, erranti quem praefers carmine, miles
Assiduus nostri papilionis erat.
Nos quoque possemus longas conscribere turmas,
Si numero starent praelia, non animis.
Primus adest nobis, Pharisaeis omnibus hostis,
Christus Apostolici cinctus amore gregis.
Tu geminas belli portas, o *Petre*, repandis,
Dum gladium stringens *Paulus* ad arma vocat.
Inde Patres pergunt quadrati, & tota Vetustas.
Nempe Nouatores quis Veteranus amat?
Iam *Constantinus* multo se milite miscet;
Inuisámque tuis erigit hasta Crucem.
Hipponensis adest properans, & torquet in hostes
Lampada, quâ studijs inuigilare solet.
*Té*que *Deum* alternis cantans *Ambrosius* iram,
Immemor antiqui mellis, eundo coquit.

XXXII. 7 contineri *Ed*: continere *D*
XXXIII. 1 nobis, 6 nostri *Ed*: nostrae *D* 8 praelia

Haec etiam ad pugnam praesens, quâ viuimus, aetas
Innumeram nostris partibus addit opem.
Quos inter plenúsque Deo genióque Iacobus
Defendit veram mente manúque *fidem.*
Interea ad sacrum stimulat sacra Musica bellum,
Quâ sine vos miseri lentiùs itis ope.
Militat & nobis, quem vos contemnitis, Ordo;
Ordine discerni maxima bella solent.
O vos inualidos! Audi quem talibus armis
Euentum Naso vidit et admonuit;
Vna dies Catharos ad bellum miserat omnes:
Ad bellum missos perdidit vna dies.

XXXIV. *De auri sacrâ fame.**

* *Vers.* 201

CLaudis auaritiâ Satyram; statuísque sacrorum
Esse recidendas, Aeace noster, opes.
Caetera condonabo tibi, scombrísque remittam:
Sacrilegum carmen, censeo, flamma voret.

XXXV. *Ad Scotiam. Protrepticon ad Pacem.*

SCotia quae frigente iaces porrecta sub Arcto,
Cur adeò immodicâ relligione cales?
Anne tuas flammas ipsa Antiperistasis auget,
Vt niue torpentes incaluêre manus?
Aut vt pruna gelu summo mordaciùs vrit,
Sic acuunt zelum frigora tanta tuum?
Quin nocuas extingue faces, precor: vnda propinqua est,
Et tibi vicinas porrigit aequor aquas:
Aut potiùs Christi sanguis demissus ab alto,
Vicinúsque magìs nobiliórque fluit:
Ne, si flamma nouis adolescat mota flabellis,
Ante diem vestro mundus ab igne ruat.

24 mente, 27 Ordo,

XXXVI. *Ad seductos innocentes.*

INnocuae mentes, quibus inter flumina mundi
Ducitur illimi candida vita fide,
Absit vt ingenuum pungant mea verba pudorem;
Perstringunt vestros carmina sola duces.
O vtinam aut illorum oculi (quod comprecor vnum)
Vobis, aut illis pectora vestra forent.

XXXVII. *Ad Melvinum.*

ATqui te precor vnicè per ipsam,
Quae scripsit numeros, manum; per omnes
Musarum calices, per & beatos
Sarcasmos quibus artifex triumphas;
Quin per Presbyteros tuos; per vrbem
Quam curto nequeo referre versu;
Per charas tibi nobilésque dextras,
Quas subscriptio* neutiquam inquinauit; * *Vers.* 215
Per quicquid tibi suauiter probatur;
Ne me carminibus nimis dicacem,
Aut saeuum reputes. Amica nostra est
Atque edentula Musa, nec veneno
Splenis perlita contumeliosi.
Nam si te cuperem secare versu,
Totámque euomerem potenter iram
Quam aut Ecclesia despicata vobis,
Aut laesae mihi suggerunt Athenae,
(Et quem non stimularet haec simultas?)
Iam te funditus igneis Camoenis,
Et Musâ crepitante subruissem:
Omnis linea sepiam recusans
Plumbo ducta fuisset aestuanti,
Centum stigmatibus tuos inurens
Profanos fremitus bonásque sannas:
Plùs charta haec mea delibuta dictis
Haesisset tibi, quàm suprema vestis

XXXVII. 7 tibi, 18 simultas

Olim accreuerit *Herculi* furenti:
Quin hoc carmine Lexicon probrorum
Extruxissem, vbi, cùm moneret vsus,
Haurirent tibi tota plaustra Musae.
  Nunc haec omnia sustuli, tonantes
Affectus socijs tuis remittens.
Non te carmine turbidum[1] vocaui,
Non deridiculúmue, siue ineptum,[2]
Non striges,[3] magiámue,[4] vel rotatus,
Non fastus[5] tibi turgidos[6] repono;
Errores,[7] maculas,[8] superbiámque,[9]
Labes,[10] somniáque,[11] ambitúsque diros,[12]
Tinnitus *Berecynthios*[13] omittens
Nil horum regero tibi merenti.
  Quin te laudibus orno: quippe dico,
Caesar sobrius ad rei Latinae
Vnus dicitur aduenire cladem:
Et tu solus ad *Angliae* procellas
(Cùm plerumque tuâ sodalitate
Nil sit crassius, impolitiúsue)
Accedis bene doctus, et poeta.

[1] *Vers.* 29
[2] 22
[3] 33
[4] 30
[5] 21
[6] 194
[7] 178
[8] 23
[9] 189
[10] 23
[11] 59
[12] 202
[13] 53

XXXVIII. *Ad Eundem.*

INcipis irridens; stomachans in carmine pergis;
  Desinis exclamans: tota figura, vale.

XXXIX. *Ad Seren. Regem.*

ECce pererratas, Regum doctissime, nugas,
  Quas gens inconsulta, suis vexata procellis,
Libandas nobis absorbendásque propinat!
O caecos animi fratres! quis vestra fatigat
Corda furor, spissâque afflat caligine sensus?
Cernite, quàm formosa suas Ecclesia pennas
Explicat, & radijs ipsum pertingit Olympum!
Vicini populi passim mirantur, & aequos

XXXVII. 33 *Grosart inadvertently omits this line*
XXXVIII. 2 figura
XXXIX. 1 nugas. 3 nobis,

Mentibus attonitis cupiunt addiscere ritus:
Angelicae turmae nostris se coetibus addunt:
Ipse etiam Christus coelo speculatus ab alto,
Intuitúque vno stringens habitacula mundi,
Sola mihi plenos, ait, exhibet *Anglia* cultus.
Scilicet has olim diuisas aequore terras
Seposuit Diuina sibi, cùm conderet orbem,
Progenies, gemmámque suâ quasi pyxide clausit.
O qui *Defensor Fidei* meritissimus audis,
Responde aeternùm titulo; quóque ordine felix
Coepisti, pergas simili res texere filo.
Obrue feruentes, ruptis conatibus, hostes:
Quásque habet aut patulas, aut caeco tramite, moles
Haeresis, euertas. Quid enim te fallere possit?
Tu venas laticésque omnes, quos sacra recludit
Pagina, gustâsti, multóque interprete gaudes:
Tu Synodósque, Patrésque, & quod dedit alta vetustas
Haud per te moritura, Scholámque introspicis omnem.
Nec transire licet quo mentis acumine findis
Viscera naturae, commistúsque omnibus astris
Ante tuum tempus coelum gratissimus ambis.
Hâc ope munitus securior excipis vndas,
Quas Latij Catharíque mouent, atque inter vtrasque
Pastor agis proprios, medio tutissimus, agnos.
Perge, decus Regum; sic, Augustissime, plures
Sint tibi vel stellis laudes, & laudibus anni:
Sic pulsare tuas, exclusis luctibus, ausint
Gaudia sola fores: sic quicquid somnia mentis
Intus agunt, habeat certum meditatio finem:
Sic positis nugis, quibus irretita libido
Innumeros mergit vitiatâ mente poetas,
Sola *Iacobaeum* decantent carmina nomen.

XL. *Ad Deum.*

QVem tu, summe Deus, semel
Scribentem placido rore beaueris,
Illum non labor irritus

16 Progenies 22 Haeresis 23 venas, omnes 24 Pagina 30 vndas 31 Latji, 33 Perge sic

Exercet miserum; non dolor vnguium
  Morsus increpat anxios;
Non maeret calamus; non queritur caput:
  Sed faecunda poësεως
Vis, & vena sacris regnat in artubus;
  Qualis nescius aggerum
Exundat fluuio Nilus amabili.
  O dulcissime Spiritus,
Sanctos qui gemitus mentibus inseris
  A Te Turture defluos,
Quòd scribo, & placeo, si placeo, tuum est.

FINIS

XL. 11 spiritus

PASSIO DISCERPTA

I. *Ad Dominum morientem.*

CVm lacrymas oculósque duos tot vulnera vincant,
Impar, & in fletum vel resolutus, ero;
Sepia concurrat, peccatis aptior humor,
Et mea iam lacrymet culpa colore suo.

II. *In sudorem sanguineum.*

QVò fugies, sudor? quamuìs pars altera Christi
Nescia sit metae; venula, cella tua est.
Si tibi non illud placeat mirabile corpus,
Caetera displiceat turba, necesse, tibi:
Ni me fortè petas; nam quantò indignior ipse,
Tu mihi subueniens dignior esse potes.

III. *In eundem.*

SIc tuus effundi gestit pro crimine sanguis,
Vt nequeat paulò se cohibere domi.

IV. *In latus perfossum.*

CHriste, vbi tam duro patet in te semita ferro,
Spero meo cordi posse patere viam.

V. *In Sputum & Conuicia.*

O Barbaros! sic os rependitis sanctum,
Visum quod vni praebet, omnibus vitam,
Sputando, praedicando? sic Aquas vitae
Contaminatis alueósque caelestes

Passio Discerpta. *From* MS. Jones B 62 *in Dr. Williams's Library* (*here cited as W*). *All footnotes refer to W, unless any other source is stated. First printed by Grosart in 1874*

I. 1 lacrymas, 2 Impar &, 4 culpa, Colore
II. 1 fugies 3 corpus 5 ipse III. 1 sanguis 2 paulò,
V. 2 vitam 4 Contaminatis,

Sputando, blasphemando? nempe ne hoc fiat
In posterum, maledicta Ficus arescens
Gens tota fiet, atque vtrinque plectetur.
Parate situlas, Ethnici, lagenásque,
Graues lagenas, Vester est Aquae-ductus.

VI. *In Coronam spineam.*

CHriste, dolor tibi supplicio, mihi blanda voluptas;
Tu spinâ miserè pungeris, ipse Rosâ.
Spicula mutemus: capias Tu serta Rosarum,
Qui Caput es, spinas & tua Membra tuas.

VII. *In Arund. Spin. Genuflex. Purpur.*

QVàm nihil illudis, Gens improba! quàm malè cedunt
Scommata! Pastorem semper Arundo decet.
Quàm nihil illudis! cùm quò magìs angar acuto
Munere, Rex tantò verior inde prober.
Quàm nihil illudis flectens! namque integra posthâc
Posteritas flectet córque genúque mihi.
Quàm nihil illudis! si, quae tua purpura fingit,
Purpureo meliùs sanguine Regna probem.
At non lusus erit, si quem tu laeta necasti
Viuat, & in mortem vita sit illa tuam.

VIII. *In Alapas.*

AH! quàm caederis hinc & inde palmis!
Sic vnguenta solent manu fricari:
Sic toti medicaris ipse mundo.

6 Ficus, 8 situlas
VI. 1 voluptas VII. 1 illudis 2 Scommata? 3 illudis?
5 flectens? 7 illudis? Si, 8 sanguine, 9 si, VIII. 1 palmis?

IX. *In Flagellum.*

CHriste, flagellati spes & victoria mundi,
 Crimina cùm turgent, & mea poena prope est,
Suauiter admoueas notum tibi carne flagellum,
 Sufficiat virgae saepiùs vmbra tuae.
Mitis agas: tenerae duplicant sibi verbera mentes,
 Ipsáque sunt ferulae mollia corda suae.

X. *In vestes diuisas.*

SI, Christe, dum suffigeris, tuae vestes
 Sunt hostium legata, non amicorum,
Vt postulat mos; quid tuis dabis? Teipsum.

XI. *In pium Latronem.*

O Nimium Latro! reliquis furatus abundè,
 Nunc etiam Christum callidus aggrederis.

XII. *In Christum crucem ascensurum.*

ZAcchaeus, vt Te cernat, arborem scandit:
 Nunc ipse scandis, vt labore mutato
Nobis facilitas cedat & tibi sudor.
Sic omnibus videris ad modum visûs.
Fides gigantem sola, vel facit nanum.

XIII. *Christus in cruce.*

HIc, vbi sanati stillant opobalsama mundi,
 Aduoluor madidae laetus hiánsque Cruci:
Pro lapsu stillarum abeunt peccata; nec acres
 Sanguinis insultus exanimata ferunt.
Christe, fluas semper; ne, si tua flumina cessent,
 Culpa redux iugem te neget esse Deum.

IX. 2 est. 5 mentes 6 ferulae, mollia corda, X. 1 Si Christe 2 legata XII. scandit] scandet *Grosart* XIII. 5 Christe

XIV. *In Clauos.*

QValis eras, qui, ne melior natura minorem
  Eriperet nobis, in Cruce fixus eras;
Iam meus es: nunc Te teneo: Pastórque prehensus
  Hoc ligno, his clauis est, quasi Falce suâ.

XV. *Inclinato capite.* Joh. 19.

VVlpibus antra feris, nidíque volucribus adsunt,
  Quodque suum nouit strôma, cubile suum.
Qui tamen excipiat, Christus caret hospite: tantùm
  In cruce suspendens, vnde reclinet, habet.

XVI. *Ad Solem deficientem.*

QVid hoc? & ipse deficis, Caeli gigas,
  Almi choragus luminis?
Tu promis Orbem manè, condis vesperi,
  Mundi fidelis clauiger:
At nunc fatiscis. Nempe Dominus aedium
  Prodegit integrum penu,
Quámque ipse lucis tesseram sibi negat,
  Negat familiae suae.
Carere discat verna, quo summus caret
  Paterfamilias lumine.
Tu verò mentem neutiquam despondeas,
  Resurget occumbens Herus:
Tunc instruetur lautiùs radijs penu,
  Tibi supererunt & mihi.

XVII. *Monumenta aperta.*

DVm moreris, Mea Vita, ipsi vixere sepulti,
  Próque vno vincto turba soluta fuit.
Tu tamen, haud tibi tam moreris, quàm viuis in illis,
  Asserit & vitam Mors animata tuam.

XIV. 2 eras.
XVI. 6 penu. 8 Negat familiae [jam] suae *conj. Grosart* 10 lumine *Grosart*: luminis *W*

Scilicet in tumulis Crucifixum quaerite, viuit:
Conuincunt vnam multa sepulcra Crucem.
Sic, pro Maiestate, Deum, non perdere vitam
Quam tribuit, verùm multiplicare decet.

XVIII. *Terrae-motus.*

TE fixo vel Terra mouet: nam, cum Cruce, totam
Circumferre potes; Sampson vt antè fores.
Heu stolidi, primùm fugientem figite Terram,
Tunc Dominus clauis aggrediendus erit.

XIX. *Velum scissum.*

FRustra, Verpe, tumes, propola cultûs,
Et Templi parasite; namque velum
Diffissum reserat Deum latentem,
Et pomoeria terminósque sanctos
Non vrbem facit vnicam, sed Orbem.
Et pro pectoribus recenset aras,
Dum cor omne suum sibi requirat
Structorem, & Solomon vbique regnet.
Nunc Arcana patent, nec inuolutam
Phylacteria complicant latrîam.
Excessit tener Orbis ex Ephebis,
Maturúsque suos coquens amores
Praeflorat sibi nuptias futuras.
Vbique est Deus, Agnus, Ara, Flamen.

XX. *Petrae scissae.*

SAnus Homo factus, vitiorum purus vterque;
At sibi collisit fictile Daemon opus.
Post vbi Mosaicae repararent fragmina Leges,
Infectas tabulas facta iuuenca scidit.

XVII. 5 tumulis, XVIII. 2 ante, XIX. 1 Frustrà Verpe
XX. 3 Leges] Legis *Grosart*

Haud aliter cùm Christus obit, prae funere tanto
  Constat inaccessas dissiluisse petras.
Omnia, praeter corda, scelus confregit & error,
  Quae contrita tamen caetera damna leuant.

XXI. *In Mundi sympathiam cum Christo.*

NOn moreris solus: Mundus simul interit in te,
  Agnoscítque tuam Machina tota Crucem.
Hunc ponas animam mundi, Plato: vel tua mundum
  Ne nimium vexet quaestio, pone meam.

XXI. 3 mundi Plato :

LUCUS

I. *Homo, Statua.*

SVm, quis nescit, Imago Dei, sed saxea certè:
Hanc mihi duritiem contulit improbitas.
Durescunt proprijs euulsa corallia fundis,
Haud secus ingenitis dotibus orbus Adam.
Tu, qui cuncta creans docuisti marmora flere,
Haud mihi cor saxo durius esse sinas.

II. *Patria.*

VT tenuis flammae species caelum vsque minatur,
Igniculos legans, manserit ipsa licet;
Sic mucronatam reddunt suspiria mentem,
Votáque scintillae sunt animosa meae.
Assiduo stimulo carnem Mens vlta lacessit,
Sedula si fuerit, perterebrare potest.

III. *In Stephanum lapidatum.*

QVi silicem tundit, (mirum tamen) elicit ignem:
At Caelum è saxis elicuit Stephanus.

IV. *In Simonem Magum.*

ECquid emes Christum? pro nobis scilicet olim
Venditus est Agnus, non tamen emptus erit.
Quin nos Ipse emit, precioso faenora soluens
Sanguine: nec precium merx emit vlla suum.
Ecquid emes Caelum? quin stellam rectiùs vnam
Quo precio venit, fac, liceare priùs.
Nempe graui fertur scelerata pecunia motu,
Si sursum iacias, in caput ipsa ruit.
Vnicus est nummus, caelo Christóque petitus,
Nempe in quo clarè lucet Imago Dei.

Lucus. *Sources as for* Passio Discerpta (*see p.* 404)
I. 5 flere II. 2 ipsa, licet. 3 mentem IV. 8 ipsa] ipse *Grosart*

V. *In S. Scripturas.*

HEu, quis spiritus, igneúsque turbo
Regnat visceribus, meásque versat
Imo pectore cogitationes?
Nunquid pro foribus sedendo nuper
Stellam vespere suxerim volantem,
Haec autem hospitio latere turpi
Prorsùs nescia, cogitat recessum?
Nunquid mel comedens, apem comedi
Ipsâ cum dominâ domum vorando?
Imò, me nec apes, nec astra pungunt:
Sacratissima Charta, tu fuisti
Quae cordis latebras sinúsque caecos
Atque omnes peragrata es angiportus
Et flexus fugientis appetitûs.
Ah, quàm docta perambulare calles
Maeandrósque plicásque, quàm perita es!
Quae vis condidit, ipsa nouit aedes.

VI. *In pacem Britannicam.*

ANglia cur solùm fuso sine sanguine sicca est,
Cùm natet in tantis caetera terra malis?
Sit licet in pelago semper, sine fluctibus illa est,
Cùm qui plus terrae, plus habuere maris.
Naufragij causa est alijs mare, roboris Anglo,
Et quae corrumpit moenia, murus aqua est.
Nempe hìc Religio floret, regina quietis,
Túque super nostras, Christe, moueris aquas.

VII. *Auaritia.*

AVrum nocte videns, vidisse insomnia dicit:
Aurum luce videns, nulla videre putat.
O falsos homines! Vigilat, qui somniat aurum,
Plúsque habet hic laetus, quàm vel Auarus habet.

V. 4 Nunquid, 10 pungunt, 11 Charta 16 Maeandrósque,
VI. 7 quietis 8 nostras Christe

VIII. *In Lotionem pedum Apostolorum.*

SOlem ex Oceano Veteres exurgere fingunt
  Postquam se gelidis nocte refecit aquis:
Veriùs hoc olim factum est, vbi, Christe, lauares
  Illos, qui mundum circumiere, pedes.

IX. *In D. Lucam.*

CVr Deus elegit Medicum, qui numine plenus
  Diuinâ Christi scriberet acta manu?
Vt discat sibi quisque, quid vtile: nempe nocebat
  Crudum olim pomum, tristis Adame, tibi.

X. Papae titulus
Nec Deus Nec Homo.

QVisnam Antichristus cessemus quaerere; Papa
  Nec Deus est nec Homo: Christus vterque fuit.

XI. *Tributi solutio.*

PIscis tributum soluit; & tu Caesari:
  Vtrumque mirum est: hoc tamen mirum magìs,
Quòd omnibus tute imperes, nemo tibi.

XII. *Tempestas Christo dormiente.*

CVm dormis, surgit pelagus: cùm, Christe, resurgis,
  Dormitat pelagus: Quàm bene fraena tenes!

XIII. *Bonus Ciuis.*

SAgax Humilitas, eligens viros bonos
  Atque euehens, bonum facit faecundius,
Quàm si ipse solus omnia interuerteret,
Suámque in alijs possidet prudentiam.

VIII. 3 vbi Christe IX. 2 manu. XI. 2 magìs XII. 1 cùm Christe resurgis 2 tenes? XIII. 1 Humilitas

XIV. *In Vmbram Petri.*

PRoduxit Vmbram corpus, Vmbra corpori
Vitam reduxit: ecce gratitudinem.

XV. *Martha: Maria.*

CHristus adest: crebris aedes percurrite scopis,
Excutite aulaea, & luceat igne focus.
Omnia purgentur, niteat mihi tota supellex,
Parcite luminibus, sítque lucerna domus:
O cessatrices! eccum puluisculus illìc!
Corde tuo forsan, caetera munda, Soror.

XVI. *Amor.*

QVid metuant homines infrà, supráue minentur
Sydera, pendenti sedulus aure bibis:
Vtque ouis in dumis, haeres in crine Cometae,
Sollicitus, ne te stella perita notet:
Omnia quaerendo, sed te, super omnia, vexas:
Et quid tu tandem desidiosus? Amo.

XVII. *In Superbum.*

MAgnas es; esto. Bulla si vocaberis,
Largiar & istud: scilicet Magnatibus
Difficilis esse haud soleo: nam, pol, si forem,
Ipsi sibi sunt nequiter facillimi.
Quin, mitte nugas; téque carnem & sanguinem
Communem habere crede cum Cerdonibus:
Illum volo, qui calceat lixam tuum.

XVIII. *In eundem.*

VNusquisque hominum, Terra est; & filius arui.
Dic mihi, mons sterilis, vallis an vber eris?

XV. 1 scopis 4 lucerna, 6 Soror *distinguished by large letters in W*: *cf.* XVI. 6 XVI. 5 Omnia, quaerendo: XVII. 3 nam pol XVIII. 2 mihi eris.

XIX. *Afflictio.*

QVos tu calcasti fluctus, me, Christe, lacessunt,
Transiliúntque caput, qui subiere pedes.
Christe, super fluctus si non discurrere detur:
Per fluctus saltem, fac, precor, ipse vadem.

XX. *In* κενοδοξίαν.

QVi sugit auido spiritu rumusculos
Et flatulentas aucupatur glorias,
Foelicitatis culmen extra se locat,
Spargítque per tot capita, quot vulgus gerit.
Tu verò collige te, tibíque insistito,
Breuiore nodo stringe vitae sarcinas,
Rotundus in te: namque si ansatus sies,
Te mille rixae, mille prensabunt doli,
Ducéntque, donec incidentem in cassidem
Te mille nasi, mille rideant sinus.
Quare, peritus nauta, vela contrahas,
Famámque nec difflaueris, nec suxeris:
Tuásque librans actiones, gloriam
Si ducat agmen, reprime; sin claudat, sinas.
Morosus, oxygala est: leuis, coagulum.

XXI. *In Gulosum.*

DVm prono rapis ore cibos, & fercula verris,
Intra extráque graui plenus es illuuie.
Non iam ventriculus, verùm spelunca vocetur
Illa cauerna, in quâ tot coiere ferae.
Ipse fruare, licet, solus graueolente sepulcro;
Te petet, ante diem quisquis obire cupit.

XXII. *In Improbum disertum.*

SEricus es dictis, factis pannusia Baucis:
Os & lingua tibi diues, egena manus:
Ni facias, vt opes linguae per brachia serpant,
Aurea pro naulo lingua Charontis erit.

XIX. 1 me Christe 4 vadem *Ed*: vader *W* XX. 7 sies
XXI. 2 Intra, 5 sepulcro XXII. 4 Aurea, pro naulo,

XXIII. *Consolatio.*

CVr lacrymas & tarda trahis suspiria, tanquam
 Nunc primùm socij mors foret atra tui?
Nos autem, à cunis, omnes sententia Mortis
 Quotidie iugulat, nec semel vllus obit.
Viuimus in praesens: hesternam viuere vitam
 Nemo potest: hodie vita sepulta prior.
Trecentos obijt Nestor, non transijt annos,
 Vel quia tot moritur, tot viguisse probes.
Dum lacrymas, it vita: tuus tibi clepsydra fletus,
 Et numerat mortes singula gutta pares;
Frustra itaque in tot funeribus miraberis vnum,
 Sera nimis lacryma haec, si lacrymabis, erit.
Siste tuum fletum & gemitus: namque imbribus istis
 Ac zephyris, carnis flos remeare nequit.
Nec tu pro socio doleas, qui fugit ad illud
 Culmen, vbi pro te nemo dolere potest.

XXIV. *In Angelos.*

INtellectus adultus Angelorum
 Haud nostro similis, cui necesse,
Vt dentur species, rogare sensum:
Et ni lumina ianuam resignent,
Et nostrae tribuant molae farinam,
Saepe ex se nihil otiosa cudit.
A nobis etenim procul remoti
Labuntur fluuij scientiarum:
Si non per species, nequimus ipsi,
Quid ipsi sumus, assequi putando.
Non tantum est iter Angelis ad vndas,
Nullo circuitu scienda pungunt,
Illis perpetuae patent fenestrae,
Se per se facili modo scientes,
Atque ipsi sibi sunt mola & farina.

XXIII. 8 quià, XXIV. 2 necesse 11 undas

XXV. *Roma. Anagr.*

Oram. Maro.
Ramo. Armo.
Mora. Amor.

ROMA, tuum nomen quam non pertransijt ORAM,
 Cùm Latium ferrent secula prisca iugum?
Non deerat vel fama tibi, vel carmina famae,
 Vnde MARO laudes duxit ad astra tuas.
At nunc exucco similis tua gloria RAMO
 A veteri trunco & nobilitate cadit.
Laus antiqua & honor perijt: quasi scilicet ARMO
 Te deiecissent tempora longa suo.
Quin tibi tam desperatae MORA nulla medetur,
 Quâ Fabio quondam sub duce nata salus.
Hinc te olim gentes miratae odere vicissim;
 Et cum sublatâ laude recedit AMOR.

XXVI. *Vrbani VIII Pont. Respons.*

CVm Romam nequeas, quod aues, euertere, nomen
 Inuertis, mores carpis & obloqueris:
Te Germana tamen pubes, te Graecus & Anglus
 Arguit, exceptos quos pia Roma fouet:
Hostibus haec etiam parcens imitatur Iesum.
 Inuertis nomen. Quid tibi dicit? AMOR.

XXVII. *Respons. ad Vrb. VIII.*

NOn placet vrbanus noster de nomine lusus
 Romano, sed res seria Roma tibi est:
Nempe Caput Romae es, cuius mysteria velles
 Esse iocum soli, plebe stupente, tibi:
Attamen VRBANI delecto nomine, constat
 Quàm satur & suauis sit tibi Roma iocus.

XXV. *Included also in Duport's* Ecclesiastes Solomonis (*here cited as D*) *and in* B.M. Add. MS. 4275 (*cited as BM*). *Title in D*: Roma dabit Oram, Ramo, &c. 2 iugum. *W* 3 deerat] deerint *BM* 7–8 perijt . . . deiecissent] perierunt, te velut Armo Jam deturbârunt *D* 9 tam] jam *D* medetur *W* 10 Quae Fabio quondam sub duce tuta fuit. *BM* 11 vicissim *W* XXVI. 4 exceptos,

XXVIII. *Ad Vrbanum VIII Pont.*

POntificem tandem nacta est sibi Roma poetam:
  Res redit ad vates, Pieriósque duces:
Quod Bellarminus nequijt, fortasse poetae
  Suauiter efficient, absque rigore Scholae.
Cedito Barbaries: Helicon iam litibus instat,
  Squalorémque togae candida Musa fugat.

XXIX. Λογικὴ Θυσία.

ARarúmque Hominúmque ortum si mente pererres,
  Cespes viuus, Homo; mortuus, Ara fuit:
Quae diuisa nocent, Christi per foedus, in vnum
  Conueniunt; & Homo viua fit Ara Dei.

XXX. *In Thomam Didymum.*

DVm te vel digitis minister vrget,
  Et hoc indicium subis, Redemptor?
Nempe es totus amor, medulla amoris,
Qui spissae fidei breuíque menti
Paras hospitium torúmque dulcem,
Quô se condat & implicet volutans
Ceu fidâ statione & arce certâ,
Ne perdat Leo rugiens vagantem.

XXXI. *In Solarium.*

COniugium Caeli Terraéque haec machina praestat;
  Debetur Caelo lumen, & vmbra solo:
Sic Hominis moles animâque & corpore constat,
  Cuius ab oppositis fluxit origo locis.
Contemplare, miser, quantum terroris haberet
  Vel sine luce solum, vel sine mente caro.

XXX. 2 indicium subis] judicium jubes *Grosart* 4 fidei, 5 dulcem
XXXI. 5 Contemplare 6 solum :

XXXII. *Triumphus Mortis.*

O Mea suspicienda manus, ventérque perennis!
Quem non Emathius torrens, non sanguine pinguis
Daunia, non satiat bis ter millesima caedis
Progenies, mundíque aetas abdomine nostro
Ingluuiéque minor. Quercus habitare feruntur
Prisci, crescentésque vnà cum prole cauernas:
Nec tamen excludor: namque vnâ ex arbore vitam
Glans dedit, & truncus tectum, & ramalia mortem.
Confluere intereà passim ad Floralia pubes
Coeperat, agricolis mentémque & aratra solutis:
Compita feruescunt pedibus, clamoribus aether.
Hìc vbi discumbunt per gramina, salsior vnus
Omnia suspendit naso, sociósque lacessit:
Non fert Vcalegon, atque amentata retorquet
Dicta ferox: haerent lateri conuitia fixo.
Scinditur in partes vulgus ceu compita: telum
Ira facit, mundúsque ipse est apotheca furoris.
Liber alit rixas: potantibus omnia bina
Sunt, praeter vitam: saxis hic sternitur, alter
Ambustis sudibus: pars vitam in pocula fundunt,
In patinas alij: furit inconstantia vini
Sanguine, quem dederat, spolians. Primordia Mortis
Haec fuerant: sic Tisiphone virguncula lusit.
Non placuit rudis atque ignara occisio: Morti
Quaeritur ingenium, doctúsque homicida probatur.
Hinc tyrocinium, paruóque assueta iuuentus,
Fictáque Bellona & verae ludibria pugnae,
Instructaéque acies, hyemésque in pellibus actae,
Omniáque haec vt transadigant sine crimine costas,
Artificésque necis clueant, & mortis alumni.
Nempe & millenos ad palum interficit hostes

XXXII. *Printed also, under the title* Inventa Bellica (*cited here as IB*), *by Pickering in 1836 from a MS. in his possession* 1 Oh Mortis longaeva fames, venterque perennis! *IB* 4 nostro] tanto *IB* 7 Hinc tamen excludi mors noluit, ipsaque vitam *IB* 17 furoris 21 In patinas alij :] Bacchantur Lapithae, *IB* 22 Mortis] belli *IB* 28 actae 29 costas 30 Artificesque *IB* : Artifesque *W*

Assiduus tyro, si sit spectanda voluntas.
Heu miseri! Quis tantùm ipsis virtutibus instat
Quantùm caedi? adeón' vnam vos pascere vitam,
Perdere sexcentas? crescit tamen hydra nocendi
Tristis, vbi ac ferrum tellure reciditur imâ,
Faecundúsque chalybs sceleris, iam sanguine tinctus,
Expleri nequit, & totum depascitur Orbem.
Quid memorem tormenta, quibus prius horruit aeuum;
Balistásque Onagrósque & quicquid Scorpio saeuus
Vel Catapulta potest, Siculíque inuenta magistri,
Anglorúmque arcus gaudentes sanguine Galli,
Fustibalos fundásque, quibus, cum Numine, fretus
Strauit Idumaeum diuinus Tityrus hostem?
Adde etiam currus, & cum temone Britanno
Aruiragum, falcésque obstantia quaeque metentes.
Quin Aries ruit, & multâ Demetrius arte:
Sic olim cecidere.
Deerat adhuc vitijs hominum dignissima mundo
Machina, quam nullum satìs execrabitur aeuum;
Liquitur ardenti candens fornace metallum,
Fusáque decurrit notis aqua ferrea sulcis:
Exoritur tubus, atque instar Cyclopis Homeri
Luscum prodigium, medióque foramine gaudens.
Inde rotae atque axes subeunt, quasi sella curulis
Quâ Mors ipsa sedens hominum de gente triumphat.
Accedit Pyrius puluis, laquearibus Orci
Erutus, infernae pretiosa tragemata mensae,
Sulphureóque lacu, totâque imbuta Mephiti.
Huic Glans adijcitur (non quam ructare vetustas
Creditur, ante satas prono cum numine fruges)
Plumbea glans, liuensque suae quasi conscia noxae,
Purpureus lictor Plutonis, epistola Fati
Plumbis obsignata, colósque & stamina vitae
Perrumpens, Atropi vetulae marcentibus vlnis.

33 Heu miseri!] O superi! *IB* 34 vos pascere] nos vivere *IB* 35 crescit] crescet *IB* 36 imâ] una *Grosart* 38 &] at *IB* 42 Anglorúmque arcus] Angligenûmque arces *IB* 43 Fustibalos] Fustibales *IB* 49 hominum] nostris *IB* 55 axes] axis *IB* 58 Erutus] Exulis *IB* 59 sulphureoque *Grosart* : sulphureâque *W IB* 60 Huic] Hinc *IB* 61 numine] vertice *IB*

Haec vbi iuncta, subit viuo cum fune minister,
Fatalémque leuans dextram, quâ stupeus ignis
Mulcetur vento, accendit cum fomite partem
Pulueris inferni; properat datus ignis, & omnem
Materiam vexat: nec iam se continet antro
Tisiphone; flammâ & fallaci fulmine cincta
Euolat, horrendúmque ciet bacchata fragorem.
It stridor, caelósque omnes & Tartara findit.
Non iam exaudiri quicquam vel Musica caeli
Vel gemitus Erebi: piceo se turbine voluens
Totámque eructans nubem, Glans proruit imo
Praecipitata; cadunt vrbes, formidine muri
Diffugiunt, fragilísque crepant coenacula mundi.
Strata iacent toto millena cadauera campo
Vno ictu: non sic pestis, non stella maligno
Afflatu perimunt: en, Cymba Cocytia turbis
Ingemit, & defessus opem iam Portitor orat.
Nec Glans sola nocet; mortem quandoque susurrat
Aura volans, vitámque aer, quam pauerat, aufert.
Dicite, vos Furiae, quâ gaudet origine Monstrum.
Nox Aetnam, noctémque Chaos genuere priores.
Aetna Cacum igniuomum dedit, hic Ixiona multis
Cantatum; deinde Ixion cum nubibus atris
Congrediens genuit Monachum, qui limen opacae
Triste colens cellae, noctúque & Daemone plenum,
Protulit horrendum hoc primus cum puluere monstrum.
Quis Monachos mortem meditari, & puluere tristi
Versatos neget, atque humiles, queîs talia cordi
Tam demissa, ipsámque adeò subeuntia terram?
Nec tamen hìc noster stetit impetus: exilit omni
Tormento peior Iesuita, & fulminat Orbem,
Ridens Bombardas miseras, quae corpora perdunt
Non animas, raróque ornantur sanguine regum
Obstreperae stulto sonitu, criménque fatentes.

66 iuncta] vincta *IB* 69 inferni. properat datus *W*: inferni, properat, datur *IB* 74 caeli] sphaerae *IB* 77 urbes, formidine] urbes formidine, *IB* 78 fragilísque] fragilesque *Grosart* 85 Dicite 87 multis] Graecis *IB* 90 cellae] sellae *IB* (*cf. l.* 55) 91 primus] primum *IB* 94 Tam] Jam *Grosart* 95 noster stetit impetus :] mortis rabies stetit ; *IB*

Imperij hìc culmen figo: mortalibus actum est
Corporéque atque animo. Totus mihi seruiat Orbis.

XXXIII. *Triumphus Christiani. In Mortem.*

AIn' verò? quanta praedicas? hercle aedepol,
Magnificus es screator, homicida inclytus.
Quid ipse faciam? qui nec arboreas sudes
In te, nec arcus, scorpionésue, aut rotas,
Gladiósue, Catapultásue teneam, quin neque
Alapas nec Arietes? Quid ergo? Agnum & Crucem.

XXXIV. *In Johannem* ἐπιστήθιον.

AH nunc, helluo, fac, vt ipse sugam:
Num totum tibi pectus imputabis?
Fontem intercipis omnibus patentem?
Quin pro me quoque sanguinem profudit,
Et ius pectoris inde consecutus
Lac cum sanguine posco deuolutum;
Vt, si gratia tanta copuletur
Peccati veniae mei, vel ipsos
Occumbens humero Thronos lacessam.

XXXV. *Ad Dominum.*

CHriste, decus, dulcedo, & centum circiter Hyblae,
Cordis apex, animae pugnáque páxque meae,
Quin, sine, te cernam; quoties iam dixero, cernam;
Immoriárque oculis, o mea vita, tuis.
Si licet, immoriar: vel si tua visio vita est,
Cur sine te, votis immoriturus, ago?
Ah, cernam; Tu, qui caecos sanare solebas,
Cùm te non videam, méne videre putas?
Non video, certum est iurare; aut si hoc vetuisti,
Praeuenias vultu non facienda tuo.

FINIS

Soli Deo Gloria.

XXXII. 100–1 Sistimus hic, inquit fatum, sat prata biberunt
Sanguinis, innocuum tandem luet orbis Abelum. *IB*

XXXIII. 4 rotas 6 Alapas *Ed* (*cf.* Passio Discerpta VIII): Alopos *W*: Alopas *Grosart* XXXIV. 1 sugam XXXV. 5 visio, 9 vetuisti

MEMORIAE MATRIS SACRUM

I.

AH Mater, quo te deplorem fonte? Dolores
  Quae guttae poterunt enumerare meos?
Sicca meis lacrymis Thamesis vicina videtur,
  Virtutúmque choro siccior ipse tuo.
In flumen moerore nigrum si funderer ardens,
  Laudibus haud fierem sepia iusta tuis.
Tantùm istaec scribo gratus, ne tu mihi tantùm
  Mater: & ista Dolor nunc tibi Metra parit.

II.

COrneliae sanctae, graues Semproniae,
  Et quicquid vspiam est seuerae foeminae,
Conferte lacrymas: Illa, quae vos miscuit
Vestrásque laudes, poscit & mixtas genas.
Namque hanc ruinam salua Grauitas defleat,
Pudórque constet vel solutis crinibus;
Quandoque vultûs sola maiestas, Dolor.
  Decus mulierum perijt: & metuunt viri
Vtrumque sexum dote ne mulctauerit.
Non illa soles terere comptu lubricos,
Struices superbas atque turritum caput
Molita, reliquum deinde garriens diem
(Nam post Babelem linguae adest confusio)
Quin post modestam, qualis integras decet,
Substructionem capitis & nimbum breuem,
Animam recentem rite curauit sacris
Adorta numen acri & igneâ prece.
  Dein familiam lustrat, & res prandij,

Memoriae Matris Sacrum. *From* A Sermon of Commemoration of the Lady Dāuers. By Iohn Donne. Together with other Commemorations of Her; By her Sonne G. Herbert. London, Printed by I. H. for Philemon Stephens, and Christopher Meredith. 1627. *The readings in the footnotes are from 1627, unless otherwise stated.*

I. 4 siscior II. 1–51 *in* Bodl. MS. Rawlinson Poet. 62 (*no important variations*) 18 prandij

Horti, colíque distributim pensitat.
Suum cuique tempus & locus datur.
Inde exiguntur pensa crudo vespere.
Ratione certâ vita constat & domus,
Prudenter inito quot-diebus calculo.
Totâ renident aede decus & suauitas
Animo renidentes priùs. Sin rarior
Magnatis appulsu extulit se occasio,
Surrexit vnà & illa, seséque extulit:
Occasione certat, imò & obtinet.
Proh! quantus imber, quanta labri comitas,
Lepos seuerus, Pallas mixta Gratijs;
Loquitur numellas, compedes & retia:
Aut si negotio hora sumenda est, rei
Per angiportus & maeandros labitur,
Ipsos Catones prouocans oraculis.
Tum quanta tabulis artifex? quae scriptio?
Bellum putamen, nucleus bellissimus,
Sententiae cum voce mirè conuenit,
Volant per orbem literae notissimae:
O blanda dextra, neutiquam istoc pulueris,
Quò nunc recumbis, scriptio merita est tua,
Pactoli arena tibi tumulus est vnicus.
   Adde his trientem Musices, quae molliens
Mulcénsque dotes caeteras visa est quasi
Caelestis harmoniae breue praeludium.
Quàm mira tandem Subleuatrix pauperum!
Languentium baculus, teges iacentium,
Commune cordis palpitantis balsamum:
Benedictiones publicae cingunt caput,
Caelíque referunt & praeoccupant modum.
Fatisco referens tanta quae numerant mei
Solùm dolores, & dolores, stellulae.
   At tu qui ineptè haec dicta censes filio,
Nato parentis auferens Encomium,
Abito, trunce, cum tuis pudoribus.
Ergo ipse solùm mutus atque excors ero
Strepente mundo tinnulis praeconijs?

II. 28 certat   29 comitas   40 tua   43 caeteras,   53 Encomium

Mihíne matris vrna clausa est vnico,
Herbae exoletae, ros-marinus aridus?
Matríne linguam refero, solùm vt mordeam?
Abito, barde. Quàm piè istic sum impudens!
Tu verò mater perpetim laudabere
Nato dolenti: literae hoc debent tibi
Queîs me educasti; sponte chartas illinunt
Fructum laborum consecutae maximum
Laudando Matrem, cùm repugnant inscij.

III.

CVr splendes, O Phoebe? ecquid demittere matrem
Ad nos cum radio tam rutilante potes?
At superat caput illa tuum, quantum ipsa cadauer
Mens superat; corpus solùm Elementa tenent.
Scilicet id splendes: haec est tibi causa micandi,
Et lucro apponis gaudia sancta tuo.
Verùm heus, si nequeas caelo demittere matrem,
Sítque omnis motûs nescia tanta quies,
Fac radios saltem ingemines, vt dextera tortos
Implicet, & matrem, matre manente, petam.

IV.

QVid nugor calamo fauens?
Mater perpetuis vuida gaudijs,
Horto pro tenui colit
Edenem Boreae flatibus inuium.
Quin caeli mihi sunt mei,
Materni decus, & debita nominis,
Dúmque his inuigilo frequens
Stellarum socius, pellibus exuor.
Quare Sphaeram egomet meam
Connixus, digitis impiger vrgeo:
Te, Mater, celebrans diu,
Noctu te celebrans luminis aemulo.

III. 3 ipse cadauer, 5 micandi 8 nescia, IV. 8 Exuor. 11 diû

Per te nascor in hunc globum
Exemplóque tuo nascor in alterum:
Bis tu mater eras mihi,
Vt currat paribus gloria tibijs.

V.

HOrti, deliciae *Dominae*, marcescite tandem;
Ornâstis capulum, nec superesse licet.
Ecce decus vestrum spinis horrescit, acutâ
Cultricem reuocans anxietate manum:
Terram & funus olent flores: Dominaéque cadauer
Contiguas stirpes afflat, eaéque rosas.
In terram violae capite inclinantur opaco,
Quaéque domus Dominae sit, grauitate docent.
Quare haud vos hortos, sed coemeteria dico,
Dum torus absentem quisque reponit heram.
Eugè, perite omnes; nec posthâc exeat vlla
Quaesitum Dominam gemma vel herba suam.
Cuncta ad radices redeant, tumulósque paternos;
(Nempe sepulcra Satis numen inempta dedit.)
Occidite; aut sanè tantisper viuite, donec
Vespere ros maestis funus honestet aquis.

VI.

GAlene, frustra es, cur miserum premens
Tot quaestionum fluctibus obruis,
Arterias tractans micantes
Corporeae fluidaéque molis?
Aegroto mentis: quam neque pixides
Nec tarda possunt pharmaca consequi,
Vtrumque si praederis Indum,
Vltrà animus spatiatur exlex.
Impos medendi, occidere si potes,
Nec sic parentem ducar ad optimam:
Ni sanctè, vtì mater, recedam,
Morte magìs viduabor illâ.

V. 16 Vespere, VI. 1 es 6 consequi 7 Indum 9 potes

Quin cerne vt erres, inscie, brachium
Tentando sanum: si calet, aestuans,
Ardore scribendi calescit,
Mater inest saliente venâ.
Si totus infler, si tumeam crepax,
Ne membra culpes, causa animo latet
Qui parturit laudes parentis:
Nec grauidis medicina tuta est.
Irregularis nunc habitus mihi est:
Non exigatur crasis ad alterum.
Quod tu febrem censes, salubre est
Atque animo medicatur vnum.

VII.

PAllida materni Genij atque exanguis imago,
In nebulas similésque tui res gaudia nunquid
Mutata? & pro matre mihi phantasma dolosum
Vberáque aerea hiscentem fallentia natum?
Vae nubi pluuiâ grauidae, non lacte, meásque
Ridenti lacrymas quibus vnis concolor vnda est.
Quin fugias? mea non fuerat tam nubila Iuno,
Tam segnis facies aurorae nescia vernae,
Tam languens genitrix cineri supposta fugaci:
Verùm augusta parens, sanctum os caelóque locandum,
Quale paludosos iamiam lictura recessus
Praetulit Astraea, aut solio Themis alma vetusto
Pensilis, atque acri dirimens Examine lites.
Hunc vultum ostendas, & tecum, nobile spectrum,
Quod superest vitae, insumam: Solísque iugales
Ipse tuae solùm adnectam, sine murmure, thensae.
Nec querar ingratos, studijs dum tabidus insto,
Effluxisse dies, suffocatámue Mineruam,
Aut spes productas, barbatáque somnia vertam
In vicium mundo sterili, cui cedo cometas
Ipse suos tanquam digno pallentiáque astra.
Est mihi bis quinis laqueata domuncula tignis
Rure; breuísque hortus, cuius cum vellere florum
Luctatur spacium, qualem tamen eligit aequi

VII. 1 imago 7 Iuno 14 tecum nobile spectrum 18 Mineruam

Iudicij dominus, flores vt iunctiùs halent
Stipati, rudibúsque volis imperuius hortus
Sit quasi fasciculus crescens, & nidus odorum.
Hìc ego túque erimus, variae suffitibus herbae
Quotidie pasti: tantùm verum indue vultum
Affectûsque mei similem; nec languida misce
Ora meae memori menti: ne dispare cultu
Pugnaces, teneros florum turbemus odores,
Atque inter reliquos horti crescentia foetus
Nostra etiam paribus marcescant gaudia fatis.

VIII.

PAruam piámque dum lubenter semitam
   Grandi reaéque praefero,
Carpsit malignum sydus hanc modestiam
   Vinúmque felle miscuit.
Hinc fremere totus & minari gestio
   Ipsis seuerus orbibus;
Tandem prehensâ comiter lacernulâ
   Susurrat aure quispiam,
Haec fuerat olim potio Domini tui.
   Gusto probóque Dolium.

IX.

HOc, Genitrix, scriptum proles tibi sedula mittit.
   Siste parum cantus, dum legis ista, tuos.
Nôsse sui quid agant, quaedam est quoque musica sanctis,
   Quaéque olim fuerat cura, manere potest.
Nos miserè flemus, solésque obducimus almos
   Occiduis, tanquam duplice nube, genis.
Interea classem magnis Rex instruit ausis:
   Nos autem flemus: res ea sola tuis.
Ecce solutura est, ventos causata morantes:
   Sin pluuiam, fletus suppeditâsset aquas.
Tillius incumbit Dano, Gallúsque marinis,
   Nos flendo: haec nostrûm tessera sola ducum.

VII. 25 dominus   VIII. 2 praefero.   6 orbibus   IX. 1 Hoc Genitrix   3 sanctis   10 pluuiam :   11 Dano :   marinis :

Sic aeuum exigitur tardum, dum praepetis anni
Mille rotae nimijs impediuntur aquis.
Plura tibi missurus eram (nam quae mihi laurus,
Quod nectar, nisi cum te celebrare diem?)
Sed partem in scriptis etiam dum lacryma poscit,
Diluit oppositas candidus humor aquas.

X.

NEmpe huc vsque notos tenebricosos
Et maestum nimio madore Caelum
Tellurísque Britannicae saliuam
Iniustè satìs arguit viator.
At te commoriente, Magna Mater,
Rectè, quem trahit, aerem repellit
Cum probro madidum, reúmque difflat.
Nam te nunc Ager, Vrbs, & Aula plorant:
Te nunc Anglia, Scotiaéque binae,
Quin te Cambria peruetusta deflet,
Deducens lacrymas prioris aeui
Ne serae meritis tuis venirent.
Non est angulus vspiam serenus,
Nec cingit mare, nunc inundat omnes.

XI.

DVm librata suis haeret radicibus ilex
Nescia vulturnis cedere, firma manet.
Post vbi crudelem sentit diuisa securem,
Quò placet oblato, mortua fertur, hero:
Arbor & ipse inuersa vocer: dúmque insitus almae
Assideo Matri, robore vinco cedros.
Nunc sorti pateo, expositus sine matre procellis,
Lubricus, & superans mobilitate salum.
Tu radix, tu petra mihi firmissima, Mater,
Ceu Polypus, chelis saxa prehendo tenax:
Non tibi nunc soli filum abrupere sorores,
Dissutus videor funere & ipse tuo.
Vnde vagans passim rectè vocer alter Vlysses,
Alteráque haec tua mors, Ilias esto mihi.

X. 1 huc vsque] hujusque *Grosart* XI. 3 securem 5 vocer *conj. Ed* (*cf. l.* 13) : vocor *1627* 9 firmissima Mater 11 so[illegible]es

XII.

FAcesse, Stoica plebs, obambulans cautes,
Exuta strato carnis, ossibus constans,
Iísque siccis adeò vt os Molossorum
Haud glubat inde tres teruncios escae.
Dolere prohibes? aut dolere me gentis
Adeò inficetae, plumbeae, Meduseae,
Ad saxa speciem retrahentis humanam,
Tantóque nequioris optimâ Pirrhâ?
At fortè matrem perdere haud soles demens:
Quin nec potes; cui praebuit Tigris partum.
Proinde parco belluis, nec irascor.

XIII.

EPITAPHIUM

HIc sita foeminei laus & victoria sexus:
Virgo pudens, vxor fida, seuera parens:
Magnatúmque inopúmque aequum certamen & ardor:
Nobilitate illos, hos pietate rapit.
Sic excelsa humilísque simul loca dissita iunxit,
Quicquid habet tellus, quicquid & astra, fruens.

XIV.

Ψυχῆς ἀσθενὲς ἕρκος, ἀμαυρὸν πνεύματος ἄγγος,
Τῷδε παρὰ τύμβῳ δίζεο, φίλε, μόνον.
Νοῦ δ' αὐτοῦ τάφος ἐστ' ἀστήρ· φέγγος γὰρ ἐκείνου
Φεγγώδη μόνον, ὡς εἰκός, ἔπαυλιν ἔχει.
Νῦν ὁράας, ὅτι κάλλος ἀπείριτον ὠπὸς ἀπαυγοῦς
Οὐ σαθρόν, οὐδὲ μελῶν ἔπλετο, ἀλλὰ νόος·
Ὃς διὰ σωματίου πρότερον καὶ νῦν δι' Ὀλύμπου
Ἀστράπτων, θυρίδων ὡς δία, νεῖμε σέλας.

XV.

Μῆτερ, γυναικῶν αἴγλη, ἀνθρώπων ἔρις,
Ὄδυρμα Δαιμόνων, Θεοῦ γεώργιον,
Πῶς νῦν ἀφίπτασαι, γόου καὶ κινδύνου
Ἡμᾶς λιποῦσα κυκλόθεν μεταιχμίους;

XII. 1 cautes. 8 Pirrhâ. XIII. 2 parens. 6 tellus XV. 1 ἄγλη,

Μενοῦνγε σοφίην, εἰ σ' ἀπηλλάχθαι χρεών,
Ζωῆς ξυνεργὸν τήνδε διαθεῖναι τέκνοις
'Εχρῆν φυγοῦσα, τήν τ' ἐπιστήμην βίου.
Μενοῦν τὸ γλαφυρόν, καὶ μελίῤῥοον τρόπων,
Λόγων τε φίλτρον, ὥσθ' ὑπεξελθεῖν λεών.
Νῦν δ' ὤχου ἔνθενδ' ὡς στρατὸς νικηφόρος
Φέρων τὸ πᾶν, κἄγων· ἢ ὡς 'Απαρκτίας
Κήπου συνωθῶν ἀνθινὴν εὐωδίαν,
Μίαν τ' ἀταρπὸν συμπορεύεσθαι δράσας.
'Εγὼ δὲ ῥινὶ ξυμβαλὼν ἰχνηλατῶ
Εἴ που τύχοιμι τῆσδ' ἀρίστης ἀτραποῦ,
Θανεῖν συνειδὼς κρεῖττον, ἢ ἄλλως βιοῦν.

XVI.

Χαλεπὸν δοκεῖ δακρῦσαι,
Χαλεπὸν μὲν οὐ δακρῦσαι·
Χαλεπώτερον δὲ πάντων
Δακρύοντας ἀμπαύεσθαι.
Γενέτειραν οὔ τις ἀνδρῶν
Διδύμαις κόραις τοιαύτην
'Εποδύρεται πρεπόντως.
Τάλας, εἴθε γ' Ἄργος εἴην
Πολυόμματος, πολύτλας,
Ἵνα μητρὸς εὐθενούσης
'Αρετὰς διακριθείσας
'Ιδίαις κόραισι κλαύσω.

XVII.

Αἰάζω γενέτειραν, ἐπαιάζουσι καὶ ἄλλοι,
Οὐκ ἔτ' ἐμὴν ἰδίας φυλῆς γράψαντες ἀρωγόν,
Προυνομίῳ δ' ἀρετῆς κοινὴν γενέτειραν ἑλόντες.
Οὐκ ἔνι θαῦμα τόσον σφετερίζειν· οὐδὲ γὰρ ὕδωρ,
Οὐ φέγγος, κοινόν τ' ἀγαθόν, μίαν εἰς θύραν εἴργειν
Ἧ θέμις, ἢ δυνατόν. σεμνώματος ἔπλετο στάθμη,
Δημόσιόν τ' ἴνδαλμα καλοῦ, θεῖόν τε κάτοπτρον.

XV. 5 *εἰ δ'* 6 *σῆνδε* 9 *ὥστ'* XVII. 2 *ἐθ'* 5 *εἴργειν* *Grosart*

Αἰάζω γενέτειραν, ἐπαιάζουσι γυναῖκες,
Οὐκ ἔτι βαλλομένης χάρισιν βεβολημέναι ἦτορ,
Αὖταρ ἄχει μεγάλῳ κεντούμεναι· εὖτε γὰρ αὖται
Τῆς περὶ συλλαλέουσιν, ἑοῦ ποικίλματος ἄρδην
Λήσμονες, ἡ βελόνη σφαλερῷ κῆρ τραύματι νύττει
Ἔργου ἁμαρτηκυῖα, νέον πέπλον αἵματι στικτὸν
Μητέρι τεκταίνουσα, γόῳ καὶ πένθεσι σύγχρουν.
Αἰάζω γενέτειραν, ἐπαιάζουσιν ὀπῶραι,
Οὐκ ἔτι δεσποίνης γλυκερᾷ μελεδῶνι τραφεῖσαι·
Ἧς βίος ἠελίοιο δίκην, ἀκτῖνας ἱέντος
Πραεῖς εἰαρινούς τε χαραῖς ἐπικίδνατο κῆπον·
Αὖταρ ὅδ' αὖ θάνατος κυρίης, ὡς ἥλιος αὖος
Σειρίου ἡττηθεὶς βουλήμασι, πάντα μαραίνει.
Ζῶ δ' αὐτός, βραχύ τι πνείων, ὥστ' ἔμπαλιν αὐτῆς
Αἶνον ὁμοῦ ζώειν καὶ πνεύματος ἄλλο γενέσθαι
Πνεῦμα, βίου πάροδον μούνοις ἐπέεσσι μετρῆσαν.

XVIII.

Κύματ' ἐπαφριοῶντα Θαμήσεος, αἴκε σελήνης
Φωτὸς ἀπαυραμένης ὄγκου ἐφεῖσθε πλέον,
Νῦν θέμις ὀρφναίῃ μεγάλης ἐπὶ γείτονος αἴσῃ
Οὐλυμπόνδε βιβᾶν ὔμμιν ἀνισταμένοις.
Ἀλλὰ μενεῖτ', οὐ γὰρ τάραχος ποτὶ μητέρα βαίνῃ,
Καὶ πρέπον ὧδε παρὰ δακρυόεσσι ῥέειν.

XIX.

EXcussos manibus calamos, falcémque resumptam
Rure, sibi dixit Musa fuisse probro.
Aggreditur Matrem (conductis carmine Parcis)
Funeréque hoc cultum vindicat aegra suum.
Non potui non ire acri stimulante flagello:
Quin Matris superans carmina poscit honos.
Eia, agedum scribo: vicisti, Musa; sed audi,
Stulta: semel scribo, perpetuò vt sileam.

XVII. 10 αὔται 18 ἐπικίδνατι XVIII. 2 ἀπαυρομένης 4 ὔμμιν
XIX. 6 matris 7–8 audi Stulta semel *See note*

ALIA POEMATA LATINA

In Obitum Henrici Principis Walliae.

ITe leues (inquam), Parnassia numina, Musae,
Non ego vos posthâc hederae velatus amictu
Somnis (nescio queîs) nocturna ad vota vocabo:
Sed nec Cyrrhaei saltus Libethriáue arua
In mea dicta ruant; non tam mihi pendula mens est,
Sic quasi Dijs certem, magnos accersere montes:
Nec vaga de summo deducam flumina monte,
Qualia parturiente colunt sub rupe sorores:
Si-quas mens agitet moles (dum pectora saeuo
Tota stupent luctu) lachrymísque exaestuet aequis
Spiritus, hi mihi iam montes, haec flumina sunto.
Musa, vale, & tu Phoebe; dolor mea carmina dictet;
Hinc mihi principium: vos o labentia mentis
Lumina, nutantes paulatim acquirite vires,
Viuite, dum mortem ostendam: sic tempora vestram
Non comedant famam, sic nulla obliuia potent.
Quare age, Mens, effare, precor, quo numine laeso?
Quae suberant causae? quid nos committere tantum,
Quod non Lanigerae pecudes, non Agmina lustrent?
Annon longa fames miseraéque iniuria pestis
Poena minor fuerat, quàm fatum Principis aegrum?
Iam foelix Philomela, & menti conscia Dido!
Foelices, quos bella premunt, & plurimus ensis!
Non metuunt vltrà; nostra infortunia tantùm
Fatáque Fortunásque & spem laesêre futuram.
Quòd si fata illi longam invidêre salutem
Et patrio regno (sub quo iam Principe nobis
Quid sperare, imò quid non sperare licebat?)
Debuit ista pati prima & non nobilis aetas:
Aut cita mors est danda bonis aut longa senectus:
Sic lactare animos & sic ostendere gemmam
Excitat optatus auidos, & ventilat ignem.

In Obitum Henrici. *This and the following poem from* Epicedium Cantabrigiense, In obitum immaturum Henrici, Principis Walliae. Cantabrigiae, Ex officina Cantrelli Legge. 1612 31 lactare] laetare *Pickering, Grosart See note*

Quare etiam nuper Pyrij de pulueris ictu
Principis innocuam seruastis numina Vitam,
Vt morbi perimant, alióque in puluere prostet?
Phoebe, tui puduit quum summo manè redires
Sol sine sole tuo! quàm te tum nubibus atris
Totum offuscari peteres, vt nocte silenti
Humana aeternos agerent praecordia questus:
Tantùm etenim vestras (Parcae) non flectit habenas
Tempus edax rerum, túque o mors improba sola es,
Cui caecas tribuit vires annosa vetustas.
Quid non mutatum est? requiêrunt flumina cursus;
Plus etiam veteres coelum videre remotum:
Cur ideo verbis tristes effundere curas
Expeto, tanquam haec sit nostri medicina doloris?
Immodicus luctus tacito vorat igne medullas,
Vt, fluuio currente, vadum sonat, alta quiescunt.

INnupta Pallas, nata Diespitre,
Aeterna summae gloria regiae,
Cui dulcis arrident Camoenae
Pieridis Latiaéque Musae,

Cur tela Mortis vel tibi vel tuis
Quâcunque guttâ temporis imminent?
Tantâque propendet staterâ
Regula sanguinolenta fati?

Númne Hydra talis, tantáne bellua est
Mors tot virorum sordida sanguine,
Vt mucro rumpatur Mineruae,
Vtque minax superetur Aegis?

Tu flectis amnes, tu mare caerulum
Vssisse prono fulmine diceris,
Aiacis exesas triremes
Praecipitans grauiore casu.

35 prostet. 36 Phaebe (*but* Phoebe, *l.* 12) 37 quàm] quum *Pickering, Grosart* 46 sit] sic *Grosart*

In Obitum Henrici (II). 1 Diespitre] Diespatre *Pickering, Grosart* 9 tantaque *Pickering, Grosart*

Tu discidisti Gorgoneas manus
Nexas, capillos anguibus oblitos,
  Furuósque vicisti Gigantes,
    Enceladum pharetrámque Rhoeci.

Ceu victa, Musis porrigit herbulas
Pennata caeci dextra Cupidinis,
  Non vlla Bellonae furentis
    Arma tui metuunt alumni.

Pallas retortis caesia vocibus
Respondit: Eia, ne metuas, precor,
  Nam fata non iustis repugnant
    Principibus, sed amica fiunt.

Vt si recisis arboribus meis
Nudetur illic lucus amabilis,
  Fructúsque post mortem recusent
    Perpetuos mihi ferre rami,

Dulcem rependent tum mihi tibiam
Pulchrè renatam ex arbore mortuâ,
  Dignámque coelesti coronâ
    Harmoniam dabit inter astra.

G. Herbert Coll. Trin.

In Natales et Pascha Concurrentes.

CVm tu, Christe, cadis, nascor; mentémque ligauit
  Vna meam membris horula, téque cruci.
O me disparibus natum cum numine fatis!
  Cur mihi das vitam, quam tibi, Christe, negas?
Quin moriar tecum: vitam, quam negligis ipse,
  Accipe; ni talem des, tibi qualis erat.
Hoc mihi legatum tristi si funere praestes,
  Christe, duplex fiet mors tua vita mihi:
Atque vbi per te sanctificer natalibus ipsis,
  In vitam & neruos Pascha coaeua fluet.

19 Gigantem *Pickering*
In Natales &c. *From Duport,* op. cit.   9 vbi *conj. Ed*: ibi *D* *See note*

In Obitum Serenissimae Reginae Annae.

QVo Te, foelix Anna, modo deflere licebit?
Cui magnum imperium, gloria maior erat:
Ecce meus torpens animus succumbit vtrique,
Cui tenuis fama est, ingeniúmque minus.
Quis, nisi qui manibus Briareus, oculísque sit Argus,
Scribere, Te dignùm, vel lachrymare queat!
Frustra igitur sudo: superest mihi sola voluptas,
Quòd calamum excusent Pontus & Astra meum:
Namque Annae laudes coelo scribuntur aperto,
Sed luctus noster scribitur Oceano.

G. Herbert Coll. Trin. Soc.

Ad Autorem Instaurationis Magnae.

PEr strages licet autorum veterúmque ruinam
Ad famae properes vera Tropaea tuae,
Tam nitidè tamen occidis, tam suauiter, hostes,
Se quasi donatum funere quisque putat.
Scilicet apponit pretium tua dextera fato,
Vulneréque emanat sanguis, vt intret honos.
O quàm felices sunt, qui tua castra sequuntur,
Cùm per te sit res ambitiosa mori.

Comparatio inter Munus Summi Cancellariatus et Librum.

MVnere dum nobis prodes, Libróque futuris,
In laudes abeunt secula quaeque tuas;
Munere dum nobis prodes, Libróque remotis,
In laudes abeunt iam loca quaeque tuas:
Hae tibi sunt alae laudum. Cui contigit vnquam
Longius aeterno, latius orbe decus?

In Obitum Annae. *From* Lacrymae Cantabrigienses: In obitum Reginae Annae. Ex Officina Cantrelli Legge, Almae Matris Cantabrigiae Typographi. 1619.

Ad Autorem &c. *From Duport,* op. cit. (*D*) *Also found in* Bodl. MS. Rawlinson Poet. 246 (*R*) 1 Ruinas *R* 2 properas *R* 3 suaviter, *R*: suaviter *L* 8 sit res] res sit *R*

Comparatio &c. *From Duport,* op. cit. *Also in* Bodl. MS. Rawlinson Poet. 246 (*R*) 2 *and* 4 abeunt] properant *R* 5 laudis *R*

In Honorem Illustr. D.D. Verulamij, Sti Albani, Mag. Sigilli Custodis post editam ab eo Instaurationem Magnam.

QVis iste tandem? non enim vultu ambulat
Quotidiano! Nescis, ignare? Audies!
Dux Notionum; veritatis Pontifex;
Inductionis Dominus, & Verulamij;
Rerum magister vnicus, at non Artium;
Profunditatis pinus, atque Elegantiae;
Naturae Aruspex intimus; Philosophiae
Aerarium; sequester expèrientiae,
Speculationísque; Aequitatis signifer;
Scientiarum, sub pupillari statu
Degentium olim, Emancipator; Luminis
Promus; Fugator Idolûm, atque nubium;
Collega Solis; Quadra Certitudinis;
Sophismatomastix; Brutus Literarius,
Authoritatis exuens tyrannidem;
Rationis & sensûs stupendus Arbiter;
Repumicator mentis; Atlas Physicus,
Alcide succumbente Stagiritico;
Columba Noae, quae in vetustis artibus
Nullum locum requiémue cernens perstitit
Ad se suaéque matris Arcam regredi:
Subtilitatis Terebra; Temporis Nepos
Ex Veritate matre; Mellis alueus;
Mundíque & Animarum sacerdos vnicus;

In Honorem Verulamii. *From* R. P. Emanuelis Thesauri Caesares. Editio Secunda. Oxonii, L. Lichfield. 1637. *Also in Bacon,* Of the Advancement of Learning, ed. Wats, 1640, *in* Herbert's Remains, 1652, *and in Duport,* op. cit., 1662. *MS. copies in* Bodl. MS. Rawlinson Poet. 246 (*R*), *on a leaf pasted over the title-page of* MS. Hardwick 72 A *in the Duke of Devonshire's library* (*D*), *and, according to Grosart* (Miscellanies, vol. I., 1870), *on the flyleaf of Mrs. Seaman's copy of Bacon's* Certaine Psalmes, 1625 (*S*) 3 Notionum] Nationum *1652* 5 at] *om. R.* 6 pinus] Cinnus *R* 12 Idolûm, atque] Idolorum & *R* 14 Mastix *1640 1652 1662 R S* : Matrix *1637 D* 16 stupendus] peritus *1662* 19 vetustis] vetustatis *D* : vetustate *1652* 20 requiémue] requiemque *R S* perstitit *1662 R D* : praestitit *1637 1640 1652* 21 suaéque *conj. Ed* : suamque *1637 1640 1662 R D S* : suumque *1652* matris] mentis *R*

Securis errorum; ínque Naturalibus
Granum Sinapis, acre Alijs, crescens sibi:
O me probè lassum! Iuuate, Posteri!

G. HERBERT Orat. Pub. in *Acad. Cantab.*

Aethiopissa ambit Cestum Diuersi Coloris Virum.

QVid mihi si facies nigra est? hoc, Ceste, colore
Sunt etiam tenebrae, quas tamen optat amor.
Cernis vt exustâ semper sit fronte viator;
Ah longum, quae te deperit, errat iter.
Si nigro sit terra solo, quis despicit aruum?
Claude oculos, & erunt omnia nigra tibi:
Aut aperi, & cernes corpus quas proijcit vmbras;
Hoc saltem officio fungar amore tui.
Cùm mihi sit facies fumus, quas pectore flammas
Iamdudum tacitè delituisse putes?
Dure, negas? O fata mihi praesaga doloris,
Quae mihi lugubres contribuere genas!

Dum petit Infantem.

DVm petit Infantem Princeps, Grantámque Iacobus,
Quisnam horum maior sit, dubitatur, amor.
Vincit more suo Noster: nam millibus Infans
Non tot abest, quot nos Regis ab ingenio.

25 Securis] Securique *1652* : Securisque *S* : Securus *R* Naturalibus] Natalibus *1640 1652 S* 27 probè] prope *1640 1652 1662 S*

Aethiopissa ambit &c. *From Duport*, op. cit. *Also in* B.M. MS. 22602 (*BM*) *and* Bodl. MS. Rawlinson Poet. 246 (*R*) 4 quae] qua *BM* : qui *R* (*with footnote* '*forte*, quae') errat] ambit *BM* 7 cernes] cernis *BM* 10 putes] putas *BM* 11 Ah! metuo ne me ad luctus mea fata crea'rint *R*

Dum petit Infantem. *From* True Copies Of all the Latine Orations, made on the 25. and 27. of Februarie 1622. London, 1623. (*see fuller description*, *p.* 440) *Pickering printed it in 1835* 'from an autograph in the hands of the publisher', *which is now in Harvard College Library. J. Mede quoted it, from a friend's report, in a letter of 22 March 1622/3* (B.M. MS. Harl. 389). *Quoted also in Bishop Overall's collections* (Cam. Univ. Libr. MS. Gg. I. 29) 1 Dum] Cum *Harvard* Infantem] Hispanam *Overall* : *for the common misprint* Infantam *see note* 2 Quisnam horum] Cujusnam *Mede* 3 Vincit] Vicit *Mede*

While Prince to Spaine, and King to Cambridge goes,
The question is, whose loue the greater showes:
Ours (like himselfe) o'recomes; for his wit's more
Remote from ours, then Spaine from Britains shoare.

In obitum incomparabilis Francisci Vicecomitis Sancti Albani, Baronis Verulamij.

DVm longi lentíque gemis sub pondere morbi
Atque haeret dubio tabida vita pede,
Quid voluit prudens Fatum, iam sentio tandem:
Constat, *Aprile* vno te potuisse mori:
Vt *Flos* hinc lacrymis, illinc *Philomela* querelis,
Deducant *linguae* funera sola tuae.

GEORGIVS HERBERT.

In Sacram Anchoram Piscatoris G. Herbert.

QVod Crux nequibat fixa, Clavíque additi,
(Tenere Christum scilicet, ne ascenderet)
Tuíue Christum deuocans facundia
Vltra loquendi tempus; addit Anchora:
Nec hoc abundè est tibi, nisi certae Anchorae
Addas sigillum: nempe Symbolum suae
Tibi debet Vnda & Terra certitudinis.

Munde, fluas fugiásque licet, nos nostráque fixi:
Deridet motus sancta catena tuos.

5–8 *From* True Copies

In obitum incomparabilis &c. *From* Memoriae Francisci, Baronis de Verulamio, Vice-Comitis Sancti Albani Sacrum. Londini, In Officina Johannis Haviland. 1626. *Also in* Herbert's Remains. 2 pede ;

In Sacram Anchoram. *From* Poems, By J. D. *1650*. *Reprinted with only insignificant changes, in the 1654 and 1669 editions of Donne's* Poems. *Also in* Herbert's Remains. *1652*. 'Quod Crux . . . Tuive Christum' (*ll.* 1–3) *in Walton's* Life of Donne, *1658, and in collected* Lives, *1670 and 1675*. Title : To Doctour *Donne* upon one of his Seales : The *Anchor*, and *Christ*. In Sacram Anchoram Piscatoris. *1652*. 2 *not bracketed 1658 1670 1675* 8, 9 *These lines are placed at the end of the poem 1650 1652 1654 1669 : for the order adopted here see note.*

Quondam fessus Amor loquens Amato,
Tot & tanta loquens amica, scripsit:
Tandem & fessa manus, dedit sigillum.

Suauis erat, qui scripta dolens lacerando recludi,
Sanctius in Regno Magni credebat Amoris
(In quo fas nihil est rumpi) donare sigillum.

ALthough the Crosse could not Christ here detain,
Though nail'd unto't, but he ascends again,
Nor yet thy eloquence here keep him still,
But onely while thou speak'st; This Anchor will.
Nor canst thou be content, unlesse thou to
This certain Anchor adde a Seal, and so
The Water, and the Earth both unto thee
Doe owe the symbole of their certainty.
Let the world reel, we and all ours stand sure,
This holy Cable's of all storms secure.

When Love being weary made an end
Of kinde Expressions to his friend,
He writ; when 's hand could write no more,
He gave the Seale, and so left o're.

How sweet a friend was he, who being griev'd
His letters were broke rudely up, believ'd
'Twas more secure in great Loves Common-weal
(Where nothing should be broke) to adde a Seal.

Another version.

WHen my dear Friend, could write no more,
He gave this *Seal*, and, so gave ore.

When winds and waves rise highest, I am sure,
This *Anchor* keeps my *faith*, that, me secure.

Although the Crosse &c. *From* Poems, by J. D. *1650*. *Reprinted in Donne's* Poems *1654 and 1669*. *Also in Walton's* Life of Donne, *1658, and in* Lives, *1670 and 1675*. 2 Though] When *1658 1670 1675* 4 while] whilst *1658 1670 1675* 10 of] from *1658 1670 1675* 11–14 *om*. *1670 1675* 11 Love neere his death desir'd to end *1658* 12 Of] With *1658* 14 He gave his soul, and so gave o're. *1658* 15–18 *om*. *1658 1670 1675*

Another version. From Walton's Lives, *1670*. *Also in* Lives *1675 and in Life in the 1674 edition of* The Temple. 3 rise] rose *Grosart*

ORATIONES

I. *Oratio Domini Georgij Herbert, Oratoris Academiae Cantabrigiensis, habita coram Dominis Legatis cùm Magistro. in Artib. titulis insignirentur.*

27. *Febr.* 1622. [i.e. 1622/3]

Excellentissimi Magnificentissimi Domini,

POST honores eximios, praefecturas insignes, Legationes Nobilissimas, aliósque titulos aequè nobis memorantibus, ac merentibus vobis gratissimos, Saluete tandem Magistri Artium, & quidem omnium Aulicarum, Militarium, Academicarum. Cuius noui tituli accessionem summè gratulantur Excellentijs Vestris Musae omnes, Gratiaéque, obsecrantes, vt deponatis paulisper vultus illos bellicos, quibus hostes soletis in potestatem redigere, leniorésque aspectus, & dulciores assumatis; nos etiam exuentes os illud, & supercilium quibus caperatam seueriorémque Philosophiam expugnare nouimus, quicquid hilare est, laetum, ac lubens, vestram in gratiam amplectimur. Quid enim iucundius accidere potest, quàm vt ministri Regis Catholici ad nos accedant? cuius ingens gloria aequè rotunda est atque ipse orbis: qui vtrasque Indias Hispaniâ suâ quasi nodo connectens, nullas metas laudum, nullas Herculeas columnas, quas iam olim possidet, agnoscit. Iamdudum nos omnes, nostrúmque regnum gestimus fieri participes eius sanguinis, qui tantos spiritus solet infundere. Et quod obseruatione cum primis dignum est, quò magìs amore coalescamus, vtraque gens Hispanica, Britannica, colimus Iacobum. Iacobus tutelaris Diuus est vtrique nostrum; vt satìs intelligatis, Excellentias vestras tantò

I. *The Oration and translation from* True Copies Of all the Latine Orations, made at *Cambridge* on the 25. and 27. of Februarie last past 1622. *With their translations into English.* London, Printed by *W. Stansby* for *Richard Meighen.* 1623. 15 Catholica 17 nodo *Ed*: *misprinted* modo (*see translation*)

chariores esse, cùm eo sitis ordine atque habitu, quo nos in hoc regno omnes esse gloriamur. Quin & Serenissimae Principis Isabellae laudes, virtutésque, vicinum fretum quotidie transnatantes, litora nostra atque aures mirè circumsonant. Necesse est autem vt foelicitas tantorum Principum etiam in ministros redundet, quorum in eligendis illis iudicium iampridem apparet. Quare Excellentissimi, Splendidissimi Domini, cùm tanti sitis & in Principibus Vestris, & in vobismetipsis, veremur ne nihil hìc sit, quod magnitudini praesentiae vestrae respondeat. Quis enim apud nos splendor, aut rerum, aut vestium? quae rutilatio? certè cùm duplex fulgor sit, qui mundi oculos perstringat, nos tam defecimus in vtroque quàm Excellentiae Vestrae abundant. Quinimo Artes hìc sunt quiete & silentio cultae, tranquillitas, otium, pax omnibus praeterquam tineis, paupertas perpetua, nisi vbi vestrae adsunt Excellentiae. Nolite tamen contemnere has gloriolas nostras quas è chartis & puluere eruimus. Quomodo possetis similes esse Alexandro Magno nisi eius res gestas tradidisset historia? Seritur fama in hoc saeculo, vt in sequenti metatur: prius Excellentijs Vestris curae erit; posterioris largam messem Vobis haec tenuia boni consulentibus, vouemus.

The Oration of Master George Herbert, Orator of the Vniuersitie of Cambridge, when the Ambassadours were made Masters of Arts.

27. *Feb.* 1622

Most Excellent and most Magnificent Lords:

AFTER many singular honors, remarkable commands, most noble Ambassages, and other titles most pleasing, as well to vs remembring, as to you deseruing them, Wee at last salute you Masters of Arts; yea, indeed of all, both Courtly, Militarie, Academicall. The accession of which

14 quiete *Ed*: *misprinted* quietae (*see translation*)
26 them. Wee

new title to your Excellencies, all the *Muses* and *Graces* congratulate; entreating that you would a while lay aside those warlike lookes, with which you vse to conquer your enemies, and assume more mild and gracious aspects; and wee also putting off that countenance and grauitie, by which we well know how to conuince the sterne, and more austere sort of Philosophie, for respect to you, embrace all that is cheerefull, ioyous, pleasing. For, what could haue happened more pleasing to vs, then the accesse of the Officers of the Catholike King? whose exceeding glory is equally round with the world it selfe: who tying, as with a knot, both *Indias* to his *Spaine*, knowes no limits of his praise, no, not, as in past ages, those Pillars of *Hercules*. Long since, all we and our whole Kingdome exult with ioy, to bee vnited with that bloud, which vseth to infuse so great and worthie Spirits. And that which first deserueth our obseruation, to the end, wee might the more by loue grow on, both the *Spanish* and *Brittish* Nation serue and worship *Iames*. *Iames* is the protecting Saint vnto vs both; that you may well conceiue, your Excellencies to bee more deare vnto vs, in that you are of the same order and habit, of which wee all in this Kingdome glorie to be. The praises also and vertues of the most renowned Princesse *Isabel*, passing daily our neighboring Sea, wondrously sound through all our Coasts, and eares. And necessarily must the felicitie of so great Princes redound also to those seruants, in the choice of whom their iudgement doth euen now appeare. Wherefore most Excellent, most Illustrious Lords, since you are so great both in your Princes, and your selues, wee iustly feare that there is nothing here answerable to the greatnesse of your presence. For amongst vs what glorious shew is there, either of garments, or of any thing else? what splendor? surely, since there is a two-fold brightnesse which dazeleth the eyes of men, we haue as much failed, as your Excellencies doe excel, in both. But yet the Arts in quietnes and silence here are reuerenced, here is tranquilitie, repose, peace with all but Booke-wormes, perpetuall pouertie, but when your Excellencies appeare. Yet doe not yee contemne these our slight

27 Exccellent,

glories, which wee raise from bookes, and painefull industrie. How could you bee like great *Alexander*, vnlesse Historie deliuered his actions? Fame is sowne in this age, that it may be reaped in the following; let the first be the care of your Excellencies; we for your gracious acceptance of these poore duties wish, and vow vnto you of the last a plenteous Haruest.

II. *Oratio in Discessum Regis ab Academiâ Cantabrigiae habita* 12° *die Martij* 1622 [i.e. 1622/3]

AVGVSTISSIME MONARCHA,

SI per haec ludicra nostra pars aliquis eius laetitiae, quâ perfundis nos omnes quotidianis beneficijs, redundarit in authorem; si spinula vlla Coronae Regiae emollita sit vel retusa; O beatos nos! o foelices! Optamus quidem vt Maiestatis vestrae gaudia responderint aut nostris votis aut virtutibus vestris, quarum enumerationi nulla vnquam vis, nulla latera sufficere possunt. Quid memorem prudentiam vestram incomparabilem, quâ optimè ostendis te eius vicarium qui omnia disponit suauiter? Quid eruditionem, quae tanta est vt, nisi Rex esses in ciuili Republicâ, eligereris in Literariâ? Non à nobis vapulant Iesuitae, sed à scriptis vestris, quae ingenti cum lucro quotidie legimus. Quid fauores erga hanc Academiam inenarrabiles, cùm non solùm tuearis nos à maleuolorum insidijs, sed etiam doceas tanquam communis defensor fidei et Academiae, sed etiam doceas, viam aperiens & methodum in studijs adhibendam, etiam libros indicans ad Theologiam expeditissimos, tanto ac tam stupendo iudicio, vt, nisi tot negotijs distractus esses, conflueremus omnes ad Aulam, atque ab eo consilium peteremus à quo et fortunas? Quid innumera alia, quae, si per tempus liceret effari, non licet per multitudinem, imò per modestiam vestram? Hocine accedit ad incredibiles laudes vestras quòd quae nos audiamus summo cum gaudio ea Maiestas vestra

II. *From* State Papers Domestic, 14. cxxxix. 90, *in the Public Record Office.*

summâ cum molestiâ? Hoc vno Rex et populus dissentimus. Quare, vt miraculis vestris nostra occurrant, oratio nostra est silentium, atque eloquentia, stupor.

Tu verò, Deus omnipotens, conserues nobis haec gaudia, imbuas cor Regium vigore, animum clementiâ, vt frequenter nos inuisat, à re instructus nos doceat, tuósque fauores populo tuo communicans coelum ac terram minori quàm cernimus interuallo connectat. Tangas, Domine, cor sacrum, sentiátque Rex ipse nos haec intimè precari.

DIXI.

III. *Oratio Quâ auspicatissimum Serenissimi Principis Caroli Reditum ex Hispanijs celebrauit Georgius Herbert Academiae Cantabrigiensis Orator.*

Veneranda Capita,
Viri grauissimi,
Pubes lectissima.

POLYCRATES cùm annulum sibi dilectum in mare dimisisset, eundémque retulisset captus piscis, foelicissimus mortalium habitus est. Quantò foeliciores nos omnes, Corona Musica, qui optimum Principem spe nuptiarum mari nuper tradentes, & ipsum accepimus saluum & annulum, annulum Coniugalem, nunc denuò nostrum, atque vbiuis terrarum pro iudicio prudentissimi Regis, & in rebus humanis diuinísque exercitatissimi, de integro disponendum. Redijt! redijt CAROLVS, & cum eo vita nostra atque calor, longo animi deliquio fugitiuus ac desertor. Quid iactas mihi aromata Orientis? Quid Theriacas peregrinas? asserunt Medici vnamquamque regionem sua sibi sufficere, neque externis indigere auxilijs atque antidotis: certè nostrate Principe nusquam praesentius Balsamum, nusquam benignius, soluens obstupefactos artus, atque exhilarans,

III. *From* Oratio Quâ &c. (*as above*). Ex Officina Cantrelli Legge, Almae Matris Cantabrigiae Typographi. 1623. 21 exercitatissimi 22 Redijt? redijt 25 sua *conj. Ed*: suam *1623*

ORATIO

Quâ auſpicatiſsimum Sereniſsimi

PRINCIPIS

CAROLI,

Reditum ex Hiſpaniĳs celebrauit

GEORGIVS HERBERT

Academiæ Cantabrigienſis

ORATOR.

Ex Officina CANTRELLI LEGGE, Almæ

Matris Cantabrigiæ *Typographi*.

1623.

tumentibus iam venis, arterijs micantibus, spiritibúsque tabellarijs laetum hunc nuncium vbique deferentibus, vt nullus sit angulus corporis, nulla venula, vbi non adsit Carolvs. Quàm facilè sentiuntur boni Principes! Vt natura omnis suos habet anteambulones, vnde pluuia futura, an sudum, facilè conijcitur ex coelo, ex garritu auium, ex lapidum exhalatione: sic bonorum Principum facilis Astrologia: quorum aduentum ipsi lapides, ipsa durissima ingenia, meum praesertim, celare non possunt: quantò minùs tacebunt lusciniae nostrae disertae, miniméque omnium coelestiores animi, quorum pietatis interest non silere.

Quae enim vspiam gens, quod vnquam seculum meliorem habuit Principem? percurrite Annales regnorum, excutite scrinia politiarum omnium; vos, vos, inquam, excutite, quorum aetas teritur in libris: non rusticis loquor aut barbaris, quos magnificentiâ promissi circumscribere in promptu erat, rudésque animos vi verborum percellere: vestra est optio, vestra disquisitio, qui tineae estis & helluones chartacei; date mihi Carolvm alterum, quamlibet *Magnum*, modò detis eum in flore, in vaginâ, in herbescenti viriditate; nondum ad spicam barbámque adultum. Non rhetoricor, Academici, non tinnio: ὑλομανίαν illam & inanem verborum strepitum iamdudum deposui: bullae & crepitacula puerorum sunt, aut eorum certè, qui cymbala sunt fanaticae iuuentutis: ego verò sentio, & quis sum ipse (barbam, hui, tam grauem) & apud quos dico, viros limatae auris atque tersae, quorum grauitate ac purpurâ non abutar.

Quare vt parciùs agam vobiscum, simúlque & laboribus meis, & vestrae fidei consulam, quemadmodum artifices non omnes licitantibus producunt merces, sed specimen tantùm: sic & ipse excerpam è Principis rebus gestis pugillum, vnam actionem è multis seligam, quam vobis amplectendam dissuauiandámque praebebo: esto autem hoc ipsum iter, quod nuper emensus est, vt sciatis omnes quàm nudè, quàm simpliciter vobiscum agam, quàm non longè abeam Oratorum more, qui nullum non angulum verrunt (ac si perdiderint ingenium) vt Spartam exornent suam: Ego verò non dicam vobis quod factum est ante seculum vestrum, aut

18 tineae *Grosart*: lineae *1623*, *Pickering*, *Willmott* 21 spicam,

apud Indos; vnicum hoc iter nuperum explicabo, in quo longè vberrimam gloriae segetem perspicio, nullâ verborum, nullâ temporis falce demetendam.

Non vnum quid spectant aut singulare Magni animi, sed varia solent esse eorum consilia, finésque multiplices & polymiti, vt si minùs id assequantur, quod primùm intendunt, saltem in secundis aut tertijs consistant. Quare & Principis iter multiplicem nobis exhibet prudentiam; primò nuptias ipsas spectate. Quid autem? Ergón' amauit Princeps? Quippini; homo est, non statua; Sceptriger, non sceptrum: aequúmne est vt tot labores & sollicitudines Principum sine condimento sint atque embammate? Quid si cochleas colligeret cum Caligulâ, praesertim cùm possit in eodem litore? Quid si muscas captaret cum Domitiano? at ille ambiuit nobilissimam Austriacam familiam, Aquilámque illam, quae non capit muscas. Nihil habet humana vita maioris momenti aut ponderis, quàm Nuptiae, quas adeò laudant Poetae, vt in coelum transtulerint: *Εἰ ἓν ἦν ὁ ἄνθρωπος*, inquit Medicorum Alpha, *οὐκ ἂν ἤλγεεν*. Hinc Thraces dicti sunt *ἄβιοι*, & Licurgus magnus Legislator *ἀτιμίαν προσέθηκε τοῖς ἀγάμοις*. Absque nuptijs foret populus virorum, essemus vnius seculi; hâc re solùm vlciscimur mortem, ligantes abruptum vitae filum, vnde consequimur, vel inuitis Fatis, quasi nodosam aeternitatem.

Non ignoro apud quos haec dico, eos scilicet, qui innuptam Palladem colunt, Musásque coelibes, qui posteros libris non liberis quaeritis. Nolite tamen nimiùm efferre vos, cùm Virginitas ipsa fructus sit Nuptiarum: quod pereleganter & supra barbariem seculi innuebant Maiores nostri, qui olim glasto se inficientes, in vxorum corporibus, Solem, Lunam, & Stellas; in virginum, flores atque herbas depinxere: vt enim Vxores, Virgines; ita Sol & Coelum producunt flores, qui symbola sunt spei, quoniam à floribus fructus sperantur.

Quòd si Nuptiae in se graues sunt, quantò magìs Principum, cùm, quò eorum conditio sublimior, eò maior cura adhibenda sit. Deus ipse cùm crearet hominem, mundi regem, consilio vsus est. Quare operosior in eo structura, & praerogatiuae regiae emicant. Soli homini dantur manus, soli caput

2 segetem, 4 spectant, 11 sollicitudnes 23 Fatis 38 manus

rotundum & coeleste, soli facies tanquam vestibulum magni palatij. Iam verò, vt Rex animalium fiat Rex hominum, apponimus nos manibus Sceptrum, capiti & faciei coronam, significantes oportere Reges ijs partibus antecellere homines, quibus homo bruta, iustitiâ scilicet & prudentiâ. *Goropius Becanus* ait vetus vocabulum nostrum, **Koning**, & contractè **King**, à *Con* verbo deduci, quòd tria complectitur, *Possum*, *Scio*, *Audeo:* cernitis Regem & nomine & re magnum quid polliceri, ideóque ex quolibet ligno, quâlibet vxore non esse fingendum: neque enim minùs refert, qualis quaeque sit mater, è quâ liberi quaerantur, quàm qualis terra, è quâ arbores. Apud Iuris-consultos, partus sequitur ventrem: quibus accedunt Poetae,

Ὅταν δὲ κρηπὶς μὴ καταβληθῇ γένους
Ὀρθῶς, ἀνάγκη δυστυχεῖν τοὺς ἐκγόνους.

Nam vt educationem liberorum mittam, quâ in re celebris est Gracchorum mater, ingenium ipsum atque indoles (veluti Conclusio sequitur infirmiorem partem) plerumque matrissat: hinc contigisse arbitror apud Romanos, quòd nonnullae familiae semper mites essent, vtì Valerij, aliae contrà semper pertinaces ac tribunitiae, vtì Appij. Quare noluit Princeps optimus, in delectu vxoris, re vnâ omnium grauissimâ, alienis oculis iudicióque inniti; Ipse, ipse profectus est, vt ingenti labore suo & periculo consuleret & praesenti Reipublicae & futurae; neque vnius seculi Princeps, sed & omnium, quae ventura sunt, haberetur. Neque in hisce Nuptijs posteritati tantùm prospexit suauissimus Princeps, verùm etiam praesenti seculo, dum pacem, quâ tot iam annis impunè fruimur, hoc pacto fundatam cupit & perpetuam; quod quidem vbi gentium si non ab Hispano sperandum? *Ὅταν νομεὺς ἀγαθὸν κύνα ἔχῃ, καὶ οἱ ἄλλοι νομεῖς βούλονται πλησίον αὐτοῦ τὰς ἀγέλας ἱστάναι.* Scio Belli nomen splendidum esse & gloriosum: dum animus grandis, suíque impos, triumphos & victorias quasi fraena ferox spumantia mandit, iuuat micare gladio & mucronem intueri.

2 animalium, hominum 8 Regem, 14 Ὅταν κρηπὶς μὴ καταβληθῇ τοῦ γένους 23 grauissimâ 24 consuleret, 25 Reipub. (*and thus abbreviated throughout*) 27 prospexit, 33 gloriosum, 34 victorias,

Iam nunc minaci murmure cornuum
Stringuntur aures: iam litui strepunt,
Iam fulgor armorum fugaces
Terret equos equitúmque vultus.

Cùm tamen splendida plerumque vitrea sint, claritatem fragilitate corrumpentia; neque de priuato agamus bono, sed publico; certè fatendum est, anteferendam bello pacem, sine quâ omnis vita procella, & mundus solitudo. Pace, filij sepeliunt patres; bello, patres filios: pace, aegri sanantur; bello, etiam sani intereunt: pace, securitas in agris est; bello, neque intra muros: pace, auium cantus expergefacit; bello, tubae ac tympana: pax nouum orbem aperuit; bellum destruit veterem.

Εἰρήνη γεωργὸν κἂν πέτραις τρέφει καλῶς,
Πολεμὸς δὲ κἂν πεδίῳ κακὸς ἔφυ.

Quod ad nostram Rempublicam, Academiam, pax adeò Musis summè necessaria est, vt sine eâ nihil simus. Nam primùm tota haec Pieria supellex, charta, calami, codices, quàm subitò dispereunt, simul ac concrepuit incendium militare: quid proderunt scalpella vestra, quando ipsae hae turres & beatae fabricae, vnico ictu sulphurei tubi, vnicâ liturâ delentur? Dein quid Musis cum tumultu? Otium poscunt artes, mentem tranquillam, serenam, sudam: lucos aestate, pinguem togam hyeme: delicata res est eruditio & tenera, tanquam flos molliculus rudiore Centurionis manu tactus flaccescit. Tu, qui Philosophiae incumbis, cùm corporis cum animâ vinculum impedimento esse ad contemplandum causaris, irruit Miles in Musaeum tuum, & gladio te liberat. Tu, qui astra scrutaris, dum globos tractas & coelos fictitios, perrumpit primipilus, & te cum coelis tuis ad inferos deturbat. Sensit hoc Archimedes, figuras iam nunc pulueri inscriptas corpore confosso obliterans. Quare cauendum, ne pacem, quae sola incubat artibus, & obstetricatur, minùs quàm par est, aestimemus. Quod aliae gentes manibus in coelum sublatis, lachrymis in terram manantibus, ieiunae, squalidae, perdiae, pernoctes flagitant, cauendum ne id nobis

12 pax, 16 Rempub. 17 simus, 21 tubi 27 animâ] animo *Willmott, Grosart* 32 inscriptas, 36 perdiae] perdies *Willmott*

nauseam moueat, aut tanquam oues taedulae & fastidiosae, cibum respuamus. Ecquid nescitis miserias Belli? consulite historias; illic tuta cognitio est, atque extra teli iactum. Ecce lanienas omnimodas, truncata corpora, mutilatam imaginem Dei, pauxillum vitae, quantum satìs ad dolendum, vrbium incendia, fragores, direptiones, stupratas virgines, praegnantes bis intersectas, infantulos plus lactis quàm cruoris emittentes; effigies, imò vmbras hominum fame, frigore, illuuie, enectas, contusas, debilitatas. Quàm cruenta gloria est, quae super ceruicibus hominum erigitur? vbi in dubio est, qui facit, an qui patitur, miserior.

Non nego bellum aliquando necessarium esse, bellíque miserias gratas, praecipuè vbi velut ex continentibus tectis ad nos traiecturum est incendium: *Σωφρόνων ἐστὶ μὴ περιμένειν, ὅτε πολεμεῖν ὑμῖν ὁμολογήσει*, dixit Mithridates. Sed non est nostri bellum indicere: prudentissimus Rex maturè prospiciet: vbi ille signum sustulerit, Leones Britannici (è quorum ossibus collisis ignis elicitur) qui nunc mansueti sunt, abundè rugient. Interim curiositas absit, neque eorum satagamus, quae ad nos non spectant; sed velut Romani lacum, cuius altitudo ignota erat, dedicabant victoriae; pariter & nos consilia regia, tanquam gurgitem imperuestigabilem, victoriae nuncupemus: praesertim cùm futura incerta sint, & nullis perspicillis, ne Belgicis quidem, assequenda: apud poetas deorum pharetrae operculum habuere, humanae non item: patent enim consilia nostra, absconduntur Diuina & Regia, praecipuè pharetrata, quae ad poenam gentium & Bellum spectant. Sunt tamen acuti quidam & emuncti, qui omnia praeuident: nihil eos latet, ac si Fatis à fuso essent atque consilijs, sine quibus ne vnum quidem filum torquerent: nobis non licet esse tam perspicacibus, quamuìs rationi consonum videtur, vt qui hìc in Musarum monte editissimo, in ipso Parnasso siti sumus, liberiorem, quàm alij, prospectum habeamus. Illud autem, quod cuiuis clarissimè patet, etiam lusco, nunquam intueri satìs vel mirari possumus, nimirum infinitum Principis in suam gentem amorem, cui pacem quaesiuit suo capite, periculis suis.

17 prospiciet, 21 erat 24 quidem 33 in ipso] et ipso *Willmott, Grosart*
37 cui] qui *Grosart*

Rectè facitis, Academici, attollentes oculos cum stupore; laudo vos, neque enim quicquam hoc itinere mirabilius, cuius tamen fructum omnem nondum habetis enucleatum. Quid enim si praeter Nuptias, prolem, tranquillitatem, etiam & scientiae augmentum ex hoc itinere captauit solertissimus Princeps? nihil ad cognitionem acquirendam peregrinatione conducibilius esse nouistis omnes, vnde cuncti antiqui Philosophi peregrinati sunt, existimantes Τυφλοὺς εἶναι πρὸς ὀξὺ βλέποντας, ἀναποδημήτους πρὸς ἐκδεδημηκότας. Quamuìs res haec Principibus vt vtilissima ita difficillima factu, cùm quantò plus possint in suâ terrâ, tantò minùs in alienâ. Omne regnum suo Principi carcer est, aut si excedat, alienum: at Noster difficultatem superans, fructum consecutus est: quid enim vtilius quàm ex obseruatione exterarum Legum ac morum, patriam ditare? Catonianum praeceptum est: Vicini quo pacto niteant, id animum aduertito; adde quòd angusti est animi aut superbi sua tantùm nosse, praesertim cùm in vno regno non sint omnia: diuisit Natura suas dotes, vt indigentia singularum regionum omnes connectat: etenim abundantia morosa est & sternax, vnde diuites syluas ac saltus quaerunt vbi aedificent, ac si non gregaria essent animalia, sed tigres aut vrsi. Quamobrem optimè consuluit gentibus natura, cùm paupertatem daret tanquam catenam, quâ dissitas nationes ac superbas constringeret. Porro si Politicos audiamus, salus regnorum pendet à vicinis, quorum consilia, apparatus, foedera, munitiones, aequè ac nostra spectari debent: incumbant sibi inuicem imperia, tanquam ligna obliqua, aliter magna haec mundi domus corrueret: hinc Reges Legatos habent statarios ac resides, quem locum Noster suauissimus impleuit, ipse egit oratorem, vt & ego aliquantulum hoc nomine glorier.

Neque alienas tantùm ex hoc itinere cognouit Respublicas sed quod plus est, suam; absentiâ magìs quàm praesentiâ. Nunc enim exploratos habet nostros in se affectus, timores, suspiria, expostulationes, iras, amorem rursus. Deus bone! qui tum rumores? quae auditiones? qui susurri? Heus, abijtne Noster? miseros nos; nunquam frigidiorem aestatem

2 Laudo   11 factu *Grosart*: facta *1623*   19 vt] et *Grosart*
20 connectit: 21 syluas,   25 Salus   35 bone?

sensimus; at quò tandem? Madritum? hui! iter bene longum! Quid autem illic? sterilem aiunt regionem: Falleris, nusquam plura bona, cùm etiam mala illic sint aurea: nihil inaudisti de Tago, Pactolo? apud nos agri tantùm sunt fertiles, illic etiam arenae. Dij te perdant, cum malis tuis & arenâ sine calce; at ego Principem vellem, CAROLVM, CAROLVM; siccine abijsti solus? cur non nos omnes tecum? cur non vt elephanti turres, ita tu patriam tecum portasti? Sic tunc omnes strepebant: huiusmodi lamentis & quiritationibus plena erant fora, nundinae, conciliabula, angiportus, Maeandri. Dicam vobis, Academici; ego tunc temporis liberior eram, huc illuc pro libitu circumcursitans: inspexi facies hominum ac vultus curiosiùs tanquam emptor; ita me ametis omnes, vt ego nihil vspiam laetum, nihil candidum expiscari possem; oculi omnium deiecti, humile os, collum pensile, manus decussatae, ipsae mulieres inelegantes, nulla pulchritudo per vniuersam Britanniam, disparuit forma, Albion nomine excidit: ipsum coelum nubilum semper, & poeta stultus qui dixerat,

Minimâ contentos nocte Britannos.

Inde ego sic mecum: gaudeo quidem de ingenti amore in Principem, cui nulla dilectio par esse potest; at cur adeò dolent? cur ringuntur? num diffidùnt prudentiae Regis? annon eius consilio res gesta est? Scio Hispanum versutum, callidum, artis & aucupij apprimè gnarum: at IACOBVS à nobis est: hìc ego me erexi & de dolore remisi plurimum, de desiderio nihil. Atque hoc quidem statu res erant, Suauissime CAROLE, cùm tu aberas; ex quo facile collectu erat, quantum deperimus te; quàm stultè de te rixamur: vt aliquando existimem id egisse prudentissimum Patrem tuum, cùm dimitteret te in Hispaniam, quod Romani Imperatores in bello, qui solebant signa in hostes inijcere, vt milites acriùs ea repeterent: certè nos te absentem omnes acerrimè concitatissiméque desiderauimus.

Ecquid videtis tandem quàm vtile hoc iter, per quod optimus Princeps non tantùm exteras regiones habuit per-

2 longum : *Willmott* 13 emptor, 15 possem, 28 collectu] collectum

spectas, verum etiam suam? Quid si hìc lateat etiam Temperantia, rara in Principibus virtus, & cui cum sceptro lites saepiùs intercedunt? Quid enim? adeón' nihili videtur res, Principem omnibus delicijs abundantem, obseptum illecebris, voluptatibus quasi fascijs circumdatum, enatare è delicijs, transilire sepes, rumpere fascias cum Hercule, serpentésque interficere voluptatis, vt iter tantum, tantis laboribus, periculis obnoxium, susciperet? Quàm pudet me delicatorum Caesarum, qui cupiditatibus immersi, aut vno semper saginantur in loco, vtì anguillae, aut si mutant locum, gestantur, tanquam onera, circumferuntur mollissimis lecticis, indicantes, se non amare patriam terram, à quâ adeò remouentur. Sic pascunt se indies, ac si corpora sua non abirent olim in elementa, sed in bellaria aut tragemata: cùm tamen in resolutione illâ vltimâ, nulla sit distinctio populi aut principis: nulla sunt sceptra in elementis, nulli fasces aut secures: vapores seruiles ad nubes educti aequè magnum tonitru edent ac regij. Quid ego vobis Neronum aut Heliogabalorum ingluuiem memorem? quid ructus crapulae solium possidentis? Dies me deficeret (& quidem nox aptior esset tali historiae) si Romanorum Imperatorum incredibilem luxum à Tiberio Caesare ad Constantinum magnum aperirem, quorum imperium gulae impar erat, vt interdum putem, optimè consuluisse Deum orbi terrarum lapides & metalla ei inserendo, aliter mundus iam diu fuisset deuoratus. Nota sunt *ταριχεύματα* Aegyptiorum, qui antequam condiebant corpora Nobilium, solebant ventres eximere, quos in arcâ repositos abijciebant in fluuium, his verbis: *Ὦ δέσποτα ἥλιε καὶ θεοὶ πάντες, εἴ τι κατὰ τὸν ἐμαυτοῦ βίον ἥμαρτον, ἢ φαγὼν ἢ πιὼν, ὧν μὴ θεμιτὸν ἦν, οὐ δι' ἐμαυτὸν ἥμαρτον, ἀλλὰ διὰ ταῦτα.* At Noster, spretis voluptatibus, illecebris *μελιταίαις ἀγχόναις* abiectis, iter aggreditur & labores, haud ignarus, ignem vitae augeri ventilatione, desidiâ corrumpi, neminémque esse sui negligentiorem, quàm qui sibi parcat. Quin exuit personam Principis, deponit Maiestatem, virgam cum sceptro commutans, vt quid priuata habeat in se vita commodi aut voluptatis, experiretur. Nihil vtilius Regi quàm aliquando non regnare:

5 è] *om. Willmott* 8 obnoxium 17 Vapores educti, 31 noster

hoc enim fastum amputat, affectus explorat, adulationem ventilat, & adulatores, qui semper titillant aures Principum, Ὥσπερ τοῖς πτεροῖς κνώμενοι τὰ ὦτα. Elfredus, nobilissimus Saxonum nostrorum Princeps, sub ementito habitu fidicinis castra hostium ingressus, ipsúmque Praetorium, fidibus canendo, omnia Danorum expiscatus consilia, victoriam celebrem consecutus est. Notissimus est Codri amor, cuius manifestationem in gentem suam priuatae personae & habitui debuit. Porro, est etiam interdum satietas quaedam honoris, quem ad tempus deponere famem excitat: non minùs vitae inaequalitas delectat, quàm terrae, quam Natura montibus vallibúsque sublimitate atque humilitate distinxit: quin & venti imperant pelago, vt laeuitatem illam aequabilem atque politiem perturbent. In picturis locus est vmbris & recessibus, etiam si quis Principem pingat. Amat varietatem Natura omnis, flores, animalia, tum maximè homo, cui soli ideò insunt oculi variegati, cùm caetera animantia vnicolores habeant. Quamobrem non est mirandum, si Reges ipsi quandoque suauitates suas populari aceto condiant.

Accepistis, Viri attentissimi, causas itineris huius, quantum quidem ego homuncio ac nanus coniectando assequor. Quare nunc vobis ex pede Herculem, ex itinere Principem metiri licet, quod sanè adeò nobile fuit & honorificum, vt nihil habeat Inuidia ipsa, quod contra hiscat aut mussitet. Adest tamen anus illa querula, & φιλεγκλήμων, quam audire videor dicentem, Pulchrum quidem iter & Amante dignum; siccine pessima? at fuerit; si amor virginis eò pertraxit Principem, quò tandem ducet amor Patriae? eadem acies & stipulam secat & lignum: idem feruor qui impar sub amoris signo meritus est, ad vera castra traductus, hostem interficiet: idem impetus, qui peragrauit Hispaniam, si opus sit, superabit; praesertim cùm amico fidere periculosius sit, quàm hostem superare. Protagoras cùm eleganter admodum caudices ligni fasciculo vinxisset, cum grandi atque impedito onere facillimè incedens, occurrit ei Democritus, & ingenium admirans, domum secum duxit, & erudiuit artibus; qui inde è baiulo euasit Philosophus, eodem ingenio vsus in lignis & literis: quis scit an & amoris onus scitè vinctum

2 Principum. 3 Elfredus 8 suam, 34 fafciculo

ligatúmque, & per tot milliaria facilè transmissum, mentem maiorum capacem indicet? Florent apud nos artes omnes, inter quas & Mathematicae, quae licèt versentur in figuris describendis, quibus nihil imperito vanius inutiliúsue videatur, vbi tamen ad vsum tralatae fuerint, machinas conficiunt ad defensionem Reipublicae mirabiles: sic idem animus, qui nuper versatus est in formâ & figuris vultûs, vbi res postulat, regnum tuebitur: imò in vniuersum, si quis de Principe aliquo, quis sit futurus aut qualis, rectè diuinaret, non respiciat materiam actionum, sed quo spiritu, quâ arte, quanto impetu atque vigore res aggrediatur: quemadmodum in Cometae praesagio, non respicitur, quae materia sit, coelestis an sublunaris, sed quae signa, quo motu transeat.

Verùm mittamus inuidos & inuidiam, quae semper se deuorat primùm, vtì vermis nucleum, è quo nascitur; non est tanti respondere latratibus maleuolorum; licèt celebres sint canes Britannici, & plùs iusto celebres, cùm leunculum & dominum suum contra naturam adoriantur: in Geoponicis dicitur, *Κάτοπτρον ἐὰν ἐπιδείξῃς τῷ ἐπικειμένῳ νέφει, παρελεύσεται ἡ χάλαζα*: quantò citiùs fugient calumniae, si speculum Inuidiae ostendas, quo deformitatem suam intueatur! Nos verò, flores Parnassi, gaudia praestolantur, quae iamdudum annuunt mihi vt perorem. Hilaris haec sumenda est dies. Quare prodite, tenebriones literarij, è gurgustijs vestris, vbi trecenta foliorum iugera vno die sedentes percurritis; prodite omnes. Quid noui? Quid noui, stupide? Redijt Princeps, CAROLVS redijt, honore grauidus, grauidus scientiâ, cruribus thymo plenis: vt enim vapor, qui furtim ascendit ad nubes, vbi iam ingrauescit humore, relabitur in terram, quâ ortus est, eíque cum foecundiâ remuneratur: sic & Noster qui clanculum exijt, vsque ad Pyrenaeas nubes conscendens, reuersus per mare, gloriâ, prudentiâ auctior, ditat patriam, suámque absentiam cum foenore compensat. Quamobrem abijcite quisque libros, non est locus grauitati, neque apud vos: tripudiet Alma Mater licèt aetate prouectior, etiam anus subsultans multùm excitet pulueris: Arionem Delphino reuectum excepere arbores tripudiantes, & Vos statis?

Tantùm precemur Deum immortalem, vt Princeps opti-

24 prodite literarij 25 iugera, 26 noui stupide?

mus nulla secunda itinera meditetur; posthac contineat se patriâ, cuius arctis amplexibus nunquam se expediet. *Gulielmus Victor* descensurus primùm è nauibus in terram hanc, incidit in coenum, quod innuebat eum hìc mansurum: vtinam & nunc sit tanta patriae tenacitas, vt nunquam Princeps se extricet: satìs virtuti datum est, satìs Reipublicae. Quod si necesse sit iterum exire patriâ, qui nunc inuenit viam, proximo itinere faciat. Apollo olim depositis radijs Daphnen deperijt, at illa mutata est in arborem triumphantium propriam: Noster etiam Princeps habuit Daphnen suam, cuius amor deinceps in triumphos & laurus mutabitur.

Nos vero, Auditores, diu iam peregrinati cum Principe, commodè peruenimus ad laurum hanc, vbi sub vmbrâ eius paulisper requiescamus: praesertim donec transeat nubes illa, quae vicinos adeò infestat: hìc enim securi sumus à pluuiâ, imò à fulmine: Obsecremus eum tantùm vt permittat nostram hanc

Inter victrices hederam sibi serpere Lauros.

Dixi.

8 radijs, 12 vero

EPISTOLAE

I. *Ad Buckingh. C.*

Gratulatio de Marchionatu

A.D. 1619 [Jan. 1617/18]

Illustrissime Domine.

ECQVID inter tot gloriae titulos caput vndique munientes meministi Magistrum Te esse Artium? an inter lauros principis hederae nostrae ambitiosae locus est? hunc quidem gradum pignus habes amoris nostri, haec est ansa quâ prehendimus Te, et tanquam Aquilam inter nouas honorum nubes è conspectu nostro fugientem reuocamus. Tu vicissim abundè compensas nos, gratissimóque Almam Matrem prosequeris animo: proin vt Fluuij quas aquas à Fonte accipiunt non retinent ipsi, sed in mare dimittunt; sic Tu etiam dignitates ab optimo Rege desumptas in vniuersam Rempublicam diffundis: per Te illucet nobis Iacobus noster. Tu aperis illum populo, & cùm ipse sis in summâ arbore alterâ manu prehendis Regem, alteram nobis ad radices haerentibus porrigis. Quare, meritissime Marchio, Tuam gloriam censemus nostram, et in honoribus Tuis nostro bono gratulamur; quanquam quem alium fructum potuimus expectare ab Eo, in quem fauor Regius, nostra vota, virtutes tantae confluxerunt? inter quae etiam certamen oritur et pia contentio, vtrum gratia Principis virtutes tuas, aut nostra vota gratiam Principis, aut Tuae virtutes et vota nostra et Principis gratiam superarent. Nimirum vt lineae, quamuìs diuersâ viâ, omnes tamen ad centrum properant; sic disparatae foelicitates hinc à populo, illinc à Principe, in Te conueniunt, et confabulantur. Quare quomodo alij

I–XVI *from* The Orator's Book, vol. II, *a manuscript collection in the Registry of the University of Cambridge. T. Zouch printed* III *and* VIII *in his edition of* Walton's Lives (1796). *All were printed by Pickering* (1836), *Willmott* (1854), *and Grosart* (1874).

I. *Title: for date see note* 3 magistrum 10 dimittunt: 15 Quare 17 gratulamur. 19 confluxerunt. 21 virtutes, 22 nostra, nimirum vt lineae 23–4 properant. Sic molem hanc laetitiae suae exprimant, ipsi viderint: nos certè precamur, vt neque virtutibus tuis desint honores neque vtrisque vita, vsquedum, postquam omnes honorum gradus hìc percurreris, aeternum illud praemium consequare, cui neque addi quicquam potest, neque detrahi.

II. *Ad R. Naunton*

Gratiae de Fluuio et de tegendis Tectis stramineis

[June, 1619]

Vir Honoratissime.

EXIMIA tua in nos merita frequentiorem calamum postulant, si tantum Honori Tuo superesset otij ad legendum, quantum à nobis ad scribendum, cùm humanitatis Tuae, tum gratitudinis nostrae ratio postulat. Sed veremur, ne literae nostrae animo Tuo tot negotijs meritissimè distincto, tempore non suo obrepant: tibíque non tam auidè veterum beneficiorum memoriam recolenti, quàm cogitanti noua, improbè molestiam creent. Quare coniunximus nunc officia nostra, tuósque fauores temporibus et diligentiâ diuisos in gratijs nostris copulauimus. Nam vtramque illam curam insignem, tam de conseruando Fluuio nostro, quàm de muniendis contra grassantes flammas aedificijs Honori Tuo acceptam ferimus: plurimúmque suspicimus cumulum amoris Tui, qui vtrumque curasti, vt neque sitirent Musae, neque flagrarent. Quòd si tam integrum tibi esset gratificari nobis in terrâ & aere, quàm in aquâ & igne fecisti, non dubitamus quin benignitas tua omnia elementa percurreret. Tu verò macte honoribus, gloriâ, id enim nostrâ interest, vt hoc precemur, aut enim miserè fallimur, aut tantum de nullo vnquam Filio Alma Mater, quantum de Te sibi polliceatur.

II. 13 noua 16 nam 19 ferimus. 21 quod 26 mater,

III. *Ad Iacobum Regem*

Gratiae de Scriptis suis Academiae donatis

18 Maij, 1620

Serenissime Domine noster, Iacobe Inuictissime.

ECQVID inter tantas mundi trepidationes nobis & Musis vacas? O prudentiam incomparabilem, quae eodem vultu et moderatur mundum et nos respicit. Circumspice, si placet, Terrarum Reges, mutus est mundus vniuersus, vestra solùm dextra (quamuìs à scriptione terrestribúsque istis sublimitate solij asserta) vitâ et actione orbem vegetat. Angustior erat Scotia, quàm vt pennas nido plenè explicare posses: quid Tu inde? Britannicas insulas omnes occupasti. Hoc etiam imperium tenuius est quàm pro amplitudine virtutum vestrarum: nunc itaque Liber hic vester dilatat pomoeria, summouet Oceanum ambientem, adeò vt qui non subijciuntur ditioni, eruditioni vestrae obtemperent: per hunc imperas orbi vniuerso, victoriaéque gloriam absque crudelitate effusi sanguinis delibas. Haec vestra spolia actósque ex orbe triumphos communicas cum Almâ Matre, vtrumque splendorem cum beneficio nostro coniungis. Sanè, gestabaris antea in cordibus nostris; sed Tu vis etiam manibus teri, semotâque Maiestate, chartâ conspiciendum Te praebes, quò familiariùs inter nos verseris. O, mirificam Clementiam! Aedificârunt olim nobis Serenissimi Reges Collegia, eáque fundârunt amplissimis praedijs, immunitatibus: etiam libros dederunt, sed non suos: aut si suos, quia dederunt, non à se compositos, scriptos, editósque: quum tamen Tu inuaseris eorum gloriam conseruando nobis quae illi dederunt, etiam augendo; interim vestrâ hâc scribendi laude intactâ manente atque illibatâ. Cuius fauoris magnitudo ita inuoluit nos, vt etiam rependendi vias omnes praecludat. Quae enim alia spes reliqua erat, quàm vt pro infinitis vestris in nos beneficijs Maiestatem vestram aeternitati in scriptis nostris certissimè

III. *Title*: Ad Iacobum Regem *not in MS.* 10 hoc 17 vtrumque] vestrumque *Cole* (*See p.* 603) 18 sanè, 21 Clementiam? 23 immunitatibus (*no stop decipherable at the edge of the MS.*)

traderemus? Nunc verò Ipse scribendo irrupisti in compensationes nostras, et abstulisti: adeón' es praedo omnis gloriae, vt ne gratitudinis laudem nobis reliqueris? Quid agimus? hoc saltem solutio est; Nos nunc conspersi atramento regio, nihil non sublime et excelsum cogitabimus, perrumpemus controuersias omnes, superabimus quoscunque. Iam dari nobis vellemus Iesuitam aliquem, vt ex affrictu Libri vestri hominem illico contundamus. Quare amplectimur, fouemus, exosculamur, hunc foetum vestrum, hunc alterum Carolum, hunc fasciculum Prudentiae, positum extra mortalitatis aleam, et quò magìs Tuum agnoscas, in ipso partu, Librorum regem creatum. Diruuntur aedificia, corrumpuntur statuae, haec imago atque character, tempore melior, iniurias seculi scriptáque hâc illâc pereuntia securiùs praeterit. Si enim in regno vestro Hibernico lignum nascitur permanens, contra omnia venena validum: quantò magìs virtutes istae in Dominum agri transferendae sunt, vt sic scripta vestra omni dente, tum edacis temporis, tum venenatorum haereticorum, insitâ vi suâ liberentur. Quod superest, precamur S.S. Trinitatem, vt vestrae coronae ciuili & literariae tertiam Coelestem serò adiungat.

Humillimi serui subditíque vestri
Procancellarius
Reliquúsque Senatus
Cantabrigiensis.

Datae freq: Senatu
xiii° Cal. Jun. A.D.
CIↃ. IↃ. CXX.

Peregrinis Academiam nostram inuisentibus

Quid Vaticanam Bodleiúmque obijcis, Hospes?
Vnicus est nobis Bibliotheca Liber.

10 Carolum 14 seculi, 15 securiùs] securus *Pickering*, *Grosart* 21 literariae, 22 serui, 30 Vaticanam, Bodleiúmque] Bodleianamque *Walton's* Lives (1670) *and Duport's* Musae Subsecivae (1676) *See note* 31 Vnicus, Bibliotheca,

IV. *Ad Iacobum Regem*

Gratiae de Fluuio contra Redemptores

14 Jun., 1620

Serenissime Domine noster, Iacobe Potentissime.

INFINITA vestra in nos Beneficia non solùm verba omnia, sed etiam cogitationes nostras exhauriunt. Quis enim impetus animi celeritatem tantae munificentiae assequi potest? quippe qui vniuersum tempus nostrum (forsitan quò alacriùs illud impenderemus Doctrinae) beneficijs etiam obligasti. Nuper enim dedisti nobis Librum, plenissimum Musarum, quae cùm olim gauderent Fluuijs, nunc etiam aquas, in quibus habitant, impertis! Quanta rotunditas Clementiae vestrae, quae ab omni parte nobis succurrit! Quòd si Artaxerxes olim paululum aquae à Sinaetâ, subiecto suo, laetissimè sumeret, quantò magìs par est, nos humillimos subiectos, integro Fluuio à Rege nostro donatos, triumphare? Tantùm Maiestatem vestram subiectissimè oramus, vt si officia nostra minùs respondeant magnitudini beneficiorum, imbecillitati id nostrae, quae fastigium regiarum notionum aequare nunquam potest, non voluntati tribuendum existimes.

V. *Ad F. Bacon, Cancell.*

Gratiae de Fluuio

[14 Jun., 1620]

Illustrissime Domine.

SICCAM animam sapientissimam esse dixit obscurus ille philosophus; sanè exorti sunt nuperi quidam homines, qui libenter sapientiores nos redderent: sed si ablatus fuisset Fluuius noster, per quem vicini agri opulentiâ fruimur, veremur ne non tam sapientes nos, quàm obscuros philo-

IV. *Title*: Ad Iacobum Regem *not in MS.* 9 impertis? 10 succurrit? 11 Sinaetâ] Linaeta *Pickering, Willmott* 12 suo
V. *Title. Date not in MS. but inferred from the preceding letter.*

sophos reddidissent. Quis enim tunc inuiseret Almam Matrem destitutam omni commeatu? opportunè his tenebris Fauor Tuus occurrit, illustrans nos omnes, luménque accendens de suo lumine,

Vt nihilo-minus Tibi luceat, cùm nobis accenderit.

Neque enim passus es illum Fluuium, qui tantae poeticae, tantae eruditionis nobis conscius est, palustri opere & vliginoso intercipi: cùm non est tanti totus ille maritimus tractus (Oceani praeda et deliciae) vt irrigui Musarum horti, floribus suis sternentes Rempublicam, prae ariditate flaccescerent. Sed siccitas anni huius derisit incoeptum et plus effecit quàm mille Redemptores exequi possent. Quanquam non mirari non possumus, vnde fit vt nullus ferè elabatur dies, qui non hostes aliquos nobis aperiat: quidam stomachantur praedia, alij immunitates carpunt, nonnulli Fluuium inuident, multi Academias integras subuersas volunt, neque illi è faece vulgi tantùm qui eruditionem simplicitati Christianae putant aduersam, sed homines nobilioris ignorantiae, qui literas imminuere spiritus, generosósque animos frangere et retundere clamitant. Tu verò, Patrone noster, qui elegantias doctrinae nitorémque spirans purpuram et eruditionem miscuisti; dilue, fuga hos omnes, praesertim sericatam hanc stultitiam contere, Academiaéque iura, dignitatem, Fluuium placidissimo fauorum tuorum afflatu nobis tuere. Quod quidem non minus expectamus à Te, quem singularis doctrina exemit à populo, & quasi mixtam personam reddidit quàm si Episcopi more pristino Cancellis praeficerentur.

VI. *Ad R. Naunton, Secret.*

Gratiae de Fluuio

Vir Honoratissime.

QVANTA hilaritate aspicit Alma Mater filios suos iam emancipatos, conseruantes sibi Illos Fontes, à quibus ipsi olim hauserunt? Quis enim sicca vbera et mammas

4 lumine. 6 es, 16 Multi 18 nobiliores *written first, then corrected to* nobilioris : *all modern editions read* nobiliores 20 verò VI. 30 Hilaritate

arentes tam nobilis parentis aequo animo ferre posset? neque sanè dubitamus vlli, si prae defectu aquae, commeatûsque inopiâ, desererentur collegia, pulcherrimaéque Musarum domus tanquam viduae effoetae, aut ligna exucca & marcida, alumnis suis orbarentur, quin communes Reipublicae lachrymae alterum nobis Fluuium effunderent. Quare plurimum debemus constantiae fauoris tui, qui restinxisti sitim exarescentium Musarum, et Xerxes istos, alterósque maris quasi Flagellatores expugnatos fusósque nobis dedisti. Quid enim inuident aquas, quas non nobis habemus sed irrigati ipsi vniuersum regnum aspergimus? Sed aliorum iniuriae tuarum virtutum pabula sunt, qui lemas istas et festucas, Reipublicae oculo haerentes, tam diligenter amoues; certè adeò festinasti ad gratitudines tuas cum emolumento nostro coniunctas, vt iam compensemur abundè, neque ampliùs quaerendum sit Tibi, Almae Nutrici quid reponas.

VII. *Ad Ful. Grevil*

Gratiae de Fluuio

Vir Honoratissime.

SCITE et appositè fecisti Fluuium nostrum conseruans altero eloquentiae Fluuio, paludúmque istos siccatores (solem officio suo priuantes) vi verborum Tuorum obruens. Neque sanè quispiam incedit Te instructior ad omnem causam, paratiórue siue à doctrina, siue ab vsu; vtrinque mirus es et exercitatissimus. Quare nos tertium praedictis adiungimus Gratiarum Fluuium, de humanitate tuâ singulari, studióque in nos iam olim perspectissimo, quippe qui eximiè semper fouisti literatos, eósque cum tineis et blattis rixantes, exuens puluere, in theatrum et lucem produxisti. Tantùm rogamus, vt pergas, & inter nouos honorum cumulos, quod expectamus indies futurum, Almae Matris amorem tecum simul euehas. Interim, si qui alij exurgant promissores magnifici et hiantes, qui, sub specie publici commodi, Academiae

VI. 1 parentis, 5–6 Lachrymae 8 exarscentium 11 aspergimus. 13 haerentes

VII. 19 siccatores, 22 vsu, 23 quare 29 matris 31 qui

incommodum videntur allaturi; os importunorum hominum Authoritate tuâ plurimâ & Eloquentiâ non minori nobis obstrue.

VIII. *Ad F. Bacon, Cancell.*

Gratiae de Instaurationis Libro Academiae donato

4° Nov. 1620

Illustrissime Domine.

PROLEM Tuam suauissimam, nuper in lucem publicam, nostrámque praesertim, editam, non gremio solùm (quod innuis) sed et ambabus vlnis osculísque ei aetati debitis excipientes, protinus tanquam Nobilem Filium (more nostro) Magistrum Artium renunciauimus. Optimè enim hoc conuenit Partui tuo, qui nouas scientiarum regiones terrásque veteribus incognitas primus demonstrat: ex quo illustrius assecutus es nomen, quàm Repertores Noui Orbis comparârunt. Illi terram inuenerunt, crassissimum elementum, Tu subtilitates Artium infinitas. Illi barbara omnia, Tu non nisi cultissima, elegantiásque ipsas exhibes. Illi magneticâ acu freti sunt. Tu penetrantiori intellectûs acumine; cuius nisi incredibilis fuisset vis, nunquam in tantis negotijs, quibus meritissimè districtus es, ea, quae fugerunt tot philosophos vmbrâ et otio diffluentes, eruisses. Quare multiplex est laetitia nostra: primò gratulamur optimo Regi nostro, qui prospicit, vt cùm ipse eruditionis Princeps sit, illi etiam honores qui finitimi sunt, et quasi accolae Maiestatis, literaturae suae et vicinitati respondeant: dein Hon. Tuo gratulamur, qui filio auctus es tali ingenio praedito: tum Academiae nostrae, quae per Tuum Partum, ex Matre nunc Auia facta est: denique huic aetati quae talem virum protulit, cum quinque millibus annorum de palmâ certantem. Id vnum dolemus, Bibliothecam nostram rudiorem esse impexiorémque, quàm vt tantum Hospitem excipiat: vtcumque, cùm olim ab *Archiepiscopo Eboracensi Summo Angliae Cancellario extructa fuerit, illam nunc denuò ex

* Rotheram (*marginal note in MS.*)

VIII. 9 artium 12 noui 13–14 elementum. 18 ea 22 sit; 23 suae, 31 fuerit:

aedibus Eboracensibus ab altero Cancellario INSTAVRARI, inter Arcana Prouidentiae planè reponimus. Faxit Deus vt quos profectus feceris in Sphaerâ Naturae, facias etiam in Gratiae: ѵ́tque maturè absoluas quae complexus es animo, ad eius gloriam, Reipublicae emolumentum, aeternitatem nominis Tui subsidiúmque

Magnificentiae Tuae deuotissimorum
Procancellarij
Reliq.

IX. *Ad Mounteg., Thesaurar.*

Gratulatio

18 Dec. 1620

Illustrissime Domine.

PENDVLAM hanc dignitatem diu expectantem magnas aliquas virtutes tandem meritis tuis votísque nostris conspirantibus obtinuisti. Quis enim rectiùs Thesauris Regijs praefici possit quàm qui, Iustitiam priùs tanto cum honore atque acclamatione administrans, distribuendi modum omnem rationémque callet? Et licet, quò proprior sis Regi, eò videaris nobis remotior, confidimus tamen vt arbores, quantò altiùs crescunt, tantò etiam altiùs agunt radices: sic merita tua ita ascensura, vt eorum vis et virtus ad nos descendat. Quare summè gratulamur tibi de nouo hoc cumulo honorum, qui tamen votis nostris nondum respondent. Ea est enim pertinacia desideriorum nostrorum, atque immortalitas, vt semper post nouas dignitates, alias tibi quaerant et moliantur. Nimirum id assecuta sunt merita Tua maxima, vt Almam Matrem spe nouâ grauidam semper atque praegnantem effecerint. Tantùm quocunque, Domine, ascendas, sume tecum amorem illum quo soles beare

Amplitudini tuae deuotissimos
Procancellarium
Rel.

9 *For unabbreviated form see end of* III.
IX. 12 tuis, 14 qui 17 arbores 21 honorum 24 nimirum 25 grauidam, 26 praegnantē *MS.* (*misread* praegnante *in modern editions*)

X. *Ad R. Naunt. Burgen. Elect.*

13 Jan. 1620 [i.e. 1620/1]

Honoratissime Domine.

TAM eximiè de nobis meritus es, vt res nostras omnes cum Honore Tuo coniunctas esse velimus. Quare frequentissimo Senatu, plenissimis suffragijs elegimus Te tribunum Parlamentarium, nos nostráque omnia priuilegia, fundos, aedificia, vniuersam Musarum supellectilem, etiam Fluuium non minùs de praeterito gratum, quàm de futuro supplicem, integerrimae tuae fidei commendantes. Magna est haec, neque quotidianae virtutis prouincia gerere personam Academiae, omniúmque Artium molem et pondus sustinere, sed perspectissimus tuus in nos amor, praestantissimaéque animi dotes effecerunt, vt Alma Mater libentissimè caput reclinet in tuo sinu, oculúsque Reipub: postquam circumspiciens reperisset Te, quasi in tuis palpebris acquiescat. Quare nos omnes ad prudentiae eloquentiaéque tuae praesidium festinantes excipe: Antiquitas praeripuit Tibi gloriam extruendae Academiae, reliquit conseruandae. Deus faueat Tibi & concedat vt terrestres tui honores cum coelestibus certent, et superentur.

XI. *Ad T. Coventry, Attorn. Cognitorem*

Gratulatio

29 Jan. 1620 [i.e. 1620/1]

Clarissime Vir.

PERMITTE vt nos etiam in praedam partémque tecum veniamus: neque enim sic effugies cum honoribus, quin laetitia nostra te assequatur. Certè non diu est ex quo gratulati sumus tibi: eccum nunc altera occasio, adeò festinat virtus tua: quòd si tertia detur et quarta, paratos nos habebis ad gratulationem, vt sic vnâ operâ vtriusque Reipublicae

X. 5. *After* tribunum *the word* Burgensem *was written in the MS., and then crossed through* 15 prudentiae, XI. 23 assequetur.

calculum et ciuilis et literariae adipiscaris. Tu verò promptitudinem amoris nostri, non passim expositam, boni consulas, curésque vt tuus in nos amor, antehac satìs perspectus, nunc cum honore geminetur. Quòd si forense quippiam nos spectans, dum incumbis muneri, occurrat, nos chartis et aeternitate occupatos, temporarijs hísce negotiolis libera. Haud frustra impendes operam nobis omnia fauorum tuorum momenta apicésque perpensuris et compensaturis.

XII. *Ad Heath, Sollicitorem Procuratorem*

Gratulatio

29 Jan. 1620 [i.e. 1620/1]

Vir Dignissime.

SIC à Natura comparatum est, Ignis et Virtus semper ascendunt, vtriusque enim splendor et claritas humilia loca deprecantur. Quare optimè fecit Rex Serenissimus, qui virtutes tuas magnis negotijs pares prouexit, noluítque vt minori sphaerâ quàm pro latitudine meritorum tuorum circumscribereris. Nos verò de hoc tuo progressu non minus Reipublicae gratulamur quàm tibi, rogamúsque vt quando beneficia tua peruagantur Angliam, nos etiam inuisant: ita excipiemus illa, vt benignius hospitium, et erga te propensius, haud vsquam forsitan reperias.

XIII. *Ad Archiep. Cantuar.*

De Bibliopolis Lond.

29 Jan. 1620 [i.e. 1620/1]

Sanctissime Pater.

CVM caeterae ecclesiae tam perspicaci diligentiâ incubes, concede vt nos etiam benignitate alarum tuarum et virtute fruamur. Praesertim hoc tempore, in quo paucorum

XI. 2 expositam 3 amor 5 muneri

XII. *Title: the marks of abbreviation* Sollicitorē Procuratorē *in the MS. have been overlooked by modern editors* 13 et *wrongly inserted after* negotijs *in modern editions*

auaritia liberalibus artibus dominatura est, nisi humanitas tua*, superiori aestate sponte suauitérque patefacta, nunc etiam laborantibus Musis succurrat. Ferunt enim Londinenses Bibliopolas suum potius emolumentum quàm publicum spectantes (quae res et naturae legibus et hominum summè contraria est) monopolijs quibusdam inhiare, ex quo timemus Librorum precia auctum iri, et priuilegia nostra imminutum. Nos igitur hoc metu affecti, vtì sanguis solet in re dubiâ ad cor festinare, ita ad Te confugimus primariam partem ecclesiastici corporis, orantes vt quicquid consilij auaritia ceperit aduersus aut immunitates nostras aut commune literarum et literatorum commodum, id omne dexterrimâ tuâ in obeundis rebus prudentiâ dissipetur. Deus Opti: Max: tua beneficia, quae nos soluendo non sumus, in suas tabulas accepti transferat.

XIV. *Ad Fr. Bacon, Cancell.*

De Bibliop. Lond.

29 Jan. 1620 [i.e. 1620/1]

Illustrissime Domine.

TV quidem semper Patronus noster es, etiam tacentibus nobis, quantò magìs cùm rogamus, ídque pro Libris, de quibus nusquam rectiùs quàm apud Te agitur. Accepimus enim Londinenses Librarios omnia transmarina scripta ad monopolium reuocare moliri, neque ratione habitâ Chartae nostrae à Serenissimo Principe Henrico 8° indultae, neque Studiosorum Sacculi, qui etiam nunc maeret et ingemiscit. Ecquid permittis, Domine? Curasti tu quidem *Instauratione* tuâ, quò minùs exteris Libris indigeremus, sed tamen comparatio & in honorem tuum cedet, nostrúmque emolumentum. Quare vnicè obsecramus, vt qui tot subsidia attuleris ad progressum doctrinae, hâc etiam in parte nobis opituleris. Aspicis multitudinem Librorum indies gliscentem, praesertim in Theologiâ, cuius Libri si alij alijs (tanquam montes

* ferina missa (*marginal note in MS.*)

XIII. 2 tua aestate, sponte, 4 emolumentum, 5 spectantes,

olim) imponerentur, verisimile est, eos illuc, quò cognitio ipsa pertingit, ascensuros. Quòd si et numerus Scriptorum intumescat, et precium, quae abyssus crumenae tantos sumptus aequabit? Iam verò miserum est, pecuniam retardare illam, cui natura spiritum dederit feracem gloriae, et coeleste ingenium quasi ad metalla damnari. Qui augent precia Librorum, prosunt vendentibus Libros non ementibus, hoc est cessatoribus non studiosis. Haec tu omnium optimè vides, quare causam nostram nósque ipsos Tibi, Téque Deo Opti: Max: intimis precibus commendamus.

XV. *Ad J. Leigh, Capitalem Iustitiarium Angl. (Camden)*

Gratulatio

6 Feb. 1620 [i.e. 1620/1]

Honoratissime Domine.

FAMA promotionis tuae gratissimè appulit ad nos omnes haud ita certè studijs chartísque obuolutos, quin aures nostrae tibi pateant. Imò prorsus censemus permultum interesse alacritatis publicae, vt bonorum praemia citissimè promulgentur, quò suauiùs virtutibus, tuo exemplo compensatis, ad vnum omnes incumbamus. Quare tam verè quàm libenter gratulamur tibi, nec minùs etiam Reipublicae, quam nunc pleno gradu ingrediens beneficijs tuis percurres. Nos etiam haud minimam fauoris tui partem speramus, orantes vt immunitates nostrae à Serenissimis Regibus concessae ab Augustissimo Iacobo auctae tuâ operâ conseruentur; eadem manus et tuum tibi largita est honorem, et priuilegia nostra confirmauit; in quâ dextrâ et fide coniuncti, in caeteris haud diuellamur. Quòd si oppidani nostri (more suo) Musarum iura et diplomata arrodant; tuus amor

XIV. 3 precium 4 aequabit. 5 dederit,
XV. *Title*: J. Leigh *MS.*: *misread by modern editors* F. Leigh 17 ad] *om. Pickering, Willmott* 19 nunc] hunc *Pickering, Willmott*: hinc *Grosart* 23 manus, largitus

et authoritas istos sorices nobis abigat. Demosthenes Atheniensis doluit se victum opificum antelucanâ industriâ, nostrae etiam Athenae artésque obscuris opificum artibus superari dolebunt. Sed tua humanitas haec nobis expediet. Deus fortunet tibi hunc honorem, et faxit, vt tibi gloriae sit, omnibus saluti.

XVI. *Ad Cranfield, Thesaurar.*

Gratulatio

8 Octob. 1621

Illustrissime Domine.

CONCEDE vt Honoribus nuperis, tanquam partubus Virtutum Tuarum, Alma Mater accurrens gratuletur: solent enim Studiosorum suffragia enixus gloriae, sollicitudine in futurum plenos, haud parum leuare; praesertim quum ipsi non solùm rectum de Bene-merentibus iudicium hausisse ab Antiquis, sed et ad Posteros transmissuri videantur. Quare post Principis manum honoribus refertam, non est quòd nostram quoque, cum amoris symbolo festinantem, recuses. Sic apud veterum aras, post ingentes Hecatombas, exiguam thuris micam adoleri legimus. Tu, Domine, vicisti; tuere nos ita vt fortunae nostrae, intra ambitum amplexúsque foelicitatis Tuae receptae, communi calore foueantur. Et cùm ob perspicacitatem singularem iam olim Regi notam atque signatam dignissimè praeficiaris Fisco, etiam Academiam in Thesauris habe: iustissimè potes sub hoc Principe, in quo doctrinae fructus atque vsus mirificè relucet. Certè, si quantum eruditio Regis profuerit Reipublicae, tantum fauoris nobis impertias, abundè succurres

Magnificentiae tuae addictissimis
Procancellario
Rel.

3 Athenae,

XVI. 9 Tuarum gratuletur. 10 gloriae 17 vicisti *stop undecipherable in MS.: Pickering and Willmott print* vicisti? 23 fructus,

XVII. *Ad R. Creighton*

[6 May, ?1627]

Erudite Cr[n].

COMITER scribis atque eleganter; quae est vestra felicitas qui puro Academiae farre vtimini. Ego hìc pultibus vescor et glande, more maiorum, multos iam annos Anglicè viuens garriénsque. Verùm, quod rem spectat, si placeat vices meas tantisper supplere donec Academia orationem tuam imbibat probétque, per me non stabit quò minùs, spe prouectâ atque adultâ, ipsam possessionem adeas, ἀγαθῇ γε τύχῃ. Proin iube Thorndick nostrum, ni graue est, librum tibi Oratorium lampadémque tradat. Verùm heus! cautè incipe, cohibens adeò stylum ingeniúmque; non quod nunc indulgeas alterutri, sed quod deinceps indultum nollem. Perpende, non tam quod tibi conueniat scribenti, quàm quod Academiae tuo calamo scribenti: multa Critt[i] meo quadrabunt, quae almae matri inconcinna erunt atque enormia. Quare scripturus, finge tibi matronam sanctam, venerandam, oris prisci atque augusti; huius tu es commotria atque ornatrix. Iam si inter commendandum adhibeas ei calamistros vtì iuuenculae, ὀφθαλμῶν ὑπογραφὰς καὶ ἐπιτρίμματα παρειῶν inducens; certè non tam ornas illam, qui infers manum grauitati. Quin nec demisso, quando ad magnates cogitas, stylo vtare, sed modestè grandi; etsi tu qui scribis (vtì quiuis priuatus) inferioris sis subsellij, Academia vniuersim sumpta vna est è proceribus, inter patritios sedens et praetextatos. Quare et Procancellarius Academiam simulans vel maximos magnatum inter eundum summouet: tu hanc personam indue scripturus, tuúmque iudicium tibi Lictor esto. Dein, oratio clara sit, perspicua, pellucens. Obscurus sermo negotijs ineptus; quae cùm plerumque implicata sint, nisi candidâ phrasi telam explices, perit negotium quasi ex nubibus Ixionis congressus. Tandem, ne et ipse peccem, breuis sit sermo, atque pressus. Aliud oratio, aliud

XVII. *From a copy, not autograph, in* MS. Jones B 57 *in Dr Williams's Library. First printed by Grosart in 1874* 8 minùs 10 Oratorium, 11 incipe ingeniúmque, 14 scribenti, 17 augusti, 19 ὑπογραφαὶ *Grosart* 26 eundem 31 Ixionis congressus *conj. Ed*: Ixioneis congressum *MS.*

epistola. Parce doctrinae in epistolis; perorans, paululùm indulge: ne tum quidem multùm, neque nostrae matronae conuenit, cui tu es ab ornatu. Vt semel dicam; Oratio perfecta, vtì vir, *τετράγωνος* est, grauis, nobilis, perspicua, succincta. Haec tu optimè nosti; neque eò dico: sed lubet garrire paulò. Iupiter! o quot iam anni sunt ex quo vel apicem Latinum pertuli! Et amor alioqui loquax est; vtì etiam senectus, quam aetatem in hâc palaestrâ consecutus mihi videor. Proinde audi Platonem: *Δοκεῖ μοι χρῆναι παρὰ τῶν πρεσβυτῶν πυνθάνεσθαι, ὥσπερ τινὰ ὁδὸν προεληλυθότων, ἣν καὶ ἡμᾶς ἴσως δεήσει πορεύεσθαι, ποία τίς ἐστι.*

Tu vero vale, mi proorator, amáque
Tuum G. H.

II Nonas V̄.
è Chelsiano.

XVIII. *Ad Lanc. Andrewes, Episc.*

Sanctissime Pater,

STATIM à solatio aspectûs Tui, Ego auctior iam gaudio atque distentior, Cantabrigiam redij. Quid enim manerem? Habui viaticum fauoris Tui, quod longiori multò itineri sufficeret. Nunc obrutus Academicis negotijs, aegrè hoc tempus illis succido: non quin pectus meum plenum Tui sit, atque effusissimum in omnia officia, quae praestet mea paruitas; sed vt faciliùs ignoscas occupato calamo, qui etiam ferians nihil Tuâ perfectione dignum procudere possit. Vtcunque Tua lenitas non ita interpretabitur mea haec scribendi interualla, ac si iuuenili potius impetu correptus, quàm adductus maturo consilio, primas dedissem literas, ideóque *praeferuida illa desideria silentio suo sepulta nunc languescere, vt halitus tenuiores solent, qui primo caloris suasu excitati atque expergefacti, vbi sursum processerint paulò, frigefacti demum relabuntur.* Hoc

6 quot] *marginal note* octo 8 etiam *altered in MS. from* jam 9 χρῆναι] χρηστὸν *Grosart* 15 *The copyist has added what could not have been in Herbert's original,* 'circa ann. 1627'

XVIII. *From the original autograph in* B.M. MS. Sloane 118 ff. 34–5 *Printed first by Pickering in 1836* 17–19, 27–30, *and* 472 8–10 : *words here italicized are underlined in the MS.*

quidem illis accidere amat, qui celeritatem affectuum raptìm sequentes, ad omnem eorum auram vacillant. Ego, non nisi meditatò, obrepsi ad fauorem Tuum; perfectionibus Tuis, meis desiderijs probè cognitis, excussis perpensísque. Cùm enim vim cogitationum in vitam meam omnem conuertissem, & ex alterâ parte acuissem me aspectu virtutum Tuarum; huc, illuc commeando, eò deueni animo, vt nunquam cessandum mihi ducerem, *nunquam fatiscendum, donec lacteam aliquam viam ad candorem Mentis Tuae ducentem aut reperissem aut fecissem.* Neque quòd ignotior eram, retundebatur vnquam impetus: quippe, qui sic colligebam; si tam abiectus sim, vt laboribus meis plurimis atque assiduâ obseruantiâ, ramenta quaepiam ex tantâ Humanitatis massâ, quae apud Te visitur, abscindere non possim, absque molestâ aliorum ac frigidâ commendatione, si huc reciderit omnis studiorum spes fructúsque:

Cur ego laborem notus esse tam prauè,
Cùm stare gratis cum silentio possim?

Quòd tamen haec omnia succedant ex voto, quòd reclusae sint fores, receptúsque sim in aliquem apud Honorem Tuum locum, magìs id adeò factum esse mansuetudine Tuâ incomparabili, quàm meis meritis vllis, semper lubentissiméque agnoscam: imò precabor enixè, me tum priuari tam communi hâc luce, quàm Tuâ, cùm id agnoscere vnquam desinam. Quanquam, cùm grauibus duobus muneribus fungar apud Meos, Rhetoris in hunc annum, & in plures Oratoris, permitte, Pater, hoc impetrem, vt cedam aliquantisper expectationi hominum, rariúsque paulò fodiam in Vintoniensi agro, dum Rhetorici satagam: quamuìs enim sexcenta huiusmodi praediola Tuâ gratiâ permutare nolim, maius tamen piaculum reor, deesse publico muneri, quàm priuato, latiúsque manare iniustitiae peccatum, quàm negligentiae. illic constringor debito; hìc etiam teneor, sed laxioribus vinculis, quaéque amor saepe remittit: illud necessarium magìs factu, hoc verò longè iucundius, nobiliúsque: vt quod Philosophus de Tactu & Visu, id appositè admodum huc

3 meditatò] meditate *Grosart* 4 cogniti 20 Honorem Tuum *abbreviated* H.T. *in MS.*: *also in* 473.2 22 semper, 26 plures, 30 praediola. nolim; 36 visu,

transferatur. Appetit tempus, cùm excusso altero iugo, dimidiâque operis parte leuatus, ad mea in Honorem Tuum officia erectior solutiórque redibo, ex ipsâ intermissione animos ducens. Interim, sic existimes nihil Mortalium firmiori flagrare in Te desiderio, quàm meum pectus; neque vlla negotia (quippe quae caput petant, non cor) Tui in me dominij ius imminuere posse, nedum rescindere. Vnà cum promotionibus Academicis maternísque, assumsi mecum propensionem in Patrem. Crescent illae, crescetis amores. Cui sententiae si fidem adhibeas, assensúmque Tuum veritati omni familiarem largiaris, *σὺν τῇ εὐλογίᾳ σοῦ προσεπιμετρουμένῃ* beabis

Filium tuum obsequentissimum
GEORGIUM HERBERT.

Ignosce (Heros illustrissime) quòd pronomina mea adeò audacter incedant in hâc epistolâ: potui refercire lineas Honoribus, Magnif., Celsitud., sed non patitur, vt mihi videtur, Romana elegantia, periodíque vetus rotunditas. Quare malui seruire auribus Tuis, creberrimâ Antiquitatis lectione tersis atque expolitis, quàm luxuriae saeculi, ambitionísque strumae, non adeò sanatae ab optimo Rege nostro quin turgescat indies, atque efferat se, indulgere.

To the right honourable and reverend Father in God, my L. Bishop of Winchester, one of the Kings most honorable privy-Counsaile.

8 Academicis, 11 *εὐλογία* 17 Magnif. Celsitud. 23–5 *Address on back of letter*

COMMENTARY

THE TEMPLE

General Note

THE basis of the present text is the *editio princeps* of 1633, and every deviation is recorded in the Apparatus Criticus. A single square bracket following any word in the footnotes, e.g. bone], indicates that that is the reading of *1633*, the MSS. agreeing with it unless otherwise stated. All the variant readings of *B* and *W* (see pp. l–lvi) are recorded except such varieties in spelling and punctuation as are without significance.

There is no uniformity, either in the MSS. or in *1633*, in the use of initial capitals for pronouns referring to God, and the practice of *1633* is followed in our text, except where otherwise noted.

It was evidently the intention of the printer of the first edition to use the consonantal *v* instead of *u*, as is also generally done, though with less consistency, in the MSS., but seven instances of consonantal *u* occur in the text of *1633*. This was clearly an oversight (e.g. in *The Priesthood*, l. 28, *conuey* and *conveys* are found in the same line), as all seven were corrected to *v* in the second edition. It was also his intention to use the consonantal *j*, but two instances (*iudgement*, *Ieat*) escaped his eye in the first edition and were corrected in the second. All these corrections are adopted in the present text.

The preterite and participial *-ed* is always to be scanned as a separate syllable, except where the abbreviation *'d* is found. The MSS. almost always observe this distinction, which is uniformly observed in *1633*. The only possible exception is at the end of a line, where a feminine ending may or may not be intended. *Prayer* is always scanned as two syllables, but *power* and *flower* as one.

The form *its* is found twice only in *B*, in *The Church-porch*, l. 266 (where *W* has *it's*) and *Josephs coat*, l. 3 (the poem is not in *W*); *1633* follows *B* in these two instances, and has *its* also, where *B* has *his*, in *Vertue*, l. 7. Everywhere else the modern *its* is represented by *his* or *her*. The conjunction *than* is always printed *then*. The modern distinction between *of* and *off* is uniformly observed in *1633*, but the form *off* is not found at all in the MSS. *1633* is more particular than the MSS. in differentiating *loose* and *lose*, but there remains an occasional ambiguity; such light as spelling can give is recorded in the footnotes.

The reader would do well to bear in mind that Herbert as often uses *grief* of physical as of mental pain, and that *still* generally means 'always'. He should also be prepared for Herbert's frequent use of *to* in the sense of 'compared with', e.g. *Providence*, l. 121: 'How harsh are thorns to pears!' and *Confession*, l. 30: 'They shall be thick and cloudie to my breast'; and *after* often means 'according to', e.g. *Sighs and Grones*, ll. 1–2: 'O do not use me After my sinnes', and *Mans medley*, ll. 17–18: 'should take place After the trimming, not the stuffe.' There is occasional ambiguity in Herbert's use of personal pronouns.

The Printers to the Reader (Page 3)

The authorship of this preface is well attested. John Ferrar in his Life of his brother (*The Ferrar Papers*, p. 59), Barnabas Oley (*Herbert's Remains*, 1652, sig. b 8ᵛ), and Walton (*Lives*, 1670, p. 76) ascribe it to Nicholas Ferrar.

PAGE 4, l. 4. *My Master*. Cf. *The Odour*, p. 174.

l. 19. *an Ecclesiasticall dignitie*. The prebend of Leighton Ecclesia in Lincoln Cathedral, the property of which was at Leighton Bromswold, Huntingdonshire (see Introduction, above, p. xxxi). John Ferrar (*The Ferrar Papers*, p. 58) confirms the statement of the preface that Herbert was anxious to have the prebend transferred to his friend Nicholas Ferrar, whose home at Little Gidding was about five miles from Leighton Bromswold, and that he was instead persuaded to undertake the repair of the ruined church. *Letters* XIV–XVI show Herbert's zeal in the restoration.

l. 28. Walton (*Lives*, p. 78) identifies the *friend* as Ferrar's first cousin, Arthur Woodnoth, who was with Herbert at his death.

The Church-porch (Page 6)

This introductory poem is to be regarded as a separate section of *The Temple*, as in both MSS. and in the early printed editions the page-heading is 'The Church-porch', which is replaced by 'The Church' for the rest of the volume, except for *Superliminare*, which has no page-heading, and *The Church Militant* at the end, which has its own page-heading. It differs, too, from the lyrical poems in being didactic, as they seldom are, except *Charms and Knots*, which resembles *The Church-porch* in manner. Donne's verse 'Letters to Severall Personages' have many gnomic lines, which may well have served Herbert for a model. The metre had been used for similar didactic purposes by Southwell, Breton, Brooke, and other Elizabethan writers. The many differences between the earlier and later MSS., and the many alterations in *W*, suggest that Herbert began this poem early and often revised it.

The long period of revision may have led to some repetition and some overlapping, but the main divisions can be thus set out: I Introduction, II–IV Chastity, V–IX Temperance, X–XII Swearing, XIII Lying, XIV–XVI Idleness, XVII–XIX Education, XX Constancy, XXI Sincerity, XXII–XXV Self-discipline, XXVI–XXX Use of Money, XXXI–XXXII Dress, XXXIII–XXXIV Gambling, XXXV–XLII Conversation, XLIII–XLV Behaviour to Superiors, XLVI Friendship, XLVII–XLVIII Suretyship, XLIX–LV Social Intercourse, LVI–LIX Purpose of Life, LX–LXI Foreign Travel, LXII Cleanliness, LXIII–LXV Almsgiving, LXVI–LXXV Public Worship, LXXVI–LXXVII Summary.

Dr. William Dillingham printed a Latin version in his *Poemata varii Argumenti* (1678). Dr. E. C. Lowe published in 1867 a useful annotated edition of *The Church-porch*.

The title *Perirranterium* was prefixed in *W* to the quatrain beginning 'Thou, whom the former precepts have Sprinkled' (p. 25), but was transferred in *B* to its present position. There is nothing in the formal arrangement in *B* or *1633* to corroborate Palmer's view (*The English Works of Herbert*, ii. 118) that the word applies to the first stanza only of *The Church-porch*, and the whole poem is better regarded as the preparation of the reader for going on into 'The Church'. *Perirrhanterium* (the *h* was added with a caret in *B*) is the Greek term (Lat. *aspergillum*) for an instrument for sprinkling holy water.

l. 2. *rate and price*. Again in *The Pearl*, p. 89, l. 35.

l. 3. *Verser*, like 'versifier', a more modest claim than poet for the writer of the didactic introduction. Jonson, as reported by Drummond, 'thought not Bartas a poet, but a verser; because he wrote not fiction'.

l. 4. Cf. R. Southwell, 'Fortunes Falsehoode', l. 2: 'Sly fortunes subtilltyes, in baytes of happiness Shroude hookes', and Cic. Sen. xiii. 44: 'divine Plato escam malorum appellat voluptatem'; but Herbert, characteristically reversing the thought, uses pleasure to allure to good.

l. 9. *thy lesson*. So *B* and the first four editions (the line is differently worded in *W*), but from 1638 *the lesson*, which is perhaps what the author intended.

l. 17. *his*: its. See General Note, p. 475.

l. 18. Lowe finds a reference to Prov. xii. 4: 'A vertuous woman is a crowne to her husband: but she that maketh ashamed, is as rottennesse in his bones.'

ll. 19–20. If there had been no divine precept of monogamy, man's acquisitiveness would have led him to appropriate woman, just as the landlords of Herbert's day were enclosing the common lands.

l. 24. *crosse*: perverse, contrarious. Again in l. 395.

l. 25. *the third glasse*. Burton (*Anat. of Melan.*, 'Democritus to the Reader', p. 44) cites 'Panyasis the poet' on the fourth glass making men mad, but actually Panyasis, like Herbert, attributes this to the third.

l. 30. *keep the round*: i.e. refill my glass each time the bottle comes round.

l. 33. *W* has *all kinds*, but *all kinde* (*B* and *1633*) was in common use.

l. 35. *devest*: alienate or convey away a vested right.

l. 37. *wine-sprung*: intoxicated. William Gurnall uses the word in *The Christian in Complete Armour* (1658) of a man who thinks 'he can skip over the Moone'.

l. 39. *his* refers to the wine-sprung man, the *another* of l. 37. 'I may not drink what the hardened drinker allows himself; need I humour him to my own undoing?' Cf. *Manchester al Mondo. Contemplatio Mortis* (1633), p. 145: 'forced healths at great feastes is a barbarous fashion: . . . the ciuility of very Pagans commanded liberty of their cuppes.'

l. 42. It is unduly modest to surrender your better judgement to a social convention for fear of discourtesy (l. 46).

l. 46. *a beast*. Cf. *Outl. Pvbs*, No. 931: 'Wine makes all sorts of creatures at table.'

l. 50. An echo of Phil. iii. 19: 'whose God is their belly, and whose glorie is in their shame.'

l. 64. Repeated in *Priest to T.*, p. 283, l. 32.

l. 66. A gaming term, or cf. Hooker, *Eccl. Pol.*, Pref. ii, § 3: 'their ministers forrein estimation hitherto hath beene the best stake in their hedge.'

l. 80. Borrowed from Donne's 'To Mr. Tilman after he had taken orders', l. 30. Again in *Priest to T.*, p. 277, l. 29.

l. 88. *Chase brave employments*. Though England was at peace in James I's reign, four of Herbert's brothers served in foreign wars (Herbert of

Cherbury, *Autobiography*, ed. S. Lee, pp. 11–14). John Wesley, in rewriting this stanza, substituted *base* for *brave*.

l. 91. *most of sloth.* Cf. *Priest to T.*, p. 274, l. 8: 'The great and nationall sin of this Land he esteems to be Idlenesse.'

l. 92. *thy flegme.* Here figuratively: phlegm was that one of the four bodily humours' which was supposed, when predominant, to cause constitutional indolence.

l. 93. *Thy Gentrie bleats.* For an appreciation of this bold phrase, see Aldous Huxley, *Texts and Pretexts* (1932), p. 159.

l. 96. *Are gone to grasse.* The phrase was already in use in Herbert's day of persons living in idleness, like horses turned out to pasture.

l. 99. *mark a partridge.* The sporting use of *mark* (mark down, watch) is found in *The Book of St. Albans* (1486).

l. 100. *Some ship them over*: i.e. send them abroad or to the colonies, with a suggestion of 'send packing, get rid of', as in *Hamlet*, IV. i. 30 and *Titus Andronicus*, I. i. 206. In *Priest to T.*, ch. XXXII, where Herbert deals with the idleness of the rich, he recommends that younger sons should improve their knowledge 'in those new Plantations' or 'travel into *Germany*, and *France*' (p. 278); but, as he points out in *Letter* XII, p. 376, l. 13, 'the time of breeding is the time of doing children good'; parents must not neglect *this art* of education.

l. 102. 'If thou art not moved by thy child being in God's image (cf. l. 379 and Gen. i. 26), be careful of him as being in thine own image.'

ll. 107–8. Cf. *Outl. Pvbs*, No. 309: 'He is not poore that hath little, but he that desireth much' and No. 403: 'Hee is rich enough that wants nothing.'

l. 117. *stowre*: stalwart, unbending. The suggestion of sturdiness follows well the physical metaphor, *knits the bones*. Wright's *English Dialect Dict.* quotes 'A staunch and stoure stickler for his lordship's politics'. Even in the seventeenth century the word was found obscure, and from 1674 was replaced by *tower*. The reading of both MSS. is *sowre*, which should be retained if a satisfactory meaning could be found for it. Grosart retains it and explains it as answering to the Scottish 'dour'; but Palmer rightly objects that, in the six instances of *sour* in *The Temple*, Herbert 'always employs it in an offensive sense'.

l. 118. *thrall*: here and in l. 286 and in *The Sacrifice*, l. 167, a noun, meaning 'thraldom' (cf. *bond* in next line). The abstract noun is used eight times by Southwell, and Milton uses *thrall* for thraldom in 'Psalm LXXXI', l. 28: 'And led thee out of thrall.'

l. 120. The sense can be inferred from the close parallel in *Miserie*, p. 102, ll. 76–8. Nature intended man to steer towards his haven like a ship, but instead he shelves himself on a rock; and this reef on which he founders is his own indulgent self. The reading of *W* is perhaps easier: 'And though hee bee a ship, is his owne shelf.' Cf. W. Habington, *Castara* (1635), 'Et Exultavit Humiles', ll. 46–9 (possibly imitating Herbert):

> Few sayle, but by some storme are lost.
> Let them themselves
> Beware, for they are their owne shelves.
> Man still himselfe hath cast away.

l. 124. The *clue* (ball of thread) comes undone.

l. 128. *sconses*: bulwarks, outworks; here, figuratively, safeguards.

l. 131. Cf. Job xxviii. 5: 'As for the earth, out of it commeth bread.'

l. 132. Quoted from the Burial Office.

l. 133. *sickly healths*: sickly states of health, rather than 'healths which are drunk, inducing sickness', as Palmer suggests, though Herbert may still have in mind the drinking customs which he condemns in stanzas v–VIII. 'Take no notice if those who have impaired their health by hard drinking scorn your temperate habits.'

l. 136. *if that thou can.* I retain the *thou* of *W*, as *you* (*B 1633*) is found nowhere else in this poem for the singular.

l. 137. Chaucer (*A Treatise on the Astrolabe*, prol. 3) mentions 'the Ecliptik lyne', the apparent orbit of the sun. Cf. Sir T. Browne, *Pseudodoxia*, VI.v.: 'If we imagine the Sun to make his course out of the Ecliptick' &c.

l. 142. *under-writes*: subscribes to, confirms by signature.

l. 148. *tumble.* Cf. *The Method*, p. 133, l. 10.

l. 149. *good-fellows*: boon companions; sometimes written as one word or with hyphen (as in *B*).

ll. 151–6. Cf. *Priest to T.*, p. 265, ll. 13–19, and *Outl. Pvbs*, No. 85: 'In spending lies the advantage.'

ll. 157–60. Youth can afford to spend all the year's income, but age must make provision for the declining years.

l. 169. *What skills it?* What difference does it make?

l. 171. Cf. *Affliction I*, p. 46, l. 11, and Luke xii. 33: 'prouide your selues . . . a treasure in the heauens that faileth not.'

l. 179. *The curious unthrift.* The spendthrift finds fault with his tailor, not with himself, for the extravagant width of his trunk-hose. The Elizabethan divine, William Perkins, calls the Prodigal Son 'the young vnthrift', and Henry Smith, the 'silver-tongued' preacher, remarks that 'Christ was not curious in his diet' (i.e. fastidious).

l. 187. *doth bear the bell*: is first, carries off the prize. Again in *The Search*, p. 163, l. 59.

l. 190. *brave*: handsome, finely dressed, like the Scotch 'braw'.

ll. 197–8. When a man's very name was passing out of local memory, a herald, making his official Visitation every thirty years or so, after some search (*at length*) finds it in a cracked church-window.

l. 211. *complexion*: disposition, temperament, resulting from the combination of the four bodily humours. Again in l. 247 and in *Employment II*, p. 78, l. 5. Lowe notes that *complexion* and *alloy* (the form which from about 1600 was replacing *allay*) are found together in Dryden's 'Heroick Stanzas on Oliver, late Lord Protector', stanza 25:

> For from all Tempers he cou'd Service draw
> The worth of each, with its Alloy, he knew;
> And, as the Confident of Nature, saw
> How she Complections did divide and brew.

l. 218. *home.* Adverbially, as in *The Quip*, p. 111, l. 24.

l. 223. *pos'd*: called in question, nonplussed. Again in *The Church Militant*, p. 191, l. 51.

ll. 223–6. Herbert's indebtedness to Bacon is clear from the following passages, which explain the reference to the web (*tela*) and identify *the great souldier* as Gonzalo Hernandez de Cordova (1453–1515), surnamed the Great Captain.

> But for this apprehension of a disgrace, that a fillippe to the person should bee a mortall wound to the reputation, it were good that men did hearken vnto the saying of *Consaluo* the great and famous commaunder, that was wont to say; A Gentlemans honor should bee, *De telâ crassiore*, of a good strong warppe or webbe that euery little thing should not catch in it, when as now it seemes they are but of copwebbe lawne, or such light stuffe, which certainly is weaknesse, and not true greatnesse of mind, but like a sicke mans body, that is so tender that it feeles euery thing. (*Speech against Duels*, 1614, pp. 20–1.)
>
> Opinion of the Touch of a Mans *Reputation*, doth multiply and sharpen *Anger*. Wherein the Remedy is, that a Man should have, as *Consalvo* was wont to say, *Telam Honoris crassiorem*. (*Essays*, 1625, No. LVII, 'Of Anger'.)

Bacon quotes Gonzalo's saying also in *The Advancement of Learning* (1603), II. xx. 12, and in *Apophthegmes*, No. 70.

l. 227. *playes*: manages, deals with. Cf. *The Familie*, p. 137, l. 10: 'Then Order plaies the soul.'

l. 228. 'To overlook trifles without incivility will not lose you credit with those whose opinion is worth most.'

l. 232. *the conceit* is the object of *advance*, as is clear from the reading of *W*, 'and thou thy mirth inhanse'. The hearers, by seeing *Thy person* in the jest, may add a point to it, which the speaker did not intend and would prefer not to be made.

l. 238. *fine*: cleared of scum; the antithesis of 'course' (l. 237).

l. 247. *sad*: grave, serious; often coupled with *wise*.

l. 248. *swallows up*. Often used of military conquest in the A.V., e.g. II Sam. xx. 19–20; it follows naturally on *leads the van*.

l. 253. *respective*: respectful (which is the reading of *W*). The Country Parson 'carryes himself very respectively . . . to his Diocesan' (p. 253, l. 5). If a man gives his superiors their due (*theirs*, l. 254), he loses no self-respect; if he is a dependant (*in service*, l. 255), his attentiveness or the reverse will accordingly (*ratably*, l. 256) make or mar his fortunes.

l. 258. *parcell*: partly; frequently used to qualify adjectives and nouns, as in 'parcel-gilt'. Cf. Lodowick Barrey, *Ram Alley* (1611): 'Parcel lawyer, parcel devil, all knave.'

l. 261. 'Do not disparage yourself or your qualities.' Cf. Herbert's advice to his younger brother Henry in *Letter* IV, p. 366, ll. 14–19.

ll. 263–4. 'Master your passions (*the beasts*) and then, like horses well broken in, they will draw you to your goal. The body is a good servant but a bad master.'

ll. 267–8. Herbert would have been familiar with Aesop's fable of the ass carrying an image and assuming the reverence of the bystanders to be paid to himself. An even closer parallel to these lines is an engraving in Alciati's *Emblems*, which shows an ass carrying a shrine of Isis to which a woman and others make obeisance; the ass is reproved by the driver with the words, 'Non es Deus tu (aselle) sed Deum vehis.'

l. 272. Cf. *Outl. Pvbs*, No. 296: 'The best mirrour is an old friend.'

l. 274. *pay down* is used figuratively by Shakespeare, *Winter's Tale*, v. i. 3.

l. 279. Cf. *Outl. Pvbs*, No. 423: 'He that hath children, all his morsels are not his owne.'

ll. 283–8. In his copy of *The Temple* Coleridge wrote 'I do not understand this stanza' (Pickering, *Works of George Herbert*, vol. ii, 1835, p. 337; by a misprint in the 2nd edn., 1838, this note was attached to stanza 52 and has misled Palmer). Where Coleridge confessed himself beaten, the present editor can hardly hope to succeed, but a partial explanation may be offered: 'If you are unmarried you may rightly pledge your estate to help your friend, and so far bring yourself *to thrall*, but it would be an excess of devotion to undertake both your own livelihood and his (*To work for two*); even love cannot make more than *one man* of me, and to attempt more would only make my inability run up a score against me.'

l. 295. Cf. *Priest to T.*, p. 260, ll. 5–7.

l. 297. *lose his rest*. O.E.D. cites Sir T. Hoby, tr. *Castigliones Courtyer* (1561), II, y iv b: '[They] fell to gamynge. And not longe after, one of the Pistoiens losinge his reste had not a farthynge left him to blesse himselfe.' In the card-game of primero, probably introduced into England in the suite of Catherine of Aragon, *the rest* was the stakes kept in reserve, which were agreed upon at the beginning of the game, and upon the loss of which the game ended. The way to win the game was to choose the right moment for declaring your hand. Herbert suggests that a man who is both proud and ignorant would sooner lose his chance of joining in conversation than show what an ill-furnished mind he has; therefore draw him out on a subject he knows (l. 295).

l. 327. *great places*: positions of political or social consequence. Herbert recognizes the counterbalancing truth in *Submission*, p. 95, ll. 15–16.

l. 334. *means*: aims at, as in *Justice I*, l. 9, *Praise III*, l. 1, *A true Hymne*, l. 2, and *The Answer*, l. 9. Herbert repeats the thought in the preface to *Priest to T.*, p. 224. Cf. Sidney, *Arcadia*, II. vi. 2: 'Who shootes at the mid-day Sunne, though he be sure he shall neuer hit the marke; yet as sure he is he shall shoote higher, then who ayms but at a bush.'

l. 341. *live alone*: i.e. can alone be said to live.

l. 348. *quit*: be an equivalent for. O.E.D. cites J. Fitzherbert, *The Boke of Husbandry* (1534), § 14: 'The roughe otes be the worste, and it quiteth not the coste to sowe them.'

l. 352. I Sam. xvii. 50: 'So Dauid preuailed ouer the Philistine with a sling.' Cf. *Praise I*, p. 61, l. 11.

ll. 353–4. Cf. *Priest to T.*, p. 228, l. 14: 'They say, it is an ill Mason that refuseth any stone', and *Outl. Pvbs*, No. 67: 'Never had ill workeman good tooles.'

l. 355. *forrain*. O.E.D., citing l. 362, explains 'not one's own', which contrasts with *thy native good* (l. 361); but the reading of *W* in ll. 367–8, 'Leave not thine owne deere-cuntry-cleanlines ffor this ffrench sluttery', makes it probable that Herbert is using *forrain* in its common sense. This also agrees closely with his advice to his brother in Paris in *Letter* iv, p. 366, ll. 5–13. He may have thought it prudent to abandon the reference to 'ffrench sluttery' after Charles I's marriage to Henrietta Maria in June 1625.

l. 368. *board*: make advances to (Fr. *aborder*).

l. 372. Cf. *Priest to T.*, p. 228, ll. 12–14: 'the purity of his mind breaking out, and dilating it selfe even to his body, cloaths, and habitation.' According to Walton (*Lives*, p. 63) it was observed of Herbert that he 'us'd to be so trim and clean', and there are many indications in his poems and prose writings of his fastidious love of neatness.

l. 373. A reproduction, as Lowe notices, of Cic. Off. i. 14. 42: 'deinde, ne maior benignitas sit, quam facultates: tum, ut pro dignitate cuique tribuatur.'

l. 383. Lowe compares Acts x. 4: 'thine almes are come vp for a memorial before God.'

l. 391. *the day*. The reading of *W*, *that day*, makes clearer the reference to Sunday, continued from l. 387. 'There are two main meals every week-day (*so oft*, l. 392, alluding to *Twice* in the line before), but on Sunday there is as well spiritual sustenance (*Thy cheere is mended*); do not perversely abstain from using it, for fasting may be *gain* any day *but then*.' (The punctuation of *W* in l. 396, recovered in *1641*, preserves the sense better than that of *B* and *1633*.) Grosart and Palmer find a reference to the sacrament in these lines, but, as its celebration was usually only once a month in Herbert's day, it is safer to take the reference to be to Morning and Evening Prayer (*Twice on the day*, l. 391): cf. 'having read divine Service twice fully' (*Priest to T.*, p. 236, l. 6).

l. 395. *the Mighty God*, the reading of both MSS., is likely to be the author's wording, and the conventional *th'Almighty God* an editorial alteration. *The mightie God* occurs again in *Sighs and Grones*, l. 5.

l. 399. *a weight*: 'an inducement or weighty argument' (Lowe). More commonly a weight is a burden, as in Shakespeare's 'waight of paine' and Prior's 'my weight of woe'. Possibly Herbert, who was a reader of St. Augustine, remembers a passage in *Conf.* xiii. ix. 10, which Quarles (*Emblems*, i. 13) translates: 'All things are driven by their own weight, and tend to their own centre; my weight is my love; by that I am driven whithersoever I am driven.'

l. 403. *bare*: bare-headed, as in *Merchant of Venice*, ii. ix. 44: 'How many then should couer that stand bare?' Donne more than once reprehended the contemporary indifference about uncovering the head 'at any part of Divine Service' (*Fifty Sermons*, pp. 470–1), and is still more severe on the neglect of kneeling (*LXXX Sermons*, pp. 72–3, 115–16).

l. 411. *Stay not for th' other pin*. Cf. *Outl. Pvbs*, No. 71: 'When prayers are done, my Lady is ready', and *Priest to T.*, p. 232, ll. 7–14.

l. 415. *seal up both thine eies*. Both here (*seale B W*, *seal 1633*) and in *The Pearl*, p. 89, l. 32 (*seeled W*, *sealed B 1633*) it cannot be determined whether the verb is *seal* (Old Fr. *seeler*) or *seel* (Fr. *siller*); nor is the spelling decisive, as contemporary use allowed many variants—*seel*, *seale*, and *sele* for *seal*; and *seal*, *sele*, *ciel*, and *cele* for *seel*. The same ambiguity attaches to *unseal* (*unseel*, *unceele*). *Seel* is a term in falconry for sewing up a hawk's eyelids, but it was also used figuratively. The fact that *seal* or *seal up* was often found with ears and lips as well as eyes makes it still more difficult to infer that 'seal the eyes' is necessarily derived from falconry. It is likely that the confusion of the two verbs even preceded Herbert's day, and that people had ceased to ask themselves whether the word they used was derived from the use of the seal or from falconry. In any case, the use here and in *The Pearl* being figurative, the sense is unaffected. In favour of *seal* is *send* (l. 416), suggesting correspondence.

l. 417. i.e. the stains which by them did rise.

l. 419. *symmetrie*: beauty of form. Ben Jonson in *Cynthias Revels* has 'a creature of her symmetry'.

l. 422. *plots*: projects, not necessarily secret or mischievous. Cf. *Businesse*, p. 113, ll. 9, 23.

ll. 423–4. Cf. Mark xi. 15–17, where Christ purges the temple and says, 'ye haue made it a den of theeues' (cf. *theeves*, l. 424).

l. 426. Cf. *Priest to T.*, p. 233, ll. 18–21.

l. 429. Cf. I Cor. i. 21: 'it pleased God by the foolishnesse of preaching, to saue them that beleeue.'

l. 430. Cf. II Cor. iv. 7: 'we haue this treasure in earthen vessels.'

l. 432. Cf. *A true Hymne*, p. 168, l. 18: 'God doth supplie the want.'

l. 443. *his condition*. Cf. ll. 265–6. Herbert may be referring to the low social standing of the clergy, which will disparage them in the eyes of the young gallant. Cf. Oley's preface to the second edition of *Priest to T.* (1671).

l. 449. *The Jews refused thunder; and we, folly*. Although the Law was promulgated on Mount Sinai amid thunder and lightning (Exod. xix. 16), the Jews soon returned to idolatry; and 'the preaching of the Crosse is to them that perish, foolishnesse' (I Cor. i. 18).

l. 450. *Though God do hedge us in*. Cf. Job iii. 23: 'whom God hath hedged in', and Lam. iii. 7.

l. 459. *lifes poore span*. Cf. Ps. xxxix. 6, B.C.P.: 'Behold, thou hast made my dayes as it were a spanne long'; A.V. has 'an hand breadth'.

ll. 461–2. For his concluding couplet Herbert has versified an epigram which has a long literary history, explored by Dr. W. A. Greenhill in his brochure, *The Contrast: Duty and Pleasure, Right and Wrong* (1874). Aulus Gellius (Noct. Attic. xvi. i. ad init.; first printed in 1469) quotes it from a speech of Cato the Censor at Numidia, 195 B.C., and adds a rather more concise Greek version by C. Musonius Rufus, a Stoic philosopher (*c.* A.D. 65). A similar Greek version appears in the commentary on Pythagoras by Hierocles (*c.* A.D. 450). Latin versions of the epigram as given by Musonius or by Hierocles appear in many books printed before Herbert's time, and Sir Humphrey Gilbert gives an English version in his *Discourse of a Discouerie* (1576: reprinted by Hakluyt in 1599): 'If through pleasure or idleness we purchase shame, the pleasure vanisheth, but the shame remaineth for ever.' In the Bodleian Library a MS. Book of Hours, given by Princess Mary, the future Queen Mary I, to one of her ladies, has a rendering of Musonius in the princess's hand: 'Yf you take labour & payne to doo a vertuous thyng, the labour goeth away, and the vertue remaynethe. Yf through pleasure you do any vicious thyng, the pleasure goeth away and the vice remaynethe' (W. D. Macray, *Annals of the Bodleian Library*, 1890, p. 53).

Superliminare (Page 25)

For the original arrangement of these quatrains in the MSS. and in *1633*, see the footnote, p. 25. They stand midway between *The Church-porch* and *The Church*, and belong to neither. They do not constitute a single poem: the first quatrain invites the reader of *The Church-porch* (*the former precepts*, l. 1) to enter *The Church*; the second, to which alone, and more appropriately, the title *Superliminare* is given in *W*, is conceived as inscribed on the lintel (cf. *superliminare* in Vulg. Exod. xii. 22), and warns off *Profanenesse* from going farther. In all editions from 1633 to 1667 there are printer's devices decorating the page, without a page-heading, and each quatrain has a large initial capital as for a complete poem. From 1674 there is substituted an elaborate engraving, which depicts the door opening from the porch into the church; the page is headed 'The Church-porch', and the two poems, with a line between them, are given in reverse order at the foot of the engraving.

l. 2. *Sprinkled* keeps up the image of Perrirhanterium.

l. 5. *Avoid*: intransitive, and addressed to *Profanenesse*; withdraw, give place. Cf. *Coventry Mysteries*, 131: 'Avoyd, seres, and lete my lorde the buschop come.' To assist the modern reader, I follow Grosart and Palmer in inserting a comma after *Avoid*.

l. 6. Cf. Rev. xxi. 27: 'And there shall in no wise enter into it any thing that defileth.'

The Altar (Page 26)

The poem, as written in the MSS. and printed in *1633*, follows the shape of a classical altar. From 1634 to 1667 the shape is further emphasized by lines drawn round the poem (cf. *this frame*, l. 11). The lines are replaced from 1674 by an engraving of a full-length Christian altar under a classical canopy, with the poem set under the canopy. A new engraving in *1703* follows the general lines of *1674*, but the canopy is more in the manner of Wren, and the altar is adorned with tear-drops or tongues of fire and with a large heart in the centre. In *1809* there is Gothic panelling and canopy-work behind a modest altar with fringed cloth, fair linen cloth, and the sacred vessels.

In *The Arte of English Poesie* (1589), attributed to George Puttenham, a chapter (Lib. II, ch. xi, a miscount for xii) is devoted to poems yielding 'an ocular representation', which are said to be 'fittest for the poetic amourets in Court'. Examples of shaped verse from 'China and Tartarie' are described, and about oval verses it is stated: 'Of this sort are diuers of *Anacreons* ditties, and those other of the Grecian Liricks, who wrate wanton amorous deuises.' Francis Davison in *A Poetical Rapsody* (1602) calls attention in his preface to poems of 'my deere friend *Anomos*', written 'almost twentie yeers since';

and among them is 'An Altare and Sacrifice to Disdaine', shaped like a pagan altar, and with lines drawn round it. The poem begins

My Muse by thee restor'd to life,
To thee Disdaine, this Altare reares.

Grosart mentions also the shaped dedicatory verses of Sylvester in *Bartas his Deuine Weekes & Workes Translated* (1605); the poem 'Lectoribus' is shaped like a pyramid, with greater help from the printer than from the poet. Although Herbert has only two examples of shaped verse, *The Altar* and *Easter-wings*, he has not escaped severe criticism (see Introduction, p. xlv). Sir Walford Davies makes a spirited defence of the most artificial examples among Herbert's poems in his preface to the Gregynog edition of *Poems of George Herbert* (1923), and Mr. T. O. Beachcroft (*The Criterion*, Oct. 1932) defends *Easter-wings*.

l. 2. *cemented*. Accented on the first syllable, as in *The Church-floore*, p. 67, l. 10, and Donne's 'The Extasie', l. 5.

l. 4. A reference to Exod. xx. 25: 'And if thou wilt make mee an Altar of stone, thou shalt not build it of hewen stone: for if thou lift vp thy toole vpon it, thou hast polluted it.'

l. 8. Cf. *The Sinner*, p. 38, l. 14: 'Remember that thou once didst write in stone.'

ll. 13–14. A reference to Luke xix. 40: 'I tell you, that if these should holde their peace, the stones would immediatly cry out.'

The Sacrifice (Page 26)

In this dramatic monologue, unlike any other of the *Temple* poems, the speaker throughout is Christ. The series of antitheses, like those in *Passio Discerpta*, suggests an early manner of Herbert; they are not, however, merely ingenious, as they support the leading idea of the poem, that the royalty of Christ, attributed to him by his persecutors in mockery, is authentic. Mr. W. Empson includes a study of this poem in his *Seven Types of Ambiguity* (1930), pp. 286–95. A Latin version is in Dillingham, op. cit. p. 24.

l. 1. *all ye, who passe by*. From Lam. i. 12. Cf. Donne's paraphrase, 'The Lamentations of *Ieremy*', and Matt. xxvii. 39.

l. 38. *the Way and Truth*. This, the reading of both MSS., as well as the parallel in l. 179 (*I, who am Truth*), establishes the allusion to John xiv. 6: 'I am the Way, the Trueth, and the Life.' All the early editions have *the way of truth*.

l. 45. They 'lay hold on eternall life' (I Tim. vi. 12), not with faith, but with physical violence.

l. 47. *who have loos'd their bands*. Cf. Ezek. xxxiv. 27: 'They shall know that I am the Lord, when I haue broken the bands of their yoke.'

l. 57. *The Priest* (the reading of *B* and *1633*): i.e. 'Caiaphas, the high Priest', who examined and then upheld the false witnesses (Matt. xxvi. 57–66). *The Priests* (*W*) agrees more closely with Matt. xxvi. 59: 'Now the chiefe Priests and Elders, and all the councell, sought false witnesse against Iesus.'

l. 63. *any robberie.* Cf. Phil. ii. 6: 'Who being in the forme of God, thought it not robbery to bee equall with God.'

l. 71. Man received the breath of life from God (Gen. ii. 7), and this is how he sends it back to him! A better way of returning it is in prayer (*Prayer I*, p. 51, l. 2): 'Gods breath in man returning to his birth' (i.e. to the place of its origin).

l. 77. *set me light*: despise, set light by me.

l. 107. *wish.* Cf. Matt. xxvii. 25: 'Then answered all the people, and said, His blood be on vs, and on our children.' Most modern editions have *with*, which is probably a misreading of *wiſh* (*1633*); both MSS. have *wish*, which is clearly right.

l. 115. *it was their own case.* Cf. *To all Angels, &c.*, p. 78, l. 20: ''Tis your own case.' Murderers themselves, they will favour Barabbas, 'who had committed murder in the insurrection' (Mark xv. 7). *case* (*W*) seems more likely to be the author's word than *cause* (*B* and *1633*).

l. 122. *He clave the stonie rock.* Although it is said of God that he 'claue' and 'smote the stonie rocke' (Ps. lxxviii. 16, 21, B.C.P.), God cannot, without too violent a transition, be the subject of l. 122. Probably the sentence is ironical: 'Caesar may have brought them wonderful material benefits, but he cannot soften their hearts, as I know by experience' ('as I by proofe doe try', *W*).

ll. 129–31. The sudden change to the third personal pronoun in both MSS. breaks the continuity, but perhaps it may be defended as heightening the insolence of the soldiers in maltreating one who is the ruler of the universe. The editor of *1633* may have shied at the departure from the first personal pronoun, although he had passed a similar reversion to the third person in l. 58.

l. 141. *abjects*: degraded persons. Cf. Ps. xxxv. 15, B.C.P.: 'yea, the very abiects came together against mee vnawares, making mowes at mee, and ceased not.'

ll. 146–7. 'In vehement shouting for my death, each one in the crowd comes near to spending his last breath (cf. 'spend my utmost breath', l. 229) and so dying before me.' Herbert uses the ambiguity of *utmost* to suggest both 'the most that one can do' and 'final'.

ll. 161–3. The same collocation of *thorns, grapes, vine*, occurs in Isa. v. 1–7, which Herbert evidently had in mind.

l. 165. 'The *curse in* Adams *fall* brought thorns upon the earth (Gen. iii. 18), and now a crown of thorns is put *unto my brows*' (l. 167).

l. 170. The same use of St. Paul's expression, 'that spirituall Rocke' (I Cor. x. 4), is made in *Love unknown*, p. 129, l. 15.

l. 179. *turn into truth their deeds.* They thought to dismiss Christ's regal claims by burlesquing them; instead, these emblems are seen to be his right.

l. 193. *ingrosse*: concentrate.

ll. 205–7. The natural world came into being by mere divine Fiat, but *a world of sinne* can only be redeemed at greater cost than *by words*.

ll. 218–19. 'Sharper nails confound my soul, namely, free-spoken reproaches against one who is bound upon a cross.' An example of such reproaches follows at once (l. 221).

l. 234. *am*, without a subject expressed, is the reading of both MSS. and of *1633*. The third edition introduced *I'm*, an abbreviation which is not found elsewhere in *The Temple*.

l. 239. Cf. Ps. lxxviii. 25: 'Man did eate Angels food: hee sent them meat to the full.'

l. 242. *which once cur'd*. Cf. Matt. xiv. 36: the sick were brought to Jesus 'that they might onely touch the hemme of his garment'.

l. 246. *I full well know*. The dying Christ can only be represented as speaking prophetically of the piercing of his side after death.

l. 247. As woman was taken from Adam's side, so from the pierced side of Jesus flowed 'bloôd and water' (John xix. 34), signifying the sacraments.

The Thanksgiving (Page 35)

l. 4. *preventest*: dost come before, excel.

l. 5. Cf. *The Sacrifice*, p. 31, l. 150: 'When all my tears were bloud.' An allusion to the bloody sweat (Luke xxii. 44 and *Affliction II*, l. 10).

l. 6. *That all thy body was one doore*. The word *doore* has been found difficult, as from 1678 it was replaced by *gore*; other emendations—e.g. *sore*, *pore*—have been suggested, but there is no need to emend. It is an outlet for the blood; cf. Shakespeare, *Julius Caesar*, III. ii. 182–4:

> And as he pluck'd his cursed Steele away:
> Marke how the blood of *Cæsar* followed it
> As rushing out of doores.

Cf. 'the doore' in Christ's pierced side in *The Bag*, p. 152, l. 38.

l. 11. The comma in *1633* after *skipping* is an unfortunate error, as the text of *B* 'skipping thy dolefull storie' is the equivalent of 'neglecting thy sad story' in *W*. The error was corrected in *1638*.

l. 13. The play on words would have been more readily apprehended in Herbert's day because of such current spelling as is found in the A.V., e.g. John xviii. 22: 'one of the officers which stood by, stroke Iesus with the palme of his hand'. Miss K. I. Barratt calls my attention to the same equivoque in F. Quarles, *A Feast for Wormes* (1620), p. 62:

> Here maist thou see, how Pray'r, and true Repentance
> Doe striue with God, preuaile, and turne his sentence
> From strokes to stroking.

l. 14. *Thy rod, my posie?* George Macdonald (*England's Antiphon*, p. 190) suggests that Herbert may have in mind 'Aarons rod that budded' (Heb. ix. 4).

l. 44. *'tis here*: i.e. in this book of poems. He at once turns to *thy book* (l. 45).

l. 48. *Victorie!* Prematurely he exclaims that, by learning from his Lord his Ars Amatoria, he has matched him, as he had assayed to do (l. 18); but the remembrance of *thy passion*, which he had postponed for later treatment (l. 29), brings him to a stand.

The Reprisall (Page 36)

The title in *W*, *The Second Thanks-giving*, makes the connexion with the preceding poem clearer; this poem takes up the theme suggested and postponed in ll. 29–30 and 49–50 of *The Thanksgiving*. It should also be compared with the discarded *W* poem, *Love* (p. 201), with which it shares some of the same ideas and phrases.

l. 6. *disentangled*. Cf. *Affliction I*, p. 47, l. 41: 'I was entangled in the world of strife', and *The Starre*, p. 74, l. 13: 'So disengag'd from sinne and sicknesse.'

l. 8. *by thy death*. 'Only in the strength given me by thy death could I die for thee.'

l. 14. *Into thy conquest*. This, the reading of both MSS., is more pointed than *Into the conquest* of *1633*, and it is closely paralleled in *Love*, p. 202, ll. 19–20:

> Let mee but once the conquest have
> Vpon the matter, 'twill thy conquest prove.

Grosart, after adopting 'Thy conquest' in his text, went back upon it in his note (i. 223) and made an interesting defence of 'the conquest'. Palmer retains 'the conquest' of *1633*, and explains: 'By conquering him whom thou dost conquer—myself—I share thy victory.'

The Agonie (Page 37)

The principal metaphor is drawn from Isa. lxiii, one of the liturgical epistles for Holy Week: 'Who is this that commeth from Edom, with died garments from Bozrah? . . . I that speake in righteousnesse, mightie to saue. . . . I haue troden the winepresse alone.' For a fuller study of this poem, see my chapter, 'George Herbert', in *Seventeenth Century Studies presented to Sir Herbert Grierson* (1938), pp. 158–60.

ll. 1–2. There must be a connexion between these lines and a passage in *Epistolae Ho-Elianae*, Letter X, Sect. 5, 2nd edn., 1650, to which Palmer calls attention: 'Philosophy hath more of reality in it than any knowledge, the Philosopher can fadom the Deep, measure Mountaines, reach the Starrs with a Staff, and bless Heaven with a Girdle.' (Note the spelling *Fadom'd* in *B*.) James Howell's letter, addressed 'To my Cosen Mr. Stgeon at Christ Church Colledge', is dated 1627, but Mr. W. G. Hiscock informs me that William St. John did not matriculate till Dec. 1628. Howell's dates are notoriously untrustworthy, and were generally absent from the first edition. Even if he saw *The Agonie* in manuscript, the poem is likely to be later than 1627, as it is not in *W*.

l. 3. *with a staffe*. A rod for measuring distances and heights, also known as a Jacob's staff. Cf. *Divinitie*, p. 135, l. 27.

l. 11. *Sinne is that presse*. Dr. B. Blackstone compares L. Andrewes, *Sermons* (1628), p. 375: 'This was the *paine* of the *Presse* (so the *Prophet* calleth it, *Torcular*:) wherewith as if He had beene in the *wine-presse*, all his *garments* were *stained* and *goared* with *bloud*.'

l. 18. A kind of inversion of the doctrine of transubstantiation: 'I receive as a refreshing cordial what was to Christ the blood of sacrifice.' Cf. *The Invitation*, p. 180, ll. 11–12: 'And drink this, Which before ye drink is bloud', and *Divinitie*, p. 135, l. 21: 'But he doth bid us take his bloud for wine.'

The Sinner (Page 38)

There are 15 sonnets in *The Temple*, besides the two New Year sonnets (see p. 206). Of these 17 six (of which two only are in *W*) are in the Shakespearian form—*abab cdcd efef gg*, the other eleven having *abab cdcd eff egg*. The present edition follows the MSS. in indentation (generally observed in *1633*), and in disregarding the practice of *1633*, which, in all but four sonnets, puts line-spaces after ll. 4, 8, 12 (after ll. 4 and 8 only in *The Holdfast*).

l. 1. Ague is again mentioned in *Affliction I*, p. 47, l. 27, and *The Crosse*, p. 165, l. 13. Masson calls it 'then the prevalent disease of the fenny Cambridge district' (*Life of Milton*, 1881, i. 167).

l. 7. *crosse to thy decrees.* Cf. J. Playford, *Psalms & Hymns* (1671), p. 19 (apostrophizing 'the World'):

> How cross art thou to that designe
> For which we had our birth?

l. 8. J. Wesley, rewriting this poem in *Hymns and Sacred Poems* (1739), has:

> Th' immense Circumference is Sin,
> A Point is all my Good.

Cf. Donne, 'The second Anniversary', ll. 436–9.

l. 9. O.E.D. states that *quintessence* was stressed on the first and third syllables from the sixteenth to the eighteenth centuries; Milton used both that and the modern pronunciation.

l. 14. *thou once didst write in stone.* Cf. Exod. xxxi. 18, and *Sepulchre*, p. 41, l. 18.

Sepulchre (Page 40)

l. 5. *our hearts good store.* Cf. *The Bunch of Grapes*, p. 128, l. 25: 'bring forth grapes good store', and M. Hanmer, *Anc. Eccles. Hist.* (1577): 'Then there were captiues great store, and cheape inough.'

l. 13. *took up stones.* Cf. John x. 31: 'Then the Iewes tooke vp stones againe to stone him.'

l. 19. *The letter of the word.* 'The Epistle of Christ' should have been written 'not in tables of stone, but in fleshy tables of the heart' (II Cor. iii. 3).

Easter (Page 41)

l. 3. *takes thee by the hand.* Cf. another Easter poem, *The Dawning*, p. 112, ll. 11–12.

l. 5. *calcined.* Cf. Browne, *Religio Medici*, i, § 50: 'I would gladly know how *Moses* with an actual fire calcin'd, or burnt the Golden Calf into powder.'

l. 13. *twist a song.* Figuratively, from the plaiting of fibres into a cord; cf. Shakespeare, *Much Ado*, I. i. 321: 'to twist so fine a story'. It is specially appropriate to polyphonic music.

l. 15. *three parts vied.* O.E.D., citing this instance, defines *vie* 'to increase in number by addition or repetition'. The heart and the lute require the

Spirit, which 'helpeth our infirmities' (Rom. viii. 26), to make the third with them to complete the common chord, and perhaps also to 'multiply' it by repeating the notes in the upper and lower scales.

l. 24. i.e. though the East give perfume. The gifts of the sun and the East are not to compare with *thy sweets* (l. 22).

l. 29. *We count three hundred.* The days of the year in round numbers; but there is only one sun-rising that brings light to all the year and through all eternity.

Easter-wings (Page 43)

'The effect of *Easter Wings* is less jejune than is sometimes supposed, for Herbert was sufficiently master of his instrument to make a double use of the pattern. The shape of the wings on the page may have nothing but ingenuity to recommend it, but the diminuendo and crescendo that bring it about are expressive both of the rise and fall of the lark's song and flight (Herbert's image) and also of the fall of man and his resurrection in Christ (the subject that the image represents).' (Joan Bennett, *Four Metaphysical Poets*, 1934, p. 66.)

l. 8. *As larks.* Cf. *Sion*, p. 107, l. 23: 'And ever as they mount, like larks they sing.'

l. 10. *Then shall the fall further the flight in me.* The paradox that Adam's sin (*felix culpa*) occasioned the glorious Redemption is familiar in St. Augustine and in medieval writers, and is still used by Milton, *P.L.* xii. 469–78.

l. 19. *imp my wing.* To imp, in falconry, is 'to engraft feathers in a damaged wing, so as to restore or improve the powers of flight' (O.E.D.).

H. Baptisme II (Page 44)

l. 10. *Behither*: short of, barring, save (O.E.D., citing this example).

l. 13. *My soul bid nothing.* The soul needs to pray for nothing but to retain its baptismal innocence. Cf. *Vanitie II*, p. 111, ll. 13–16, and H. Vaughan's 'The Retreate'.

Nature (Page 45)

l. 2. *or travell.* Walton relates that Herbert's mother 'would by no means allow him to leave the University, or to travel' (*Lives*, p. 29). Cf. H. Vaughan, 'Misery', ll. 73–4:

> I'd loose those knots thy hands did tie,
> Then would go travel, fight or die.

l. 10. *by kinde*: according to their nature, as bubbles will. Cf. *A true Hymne*, p. 168, l. 15.

Sinne I (Page 45)

Coleridge admired this sonnet 'for the purity of the language and the fulness of the sense', and quoted it in full in *Biographia Literaria*, ch. xix, and again in *Aids to Reflection*. In introducing it in the former book he describes it as 'equally admirable for the weight, number, and expression of the thoughts, and for the simple dignity of the language. Unless, indeed, a fastidious taste should object to the latter half of the sixth line.'

ll. 7–8. Cf. H. Vaughan, 'The Tempest', ll. 21–4:

> Sure, mighty love foreseeing the discent
> Of this poor Creature, by a gracious art
> Hid in these low things snares to gain his heart,
> And layd surprizes in each Element.

Affliction I (Page 46)

l. 25. *My flesh began unto my soul in pain.* Coleridge annotates: 'Either a misprint, or a noticeable idiom of the word "began"? Yes! and a very beautiful idiom it is;—the first colloquy or address of the flesh.' The only use of *begin to* noticed in O.E.D. is 'to pledge, toast'. Grosart cites for this sense Joseph Hall, *Contemplations* (1634), ii. 221: 'O blessed Saviour, we pledge thee, according to our weaknesse, who hast begun to us in thy powerfull sufferings.' But there seems to be no suggestion of pledge or challenge in Herbert's words, and a simpler explanation may serve: the flesh in pain at last begins to remonstrate with the idealizing soul, and utters its complaint in the following three lines, in which, it will be noticed, all the verbs are in the present tense.

l. 32. *my friends die.* Ludovick Stuart, 2nd duke of Lennox and Richmond, died on 16 Feb. 1623/4; James, 2nd marquis of Hamilton, on 2 Mar. 1624/5; and King James I on 27 Mar. 1625. Bacon died on 9 Apr. 1626, Andrewes on 26 Sept. 1626, and Herbert's mother in June 1627. According to Walton, 'all Mr. *Herbert's* Court-hopes' died with the death of the three first named.

l. 38. *The way that takes the town.* The phrase occurs also in the *W* version of *The Church-porch*, l. 22. Oley (*Herbert's Remains*, sig. b 7v) explains it as 'Martiall Atchievements', but it is as likely to be what Walton calls 'the painted pleasures of a Court life' or the career of a Secretary of State.

l. 47. *till I came where. W*, the only extant MS. which Herbert saw, has *where*; *B* has *neere* (with a comma), a line is drawn under it, but it is not crossed through, and above it is written *where* (without a comma) by a hand different from the copyist's and in yellower ink. The MSS. of Donne's poems show the practice of drawing a line under a cancelled word (Grierson, *Poems of Donne*, ii. 49). If, as I think likely, the printer of *1633* used *B*, he might well print *neere*, as it is not crossed out, but *where* is likely to be the author's word and it yields the better sense—'Till I came to a point or a state of mind from which I could neither bring myself to withdraw nor continue in my present course whole-heartedly.'

l. 53. *crosse-bias me*: 'give me an inclination other than my own' (Grierson, *Metaphysical Lyrics and Poems*, p. 230). The metaphor from the game of bowls is used again in *Constancie*, p. 73, l. 32.

l. 62. *must be stout.* Cf. Mal. iii. 13: 'Your words haue bin stout against me, saith the Lord.'

ll. 65–6. The passionate return to the first and only allegiance possible to him takes the form of a paradox: if he cannot hold on to his love of God even when he feels forsaken or unrewarded, he had better not hope to love at all; it is the strongest possible asseveration of his love. The amanuensis of *W*, who is capricious, as Herbert is also, in writing *u* or *v*, has 'Lett me not loue Thee, if I love Thee not'; B. G. Hall states wrongly that the second *love* is written *lowe*, which he takes to be a form of an archaic word (Fr. *louer*, Lat. *laudare*) meaning 'praise'. The question does not, however, arise, as *w* in *W* is always quite distinct from his *v*.

Repentance (Page 48)

l. 3. *momentary* and *momentarie* are the spellings of *W* and *B*, though Grosart states otherwise, but the form *momentanie* (*1633*) was still in common use and is found in Donne, Bacon, Quarles, and Burton.

l. 21. *Thy wormwood*. Cf. Jer. ix. 15: 'Behold, I will feed them, euen this people with wormewood.'

l. 22. *stay*, as often in Herbert, means 'stay away, delay coming'. Cf. note on *Home*, p. 515.

l. 25. *for sinne rebukest man*. Cf. Ps. xxxix. 12, B.C.P.: 'When thou with rebukes doest chasten man for sinne, thou makest his beautie to consume away.'

l. 29. *drop*. *B* has *drope*, which is possibly a spelling of *droop*, but O.E.D gives no instances later than the fourteenth century, while *drope* is found for *drop* till much later, and is probably so intended in *B*.

l. 32. *the broken bones may joy*. Cf. Ps. li. 8: 'that the bones which thou hast broken, may reioyce.'

l. 36. Cf. Shakespeare, *II Henry IV*, iv. i. 221–3:

> If we do now make our attonement well,
> Our Peace will (like a broken Limbe vnited)
> Grow stronger, for the breaking.

Faith (Page 49)

l. 3. *to regard his ease*. Cf. *The H. Communion*, p. 53, l. 37: 'Thou hast restor'd us to this ease.'

l. 9. *a rare outlandish root*. His *walk to heav'n* is hampered by the serpent (Gen. iii. 15) having bruised his heel (*my foot*, l. 11), but Christ provides an antidote, like the snake-root of Virginia (*Aristolochia serpentaria*).

l. 30. *a great Clerk*. Cf. Chaucer, *Reeve's Tale*, A 4054: 'The gretteste clerkes been noght wisest men.'

l. 37. *clean*. An adverb: wholly, quite, as in *Affliction I*, p. 48, l. 65: 'I am clean forgot.'

l. 38. *pricking the lookers eie*. From the many allusions to the discomfort of the eyes (e.g. *Ungratefulnesse*, l. 17; *Frailtie*, l. 16) we may infer that Herbert was specially sensitive about them.

l. 43. *an exact and most particular trust.* Cf. the injunctions about his dead wife's shrine in Henry King's 'The Exequy', ll. 65–6:

For thou must audit on thy trust
Each graine and atome of this dust.

Prayer I (Page 51)

l. 1. *Angels age* is contrasted with 'Mans age' (*Repentance*, p. 48, l. 7). 'The dayes of our age are threescore yeeres and ten' (Ps. xc. 10, B.C.P.), uncertain and troubled, but prayer acquaints man with the blessed timeless existence of the angels.

l. 3. *The soul in paraphrase.* A paraphrase does not epitomize, as Palmer suggests, but rather it clarifies by expansion; in prayer the soul opens out and more fully discovers itself.

l. 5. *Engine against th' Almightie.* Cf. *Artillerie*, p. 139, especially l. 25: 'Then we are shooters both.'

l. 7. An hour of prayer may affect a universe which took six days to set in order.

l. 12. *the bird of Paradise.* This bird may be chosen for its name, as well as for its brilliant colouring and its gaiety, but a further aptness may be discovered in John Wilkins's description (*New World*, 1640): 'The Birds of Paradise . . . reside Constantly in the Air.'

The H. Communion (Page 52)

l. 2. *a wedge of gold.* Herbert had in mind Achan's answer to Joshua (Joshua vii. 21): 'When I saw among the spoiles a goodly Babylonish garment, and . . . a wedge of gold . . ., then I coueted them, and tooke them.' A contrast is intended between the simple accessories of Anglican worship and those of the Roman Catholic rite.

l. 3. *who for me wast sold.* The reading in *B*, *for mee*, is corroborated by exact parallels in *Dialogue*, p. 114, l. 15: 'Who for man was sold', and *Antiphon II*, p. 92, l. 12: 'For us was sold.' The *from me* of *1633* affords a sharper antithesis to *To me* in l. 4, but yields a less satisfactory meaning. This part of the poem is absent from *W*.

ll. 7–9. *thy way* of l. 9 is contrasted in Herbert's manner with *my rest*, and is not a mere recapitulation of *the way* of l. 7.

ll. 13–24. The eucharistic elements can of themselves reach no farther than the door (l. 23) which gives entrance to the soul, but the grace which accompanies them (l. 19) has the key that opens to the soul's inmost recesses.

l. 15. *fleshy hearts.* This, the reading of *B*, is more likely to be right than *fleshly* (*1633*) because it is Herbert's habit to adhere closely to the text of Scripture, 'fleshy tables of the heart' (II Cor. iii. 3). 'My flesh, & fleshly villany' of the discarded *W* poem, *The H. Communion*, p. 201, l. 29, answers to the 'fleshly lusts' of I Pet. ii. 11.

l. 34. *sinne to smother.* The phrase recurs in *The Church Militant*, p. 197, l. 266.

Antiphon I (Page 53)

'Antiphon. A composition, in prose or verse, consisting of verses or passages sung alternately by two choirs in worship' (O.E.D.).

Love I (Page 54)

ll. 1–4. There are evident reminiscences of these lines, especially of 1 and 4, in the prologue of Tennyson's *In Memoriam*.

l. 1. *this great frame*. Cf. Shakespeare, *Hamlet*, II. ii. 317: 'this goodly frame, the Earth', and Milton, *P.L.* viii. 15: 'this goodly Frame, this World Of Heav'n and Earth consisting.'

l. 13. *a skarf or glove*. Cf. Aug. *Conf.* x. xxxiv. 53, and H. Vaughan, 'Idle Verse', ll. 15–16:

> The idle talk of feav'rish souls
> Sick with a scarf, or glove.

Love II (Page 54)

l. 12. *disseized*. A legal term, like *recover* in the preceding line: 'dispossess, usually wrongfully or by force' (O.E.D.). It is used again in *Submission*, p. 95, l. 12: 'Disseize thee of thy right.'

l. 14. *who did make and mend our eies*. Cf. *Love III*, p. 189, l. 12: 'Who made the eyes but I?' and *The H. Scriptures I*, p. 58, l. 9: 'mends the lookers eyes.'

The Temper I (Page 55)

Mr. Aldous Huxley, op. cit. pp. 16–17, commenting on this poem, remarks on the 'many conditional clauses in the writings of the mystics'.

l. 5. *some fourtie heav'ns*. St. Paul speaks (II Cor. xii. 2) of being 'caught vp to the third heauen'. Jewish apocalypses speak of seven heavens or of a series of heavens.

l. 10. *Those distances belong to thee*: i.e. such distances, reaching heaven and hell, as are described in the previous verse, befit thy nature; 'but do not thou stretch me so far.' Cf. *The Search*, p. 163, ll. 41–7. Perhaps there is a half-thought of the distances which duellists are required to keep.

l. 13. *Wilt thou meet arms with man?* There is a play on the word *mete* (cf. *measure*, l. 15), as of those who measure arms before fighting a duel. Herbert has other allusions to fencing, e.g. *The Church-porch*, p. 19, l. 316.

l. 20. *And I of hope and fear*. 'If, instead of attempting these distances, I may nestle contentedly under *thy roof* (cf. Ps. lxxxiv. 3) in *love and trust* (l. 27), I shall be quit of distractions, whether of hope or of fear.' Herbert often shows a fear of unlimited space and loves the shelter of an enclosure.

The Temper II (Page 56)

l. 4. *Save that, and me*. 'Spare *that mightie joy* as well as *my heart*.'

l. 7. *raise and race*. Cf. *The Sacrifice*, p. 28, l. 66: 'raz'd, and raised'. O.E.D. cites Archbishop Parker, *Psalter*, lxxix: 'Thy holy house they haue defylde, Hierusalem is raced', and gives other instances of *race*, as a form of *raze*, in Herbert's time and later.

l. 9. *thy chair of grace*: i.e. throne (cf. 'Majestie', l. 16). Similarly in *Jordan I*, p. 56, l. 5 and *Church-rents and schismes*, p. 140, l. 10.

Jordan I (Page 56)

Many explanations have been attempted of the title. Grosart suggests that Herbert, having crossed into his Promised Land, can now take Jordan for his Helicon. (This would have its dangers; Fuller remarked of Sternhold and Hopkins that their '*piety* was better than their *poetry*: and they had drank more of *Jordan*, than of *Helicon*'.) Palmer, quoting Giles Fletcher (*Christs Victorie*, pt. iv, stanza 5) on Jordan's 'crooked tide', thinks that Jordan represents 'the artificiality and the indirectness of the love-poets' and that Herbert 'calls such love-utterances Jordans'. Though it is more meandering than most rivers, so scriptural a writer as Herbert is not likely to use Jordan as a term of reproach. It is simpler to see an allusion to Elisha's counsel to Naaman the Syrian who preferred the rivers of Damascus (II Kings v. 10): 'Goe and wash in Iordane seuen times . . . and thou shalt be cleane.' This is exactly paralleled in Thomas Lodge's preface to *Prosopopeia* (1596, sig. A 8), where he prays that 'now at last after I have wounded the world with too much surfet of vanitie, I maye bee by the true Helizeus, cleansed from the leprosie of my lewd lines, and beeing washed in the Jordan of grace, imploy my labour to the comfort of the faithfull'.

'A protest, it is said, against love poems, but also, I think, against the pastoral allegorical poetry of the Cambridge Spenserians' (Grierson, op. cit. p. 230). In ll. 9–10 of this poem, and still more in the second *Jordan* (p. 102), Herbert may be expressing his attraction, for his own use at any rate, to a simpler manner of expression than the intellectual subtleties affected by Donne.

l. 5. *Not to a true, but painted chair?* H. Vaughan has the same antithesis of *true* and *painted* in *The Mount of Olives* (*Works*, ed. Martin, i. 186).

l. 7. *sudden arbours*: that appear unexpectedly, it being an aim of the designer of a garden that it should have surprises. Cf. J. Beaumont, *Psyche*, IV. lxxxviii: 'Up sprung a suddain Grove', and Addison's hymn (*Spectator*, 26 July 1712):

> The barren Wilderness shall smile
> With sudden Greens and Herbage crown'd.

l. 12. *pull for Prime*: 'to draw for a card or cards which will make the player *prime*' (O.E.D.). Cf. *The Church Militant*, p. 193, l. 134, and Donne, Satyre II, l. 86: 'men pulling prime.' For the card-game of primero, see note on *The Church-porch*, l. 297, p. 481.

Employment I (Page 57)

ll. 17–20. There are reminiscences of these lines in Coleridge's poem, 'Work without Hope'.

l. 21. *no link of thy great chain.* Donne, who specially condemned sloth, in a sermon preached at Paul's Cross in 1616/7 has the same phrase (*XXVI Sermons*, xxiv. 343): 'If thou wilt be no link of Gods Chain', &c.

l. 23. *thy consort.* O.E.D. cites R. Holme, *The Academy of Armory* (1688): 'A Consort is many Musitians playing on several Instruments.'

The H. Scriptures I (Page 58)

l. 2. *a hony gain.* Cf. Ps. cxix. 103: 'How sweet are thy words vnto my taste! yea, sweeter then hony to my mouth.'

l. 8. *thankfull*: as we say 'grateful' to-day.

l. 11. *Lidger* (Lieger *1633*², Leiger *1634*): one appointed to 'lie' or reside at a foreign court, a resident ambassador. This gives an added point to the use of the word *states* in the following line.

l. 13. *handsell*: a first instalment, a pledge of what is to follow.

The H. Scriptures II (Page 58)

Priest to T. (p. 229, ll. 4, 10) recommends 'a diligent Collation of Scripture with Scripture', and asserts 'the coherence' of a text with 'what goes before, and what follows after'.

l. 2. *configurations*: the relative positions of the celestial bodies.

l. 7. *as dispersed herbs do watch a potion.* The word *watch* was sometimes used in the sense of 'contrive', though generally of contriving mischief; but here the potion must be supposed to do good. As the verses of Scripture are said to mark one another that they may by combination guide man to salvation, so the scattered herbs are on the watch to be combined in a potion, for they 'gladly cure our flesh' (*Man*, l. 23). Dr. Dorothy L. Graham notes that Vaughan speaks of herbs watching in 'The Night', ll. 23–4 (of Jesus alone on the hill-side):

> Where *trees* and *herbs* did watch and peep
> And wonder, while the *Jews* did sleep.

Also in 'The Favour', ll. 7–8:

> Some kinde herbs here, though low & far,
> Watch for, and know their loving star.

Vaughan, and Herbert to a less extent, affect the notion of affinities existing between the lowly inanimate things of earth and the stars, and it will be noticed that allusions to the stars occur at the beginning and end of Herbert's poem. Cf. *Providence*, p. 119, ll. 73–7, especially l. 77: 'And if an herb hath power, what have the starres?' and *Employment II*, p. 79, ll. 19–20: 'the starres Watch an advantage to appeare.'

Both MSS. and all the early editions agree in reading *watch*, but Coleridge suspected 'some misprint'. None of the conjectures—*match, patch, hatch* ('to bring to full development, especially by a covert or clandestine process', O.E.D.), *destill* (replacing *do watch*: cf. *Praise I*, p. 61, l. 13: 'An herb destill'd')—is satisfactory, and no emendation appears to be needed.

l. 11. *Thy words do finde me out.* Cf. Coleridge, *Confessions of an Inquiring Spirit*, Letter II, ad init.: 'the words of the Bible find me at greater depths of my being' than those 'in all other books put together'.

Whitsunday (Page 59)

l. 14. *Hung down his head.* Repeated in *Miserie*, p. 101, l. 33.

l. 17. *those pipes of gold*: i.e. the apostles as channels of grace (perhaps, as Palmer suggests, with an allusion to 'the two golden pipes' of Zech. iv. 12).

l. 20. The martyrdom of the apostles turned to the disadvantage of those who put them to death.

l. 23. *braves*: defiant threats. Cf. Fuller, *Worthies*, i. 33: 'Bitter was the Brave which railing Rabsheca sent to holy Hezekiah.'

l. 25. Cf. R. Southwell, *S. Peters Complaint*, cxxxii. 4: 'Bee thou thyself, though changeling I offend.'

Grace (Page 60)

ll. 1–4. Cf. Job xiv. 7–9. The *stock* is the trunk of a tree.

ll. 11–12. 'Grass cannot call for dew and yet receives it, but I can and do call for the dew of thy grace; O, do thou drop it upon me.' There is a play on words; *grasse* replaces *grace*, which is found in the third line of every other verse except the last.

Praise I (Page 61)

l. 11. *with a sling.* As David slew Goliath 'with a sling and with a stone' (I Sam. xvii. 50).

ll. 13–16. The effects of the potion when drunk ascend to the brain and so dwell next door to and on the same floor as a brave soul (it being assumed that the head is the seat of the soul); if God exalts the poor, they do even better, they dwell near God. I owe this explanation to Mr. H. F. B. Brett-Smith.

Affliction II (Page 62)

ll. 4–5 'Even if, by way of paying off my debt by instalments (*in broken pay*, fractionally), I were to die once in every hour of a life as long as Methuselah's.'

l. 10. *discolour*: take the colour out of, render pallid. Cf. *Justice II*, p. 141, l. 5.

l. 15. *imprest*: a payment in advance, especially of soldiers and sailors; an earnest.

Mattens (Page 62)

The *new light* (l. 18) of each morning reveals to man the visible world and takes all his attention (l. 16), but he ought to recognize also the love of the Creator (the *workman*, l. 19).

Sinne II (Page 63)

The clue to this poem is the doctrine maintained by St. Augustine (*Conf.* VII. xi–xvi. 17–22), by St. Thomas (*Summa Theol.*, Pars II, Quaestio xlviii) and other schoolmen, that evil *non est substantia*; there is no evil substance alongside of good, as substance and goodness are interchangeable (*bonum convertitur cum ente*), but evil is a privation or corruption of good. Even the devil (ll. 2–3) is a fallen angel. Evil is a defect, and defect (though an undoubted fact) is not the presence of an additional real character in the thing, but a failure of the thing to attain the degree of positive actuality which befits it. Since, then, in this sense evil has no *being* (l. 5), man cannot see evil itself (l. 8) but only good things or spirits corrupted. In the last line of 'The Litanie' Donne says, 'As sinne is nothing, let it no where be', and he develops the theme in some of his sermons, e.g. *LXXX Sermons*, xvii. 170–1: 'You know, I presume, in what sense we say in the Schoole, *Malum nihil*, and *Peccatum nihil*, that evill is nothing, sin is nothing; that is, it hath no reality, it is no created substance, it is but a privation, as a shadow is, as sicknesse is; so it is nothing.' But, as Dr. E. M. Simpson points out (*A Study of the Prose Works of Donne*, p. 109), Donne, with his profound sense of the reality of sin, was not altogether satisfied about 'that inextricable point' (*LXXX Sermons*, xxxv. 342), and sometimes expresses himself otherwise, e.g. *Fifty Sermons*, xxi. 176–7:

> And we must not think to ease our selves in that subtilty of the School, *Peccatum nihil*. . . . This is true; but that will not ease my soul, no more then it will ease my body, that *sicknesse* is nothing, and *death* is nothing. . . . And therefore as we fear death, and fear damnation, though in discourse, and in disputation, we can make a school-shift, to call them *nothing*, and but privations, so let us fear sin too, for all this imaginary *nothingnesse*, which the heat of the School hath smoak'd it withall.

l. 10. *perspective*: 'a picture or figure constructed so as to appear distorted except from one particular point of view' (Onions). Devils are our sins seen askew; we are saved from seeing sin in its full horror, but only 'per speculum, in aenigmate'. Shakespeare has a similar metaphorical application (*Ant. and Cleop.* II. v. 115–16):

> Though he be painted one way like a Gorgon,
> The other way 's a Mars.

Even-song (Page 63)

l. 7. Cf. Ps. cxxx. 3, B.C.P.: 'If thou Lord wilt be extreme to marke what is done amisse: oh Lord, who may abide it?'

l. 8. *his sonne*. For the play on the word, see note on *The Sonne*, p. 536.

Church-monuments (Page 64)

Mr. G. Williamson (*The Donne Tradition*, p. 95) finds this poem 'an example of the charnel-house mood of Donne', but it is also characteristic of

Herbert, who uses the word *dust* 35 times in his poems, almost always in reference to man's origin and his dissolution.

The poem in both MSS. is without stanzas, and it will be noticed that there is no punctuation-mark or a comma only at the end of ll. 6, 12, and 18, but the editor of *1633* recognized that the rhyme-scheme implies a six-line stanza.

ll. 14–16. 'What shall distinguish tomb and bodies, when all are, sooner or later, commingled in one heap of dust, and when the hour-glass shall be dust like that which it now contains?' (l. 20.)

l. 23. *How tame these ashes are, how free from lust.* Cf. A. Marvell, 'To his Coy Mistress', ll. 25–32.

Church-musick (Page 65)

l. 5. *without a bodie move.* Cf. *Musae Responsoriae*, XXIII, p. 394, ll. 25–6: 'spiritum Caeno profani corporis exuens', and R. Hooker, *Eccl. Pol.* v. xxxviii. 1 (of music): 'filling the minde with an heauenly ioy and for the time in a maner seuering it from the body.' Also Spenser, 'An Hymne of Heavenly Beautie', ll. 267–8:

> Ne from thenceforth doth any fleshly sense,
> Or idle thought of earthly things remaine.

l. 8. *God help poore Kings.* 'From this height of rapt abstraction, those upon whom the burden of the world rested were but objects of distant pity' (S. R. Gardiner, *Hist. Eng.* vii, p. 270). Cf. Browne, *Religio Medici*, ii, § 15: 'I shall be happy enough to pity *Caesar*.' There is possibly a reminiscence of the last soliloquy of Richard II on his hearing music which 'mads' him (v. v. 41–64).

l. 9. *Comfort*: as an interjection, take comfort. Cf. Shakespeare, *Richard II*, III. ii. 82: 'Comfort, my liege; remember who you are.'

l. 12. Cf. *Mem. Matris Sacr.* II, p. 423, ll. 43–4: 'Musice . . . visa est quasi Caelestis harmoniae breue praeludium.'

Church-lock and key (Page 66)

This poem was entitled *Prayer* in *W* and followed *The H. Communion.* When Herbert revised it and introduced the word *locks* in the first line, he renamed it and grouped it with the poems on the monuments, music, floor, and windows of the church.

l. 5. *cold hands are angrie.* O.E.D., citing Florio's 'angrie kibes, chilblanes', gives the meaning 'inflamed, smarting as a sore', and the word is still used colloquially in this sense; but here it suggests as well an unreasonable man's laying the blame for his cold hands on a sulky fire. *Angrie* is used in a rather different sense in *Vertue*, p. 87, l. 5.

ll. 11–12. Stones in the bed of a shallow brook make the current run more noisily (cf. 'Out-crying', l. 3).

The Church-floore (Page 66)

l. 15. *the marble weeps.* Again in *Grieve not, &c.*, p. 136, l. 23. Cf. Virg. Geo. i. 480: 'Et maestum illacrimat templis ebur, aeraque sudant.'

l. 17. *Blows all the dust about the floore.* A similar idea is used with great effect by Donne, *LXXX Sermons*, xv. 148:

and when a whirle-winde hath blowne the dust of the Church-yard into the Church, and the man sweeps out the dust of the Church into the Church-yard, who will undertake to sift those dusts again, and to pronounce, This is the Patrician, this is the noble flowre, and this the yeomanly, this the Plebeian bran?

The Windows (Page 67)

l. 6. *anneal*: fix the colours, after painting, by heating the glass. Again in *Love-joy*, p. 116, l. 3.

Content (Page 68)

l. 15. *let loose to*: aim at, as one lets an arrow loose at a target.

l. 16. *Take up within a cloisters gates.* The stock example of the emperor Charles V giving up his thrones for the cloister in 1556 was a favourite topic in the Conversations of Little Gidding. For *take up*, cf. Pepys, *Diary*, 14 Oct. 1662: 'To Cambridge . . . whither we come at about nine o'clock and took up at the Beare.'

ll. 22–4. *fumes . . . from a huge King.* Cf. *Oratio* III, p. 452, ll. 16–17. Ordericus Vitalis (*Hist. Eccles.* 662 c) tells that at the burial of William the Conqueror in the abbey church at Caen, on his corpulent body being thrust into the narrow stone coffin, 'pinguissimus venter crepuit, et intolerabilis foetor circumstantes personas et reliquum vulgus implevit'.

l. 28. *rent*: intransitive verb, a variant of *rend*, tear. Books will outlast human bodies. Cf. *Priest to T.* p. 234, l. 2.

ll. 29–32. 'The reputation which you have taken so much pains to create will rest ultimately on the intelligence and appetite of those who come after your day.'

l. 33. *discoursing*: in the now obsolete sense of 'busily thinking, passing rapidly from one thought to another' (O.E.D.).

The Quidditie (Page 69)

The quiddity, properly the schoolmen's term for the nature or essence of a thing, came to be used for any over-subtle or captious distinction. Falstaff rallies Prince Hal about 'thy quips and thy quiddities' (*I Henry IV*, I. ii. 51).

l. 8. *my great stable.* The *my* of both MSS. is more vivid than the *a* which replaces it in *1633*. The owner shows off his possessions to his guests.

l. 10. *Hall*: probably the hall of a Livery Company, in which business was transacted for the sale of the members' goods.

l. 12. *most take all.* Mr. J. Middleton Murry kindly allows me to give his explanation: 'The titles to esteem which verse is not are first detailed; then it is declared that verse nevertheless is the *quiddity* of them all, in the very real sense that Herbert in his poetry comes nearest to God and most partakes of the creative power that sustains all these excellences.'

Humilitie (Page 70)

The distinctive tribute which the beasts (man's natural passions: cf. *The Church-porch*, ll. 263–4) brought were allotted, each to the Virtue best fitted by its contrary quality to use them aright: e.g. the hare's ears were given to Fortitude and the fox's brain to Justice. All went well until the Virtues *fell out* over *the Peacocks plume*; the beasts took advantage of this diversion and would have prevailed, but that Humility's tears ruined the plume, and the Virtues, having now nothing to quarrel over, joined forces against the beasts.

There is some likeness, as Palmer points out, to Sidney's poem, 'As I my little flock', in which the beasts bring each his particular quality to Jove, for him to combine them in creating man to be their ruler: 'The fox gaue craft; the dog gaue flattery: Ass patience', &c.

l. 3. *beasts and fowl.* The singular collective form, found in both MSS., is altered to *fowls* in *1633*. The collective occurs more than once in the A.V. in the same connexion, e.g. I Kings iv. 33 (of Solomon): 'hee spake also of beasts, and of foule, and of creeping things, and of fishes.'

l. 10. *giv'n to Mansuetude.* Sir Paul Rycaut's translation (1681) from the Spanish of Baltasar Gracian's *The Critick* has an almost identical phrase: 'A Lion whose fierceness had been lately turned to the Mansuetude of a Lamb.'

l. 13. The coral chiefly known in Herbert's time was red; Coverdale translates Lam. iv. 7, 'Their colour was fresh read as the Corall'. The *corall-chain*, therefore, fitly describes the turkey's red wattle, which symbolizes fleshliness. The word *jealous* was used specially of amorous rivalry.

l. 29. *bandying.* O.E.D., citing this example, defines 'to band together, league, confederate (cf. Fr. *se bander*)'. The reading in *B*, *banding*, does not scan and must be a copyist's error.

l. 31. *amerc'd*: fined, here with the penalty expressed.

Frailtie (Page 71)

l. 16. *prick*: inflame, make to smart. This sense is evident from the earlier reading in *W*, 'Troubling mine eyes'.

l. 19. *Affront*: confront, as in Milton, *P.L.* i. 391.

Constancie (Page 72)

Grosart noticed an allusion to this poem in the dedication of *The Standard of Equality* (1647) by Philo-Dicaeus to Sir John Danvers: 'it directed my thoughts unto your selfe, having heard that the Author in his lifetime had therein designed no other Title than your Character in that Description.' It little corresponds, however, to what is known of Sir John's character and career. In this poem Herbert is but following the contemporary fashion of writing Characters like Campion's 'The man of life upright' and Sir Henry Wotton's 'The Character of a Happy Life'. Wordsworth's 'Character of the Happy Warrior' owes something to Herbert's poem.

ll. 26–30. The same thought and some of the same words recur in *Letter* XII, p. 376, ll. 3–11.

ll. 31–3. The bowler is apt to *writhe* his shoulders, and to continue in a strained posture or even to strain further after discharging the ball, in a vain hope that he can twist it into a right course; so he *shares* the twistings of the ball to no purpose. Cf. Webster, *The White Devil*, I. ii:

> The Duke your maister visits me I thanke him,
> And I perceaue how like an earnest bowler
> Hee very passionatelie leanes that way,
> He should haue his boule runne.

Cf. also J. Earle, *Microcosmographie* (1628), xxx. 'A Bowl-alley': 'No antick screws men's bodies into such strange flexures', and Quarles, *Emblems*, I. x. 13–14:

> See how their curved bodies wreath, and screw
> Such antic shapes as Proteus never knew.

Affliction III (Page 73)

ll. 8–9. Herbert expresses the popular notion that a sigh diminishes man's vital strength and so shortens his life. Cf. *L'Envoy*, p. 199, l. 14, and Donne, 'A Valediction: of weeping', ll. 26–7:

> Since thou and I sigh one anothers breath,
> Who e'r sighes most, is cruellest, and hasts the others death.

God knows our allotted score (*tallies*, l. 8) and how much of life is left to us (*what's behinde*, l. 9).

ll. 17–18. 'They who praise thee only for thy death on the cross, praise thee below thy deserts, for, by sharing in the grief and sufferings of all *thy members* (ll. 2, 16), thou diest daily.'

The Starre (Page 74)

l. 30. *like a laden bee*. Cf. H. Vaughan, 'The Bee', ll. 105–6: 'like a laden *Bee*, I may fly home, and *hive* with thee.'

Sunday (Page 75)

l. 5. *cares balm and bay*. There may be, as Palmer suggests, an allusion to the notion which Browne discusses in *Pseudodoxia*, II. vi. 6, 'that *Bayes* [i.e. bay-trees] will protect from the mischief of Lightning and Thunder'; more probably *bay* here means a haven.

ll. 22–8. The words used in the comparison of Sundays and week-days with the arrangement of a garden suggest Bacon's advice (*Essays*, XLVI, Of Gardens):

> The *Garden* is best to be Square; Incompassed, on all the Foure Sides, with a *Stately Arched Hedge*. The *Arches* to be upon *Pillars*, of Carpenters Worke, of some Ten Foot high, and Six Foot broad: And the *Spaces* between, of the same Dimension, with the *Breadth* of the *Arch*.

ll. 26–8. Cf. H. Vaughan, 'The Bee', ll. 1–2:

> From fruitful *beds* and flowry *borders*
> Parcell'd to wastful Ranks and Orders.

l. 27. *that is bare*: i.e. the spaces between the flower-beds, like the intervals between Sundays, are bare.

l. 40. *took in*: enclosed, took into cultivation.

ll. 43–9. The rest-day of the Creation, the seventh day of the week, was *unhinged* by the substitution of the first day commemorating the Resurrection. The word *unhinge* means here 'to unsettle an established order of things', and as well in its primary sense it fits Samson's bearing the doors away (l. 47). The same comparison of the earthquake at the death of Christ (Matt. xxvii. 51) with Samson's overturning of the temple pillars (Judges xvi. 25–30) is made in *Passio Discerpta*, XVIII, p. 408.

l. 47. *Sampson*, though etymologically indefensible, is retained in the text, as it is the spelling in both MSS. and in Herbert's autograph of *Passio Discerpta*, XVIII (see frontispiece). The A.V., like the Geneva Bible and the Bishops', has *Sampson* in the only mention of him in the New Testament (Heb. xi. 32), but *Samson* always in Judges. Donne and others of Herbert's time often spell *Sampson*.

Avarice (Page 77)

ll. 13–14. Cf. *Providence*, p. 119, ll. 81–4, and the note, p. 519.

To all Angels and Saints (Page 77)

l. 1. *after all your bands*. If the *glorious spirits* are angels, the meaning is 'according to your ranks', with an allusion to the nine orders of angels. But, as angels are sinless and cannot know the *frown* of God, 'the spirits of just men made perfect' may be intended, who incurred the frown (cf. *The Flower*, p. 166, l. 35) by sinful acts in their earthly life, and have now received 'a crown of glory' (I Pet. v. 4): in that case *bands*, an old variant of *bonds*, means the fetters of sin (cf. Collect for Trinity XXIV in B.C.P.: 'delivered from the bands of those sins, which by our frailty we have committed', and the note on *The Sacrifice*, p. 485, l. 47).

l. 10. *Mother of my God*. Donne also calls Mary 'the Mother of God' (*LXXX Sermons*, xii. 112), 'whom no man can honour too much, that makes her not God', though he does not allow that the saints 'receive appeales from God, and reverse the decrees of God' (ibid. v. 46: cf. l. 22 of Herbert's poem). In more detail Donne discusses 'the degrees of Glory in the Saints' and their heavenly crowns in Sermon lxxiii.

ll. 11–12. *the gold, The great restorative*. Cf. Donne, Elegy xi. 112: 'Gold is Restorative, restore it then.' 'At one time when Bishop *Morton* gave him a good quantity of Gold (then a usefull token) saying, *Here Mr.* Donne, *take this, Gold is restorative*: He presently answered *Sir, I doubt I shall never restore it back again*: and I am assured that he never did' (J. Barwick, *Life of Morton*, 1660). The medicinal virtue of gold is discussed by Browne in *Pseudodoxia*, II. v. 3, and by Burton, who quotes Chaucer's 'For gold in physik is a cordial' (*Anat. of Melan.*, Part II, IV. i. 4).

Employment II (Page 78)

l. 5. *complexions*: 'bodily habit or constitution, originally supposed to be constituted by the four humours' (Onions).

l. 6. *a quick coal*: a piece of carbon glowing without flame (O.E.D.): cf. 'a liue-cole' (Isa. vi. 6), in contrast with dead 'coal', as in *Vertue*, l. 15.

l. 11. *th' elements*. 'The four elements, earth, air, fire and water; which were believed to enter into the constitution of every man, and upon a proper blending of which the temperament and character depended' (W. Aldis Wright). Fire was thought to be the highest (l. 13) and earth the lowest because the least active (l. 14).

l. 21. *Oh that I were an Orenge-tree*. 'Childish and impotent longings that his nature were of a more perfect, though lower, order' (W. J. Courthope, *Hist. of Engl. Poetry*, iii. 213).

l. 22. *That busie plant!* Busy, because it bore both fruit and blossom at the same time.

ll. 26–8. 'We excuse ourselves from beginning action on the ground that we are too young or too old for it, and so we let life slip by (*The Man is gone*, l. 27) before we have produced any *fruit for him that dressed* us.'

Deniall (Page 79)

l. 3. *my heart broken, as was my verse*. The imperfect harmony between the soul and God is figured by the unrhymed final line of each stanza until the last, where the restored harmony will *mend my ryme* (l. 30).

Christmas (Page 80)

ll. 6–7. Cf. *The Pulley*, p. 160, ll. 18–20.

l. 12. 'From being laid in *a rack* (l. 14) at birth, thou wert no stranger to the cattle.'

ll. 23–31. The meaning of *we* keeps shifting according to the context: l. 23 shepherd and flock; l. 25 he, they, and the sun; l. 28 shepherd and flock again; l. 31 he, they, and the new sun which he has gone to find (l. 27).

Ungratefulnesse (Page 82)

l. 6. Cf. Matt. xiii. 43: 'Then shall the righteous shine foorth as the Sunne', and Dan. xii. 3.

l. 7. Cf. Southwell, *S. Peters Complaint*, lx. 5: 'The cabinets of grace vnlockt their treasure.'

l. 18. A common treatment of a horse or dog with bad eyes was to blow a powder into them to clear the film.

l. 19. The Incarnation (*this box*, l. 23) contains the tender *mercies* of Christ, just as the spring is 'A box where sweets compacted lie' (*Vertue*, p. 88, l. 10). For Herbert's use of *sweets* meaning perfumes, see note on *Mortification*, l. 2, p. 511.

l. 29. *their box apart*. So in *Confession*, p. 126, ll. 2–5, there are boxes within a chest and 'in each box, a till'. In several poems Herbert shows an interest in joinery.

l. 30. *two for one*. 'Thou didst give *two rare cabinets* (l. 7) and askest only a single *heart* (l. 26) in return.'

Sighs and Grones (Page 83)

ll. 1–2. Cf. Ps. ciii. 10: 'Hee hath not dealt with vs after our sinnes.'

l. 10. *magazens*: storehouses.

l. 14. *an Egyptian night*. Exod. x. 22.

l. 20. *the turn'd viall*. Rev. xv. 7 and xvi. 1.

l. 28. Corrosive: a caustic remedy. Cf. Southwell, 'Fortunes Falsehoode', l. 11: 'With bitter corrosives her joyes are seasoned.'

The World (Page 84)

l. 7. Balcones. This Italian word, with all three syllables sounded, was commonly until the nineteenth century accented in English on the second, as in Italian.

l. 11. *Sycomore* was considered, by a mistaken etymology, to be a species of fig-tree: cf. *leaves* of l. 12 with *fig-leaves* of l. 16 in the preceding poem, in allusion to Gen. iii. 7.

l. 14. *sommers*: girders, the supporting beams.

'*Our life is hid*', &c. (Page 84)

Herbert had this text painted in Bemerton Church 'at his wive's seat' (Aubrey, *Brief Lives*, i. 310). The imagery of this poem is sustained by the motto itself running *obliquely* (l. 4) across the page. Cf. Browne, *Pseudodoxia*, VI. v, for the 'two motions' (cf. *a double motion*, l. 2) of the sun and 'an obliquity in his annual motion', and *The Church-porch*, p. 12, ll. 136–7.

Vanitie I (Page 85)

l. 5. *their dances*. Sylvester's translation of Du Bartas uses the word *dance* of the stars, and Giles Fletcher says of the star of Bethlehem (*Christs Victorie*, I. lxxxii. 6): 'A Starre comes dauncing vp the orient.' Beatrice says, 'there was a starre daunst, and vnder that was I borne' (*Much Ado*, II. i. 351).

l. 7. *aspects* (accented on the second syllable): 'the relative positions of the heavenly bodies as they appear to an observer on the earth's surface at a given time, and the influence attributed thereto' (Onions). Cf. Milton, *P.L.* x. 658, and Masson's citation *ad loc.* from Bebelius, *De Sphaera* (1582).

l. 14. *Her own destruction*. In spite of the correction in *B* of *Her* to *His*, the editor of *1633* was clearly right in retaining *Her*, or the antithesis would be lost.

ll. 15–21. The chemist in his laboratory is, as it were, *admitted to* the *bed-chamber* of the object of his inquiry, and he can there unclothe it (*devest*) and *strip* it of the feathers which disguise it (cf. *callow*, featherless), so as to discover its interior *principles*; he can give his mind to their study (l. 18) with better opportunity than those can who only see them emerge from *the doore* fully drest.

l. 22. *sought* (*1633*). *B* has *wrought*, but the theme of the poem (*surveys, fetch, did hide, finde, found, finde out*) seems to require *sought*.

Lent (Page 86)

Fasting in relation to Church authority is temperately discussed in *Priest to T.*, ch. x. Herbert's chronic ill-health interested him in matters of diet and made him willing to translate Cornaro's treatise *Of Temperance*. Cf. *Letter* III, p. 365, l. 1: 'Now this *Lent* I am forbid utterly to eat any Fish.' Oley mentions Herbert's 'carefull (not scrupulous) observation of *appointed Fasts, Lents* and *Embers*' (*Herbert's Remains*, sig. c. 1ᵛ).

l. 24. *Revenging*: exacting appropriate punishment for. Cf. Ecclus. v. 3: 'the Lord will surely reuenge thy pride.'

l. 25. *pendant profits*: 'Profits hanging like fruits, to be gathered in due season' (Willmott).

ll. 28–9. Cf. Shakespeare, *Romeo and Juliet*, II, iii. 19–20:

> Nor ought so good, but strain'd from that faire vse,
> Reuolts from true birth, stumbling on abuse.

l. 46. *revell at his doore*. Cf. *Unkindnesse*, p. 93, ll. 13–14. Herbert is evidently drawing from Isa. lviii. 6–7: 'Is not this the fast that I haue chosen? . . . Is it not, to deale thy bread to the hungry, and that thou bring the poore that are cast out, to thy house?'

Vertue (Page 87)

Ruskin makes a striking use of the last two lines (which, however, he quotes with Walton's slight variations from the original) in *A Crown of Wild Olive*, Lecture III. Coleridge gives the first three verses in *Biographia Literaria*, ch. xix.

l. 5. *angrie*. O.E.D., citing this passage, defines 'Having the colour of an angry face, red.'

l. 6. *the rash gazer*. Cf. Spenser, *F.Q.* II. iii. 23:

> So passing persant and so wondrous bright
> That quite bereau'd the rash beholders sight.

Also *The Pilgrimage to Parnassus*, ed. Macray, 1886, p. 85:

> *Draytons* sweete muse is like a sanguine dy,
> Able to rauish the rash gazers eye.

l. 7. *its* (*1633*): *his* (*B*). The form *its* was only slowly coming into use in Herbert's lifetime; it is not found at all in the A.V. of 1611. See p. 475.

l. 10. *sweets*: perfumes.

l. 11. *closes*: the musical term for a cadence. Cf. Shakespeare, *Tw. Night*, I. i. 4: 'That straine agen, it had a dying fall.'

ll. 13–16. While the day and the rose and the spring come to a natural end, virtue alone survives the general conflagration at the end of the world, which reduces all else to 'coal' (i.e. cinder, ashes).

The Pearl (Page 88)

ll. 1–2. *the head and pipes.* Probably in allusion to Zech. iv. 12: 'two oliue branches, which through the two golden pipes emptie the golden oyle out of themselues' (to feed the bowl for the seven lamps). But, as Beeching observes, it would be in Herbert's manner that the olive or wine press should suggest the printing press. Perhaps *the head* is the fountain of knowledge, the universities, and the *pipes* are those who mediate that knowledge to the world in the learned professions; thus Oley (*Herbert's Remains*, sig. a 5) writes of 'those Horns of Oyl, the two Universities'.

l. 8. '*Stock and surplus* may be the learning we inherit, and that which we add to it' (H. C. Beeching, *Lyra Sacra*).

ll. 13–17. 'I know how to gauge by the rules of courtesy who wins in a contest of doing favours; when each party is urged by ambition to do all he can by look or deed to win the world and bind it on his back' (Beeching).

l. 32. *not sealed, but with open eyes* (seeled *W*). See note on *The Church-porch*, l. 415. Cf. Peter Sterry, *The Rise, Race and Royalty of the Kingdom of God* (1683), p. 224: 'When thine Eyes shall be unsealed, how will thy Spirit within thee be amazed?'

ll. 33–40. 'I understand the conditions of sale, and the price I must pay, but, after all, it is thy guidance rather than my intelligence that brings me to thee.'

l. 38. *thy silk twist*: a thread or cord composed of fibres of silk, wound round one another. A hyphen was often used, as in *W* and *1638*. Cf. *Providence*, p. 118, l. 58.

Affliction IV (Page 89)

l. 3. *A thing forgot.* Cf. Ps. xxxi. 12: 'I am forgotten as a dead man out of minde.'

l. 4. *now a wonder.* Cf. Ps. lxxi. 7: 'I am as a wonder vnto many, but thou art my strong refuge' ('tanquam prodigium factus sum multis', Vulgate).

l. 7. *My thoughts are all a case of knives.* Walton reports of Herbert: 'he would often say, *He had a Wit, like a Pen-knife in a narrow sheath, too sharp for his Body*' (*Lives*, p. 28).

l. 12. *pink*, the reading of both MSS., is more likely to be the author's word than *prick* (*1633*), especially in relation to *Wounding* (l. 8) and to Herbert's frequent references to fencing. Cf. B. Jonson, *Ev. Man in Hum.* IV. ii: 'I will pinck your flesh, full of holes, with my rapier.' But *prick* is also suitable: cf. H. Vaughan, preface to *The Mount of Olives* (*Works*, ed. Martin, i. 141): 'If therefore the dust of this world chance to prick thine eyes, suffer it not to blinde them.'

Herbert uses a metaphor (watering-pots) within a metaphor (knives) and then gets back to knives (l. 12), the word *scatter'd* being common to the description of the effects of the knives and of the watering-pots. A similar return is found in *Artillerie*, p. 139, ll. 17–25.

Man (Page 90)

There are many resemblances, especially in verses 5–8, to Abelard's Creation hymn, 'Ornarunt terram germina'.

l. 1. *I heard this day.* The words that follow sound too formal for the language of conversation; perhaps Herbert had heard Luke xiv. 28–30 in the appointed lesson for the day or a sermon on that passage (but not, as Grosart suggests, 'by one of his Curates', as the poem, being found in *W*, was probably written before Herbert went to Bemerton). Both Herbert and Vaughan affect this casual and almost colloquial allusion to a day in the first line of a poem, e.g. *Affliction V*, p. 97, 'My God, I read this day', and Vaughan's 'I saw Eternity the other night' and 'I walkt the other day (to spend my hour)'; but Herbert generally composes at once (*this day*), while Vaughan writes in retrospect.

ll. 7–8. *Man is ev'rything, And more.* That Man is *minor mundus*, a microcosm, 'in little all the sphere' (l. 22), is a commonplace of the schoolmen, and the idea is continued into Herbert's day by Bacon, Sir John Davies, and Henry More; but Herbert urges that Man is all that *and more*. Cf. Donne, *XXVI Sermons*, xxv. 370:

> The properties, the qualities of every Creature, are in man; the Essence, the Existence of every Creature is for man; so man is every Creature. And therefore the Philosopher draws man into too narrow a table, when he says he is *Microcosmos*, an Abridgement of the world in little: *Nazianzen* gives him but his due, when he calls him *Mundum Magnum*, a world to which all the rest of the world is but subordinate.

Donne's last clause is very near to ll. 5–6 of this poem.

l. 8. *yet bears more fruit.* There is no greater textual difficulty in *The Temple* than this, and an editor, while obliged to make a decision in printing the text, ought to allow the case against his decision to be fully stated. *W*, the only surviving MS. which Herbert saw, has *more* (not *mo*, as the Nonesuch edition states), which is replaced by *no* in *B* and all the early printed texts. Grosart guessed that the copyist of *B* had *mo* before him and mistook this uncommon word for *no*; but it is unlike Herbert to use an obsolescent form, though *moe* is found in the A.V., e.g. Exod. i. 9 and Num. xxii. 15, and *mo* and *moe* are in Shakespeare. If the *no* of *B* is not a copyist's mistake or an emendation of Ferrar's, it 'represents a later stage of Herbert's thought', as Palmer believes 'on the whole', adding in explanation: 'Man does not attain the fruitfulness he should possess. In the next line it is hinted that he also fails in his appropriate superiority to the beast. Elsewhere Herbert laments that man falls short of the fruitful tree' (*Employment II*, p. 79, ll. 21–5, and *Affliction I*, p. 48, ll. 57–60). It might further be urged that Man does not quickly bear fruit and then rest content; his bearing comes late and is less directly noticeable than the fruit on the tree. All this constitutes a strong case for *no fruit*, and if it is indeed Herbert's second thought it must stand; but, in spite of this reasoning, the sense of the whole passage seems to demand *more*. Mr. John Sparrow allows me to give his comment: 'Herbert is showing that man is the noblest of creatures—man alone (l. 10) has reason and speech;

if any other animals speak (e.g. *Parrats*, l. 11), they owe it to man. He *is* a beast, but he is more than a beast. He is a tree, but—the sense demands that "he is more than a tree" should follow. Does *no fruit*, or *more fruit*, give this sense? Now, if in bearing no fruit man showed himself superior to apple trees, *no fruit* might be right. But surely Herbert is not simply saying that man is better than trees because he does not bear apples and pears; he is saying that man is better than trees because he bears more (more abundant and more various and nobler) fruit than trees bear. I therefore should read *more*.'

l. 12. *They go upon the score*: are in man's debt.

l. 16. *Each part may call the furthest, brother*. Cf. *Dooms-day*, p. 186, ll. 5–6:

While this member jogs the other,
Each one whispring, *Live you brother?*

l. 18. Refers to the notion that different parts of the body are affected by the motions of the moon and stars and planets.

l. 39. When the waters were *distinguished*, i.e. separated from the land (Gen. i. 9–10), the latter afforded a *habitation* for man.

l. 40. *above, our meat*. The rain is needed to make the earth yield her fruits.

l. 41. *Hath one such beautie?* 'If a single element, water, has such a variety of good uses, may we not expect the other elements to have a similar aptness for man's service?'

l. 45. *He treads down*, &c. Cf. Donne, *XXVI Sermons*, viii. 111 (using Clement of Alexandria's comparison): 'we tread upon many herbs negligently in the field, but when we see them in an Apothecaries shop, we begin to think that there is some vertue in them.'

l. 50. *O dwell in it*. And so fulfil the purpose (l. 3) of building such a *stately habitation* (l. 2). Cf. *The World*, p. 84, l. 1: 'Love built a stately house.'

Antiphon II (Page 92)

l. 18. *crouch*: 'Formerly often applied to the act of bowing low in reverence or deference' (O.E.D.). Cf. *Miserie*, p. 101, l. 39: 'we crouch To sing thy praises.'

l. 23. The common praise of God has united angels and men.

Unkindnesse (Page 93)

l. 1. *coy*: reserved, backward (O.E.D., citing this example).

l. 16. *pretendeth to*: aspires to, is a candidate for.

Life (Page 94)

Vaughan quotes this poem in full in *The Mount of Olives* (*Works*, ed. Martin, i. 186), introducing it with the words: 'Heark how like a *busie Bee* he *hymns* it to the *flowers*, while in a handful of *blossomes* gather'd by himself, he foresees his own *dissolution*.'

l. 15. *after death for cures.* The rose 'purgeth' (*The Rose*, p. 178, l. 18); 'the Parson useth damask or white Roses' for 'loosing' (*Priest to T.*, p. 261, l. 34); 'A rose, besides his beautie, is a cure' (*Providence*, p. 119, l. 78). Cf. Donne, 'The first Anniversary', ll. 403–4:

> Since herbes, and roots, by dying lose not all,
> But they, yea Ashes too, are medicinall.

Submission (Page 95)

l. 10. 'I resume the use of my private judgement, which I had surrendered' (l. 2).

l. 17. 'I stand by my surrender, which I threatened to take back' (ll. 10–12). Cf. Southwell, 'Dyer's Phancy', ll. 119–20:

> I gave my vow; my vow gave me;
> Both vow and gift shall stande.

Justice I (Page 95)

l. 10. *the hand hath got*: hath got the upper hand. This use of the phrase without 'upper' is not recorded in O.E.D.

Charms and Knots (Page 96)

Herbert returns for once to the didactic manner of *The Church-porch*. There are many parallels in the Book of Proverbs (e.g. iii. 9–10, xi. 24, xix. 17) and in *Outl. Pvbs*. The word *knot* is used figuratively of knotty problems: cf. *Divinitie*, p. 135, l. 20: 'Who can these Gordian knots undo?' Dillingham, op cit. p. 43, gives a Latin rendering of this poem under the title 'Gryphi'.

ll. 9–10. Cf. *Priest to T.*, p. 269, l. 13: 'he that throws a stone at another, hits himselfe', and *Assurance*, p. 156, ll. 39–40: 'for thou hast cast a bone Which bounds on thee.'

ll. 15–16. The payment of the tithe or tenth part of agricultural produce to the parish priest is repaid by his ministrations. Cf. *Jacula Prudentum*, No. 1147: 'Tithe, and be rich.'

Affliction V (Page 97)

l. 2. *planted Paradise.* Cf. Gen. ii. 8: 'And the Lord God planted a garden Eastward in Eden.'

l. 3. *As was and is thy floting Ark.* The allusion is to the Christian traditional use of the word *Ark*, as in the Baptismal Office, for 'the Arke of Christs Church'.

l. 15. *Some Angels us'd the first.* Cf. *Praise III*, p. 158, l. 21: 'Angels must have their joy.'

l. 17. *baits in either kinde*: the 'bait of pleasure' (*The Church-porch*, l. 4) and weariness, as at the end of *The Pulley*, p. 160, ll. 18–20.

ll. 21–2. A bower is a shelter, either natural or artificial, formed by branches or shrubs; cf. *Miserie*, p. 101, l. 55: 'a daintie bowre Made in the tree'. A knot is a flower-bed laid out in a fanciful or intricate design: cf. Shakespeare, *Love's Labour's Lost*, I. i. 248: 'thy curious-knotted garden'. Milton (*P.L.* iv. 241–6) contrasts the bower of natural growth with 'Beds and curious Knots' made by 'nice Art'.

l. 22. *store*, a common Elizabethan word for abundance, is used by Herbert 21 times. Grosart takes it here to be a word, now only used provincially, meaning a stake.

l. 24. *may tame thy bow*. The rainbow (Gen. ix. 12–17) follows on the mention of the Ark in l. 3, but the word *bow* is also meant to suggest the instrument of divine punishment: cf. *Discipline*, p. 179, l. 25: 'Who can scape his bow?'

Mortification (Page 98)

The same theme is developed, though with a more terrible morbidity, in Donne's last sermon, *Deaths Duell* (1632), e.g. in the following passage (pp. 11–12):

> That which we call life, is but *Hebdomada mortium*, a *weeke of death*[*s*], seauen dayes, seauen periods of our life spent in dying, *a dying seauen times ouer*, and there is an end. *Our birth dyes* in *infancy*, and our *infancy* dyes in *youth*, and *youth* and the rest *dye* in *age*, and *age* also dyes, and *determines all*.

l. 2. *a chest of sweets*. The word *sweet* is used often by Herbert (e.g. *Easter*, l. 22; *Ungratefulnesse*, l. 19; *The Odour*, ll. 17–25; *Vertue*, l. 10) in the sense of sweet odours, perfumes, fragrance; not sweetmeats.

l. 4. *Scarce knows the way*. Borrowed, as Palmer notes, from the opening line of Donne's 'Elegie on the Lord Chancellor': 'Sorrow, who to this house scarce knew the way.'

l. 5. The word *clouts* had been used, from the thirteenth century at least, specially for swaddling clothes, e.g. by Caxton (*Golden Legend*, 128. 2): 'The chyld wrapped in poure clowtes lyeng.'

l. 12. *bound for death*. The metaphor is of a passenger on board ship, borne to his destination by the *rolling waves* (l. 11).

l. 17. *the knell*. In Herbert's day the passing-bell was still rung, in accordance with the Canons Ecclesiastical (1604), No. lxvii, 'when any is passing out of this life', and not, as later, only after death. Cf. Donne, 'To Sir H. W. at his going Ambassador to Venice', ll. 15–16: 'as prayers ascend To heaven in troupes at a good mans passing bell', and Herbert's discarded poem *The Knell*, p. 204. The bell prompted the charitable to 'assist the dying Christian with prayers and tears' (Oley in *Herbert's Remains*, sig. c 1ᵛ), so that it may be said to *befriend him at the houre of death*. The reading *houre* in *W* is more likely to be intended than *house* (*B* and *1633*), which pointlessly anticipates its appropriate use in l. 30.

l. 24. *attends*: (figuratively, of things) is in store for, awaits. Cf. *Justice II* p. 141, l. 16.

l. 29. *A chair or litter.* Cf. *The Pilgrimage*, p. 142, l. 36. The use of the word *chair* has more point when it is remembered that in Herbert's day it was a symbol of old age: e.g. 'thy chair-days' in Shakespeare, *II Henry VI*, v. ii. 48, and *I Henry VI*, iv. v. 4–5:

When saplesse Age, and weake vnable limbes
Should bring thy Father to his drooping Chaire.

Herbert's thought is anticipated by Southwell, 'Upon the Image of Death', stanza 5:

The gowne that I do use to weare,
  The knife wherewith I cut my meate,
And eke the old and ancient chaire
  Which is my onely usuall seate:
All these do tel me I must die,
And yet my life amend not I.

l. 33. *herse*: bier. The word was not yet used for a funereal carriage.

Decay (Page 99)

The theme is discussed, with a repeated use of the word *decay*, in Donne's sermon of Whitsunday 1625 (*LXXX Sermons*, xxxvi. 357), e.g.

> As the world is the whole frame of the world, God hath put into it a reproofe, a rebuke, lest it should seem eternall, which is, a sensible decay and age in the whole frame of the world, and every piece thereof. . . . And the Angels of heaven, which did so familiarly converse with men in the beginning of the world, though they may not be doubted to perform to us still their ministeriall assistances, yet they seem so far to have deserted this world, as that they do not appeare to us, as they did to those our Fathers.

ll. 3–5. Moses was on such familiar terms with God, that, though he was bidden *Let me alone*, he persisted in pleading until, unable to resist his *strong complaints*, 'the Lord repented of the euill which he thought to doe vnto his people' (Exod. xxxii. 9–14).

l. 15. *to gain thy thirds.* Thirds (usually in the plural) was a legal term, specially used of the third part of a deceased husband's real property, to which the widow was entitled. Sin and Satan seek to oust God from the third part of the heart, which is all that is left to him when they are in possession, so that he must *still retreat* (l. 18).

l. 16. *when as*: (oftener printed as one word) seeing that, inasmuch as. Used again in *The Glimpse*, p. 154, l. 19, and *Love*, p. 202, l. 7.

l. 18. *Doth closet up it self.* Cf. *Whitsunday*, p. 60, l. 21: 'Thou shutt'st the doore, and keep'st within.'

Miserie (Page 100)

l. 5. Cf. Isa. xl. 6: 'All flesh is grasse.'

l. 16. Cf. Ps. cxxxix. 2, B.C.P.: 'Thou art . . . about my bed: and spiest out all my wayes.'

l. 25. *quarrell*: (transitive verb) find fault with, dispute thy right to command.

l. 35. *infection*: moral contamination. 'How shall a corrupted thing approach thy *perfect puritie?*' (l. 32) Images from the plague, which was common in that age, come naturally. Cf. *The Church-porch*, p. 16, l. 249.

l. 62. *winks*: (figuratively) closes the eyes to what he does not wish to see. Cf. *The Collar*, p. 153, l. 26.

l. 77. *shelf*: sandbank or a submerged ledge of rock; here figuratively, as in *The Church-porch*, l. 120: see note on p. 478 for the parallel from Habington's *Castara*.

l. 78. *My God*. Probably a vocative, not an exclamation.

Jordan II (Page 102)

For the meaning of the title, see note on *Jordan I*, p. 495.

l. 3. *invention*. The title of this poem in *W*. Almost a technical term in rhetoric: e.g. Obadiah Walker, *Oratory* (1659), p. 1: 'The Parts of Oratory are Invention, taking care for the Matter; and Elocution, for the Words and Style.'

l. 4. *burnish*: spread out, grow in strength and vigour; coupled with *spread* in Fuller and Dryden, as Palmer points out.

l. 5. *Curling*. Cf. *Dulnesse*, p. 115, ll. 5–8.

l. 10. *quick*: as often, in antithesis to *dead* (cf. Acts x. 42: 'the Iudge of quicke and dead'); here and in *Sion*, p. 107, l. 21, figuratively, meaning 'lively'.

l. 16. *wide*: now oftener in the phrase, 'wide of the mark'.

ll. 16–18. Cf. the opening sonnet of Sidney's *Astrophel and Stella*, ending with the line, 'Foole said my *Muse* to mee, looke in thy heart and write.' Herbert had already shown familiarity with this sonnet in his second New Year sonnet, p. 206.

Prayer II (Page 103)

l. 9. *tacks the centre to the sphere*. The sphere, the apparent outward limit of space, is at all points equidistant from its centre, which is the earth.

l. 15. *curse*. Cf. Gal. iii. 13: 'Christ hath redeemed vs from the curse of the Law, being made a curse for vs: for it is written, Cursed is euery one that hangeth on a tree.'

Obedience (Page 104)

Legal terms are used throughout, except perhaps in stanzas 5 and 6.

l. 2. *Convey*: transfer or make over by deed or other legal process.

l. 6. *On it my heart doth bleed*, &c. Cf. Marlowe, *Faustus*, II. i. 35, where Mephistophiles bids Faustus sell his soul:

> But Faustus, thou must bequeathe it solemnely,
> And write a deede of gift with thine owne blood.

l. 8. *passe*: convey legally.

l. 11. *If that*: in use for the simple *if*; cf. Shakespeare, *Lear*, v. iii. 263–4: 'If that her breath will mist or staine the stone, Why, then she lives.'

l. 13. *a reservation*: a clause of a deed by which some right or interest in property to be conveyed to another is reserved or retained for one's self.

l. 35. 'Purchase is called the possession of landes or tenementes that a man hath by his dede or by his agreemente' (*Littleton's Tenures*).

l. 42. *If some kinde man*, &c. As Miss Elizabeth Holmes points out (*Henry Vaughan and the Hermetic Philosophy*, 1932, pp. 12–13), Vaughan 'comes forward to answer the plea of Herbert's *Obedience* in his own poem *The Match*':

> Here I joyn hands, and thrust my stubborn heart
> Into thy *Deed*.

l. 43. *heav'ns Court of Rolls*. Its earthly counterpart is the Court of the Master of the Rolls for the custody of records. Herbert imagines his own Deed moving *some kinde man* to follow his example, and the conveyances of both being registered together by the recording angels.

Conscience (Page 105)

l. 8. *B* has no mark of punctuation after *sphere*, perhaps because the line reaches the extreme margin, but *1633* has a semicolon and *1634* a full stop. Some stop is needed, as rocking cannot aptly be compared to the action of a sphere.

ll. 21–2. A reminiscence of Ps. xxiii. 4–5, B.C.P.: 'thy rod and thy staffe comfort me. Thou shalt prepare a table before mee against them that trouble me.' A *bill* is a halberd.

ll. 23–4. Cf. Donne, 'The Crosse', l. 25: 'Materiall Crosses then, good physicke bee.' Mr. W. Empson discusses the imagery in *Some Versions of Pastoral* (1936), p. 79.

Sion (Page 106)

The poem is a comment on Acts vii. 47–8: 'But Solomon built him an house. Howbeit the most high dwelleth not in temples made with hands', and I Cor. iii. 16: 'Knowe yee not that yee are the Temple of God?' God abandons his *ancient claim* that Solomon should 'build an house' (II Sam. vii. 13), as the temple which he now desires *is within* (l. 12).

l. 6. Every detail revealed the builder's care and invited the beholder's attention. I retain the spelling of *B*, *seeers*, because it both helps the scansion and avoids a misunderstanding.

l. 11. *thy Architecture meets with sinne*. Man, *thy Architecture*, is 'the Temple of God' (I Cor. iii. 16), yet sin also is in him, so that *There* (l. 13) is the seat of conflict. Cf. 'the *Architect*' who could build 'in a weak heart' (*The Church-floore*, p. 67, ll. 19–20).

l. 16. *Great God doth fight*. Cf. *The Temper I*, p. 55, ll. 13–16, and *Artillerie*, p. 139, ll. 25–7.

l. 17. Solomon 'made a moulten Sea' of brass (I Kings vii. 23), and his temple 'was built of stone' (vi. 7). A *world* is used by Shakespeare and other contemporaries of a vast quantity.

l. 18. *as one good grone.* Cf. *Gratefulnesse*, p. 124, ll. 19–20.

Home (Page 107)

The allusions to *this holy season* (l. 73), to the Day of Judgement (l. 58), and to the Incarnation (l. 19), make it probable that the poem was written in Advent, although ll. 7–10 suggest Passion-tide. The word *stay*, upon which the whole poem is built, means 'delay coming, be long in coming, stay away', though Herbert also takes advantage of its ambiguity in ll. 31 and 67.

ll. 13–15. Cf. Isa. lix. 16: 'And hee [the Lord] saw that there was no man, and wondered that there was no intercessour.'

l. 19. *thy sonne.* This is a surprising turn, as the Son himself is addressed in ll. 6–10. There is a similar change from addressing the Holy Spirit to addressing the Father in *Grieve not the Holy Spirit*, p. 135, ll. 1 and 35.

l. 22. *Leave one poore apple.* Cf. 'Prayer before Sermon', p. 288, ll. 20–1: 'for an apple once we lost our God, and still lose him for no more; for money, for meat, for diet.'

l. 31. *Yet* introduces a change of emphasis: the second line of the refrain (l. 6) is now stressed instead of the first; 'if thou wilt not *show thy self to me* here, then *take me up to thee.*'

l. 39. *wink Into*: 'bring into a specified state by a glance or nod' (O.E.D., citing this passage).

l. 76. *The word is,* Stay. To rhyme with *pray* (l. 74).

The British Church (Page 109)

We might have expected *English*, but *British* had perhaps special aptness after James I had been proclaimed King of Great Britain, and after full episcopacy had been reintroduced into Scotland in 1610. The *via media* of the Anglican Church, between Rome and Geneva, both in doctrine and in worship, is often commended by Herbert, e.g. in *Musae Responsoriae*, xxv and xxx. The Country Parson desires 'to keep the middle way between superstition, and slovenlinesse' (*Priest to T.*, p. 246, l. 24.). Donne also commends 'the middle way' (*LXXX Sermons*, v. 42, and *Essays in Divinity*, pp. 106–11), though he shows uncertainty in 'Holy Sonnets', xviii, with which Herbert's poem has some verbal similarities.

l. 5. *dates her letters.* Besides retaining many of the old holy-days, the Church of England officially still reckoned the beginning of the year from Lady Day, which was also Herbert's practice in dating his letters.

ll. 10–12. Cf. T. Fuller, *Hist. of Waltham Abbey* (1655), p. 19, in commending a decent comeliness in the ornaments of the church: 'Is there no mean betwixt painting a face, and not washing it? He must have a fixt aim and strong hand, who hits decency, and misseth gaudiness and sluttery.'

l. 13. *She on the hills.* Cf. Donne, *LXXX Sermons*, lxxvi. 769:

Trouble not thyselfe to know the formes and fashions of forraine particular

Churches; neither of a Church in the lake, nor a Church upon seven hils; but since God hath planted thee in a Church, where all things necessary for salvation are administred to thee, and where no erronious doctrine (even in the confession of our Adversaries) is affirmed and held, that is the Hill, and that is the Catholique Church.

The Quip (Page 110)

l. 2. *train-bands*, a common abbreviation of *trained bands*, used of the citizen soldiery of London.

l. 15. 'I was allowed but a glimpse of Court life before my hopes of preferment were dashed.'

l. 19. *an Oration*. The initial capital in *B* may indicate a playful reference to Herbert's career as Public Orator at Cambridge.

l. 24. *home*: an adverb. Cf. *The Church-porch*, p. 15, l. 218, and the Countess of Pembroke, *Psalm* liv: 'Lord . . . pay them home, who thus against me fight.'

Vanitie II (Page 111)

l. 1. *Poore silly soul*. The poet is addressing himself, as in *Businesse*, p. 113, ll. 2 and 6: 'Foolish soul', 'poore soul'.

The Dawning (Page 112)

The dawning of Easter Day. The ideas of the poem recall those in *Easter*, p. 41, and *Easter-wings*, p. 43.

l. 9. *if thou doe not*. The alteration of *doe* (*B*) to *dost* (*1633*) is probably editorial, as the author commonly has the subjunctive form after *if*, e.g. *The Church-porch*, l. 461: 'If thou do ill.' He would also be likely to avoid the assonance of *dost* and *withstand*.

Jesu (Page 112)

The differentiation of I and J, whether in manuscript or in print, was not complete in Herbert's time: e.g. J is not found in the A.V. of 1611. In *B* the same capital letter is used for the consonant as for the vowel, but *1633* prints J for the last word of l. 5, the title, and the first and last words of the poem. The last word of l. 5 must be pronounced *I*, as it rhymes with *instantly*, while *Jesu* (ll. 1, 10) is a disyllable, with the first letter as a consonant.

Businesse (Page 113)

If one has committed sin, there is no time to lose (no *space of breath*, l. 29) before accepting Christ's offer of redemption; to repent is to be busy, to delay repentance is to be idle.

ll. 13–14. It were better to have no body to feel the pains of hell; these, however, can be escaped by enduring the *Lesser pains* of a present penitence.

l. 22. *two deaths.* The first is the natural death of the body, and 'the second death' (Rev. xx. 6, 14; xxi. 8) is eternal death, the condemnation of the lost soul after the Judgement. Cf. *Mans medley*, p. 131, l. 30: 'And he of all things fears two deaths alone', and H. Vaughan, 'Easter-day', ll. 5–8:

> Awake, awake,
> And in his Resurrection partake,
> Who on this day (that thou might'st rise as he,)
> Rose up, and cancell'd two deaths due to thee.

fee: in the now obsolete sense of reward. Cf. Spenser, *F.Q.* IV. x. 3: 'Yet is the paine thereof much greater then the fee.'

l. 28. *Two lives.* A life *in miserie*, here and hereafter, would be worse than any number of merely physical deaths.

l. 34. *a silver vein.* Cf. Job. xxviii. 1: 'Surely there is a veine for the siluer.'

Dialogue (Page 114)

ll. 1–8. 'If I thought my soul worth thy having, I would not hesitate to surrender it, but, since all my care spent upon it cannot give it worth (*gains*, l. 6), how can I expect thee to benefit by acquiring it?'

l. 4. The form *wave* is found as a variant of *waver*, but it is also an old spelling of *waive*. Either meaning is possible here, but the sustained legal metaphor in this poem is in favour of *waive*, 'decline the offer' instead of *resigning* (l. 28).

l. 20. *savour*: perception, understanding (O.E.D., citing this instance).

ll. 22–3. 'I deny all responsibility for the bargain; it was none of my making.'

ll. 25–8. 'That settles it; that resignation of yours is the end of the matter, if at least you can make it without reservation or regret. You would but be following the example of my renunciation.'

l. 30. *desert*: pronounced *desart*, as it was often also spelt, e.g. in Marvell's 'To his Coy Mistress', l. 24.

Dulnesse (Page 115)

'The peculiarity of this poem is not so much that it offers God the adoration of a lover—other religious poets and mystics have done that—as that on Herbert's lips such language sounds perfectly natural and appropriate, suggesting neither an uncommon state of mystical exaltation nor a tendency to weakness or sentimentality. There is that same blend of wit and tenderness which is characteristic of some of the best love-poetry of his age—even that conceit about red and white, which many would find offensive, seems to me, I must admit, entirely in keeping with the whole tone of the poem, and not at all extravagant' (J. B. Leishman, *The Metaphysical Poets*, 1934, p. 137).

ll. 13–14. 'All perfections are assembled in one, and that single perfection is made up of the many perfections exhibited together in thy form only.'

l. 18. *window-songs*: serenades.

l. 19. *pretending*: in the old sense of making suit for, wooing. Cf. *The Size*, p. 138, l. 36.

l. 25. *cleare*: discharge a debt or promise. 'Give me *quicknesse*, the liveliness of mind, for which I asked thee' (l. 3).

Love-joy (Page 116)

The vine suggests both Christ 'the true vine' and the joy of feasting, with a thought also of the sacrament of love. The tendrils appear to take the shapes of *J* and *C*.

l. 5. *spend*: utter, with a suggestion of uttering needlessly or squanderingly.

l. 6. The *bodie* of a tree is the stem or main part; Defoe says of Robinson Crusoe that 'he got into the body of the tree'.

Providence (Page 116)

There are many echoes of Psalm civ, which is headed in A.V. 'A meditation vpon the mighty power and wonderfull prouidence of God'. There are also resemblances to the thought and expressions of Donne, especially in ll. 8, 21–4, 51, 59–60, 85, 140. A Latin version is in Dillingham, op. cit. p. 35.

ll. 1–2. Cf. Wisdom viii. 1: 'Wisdome reacheth from one ende to another mightily: and sweetly doeth she order all things.' Repeated in ll. 31 and 39.

l. 9. *birds dittie to their notes*. Birds would fain fit words to their song.

l. 12. *lame*: i.e. the fingers cannot handle the pen (l. 7). Dr. Johnson writes of 'lame fingers'.

l. 13. *Man is the worlds high Priest*. Cf. 'Quis iste tandem', p. 436, l. 24, and Henry More, *An Anti-dote against Atheism* (1653), p. 85:

> One singular End of man's creation is that he may be a *Priest* in this magnificent *Temple* of the *Universe*, and send up Prayers and praises to the great Creator of all things in behalf of the rest of the Creatures.

ll. 21–4. Cf. Donne, 'Holy Sonnets', xii. 1–8.

l. 23. *Pull*: used of plucking fruit.

l. 36. *stealing pace*. Cf. P. Fletcher, *The Purple Island* (1633), VI. lxxvii: 'But see, the stealing night with softly pace . . . creeps up the East.'

l. 39. *temper'st*. As *tun'd* precedes and *musick* follows, it is likely that Herbert has in mind the musical sense of *temper*, to tune, adjust the pitch, bring into harmony.

ll. 47–8. Cf. Jer. v. 22: [I] 'haue placed the sand for the bound of the sea, by a perpetuall decree that it cannot passe it, and though the waues thereof tosse themselues, yet can they not preuaile.'

l. 51. *fishes have their net*. Perhaps an echo of Donne, 'The Progresse of the Soule', xxxiii, where the whale with 'his gulfe-like throat' is, as it were, provided with 'his owne net'.

l. 53. *prevent*: anticipate. No creature comes into existence before there is food for it.

l. 56. *their cheer*: the winter provender of those in l. 55. Cf. R. Knolles, *History of the Turks* (1621), p. 713: 'their cheere was only rice and mutton.'

l. 71. *vent*: discharge (O.E.D., citing this instance), though perhaps the following words, *expense* and *store*, intentionally bring to mind a different verb *vent*, meaning 'sell': cf. *Sinnes round*, p. 122, l. 9.

l. 74. *vertues*: healing properties. The word is specially used (e.g. in Gerarde's *Herball*) of the efficacy of plants to affect the human body beneficially.

l. 76. *expressions*: literally used of juices squeezed out or expressed (cf. *expresse*, l. 73), but Herbert may as well be playing with its other meaning, as used in l. 142 ('None can expresse thy works').

l. 80. *Are there.* Our fortunes are determined in the stars, which have *power* (l. 77) over men's lives, but *our art* of interpreting them is not to be relied on. Cf. *Outl. Pvbs*, No. 641: 'Astrologie is true, but the Astrologers cannot finde it.'

l. 81. *Thou hast hid metals.* Cf. Hor. C. III. iii. 49: 'Aurum irrepertum et sic melius situm'; Milton, *P.L.* i. 687–8: [Men] 'Rifl'd the bowels of their mother Earth For Treasures better hid'; and Pope, *Moral Essays*, Ep. III, ll. 9–10:

Nature, as in duty bound,
Deep hid the shining mischief under ground.

l. 83. *He makes a grave.* Cf. *Avarice*, p. 77, l. 14.

l. 85. *Ev'n poysons praise thee.* As Donne suggests ('To S[r] Edward Herbert, at Iulyers', ll. 23–30), poisons 'may be good At lest for physicke, if not for our food', and he says elsewhere (*LXXX Sermons*, xvii. 170) that 'poisons conduce to Physick'.

ll. 105–8. Cf. *Priest to T.* p. 229, l. 23: 'one Countrey doth not bear all things, that there may be a Commerce', and *Oratio* III, p. 450, ll. 18–25: 'diuisit Natura suas dotes, vt indigentia singularum regionum omnes connectat. . . . Quamobrem optimè consuluit gentibus natura, cùm paupertatem daret tanquam catenam, quâ dissitas nationes ac superbas constringeret.'

l. 116. *grew*: grew into, became.

l. 126. *The Indian nut*: the current name for the coco-nut.

l. 130. *Cold fruits* is, I think, the object of *help*, not, as Grosart and Palmer print it, a genitive annexing *kernells*.

l. 133. *Thy creatures leap not.* There are gradations or links between all created things; 'Natura non facit saltus.'

l. 140. *th' Elephant leans or stands.* Donne ('The Progresse of the Soule', xxxix) remarks that the elephant 'Still sleeping stood', but Browne, discussing the same notion in *Pseudodoxia*, III. i, mentions that an elephant has been seen 'kneeling and lying down' in England 'not many years past'. The supposed fact that an elephant does not lie down at night was a common illustration in medieval preaching (G. R. Owst, *Literature and Pulpit in Medieval England*, p. 198).

l. 146. *advise*: opinion, judgement (O.E.D., citing this instance of a use now obsolete).

l. 148. *in this twice.* In this poem only, the poet offers praise both in his own person and as the spokesman or priest of all creation: cf. ll. 13–14, 25–6.

ll. 149–52. Palmer detects that this verse is an alternative for the preceding, the author perhaps having not decided which of the two to retain. This is probable, although there is no indication in the MS. that the verses are alternative.

Hope (Page 121)

The *watch* given to Hope suggests the giver's notion that the time for fulfilment of hopes is nearly due, but the *anchor*, given in return, shows that the soul will need to hold on for some time yet; the *old prayer-book* tells of prayers long used, but the *optick*, or telescope, shows that their fulfilment can only be descried afar off; *tears* receive in return only *a few green eares*, which will need time to ripen for harvest; and then the donor's patience gives out. Cf. H. Vaughan, 'Love, and Discipline', ll. 16–18.

There may be an allusion to the seals, 'to be used as *Seales*, or *Rings*', sent by Donne shortly before his death (31 Mar. 1631) to Herbert, Walton, and other friends (Walton, *Life of Donne*, 1658, p. 80). On them was engraved Christ crucified on 'an Anchor (the Embleme of hope)'; cf. Heb. vi. 19: 'Which hope we haue as an anker of the soule.' See also Herbert's poem, 'In Sacram Anchoram Piscatoris', p. 438.

Sinnes Round (Page 122)

l. 4. *cockatrice*: a fabulous creature hatched by a serpent from a cock's egg. Cf. Isa. lix. 5: the wicked 'hatch cockatrice egges . . . he that eateth of their egges dieth, and that which is crushed breaketh out into a viper', and Browne, *Pseudodoxia*, III. vii.

l. 8. *the Sicilian Hill*: Mount Etna.

l. 9. *vent*: discharge (cf. *spit it forth*, l. 8), but *wares* suggests that the different verb, *vent* 'sell', is also present to Herbert's mind. Cf. the note on *Providence*, p. 519, l. 71. To *ventilate* is to increase the flame by blowing or fanning; the cockatrice was thought to kill by its breath.

Time (Page 122)

There is a curiously light, bantering tone about this grave subject, as there is also in *Death*, p. 185, and *Dooms-day*, p. 186.

l. 7. At this point the poet resumes his remonstrance and continues to the end of l. 26, when Time interrupts and has the last word.

passe. Shakespeare also uses the word absolutely for the act of dying, e.g. *Lear*, IV. vi. 48.

ll. 25–6. The poet grudges the protraction of the earthly life that stands between him and the timeless life of eternity (Rev. x. 6); that was why he began by asking Time to sharpen his scythe (l. 2), but Time had not then seen, as he does now (l. 30), the reason for the request.

Gratefulnesse (Page 123)

l. 13. *knockings*. Cf. *The Storm*, p. 132, ll. 11–16. Miss E. Holmes, op. cit. p. 15, notes Thomas Vaughan's travesty of this stanza in his *Anima*

Magica Abscondita (1650), describing the 'magician's' preparations for the entrance of the divine spirit into matter, and his tiring him with his 'pious importunities':

> Perpetuall knockings at his Doore,
> Teares sullying his transparent Roomes,
> Sighes upon sighes: weep more and more,
> He comes.

l. 15. *much would have more*. Cf. Hor. C. III. xvi. 42–3: 'Multa petentibus desunt multa.' The English proverb is given in J. Clarke's *Paroemiologia* (1639). Cf. Drayton, *Polyolbion*, xv. 293:

> Then *Loddon* next comes in, contributing her store;
> As still we see, 'The much runs ever to the more'.

ll. 17–24. Cf. Donne, 'The Litanie', ll. 199–201:

> Heare us, O heare us Lord: to thee
> A sinner is more musique, when he prayes,
> Then spheares, or Angels praises bee.

l. 24. *take*: captivate, 'fetch'. Cf. Jonson, *Silent Woman*, I. i:

> Such sweet neglect more taketh me,
> Than all th' adulteries of art.

l. 31. Oley (*Herbert's Remains*, sig. c) notes Herbert's '*consciencious expence of Time*, which he even measured by the *pulse*, that *native watch* God has set in every of us'.

Peace (Page 124)

ll. 22–3. *a Prince of old At Salem dwelt*. It is evident from 'The Sap', a poem with many borrowings from Herbert's *Peace*, and with perhaps a reference to its author ('one who drank it', l. 45), that Henry Vaughan took Herbert here to be referring to Christ. Melchisedec, 'king of Salem, which is, king of peace' (Heb. vii. 2), who 'brought foorth bread and wine' (Gen. xiv. 18), prefigures Christ.

Confession (Page 126)

l. 12. Cf. *Outl. Pvbs*, No. 475: 'Wealth is like rheume, it falles on the weakest parts', and Bacon, *Plantation of Ireland*: 'If there be any weak or affected part, this is sufficient to draw rheums, or humours to it.'

l. 15. *foot*: seize with the claws (oftener used of birds of prey).

ll. 19–20: *an open breast Doth shut them out*. Cf. *no fastning*, l. 23. A deliberate paradox: the opening of the heart by confession, instead of exposing it to the assault of sin and grief, renders it immune.

l. 30. '*They* (*the brightest day* and *The clearest diamond*) will look cloudy compared with my breast, when it is cleared by confession.'

Giddinesse (Page 127)

l. 11. *snudge*: remain snug and quiet (O.E.D., citing this instance). But a different verb, *snudge* = to be stingy, would fit the reference to eating in the previous line: 'to snudge it; or churlishly to eat all his meat all alone' (Cotgrave).

l. 19. *like a Dolphins skinne.* Not the mammal like a porpoise, but the dorado (*Coryphaena hippuris*), popularly called a dolphin, a fish like a mackerel; its metallic colours undergo rapid changes on its being taken out of the water and about to die, but it cannot be inferred that the changes have any relation to its *desires* (l. 20).

l. 27. *Except thou make us dayly.* Cf. II Cor. iv. 16: 'though our outward man perish, yet the inward man is renewed day by day.'

The Bunch of Grapes (Page 128)

The story of the Israelites journeying from the Red Sea through the wilderness to the Promised Land is also our story, because God's righteous acts are prophetic and foreshadow our case too (ll. 11–14). And if we do not meet with their 'cluster of grapes' (Num. xiii. 23), we have Christ 'the true vine' (John xv. 1).

l. 4. *vogue*: general course or tendency (O.E.D., citing this example of a use now obsolete).

l. 10. *spann'd*: measured out, limited. Cf. Shakespeare, *Henry VIII*, I. i. 223: 'My life is spand already.'

l. 16. *Our Scripture-dew.* An allusion to Num. xi. 9: 'And when the dew fell vpon the campe in the night, the Manna fell vpon it.'

l. 17. *shrowds*: shelters, especially of a temporary kind. Cf. Milton, *Comus*, l. 147: 'Run to your shrouds, within these Brakes and Trees.'

l. 28. *pressed.* Cf. *The Agonie*, p. 37, Isa. lxiii. 3, and Quarles, *Divine Fancies* (1630), ii. 76:

> Me thinkes, the grapes that cluster from that Vine,
> Should (being prest) afford more blood then wine.

Love unknown (Page 129)

Coleridge quotes this poem in full in *Biographia Literaria*, ch. xix, as illustrating 'the characteristic fault of our elder poets', namely, 'conveying the most fantastic thoughts in the most correct and natural language'; he calls this poem 'an enigma of thoughts'. It has much in common with the emblem-poetry of Quarles, and it is likely that Herbert had some pictorial emblem in mind.

l. 5. *both lives in me.* 'I hold *some grounds* (i.e. my soul) to improve in this world and the next (*for two lives*).'

l. 15. *a great rock.* The rock struck by Moses (Exod. xvii. 6) is allegorized in I Cor. x. 4: 'our fathers . . . dranke of that spirituall Rocke that followed them: and that Rocke was Christ.' Cf. *The Sacrifice*, p. 32, l. 170.

l. 26. *fornace.* This is the spelling here of both *B* and *1633*, and it is the form found in the A.V. of the Bible, but in *Longing*, p. 149, l. 26, the *furnace* of *1633* replaces the *fornace* of *B*.

l. 34. *slipt*: inserted furtively.

l. 37. Your heart was hard. Cf. *Grace*, p. 60, ll. 17–20.

l. 43. *steal*: convey stealthily. Cf. R. North, *Autobiogr*. i. 3: 'But there was another use made of this botle, for our Mother would steal into it slices of Rubarb.'

Mans medley (Page 131)

Medley, a combination or mixture, was formerly used without a disparaging sense; the word was also used for a cloth woven in different colours, and this sense may have been in Herbert's mind when he wrote ll. 15–18. Dillingham, op. cit. p. 44, has a Latin version of this poem.

l. 10. Man alone has both joys, those of earth and heaven, whereas mere sentient creatures (*things of sense*, l. 7) have earth only, and Angels heaven only.

l. 15. *round*: a technical term to describe cloth made of thick thread.

ll. 15–18. Man should take his rank, not by the coarse material of his animal nature, but according to (*After*, l. 18) the fineness of *the trimming*, which links him with a higher destiny.

l. 18. *ground*: 'a piece of cloth used as a basis for embroidery or decoration' (O.E.D.).

l. 27. *two winters*: physical (*frosts*) and spiritual (*thoughts*).

l. 30. *two deaths*. See note on *Businesse*, p. 517, l. 22.

The Storm (Page 132)

l. 6. *Amaze*. The amanuensis of *B* probably reproduced the author's word in writing *Amuse*, which, derived from the French *amuser*, originally meant 'cause to muse, bemuse, bewilder'; thus John Hacket, Herbert's contemporary at Westminster and Trinity, said in a sermon that Christ's transfiguration 'did amuse Peter, James and John'. Cf. Donne, 'A Valediction: of the booke', ll. 32–4:

> Or, loth so to amuze
> Faiths infirmitie, they chuse
> Something which they may see and use.

But already *amuse* was being used, e.g. by Donne elsewhere, in its modern sense, and either Herbert on second thoughts or his editor substituted *Amaze*.

object: bring their guilt before them, make them conscious of their crimes.

l. 7. Stars, though they seem to represent the serenity of heaven, have their meteor-showers.

l. 17. Cf. *The Bag*, p. 151, l. 5: 'Storms are the triumph of his art.'

Paradise (Page 132)

The poet lops the rhyme-words, letter by letter, much as the divine Gardener is said to *prune and pare*. R. Seeley in his edition of *The Temple* (1894) illustrates this poem by the reproduction of an engraving of fruit-trees *in a row*, gardeners, and a pruning-knife, from *The Gardeners Labyrinth* (1577) by Didymus Mountain (pseudonym of Thomas Hill). There is another allusion to a formal garden in the fourth stanza of *Sunday*, p. 75.

The Method (Page 133)

'If God refuses your petition (l. 2), you would do well to examine your behaviour and to discover *the method* or way of procedure which will win his assent.'

l. 3. *rub*: impediment; a metaphor from an obstacle diverting a bowl on the green, as in Shakespeare, *Richard II*, III. iv. 4, and *Hamlet*, III. i. 65.

l. 6. *move*: urge, prefer a request. Cf. 'motions' (l. 19) and *Praise II*, p. 146, l. 4.

l. 10. *turn thy book*: search through it by turning the leaves; cf. *The Pilgrimage of Perfection* (1531): 'Handes . . . redy to turne theyr boke.' The *book* is the register of his life, in which the lines italicized (15–17 and 22–4) are entered: cf. *Judgement*, p. 187, l. 5: 'ev'ry mans peculiar book'. Bishop Pecock (*c.* 1449) speaks of 'the book of mannis soule'.

l. 18. *indifferents*: persons so little concerned that they do not even pay heed to their own petitions.

Divinitie (Page 134)

l. 2. *spheres*: globes showing the position and motions of the heavenly bodies.

l. 3. *a clod*: a clodhopper. Used in this sense by Jonson in *Volpone*, III. i. 9.

l. 8. *lies by*: remains unexercised.

l. 11. *jagg'd*: slashed or pinked by way of ornament.

ll. 13–16. Cf. *Priest to T.* p. 263, ll. 3–4: 'the Parson hath diligently examined . . . whether any rule in the world be obscure, and how then should the best be so, at least in fundamentall things.'

l. 25. *Epicycles*: smaller circles having their centres in the circumference of a larger circle or 'cycle'. 'In the Ptolemaic system of astronomy each of the "seven planets" was supposed to revolve in an epicycle, the centre of which moved along a greater circle' (O.E.D.).

'*Grieve not the Holy Spirit*' (Page 135)

l. 10. *part*: die, as in *The Size*, p. 137, l. 3.

ll. 23–4. *strings* are made of cat-gut: O.E.D. cites from *Liber Cocorum* (*c.* 1420): 'Harpe strynges made of bowel'. The Bible regards the bowels as the seat of the tender emotions: cf. *Longing*, p. 149, l. 19: 'Bowels of pitie, heare!'

ll. 28–32. 'I am not crystal-clear but so stained with sin that I need *endlesse tears*, which *Nature denies* me; yet *a cleare spring* runs without cease, whether I need its water or not.'

The Familie (Page 136)

The poem complains of disorderly noise which offends Herbert's musical ear and his love of 'all things neat' (*Man*, p. 92, l. 42). If only Peace and

Order were to bear rule (l. 4) in his heart, he might expect, not the intermittent, but the *constant stay* (l. 24) of the divine presence.

l. 3. *puling*. In *B* the word was first written *pulling*, but the second *l* has been erased with a pen-knife, yet so imperfectly that the correction has been overlooked or questioned by some who have examined the MS. All the early printed texts have *pulling*. It is, however, probable that the correction was rightly made. There is no satisfactory sense to be made of *pulling fears*, but whining fears, joined with *loud complaints*, add to the general disturbance of peace, where there are no sensitive *eares* and *no rule*.

l. 10. *plaies*: as on an instrument, to bring it into tune. The many musical terms in this poem make it likely that *plaies* also has a musical connotation.

l. 19. *distemper'd*: mentally deranged (O.E.D., citing this instance). Cf. Milton, *P.L.* iv. 807: 'distemperd, discontented thoughts'.

l. 20. *shrill*: poignant. Vaughan was so taken with the paradox that, after a less successful adaptation of it in 'An Epitaph upon the Lady Elizabeth', he opened his poem 'Admission' with Herbert's words almost unaltered: 'How shril are silent tears?' (J. Bennett, op. cit. pp. 89–90).

The Size (Page 137)

Similarly in *The Rose*, p. 177, l. 4, Herbert accepts 'my strict, yet welcome size', i.e. a modest status.

l. 16. Both *Enact* (*1633*) and *Exact* (*B*) give good sense, but the former is likely to be the right word as it better carries on the metaphor of the previous line (*laws of fasting disanull*).

ll. 19–22. *Great joyes* realize all that was hoped for (*have their hopes*) and leave nothing more to be expected; but *Modest and moderate joyes* (l. 2) are only an earnest of what we may hope to receive *hereafter* (l. 3), and *tice us on to hopes of more* (l. 29).

l. 22. *on score*: in debt, on credit.

ll. 25–7. M. Arnold, quoting these lines in *Culture and Anarchy*, p. 139, substituted *banished* for *sentenc'd*.

l. 36. *a pretender*: a suitor, wooer. The word was regularly used in this sense, and survives in such expressions as 'pretend to the hand'. Cf. *Dulnesse*, p. 116, l. 19: 'Lovers are still pretending.' The suitor's mind is divided between happiness and anxiety before he has achieved his marriage.

ll. 39–41. 'We should be reckoning time, not by the last great snowstorm, but by our latest joy; for joys would be as infrequent and memorable as a snowstorm, if they depended on our having earned them' (*fell according to desert*, l. 39).

l. 46. *meridian*: 'a graduated ring (sometimes a semi-circle only) of brass in which an artificial globe is suspended and revolves concentrically' (O.E.D., citing this example).

Artillerie (Page 139)

A development of the idea already found in *Prayer I*, p. 51, that prayer is an 'Engine against th' Almightie, sinners towre, Reversed thunder'. Crashaw imitates the conceit in 'On a prayer booke sent to Mrs. M. R.', l. 9: 'It is loves great Artillery.'

l. 2. *Me thoughts*: it seemed to me. An archaic impersonal verb, distinct from the common verb *think*. *Me thoughts* or *Methoughts* (again in *The Collar*, p. 154, l. 35) is an incorrect form of *methought*, on the analogy of *methinks*.

l. 8. Divine impulses, like falling stars, have the appearance of fire, and therefore suggest danger and disturbance, but in the end they bring restful thoughts.

l. 11. *ministers*. Cf. Ps. civ. 4, B.C.P.: 'He maketh his Angels spirits: and his ministers a flaming fire.'

l. 17. *shooters*: shooting stars. O.E.D. gives no other example of this sense. The *Report of the British Association*, 1857, i. 152, records 'an instance, the rare one of an *ascending* shooting star'. But when Herbert uses *shooters* of stars, he is also conscious of the relation of the word to *Artillerie* and in l. 25 he uses it in its ordinary sense.

l. 27. *thine own clay*. Cf. *Dialogue*, p. 115, l. 27: 'my clay, my creature.'

ll. 29–30. *I am thine . . . if I am mine*. This theme is developed in *Clasping of hands*, p. 157.

l. 31. *articling*: arranging by treaty or stipulation. Often found with the word *parley* (l. 27): e.g. North, *Plutarch* (1676), p. 124: 'In which parly it was articled', &c. John Howe, Cromwell's chaplain, in his *Self-dedication*, states the converse of Herbert's saying: 'God is pleased to article with dust and ashes.'

Church-rents and schismes (Page 140)

The Church is figured as 'the rose of Sharon' (Song of Songs, ii. 1) in her *chair* of authority: schisms *within you* (l. 17) harm the Church more than assaults from without (ll. 13–15), which purge her of insincere adherents.

l. 1. *chair*. *B* has *place*, which does not rhyme; *chair*, if not originally intended by the author, was inferred by the editor of *1633* from its use in l. 10. Perhaps the author intended to change *chair* in l. 10 to *place*, which suits that context better, but by inadvertence the change was made in l. 1 instead. There are instances of the copyist's inattention in this poem.

l. 10. *bitten*. *B* has *sitten*, a form of the past participle which is found in *Psalm I*, p. 214, l. 4; but *all sitten*, in spite of *chair*, makes no sense, and is probably a slip of the amanuensis.

l. 12. *And shows it so*. The Church, *my Mother*, shows that she is a rose by blushing.

l. 18. *vaded* (*B*). This variant form of *fade* was much affected by poets, at least as late as Marvell, and here it helps to make a pleasing succession of initial consonants, besides giving a tone of sadness. In the other four uses of this verb in *The Temple* both *B* and *1633* have *fade*.

l. 21. *start*: as timber is said to start, get loose.

l. 29. *With these two poore ones*: i.e. 'with the only two eyes I have, though I need for my grief *As many eyes as* there are *starres*' (l. 26). For the hyperbole, cf. *Grief*, p. 164, ll. 1–10.

Justice II (Page 141)

The justice of God, as seen in the Old Testament, has lost its terrors, now that it is viewed in the light of Christ's mediation (l. 13); but Herbert also has himself (*to me*, l. 4) passed from fear to confidence (l. 14).

ll. 7–10. The *dishes* or *scales* (l. 16) hang from the *beam* or cross-piece, the *scape* (Lat. *scapus trutinae*) being the upright shaft or tongue of the balance.

l. 10. *torturing* (*B*). *1633* prints *tort'ring*, an abbreviation *metri gratia* which is found in Pope's 'The Rape of the Lock', iv. 100.

l. 13. *Christs pure vail.* Palmer refers to II Cor. iii. 14: 'in the reading of the old testament' a veil was used which 'is done away in Christ'; but this poem affirms the presence of a veil in the Christian dispensation. For Christians it is no longer the opaque veil of the old Law 'of blue, and purple, and crimson' (II Chron. iii. 14), but *Christs pure vail*, a transparent one, 'the vaile, that is to say, His flesh' (Heb. x. 20).

ll. 16–17. *buckets, which attend.* It is tempting to suppose, with B. G. Hall, that *attend* (*B* and *1633*) is a mistake for *ascend*, but it would be an unsatisfactory rhyme to *descend*. There is possibly a play on words between the scales of the balance and Jacob's ladder (*scala* in the Vulgate version of Gen. xxviii. 12), on which the angels ascended and descended. The fact that the unusual word *interchangeably* (l. 17) occurs twice in Shakespeare's *Richard II* makes it the more likely that Herbert remembered the king's words to Bolingbroke (iv. ii. 184–9):

> Now is this Golden Crowne like a deepe Well,
> That owes two Buckets, filling one another,
> The emptier euer dancing in the ayre,
> The other downe, vnseene, and full of Water:
> That Bucket downe, and full of Teares am I,
> Drinking my Griefes, whil'st you mount vp on high.

The Pilgrimage (Page 141)

l. 10. *my houre.* Cf. *Complaining*, p. 144, ll. 17–18: 'my houre, My inch of life.' Herbert is conscious that his short span of life is slipping by with nothing accomplished.

ll. 13–14. *which Some call the wold.* For instance, the hilly tracts of Lincolnshire, which Herbert knew through his visiting his sister Frances, Lady Browne, are so called. A pun may be intended on *would* (*B*).

l. 17. *one good Angell.* A pun on the gold coin with the device of St. Michael on it, last coined in Charles I's reign. Donne carries the same pun very far in 'Elegie XI'. If Herbert is not simply thinking of his guardian angel, but, as some suppose, of his marriage to Jane Danvers, the *friend* is likely to be her kinsman Henry Danvers, earl of Danby, with whom Herbert was living at the time. When Woodnoth contemplated entering Sir John Danvers's service, Herbert advised him that 'to be a prompter of good to Sr Iohn was to be a good Angell too him' (*The Ferrar Papers*, p. 267).

l. 36. *a chair*. Cf. *Mortification*, p. 98, l. 29: 'A chair or litter shows the biere.'

The Holdfast (Page 143)

The title is probably drawn from Ps. lxxiii. 27, B.C.P.: 'But it is good for me to hold me fast by God.' The interlocutor speaks or is reported as speaking ll. 3–4, 6–7, 9–10; *a friend* speaks ll. 12 and 13–14, unless the final couplet is the poet's summary; this monitor pushes him a stage farther each time: he may *trust in* God (l. 4), but God alone gives him the power to trust (l. 6); he *must confesse* (l. 7), but the confession too is God's gift (l. 9). These divine gifts of grace are safer in Christ's keeping (l. 14) than in our own.

l. 12. *more ours by being his*. Cf. the fourth stanza of *The Discharge*, p. 144.

Complaining (Page 143)

l. 5. *thy dust that calls*. Cf. *Deniall*, p. 80, ll. 16–18:

> O that thou shouldst give dust a tongue
> To crie to thee,
> And then not heare it crying!

The Discharge (Page 144)

The word *discharge* is used for a document conveying release from an obligation; there are other words in this poem having a legal or commercial connotation—*counts*, *depart*, *right*, *fee*. 'Having once given up all to God, you should feel yourself free from anxiety; by that surrender you have committed the future to his keeping.'

l. 3. *licorous*: having a keen desire for what is pleasant.

l. 8. *with the whole depart*: part with, surrender all. Cf. Shakespeare, *John*, II. i. 562–3:

> *Iohn* to stop *Arthurs* Title in the whole,
> Hath willingly departed with a part.

l. 21. *fee*: allotted portion.

ll. 31–2. If man worries himself about the future, he violates the accepted order, namely, that the present only is his concern, and the future is God's. Cf. Shakespeare, *Ant. and Cleop.* II. iii. 6: 'I haue not kept my square', and J. Heywood, *Prouerbes*: 'An inche breaketh no square.'

ll. 36–40. Seeley, op. cit. p. 184, illustrates these lines with an engraving from Holbein's *Dance of Death*, showing an astrologer, who tries to read the future from a sphere, and is confronted by Death thrusting a skull before his eyes.

l. 45. *draw the bottome out.* Herbert uses *bottom* of a skein of thread again in *Letter* XI, p. 373, l. 6.

an end: continuously. Sometimes written as one word or with hyphen. Cf. Shakespeare, *Two Gent.* IV. iv. 68: 'A slaue that still an end turnes me to shame.'

l. 46. *God chains the dog till night.* Isaac Barrow, walking in a friend's garden before daybreak, was attacked by a watchdog, which was chained by day and let loose at night as a protection against thieves.

ll. 48–50. 'Vex yourself to-day (*now*) about to-morrow's ills, and then to-morrow grieve over them afresh.'

Praise II (Page 146)

ll. 15–16. 'Thou alone didst listen to me, when my sins still clamoured against me, after thou hadst acquitted me' (ll. 13–14).

l. 26. *enroll*: record with honour, celebrate.

ll. 27–8. Cf. the close of Addison's hymn (*Spectator*, 9 Aug. 1712):

For oh! Eternity 's too short
To utter all thy Praise.

An Offering (Page 147)

ll. 11–12. A king or other representative man may plead for a nation and ward off a pestilence, as David did. Cf. H. Vaughan, 'Rules and Lessons', ll. 63–4:

Thou mai'st in Rags a mighty Prince relieve
Who, when thy sins call for't, can fence a Curse.

l. 22. *All-heal.* Here a general term for a balsam which heals all wounds; applied specially by Gerarde to Clown's Woundwort: cf. Marvell, 'Damon the Mower', ll. 83–4:

With Shepherds-purse, and Clowns-all-heal,
The Blood I stanch, and Wound I seal.

Longing (Page 148)

l. 9. Cf. Gen. iii. 17.

l. 21. From Ps. lxxxvi. 1.

ll. 22–4. '*Thy name* is found in *my words*; why then should they be scattered?'

ll. 25–30. Mr. W. Force Stead remarks that this stanza 'with its *sorrows, furnace, flames, heats, griefs, shames,* seems an eruption from Southwell's *Burning Babe*'.

ll. 35–6. Quoted from Ps. xciv. 9.

l. 38. *it creeps.* Mr. Feeble-mind in *The Pilgrim's Progress* (Oxford edn., p. 249) says: 'this I have resolved on, to wit, to *run* when I can, to *go* when I cannot *run*, and to *creep* when I cannot *go*.' Cf. *Discipline*, p. 179, l. 15.

l. 52. *interlin'd*: come between the lines. Cf. Vaughan, 'White Sunday', ll. 37–8: 'as in nights gloomy page One silent star may interline', and Donne, *A Sermon preached at Whitehall, 4 Feb. 1625* (1626):

> What place of Scripture soever thou pretend, that place is interlined—interlined by the Spirit of God Himself with conditions and limitations and provisions,—'If thou return', 'if thou repent',—and that interlining destroys the bill.

The Bag (Page 151)

l. 1. *my gracious Lord doth heare.* An answer to the plaintive entreaty in l. 79 of the previous poem. Herbert's recovery from depression often marks the conclusion of a poem which begins in sadness; sometimes the recovery is only reached, as here, in a succeeding poem.

l. 6. *close his eyes,* as on the boat in the storm (cf. l. 4) on the Sea of Galilee (Matt. viii. 24).

l. 11. *light*: alight.

l. 13. *tire*: especially of a head-dress. Cf. Spenser, *F.Q.* I. x. 31: 'And on her head she wore a tyre of gold.'

l. 14. *the fire*: lightning.

l. 17. *He smil'd and said.* Cf. *Love III*, p. 189, l. 11: 'Love took my hand, and smiling did reply.'

The Jews (Page 152)

l. 2. *cyens* (a spelling of *scions* in common use as late as Dryden): slips for grafting. Cf. Shakespeare, *Winter's Tale*, IV. iii. 92–3: 'we marry A gentler Sien, to the wildest Stocke.' The reading of *B*, *sinnes*, is probably the copyist's misreading of an unfamiliar word; the metre requires a disyllable, and *cyens* continues the metaphor of *sap and juice*.

purloin'd: robbed. The word is similarly used in R. Surflet and G. Markham's *The Country Farme* (1616) about weeds: 'If they be suffered to grow vp, sucke, purloine, and carrie away the sap.'

ll. 5–6. The clue to these difficult lines must be found in St. Paul's contention that a Jew who rested in the old Law was 'a debtor to doe the whole Law' (Gal. v. 3), which was an impossible task; yet by still trying to keep the letter of the Law, instead of accepting Christ's deliverance from it (Rom. vii. 6), he stood to lose; *the letter* which he loses may perhaps, by a play on the word, stand also for the New Testament. Cf. Rom. ii. 17–29.

l. 12. Cf. Job xiv. 7–9: 'For there is hope of a tree, if it be cut downe, that it will sprout againe . . . though the stocke thereof die in the ground: Yet through the sent of water it will bud, and bring forth boughes like a plant.'

The Collar (Page 153)

M. Pierre Legouis (*André Marvell*, 1928, p. 168) comments on the *audaces* of Herbert in this early example of *vers libres*, with the varying length of the lines and the wide spacing of the rhymes; he thinks that Marvell in his poem 'On a Drop of Dew' is following the lead of *The Collar*.

The collar was in common use to express discipline, and 'to slip the collar' was often used figuratively. Preachers would use the word *collar* of the restraint imposed by conscience; for example, Daniel Dyke (ob. 1614) says that religion 'will not teach thy servant to slip his neck out of the collar, and to deny thee service and subjection'.

l. 6. 'Am I always to be doing suit and service to another, instead of taking my own line?'

ll. 33–6. There is a similar end to *Mem. Matris Sacr.* VIII, p. 427, ll. 7–10.

The Glimpse (Page 154)

l. 5. The MS. reading *to my heart* is preferable to *for my heart* (*1633*), as it avoids the repetition of *For* from the previous line.

ll. 11–15. 'The addition of water only increases the *inward heat* of the quicklime; so *Thy short abode* is tantalizing and only increases my desire for an enduring union.' The words 'of old, they say' suggest that Herbert is alluding to a fable or allegory; there is some resemblance to No. LXXV of the *Aenigmata* of Symphosius with the title of *Calx* (Baehrens, *Poet. Lat. Min.* iv. 379):

> Euasi flammas, ignis tormenta profugi:
> Ipsa medella meo pugnat contraria fato;
> Infundor lymphis: gelidis incendor ab vndis.

I have to thank Professor L. C. Martin for this parallel.

l. 20. An Italian proverb, translated in *Outl. Pvbs*, No. 726.

ll. 23–5. 'Though *thy heap* or store of heavenly things is rightly kept under lock and key for future use, occasional *droppings* from it, like "the crummes which fall from their masters table" (cf. l. 17), may be allowed to reach me, without breaking the lock and touching the main *stock*.'

ll. 26–7. The difficulty of interpreting these lines turns on the ambiguity of the word *stay*. If, as in l. 11, it means 'staying here', it is not complimentary to say that the presence of delight would seem short because I was busy spinning. If, as seems more likely from *thy coming* in l. 30 referring apparently to the future, *stay* means 'staying away, absence' (as in *Home*, p. 108, l. 31), the sense is: I will spin so busily that the time of thy staying away will seem short; or, I will contentedly keep the wheel going, and not let grief and sin interrupt my work, provided (*so that*, l. 26) thy absence does not last too long.

ll. 29–30. 'Do not by thy absence give grief and sin an occasion to jeer at me, whereas *thy coming* would transform my heart into *a court*.' The antecedent of *Who* is *me*

Assurance (Page 155)

ll. 32–3. *while rocks stand, And rivers stirre*: i.e. so long as the world lasts. Cf. Vaughan, 'To the River *Isca*', l. 34: '"Till *Rivers* leave to *run*.'

l. 39. 'Thou *foolish thought*, thou hast tried to sow discord *Betwixt my*

God and me (l. 9), but the bone will rebound and stick in thy throat.' Cf. J. Heywood, *Prouerbes*: 'The diuell hath cast a bone (said I) to set stryfe Betweene you.'

The Call (Page 156)

l. 2. Most journeyings put us out of breath, but this gives us the breath of life. Cf. *Priest to T.* p. 257, l. 34: 'for thou art not only the feast, but the way to it.'

ll. 6–8. The divine light sets off the festal scene; it is a feast which improves as it goes on (cf. John ii. 10: 'but thou hast kept the good wine vntill now'); and the eucharistic feast is for 'the strengthening and refreshing of our soules'. Cf. *Priest to T.* p. 259, l. 14: 'Hee that comes to the Sacrament, hath the confidence of a Guest.'

l. 10. *move*: take away. Cf. *The 23d Psalme*, p. 173, l. 23: 'And as it never shall remove', and John xvi. 22: 'your ioy no man taketh from you.'

Clasping of hands (Page 157)

Dr. Mario Praz gives many contemporary examples of such verbal play in *A Garland for John Donne* (1931), p. 62.

ll. 12–13. 'I dare to think that thou art somehow more mine than thine own.' Cf. H. Vaughan, 'Love-sick', ll. 18–22.

l. 20. Cf. *Theologia Germanica* (tr. S. Winkworth), ch. xliii: 'Where this Light is, the man's end and aim is not this or that, Me or Thee, or the like, but only the One, who is neither I nor Thou, this nor that, but is above all I and Thou, this and that; and in Him all Goodness is loved as one Good.'

Praise III (Page 157)

l. 15. The classical name *Albion* for Britain was familiar from its use by Drayton, Shakespeare, and Camden; Herbert uses it in *Oratio* III, p. 451, l. 18. It was, perhaps, congenial to James I; a Roman Catholic petition to him for toleration has the words, 'your blessed Mothers right unto the Scepter of *Albion*' (*Scrinia Sacra*, ii. 82). The phrase here is like 'All the king's horses and all the king's men' in the nursery rhyme.

l. 17. Cf. Exod. xiv. 25: 'the Lord . . . tooke off their charet wheeles, that they draue them heauily.'

l. 23. *stint*: limitation, due measure.

l. 27. *a bottle*. Cf. Ps. lvi. 8: 'Thou tellest my wanderings, put thou my teares into thy bottle: are they not in thy booke?'

l. 28. Canon lxxxiv orders the provision of 'a strong Chest' in every church 'to the intent the Parishioners may put into it their alms for their poor neighbours'.

l. 33. *like streamers*. Flags, which were hung from church towers after a victory, would 'stream' in the wind. R. Seeley, op. cit. p. x: 'The comparison seems very forced and artificial; but in a rudely-coloured German woodcut preserved in the British Museum, the drops of blood have just the appearance of red pennons, and the same effect may have been sometimes seen in stained glass windows.'

l. 35. *bloudie battell.* Cf. Christ's 'bloudie fight' in *Good Friday*, p. 39, l. 22.

l. 38. *Though press'd.* See l. 5.

l. 40. *at use*: at interest.

Josephs coat (Page 159)

Like the 'coat of many colours' (Gen. xxxvii. 3) life is variegated by joy and pain and by different forms of pain. The poet gets relief by making music of all his chequered experiences; for, if he were to allow a single grief to absorb him, it would claim both heart and body as its prey. In l. 8 *both* means *one grief and smart* (a single conception, followed by singular pronouns, *his*, *it*) and *my heart*, but in l. 9 *both* appears to be *my heart* and *the bodie*.

l. 6. *had his full career.* Cf. *The Glance*, p. 172, ll. 11–12:

> Had the malicious and ill-meaning harm
> His swing and sway.

l. 9. *due to grief.* There is perhaps a reminiscence of Aesop's fable, 'Grief and his Due': Grief having been absent when Jupiter allotted privileges, there was nothing left for him until Jupiter 'at last decided that to him should belong the tears that were shed for the dead'.

l. 10. *he hath spoil'd the race.* God mercifully frustrates this precipitate impulse of grief and the heart to kill the body, by his tempering pain with joy and by teaching the sufferer to make songs of his grief (l. 14).

The Pulley (Page 159)

Herbert refashions a later version of the story of Pandora, the first mortal woman. Jupiter gave her a box containing the blessings of the gods, but on its being opened they all slipped out and were lost except Hope, which lay at the bottom.

l. 15. *both*: i.e. God and man.

l. 16. *the rest.* Alice Meynell regretted that Herbert did not avoid 'this rather distressing ambiguity', but some readers take pleasure in the play on the words *rest* (ll. 10, 16) and *restlesnesse* (l. 17).

l. 20. *tosse.* The word is used in a similar context by Crashaw in 'To the same party Councel concerning her choise', l. 49.

The Priesthood (Page 160)

l. 10. *compositions*: states of the body, or of body and mind combined. Cf. Shakespeare, *Richard II*, II. i. 73–4:

> Oh how that name befits my composition:
> Old *Gaunt* indeed, and gaunt in being old.

l. 16. *That earth is fitted by the fire.* Cf. 'I but earth and clay' (l. 8) and 'thou art fire' (l. 7). The Creator working like the potter on the clay is a familiar Biblical image, e.g. Isa. lxiv. 8, Jer. xviii. 6, Rom. ix. 21–3; and St. Paul is called 'a chosen vessell vnto me' in Acts ix. 15.

l. 29. Cf. *Imitatio Christi*, iv. xi. 4: 'O quam magnum et honorabile est officium sacerdotum: quibus datum est Dominum majestatis verbis sacris consecrare, labiis benedicere, manibus tenere! . . . O quam mundae debent esse manus illae!'

l. 32. *To hold the Ark*. As Uzzah rashly did (II Sam. vi. 6).

ll. 39–42. Herrick quotes the proverb, 'Manners know distance'. The modest by observing a respectful deference pay a better homage than the proud who seek to keep up their state by a rival magnificence. Herbert may hope to commend himself for the priesthood by his humility.

The Search (Page 162)

l. 3. *my daily bread*. Cf. Ps. xlii. 3, B.C.P.: 'My teares haue beene my meat day and night: while they daily say vnto me, where is now thy God?'

l. 14. *Simper*: glimmer, twinkle.

l. 24. *all was one*. 'It came to the same thing; my second attempt was as fruitless as my first.'

ll. 25–8. 'Art thou absorbed in creating a new world, giving up the old one in despair?'

l. 33. *that of any thing*. 'Above all, let it not be *thy will* (l. 32) that keeps thee from me.'

l. 35. *ring*: ring-fence; cf. 'these barres' (l. 49).

l. 42. *to it*. In comparison with that distance, other distances are as nothing.

l. 47. *charge*: burden, my load of trouble.

Grief (Page 164)

l. 10. *a lesse world*: man, the microcosm (cf. *Man*, p. 92, l. 47). Yet even the world, though greater than man, is *but small*.

l. 15. *your feet*. Herbert puns on the metrical feet and the eyes running with tears.

The Crosse (Page 164)

The title is explained by the last stanza. Sir Herbert Grierson compares with this poem the latter part of Donne's poem with the same title. Herbert has reached *this deare end*, the priesthood (cf. *Letter* iii, p. 364, l. 27: 'my journies end'), but is soon after incapacitated by failing health.

l. 13. *ague*. See note on *The Sinner*, p. 489.

ll. 17–18. 'I am altogether weak except when I contemplate the cross; but its strength spurs me to action.'

l. 23. *sped*: brought to a successful issue.

l. 29. *delicates*: delights, luxuries.

l. 36. *my words*: i.e. thine adopted as my own.

The Flower (Page 165)

l. 3. *demean*: bearing (like the similar word *demeanour*); but it is also found as a variant form of *demesne*, 'estate'. The meaning is little affected: the spring flowers not only have their own intrinsic beauty, but they are also welcome as a sign of the passing of winter; so are the *returns* of grace the more welcome after a time of spiritual aridity.

ll. 10–14. Cf. *Mem. Matris Sacr.* v, p. 425, l. 13, and Donne, 'A Hymne to Christ', ll. 13–16:

> As the trees sap doth seeke the root below
> In winter, in my winter now I goe,
>   Where none but thee, th' Eternall root
>   Of true Love I may know.

ll. 15–17. Imitated by Keble in the second stanza of 'Sixth Sunday after Trinity' in *The Christian Year*.

l. 18. *a chiming*. Instead of the single-toned *passing-bell*, there is the pleasing and varied sound of the bells being chimed, i.e. swung just enough to make the clappers strike. Palmer suggests 'a bridal peal', but marriage bells are rung, i.e. swung right up on end.

l. 20. '*Is*, i.e. is in itself, or unchangeably; it is what it is by God's immediate ordinance' (H. C. Beeching, *Lyra Sacra*, p. 95).

l. 25. *Offring at*: aiming at. Cf. *The Knell*, p. 204, l. 5.

ll. 32–5. 'There is no frost to compare with that which is caused by thy *least frown*; Arctic cold is nearer to the heat of the torrid zone than to such a frost.'

l. 44. *glide*: slip away gently and imperceptibly.

Dotage (Page 167)

l. 1. *casks of happinesse*. The word *cask* was sometimes used for *casket* (e.g. Shakespeare, *II Henry VI*, III. ii. 409), and may here suggest valuable cases with nothing of worth inside them.

l. 2. *Foolish night-fires*. O.E.D., citing this example only, defines 'An ignis fatuus, will o' the wisp'.

l. 4. *in a career*: as we say 'in full career'. Cf. *Josephs coat*, p. 159, l. 6.

l. 5. *nothing between two dishes*. A Spanish proverb. The upper or covering dish being removed, nothing is found in the lower one. Cf. Walton, *Lives*, p. 68: 'Mr. *Farrer*, having seen the manners and vanities of the World, and found them to be, as Mr. *Herbert* sayes, *A nothing between two Dishes*.'

l. 8. *in grain*: fast dyed; often, as here, figuratively, for 'firmly established, ineradicable'.

The Sonne (Page 167)

l. 3. *coast*: region, country, as often in the A.V. of the Bible.

l. 8. *Chasing*: dispelling. As the father's light grows dim, the son carries forward the *vitai lampada*.

l. 12. The pun proved irresistible to many writers of the time, e.g. Donne, 'A Hymne to God the Father', ll. 15–16: 'at my death thy sonne Shall shine as he shines now.'

A true Hymne (Page 168)

l. 14. *behinde*: still to come, lacking. Cf. *Affliction III*, p. 73, l. 9; *L'Envoy*, p. 199, l. 16; Col. i. 24; and Shakespeare, *Measure for Measure*, v. i. 540–1:

> So bring vs to our Pallace where wee'll show
> What's yet behinde, that's meete you all should know.

The Answer (Page 169)

l. 3. *bandie*: toss to and fro, like a tennis-ball.

l. 4. *summer friends*. Cf. Quarles, *Job Militant* (1624), Digestion iv: 'If Winter fortunes nip thy Summer Friends', and Massinger, *Maid of Honour* (1632), III. i. 222–5:

> ô summer friendship,
> Whose flattering leaves that shaddowed us in
> Our prosperity, with the least gust drop off
> In th' Autumne of adversity!

So long as men possess their *estates*, and the sun shines upon them, the *summer friends* swarm about them and settle on them like *Flyes*.

l. 8. *exhalation*: a vapour rising from the damp ground. Herbert uses the same simile in *Epistola* XVIII, p. 471, ll. 28–30.

l. 10. *pursie*: puffy, swollen. Cf. Vaughan, 'The Dawning', l. 21: 'The pursie Clouds disband, and scatter.'

A Dialogue-Antheme (Page 169)

A similar bantering of Death is found in *Death*, p. 185, *Dooms-day*, p. 186, and in Donne's sonnet, 'Death, be not so proud'.

l. 6. *Thy curse*. The allusion is to Gal. iii. 13. Cf. *Prayer II*, p. 103, l. 15.

l. 7. *Let losers talk*. *Outl. Pvbs*, No. 602.

Self-condemnation (Page 170)

l. 2. *Barrabas*. I have retained the MS. spelling, though etymologically indefensible, because it represents the contemporary pronunciation and metrical stress, as well as Herbert's practice. Shakespeare (*Merchant of Venice*, IV. i. 297) and Donne (*Deaths Duell*, 1632, p. 41) spell *Barrabas*. Crashaw, though he spells *Barabbas* in 'The houres', accents the first syllable.

a murderer. Cf. Luke xxiii. 18–19: 'release vnto vs Barabbas, Who for a certaine sedition made in the citie, and for murder, was cast in prison.'

l. 6. *That choice*. 'The Jews' choice of Barabbas may repeat itself in thy life's story.'

Bitter-sweet (Page 171)

Bitter-sweet is used by Gower as the name of an apple and in Gerarde's *Herball* for the Woody Nightshade. Feltham (*Resolves*, 1628, p. 295) calls love 'a kinde of bitter-sweet'.

The Glance (Page 171)

l. 8. *take it in*: admit as a guest. Cf. Matt. xxv. 35: 'I was a stranger, and ye tooke me in.'

l. 12. *swing and sway*: i.e. had full control. Cf. *Josephs coat*, p. 159, l. 6, and Massinger, *The Emperor of the East*, iv. i.: 'That shee might still continue Her absolute sway, and swing ore the whole state.'

l. 16. *got the day*. Cf. Tusser, *Hundred Points of Husbandry*, xci: 'The battell is fought, thou hast gotten the daye.'

The 23d Psalme (Page 172)

In his quotations from the Psalms Herbert shows a greater familiarity, as might be expected of a churchman, with Coverdale's version in the B.C.P. than with the A.V. In this paraphrase he draws from both: the influence of the A.V. is shown in *want*, *gently passe*, *in my enemies sight*, *Runnes*; but he follows the B.C.P. in *convert* (Vulgate, *convertit*), where the A.V. has *restoreth*. The metrical version of Sternhold and Hopkins, generally bound at the end of the B.C.P., must also have been familiar to him. Two versions of this psalm are given there: the first, by W. W., contains 'And he that doth me feed' and 'the tender grasse'; the second, by Thomas Sternhold, has the line 'And brought my mind in frame'.

William Barton in the second edition (1645) of *The Book of Psalms in metre*, 'Printed by Order of Parliament', introduced Herbert's version, with a few changes, but without naming the author. As there were many subsequent editions, Herbert's version must have become widely known.

l. 9. *convert*. O.E.D. cites this instance, not in the theological sense, but in the literal meaning 'cause to return' (cf. *stray* in the previous clause).

l. 10. *in frame*: into a suitable disposition. The Country Parson says that it is easy for his flock on Sundays 'to compose themselves to order, which they put on as their holy-day cloathes, and come to Church in frame' (*Priest to T.* p. 247, ll. 8–10).

l. 22. *measure*: be commensurate with (O.E.D., citing this example).

l. 24. *my praise*. This, the reading of all early printed texts, replaces *thy praise*, the reading of *B*, which is not recorded by Grosart, Palmer, and the Nonesuch edition. The sense is unaffected, as *thy praise* here can only mean 'my praise of thee', but *my praise* expresses this more naturally, and it also makes the patterned opposition to *thy sweet and wondrous love*.

Marie Magdalene (Page 173)

The identification of the unnamed 'woman in the citie which was a sinner', who anointed Jesus' feet (Luke vii. 37–8), with Mary Magdalene was generally accepted in the medieval Church and later.

l. 14. *dash*: splash, bespatter.

Aaron (Page 174)

'Each verse of Herbert's poem suggests metrically the swelling and dying sound of a bell; and, like a bell, the rhymes reiterate the same sound' (Grierson, op. cit. pp. 231–2).

Aaron's priestly garments, as described in Exod. xxviii, included a mitre with a gold plate engraved with the words 'Holiness to the Lord', a breastplate or pouch containing the Urim and the Thummim ('That is, *the Lights and the Perfections*', R.V. margin), and a robe with pomegranates and golden bells alternately at the hem.

l. 8. *A noise*, being contrasted with *Another musick* (l. 13), may suggest the special meaning of *noise* as 'a band of musicians'. Cf. *The Familie*, p. 136, l. 1.

l. 18. *striking*: as the clapper strikes the bell.

The Odour (Page 174)

l. 2. *Amber-greese*. French *ambre gris* (cf. Pomander, *pomme d'ambre*, l. 16): a secretion of the sperm-whale, found floating in tropical seas, and used in perfumery and in cookery.

l. 7. 'I thrust my mind into the two words, *My Master*, so as to discover their charm, as one thrusts the nose into a bouquet.'

l. 13. As welcome as man can be to God.

l. 16. *Pomander*: a scent ball, which gives out its odour when it is warmed by the hand or squeezed; cf. *The Banquet*, p. 181, l. 27: 'Yet being bruis'd are better sented', and *Passio Discerpta*, VIII. 2: 'Sic vnguenta solent manu fricari.' The ball of ambergris or other scent in a silver container was hung at the girdle or on a chain round the neck.

The Foil (Page 175)

The foil, a thin leaf of metal, is placed under a jewel to set it off: so the stars set off the virtues, and the griefs which follow sinning show sin up for what it is (cf. *The Invitation*, p. 180, ll. 14–16: 'pain Doth arraigne, Bringing all your sinnes to sight'). 'Yet we behave as if we had not the eyes to see that virtue is as attractive (*winning*) as grief is repellent (*foul*).' Herbert oftener uses *grief* of physical than of mental pain; it is unlikely that he would call sorrow *foul*. The antithesis would, however, be more logically stated if, as Palmer suggests, *sin* were read for *grief* in l. 8.

The Forerunners (Page 176)

Harbingers were sent in advance of a royal progress to purvey lodgings by chalking the doors (cf. l. 35). Death's harbinger already marks the poet's head with the whitening of the hair (l. 2): must intellectual decay follow (ll. 3–5)?

l. 3. *dispark*, for *disimpark*, turn out of a park. Again in *The Church Militant*, l. 147. Cf. Dekker, *Gulls Horne-book*, 81: 'The spending Englishman . . . disimparks the stately swift-footed wild deer.' So the *notions*, *bred* in *my brain*, may be evicted.

l. 6. Cited from Ps. xxxi. 14, though *still* (= always, now as before) is not in the A.V. or B.C.P. rendering.

l. 9. *I passe not*: I reck not. Again in l. 31. Cf. *Outl. Pvbs*, No. 35: 'Hee looseth nothing, that looseth not God.'

l. 10. *out of fear*: in no danger of being taken from me.

l. 11. The word *dittie* was used, not only of the music of a song, but also of its theme or burden: cf. *The Banquet*, p. 182, l. 50, and Sir T. Browne, *Letter to a Friend*, § 25: 'to be dissolved, and be with Christ, was his dying Ditty.'

ll. 14–17. Cf. *Jordan II*, p. 102, and Vaughan's tribute to Herbert in the preface to *Silex Scintillans*. Herbert sought at first to dedicate to sacred use the language which before had been used by others in the service of Venus.

l. 26. Canvas was still used for clothes. O.E.D. cites Robert Boyle's *Occasional Reflections* (1675) on the fashion that 'allows our Gallants to wear fine Lace upon Canvass and Buckram'.

The Rose (Page 177)

The thought of this poem is also found in *Life*, p. 94, and there are many resemblances to *The Size*, p. 137 (e.g. *size*, l. 4, and *sentence*, l. 25). Vaughan borrows from it in *The Mount of Olives* (*Works*, ed. Martin, i. 185–6):

> I shall hold it no *Paradoxe* to affirme, *there are no pleasures in this world*. Some *coloured griefes* and *blushing woes* there are, which look so clear as if they were *true complexions*; but it is a very sad and a tryed truth that they are but *painted*.

l. 6. *Colour'd*: made to look something that they are not, with an obvious allusion to the literal sense (cf. Blushing, l. 7).

l. 12. *pass'd my right away*. Cf. *Obedience*, p. 104, l. 8.

l. 18. *it purgeth*. See note on *Life*, p. 510, l. 15.

l. 20. *forbearance*: abstinence. John Canne in *A Necessitie of Separation* (1634) commends 'Daniel's forbearance of the King's meats'. *Physick* is for occasional use only (l. 29).

Discipline (Page 178)

l. 1. Cf. Jonson, 'An Hymn to God the Father,' and Southwell, 'S. Peters Remorse', ll. 25–8:

> But Mercye may relente,
>   And temper Justice' rodd,
> For mercy doth as much belong
>   As justice to a Godd.

l. 22. *a man of warre*. From Exod. xv. 3. Perhaps also Herbert remembers that the Greek god of love has *his bow* (l. 25).

The Invitation (Page 179)

'I have invited all' (l. 31) may indicate that Herbert is already a priest.

l. 3. *Save your cost.* A reminiscence of Isa. lv. 1–2: 'Ho, euery one that thirsteth, come ye to the waters, and he that hath no money: come ye, buy and eate, yea come, buy wine and milke without money, and without price. Wherefore doe yee spend money for that which is not bread?'

ll. 5–6. *the feast, God.* Cf. *The Priesthood,* p. 161, l. 27, and *Priest to T.* p. 257, l. 30.

l. 8. *define*: characterize (O.E.D., citing this example). Cf. Milton, *Tenure of Kings,* p. 55: 'Being lawfully depriv'd of all things that define a magistrate.'

ll. 13–15. 'It is pain, coming in the wake of sin, which makes you recognize that you have sinned.' Cf. *Miserie,* p. 100, ll. 21–2, and *The Foil,* p. 176, l. 6.

ll. 22–4. *Drowning* is used in *Priest to T.* p. 275, l. 24, of the deliberate flooding of meadows to improve their cultivation.

The Banquet (Page 181)

A free rewriting of this poem in octosyllabic lines appears in Bishop Simon Patrick's posthumous *Poems upon Divine and Moral Subjects* (1719).

l. 14. *Made a head*: pressed forward in opposition. Cf. *The Sacrifice,* p. 26, l. 5, and 'To the Queene of Bohemia', p. 213, l. 59.

l. 31. *my birth*: i.e. my heavenly birth. Cf. 'born on high' (*Vanitie II,* p. 111, l. 13).

l. 43. Cf. *Praise I,* p. 61, ll. 5–6: 'help me to wings, and I Will thither flie'

l. 45. *I wipe mine eyes.* Cf. *Vertue,* p. 87, l. 6.

l. 49. *his pitie* (*B*) is perhaps preferable to *this pitie* (*1633*), and it is parallel with 'thy pitie' in *Home,* p. 107, l. 13.

The Posie (Page 182)

On the use of mottoes inscribed on rings and window-panes see Joan Evans, *English Posies and Posy Rings* (1931). Herbert's motto is alluded to in 'The Printers to the Reader' (above, p. 4), Oley's 'Prefatory View' in *Remains* (c 4[v]) and Walton's *Lives,* p. 74.

ll. 3–4. Cf. Gen. xxxii. 10: 'And Iacob said . . . I am not worthy of the least of all the mercies, and of all the trueth, which thou hast shewed vnto thy seruant.' St. Paul calls himself 'lesse then the least of all Saints' (Eph. iii. 8).

l. 8. *dictate.* Accenting the second syllable is modern: 'The poets from G. Herbert to Byron and Shelley have only di·ctate' (O.E.D.).

A Parodie (Page 183)

This seems to fit Dryden's description of parodies (*Juvenal,* Dedication, p. 34) as 'Verses patch'd up from great Poets, and turn'd into another Sence than their Author intended them'; it is not Herbert's intention to travesty the original, but to convert the profane to sacred use. His adaptation does not extend beyond the opening lines:

Soules joy, now I am gone,
And you alone,
(Which cannot be,
Since I must leave my selfe with thee,
And carry thee with me)
Yet when unto our eyes
Absence denyes
Each others sight,
And makes to us a constant night,
When others change to light.

Lansdowne MS. 777 has for the first line 'Soules joy, when I am gone', which is nearer Herbert's line. The poem is included in every early edition, except that of 1633, of Donne's *Poems*, but it is also found in *Poems by the Earle of Pembroke and Sr Benjamin Ruddier* (1660) and in Lansdowne MS. 777, in both these latter cases being attributed to William Herbert, 3rd earl of Pembroke. E. K. Chambers (*Poems of John Donne*, i. 230) states that he has 'very little doubt' that it is Donne's, but Grierson (*The Poems of John Donne*, 1912, ii, pp. cxxxv–vi) thinks it is 'most probably by the Earl of Pembroke'.

ll. 20–30. 'My faltering sense of thy continued presence gives Sin occasion to say *that thou art not here*, and that, though I may be seeking thee, *thou art lost* to me, so that *I half beleeve, That Sinne sayes true*, until thou comest to relieve me (l. 30). Thou alone knowest *what life I have* (l. 21), in spite of Sin's denial.' Cf. *Assurance*, p. 155, ll. 7–12.

The Elixir (Page 184)

No poem of Herbert's better shows his skill in revision. As first written in *W*, it is lifeless and awkward, but it is brought to life by the new verse, inserted in *W* in Herbert's hand, introducing the idea of the elixir. Further improvements are made, both in *W* and in the final form in *B*, as may be seen in the Apparatus Criticus on pp. 184–5.

The elixir is here identified with *the famous stone* (l. 21), as in Chaucer's 'The philosophres stoon, Elixir clipt', supposed by the alchemists to have the property of turning other metals to gold.

l. 7. *still to make thee prepossest*: always to give thee a prior claim.

l. 8. *his*: its. Again in l. 15.

l. 14. *Nothing can be so mean*. The Country Parson 'holds the Rule, that Nothing is little in Gods service: If it once have the honour of that Name, it grows great instantly' (*Priest to T*. p. 249, ll. 1–3).

l. 15. Tincture is a technical term in alchemy for 'a supposed spiritual principle or immaterial substance whose character or quality may be infused into material things' (O.E.D.); *for thy sake* is the tincture which can brighten and purify any action.

l. 23. The word *touch* was used of testing the fineness of gold by rubbing it with the touchstone; also of officially marking metal as of standard quality after it had been tested. What God has 'touched' and approved as gold, no one may rightly reckon *for lesse*. Cf. Shakespeare, *Timon*, III. iii. 6: 'They haue all bin touch'd, and found Base-Mettle.'

A Wreath (Page 185)

For such inweaving compare the first stanza of *Justice I*, p. 95, and *Sinnes round*, p. 122, where, as here, the poem works round till it ends where it began. Cf. R. Southwell, *S. Peter's Complaint*, stanza ciii.

l. 5. *life is straight*. Repeated from *Our life is hid*, p. 84, l. 3.

Death (Page 185)

ll. 13–14. Cf. *Church-rents and schismes*, p. 140, ll. 12–13.

ll. 17–18. Cf. *Home*, p. 108, l. 58: 'The last and lov'd, though dreadfull day.'

Dooms-day (Page 186)

ll. 5–6. Crashaw says of the waves ('Against Irresolution, &c.', ll. 43–4):

Each bigge with businesse thrusts the other,
And seems to say, Make haste, my Brother.

l. 12. *Tarantulas raging pains*. Tarantism, an hysterical malady, was supposed to be caused by the bite of the wolf-spider or tarantula and to be cured by music and wild dancing. Cf. R. Greene, *Philomela* (sig. G 3^{v}): 'such as are stung by the Tarentula, are best cured by Musicke.'

ll. 15–18. If the graves are not obliged to disgorge at once, they may later claim a prescriptive right to retain the bodies; and they may have learnt such obstinacy from human example.

ll. 21–4. Bodies turning to dust may be scattered by winds which bring mortals to shipwreck, or turning to gases they may spread a pestilence. Vaughan imitates in his 'Buriall', ll. 25–8:

(thus crumm'd) I stray
In blasts,
Or Exhalations, and wasts
Beyond all Eyes.

Both MSS., as well as all printed texts, have *windes* or *winds*, but B. G. Hall thought it was a misreading of *wines*, and took *noisome vapours* to refer to the use of tobacco; he overlooked the fact that the whole poem refers to dead bodies, not to the habits of the living.

Judgement (Page 187)

l. 10. *in merit shall excell*. Coleridge was misled by the reading in all editions 1660–1799 of *here* for *heare* in l. 7 into supposing that Herbert approved the doctrine of merit, which is repugned in the XXXIX Articles of

Religion; on the contrary, he *declines* it (l. 12), for himself at least, and trusts to St. Paul's doctrine of Christ having taken men's sins upon himself (l. 15); cf. *Love III*, p. 189, l. 15: 'And know you not, sayes Love, who bore the blame?'

Heaven (Page 188)

Lord Herbert of Cherbury wrote four echo-songs, one of which, 'Echo in a Church', according to Professor G. C. Moore Smith, 'might well have been written by George Herbert'.

Love III (Page 188)

ll. 7–12. Cf. Southwell, *S. Peters Complaint*, cxviii:

At sorrowes dore I knockt, they crau'd my name;
I aunswered one, vnworthy to be knowne;
What one, say they? one worthiest of blame.
But who? a wretch, not Gods, nor yet his owne.
A man? O no, a beast; much worse: what creature?
A rocke: how cald? the rocke of scandale, Peter.

The Church Militant (Page 190)

This long poem stands apart in both MSS. from the lyrical poems which have *Finis* at the end of the section called 'The Church'. All the internal evidence points to an early date for the inception of this poem. The complimentary references to Spain (ll. 89, 265) and the depreciatory references to France (ll. 241–6) suggest that Herbert was at work upon it before Prince Charles exchanged the hope of a Spanish for a French betrothal. The allusions to the hopes of evangelizing the American colonies bear some relation to the projects of Ferrar and other members of the Virginia Company, which was deprived of its patent in 1624. The anti-Roman animus is characteristic of Herbert's early and more controversial mind. The influence of Donne is still strong; both in the theme and in the manner of its treatment *The Church Militant* resembles such a comprehensive survey as Donne's 'The Progresse of the Soule'. Herbert perhaps came to recognize that his lyrical gift was not well fitted for ambitious attempts of this kind.

The theme is logically developed. The Christian Church followed the course of the sun westward. Beginning in the East, it travelled to Egypt, Greece, Rome, Germany, Britain. But Sin followed in its wake (l. 101) and particularly established itself in Rome, which is called *Western* Babylon (l. 211). Even *the late reformation* (l. 226) was disappointing in its results, and now the best hope for religion is that it should win fresh triumphs in the American colonies (l. 236), though there too *Sinne shall trace and dog her instantly* (l. 260). Going ever westward like the sun, the Church and Sin shall at last circle the globe and arrive where they started, and there be judged (l. 277).

H. Vaughan summarized Herbert's poem in 'To Christian Religion', ll. 9–14:

> A *Seer*, that observ'd thee in
> Thy Course, and watch'd the growth of Sin,
> Hath giv'n his Judgment and foretold,
> That *Westward* hence thy *Course* will hold:
> And when the day with us is done,
> There fix, and shine a glorious Sun.

l. 12. *indeare*. O.E.D. cites this example of a sense, now obsolete, 'to bind by obligations of gratitude'.

l. 15. Noahs *shadie vine*. Gen. ix. 20. Cf. *The Bunch of Grapes*, p. 128, l. 24.

ll. 19–22. These lines are obscure through their compression and allusiveness. The wanderings of Noah's ark and of Moses' ark are ingeniously brought into relation with one another. The former came to rest 'vpon the mountaines of Ararat' (Gen. viii. 4), and *the other Ark* was carried by the descendants of Abraham into battle against the Philistines and taken by the enemy *from Canaan* into the Philistines' land (I Sam. v. 1), until in David's day it was brought back and found a final resting-place in the temple which Solomon built 'in Mount Moriah' (II Chron. iii. 1). Abraham also had gone *from Canaan* and 'soiourned in the Philistines land' (Gen. xxi. 34), and was bidden to go thence to a mountain in 'the land of Moriah' (Gen. xxii. 2) to sacrifice Isaac. The reading of *W*, *to Canaan*, would be explained by Abraham and his family leaving Ur of the Chaldees when they 'went foorth to goe into the land of Canaan' (Gen. xii. 5).

l. 22. *Religion*, found nine times in this poem, but nowhere else in *The Temple*, is scanned here and in l. 212 as having four syllables, but the other seven times it is trisyllabic.

ll. 23–4. The same conceit is elaborated in *Passio Discerpta*, XVIII, 'Terraemotus', p. 408. Cf. Eph. ii. 14 for *the partition-wall*.

l. 28. *alone*. Religion now carries *the crosse* only, and is without the *glorie* (l. 27) which the Jewish religion could once boast.

l. 41. Macarius and Anthony, hermits of the Thebaid in Upper Egypt in the fourth century.

l. 42. *changing th' historie*. When Moses brought the plague of darkness over Egypt, 'all the children of Israel had light in their dwellings' in 'the lande of Goshen' (Exod. x. 21–3, viii. 22, ix. 26). Now all is reversed: instead of bringing forth frogs (viii. 6), the Nile brings forth Christians baptized in its waters by the saints of the desert.

l. 44. *for*: instead of. Again in ll. 46 and 127.

ll. 47–8. The refrain is from Ps. cxxxix. 17 and lxxxix. 6, B.C.P.

l. 51. *pos'd*. To appose or pose was the scholastic word for examining by oral questions, often with the further sense of 'nonplus'. Cf. *The Church-porch*, p. 15, l. 223.

set: 'puzzle, nonplus, "stump"' (O.E.D., citing this example of a sense now found only in Northern dialect).

l. 54. *Christ-Crosse*, or criss-cross-row, was a name for the alphabet, because a cross was prefixed to it in the horn-books: cf. Overbury, *A Wife*, p. 181: 'A Horne-book without a Christ-Crosse afore it.' Philosophers must go back to their lessons from the start.

l. 63. *resounds*: proclaims, celebrates.

l. 69. *pierce again*: i.e. repeat the act of the Roman soldier who, when Christ hung on the cross, 'with a speare pierced his side' (John xix. 34).

l. 72. Grosart and Palmer refer to Pope Gregory XIII's reform of the calendar in 1582, but the context seems to require some event of the early Christian centuries, such as the provision of the ecclesiastical year with feasts and saints' days, replacing the pagan festivals.

ll. 73–4. Although Alexander's empire had broken up, the glory was revived when Constantine moved his capital from Rome to Byzantium in 330.

l. 76. *against*: before, by the time that. Cf. Gen. xliii. 25: 'And they made ready the Present against Ioseph came at noone.'

l. 81. Germany, like Spain, is mentioned because of its connexion with the Holy Roman Empire (l. 89). The association of Germany with art in the following lines may be connected in Herbert's mind with the engravings of sacred subjects by Holbein, Dürer, and other German artists, which Ferrar used for the Little Gidding Concordances, one of which was made for Herbert. Ferrar in his travels abroad 'bought also a very great number of Prints engraved by the best masters of that time; all relative to historical passages of the old and new Testament' (P. Peckard, *Nicholas Ferrar*, p. 88).

l. 88. Then Religion waters the garden.

ll. 90–3. Constantine, son of the emperor Constantius and of Helena, who was reputed to be of British birth, was proclaimed emperor by the soldiers at York on his father's death there in 306. By his being the first emperor to profess the Christian faith, he set a precedent for the royal protection of the Church, which may be said to have been given *a crown to keep her state*.

l. 94. *this mysterie*, of the connexion of Church and State, is probably an allusion to the so-called Donation of Constantine, professing to grant temporal power and estates to the Church; it was held by writers of the Renaissance period to be a forgery of the eighth century.

l. 98. *meridian*: the point at which the sun reaches its highest altitude; here, figuratively, for the point of highest development, after which decline sets in.

l. 110. *sallet* (obsolete form of *salad*): vegetable eaten raw.

l. 112. *Adoring garlick*. Cf. Donne, 'The second Anniversary', ll. 427–8: 'For as the Wine, and Corne, and Onions are Gods unto them.' The Israelites, regretting the food which they 'did eate in Egypt freely', named expressly 'the leekes, and the onions, and the garlicke' (Num. xi. 5). Cf. Juv. xv. 9–11.

l. 118. *adores his broom*. The besom was originally made of twigs of broom and other plants. This worshipper of vegetable gods neglects to use what would have kept his house clean.

l. 127. *for*: instead of the vegetable gardens which served him in Egypt (l. 108).

l. 131. *a poet.* Because Greek oracles were often given in verse. The poison of the *sublimate* (mercuric chloride) in the medicinal *conserve* is concealed by the sugar coating of the pill. Cf. Jonson, *Silent Woman*, II. ii: 'Take a little sublimate and goe out of the world, like a rat.'

l. 134. *pull*: draw from the pack. Cf. *Jordan I*, p. 57, l. 12.

ll. 137–8. *to discredit those*, &c. Palmer thinks that the allusion is to the Sibylline oracles which were long regarded as testifying to Christ (cf. the hymn 'Dies Irae', l. 3: 'teste David cum Sibylla'); but l. 147, which credits 'our Saviour' with 'Disparking oracles', hardly seems to support this view.

l. 149. Mahomet, and the Koran's promise of heavenly pleasures.

l. 169. An allusion to the patronage of secular art by some Popes of the Renaissance.

l. 174. *Christs three offices*: i.e. as prophet, priest, and king; caricatured by Sin in ll. 171–3, 177–80, 187–8. All three offices, instead of being prosecuted by Sin in three places successively, are now discharged simultaneously at Rome alone (l. 176).

l. 178. A line of six feet, unless there are double elisions.

l. 184. *make that name good.* The old Babel (Gen. xi. 9) scattered the nations, but now *All poste to* Rome (l. 195), the *Western* Babylon (l. 211).

l. 190. Imitated by Vaughan in 'The World', ll. 44–5:

> And poor, despised truth sate Counting by
> Their victory.

Both Vaughan and Herbert represent Truth as reduced to sitting helplessly by and reckoning up Sin's triumphs.

l. 192. *captivate*: in the original sense 'make captive', the Jews being deported to Babylon.

l. 198. Fur befits the inactive, as in *Employment II*, p. 78, l. 4.

l. 204. *the Popes mule. La mule du pape* is used of his shoe. The English word, derived from the French, was sometimes used to 'render the like-sounding Latin *mulleus*' (O.E.D.), a purple slipper worn only by the three highest magistrates of ancient Rome. The allusion here is to the reverence paid *t' his publick foot* (l. 196).

l. 219. *double crest.* As a person may, by special grant of the Crown, bear the surname and arms of another family in addition to his own.

ll. 225–8. *The late reformation* fell as far short of the primitive Church as *The second Temple* did of the first, and is equally a matter for tears (Ezra iii. 12).

ll. 232–4. The Church will have shrunk by the time of *Christs last coming* in the same *proportion* as it has grown since its first beginnings within the limits of *Jurie.*

ll. 235–6. These famous lines arrested attention, but it is not certain that the idea originated with Herbert. The following extract from a letter, dated 4 March 1634, from Dr. William Twisse to Joseph Mede, suggests that the idea was very much in the air at that time: 'And then considering our English plantations of late, and the opinion of many grave divines concerning the Gospel's fleeting westward, sometimes I have had such thoughts, why may not that be the place of New Jerusalem? But you have handsomely and fully cleared me from such odd conceits' (Mede, *Works*, p. 799). Nearly a century later George Berkeley, the future bishop, in 'Verses on the prospect of planting Arts and Learning in America', foresaw 'another golden age' and a race of men 'not such as Europe breeds in her decay', and ended with words which may be a reminiscence of Herbert's:

> Westward the course of empire takes its way;
> The four first Acts already past,
> A fifth shall close the Drama with the day;
> Time's noblest offspring is the last.

Berkeley's poem probably belongs to the time of his *Proposal* (1725) for erecting a college in Bermuda, about which he remarks: 'In Europe the protestant religion hath of late years considerably lost ground, and America seems the likeliest place wherein to make up for what hath been lost in Europe, provided the proper methods are taken' (*Works*, ed. Fraser, 1871, iii. 224 and 232). Cf. Rushworth, *Hist. Coll.* ii. 301.

Walton's statement that the Cambridge Vice-Chancellor hesitated about licensing *The Temple* because of these lines is more precise than anything found in earlier accounts. Oley (*Herbert's Remains*, 1652, sig. b 1–4), though he mentions a licence being refused to Ferrar for his translation of Carbo, says nothing about any difficulty over *The Temple*. He quotes in full ll. 235–59, and comments: 'I pray God he may prove a true prophet for *poor America*, not against *poor England*.' John Ferrar, in his Life of his brother (*The Ferrar Papers*, p. 59), states that *The Temple* 'was licensed at Cambridge (with some kind of Scruple by some, if I was not misinformed) only for those his Verses upon America &c.: But it did pass, with the epistle that N.F. made to it.' Walton's fuller statement (*Lives*, p. 75) may owe something to his desire to improve the occasion:

> And this ought to be noted, that when Mr. *Farrer* sent this Book to *Cambridge* to be Licensed for the Press, the *Vice-Chancellor* would by no means allow the two so much noted Verses
>
> *Religion stands a Tip-toe in our Land,*
> *Ready to pass to the* American *Strand.*
>
> to be printed; and, Mr. *Farrer*, would by no means allow the Book to be printed, and want them: But after some time, and some arguments for, and against their being made publick, the *Vice-Chancellor* said, *I knew Mr.* Herbert *well, and know that he had many heavenly Speculations, and was a Divine Poet; but, I hope the World will not take him to be an inspired Prophet, and therefore I License the whole Book.*

l. 241. Sein *shall swallow* Tiber. Perhaps a reminiscence of Juv. Sat. iii. 62: 'Iam pridem Syrus in Tiberim defluxit Orontes.'

l. 256. *her ancient place* (the reading of both MSS.): i.e. the place where Grace has hitherto dwelt. This gives a more satisfactory sense than ***our ancient*** *place* (*1633*). England gets gold from America; America gets the Gospel from England, and has the better of the exchange (l. 254).

l. 265. Spain *hath done one*. Spain illustrates the one process by using her empire (cf. l. 89) to *usher* the Gospel into South America, with a suggestion in the next line that such work done by *the Empire and the Arts* will not withstand the assault of Sin.

l. 268. *sound*: an inlet of the sea, affording a haven, like Plymouth Sound.

L'Envoy (Page 199)

l. 2. *make warre to cease*. Cf. Ps. xlvi. 9: 'He maketh warres to cease.' Herbert commonly follows scriptural precedent so closely that *warrs* (*W*) is more likely to be right than *warre* (*B* and *1633*); if he, and not his editor, made the change, it may have been in order to reduce the sibilants in this line and the next.

ENGLISH POEMS IN THE WILLIAMS MS. NOT INCLUDED IN *THE TEMPLE*

Six of the English poems in the Williams MS. were excluded from the Bodleian MS., and therefore from the printed text of *The Temple*, presumably because of the author's dissatisfaction with them. He substituted new poems entitled 'The H. Communion' and 'Even-song'. He could discard 'Love' because its theme and some of its characteristic phrases, e.g. 'There is no dealing with thee' and 'thy conquest', occur in 'The Reprisall'. 'Trinity Sunday' could be spared, as another poem with that title is found in both MSS. For the positions of these poems in the Williams MS., see the Introduction, pp. liv–lv. Grosart had no authority for entitling them 'Lilies of the Temple'.

The H. Communion (Page 200)

l. 6. Either the divine Presence causes the Bread, *thy poore creature*, to cease to be there (cf. l. 8), or the Bread stays (l. 7).

ll. 13–18. 'The road is longer (*more*, l. 18) if thou comest first into the Bread and then into me, but equally I am the gainer and am unaffected whether there are two stages (*stations*, l. 16) or one only in thy coming.' This indifference to the manner of Christ's Presence in the sacrament was a typically Anglican position, as Gibson illustrates from Bishop Andrewes's *Responsio ad Apologiam Cardinalis Bellarmini*, p. 13: 'Praesentiam credimus non minus quam vos veram: de modo praesentiae nihil temere definimus, addo, nec anxie inquirimus.' Cf. Hooker, *Eccl. Pol.* v. lxvii. 12 and Donne, *LXXX Sermons*, xxx. 301 and iv. 34: 'But for the manner, how the Body and Bloud of Christ is there, wait his leisure, if he have not yet manifested that to thee: Grieve not at that, wonder not at that, presse not for that; for hee hath not manifested that, not the way, not the manner of his presence in the Sacrament, to the Church.'

l. 25. *an Impanation*: a eucharistic theory attributed by some medieval writers to the followers of Bérenger de Tours (998–1088), though it was certainly not his view. Dr. J. H. Srawley defines it: 'As Christ took human nature into personal union with Himself and became incarnate, so in the Sacrament He takes bread and wine into the same kind of union, and may be said to be impanate and invinate' (Hastings, *Dict. of Rel. and Eth.* v. 557). It is the obverse of transubstantiation, which affirms the conversion of the *substantia* of the elements into the Body and Blood, its accidents alone remaining.

l. 41. *bounds & meres.* The words are often found together, e.g. in Holland's *Livy*, p. 1403: 'The god of Meeres and Bounds, *Terminus*.' A mere is a boundary or landmark.

Love (Page 201)

l. 8. *shrodely*: shrewdly.

l. 13. *when thou didst sleep*: on the Sea of Galilee while 'the waues beat into the ship' (Mark iv. 37).

Trinity Sunday (Page 202)

l. 12. *the first Theefe.* So Milton (*P.L.* iv. 192) calls Satan 'this first grand Thief'.

Euen-song (Page 203)

l. 13. *thou art Light & darknes.* Cf. H. Vaughan, 'The Night', ll. 49–50:

There is in God (some say)
A deep, but dazling darkness.

The Knell (Page 204)

l. 3. *wishly*: wistfully.

l. 17. *Julips*: medicated drinks, comforting mixture.

Perseverance (Page 204)

l. 12. *forbid the banes.* Banes (pronounced with a long *a*) was the spelling of banns of marriage in the Book of Common Prayer of Herbert's time.

POEMS FROM WALTON'S *LIVES*

Sonnets (Page 206)

These sonnets, with an accompanying letter (see above, p. 363), were 'in the first year of his going to *Cambridge* sent his dear Mother for a New-years gift' (*Lives*, p. 19). Herbert was matriculated on 18 Dec. 1609; he was therefore near his seventeenth birthday when he wrote them.

i. l. 4. *Venus Livery.* Cf. R. Southwell's second set of prefatory lines to *S. Peters Complaint*, ll. 15–16:

Christs thorn is sharp, no head his garland wears;
Still finest wits are 'stilling Venus rose.

ll. 8–9. *Cannot thy Dove Out-strip.* Cf. 'Grace', p. 60, l. 10: 'And shall the dew out-strip thy Dove?'

l. 11. *run smooth.* Cf. Shakespeare, *II Henry VI*, III. i. 53: 'Smooth runnes the Water, where the Brooke is deepe.'

II. l. 14. *discovery*: in the older sense of uncovering, disclosing.

To my Successor (Page 207)

After rebuilding Bemerton Rectory Herbert 'caus'd these Verses to be writ upon, or ingraven in the Mantle of the Chimney in his Hall' (*Lives*, p. 46). In a modern restoration of the hall to its previous state 'the massive chimney mantel' was retained, 'but on removing the plaster no indication could be found of any inscription' (F. Warre, *A Collection of Papers relating to Bemerton*. Salisbury, 1893). Fuller introduced his version of the lines, without naming Herbert, in his character of The Faithful Minister with the words: 'A Clergieman who built his house from the ground wrote in it this counsell to his successour' (*The Holy State*, 1642, Book II, ch. ix).

DOUBTFUL POEMS

On Sir John Danvers (Page 208)

The attribution of these lines to Herbert rests solely on Aubrey, who states that they were 'pinned on the curtaine of the Picture of the old S[r] John Danvers, who was both a handsome and a good man' (*Wiltshire Collections*, 1862, p. 225). Herbert cannot have known Sir John, who died in 1594, but he may have heard much of him from his son Henry, earl of Danby, in whose house at Dauntsey he 'lived a yeare or better' (Aubrey). The lines, if Herbert's, are a courtly compliment to his host.

Sir John Danvers (1540–94), of Dauntsey, married Elizabeth Nevile, fourth daughter and co-heiress of John, last Baron Latimer. Their children included Charles, Henry, John (Magdalen Herbert's second husband), Katharine Lady Gargrave, and Dorothy Lady Osborne, mother of the Dorothy Osborne who married Sir William Temple.

l. 15. *to a sonne*: to be compared with a son.

l. 16. *Reade him there*: i.e. in his son, Lord Danby, who reproduces his worth better than any monument or verse can do.

On Henry Danvers, earl of Danby (Page 208)

The verses are engraved on the east side of Danby's tomb in Dauntsey Church, and appear, by their lettering, spelling, and general character, to be contemporary with the other inscriptions on the tomb. The name 'G: HERBER[T].' is in the same lettering. As Danby, who was twenty years Herbert's senior, outlived him by nearly eleven years, it is improbable that Herbert wrote this epitaph for his host; but they are almost impersonal and may have been written by him for another occasion or even without any particular person in mind. Danby 'lov'd Mr. *Herbert* much' (Walton, *Lives*, p. 36), and, as he gave directions in his will for the making of the great altar tomb in white marble, he may also have directed that his friend's verses should be inscribed on it.

Henry Danvers (1573–1644) served in the Low Countries as page to Sir Philip Sidney. He and his brother Charles were outlawed in 1594 for a murderous affray with the Longs of Corsham, and served in arms in France under Henri IV, who helped to procure their pardon in 1598. They then served under the earl of Essex in Ireland, and Charles was attainted and beheaded in 1601 for complicity in Essex's rebellion. Henry was created Baron Danvers of Dauntsey in 1603 and earl of Danby in 1626. He presented the Physic or Botanic Garden to the university of Oxford and his name is inscribed on the gatehouse.

George Herbert was doubly connected with the Danvers family, through his mother's marriage in the spring of 1608/9 to the younger Sir John, and through his own marriage twenty years later to Jane Danvers.

l. 5. *hee*: i.e. Time (l. 4).

ll. 6–7. *if the teares Are shed*: i.e. if the tears which are shed for him should dissolve the tomb.

To the L. Chancellor Bacon (Page 209)

In all the three MSS., in which this English poem is found, it is accompanied by the Latin poem, 'Aethiopissa ambit Cestum' (see above, p. 437), which is printed as Herbert's in Duport's *Ecclesiastes Solomonis* (1662), and which is assigned to Herbert in B.M. Add. MS. 22602. In Bodl. MS. Rawl. Poet. 246, which is a collection mostly of Eton and Cambridge poems, 'My Lord. A diamond' follows four Latin poems, without author's name, in honour of Bacon; all but the first of these Latin poems are printed as Herbert's by Duport. The English poem precedes 'Aethiopissa' and evidently refers to it; the *Blackamore* which the writer presents in return for the *diamond* is the Latin poem 'Aethiopissa'. If Duport was right in ascribing 'Aethiopissa' to Herbert, the English poem accompanying it is likely to be his also. In the unnamed MS. used by Fry (*Bibliographical Memoranda*, 1816) they are both attributed to A. Melvin (Andrew Melville: see below, p. 587); but, apart from other improbabilities of such authorship, by the time that Bacon was chancellor (1618–21) Melville was living abroad and near the end of his long life. Fry suggests that the *diamond* was a copy of Bacon's *Essays*, but no edition appeared between 1614 and 1624; the only work published by Bacon while he was chancellor was *Instauratio Magna* (1620).

A Paradox (Page 209)

Pickering, Grosart, and Palmer followed the text of Bodl. MS. Rawl. Poet. 147, a collection consisting mostly of Cambridge poems, probably compiled between 1647 and 1658. They did not use B.M. Add. MS. 25303 and Harl. 3910. These two MSS. agree closely; they have erratic spelling, but they preserve the right reading in ll. 14 and 39, and the right scansion in l. 9, where *Rawl* is a foot short. In all three MSS. there is a departure from the rhyme-scheme in the third stanza. *Rawl* alone preserves the rhyme in l. 25. *Harl* and *Rawl* assign the poem to Herbert, but *25303* gives no author's name.

Pickering, in his 2nd edition (1838), compared 'A Paradox. *The worse the better*' in *The Synagogue*, which may indicate that Christopher Harvey took Herbert, whom he was imitating throughout his book, to be the author of 'You whoe admire'.

Herbert's constant lack of full health (cf. l. 12, *Mediocritie*, a middling state of health) fits the subject of the poem, and the phrase *and more* (l. 10) is very often found in *The Temple*, but there is little else to suggest his authorship of this poem. For the thought cf. Donne, 'The first Anniversary', ll. 91–2:

> There is no health; Physitians say that wee,
> At best, enjoy but a neutralitie.

l. 14. *Wheare*. The reading *wch* in *Rawl* led earlier editors to suspect a mistake. Grosart's conjecture *Where* is now confirmed by its being found in the two MSS. which he did not see.

l. 39. *Wayle*, the reading of *25303* and *Harl*, is preferable to *plaint* (*Rawl*). O.E.D. gives no example of *plaint* as a transitive verb; perhaps the copyist took the word unwittingly from the preceding line.

To the Queen of Bohemia and *L'Envoy* (Page 211)

The two pieces may be regarded as one poem and have evidently the same author. MS. Harl. 3910 has the initials 'G H' at the head of the first piece, which is followed on the same page by 'L'Envoy'. The undescribed MS., which H. Huth used for his edition, has 'G.H.' at the end of the second piece only. Neither MS. gives the surname Herbert, but the poem preceding 'To the Queene of Bohemia' in *Harl* is an Ode on Prince Henry 'by Sr Ed: Her:', which appeared with Sir Edward Herbert's name in the 3rd edition of Sylvester's *Lachrymae Lachrymarum* in 1613 (*The Poems of Lord Herbert of Cherbury*, ed. G. C. Moore Smith, p. 127). We have not enough authentic examples of George Herbert's secular verse to judge securely of poems of that kind attributed to him on slender evidence. The hyperbolic compliments are not unsuitable to the courtly Herbert of the Latin letters, but the vindictive passage (ll. 47–54) does not seem to be in character. The diction is rather in favour of his authorship. Many favourite words of his occur: *curious, beam, sphere, thrall, native*; and phrases which are found in *The Temple*: *making a Head, close sit, when as, Great God*. When we consider the unlikeness of the subject, it is remarkable that so few words occur which do not find a place in *The Temple*: some of them are homely words—*clip, peck, brinish, bout*—such as he might well have used, and the most striking of the rest are *self-sufficient, maugre, sublunary, rauening Harpyes*. If the reference in l. 34 to Elizabeth's *vndiuided Maiestye* means that she is by now a widow, the poem can hardly be Herbert's, since the Elector died on 29 Nov. 1632, only thirteen weeks before Herbert's death.

Elizabeth, the eldest daughter of James I, was married in 1613 to Frederick V, Elector Palatine, head of the Protestant Union of Germany. The Bohemian Estates on 26 Aug. 1619 deposed their king, Ferdinand of Styria, and elected Frederick in his place. 'The Winter King' enjoyed his Bohemian throne for little more than a year. Ferdinand, elected emperor two days after Frederick became King, soon struck at his rival. The Catholic League army under Tilly defeated Frederick at the battle of the White Hill on 8 Nov. 1620, and he was obliged to flee the kingdom. He could not even retain his hereditary dominions, as Spanish troops (cf. 'L'Envoy', l. 9) conquered the Upper Palatinate, while Maximilian, duke of Bavaria, took the Lower, and the electoral dignity was transferred to Maximilian. Frederick's chief opponents, Ferdinand and Maximilian, had been pupils of the Jesuits (cf. 'L'Envoy', l. 9), who encouraged the formation of the Catholic League. The poem clearly refers to Elizabeth's time of exile in Holland.

l. 8. *ten spheres*: the ten spheres of the Ptolemaic astronomy. Sir Thomas Browne alludes to 'the tenth Spheere' (*Religio Medici*, i, § 49).

l. 13. *optick*: as in 'Hope', l. 4, for a magnifying glass or telescope.

l. 17. *black tiffany*. O.E.D. cites from the *London Gazette* for 1635 '33 yards of Black Tiffaney for Mourning Scarves'.

ll. 32–3. *the thrall Of thousand harts*. The sense requires that the queen should take the hearts of others captive, not that she should be their subject; *thrall* must therefore be used here, as elsewhere in Herbert, to mean thraldom.

l. 42. *Children for kingdomes*. Elizabeth had a large family, including Prince Rupert and Sophia, mother of George I.

l. 47. *the Eagles winges*. An allusion to the insignia of the Imperial House.

l. 51. *Paris garden*: a place on Bankside, Southwark, where bears were kept and baited; here figuratively, as we should speak of a bear-garden.

l. 64. *thy Rhenish wine:* i.e. Rhinish. Elizabeth resided chiefly at Rhenan, near Arnheim, on the Rhine.

L'Envoy (Page 213)

l. 2. *Like Dauid's tree*. Ps. i. 3: 'And he shalbe like a tree planted by the riuers of water, that bringeth foorth his fruit in his season.'

l. 10. *saile into the Maine*: i.e. into the open sea, the English Channel, though perhaps not without a thought of the Maine being a principal river of the Palatinate.

The Convert (Page 213)

Nahum Tate, compiling his anthology sixty-three years after the publication of *The Temple*, gives no authority for his calling this poem 'An Ode, written by Mr. George Herbert'. The coincidence of the clause and the line, the straightforward statement without any use of inversions, and the diction suggest a later generation than Herbert's. Such a line as 'A Deluge on my sensual Flame' is not in his manner, and many of the words in this short poem—*averse*, *penitential*, *sensual*, *Syrens*, *treacherous*—are not found in his authentic poems. The title also is unlike Herbert's, and there is no instance of his using the noun *convert*. He has nowhere expressed regret at having written 'foolish Lays' about 'Frail Beauty's Charms', and there is no evidence of his having been unfaithful to the resolve, which he had declared in his youthful sonnets, to forswear love-poetry.

Psalms (Page 214)

The attribution to Herbert of these metrical paraphrases of the first seven Psalms rests solely on Playford's testimony, and, as will be seen, he gives it hesitatingly. John Playford (1623–86?), the most successful music publisher of his day in London, in his preface to *Psalms & Hymns in Solemn Musick* (1671), shows a marked devotion to Herbert and quotes his 'Antiphon' in full. He prints a musical setting of his own for 'Voce Sola' of 'The Altar, by Mr. George Herbert', and includes among the Psalms the version of Ps. xxiii from *The Temple*. The Psalms are mostly taken from the authorized collection of Sternhold and Hopkins, but Playford regrets their 'Course and Threadbare Language', and expresses a wish that one of the recently published 'more refin'd Translations' might be 'allowed and used in Churches', commending specially the translations of 'Dr. *Henry King*, late Lord Bishop of Chichester' and of 'Mr. *Miles Smith*, yet living'. 'Some few Psalms out of these two Translations I have made use of in this Book; and some other excellent Translations of several Psalms which were never printed till now. To those which are Bishop *Kings* there is *H.K.* Those of Mr. Smiths, *M.S.* Those with *G.H.* are supposed to be Mr. *George Herberts*.'

After giving the old version of Ps. c to the Common Tune (now known as the Old Hundredth), Playford has the heading 'Two other Psalms to this Tune, of a new Translation' and under it gives versions of Pss. i and ii, with the initials G.H. after the second; the presumption is that both these Psalms from 'a new Translation' are by the same hand, and Grosart accordingly prints them both, but Palmer omits Ps. i. Versions of Pss. iii–vii are printed by Playford with the initials G.H. after each of them, but Palmer omits Ps. v, although the evidence for it is precisely the same as for the others. Already, before these modern editors, Edward Farr had included Ps. v in his *Select Poetry chiefly sacred of the Reign of King James I* (1847): a note there asserts that Playford had attributed seven Psalms to Herbert, but erroneously adds 'One of these is given under his name', although Playford's only use of Herbert's surname, after the preface, is in the titles of 'The Altar' and Ps. xxiii from *The Temple*.

A doxology is added in italic to Ps. xxiii, but, as it is also appended to a hymn which is certainly not Herbert's, it may be taken to be Playford's editorial addition. An italicized doxology appears at the end of Ps. vi also, but it is found after two other Psalms, to which the initials G.H. are not attached, and it may be assumed that the author of the paraphrase of Ps. vi is not responsible for it.

Since so many genuine poets of the sixteenth and seventeenth centuries—among them Wyatt, Surrey, Sidney, Phineas Fletcher, Milton, Crashaw, Vaughan—tried their hand, though with indifferent success, at metrical paraphrases of the Psalms, it would be rash to conclude that the devout Herbert escaped the fashion, but the Psalms signed G.H. in Playford's collection have none of the felicity which distinguishes Herbert's authentic version of Ps. xxiii. They may possibly be early experiments of his, which he was too well advised to continue or to publish, but the evidence for assigning them to him is happily slender.

Psalm II (Page 215)

l. 13. Playford's text *But I by God and seated King* clearly needed correction; but Grosart's conjecture *But I am God* overlooks the fact, which is evident from *his sacred will* (l. 16), that God is not the speaker. The simple alteration of *and* to *am* brings the amended line *But I by God am seated King* into exact correspondence with the Vulgate rendering: 'Ego autem constitutus sum rex ab eo super Sion montem sanctum eius.'

l. 29. *lest he be wrath.* Shakespeare uses the adjective *wrath* once (*Mids. N. Dr.* II. i. 20: 'For *Oberon* is passing fell and wrath'), but *wroth* never. The Douai Bible sometimes has *wrath* as adjective, but the A.V. consistently uses *wroth*. Milton ('On the Morning of Christ's Nativity', l. 171) has *wrath* adjectivally.

OTHER POEMS ATTRIBUTED TO HERBERT

Mr. Norman Ault called my attention to a poem in a manuscript collection (B.M. Add. MS. 18220, f. 80). The unidentified compiler has a note 'Communicated to the writer by Ben Watson and Rob. Peachy A.M.' concerning the poem headed 'An Answer to Anacreon (suppos'd) By Mr. Geo: Herbert Against Drinking', beginning 'The parched earth, when one would think'. It is evidently an answer, not to a Greek original, but to the poem 'Drinking' in Cowley's *Anacreontiques*. There are many direct citations of Cowley's poem, and the last line, 'Why, man of more-ale? tell me why', is an obvious retort to Cowley's last line, 'Why, man of morals, tell me why'. As Cowley's poem was not written till after Herbert's death, the Answer cannot be his.

In *England, my England: a War Anthology* (1914), edited by George Goodchild, there appeared a spirited ballad of ten verses, entitled 'The Spanish Armado', and assigned by the editor to George Herbert. Its opening words, 'Some years of late, in eighty-eight, As I do well remember', do not fit Herbert, who was not born till five years after the Armada, nor is there anything in the poem which suggests his manner.

An article by Miss Alice Law, 'A New Caroline Commonplace Book', in *The Fortnightly Review*, Sept. 1899, describes a manuscript collection with the entry 'Elizabeth Statham (? Stalham) Her Book 16670' (i.e. 1670), and other entries with the surname Choate. After a medley of Latin and English verses and medical and cookery recipes, there is at the end a set of seven hymns without author's name. Miss Law suggests Herbert for their author, but, as she prints them in full, she leaves others to form their own judgement. I find nothing of Herbert's wit and neatness and none of his conceits and surprises in these lame efforts. The expression in the last hymn, 'We live in warr yet have we peace through Christ', suggests that it was written during the Civil War.

A PRIEST TO THE TEMPLE (Page 223)

This treatise was first 'exposed to publick light' nineteen years after the author's death in *Herbert's Remains* (1652), of which it formed the major part. It was published separately as 'The second Edition' in 1671, and again in 1675 and 1701. Its probable editor, Barnabas Oley (1602–86), was admitted to Clare Hall in 1617 and was a fellow from 1623 until his death, except for the years from his ejection by the earl of Manchester in 1644 till the Restoration; he was, therefore, living in Cambridge for a large part of Herbert's years of residence and must have known him well by repute, if not personally. Walton's account of the book in his *Lives* (1670, p. 49) is: 'At the Death of Mr. *Herbert*, this Book fell into the hands of his friend Mr. *Woodnot*; and he commended it into the trusty hands of Mr. *Bar. Oly* who publish't it with a most consciéntious, and excellent Preface.' In the 1671 edition of *A Priest to the Temple* Oley corrects Walton's story of the manuscript; after admitting that he was the author of the unsigned 'Prefatory View of the Life of the Authour', he gives as the second reason for his writing a new Preface: 'To do a Piece of Right, an office of Justice to the Good man that was possessor of the Manuscript of this Book and transmitted it freely to the Stationer who first printed it. . . . He was Mr. *Edmund Duncon* Rector of *Fryarn-Barnet*.' According to Walton, Duncon had come, at Ferrar's request, to visit Herbert in his last sickness, and had received from the dying man's hands the manuscript of *The Temple*. He may at the same time have been given the manuscript of *A Priest to the Temple*, or Arthur Woodnoth, who was also at Bemerton at the time, may have received it and left it at his death about 1650 to Duncon, who lived till 1673. In any case Oley must be right in saying that it was in Duncon's possession when it was first sent to the printer. Walton did not make any corrèction on this point in the reissues of the *Life* in 1674 and 1675.

The treatise was carelessly printed in 1652; some obvious slips were corrected in the second edition, and the punctuation of one straggling sentence (see pp. 249–50) was drastically altered in the third edition.

PAGE 224, l. 5. *the argument.* John xxi. 15–17.

l. 7. *a Mark to aim at.* At Herbert's induction in Bemerton Church '(as he after told Mr. *Woodnot*) he set some Rules to himself, for the future manage of his life' (Walton, p. 42).

l. 16. *Pastorall*: 'A book relating to the cure of souls' (Johnson's *Dictionary*).

PAGE 225, l. 1. *reducing*: in the older sense, now obsolete, of bringing back from error. Cf. p. 262, l. 21.

l. 6. *revoking*: recalling to a right way of life or belief.

l. 10. *the first to the* Colossians. The first chapter (i. 24) must be intended, as there is only one epistle.

PAGE 228, l. 23. *There he sucks.* Cf. 'The H. Scriptures' I, p. 58, l. 2: 'Suck ev'ry letter.'

l. 31. *they feel them not.* Cf. Coleridge, 'Dejection', l. 38, referring to the beauties of nature: 'I see, not feel, how beautiful they are.'

PAGE **229**, l. 7. *comparing of place with place.* Cf. 'The H. Scriptures' II, p. 58, ll. 1–8.

l. 12. *the scope of the Holy Ghost.* Cf. Hobbes, *Leviathan*, ch. xliii ad fin.: 'For it is not the bare words, but the scope of a writer, that giveth the true light by which any writing is to be interpreted, and they that insist upon single texts, without considering the main design, can derive nothing from them clearly.'

l. 24. *a Commerce*: intercourse or dealings. A favourite word and idea of Herbert: cf. 'Giddinesse', p. 127, l. 22, 'The Odour', p. 175, l. 29, and 'Providence', p. 120, ll. 105–8.

PAGE **230**, l. 13. *Catechizing . . . required under Canonicall obedience.* Canons Ecclesiastical of 1604, No. lix. See further note on p. 560.

l. 19. Anglican divines, e.g. Taylor and Sanderson, wrote on casuistry.

l. 32. *bane*: poison. Cf. p. 265, l. 22, 'baned meat'.

PAGE **231**, l. 17. *treatable*: deliberate, distinct. Bishop Parkhurst in his Injunctions of 1561 inquired whether the parson 'doth reade the common service with a lowde, distinct, and treatable voyce'.

l. 30. *in a hudling, or slubbering fashion.* Gervase Babington (*Commandements*, 1583) urged that it should be an offence if judges 'should minister oaths in such hudling, posting, and unreverent manner, as that a man can scarce tell what he saith'.

PAGE **232**, l. 13. *to be presented.* Canon cxi orders the churchwardens to present the names of any disturbers of divine service at the next visitation of the bishop or archdeacon, but 'because it often cometh to pass that the Churchwardens . . . do forbear to discharge their duties therein, either through fear of their superiors, or through negligence' (Canon cxiii), the minister may himself present.

l. 16. *let the world sinke.* Repeated at the end of ch. XXIX. Cf. Browne, *Religio Medici*, pt. II, sect. 11: '*Ruat coelum, Fiat voluntas tua*, salveth all', and *Outl. Pvbs*, No. 818: 'Doe what thou oughtest, & come what come can.'

PAGE **233**, l. 6. *he serves himselfe of*: make use of, avail oneself of (*Fr.* se servir de). Used in the A.V. in Jer. xxv. 14, xxvii. 7; and earlier in the Geneva Bible.

l. 24. Hermogenes. 'A rhetorician of Tarsus in the reign of Marcus Aurelius. He describes and gives "precepts" for seven "characters" of good oratory, such as perspicuity, elegance, &c. A good edition by Laurentius had appeared in 1614' (Beeching).

PAGE **235**, l. 6. *crumbling a text.* Herbert's is one of the earliest criticisms of the prevalent practice, illustrated in Andrewes's *Sermons* (1628), in which sometimes each word of the preacher's text is separately considered for a page or more apiece. The Calvinist divine, John Edwards, making a similar criticism so long after as 1705 (*The Preacher*, i. 202), remarks that the practice would not have survived 'if *Mr. Herbert* had been attended to' (cit. ap. W. Fraser Mitchell, *English Pulpit Oratory*, 1932, p. 362).

PAGE **236**, l. 2. *induce*: bring in by way of illustration.

l. 4. *at his first entrance* humbly adoring. Canon vii of 1640 commends 'to all good and well-affected people, members of this church' the practice of 'doing reverence and obeisance both at their coming in and going out of' church 'according to the most ancient custom of the Primitive Church in the purest times, and also of this Church'.

l. 29. *like hindes feet ever climbing.* Cf. Ps. xviii. 33 (A.V.) and 'The Pearl', p. 89, l. 40.

l. 31. *virginity is a higher state.* The use of italics in this chapter (if they were intended by the author) marks Herbert's strong feeling. Cf. 'The Church-porch', p. 6, l. 15 (*W* version): 'If this seeme Monkish', &c.

PAGE **237**, l. 18. Herbert evidently had I Cor. vii in his mind throughout this chapter. He takes the A.V., 'he will keep his virgin' (verse 37), as Taylor appears to do (*The Great Exemplar*, I. viii. 12), to mean 'he will keep himself a virgin'. Margaret Blagge, at one time resolving not to marry Sidney Godolphin, writes, 'I will keepe my *Virgin*' (J. Evelyn, *Life of Mrs. Godolphin*, ed. H. Sampson, p. 42).

PAGE **238**, l. 15. under colour of accommodation. Cf. 'Submission', p. 95, especially the second stanza.

l. 21. experiment: as transitive verb, to have experience of.

l. 26. *choyce of his wife . . . by his eare.* This lends a little colour to Walton's account of what led to Herbert's marriage to Jane Danvers. Walton also states that Herbert made his wife his almoner. (*Lives*, pp. 37, 64; cf. Herbert's Will, p. 382, ll. 16–18.)

PAGE **239**, l. 31. *the prerogative of*: a prior claim to.

l. 32. *happily*: haply. Cf. *Taming of the Shrew*, IV. iv. 54: 'And happilie we might be interrupted.'

l. 33. *prentices.* The abbreviated form was still printed in the contemporary Prayer Book.

PAGE **240**, l. 9. *Chamber of* London: the City Chamberlain's office or treasury (*camera*). Thomas Sutton, the founder of the Charterhouse, in 1611 left large sums for charitable purposes to the Chamber of London, which was regarded as specially good security.

l. 10. *Good deeds, and good breeding.* Cf. *Outl. Pvbs*, No. 107: 'Vertue and a Trade are the best portion for Children'; and No. 953: 'The best bred have the best portion.'

l. 23. *Even the wals are not idle.* Cf. the decoration with texts and mottoes of the walls at Little Gidding (*Nicholas Ferrar*, ed. Mayor, pp. 124–5).

PAGE **241**, l. 11. *boards a child*: borders on (*Fr.* aborder), approaches to the status of a son of the house.

l. 19. *back-side*: back-garden. Pickering altered to *yard.*

l. 25. *providence . . . of the great householder of the world.* This theme is developed along similar lines in 'Providence', p. 116.

PAGE **242**, l. 9. *had not Authority interposed.* Cf. 'Lent', p. 86, ll. 1–12.

l. 31. *diseases of exinanition.* Cf. p. 267, l. 14, and *Letter* III, p. 365, on his dieting himself, and his translation of Cornaro.

PAGE **244**, l. 22. *that excellent statute.* The Poor Law Act of 1601 required the churchwardens and elected householders, called the overseers of the poor, 'to set the poor on work' and to relieve those 'not able to work' from local rates.

Page **245**, l. 16. *most charged*: burdened with liabilities or expenses.

Page **246**, l. 2. *that all things there be decent*. Most of the details which follow are prescribed, largely in the words here used by Herbert, in the rubrics of the Prayer Book, the Canons of 1604, or the Visitation Articles of contemporary bishops, but the direction about the decorating and censing of the church 'at great festivalls' seems to be Herbert's own.

l. 13. *foolish anticks*: grotesque representations of animals and flowers. Cf. Evelyn, *Diary*, 18 Jan. 1645: 'The walls and roofe are painted, not with antiques and grotescs, like our Bodleian at Oxford, but emblems, figures, diagrams.'

l. 16. *Cloth* of fine linnen. Cf. Canon lxxxii: 'covered, in time of Divine Service, with a carpet of silk or other decent stuff... and with a fair linen cloth at the time of the Ministration.'

l. 19. a Chalice, and Cover. Cf. Bishop Cosin's Articles of Visitation, 1627: 'Have you a fair *chalice* ... with a large cover or *paten* for the bread?'

l. 21. a Poor-mans Box. Prescribed by Canon lxxxiv. Cf. 'Praise' III, p. 158, l. 28: 'As we have boxes for the poore.'

Page **247**, l. 6. *wallowing*: immersed or engrossed in some occupation; a shade less contemptuous than its modern use.

l. 11. *first he blesseth it*. As is prescribed in the Order for the Visitation of the Sick in the Prayer Book.

l. 32. like brute beasts. Cf. 'The Elixir', p. 184, l. 5: 'Not rudely, as a beast'. Walton (*Lives*, p. 59) tells how the peasants in the fields were encouraged to sanctify their labours 'when Mr. *Herberts Saints-Bell* rung to Prayers'.

Page **248**, l. 27. *our Saviours rule*. Matt. xviii. 15.

Page **249**, l. 2. *Nothing is little in Gods service*. Cf. 'The Elixir', p. 184, ll. 14–16.

l. 8. *comfortable*: affording comfort; cf. 'the most comfortable Sacrament' in the Prayer Book.

l. 34. at that time especially. Cf. The Order of the Visitation of the Sick: 'The Minister may not forget, nor omit to mooue the sicke person (and that most earnestly) to liberalitie toward the poore.' But the third edition (1675), by its change in the punctuation (see footnote, p. 250), perhaps rightly, attaches this clause to the following words, 'to the participation of the Holy Sacrament'.

Page **250**, l. 4. the disaffected: probably in the old sense of being affected with disease, rather than evilly affected or estranged.

Page **251**, l. 2. *those he meets on the way*. Walton illustrates Herbert's own practice (*Lives*, pp. 60–3).

l. 7. *joyne . . . to the company*. This absolute use of *join*, without *himself* being expressed, is noted in O.E.D.; cf. W. Penn, *Address to Protestants*, ii. 27: 'Philip joyn'd to him & askt him, If he understood what he read.'

l. 20. *Buttery*: (*Fr.* boterie, bouteillerie), a storeroom for liquor and other provisions.

Page **252**, l. 3. *censure*: judgement, not necessarily adverse; cf. Jackson's 'censure' of Valdesso (see below, p. 567).

l. 8. *suppling words.* For this figurative use O.E.D. instances R. Southwell, *S. Peters Complaint*, lxxx: 'Pour suppling showers upon my parched ground.' Cf. 'Grace', p. 60, l. 19.

l. 26. *set at*: assessed at for military service.

PAGE 253, l. 6. *respectively*: respectfully. Cf. the note on 'The Church-porch', l. 253.

l 30. *he expects no Briefe*: he does not wait to receive letters patent authorizing a collection to be made in parish churches. John Ferrar (*The Ferrar Papers*, p. 58) states that 'there had been gotten a Brief for the repairing of' Leighton Bromswold Church.

PAGE 254, l. 14. *a tester*: a corruption of *teston*, a shilling or, by Herbert's day, a half-shilling.

PAGE 255, l. 1. *values Catechizing highly.* Throughout the book Herbert insists upon the value of this teaching method. Besides the directions in the Prayer Book and Canons lix and lxxix, Archbishop Abbot, acting on James I's instructions, wrote to the bishops on 15 Aug. 1622 'that those Preachers be most encouraged and approved of who spend their afternoons exercises in the examination of Children in their Catechism, which is the most antient and laudable custom of teaching in the Church of England'. Ferrar sent to Herbert a translation he had made of a work on catechizing by Ludovicus Carbo (Venice, 1596); it was 'well approved' by Herbert, but was refused publication by the Cambridge licensers (Oley in *Remains*, sig. b1^{v} and Mayor, op. cit. pp. 51, 302).

l. 16. *preferreth the ordinary Church-Catechism.* Many unauthorized catechisms, mostly Calvinistic, were in use in Herbert's day.

l. 20. *give the word*: the pass-word, as in *Lear* IV. vi. 94–6.

PAGE 256, l. 23. *found Philosophy in silly Trades-men.* Socrates' 'midwifery' arts of extracting knowledge from the unlearned (*silly*) are described in Plat. Theaet. 151*c* and Meno 80*d*–86*c*; he claims to have elicited the demonstration of a geometrical theorem from a slave boy who had never learnt geometry. In Xen. Mem. III. x he is described as paying visits to tradesmen, whom he helps to realize the general principles of their crafts which had not occurred to them before.

l. 35. *in vertue*: virtually. O.E.D. gives this instance only.

PAGE 257, l. 12. *a hatchet.* Actually this word is not found in the A.V., which always has *axe*; nor is it in the Geneva or the Bishops' Bible.

PAGE 258, ll. 3–4. *Hee admits no vaine or idle names.* The Constitutions of Archbishop Peckham (1281) ordered that priests should refuse wanton names at baptism, especially for female children.

PAGE 259, l. 9. *loosely and wildely*: 'neither in set form nor sequence' (Grosart).

l. 25. *to present all that receive not.* Canon cxii orders that the minister and wardens are within forty days of Easter to present to the bishop or his chancellor the names of all parishioners who 'received not the Communion at Easter before'. For *frequency* (l. 19) see note on 'The Church-porch', l. 391.

PAGE 260, l. 2. Michael Dalton's *The Countrey Justice*, first published in 1618, was a popular book which continued to be printed for a century. The fourth edition, revised and corrected, appeared in the year that Herbert went to Bemerton.

l. 36. *in tickle cases* (altered in 2nd edition to *ticklish*): needing cautious handling.

PAGE **261**, l. 4. *one Anatomy*: either a dissected body or a model of such.

l. 5. The *Universa Medicina* (1586) and other treatises of Jean François Fernel, physician to Henri II, were frequently reprinted in Herbert's lifetime. Herbert of Cherbury writes: 'I do especially commend ... Fernelius' (*Autobiog*. p. 30); he left three works of this author to Jesus College, Oxford.

l. 34. *Bolearmena* (βῶλος, a lump of earth): an astringent earth from Armenia.

l. 34. *Roses*. Cf. 'Providence', l. 78: 'A rose, besides his beautie, is a cure', and 'The Rose', p. 178, ll. 17–20.

PAGE **262**, l. 2. *savoury*. Mountain or Winter Savory, a perennial, was used for flavouring in cookery.

l. 5. *hyssope, valerian*, &c. The medicinal properties of these plants are described in the popular *Herball* of John Gerarde (1597). The pot-herb All-good was also known as the English Mercury. Gerarde names the Water Milfoil and Water Yarrow. The dried flowers of the Yellow Melilot were used in making poultices. Smallage was also known as Wild Celery or Water Parsley.

l. 31. As appears from the sentences which follow, *scandall* is used in the New Testament sense (e.g. Matt. xviii. 7) of a cause of offence or stumbling; here it is something which, rightly or wrongly, leads the objector to refuse conformity. Cf. 'Lent', p. 86, l. 11.

PAGE **263**, l. 17. *unmoved in arguing*. Cf. 'The Church-porch', p. 18, ll. 307–12.

l. 25. *consters*: common for *construes* until the nineteenth century, and so pronounced even when *construes* became the more usual spelling.

PAGE **264**, l. 13. *witty to others*. Here and p. 275, l. 6, *witty* has the now obsolete sense of pert, censorious: cf. *All's Well*, II. iv. 32: 'Go to, thou art a wittie foole.'

PAGE **267**, l. 7. *disgest*. This form kept its place in the seventeenth century, although the form *digest*, as on p. 230, l. 24, eventually displaced it.

l. 12. Gerson, *a spirituall man*. Jean Charlier de Gerson (1363–1429), chancellor of the university of Paris, a mystic and reformer. 'The fact that he has been regarded as a probable author of the *Imitatio* indicates the character and tone of his spirituality' (E. Underhill in *Cam. Medieval Hist*. vii. 810).

l. 29. *defixed on it with those nailes*. This, the correction in the 3rd edition of *defixed on, and with those nailes*, is probably right, as so sober a Christian as Herbert would not be likely to advise an intent gazing upon *those nailes* rather than on *it* (i.e. *the Crosse of Christ*, l. 28).

PAGE **268**, l. 17. *the Apostles rule*. I Tim. iv. 12.

PAGE **269**, l. 14. *hits himselfe*. The same proverbial expression occurs in 'Charms and Knots', p. 96, ll. 9–10, and in 'Assurance', p. 156, ll. 39–40.

PAGE **270**, l. 1. *enabled*: legally empowered.

l. 12. According to Canon cxix the bishop, on summoning to a visitation, shall cause 'books of articles' to be delivered to the churchwardens, to give them the grounds of any presentments they ought to make. Before making any such presentments they must be sworn (cf. *keep their oath*, l. 16).

l. 26. *soyle*: manure.

PAGE **271**, l. 30. *cock-sure*. G. M. Young, in a letter to *The Times Literary Supplement* of 29 Dec. 1932, quotes this instance in support of his suggested derivation of the word; it 'will mean (objectively) the state of the hay, (subjectively) the state of the mind of the farmer when there is no sign of any break of the weather before the hay is cocked'. The word *cock*, though oftener used of hay, was also used of corn.

PAGE **272**, l. 3. *utter*: put upon the market, sell.

l. 33. *the exigent*: the emergency.

PAGE **274**, l. 8. *The great and nationall sin*. Cf. 'The Church-porch', p. 10, l. 91: 'O England! full of sinne, but most of sloth.' Herbert constantly denounces idleness and presses 'the necessity of a vocation' as a debt owed to the commonwealth.

PAGE **275**, l. 24. *drowning*: intentional flooding.

l. 36. *they are least there*. Charles I, following his father's example, put out in 1630 a proclamation requiring the gentry to reside upon their estates; it was the occasion of Richard Fanshawe's 'Ode on the Proclamation'.

PAGE **276**, l. 8. *nothing to that*: nothing to compare with that; cf. p. 277, l. 10: 'there is no School to a Parliament.'

l. 35. *the Statutes at large*. Cf. *Love's Labour's Lost*, I. i. 154: 'So to the Lawes at large I write my name.'

PAGE **277**, l. 1. *Sizes*. Altered to *Assizes* in 3rd edition, but the abridged form is used by Beaumont and Fletcher, and Donne, and even by Temple and Defoe.

l. 10. *a Knight or Burgess there*: i.e. a county or borough Member of Parliament.

l. 16. *ride the Great Horse*. A charger needed to be heavily built to carry a rider in full armour. Herbert of Cherbury 'spent much time also in learning to ride the great horse', and has much to say of the exercise (*Autobiog*. pp. 37, 39–41, 52). See also the quotation from Evelyn in the note below on p. 278, l. 2.

l. 17. *now weakned*, the reading of the 2nd edition, is preferable to *not weakned*, as Herbert has already declared against the idleness and sedentary lives of the gentry.

l. 23. *squared out to*: gave appropriate advice to, apportioned duties to.

l. 29. *in dressing, Complementing*, &c. Repeated from 'The Church-porch', p. 9, l. 80.

PAGE **278**, l. 2. *Fortification*. Evelyn, visiting Paris as a young man, describes a curriculum, very like Herbert's, which he found there (*Diary*, 6 Apr. 1644): 'Here I also frequently went to see them ride and exercise the great horse . . . and here also young gentlemen are taught to fence, dance, play on music, and something in fortification and the mathematics.'

l. 5. *those new Plantations, and discoveryes*. Cf. p. 282, ll. 31–5. Several of Herbert's friends, including Bacon, Donne, Danvers, and Ferrar, were interested in the American colonies. As to the plantations affording *a religious imployment*, Ferrar was keenly alive to the opportunity of 'the planting of Christian religion in the new world' (Mayor, op. cit. pp. 12, 202–5, 250, 339–41), and one of the few sermons published by Donne in his lifetime was *A Sermon preach'd to the honourable Company of the Virginian Plantation* (1622).

PAGE 278. Chap. XXXIII. *The Parson's Library*. The contents correspond so little with the title, except for elaborating a paradox, that the chapter is possibly misnamed. Elsewhere in this book Herbert commends the reading of many books—the Fathers and Schoolmen, the lives of the saints, Plato and Latin classical writers; and his Cambridge letters show his appetite for books. Books are also expressly named among his effects in his will (p. 382, ll. 4, 18–21).

PAGE 281, l. 24. *earing and harvest*. The old word for ploughing is found in the A.V., e.g. Exod. xxxiv. 21: 'in earing time and in haruest.'

l. 26. *wherewith also a careful* Joseph *might meet*: i.e. might provide for, take precautions against.

PAGE 283, l. 7. *the boundlesse Ocean of Gods Love*. Archbishop Alexander says of the last part of this chapter: 'For broken and contrite hearts he has some of the most consolatory words which were ever uttered by mortal lips' (preface to *Poems by George Herbert*, 1905).

l. 16. *needed not*: was not needful.

l. 26. *makes us onely not embraced*. It is only our rejection of his arm which can prevent our being embraced.

PAGE 284, l. 2. *he loves Procession*. During the Rogation Days it was usual for priest and people to beat the bounds of the parish and to invoke the Divine blessing on the growing crops, the Litany and appropriate Psalms being sung in procession.

PAGE 285, ll. 23–4. *ill Priests may blesse*. Cf. Articles of Religion, No. XXVI, 'Of the Unworthiness of the Ministers, which hinders not the effect of the Sacrament.'

PAGE 286, l. 26. *in writing Letters also*. All Herbert's Bemerton letters, except a very short one, contain a blessing, and a specially attractive example is in his letter to Anne, Countess of Pembroke (p. 376).

PAGE 288, ll. 6–7. *even God himself hath forgotten*. A characteristically daring, if doubtfully orthodox, sentence with which to end the Pastoral.

THE AUTHOUR'S PRAYERS BEFORE AND AFTER SERMON (Page 288)

J. Yeowell (*Notes and Queries*, 31 Jan. 1857) questioned Herbert's authorship on the ground that one so scrupulous in following canonical rule would not have used unauthorized prayers in divine service, but Canon lv (1604), which gives a form of Bidding Prayer leading up to and 'always including the Lord's Prayer', expressly allows some latitude to the preacher; he is to use a Prayer 'in this form, or to this effect'. J. E. B. Mayor (ibid. 14 Feb. 1857), in reply to Yeowell, held that Herbert was unlikely to have had any such scruple, and that the prayers 'seem to be altogether in his tone'. When, however, Mayor went on to suggest that the prayers were perhaps 'intended for private use', he overlooked such expressions as 'we stand here', 'here assembled together', and 'we say', and still more the fact that at its close the prayer before sermon invites the congregation, in the authorized way, to join in saying the Lord's Prayer.

At their first printing in 1652 the prayers are in italic, but certain words (see p. 288, note) are in roman, for so little apparent reason that they are likely to be printer's oversights in a carelessly printed book. The punctuation of 1652 is retained, because it probably represents the author's intention of marking the division of clauses for speaking aloud (cf. P. Simpson, *Shakespearian Punctuation*).

l. 15. *another to serve us*. Cf. 'Man', p. 92, ll. 47–8.

l. 19. *for an apple*. Cf. 'Home', p. 107, l. 22.

PAGE 289, l. 23. *Ride on*, &c. Quoted from Ps. xlv. 5 (B.C.P.).

CORNARO'S TREATISE OF TEMPERANCE (Page 291)

Luigi Cornaro, a Venetian of noble birth, wrote at the age of 83 *Trattato de la vita sobria* (Padua, 1558), later adding three further discourses on the same theme, and died at Padua on 26 Apr. 1566. It has escaped the notice of previous editors that Herbert made his translation of Cornaro's first treatise, not from the original, but from the Latin version made by Leonard Lessius, of the Society of Jesus, a professor at Louvain, who appended it to his own Latin treatise *Hygiasticon* (Antwerp, 1613; later editions in 1614 and 1623). Not only does Herbert follow Lessius's abbreviations of Cornaro's garrulous narrative, and adopt his occasional paraphrases, but he owes to him many of the Latinisms in his translation, e.g. 'that the patient might be proportionate to the agent', 'and those divers', 'of inferior condition'. As there is evidence of Herbert knowing Italian ('He sayth he doth Vnderstand Italian a lyttle', Letter of Woodnoth in *The Ferrar Papers*, p. 268), he may have consulted the original, but the basis of his translation is certainly Lessius's version.

There is a conflict of evidence as to who it was that conceived the idea of presenting the same two works together in an English dress and as to whether the English translation of Lessius's own treatise preceded or followed Herbert's translation of Cornaro's treatise. John Ferrar, writing the life of his brother about 1655, says of Nicholas's literary relations with Herbert (ibid., p. 59):

> And as N.F. communicated his heart to him, so he made him the Peruser, & desired the approbation of what he did, as in those three Translations of Valdezzo, Lessius, & Carbo. To the first M[r] Herbert made an Epistle, To the second, he sent to add that of Cornarius temperance, & well approved of the last.

But John Ferrar, never much of a scholar, and with his memory perhaps failing him, probably overstated the responsibility of his brother for the book. More weight must be given to the preface to the English *Hygiasticon*, signed

'T.S.', where it is said of Cornaro's treatise that 'as it was first written in order of time, so it was in translation', and the origin of the English publication is thus described:

> Master *George Herbert* of blessed memorie, having at the request of a Noble Personage translated it into English, sent a copie thereof, not many moneths before his death, unto some friends of his, who a good while before had given an attempt of regulating themselves in matter of *Diet*. . . . Not long after, *Lessius* his book . . . came to their hands: Whereby receiving much instruction and confirmation, they requested from me the Translation of it into English. Whereupon hath ensued what you shall now receive.

The 'Noble Personage' who requested Herbert to translate Cornaro may have been Bacon, who had called attention to 'the Regiment and Diet which the *Venetian Cornarus* used' in his *Historia Vitae et Mortis* (1623); and it is significant that a translation of this passage from the *Historia Vitae* is given among the preliminary pages of the English *Hygiasticon*.

'T.S.', in his preface, claims to be the translator of Lessius's original work, as well as of the third piece in the English volume, 'A Paradox' by 'an *Italian* of great reputation, living in the same age which *Cornarus* did'. It is probable that the friends interested in diet to whom Herbert sent his Cornaro in manuscript were the Ferrars, and that they subsequently invited 'T.S.' to translate Lessius's treatise. Mr. John Hodgkin (*The Times Literary Supplement*, 28 June 1917) suggests that 'T.S.' is Thomas Sheppard, a London merchant and a friend of the Ferrars, though he does not give any evidence of Sheppard's literary qualifications and experience. Barnabas Oley, who had contributed to *Hygiasticon* complimentary verses 'To the Translatour', stated in his 'Prefatory View' in *Herbert's Remains* (1652) that Nicholas Ferrar 'help'd to put out Lessius', and this modest statement is not inconsistent with what 'T.S.' wrote of his own part in the book.

Ferrar's interest in Cornaro would be the more readily engaged because, on his travels abroad as a young man, he was dangerously ill at Padua, and 'a very old physician' persuaded him that 'he was his own best physician', and that he would live 'healthfuller every day than other', if he 'observed a regularity in his diet' (Mayor, op. cit. 189–91). Ferrar may well have noticed the fine Palazzo Cornaro in Padua and heard of the famous old man who had died there fifty years before. Herbert, also, had need throughout life to pay attention to diet; Walton tells how by 'a spare diet' Herbert sought to cure his constitutional weakness, and how he 'became his own Physitian, and cur'd himself of his Ague' (*Lives*, p. 35).

Herbert has sensibly abbreviated Cornaro, even more than Lessius had done. With English readers in mind, he omits topical allusions, e.g. a passage in which the author apostrophizes 'unhappy Italy' for three innovations—sycophancy, Lutheranism, and drunkenness. There are no omissions, as 'T.S.' remarks, of 'any thing appertaining to the main subject of the book'.

Among the complimentary verses at the beginning of the English *Hygiasticon* is a poem by 'R. Crashaw, Pemb.', which later appeared, in a slightly enlarged and altered form, in the second part of *Steps to the Temple* (1646) under the heading 'In praise of *Lessius* his rule of health'. Addison wrote about Cornaro in *The Spectator* of 13 Oct. 1711, and he is described in an article, 'A great Venetian Gentleman', in *The Times Literary Supplement* of 31 May 1917.

PAGE **292**, l. 18. *abhorring from*: cum abhorrerem a (Lessius). Cf. J. Hales, *Golden Remains*, p. 423: 'They abhorr'd from the conceit of many men.'

PAGE **293**, l. 34. *I preserved me from*: servavi me ab (Lessius).

PAGE **294**, l. 33. A *squat* is a heavy fall or bump: still found in Northern dialect.

PAGE **295**, l. 21. *stint*: measure (mensura). Cf. 'Praise' III, p. 158, l. 23.

l. 34 and note. Lessius gives the proverbs in Latin only, Herbert gives English versions and also the Italian proverbs in a neater form than in Cornaro.

PAGE **296**, l. 19. *Upon the neck of it*: i.e. immediately after. Cf. Sir W. Temple, *Works*, i. 376: 'This Offer coming upon the Neck of the Parliament's Advice to his Majesty.'

PAGE **298**, l. 17. *like a Lamp* &c. Herbert takes this simile from an earlier paragraph of Cornaro which he has omitted.

PAGE **299**, l. 1. Alessandro Farnese, elected Pope as Paul III in 1534, died in 1549 at the age of 83. Pietro Bembo, made cardinal by Paul III, settled at Padua, where he formed a great library and died in 1547 at the age of 76.

l. 2. *Landus*: misprinted *Laudus* in all English editions of *Hygiasticon*. Pietro Lando was elected 78th Doge of Venice in 1539 and died in 1545 at the age of 85. He was succeeded by Francesco Donato, who died in 1553, also aged 85.

PAGE **300**, l. 4. *by all means*: perhaps a misprint for *by all men*. Cornaro has 'deve da ogni uno essere sequita', which Lessius translates 'digna est quam omnes amplectantur'.

PAGE **301**, l. 15. *and those divers*: iisque diversis (Lessius). From 1700 the spelling of the word in this sense has been 'diverse'.

l. 19. *village*: perhaps a misprint for *villa*. Cornaro has 'la mia Villa di piano', which Lessius translates 'villa mea in pleno'. Lessius renders *villagio* by *vicus*.

l. 25. *manured*: in the older sense of 'cultivated'.

PAGE **302**, l. 15. *untoiled*: untilled.

l. 19. (*which in* Italie *is very great*). This explanation for the English reader's benefit is not in the original or in Lessius's translation.

l. 33. *a* Greek Poet *of old*. Euripides produced his last play *Orestes* in 408 B.C. at the age of 73, and died two years after.

PAGE **303**, l. 5. *well given*: well disposed, inclined. Cf. Holland, *Pliny*, ii. 118: 'What man is there well giuen and honestly minded?'

l. 26. *resolution*: dissolution. Cf. II Tim. iv. 6, Vulg.: 'tempus resolutionis meae instat', and Rheims New Test.: 'The time of my resolution is at hand.'

VALDESSO'S *CONSIDERATIONS* (Page 304)

Walton's account of Valdesso, which he says that he had 'from a Friend, that had it from the mouth of Mr. *Farrer*', seriously confuses him with his brother Alonso, who was knighted in the service of the emperor Charles V and died in 1532. The most recent and authoritative account of John Valdesso is in M. Marcel Bataillon's introduction to his edition of the *Dialogo de Doctrina Cristiana* (Coimbra, 1925). Juán de Valdés (the name is Italianized as Valdesso, and appears in the French translation as Ian de Val d'esso), of a Castilian noble family, studied at the university of Alcala, where the influence of Erasmus on Biblical studies had penetrated. In 1524 Valdesso passed into the service of the marquis of Villena, at whose house the Illuminés would often meet to read the Scriptures and discuss the spiritual life. Shortly before the marquis's death in 1529 Valdesso dedicated to him his anonymous *Dialogo*, which was modelled on the *Colloquia* of Erasmus. There are extant three letters of Erasmus to him in the years 1528–30 (*Letters of Erasmus*, ed. Allen, vii. 340, viii. 96, 320). By August 1531 we find Valdesso in Rome, where he was for a short while chamberlain to Clement VII. By 1534 he had settled in Naples, where he lived until his death in 1541. Here he was a leading member of a religious coterie, which included Vittoria Colonna and Julia de Gonzala; he dedicated to the latter his commentary on the Romans in a letter which Ferrar included in his edition of the *Considerations*.

The Hundred and Ten Considerations was written in Spanish, but the original was probably never printed and is no longer extant, except for about a quarter of the work. About nine years after Valdesso's death Pietro Paolo Vergerius, who had given up the bishopric of Capo d'Istria to join the reformed faith, brought to Basel a MS. of the original or an Italian version of the *Considerations* and gave it to Coelius Secundus Curio to publish. The Italian translation (Basel, 1550) was soon followed by a French translation from the Italian by Claude de Kerquefinem (Lyons, 1563; 2nd edition, Paris, 1565). As the title-page of Ferrar's English translation (1638) shows, he made it from the Italian, though he or Herbert consulted also the French version, as two notes on the 37th and 65th Considerations, among Herbert's 'Briefe Notes', are described in the margin as the French translator's; as they are not Herbert's, they are not included in the present edition. Walton says that Ferrar met with Valdesso's book 'in his Travells', which is probable enough, as he collected many religious books during his journeys (Peckard, *Memoirs of N. Ferrar*, p. 88).

On 29 Sept. 1632, five months before his death, Herbert returned to Ferrar 'your Valdesso', with a commendatory letter and 'Briefe Notes', but the book was not published till some months after Ferrar's own death which occurred on 4 Dec. 1637. It included the 'censure' of Dr. Thomas Jackson, President of Corpus, who examined the work at the instance of the Vice-Chancellor of Oxford before it was issued by the university printer. He was able to 'approve and commend the greatest part of it', but added:

> There be some passages obscure, dubious, and offensive, wherein notwithstanding, the Publisher has given me satisfaction, and I doubt not but his Annotations in the Preface together with M. *Herberts* Apologie for the offensive places will doe the like to every unpreiudicate and unpartiall Christian Reader.

Another edition under the title *Divine Considerations* was printed by the university printer at Cambridge in 1646. Its editor, whose name does not appear, showed less courage and less literary propriety than Ferrar, who had given Valdesso's work 'without any alteration at all from the Italian copy'; in the 51st Consideration where the author had drawn upon his experience as a papal chamberlain to describe the 'prudence, bounty, liberality and iustice' with which the Pope ruled his household, the editor of 1646 substitutes 'the Prince' for 'the Pope'. Of Herbert's 'Briefe Notes' he discards seven, and alters or adds to some others, and introduces five new notes. As it is unlikely that these alterations and additions are Herbert's, they are in the present edition relegated to the footnotes.

Letter to the Translator (Page 304)

The year is missing from the date of the letter as printed in 1638, but '1632' is given in all subsequent printings of it. The date is corroborated by Peter Peckard (op. cit. p. 212 and p. 215), who, with the original in his possession, printed its subscription as 'Bemerton, Sep. 29, 1632'. The copy of the 1638 edition in the Cambridge University Library (Syn. 7. 73. 370) has a manuscript note on the fly-leaf certifying Ferrar to be the translator, signed 'P. P.', and at the end of Herbert's letter another note, in the same handwriting but without the initials: 'The Orig[l] M.S. of this Letter is dated Sep. 29, 1632.' It is possible that these two notes were not written by Peckard but by someone who drew his information from Peckard's *Memoirs*; the handwriting is, however, very like Peckard's. One further doubt may be removed. Mr. J. E. Butt in his 'Bibliography of Walton' in the *Proceedings of the Oxford Bibliographical Society*, 1933, p. 333, describes the Bodleian copy (Wood 229) of Walton's *Lives* (1670) as having the 'date deleted'; but the tops of the figures are decipherable, and it cannot be a deliberate cancellation, but is merely a piece of defective printing. Other copies of this edition, including the British Museum one (C 45 b 8) and my own, have the full date clearly printed.

l. 4. *griefes*: as often in Herbert, physical sufferings. He was in his last sickness and died just five months after writing this letter.

PAGE **309**, l. 29. *bark*. This is the reading of 1638 and 1646, but the third letter is blurred in some copies of the latter, and Pickering, who printed the 'Briefe Notes' from 1646, has *back*. O.E.D. gives, as an example of the figurative use, John Jackson, *The True Evangelical Temper* (1641), i. 68: 'The Jews . . . stick in the barke, and expound the text to be fulfilled to the very letter of it.'

PAGE **320**, l. 1. *analogat*: analogous. A form not recorded in O.E.D.

OUTLANDISH PROVERBS (Page 321)

The Question of Herbert's Connexion with the Book

The complicated bibliography of *Outlandish Proverbs* must be fully set out because of its bearing on the disputed question of Herbert's part in the collection. In the Stationers' Register Matthew Simmons 'entred for his copie . . . a booke called *Outlandish Proverbs* selected by G. H.' on 24 Sept. 1639. On 15 Oct. following Humphrey Blunden entered for 'a book called *Wits Recreations* . . . with *a thousand outlandish proverbs*'. The former appeared as a separate publication, printed by T. P[aine] for Humphrey Blunden, 1640, and the proverbs appeared also in identical form, with the signatures unchanged, as the second part of *Witts Recreations* in the same year. The latter composite volume has an engraved title-page 'Witts Recreations . . . With A Thousand outLandish Proverbs. Printed for Humph: Blunden. 1640'; it has a separate title-page for the first part 'Printed by R. H[odgkinson] for Humphry Blunden, 1640', and another for the second part identical with that of the separate issue of *Outlandish Proverbs*. Although Simmons entered for the proverbs, Blunden's name only appears as publisher on all these title-pages, and there is a different printer for each part of *Witts Recreations*. Blunden was also responsible for the second edition, 1641, but Simmons for that of 1650; no edition except the first contained the proverbs, and accordingly no mention is made of them on the revised title-page. It is unfortunate that in the reprint of *Witts Recreations* and other works in *Facetiae: Musae Deliciae*, 1817, edited by Edward Dubois, *Witts Recreations* was printed from a defective copy of the first edition without the engraved title-page, and its place was taken by the title-page of 1641, which does not mention the proverbs. This has misled some bibliographers. It was also without the last three pages of the proverbs, which therefore end at No. 910. In the first edition the proverbs are numbered from 1 to 1032, but one of the two copies of *Witts Recreations*, 1640, in the British Museum (C 65 c 6) has a cancel leaf of E^3, giving proverbs 1003–10 reset and followed by 'Finis' and '1639. *Imprimatur*. Matth. Clay'. (This Imprimatur, with the addition of 'Octob. 8', is generally found at the end of the previous section of the book.) The other copy of *Witts Recreations*, 1640, in the British Museum (1076 f 16), like the Bodleian copy of the separate issue of *Jacula Prudentum*, 1651 (Malone 895), has the words on the title-page 'By M^r. *G. H.*' heavily scored through by hand in a brownish ink, though perhaps W. C. Hazlitt was hardly warranted in saying of the Bodleian erasure that it was made 'by some one at the time, as if he knew Herbert not to be the author' (*Collections and Notes, 1867–76*, 1876). James Yeowell, who re-edited Pickering's *Works of Herbert* for Messrs. Bell and Daldy in 1859–60, also called attention to the Bodleian erasure in *Notes and Queries* of 31 Jan. 1857, but neither he nor Hazlitt noticed the similar erasure in the British Museum copy. In any case it is unlikely that the initials only would have had much selling value, as few buyers would have recognized in them the author of the popular *Temple*.

The next appearance of the proverbs after their first appearance in 1640 is as a separate reissue of T. Paine's printing of them with a new title-page, 'Jacula Prudentum Or, *Outlandish* Proverbs, Sentences, &c. Selected by Mr. *George Herbert*, Late Orator of the Universitie of Cambridg. London, Printed by T. M[axey] for T. Garthwait. 1651.' The text of 1640 is not reset, as may be seen by the repetition of the old defects—a wrong signature (D^2 for E^2), misspellings (e.g. 25 *waights*, 183 *Shcoller*, 460 *dsepise*), and failures of alinement. The page-headings continue to be 'Outlandish Proverbs', as in 1640. The title-page differs only slightly (e.g. an additional comma, a different arrangement of the lines of imprint, and the use of initial only for Maxey's surname) from that found in the separate title-page for 'Jacula Prudentum', also dated 1651, in *Herbert's Remains* (1652). There is a stub between A⁷ and A⁸, conjugate with the title-page, which is likely to be a cancel. There appears to be no copy of this made-up book except Malone 895.

Maxey was the printer for Garthwait of the whole of *Herbert's Remains*. The erratic pagination (see Introduction, p. lxiv) gives a suspicious appearance to 'Jacula Prudentum' as if it had been an insertion not at first intended; the proverbs are not mentioned on the initial title-page nor in Oley's 'Prefatory View'. Yeowell gives no evidence for his suggestion that the first appearance of 'A Priest to the Temple' was unaccompanied by 'Jacula Prudentum', and no copy of *Remains* has been found without the proverbs. J. E. B. Mayor in answer to Yeowell (*Notes and Queries*, 14 Feb. 1857) remarked that irregular pagination was common in books of the period, and that neither Oley nor Walton professed to give a complete list of Herbert's works. 'Jacula Prudentum' in *Remains*, besides giving the 1,032 proverbs of the 1640 book, intersperses six new ones in the first few pages, and adds 152 at the end, without any indication that they are an addition; the proverbs throughout are unnumbered. It is probable that this enlarged form of 'Jacula Prudentum' had an independent existence as a separate publication in 1651, though it must be distinguished from the *Jacula Prudentum* of the same year using Paine's text, already described (Malone 895). There is, indeed, a copy (B.M. 1070 h 4) of *Jacula Prudentum*, of Maxey's printing (1651), without 'A Priest to the Temple', but, since it includes the miscellaneous matter, paged 171–94, as in *Remains*, it looks as if it were merely an incomplete copy of *Remains*; otherwise there is no accounting for the pagination of the last section. Some copies only have 'June 30. 1651. *Imprimatur*, Jo. Downham' on p. 194.

If the bibliographical evidence for Herbert's connexion with *Outlandish Proverbs* is inconclusive, the case for his having formed at least the nucleus of the collection and for his being the translator of many foreign proverbs is very strong, and is supported by much evidence, some of which was not available when Yeowell and Hazlitt expressed their doubts. This evidence mainly derives from Little Gidding where Herbert's reputation as a writer was jealously cherished. The Rev. John Jones (1700–70), who served parishes in Huntingdonshire and neighbouring counties, was an industrious annalist, specially interested in Gidding. From Hugh Mapletoft, a descendant of the Ferrars, he had received the early draft of Herbert's poems, which is now in Dr. Williams's Library (see Introduction, p. lii). To the same library came a large collection of Jones's notes. In MS. Jones B 87 there are lists of 'Books and MSS. belonging to Mr. John Mapletoft' (1687–1763, vicar of Byfield, near Daventry, son of another John, 1631–1721; the older John was a great-nephew of Nicholas Ferrar and was brought up at Gidding after his father Joshua's death in 1635). Jones's lists include some Gidding manuscripts 'At Mr. Mapletoft's at Bifield' and others 'At Mr. Bunbury's of Catworth' (William Bunbury, rector of Great Catworth, Huntingdonshire, 1704–48). Among the latter, besides other folios, Jones notes (f. 43):

And large Book of Stories—with Outlandish Proverbes at the end englished by Mr George Herbert. 1. I wept wh^n^ born & ev. D. shewes why. Pvbs. In all 463 Proverbs. ult. A piece of Ch. yd fits ev. bod . . . One Story Book begins with The Chief Care of Parents ought to be good Educ^n^ of Children. 2. Examples of Good Children. This is the St.B. with Proverbs, &c.

The two proverbs which are here said to begin and end the collection of 463 proverbs are found as No. 199 and No. 1027 in *Outlandish Proverbs* (1640).

A Story Book beginning with the words 'The Chief Care of Parents' cannot now be traced, but I have recently, by the kindness of the owner, the Hon. Lady Langman, a descendant of John Ferrar, examined one which has an evident relation to it. This Story Book is described on the first page: 'N.3. Transcribed from Number Tow. N.B. This *Numb.* 3 is a Copy of ye first Halfe of N.2', and it is, in fact, a duplicate of the first part of vol. ii, now in the British Museum (Add. MS. 34658). The B.M. volume has no proverbs, but Lady Langman's has a collection of 204 on the first three pages, not in the recognizable Gidding hand in which the following dialogues are written, but in a rather untidy hand. The words 'englished by Mr George Herbert' are not found, the only heading being 'In the Name of God. IHS. Amen. Proverbs'. The first is 'I wept when I was borne and euery day shews why', but the last is not 'A piece of Churchyard fits euery body', perhaps because the transcript was not finished. The copy was evidently not made from a printed book as the copyist twice leaves a blank for a word which he presumably could not decipher. All but three of the 204 proverbs are found in *Outlandish Proverbs* (1640). Of these three one, 'The longest day hath an euening', is among the two in Sir Henry Herbert's transcript, to be described later, which are absent from *Outlandish Proverbs*. The readings that differ from the printed book generally agree with Sir Henry Herbert's.

Francis Peck (1692–1743), rector of Goadby-Marwood, and, like Herbert, a prebendary of Lincoln, was engaged in compiling a life of Ferrar, which Peter Peckard, husband of Martha Ferrar, was later to use for his *Memoirs of the Life of Mr. Nicholas Ferrar* (1790). John Jones helped Peck with materials, including lists of Gidding MSS. similar to those already described, and notes of his own; these lists appear in Middle Hill MS. 9527, now in Clare College Library. From the Middle Hill MS. Mayor reproduced in part the lists of manuscripts formerly at Byfield and Catworth in his *Nicholas Ferrar* (1855), pp. 300–3, but the Middle Hill MS. does not mention the two proverbs cited in MS. Jones B 87, or Mayor could have strengthened his case against Yeowell.

The ascription of proverbs to Herbert in the Gidding community is corroborated by an undated letter (*The Ferrar Papers*, 1938, p. 303) from John Ferrar to his son, recommending him, when he comes into his inheritance, to devote a twentieth part of it to God:

Remembring daly those tow Divine Verses of your Vnkells most Deare freind (of whom it was Said by them that knewe them booth there was one Soule in twoe Bodys)—

Greate Almes Giving lessens noe mans livinge
By Givinge to the Poore we Increase our Store

And I shall leaue you a Table to be hunge up in the house where in these Verses shalbe written.

These two proverbs are Nos. 190 and 191 in *Outlandish Proverbs*, the second being slightly altered.

A further link between Herbert and *Outlandish Proverbs* has recently been made known in Professor H. G. Wright's article, 'Was George Herbert the Author of *Jacula Prudentum*?' in *The Review of English Studies*, Apr. 1935. The National Library of Wales has acquired some manuscripts formerly in the possession of the Herbert family (H. G. Wright in *Mod. Lang. Review*, July 1933); among them is MS. 5301 E, which includes, in the handwriting of George Herbert's brother Henry, 'Outlandishe Prouerbs selected out of seuerall Languages & enterd here the vi. August 1637. At Ribsford. H. H.' The manor of Ribbesford, Worcestershire, was owned by Sir Henry Herbert and his descendants for about 150 years. The list in the writing of H. H. is, with two exceptions, identical with the first 72 in *Outlandish Proverbs*, published three years later. The slight variants are noted above on pp. 321–3; in at least two cases the text is obviously better presented in the Ribbesford MS. than in the book.

There is also the corroborative evidence of George Herbert's use of proverbs in his writings and letters. He uses the word *outlandish* twice in *The Temple* and twice in *A Priest to the Temple*, always in the sense of 'foreign' and twice in reference to a proverb. In *A Priest to the Temple* (p. 251) he quotes 'the outlandish proverb, that *Prayers and Provender never hinder journey*'. This is a Spanish proverb, No. 277 in *Outlandish Proverbs*. In a letter to his brother Henry (p. 376, ll. 16–18), written from Bemerton, he advises him: 'But take this rule, and it is an outlandish one, . . . "the best-bredd child hath the best portion".' This is No. 953. Herbert's fondness for proverbs is evident in all his writings, both public and private, but it is likely to be more than coincidence that he uses so many of those to be found in *Outlandish Proverbs*, especially as his instances are all but one of foreign origin and mostly unfamiliar in English. He uses No. 475 in 'Confession', l. 12, No. 602 in 'A Dialogue-Antheme', l. 7, No. 726 in 'The Glimpse', l. 20, and Nos. 223 (adapted), 277, 419, and 427 in *A Priest to the Temple* (pp. 240, 251, 275, 268). He quotes none of those added in *Jacula Prudentum*. On all these grounds Herbert may with some confidence be accounted the collector and the skilful translator of at any rate a considerable part of *Outlandish Proverbs*, though it is unlikely that he had any responsibility for the proverbs added in 1651.

An interest in foreign proverbs had been created by the *Adagia* of Erasmus, a popular book in England, and the interest was at its height in the Elizabethan age. Sanford (1573) and Florio (1578) introduced many Italian proverbs to English readers, and the compilers of French and Spanish grammars and dictionaries for English students paid much attention to proverbs. Cotgrave's *A Dictionarie of the French and English Tongues* (1611) quoted a large number of French proverbs with English translations or equivalents; of the first ninety of *Outlandish Proverbs* all but two are found in Cotgrave, which is likely to have been one of the compiler's sources, though his translations often differ from Cotgrave's. A collection of English proverbs was begun by John Heywood in 1546 and subsequent editions made large additions to the number; other collectors were James Sanford (1573) and Thomas Draxe (1616). We may also note that two writers for whom Herbert had respect were collectors of proverbs: Bacon compiled in 1594 *A Promus of Formularies and Elegancies*, and William Camden, a famous name at Westminster School, included in the second edition of his *Remaines* (1614) nearly 400 proverbs.

The title *Outlandish* is more fully justified than might have been expected until an analysis was made of the collection. I have found French, Italian, or Spanish originals or equivalents of more than six-sevenths of *Outlandish Proverbs*. I have not overlooked the fact that very similar proverbs originate independently in different countries besides others that are carried from country to country, but the versions in *Outlandish Proverbs*, e.g. Nos. 142 and 872, are often nearer to a foreign than to the familiar English form. Nos. 2–90 and 792–883 are mainly French, Nos. 91–388 Spanish, and 389–751 Italian, while there is greater mixture in the other sections. There are not enough proverbs of German or Dutch origin to make it safe to infer that the compiler knew the Teutonic languages. Most of these proverbs had not appeared in English dress before, as may be seen from *The Oxford Dictionary of English Proverbs* and G. L. Apperson's *English Proverbs and Proverbial Phrases: a Historical Dictionary*, and comparatively few of them have established themselves in popular use. Some of them are rather *sententiae* of the learned than the wisdom of the people, e.g. No. 773, and justify the use of the word 'Sentences' in the sub-title of *Jacula Prudentum*. Sometimes alternative versions of the same proverb are given together, e.g. Nos. 157–8, 189–91, 330–1, 919–20, as though the compiler had not yet decided between them, and sometimes also an explanation is numbered as if it were a fresh proverb, e.g. Nos. 192–3. Many are rhymed, as often in the foreign originals, but from the first they were printed straight out.

16. Cotgrave explains: 'One knave can easily get at the drift of another.'

19. *a staffe*: a staff of office (*la baguette*), as Bacon renders it (*Promus*, No. 1583).

30. *man*: in falconry, to accustom to man's presence, and so to tame. Cf. Shakespeare, *Tam. Shrew*, IV. i. 196:

> Another way I haue to man my Haggard,
> To make her come, and know her Keepers call.

Cotgrave explains: 'A well bred person needs not much tutoring.'

38. Cotgrave explains: 'He that offers me all, means to give me nothing.'

57. *needes a Dog for his man*: so Cotgrave renders 'porte le chien sous l'hocton' (*hoqueton*, sleeved gown).

63. *bable*: a wooden mace or baton.

87. *miscarry*: 'iamais ne tombe de la main' (Cotgrave).

90. *buzzard*: 'a stupid fellow' (O.E.D.). The French proverb has 'un jeune coquerel'.

95. *attends*: i.e. awaits the attack, rather than rushes in.

99. *no Chimney*. The Spanish proverb has 'there are not even hooks' for the bacon.

101. *Presse* (all editions) is a misprint for *Dresse*. Cf. Jonson, *Underwoods*, Celebr. Charis ix:

> Dressed, you still for man should take him!
> And not think h'had eat a stake.

102. The tongue goes to where the tooth aches.

131. A literal translation of a Spanish proverb, which appears to mean that a horse who has to get home in the rain will go as fast as if he had had a good meal: i.e. difficulties spur one on.

134. *advise*: here and in No. 273 in the old sense of 'deliberate, reflect'.

142. Torriano (*Piazza Universale*, London, 1666) translates: 'A morsel once swallowed begets not friends.' Minsheu and Camden have the more familiar 'Eaten bread is forgotten'.

172. Do not dwell in a newly built house; let somebody else put it to the test. Cf. 'Finita la casa, entra morte' (*Notes and Queries*, 3 Mar. and 12 May 1900).

198. A man plants a tree at his own expense, but its slow growth brings the benefit to his successor only. Cf. Virg. Geo. ii. 58.

203. Rub your sore eye with the elbow only (which you cannot do). Cf. No. 837.

205. The Bodleian copy of *Jacula Prudentum* (1651) has a correction made by hand to 'A gentleman, a grayhound', and this is the form found in H. Mapletoft's *A Select Collection of Proverbs* (1707).

276. Perhaps omit *then*, as the Spanish proverb ends: 'but more spends he who abides.'

284. *bribe*. The Spanish proverb runs: 'Neither take bribes nor lose thy right.'

285. *In the world*. The French and Spanish versions begin 'The world is round'.

295. *groundsell*: door-sill, threshold. Cf. Milton, *P.L.* i. 460.

310. The Spanish proverb has 'drink of this water', sometimes adding 'however foul it be'.

317. The Little Gidding MS. cites Hor. C. III. xvi. 9–11.

335. Spanish. Your household expenses must match the year's harvest.

400. 'Vecchio amico, casa nuova', which Torriano translates 'An old friend, but a new house.' The meaningless *is* of O.P. is probably a misprint.

405. 'Bel colpo non ammazzo mai uccello' (of a boasting sportsman). Probably *Farre* is a misprint for *Faire*.

406. *upbraided*: regurgitated. An Italian proverb.

414. *one of debts*. The Italian has 'one ounce of debts', and so Camden gives it (*Remaines*, p. 303).

445. Pescetti (*Proverbi Italiani*, 1618, f. 223) has 'non fà mai roba', but the compiler of O.P. appears to translate 'ruba'.

461. *that out of doores*: i.e. over the threshold. A Latin proverb, 'Porta itineri longissima' (Varro R.R. I. ii. 2), found in Italian and German.

522. 'Un bel morir tutta la vita onora' (Petrarch, *Rime*, ccvii, l. 65).

589. 'Grande forza è nascosta in dolce impero.' Pettie's *Guazzo* (1586) introduces with the words, 'as the Poet saith'.

610. *Counters* was the common name for the sheriffs' prisons in London. In *Proverbs Englished by N. R.* (1659) the proverb is given thus: 'The slothfull is the Servant of a Prison.'

635. The Italian proverb ends 'e la mattina l'hoste', which Torriano translates 'and the morning mine Host'. The *frost* of O.P. is probably a misprint.

641. *cannot finde it*: rather, as Torriano renders it, 'but the Astrologer is hard to find' ('l'Astrologo non si truova'). Bacon gives it in Italian only (*Promus*, No. 111).

647. *scald*: affected with the scall, scabby.

669. *habit*: dress. Cf. *Rom. Rose*, l. 6192: 'Habite ne maketh monk ne frere.'

692. Cf. Fuller, *Holy State* (1642), II. xxiv: the University man 'knowes well that cunning is no burthen to carry, as paying neither portage by Land, nor pondage by Sea.'

762. *an eele in a sacke.* Cotgrave has 'On ne cache point aiguilles en sac', the equivalent of our 'needle in a bottle of hay' (a French variant has 'une botte de foin'). It is tempting to suppose that the compiler of O.P. used a text where the word was printed *anguilles* (eels), although T. Fuller (1732) has a proverb, 'He is as much out of his element as an eel in a sandbag.'

785. *bending*: *sc.* his bow; will ever be shooting.

811. *Weening*: guessing. Cf. *Piers Plowman*, xx. 33: 'Wenynge is ne wysdome ne wyse ymagynacioun.'

867. 'A brebis tondue Dieu mesure le vent': given in slightly different form in H. Estienne, *Les Prémices* (1594). Best known in English in the form given to it by Sterne (*Sentimental Journey*, ii. 175): 'God tempers the wind, said Maria, to the shorn lamb.'

869. 'A un pauvre homme sa vache meurt, et au riche son enfant.' Cotgrave has a variant, 'La vache du riche velle (calves) souvent, celle du povre avorte.'

878. *assault*: assault at arms (*assaut d'armes*). An earlier example of this special sense than any given in O.E.D.

893. *to maintaine one.* The German proverb is clearer: 'than to keep fire on one' ('als auf einem immer Feuer haben').

903. The reverse of the proverb found in Italian and French: 'One sees more old drunkards than old physicians.'

910. The Little Gidding MS. cites Hor. Ep. I. i. 41–2.

933. Gives no sense as it stands: perhaps the original represented something like 'Trees eat but in one place.' Cf. M. K. Rawlings, *The Yearling*, 1938, p. 3: 'Dogs were the same everywhere, and oxen and mules and horses. But trees were different in different places. "Reckon it's because they can't move none", he decided. They took what food was in the soil under them.'

943. The whitethorn tree, which promises so much from its wealth of blossom, yields poor fruit, even compared with the sloes of the blackthorn. I owe the explanation of this proverb and of Nos. 198 and 933 to the Director of the Royal Botanic Gardens, Kew.

955. *wimble*: gimlet.

1020. *the bone in the legge*: a feigned excuse for idleness. Cf. Swift, *Polite Conv.* iii: 'I can't go, for I have a bone in my leg.'

JACULA PRUDENTUM (Page 356)

These additions to *Outlandish Proverbs* are not likely to be Herbert's. Some of them are taken from John Minsheu's *A Spanish Grammar* (1599), e.g. Nos. 1148–55, and others from Bacon's *Apophthegmes* (1625), e.g. Nos. 1157–61, including the bracketed explanations. Many, especially those at the end, answer better to the description 'Sentences' than to that of proverbs. The proportion of foreign proverbs is still high, but lower than in the earlier collection.

1036. The Fox is Louis XI, who took Amiens in 1471, and the Lion is his rival, Charles the Bold.

1040. In the old French province of Berri, according to Howell (*Proverbs*, 1659), the sheep have scurf on the nose, because they feed on thyme.

1058. *incompossible*: a scholastic term for 'that cannot exist together, incompatible'.

1073. A punning French proverb: 'Chercher noises pour noisettes.' Cotgrave explains: 'to pick a quarrel on a small occasion.'

1085. *rock*: distaff.

1137. Wotton's epitaph: 'Hic jacet hujus sententiae primus author disputandi pruritus, ecclesiarum scabies.' Cf. *Herbert's Remains*, p. 193, and *Reliquiae Wottonianae* (1651), p. 145.

1138. Raleigh used it in the preface to *Hist. of World* (1614).

1156. Cf. John Northbrooke, *Dicing Reproved* (1579): 'I pray God the olde proverb be not found true, that gentlemen and rich men are venison in Heauen (that is), very rare and daintie to haue them there.'

1157–61. Bacon attributes No. 1157 to Wotton, 1158 to Alonso of Aragon, 1159 to Alexander, 1161 to Sir Amyas Paulet.

LETTERS (Page 363)

No autograph English letter of Herbert's appears to be extant now except the one to Sir Robert Harley (No. VI), which is in the Harley Papers at Welbeck Abbey, and the advice to Woodnoth (No. XIX), which Dr. B. Blackstone recently found in the library of Magdalene College, Cambridge. Dr. Peter Peckard, Master of Magdalene, stated (*Memoirs of Nicholas Ferrar*, 1790, p. 212) that the letter to the translator of Valdesso (No. XVIII), then in his possession, 'is precisely the same with that prefixed to' Ferrar's translation printed in 1638, but the original cannot now be traced. The other two letters to Ferrar (Nos. XV, XVI) are here printed from the transcript made by Thomas Baker (1656–1740) of John Ferrar's life of his brother; Mayor used the same source for his *Nicholas Ferrar: Two Lives* (1855). Miss Rebecca Warner of Bath printed Nos. IV, XII, XIV, and XVII in *Epistolary*

Curiosities: Unpublished Letters, Illustrative of the Herbert Family (1818) from the originals lent to her for the purpose by the heir of Francis Ingram of Ribbesford, Worcestershire. Ingram in 1787 acquired many Herbert papers with the house, which Sir Henry Herbert had bought from his brothers Edward and George in 1627; these letters cannot be traced. For all the other letters except XVIII and XIX we are dependent on Walton. He included No. I in the 1670 editions of his life of Herbert, and added No. XI in 1674. In the appendix of the 1670 editions he printed eight letters in the following order—Nos. XVIII, II, X, III, VII, IX, VIII, V, and he added No. XIII in 1675. Walton arranged them with little regard for chronological order, as the dates and internal evidence make clear.

The nineteen letters fall into two main groups and represent only particular periods of Herbert's life. After the fragment of a letter written in his 17th year there are nine belonging to his Cambridge time, written between the ages of 24 and 27, then the letter to his mother in her sickness, written in his 30th year, and, after a gap of eight years, eight letters written at Bemerton. There is no clearer evidence of the development of his character than the difference between the Cambridge and the Bemerton letters.

The contents of two other letters of Herbert to Ferrar are given in Bodl. MS. Rawlinson D 2, a collection of the materials of Dr. Francis Turner for a life of Nicholas Ferrar, which he contemplated publishing about 1681. The materials include a transcript of a substantial part of John Ferrar's life of his brother; after the description, which Baker included in his transcript, of the making of Concordances at Little Gidding with scissors and paste, there is a passage (f. 41) which Baker omits:

> One of these Books was sent to Mr Herbert, wch he sayd, he prized most highly, as a rich jewel worthy to be worne in ye heart of all Xtians, & in his letter to them expresses himself thus, y^{t} he most humbly blessed God, y^{t} he had lived now to see womens scizzers brought to so rare an use as to serve at Gods altar, & incouraged them to proceed in ye like works as y^{r} most happy employment of theyr times, & to keep y^{r} Book allwayes wthout Book in their hearts, as well as they had it in their heads, memories, & tongues dayly.

And on f. 44^{v} is the following (also omitted by Baker):

> Mr Herbert writes to Mr. N. F. Letter of great affection, much commendation, free & Xtian Counsill. That they would proceed in their well begun Devotions & Exercises, humbly, Thankfully, Constantly, to inflame their hearts every day more & more with ye love of God & his holy & sweet Word & Sacrament. To attend to the great Christian duty of Mortification, & with true humble contempt of the world: not to be frighted with the suspitions, slanders & scornes wch worldly persons would throw uppon them. To read often the Lives of the Saints and Martyrs in all Ages, To have ever in their minds the 11th to the Hebr. the cloud of Witnesses & noble Army of Martyrs, Virgins, Sts, Looking unto our sweetest Jesus, *the Author & Finisher of our Faith*, & finally to have a very constant due regard and circumspection to their health.

Musick Good Diet & moderate Exercises he recommended to the Virgin Sisters.

He presented you with the noble Italian Cornaro in English.

I (Page 363)

In view of the freedom with which Walton altered and paraphrased some of Donne's letters in the text of the *Life* (1658), we cannot be sure that we have Herbert's exact words in this reported early letter. Cf. R. E. Bennett, 'Walton's Use of Donne's Letters in *Lives* (1670)', *Philological Quarterly*, Jan. 1937, and John Butt, 'Izaak Walton's Methods in Biography', *Engl. Assoc. Essays*, XIX, 1934.

II (Page 363)

This undated letter probably precedes only by a short time No. III, in which Herbert alludes to his taking horse-exercise.

l. 22. *a Horse-back*. Cotgrave quotes a proverb: 'Diseases come a horse-backe, and returne on foot.'

III (Page 364)

l. 27. *my journies end*: i.e. the priesthood. Cf. 'The Crosse', p. 164, l. 8: 'this deare end, So much desir'd.'

PAGE 365, l. 6. *to* New-market, *and there lie a day or two*. Palmer and others have rashly inferred that Herbert, at the age of 24 and with little income, had a house there.

l. 20. *engaging*: pledging, mortgaging. In No. V, l. 8, Herbert proposes that his annuity should be doubled until he has ecclesiastical preferment. Here he asks his step-father to use his influence with the trustees of his father's estate. His eldest brother states: 'to gratify my mother, as well as those so near me, I was voluntarily content to provide thus far, as to give my six brothers thirty pounds apiece yearly, during their lives' (*Autobiog*. p. 43). In a letter dated 12 May 1615 from Lady Danvers to Sir Edward Herbert, then abroad, she writes (*Collections for Montgomeryshire*, xx. 85): 'Now for your Baylifs I must tell you they have not yet payed your brothers all their Annuities due at Midsom'er past, and but half due at Christmas past and no news of the rest: ... it is ill for your Brothers, and very ill you have such officers.'

IV (Page 365)

The fact that George was two years older than Henry accounts for the tone of elder brother. Henry spent the whole of 1618 in France.

PAGE 366, l. 7. *Bee covetous* &c. This corresponds with the advice given in 'The Church-porch', p. 20, ll. 355–66.

ll. 13–19. Cf. 'The Church-porch', p. 19, ll. 331–42.

l. 24. Sir Edward, returning from the Low Countries, was in London from the beginning of 1618 until he left on 13 May 1619 to be ambassador in Paris. Though suffering almost all the time from a quartan ague (*Autobiog*. p. 97), he was not yet cured of his quarrelsomeness and addiction to duelling (pp. 98–101). He admits (p. 11) that 'passion and choler' were 'infirmities to which all our race is subject'.

V (Page 366)

This undated letter must belong to 1618, when Henry Herbert was in Paris.

PAGE **367**, l. 7. *my old ward*: a fencing term for a posture of defence. O.E.D. cites R. L. Stevenson, *In South Seas*: 'He hastily returned to his old ward. "I don't deny I could if I wanted", said he.'

l. 21. *my dear sick Sister*. Elizabeth Lady Johnes. See note to No. X.

l. 23. *my Brothers Letter*. Evidently a letter to Edward, now in London.

VI (Page 367)

Sir Robert Harley (1579–1656) of Brampton Bryan, Herefordshire, was Herbert's first cousin by marriage. His second wife, alive at the time of this letter, was Mary, daughter of Sir Francis Newport, Magdalen Herbert's brother. Sir Francis, writing to his nephew, Sir Edward Herbert, in 1615 mentions 'mye daughter Harley' (*Coll. Montg.* xx. 87): she is wrongly described in the D.N.B., s.v. Robert Harley, as a daughter of Sir Richard Newport, Sir Francis's father.

PAGE **368**, ll. 2–4. 'Sir John's affection for you suffers him not to defer communicating with you until there is more interesting news to tell after Christmas.'

ll. 4–16. The East India Companies of England and Holland were constantly at feud, and the Dutch had recently captured two English ships and put their crews in irons. The States-General of Holland, desiring to avoid open rupture, sent commissioners who reached London on 29 Nov. 1618. James I took advantage of the occasion to press for the removal of other English grievances, especially the claim of the Dutch to fish for herrings off the British coast. The commissioners replied that they had no instructions from home on this matter, and there was considerable delay before a treaty was eventually signed in the following summer.

l. 16. Buckingham was rising rapidly; a month later he was appointed lord high admiral.

l. 19. *his Lady*. Mary, the daughter of Sir John Fitz of Fitzford, Devon, a wealthy heiress who carried things with a high hand, married four knights in succession, outlived the last of them, and died in 1671. In 1612 she married as third husband Sir Charles Howard, fourth son of Thomas, first earl of Suffolk. Three weeks before the date of Herbert's letter Howard had written to Harley (Hist. MSS. Comm. *14th Report*, 1894, p. 8).

l. 26. *a treatise*. Thomas Lorkin, writing ten days later than Herbert to Sir Thomas Puckering, evidently alludes to the same book (*Court and Times of James I*, ii. 119):

There hath been lately presented to his majesty a book of no small contentment, which was printed at Toledo, *cum privilegio*, and written by commandment of the king of Spain, wherein the Pope's encroachments upon princes is largely opposed, and the temporalities of kings, against all the Pope's usurpations, notably defended.

With Lorkin's more precise reference the book can be identified: Hieronymo de Cevallos, *Tractatus de cognitione per viam violentiae in Causis Ecclesiasticis*, Toledo, 1618. It is dedicated to Philip III, and maintains that the sovereign 'in his own kingdom is subject to no one in temporalities'.

l. 30. The literary connexions of France with England are discussed by G. Ascoli in *La Grande Bretagne devant l'opinion française au XVIIe siècle* (1930). The reputation of James I as a Maecenas attracted several French poets to England: e.g. Jean de Schelandre procured from the duke of Lennox an introduction to the king, but he had left this country by 1610. An epigram on not being received by 'Jacques, le roi du savoir' is attributed to Théophile (1590–1626), but he is not likely to be the poet referred to by Herbert. Lorkin, in the letter cited above, has the same story of 'a certain Frenchman', who had been rewarded, for a writing he presented to the king, 'according to the quality of his desert, though not to his content', and, because of his threatening attitude, had been 'committed a close prisoner'.

VII (Page 369)

The date of this letter can be inferred with some exactness. It was written after the news had reached Cambridge of Nethersole being knighted at Theobalds on 19 Sept. 1619 and before 29 Sept. (cf. l. 12, *presently after* Michaelmas). On 21 Oct. a Grace was passed allowing Nethersole to appoint Herbert as his deputy on his going abroad on the king's business. Herbert already knows that Nethersole is intending to resign the Oratorship, as he actually did on 18 Jan. following. He is expecting to deliver an Oration soon after the beginning of the Michaelmas Term.

l. 14. *my* Lincoln *journey*. This can be safely identified with the allusion in the postscript of the next letter. His third sister Frances was wife of Sir John Browne of East Kirkby, Lincolnshire. A letter of Sir John Danvers, dated 19 Nov. 1631, mentions that his godson, Sir John Browne's son and heir, is being sent to be educated at Little Gidding (*The Ferrar Papers*, p. 4).

l. 15. At Bugden or Buckden, Huntingdonshire, was a palace of the bishop of Lincoln. Probably Sir John Danvers wished Herbert to deliver in person a letter to the bishop, George Montaigne, a Cambridge man, soliciting his support of Herbert's candidature for the Oratorship.

l. 21. *ancient acquaintance*. Nethersole was elected a major fellow of Trinity a few months after Herbert was elected a scholar.

l. 25. *our Master*. John Richardson, Master of Trinity 1615–25.

l. 30. *The Orators place*. The University Statutes ruled that the Public Orator, if a Master of Arts, should have precedence of all others of that degree. He had also the privilege of voting either with the Regent or with the Non-Regent House. Herbert as a Master of less than five years' standing was a Regent.

PAGE 370, l. 7. *work the heads*. On the day preceding the election the Heads of Colleges were to meet and nominate two persons, one of whom was to be elected by the Senate (H. Gunning, *Ceremonies observed in the Senate House of the University of Cambridge*).

VIII (Page 370)

Some confusion has been caused in the account of Herbert's candidature by this letter being printed after No. IX in every edition from Walton to Palmer, although the contents of IX show that Herbert, in dating the letter, reckoned the year from Lady Day.

l. 19. *this place being civil*. Both Nethersole and his predecessor, Sir Robert Naunton, found the Oratorship a stepping-stone to the office of a secretary of state.

l. 30. Sir Benjamin Rudyard (1572–1658), a poet and a friend of poets, was on intimate terms with William Herbert, 3rd earl of Pembroke (who may be *my Lord* of l. 29). The younger Donne published together poems by Pembroke and Rudyard in 1660.

IX (Page 371)

l. 12. *her Son, and my charge*. Lady Johnes had, besides daughters, one son (Herbert of Cherbury, *Autobiog*. p. 14), who was afterwards Sir Henry Johnes, baronet. He was dead before 26 July 1655 when his widow and Magdalen Vaughan, Herbert's niece, were godmothers at the christening of Magdalen, daughter of Sir Henry Herbert (Warner, op. cit. p. 5). 'My charge' suggests that George Herbert was godfather of Henry Johnes, whose father was still alive thirteen years after this.

l. 17. *the next* Friday. Herbert is writing on Wednesday 19 Jan. 1619/20, the day after Nethersole's resignation, and on Friday 21 Jan. he was elected Orator.

X (Page 371)

Elizabeth, Herbert's eldest sister, ten years older than himself, married Sir Henry Johnes of Abermarles, Carmarthenshire. (He is wrongly identified by Sir Sidney Lee in his annotated edition of the *Autobiography of Lord Herbert of Cherbury*, p. 14, with an earlier Sir Henry, sheriff of Carmarthenshire in 1574, who married Elizabeth, daughter of Matthew Herbert of Swansea.) Lady Johnes was living for many years with her mother in London, in order to have better medical attendance during a long wasting sickness. Her brother Edward, writing from the British embassy in Paris in Sept. 1619 to Sir Robert Naunton, asks him to get Theodore de Mayerne, first physician to James I, 'to look to my sick sister, who hath long been his patient' and 'to oblige him the more to procure her health' (*Autobiog*. p. 194). He says of her (p. 14): 'for the space of about fourteen years she languished and pined away to skin and bones, and at last died in London.' Her husband, writing from

Abermarles on 27 Feb. 1633/4 to his 'brother', Sir Henry Herbert, evidently expects her end to be not far off (Warner, op. cit. p. 18). She outlived her brother George by at least a year; the symptoms of her disease resemble his.

XI (Page 372)

According to Walton, who added this letter to the text of his Life of Herbert in *The Temple* (1674), the bearer of it was Woodnoth. Lady Danvers lived another five years, but her health was failing, and the low spirits which Herbert tries to allay in this letter find corroboration in Donne's sermon in commemoration of her, pp. 135–6:

> And for her, some sicknesses, in the declination of her yeeres, had opened her to an ouerflowing of *Melancholie*; Not that she euer lay vnder that *water*, but yet, had sometimes, some high tides of it; and, though this distemper would sometimes cast a cloud, and some half damps vpon her naturall cheerfulnesse, and sociablenesse, and sometimes induce darke, and sad apprehensions, *Neverthelesse*, who euer heard, or sawe in her, any such effect of *Melancholy* as to murmure, or repine?

l. 15. *my self.* Three months before, on 16 Feb. 1621/2, Joseph Mede, writing from Christ's College to Sir Martin Stutevile (B.M. MS. Harl. 389 f. 146v), reported 'our Orator' to be 'at death's dore'. It is, however, probable that Mede refers to the previous Orator, as in his next letter, dated 23 Feb., he states, 'Sr Francis Nethersole (that was once our Orator) is dead in Germany'; actually Nethersole lived till 1659.

l. 20. *Commencement* is the Cambridge term for the ceremony of conferring degrees at the end of the academical year. The Orator had a prominent part.

PAGE 373, l. 6. The *bottom* (used also in 'The Discharge', p. 145, l. 45) is a skein or ball of thread. For its figurative use O.E.D. cites Samuel Clarke, *Scripture-Justification* (1698), p. 112: 'It's high Time now to wind up my Bottoms.'

l. 9. *unable to perform.* Cf. the sad complaint of 'The Crosse', p. 164, ll. 7–12.

XII (Page 375)

This undated letter must have been written after Herbert was settled at Bemerton rectory, which, according to Walton, had needed to be 'almost three parts' rebuilt. It was also before he had recovered from the expenses of building (p. 376, l. 2), and before he had received any tithe (ibid.), which was paid half-yearly. This suggests the late summer or autumn of 1630.

Herbert's second sister Margaret married in 1606 John Vaughan, son and heir of Owen Vaughan, of Llwydiarth, Montgomeryshire. Sir Francis Newport, writing in 1615 from Eyton, Shropshire, to Sir Edward Herbert, tells him: 'Mye syster y'r mother is confident to take a iourney into these pts this somer, the rather I think because yo'r brother Vaugh'n is dead' (*Coll. Montg.* xx. 87). As Vaughan had daughters only, the estate passed to heirs male (ibid. vii. 135). His widow died on 14 Aug. 1623 at Llanerfyl, Montgomeryshire, and was buried among her kinsfolk in Montgomery Church.

By her will (ibid. xxi. 243–4) she left the residue of her property in equal parts to her three daughters, Dorothy, Magdalen, and Catharine, and assigned the rights of wardship to her brother Edward. This letter shows that Edward had been urging George, now that he had a home of his own, to adopt one of the nieces, and that George, with great discernment, had agreed to take two or none. He had accordingly received the two elder nieces at Bemerton. There remained the youngest: George has asked Henry to have her, but is now willing to have her as well, although his finances are at present low.

Dorothy died about six months before George Herbert (see below, p. 586). Magdalen was alive and unmarried in 1655 (Warner, op. cit. p. 5). William Cole, the antiquary, claims George Herbert as 'my Cousin' on the strength of Catharine Vaughan being his great-great-grandmother (B.M. MS. Harl. 5813 f. 110^{v}).

l. 29. *my cousin Bett.* Beatrice, the only surviving daughter of Lord Herbert of Cherbury, was now 26 years old, unmarried, and probably living with the Newports at Eyton. The word *cousin* was commonly used of nephews and nieces: e.g. Sir Francis Newport writes to his nephew, Sir Edward Herbert, in 1616 of 'Mye Cussyn Bettye yo'r daughter' (*Coll. Montg.* xx. 87). Dorothy left £40 by will to 'Mrs Beatrice Herbert'.

PAGE **376**, l. 18. *the best-bredd child* &c. *Outl. Pvbs*, No. 953.

XIII (Page 376)

The Lady Anne Clifford (1590–1676), daughter and sole heiress of the 3rd earl of Cumberland, and widow of Richard Sackville, 3rd earl of Dorset, who died in 1624, married on 1 June 1630 at the age of 40 Philip Herbert, 4th earl of Pembroke and 1st of Montgomery, a widower of 45. Philip succeeded his brother William in April of that year, and in the same month George Herbert was instituted to the rectory of Bemerton. Their early married life was spent partly at Court, where Pembroke was lord chamberlain, or at his London house, Baynards Castle, but Aubrey states that Pembroke 'commonly came to Wilton every summer'. Woodnoth mentions Herbert paying her an hour's visit at Wilton in Oct. 1631 (*The Ferrar Papers*, p. 267). In her autobiography Anne tells of her unhappy marriages and says that she took refuge in 'retiredness' and 'made good Bookes and verteous thoughts my Companions' (G. C. Williamson, *Lady Anne Clifford*, 1922, p. 174). She must have welcomed the friendship of George Herbert, who, according to Aubrey, was chaplain to Pembroke. Her second husband was coarse and violent and faithless, and she left him about 1635, fifteen years before his death. On the death of the fifth and last earl of Cumberland in 1643, she succeeded to vast estates in Westmorland and Craven, which fully employed her gift of management and her passion for building till she died in her 87th year. In 'the great picture' which she caused to be painted for Appleby Castle in 1646 her love of books is shown in the large number on the shelves and on the floor, displaying their titles; they include the poems of Herbert, Daniel (who had been her tutor), Sidney, and Donne, besides works of divinity and philosophy.

l. 30. Metheglin was a spiced variety of mead, made with herbs and honey. It was originally peculiar to Wales, but in an article entitled 'Old Wiltshire: Memories of 75 years', contributed to *The Times* of 5 Aug. 1935, the writer states that 'Metheglyn was still brewed in lonely farmhouses on the Plain'.

PAGE 377, l. 4. *the blessing of your Mother*. Anne says that she was able to come through the troubles of her married life, 'the Prayers of my Blessed Mother helping me herein' (G. C. Williamson, op. cit. p. 174). There are fine tombs of Anne and of the countess of Cumberland in Appleby Church.

XIV (Page 377)

The date of this letter and of XV can now be established from an unprinted letter from Woodnoth to N. Ferrar, received on 25 Mar. 1632, in the library of Magdalene College, Cambridge. Woodnoth relates that he and Sir Henry Herbert have recently waited on the duchess of Lennox and secured from her £100 for the repair of Leighton Church and the promise of more which she will procure from her son.

l. 19. *my Lady Duchess's forwardnes*. This is explained in the postscript of the next letter.

l. 23. Henry Montagu (1563?–1642), of Kimbolton Castle, created earl of Manchester in 1626, was likely, as lord lieutenant of Huntingdonshire, to be interested in Leighton Bromswold, and, as head of the Virginian commission in 1624, he would know Ferrar. (See note on *Epistola* IX.) Oliver St. John (1580?–1646) succeeded his father in 1618 as 4th baron St. John of Bletso, and in 1624 was created earl of Bolingbroke.

XV (Page 378)

Herbert was at one time minded to surrender his prebend in favour of Nicholas Ferrar, but Ferrar diverted 'to a much righter end his Brother Herbert's good Intentions' by proposing to him that he should make himself responsible for rebuilding the church which 'was fallen down a long time & lay in the dust, the vicar and Parish fain to use my Lord Duke's great Hall for their Prayers and preaching' (*The Ferrar Papers*, p. 58). Although Herbert was not responsible for the fabric of the church, by his own efforts and with his brother Henry's influence he raised enough money to rebuild the church and to wainscot and furnish it handsomely. Cf. Ferrar's preface to *The Temple* above, p. 4.

l. 23. *Mr W.* Arthur Woodnoth, 'a goldsmith in Foster Lane, London' and 'an old and dear friend' of Herbert, was a first cousin of Ferrar. (In the first edition of his *Life of Herbert* Walton gave Woodnoth's Christian name as John, but he corrected it to Arthur in 1674.) He kept the accounts of the building fund, and Herbert left to him as his executor £15 for the restoration of Leighton Church (see p. 382).

PAGE 379, l. 1. *the Duchess*. Katharine, only child and heiress of Sir Gervase Clifton, who was created in 1608 baron Clifton of Leighton, married Esmé Stuart (1579–1624), who succeeded his brother Ludovick, a friend of Herbert's, as 3rd duke of Lennox. Her father 'began to build a beautiful house here, but lived not to finish it' (Lysons, *Magna Brittania*, 1720, i. 1056). The duchess continued to live here after her husband's death. Their son James (1612–55), 4th duke of Lennox, was not yet of age, but later he completed the fabric of the church by building the tower 'at his own proper cost & charges' as a memorial of Herbert (*The Ferrar Papers*, p. 59).

l. 8. *our Book*. Perhaps the building plans or the list of subscriptions.

XVI (Page 379)

l. 19. *your Brother*: i.e. John Ferrar. Nicholas informed Herbert that 'he would undertake, his Brother J.F. should very carefully prosecute the business (if once begun) by three times a week attending the workmen, & providing all Materials' (ibid. p. 58). John Ferrar writes to his brother on 30 July 1632: 'We have 18 Masons and Labrores at worke at Layton Church and we shall have this weeke 10 Carpenters' (ibid. p. 276).

XIX (Page 380)

Herbert's advice to Woodnoth is among the Ferrar Papers at Magdalene College, Cambridge, and it is here reproduced with the kind permission of the college and of the Cambridge University Press. It was first printed in a letter of Dr. Bernard Blackstone to *The Times Literary Supplement* of 15 Aug. 1936, and he has since included it in *The Ferrar Papers* (Cambridge, 1938, pp. 269–70). A letter of Woodnoth to Nicholas Ferrar, dated from London on 13 Oct. 1631 (ibid. pp. 266–9), gives the occasion of Herbert's paper. Woodnoth describes his visit to Bemerton in the previous week, when he had pressed his host to advise him about his career. Although he had followed the trade of goldsmith in Foster Lane for many years, he had thought of leaving it to enter holy orders, but Ferrar and Herbert discouraged him. Now he has entered the service of Sir John Danvers, whom he had known through their association in the Virginia Company. Woodnoth writes that Herbert, after a night's thought, committed his advice to writing, and a day or two later, on Woodnoth's leaving, added the last paragraph. Sir John's extravagance, especially after his second marriage, needed the restraining force of which Herbert writes, but the task may well have made Woodnoth hesitate.

This paper resolves a difficulty in Walton's *Lives*. He there described Woodnoth as 'a useful Friend to Mr. *Herberts* Father', but Richard Herbert died in 1596 when Woodnoth was a child. The new evidence makes it clear that his service was to Herbert's step-father.

PAGE **381**, l. 3. *be without dores*: a figurative use, now obsolete, for being lost, astray.

l. 4. The epithet *blessed*, commonly reserved to the Virgin Mary, is used as here of the Magdalene in Herbert's poem, beginning 'When blessed Marie wip'd her Saviours feet' (above, p. 173).

ll. 27–30. The duty to the commonwealth is similarly urged in *Priest to T.*, p. 239, ll. 19–23: 'His children he first makes Christians, and then Commonwealths-men; the one he owes to his heavenly Countrey, the other to his earthly, having no title to either, except he do good to both.'

THE WILL OF GEORGE HERBERT (Page 382)

The date of the will is now known through a letter written by the executor to Ferrar within a few days of Herbert's death, printed for the first time in *The Ferrar Papers*, pp. 276–7: 'His will He made but Vppon munday before hee dyed', i.e. on 25 Feb. 1632/3. Woodnoth calls it 'the most imperfect act' that Herbert ever did; 'I shall not neede to say more then this He hath made mee his executor.' It was not unusual to appoint an overseer to supervise and assist the executor, and Herbert named his step-father for this purpose, just as his sister Margaret appointed her uncle Charles Herbert overseer (*Coll. Montg.* xxi. 243). The witnesses to the will were one of Herbert's curates and one of his servants. The will was proved in London before a surrogate of the Prerogative Court of Canterbury by Arthur Woodnoth on 12 Mar. 1632 'juxta cursum et computac̄onem Ecclesie Anglicane', i.e. 1632/3.

Dorothy Vaughan, the eldest of the three nieces for whom Herbert made a home at Bemerton, died about six months before him, and her will was proved on 9 Oct. 1632, Herbert, her executor, having previously sworn by commission before Nathaniel Bostock, clerk. It will be seen by the crosses affixed that the legacies to relations and servants had mostly been discharged by Herbert before his death, except for the principal sums due to the two surviving nieces, to whom Herbert leaves his own share also. For Magdalen and Catharine Vaughan see the note on *Letter* XII, p. 582.

Walton reports Herbert as saying, 'my Wife hath a competent maintenance secur'd her after my death' (*Lives*, p. 65). Woodnoth supposes that she will go to live with her mother, Mrs. Charles Danvers, at Baynton House, and he suggests to Ferrar that, if the nieces are not otherwise housed, they should be received at Little Gidding. After some years of widowhood (Walton says 'five years' in 1670 and alters this to 'about six years' in 1675), Mrs. Herbert married Sir Robert Cooke of Highnam, near Gloucester, a widower with sons; she bore him a daughter. She outlived her first husband by 28 years and her second by 18, dying herself on 27 Nov. 1661. Cooke was related to Sir Robert Harley, Herbert's first cousin; in a letter to Harley of 13 Sept. 1642 (Hist. MSS. Comm., *Portland*, iii. 98) Cooke professes himself 'ready to relieve Brampton Castle'. He died in the following June.

l. 4. The special mention of books among Herbert's effects indicates that they were of value. Walton states that Lady Cooke 'had preserv'd many of Mr. *Herberts* private Writings, which she intended to make publick; but they, and *Highnam* house, were burnt together, by the late Rebels' (*Lives*, p. 82). Aubrey's account (*Brief Lives*, i. 309) differs, but his references to Herbert's wife are apt to be malicious:

> He writt also a folio in Latin, wch because the parson of Hineham could not read, his widowe, (then wife to Sir Robert Cooke), condemned to the uses of good houswifry. This account I had from Mr. Arnold Cooke, one of Sr Robert Cooke's sonnes, whom I desired to ask his mother-in-law for Mr. G. Herbert's MSS.

l. 8. Thomas Lawley, son of Francis Lawley of Spoonhill, Shropshire, by his wife Elizabeth Newport, Magdalen Herbert's sister, was M.P. for Wenlock in 1625, and was later created a baronet. The manor of Ribbesford was granted by the Crown on 21 July 1627 to Sir Edward Herbert, George Herbert, and their first cousin Thomas Lawley; before the end of that year Sir Henry Herbert acquired it from them for £3,000.

l. 16. A *bill* was used for any formal document. O.E.D. gives an example from 1424: 'I declare my last will in this bill.'

l. 18. *Mr Hays.* Herbert's second curate cannot be identified with certainty, but he may be William Hayes, B.D. of Magdalen Hall, Oxford, who became rector of Orchard Portman, Somerset, in 1635.

l. 19. *In Sacrosancta quatuor Evangelia F. Lucae Brugensis Commentarius*, folio, 1606.

l. 20. Nathaniel Bostock, M.A. of Brasenose College, Oxford, proceeded to the B.D. degree in the year after Herbert's death, and, after being rector of Oxcombe, Lincolnshire, for three years, was appointed by Bishop Juxon vicar of Heston, Middlesex, in 1642.

ll. 22–6. Herbert had apparently in his service four maids and two men, who may not all have been indoor servants.

PAGE **383**, l. 7. *Mrs Beatrice Herbert.* See the note on *Letter* XII, p. 583, l. 29.

ll. 8–13. There are bequests not only to Mrs. George Herbert, but also to her mother, Mrs. Charles Danvers, four of her sisters—Amy, Anne, Mary, and Joan, wife of Edward Michel—and her sister-in-law Elizabeth. Cf. F. N. Macnamara, *Memorials of the Danvers Family*, 1895, p. 536.

l. 18. Judith Spencer, daughter of William Spencer of Whitton, Shropshire, by Bridget, third daughter of Edward Herbert of Montgomery, was a witness to the will of Margaret Vaughan, Dorothy's mother, in 1623 (*Coll. Montg.* xxi. 243–4).

l. 20. The two final sentences headed MS. (which may stand for *Memoriae Suae*, aids to his own memory) are evidently directions of Herbert himself, not Dorothy Vaughan's.

l. 22. Stephens was the publisher of Donne's sermon on Lady Danvers, including Herbert's 'Memoriae Matris Sacrum'.

MUSAE RESPONSORIAE (Page 384)

The writing of Andrew Melville's *Anti-Tami-Cami-Categoria*, to which Herbert's epigrams are a direct answer, undoubtedly belongs to the year 1603/4, as it was occasioned by the hostile resolutions of the two English universities against the Millenary Petition of that year. Grosart and others have stated that the *Categoria* was published in 1604, but no earlier printing of it has been discovered than David Calderwood's publication of it, without imprint, in 1620. It was, however, probably circulated from 1604 in manuscript, and it provoked many replies. Its printing in 1620 occasioned a fresh crop of replies, among which Herbert's may be reckoned.

In the first issue of his *Life of Herbert* (1670) Walton was obviously in error in giving as the occasion of Herbert's epigrams Melville's return to England from abroad 'some short time before, or immediately after Mr. *Herbert* was made *Orator*' (21 Jan. 1619/20), as Melville was continuously abroad from 1611 till his death at Sedan in 1622. In revising the *Lives* for the edition of 1675, Walton rewrote the paragraph, and now stated that Melville's verses were 'brought into *Westminster-School*, where Mr. *George Herbert* then, and often after, made such answers to them'. Herbert entered the school in 1605 at the age of twelve, and left for Cambridge at the age of sixteen. Some of the epigrams may have been written in school-days, as they are not beyond the capacity of a precocious boy, well trained in writing Latin verse, just as Crashaw may have written some of his *Epigrammata Sacra* at Charterhouse. It is more probable that the fresh attention secured for *Categoria* by its being printed in 1620 set Herbert writing or continuing his *Musae Responsoriae*. The dedicatory verses fit this later date: Charles was not Prince of Wales in Herbert's school-days, and Andrewes did not become Bishop of Winchester till Feb. 1618/19. If the fact of Melville's death in 1622 was known to Herbert, he would not have addressed verses to him. It can, therefore, be inferred that Herbert's epigrams, or at any rate most of them, were written soon after the appearance of *Categoria* in print in 1620. Herbert did not publish his epigrams, and they were not included in *Remains* (1652), perhaps because the editor did not know of their existence.

James Duport (1606–79), educated like Herbert at Westminster and Trinity, of which he became a fellow and Vice-Master, published Herbert's epigrams in his *Ecclesiastes Solomonis* (1662). In his Latin preface he states that, after he had finished writing his own part of the volume, the epigrams were put into his hands by Dr. Dillingham, Master of Emmanuel. William Dillingham (1617?–89) had shared chambers as an undergraduate with William Sancroft, the future archbishop, and maintained a close friendship with him for life. Both men were interested in Herbert's writings; Sancroft came to possess the manuscript of *The Temple* with the licensers' signatures, which is now in the Bodleian, and Dillingham, besides owning Herbert's epigrams, included his own Latin versions of 'The Church-porch' and four other poems from *The Temple* in his *Poemata varii argumenti* (1678).

Herbert's youthful reply to Melville's attack on the ceremonies and polity of the Church of England does not merit either the extravagant praise of his contemporaries or the heavy-handed reproofs of Dr. Grosart. There may be something unseemly, as Herbert himself admits (II), in the young Cambridge scholar tilting at a veteran who had reformed the Scottish universities and suffered imprisonment and exile for his indomitable courage. Yet, although Melville had denounced the Anglican rites, which were dear to Herbert, in language that was offensive, comparing a set liturgy to the magic wheel of incantation, the priest's words at infant baptism to the noises of a screech-owl, and church music to the clash of Phrygian cymbals, Herbert does not retaliate with similar wounding words. He can make fair game of the monstrous word Anti-Tami-Cami-Categoria, of the theologian choosing sapphics, a woman's metre, for his satire, and of the false quantity in latinizing Whittaker's name, but he may fairly claim that his own Muse is 'toothless and free from venom' (XXXVII. 12). He is happy to agree with two-thirds of Melville's poem (IV), with the eulogy of great theologians and the praise of the divine attributes; the latter part of the poem, he generously allows, is 'full of God'. Herbert's last long poem, directed to Melville personally, is disarming, and ends by acclaiming him as a great scholar and a poet (XXXVII. 47).

I (p. 385). Pickering was mistaken in placing at the head 'Ad Regem Epigrammata duo'. The last two words do not occur in Duport's edition, which has '*Epigr.* I' above this epigram and '*Epigr.* II' above the following epigram, 'Ad Melvinum'. Grosart followed Pickering, but contrived two epigrams to the king by making ll. 5–6 of 'Ad Regem' into a separate epigram, although the sense demands that those lines should belong to the preceding four.

III (p. 386), l. 9. *Pollubra*: laver, for which another term is *pelvis*. Andrewes observed the ceremonial washing of hands at the altar. The allusion here is to the epigram which got Melville into trouble, written after he had been obliged to attend the King's Chapel on Sunday, 28 Sept. 1606:

Cur stant clausi *Anglis* Libri duo Regiâ in ARA,
  Lumina caeca duo, Pollubra sicca duo?
Num sensum cultumque Dei tenet *Anglia* clausum,
  Lumine caeca suo, sorde sepulta suâ?
Romano an ritu dum Regalem instruit ARAM,
  Purpuream pingit religiosa Lupam?

Fuller (*Ch. Hist.*, 1655, x, p. 70) quotes Melville's lines, and regrets that 'all my industry cannot recover' Herbert's 'most ingenious retortion of this *Hexastick*', though he hopes that the *Remains* 'shortly to be put forth into Print' ('shavings of Gold are carefully to be kept') may include it. *Herbert's Remains* had, in fact, appeared three years before Fuller's book, and did not contain Herbert's epigram, which first appeared in Duport's volume of 1662.

VI (p. 387), l. 4. *Pallada gorgoneam*. The epithet γοργῶπις, used of Athena in Soph. Ajax 450, refers to her *aegis*, which had a fringe of snakes and a Gorgon's head.

IX (p. 388), l. 6. Cf. Matt. v. 18: 'iota unum aut unus apex non praeteribit a lege, donec omnia fiant.'

X (p. 389), l. 8. *Ecquis autem brachijs*, &c. Can anyone swim, without his outstretched arms suggesting the Cross?

XII (p. 390), ll. 15–16. At the Fall woman hid from God when He was angry (*commotum*); now that He is kind and she is blessed, she rightly returns to Him.

XIV, ll. 14–15. *binas homini sequendas Spiritus proponit*. Cf. Matt. x. 16: 'Ecce ego mitto vos sicut oves in medio luporum. Estote ergo . . . simplices sicut columbae.' The chapters named in Columella's De Re Rustica (*c.* A.D. 50) refer to the preference for white wool and for white pigeons.

XVII (p. 392), ll. 12–13. *pauculos Quam cunctos*. If bishops are a bad institution, it is better to have few, as the Church of England has, than to have every presbyter ranking as a bishop.

XIX, l. 6. Cf. 'doctor in utroque jure' (i.e. canon and civil).

XX, l. 9. *verum*, supplied by the editor to make up the missing foot, balances *falsum*, 'harp on what is false rather than true in your verse'. The printer might easily have dropped out *verum* before *versu*.

l. 12. Melville wrote *Strigis* with a false quantity; perhaps Herbert emphasizes it with *perhorridas*, or he may remember Ov. F. vi, 139–40.

XXIII (p. 393), l. 3. *Mutas in humanam figuram Saxa*. See note on *Mem. Matris Sacr.* xii. 8, p. 595.

PAGE 394, l. 14. *Amphionis testudine*. Cf. Hor. Ars Poet. 394–6:

> Dictus et Amphion, Thebanae conditor arcis,
> Saxa movere sono testudinis, et prece blanda
> Ducere quo vellet.

XXV (p. 395), l. 19. *Scripturae canones*. Not only should the debtor be allowed to retain his clothes (Deut. xxiv. 13), but clothes that are not his (*non suam*, l. 23) should be given to the naked (Ezek. xviii. 7).

XXVI (p. 396), l. 5. Borrowed from Hor. Sat. II. iii. 320: 'haec a te non multum abludit imago.'

XXVIII (p. 397), l. 14. *renouare*: retouch. In their dislike of set forms, Puritans would even vary Scriptural prayers.

XXIX, l. 2. Cf. Ov. Ars Am. iii. 193: 'ne trux caper iret in alas'.

XXX, ll. 4–5. *Charybdim . . . Vestramque Scyllam*. Cf. 'The British Church', p. 109.

XXXII (p. 398), l. 6. *Incalescit fabula*: the play warms up in Act IV.

XXXIII. The Oxford resolution against the Millenary Petition contained the boast that 'there are at this day more learned men in this kingdom than are to be found among all the ministers of religion in all Europe besides'. Melville replied with a catalogue of Protestant divines on the Continent and at home.

l. 16. An allusion to Constantine's *labarum*.

PAGE 399, l. 24. Herbert alludes again in XXXIX. 17 to the royal title, *Fidei Defensor*.

ll. 31–2. From Ov. Fast. ii. 235–6, Herbert substituting *Catharos* for *Fabios*.

XXXIV, l. 3. Cf. Mart. III. l. 9: 'Quod si non scombris scelerata poemata donas.'

XXXVII (p. 400), ll. 5–6. *vrbem Quam . . . nequeo referre*. Edinburgh.

PAGE 401, l. 39. *Tinnitus* Berecynthios. Cymbals were used in the orgiastic worship on Mount Berecynthus in Thessaly. Cf. Virg. Geo. iv. 64.

XL (p. 402). *Ad Deum*. Mr. Edmund Blunden gives a verse translation of this poem in his chapter 'George Herbert's Latin Poems' in *Essays and Studies by Members of the English Association*, vol. xix, 1934. He remarks that, 'in spite of this array of vast acknowledgements' to King James and other patrons, 'Herbert had praise left in him to offer to the Almighty, and his "Ad Deum", a theory of inspiration, reminds one of Vaughan's comment that "'twas not my quill".' The opening lines and the last are an imitation of Hor. C. IV. iii. 1–4 and 24, *scribo* being substituted for *spiro*.

PASSIO DISCERPTA (Page 404)

The two collections of Latin poems, *Passio Discerpta* and *Lucus*, follow the English poems in MS. Jones B 62 in Dr. Williams's Library, and, unlike the

English poems, are in Herbert's handwriting. The only corrections, except of single letters, are 'Sera nimis' in *Lucus*, XXIII. 12, and 'caecos' in XXXV. 7; they are made in the author's hand, and the words erased cannot be deciphered. A few words distinguished by larger letters are represented in the present edition by small capitals. A clue to the date of composition is afforded by the group of poems, *Lucus*, XXVI–XXVIII, on Urban VIII (Maffeo Barberini); the allusions to his election and to his assuming the name of Urban would be most naturally made soon after he was elected Pope in Aug. 1623.

V (p. 404), l. 3. *Sputando*. Mark viii. 23 and John ix. 6.

PAGE 405, l. 6. Mark xi. 21: 'Rabbi, ecce ficus, cui maledixisti, aruit.'

VI. 'Thou art pricked by the thorn, I by the rose. Yet thou art the head, and we thy members: let us exchange; be thine the rose-garlands, ours the thorns.'

VII, l. 2. For the shepherd's pipe (*arundo*), cf. Milton, *Comus*, l. 345: 'pastoral reed with oaten stops.'

l. 6. Phil. ii. 10: 'ut in nomine Jesu omne genu flectatur caelestium, terrestrium et infernorum.'

VIII. *In Alapas*. Mark xiv. 65: 'ministri alapis eum caedebant.'

XV (p. 407), l. 4. Matt. viii. 20: 'Filius autem hominis non habet ubi caput reclinet.'

XVIII (p. 408), l. 2. *Sampson vt antè fores*. The same comparison is found in 'Sunday', p. 76, ll. 43–9.

XIX, l. 11. *Excessit ex Ephebis*. The phrase is used in Ter. Andr. I. i. 24, in imitation of the Greek ἐξελθεῖν ἐξ ἐφήβων, to reach adolescence.

XX. The Devil, for his own ends (*sibi*), dashed to pieces God's creature made of clay (*fictile opus*: cf. Gen. ii. 7); and, when the Mosaic Laws were like to mend the pieces, the tables of stone made by God (*tabulas factas opere Dei*, Exod. xxxii. 16) were themselves shattered because of the man-made calf (*facta iuuenca*). Breaking was the common fate of Adam, the Ten Commandments, rocks at the Crucifixion; but contrite hearts relieve all losses. Eve is included in *vterque* (l. 1).

XXI (p. 409). 'With Christ's death all the world lost its Life: so you may keep your doctrine, Plato, of a World-Soul, if you will admit that the *Anima Mundi* you talked of is Christ.'

LUCUS (Page 410)

Lucus was used specially of a grove sacred to a deity. Cf. Sen. Herc. Oet. 956: 'nemoris sacri lucos tenere.'

I, l. 1. Gen. i. 27: 'Et creavit Deus hominem ad imaginem suam.'

l. 5. *docuisti marmora flere*. Cf. 'The Church-floore', p. 67, l. 15, and 'Grieve not &c', p. 136, l. 23.

V (p. 411), l. 4. *pro foribus sedendo nuper*. Cf. 'Artillerie', p. 139, ll. 1–2:

> As I one ev'ning sat before my cell,
> Me thoughts a starre did shoot into my lap.

l. 8. *mel comedens*. Cf. 'The H. Scriptures' I, p. 58, l. 2: 'Suck ev'ry letter, and a hony gain.'

VI, l. 2. *caetera terra*. The Thirty Years' War, beginning in 1618, quickly involved many states, while James I pursued his pacific policy.

l. 8. Cf. John vi. 19: 'vident Jesum ambulantem supra mare', and Gen. i. 2: 'Spiritus Dei ferebatur super aquas.'

XIV (p. 413). Acts v. 15.

XVI, l. 6. Cf. Ov. Am. I. ix. 46: 'Qui nolet fieri desidiosus, amet.'

XX (p. 414), l. 3. Aristotle (Nic. Eth. I. v. 4) maintains that happiness is nothing that lies outside us and that depends on others. Cf. John xvi. 22: 'your ioy no man taketh from you.'

l. 7. Cf. Hor. Sat. II. vii. 86: 'in se ipso totus, teres atque rotundus.'

l. 15. The morose man is like thick sour curds; the man easily impressed is like rennet.

XXII, l. 1. Cf. Pers. Sat. iv. 21: 'pannucea Baucis'. Philemon and Baucis, an aged couple, had but poor fare to offer Zeus and Hermes, coming to their hut incognito.

XXIII (p. 415). This *Consolatio* owes much to Sen. Ep. xxiv. 19–20: 'Memini te illum locum aliquando tractasse, non repente nos in mortem incidere, sed minutatim procedere; cotidie morimur.... Usque ad hesternum, quicquid transiit temporis, periit; hunc ipsum, quem agimus, diem cum morte dividimus. Quemadmodum clepsydram non extremum stillicidium exhaurit, sed quicquid ante defluxit, sic ultima hora, qua esse desinimus, non sola mortem facit, sed sola consummat; tunc ad illam pervenimus, sed diu venimus.' Seneca then quotes the line: 'Mors non una venit, sed quae rapit, ultima mors est.'

XXVI (p. 416). If it is Herbert who invents the reply of the newly elected Pope to the anagram *Roma*, he allows the Pope to have the better of the exchange in XXV and XXVI, and makes amends for the petulant rejoinder of XXVII by the courteous and conciliatory tone of XXVIII. Urban was addicted to writing Latin poems in classical metres on sacred themes, e.g. the Song of Simeon in sapphic strophes. Herbert plays on the meaning of *urbanus* as witty.

XXVIII (p. 417), l. 3. Andrewes engaged more than once in theological controversy with Cardinal Bellarmine (1542–1621), and so did James I.

XXIX. The title is made up of *θυσίαν ζῶσαν* and *τὴν λογικὴν λατρείαν ὑμῶν* in Rom. xii. 1.

l. 2. Cf. Hor. C. III. viii. 3: 'positusque carbo in caespite vivo.'

XXX, l. 2. 'Dost thou submit even to this proof?' The word *indicium* may suggest the finger (*index*) with which Thomas probed Christ's side. The autograph has *indicium* clearly; *iudicium* is an attractive emendation.

l. 8. Cf. 1 Pet. v. 8: 'adversarius vester diabolus tanquam leo rugiens circuit, quaerens quem devoret.' No allusion is intended to any Pope, as no recent Pope had chosen the name of Leo, except Leo XI who occupied St. Peter's chair for a few days only in Apr. 1605.

XXXII (p. 418). *Triumphus Mortis*. In the MS. from which Pickering printed this poem in 1836 it is entitled *Inventa Bellica* (here cited as *IB*), and it appears to be a revision. The awkwardness of making Death the speaker at the beginning and end of the poem, as it appears in *W*, is avoided in *IB* by slight alterations in ll. 1, 4, 7, 34, 49, 95, 100–1, which present the theme from the point of view of mortal man. If the MS. could be traced and its authenticity established, *IB* might afford a preferable text; but meanwhile it seems safer to print from Herbert's autograph version in *W*. There are some obvious slips in *IB*, some of which may be due to Pickering's faulty transcription, e.g. *arces* l. 42, *Fustibales* l. 43, *Exulis* l. 58, *sellae* l. 90. Mr. Blunden (op. cit. p. 37) has made a verse-translation from Pickering's text.

l. 2. *Emathius torrens*. Caesar defeated Pompey in the battle of Pharsalia in 48 B.C. Cf. Virg. Geo. i. 492.

l. 3. *Daunia*: i.e. Apulia, where Hannibal defeated the Romans at Cannae in 216 B.C.

l. 8. *ramalia mortem*. Probably a reference to Cain clubbing Abel, as the poem ends in *IB* with an allusion to this murder (l. 101).

l. 13. Cf. Hor. Sat. II. viii. 64: 'suspendens omnia naso.'

l. 14. Cicero uses *amentatae hastae* of oratorical shafts. The thong (*amentum*) greatly increased the 'carry' of the javelin to which it was attached.

l. 31. *ad palum*. Tilting at the quintain was still practised in Herbert's day.

PAGE **419**, l. 41. *Siculique inventa magistri*. Archimedes of Syracuse devised engines of war for the defence of his native city against the Roman attack in 214 B.C. He is alluded to again in *Oratio* III, p. 448, l. 31.

l. 44. Tityrus, the name of a shepherd in Virgil's Eclogues, is here used for the shepherd boy David. Goliath, the Philistine from Gath, is not properly called an Edomite.

l. 45. Cf. Juv. Sat. iv. 126: 'de temone Britanno excidet Arviragus.'

l. 47. *Demetrius*. A marginal note in *IB* reads 'Poliorcates, cog.'; more correctly, Poliorcetes (besieger of cities), a Greek surname (*cognomen*) given to Demetrius, king of Macedonia, for his attack on the walls of Rhodes with huge engines of war.

l. 57. *Pyrius puluis*: gunpowder. The epithet is probably coined from πῦρ. Again in 433. 33.

l. 60. *ructare*. Primitive man had coarse food and no table manners; his wife is described by Juvenal (Sat. vi. 10) as 'saepe horridior glandem ructante marito'.

l. 62. Caesar and other military writers use *glans* of the acorn-shaped ball of lead or clay which was discharged against the enemy.

PAGE **420**, l. 81. *Cocytia* is not the only false quantity in Herbert's verse, e.g. *trecentos* in *Lucus* XXIII. 7.

l. 82. *Portitor*: i.e. Charon, as in Prop. IV. xi. 7. 'And the tired boatman asks a helping hand' (Blunden).

l. 89. *Monachum*. Either Friar Bacon, the traditional inventor of gunpowder, or the German monk, Berthold Schwartz.

l. 96. A Spanish Jesuit, Mariana, in his *De Rege et Regis Institutione* (1599), defended tyrannicide. There may be an allusion (*sanguine regum*, l. 98) to the assassination of Henri III and Henri IV.

XXXIV (p. 421). *ἐπιστήθιον*. A word coined to describe the disciple of Jesus 'who leaned on his breast at supper' (*ἐπὶ τὸ στῆθος αὐτοῦ*, John xxi. 20).

XXXV, l. 3. *sine, te cernam*. Herbert puns on the imperative *sine* here and the preposition in l. 6.

MEMORIAE MATRIS SACRUM (Page 422)

Herbert's mother was buried in Chelsea parish church on 8 June 1627. Donne preached in that church on Sunday, 1 July, and on 7 July *A Sermon of commemorac̄on of the ladye Danvers by John Donne . . . with other Commemoracions of her by George Harbert* was entered at Stationers' Hall on behalf of Philemon Stephens and Christopher Meredith. The only title given by Herbert to his elegiac verses is *Memoriae Matris Sacrum*; the word *Parentalia*, which does not occur in the 1627 book, probably originated with Oley's description (*Remains*, sig. b.7). Mr. Blunden (op. cit.) gives verse-translations of I, II, V, X, and XI.

I, l. 4. Herbert's tears are as drouth compared with those of the choir of mourning Virtues. Cf. Hor. C. I. xxiv. 5–8.

l. 6. *sepia iusta*. 'The oddest figure of a man being mixed with a river to produce *ink* that ever was contrived' (Blunden). Herbert's *Mater* becomes his *Metra* (verses).

II, ll. 5–6. In face of such a loss grief may be indulged without breach of dignity and seemly reserve. Cf. Hor. C. I. xxiv. 1–2: 'Quis desiderio sit pudor aut modus tam cari capitis?'

l. 10. *comptu*. Cf. I Pet. iii. 3–4. J. R. Planché (*British Costume*, p. 331) quotes from Stubbes's *Anatomie of Abuses* a description of the 'stately turrets' which Elizabethan ladies made of their hair and its ornaments. Cf. Prudentius, Psych. v. 183: 'Turritum tortis caput accumulant in altum crinibus.'

l. 15. *nimbum*. Cf. Planché, p. 322: 'An enormous ruff, rising gradually from the front of the shoulders to nearly the height of the head behind, encircled the wearer like the nimbus or glory of a saint.'

PAGE 423, l. 21. *crudo*: early. She makes her round punctually and does not keep her servants working after the proper time.

ll. 39–41. The gentle hand that wrote so fair deserves to lie in no dust less precious than the golden sands of the Pactolus.

III (p. 424). The sunbeams remind him of Jacob's Ladder; can they bring down his mother to him? No, she must remain where she is (l. 10), but by those rays he may hope to reach her.

IV, l. 8. *pellibus exuor*. 'When I join in the music of the spheres, I cast off my slough, "this muddy vesture of decay".'

V (p. 425), l. 14. *Satis*. God gives graves without price (cf. Isa. lv. 1) to all things that grow in the earth.

VI. Herbert reproves his physician for feeling his pulse. 'I am sick, but my sickness is of the mind.'

VII (p. 426), l. 12. Astraea, daughter of Themis, was last of the immortals to leave earth at the end of the Golden Age.

l. 13. *Examine*. Themis is represented on coins with her balance.

VIII (p. 427), l. 9. Cf. Mark x. 38: 'Potestis bibere calicem quem ego bibo?'

IX, l. 7. On 27 June 1627, within a few weeks of Lady Danvers's death, Buckingham sailed from Stokes Bay with about one hundred ships and 6,000 troops for the relief of La Rochelle. The ill success of the expedition would not have been known when this poem was published. Cf. *Gallusque marinis*, l. 11.

l. 11. Count Tilly, commanding the army of the Catholic League, totally defeated Christian IV of Denmark at Lutter on 27 Aug. 1626.

l. 14. *nimijs aquis*. From this and from the next poem we may infer that it was a very rainy summer, which Herbert represents as Nature mourning for his mother.

X (p. 428), l. 9. *Scotiae binae*: Scotland and Ireland. At the time of Lady Danvers's death, her eldest son had an Irish peerage only, of Castle-island, county Kerry, from the name of an estate which was inherited by his wife, Mary, daughter of Sir William Herbert. The long residence of the Herbert family on the Welsh border explains the grief of *Cambria peruetusta*.

XII (p. 429), l. 3. *Molossorum*. Wolf-dogs used by Epirot shepherds.

l. 8. *optimâ Pirrhâ*. Medusa turned men who saw the snakes in her hair to stone; Pyrrha did the reverse. When Deucalion and Pyrrha alone survived the flood, the stones which they flung over their shoulders, in obedience to an oracle, became men and women to repopulate the earth (Ov. Met. i. 383–93).

l. 10. From *belluis* in the next line, and from *Tigris* having an initial capital, we may infer a pun on the tigress and the river. Roman interest in Stoicism dates from the visit of Diogenes Babylonius, who was sent with two other envoys from Athens in 155 B.C. Panaetius, who did much to popularize Stoicism in Rome, was his pupil. Lucian (Macr. lxii. 20) describes Diogenes as a native of Seleucia on the Tigris.

XV, l. 2. *Θεοῦ γεώργιον*. From 1 Cor. iii. 9.

XVII (p. 431), ll. 9–10. Cf. Hom. Il. ix. 9.

XIX, l. 8. A colon is needed after *Stulta* (vocative); the poet would hardly condemn his tributes to his mother as foolish things. 'You drove me to it, and I write; but hearken, foolish Muse: this once I write, but not again.'

ALIA POEMATA LATINA (Page 432)

These occasional poems are for the first time arranged chronologically. The relative order of the three poems addressed to Bacon cannot be determined, but they are not far apart in time.

In Obitum Henrici Principis (Page 432)

Henry Frederick, eldest son of James I, died of typhoid fever on 6 Nov. 1612 at the age of nineteen. Herbert, who was also nineteen, wrote these poems a few months before he took his B.A. degree; they are his first poems to be printed. Fuller (*Ch. Hist.* x, § 22), after mentioning the tributes of both universities to this promising prince, quotes lines of Giles Fletcher and continues: 'Give me leave to adde one more, untranslatable for its Elegancy, and Expressivenesse:

Ulteriora timens cum morte paciscitur Orbis.'

Fuller's marginal note reads: 'Made by Mr. *George Herbert*.'

l. 31. *lactare*. This, the reading of 1612, is corrected by all modern editors to the more familiar word *laetare*, but *lactare*, to deceive with false hopes, gives the better sense.

PAGE 433, l. 33. *Pyrij de pulueris ictu*. 'Why did the fates spare the prince in the Gunpowder Plot, if he was to die of disease before he reached manhood?'

l. 43. Taken from Virg. Ecl. viii. 4: 'Et mutata suos requierunt flumina cursus.'

In Natales et Pascha Concurrentes (Page 434)

Grosart (ii. 178) compares Donne's poem 'Upon the Annuntiation and Passion falling upon one day. Anno Dñi 1608', and suggests that Donne's and Herbert's poems 'probably both were written on the same occasion'; but this is out of the question, as Donne treats of the concurrence of Lady Day (25 Mar.) and Good Friday, and Herbert of the concurrence of his own birthday (3 Apr.) and Good Friday. Good Friday fell on 3 Apr. in 1607, when Herbert was 14, and again in 1618 and 1629; 1618 seems the most likely date for this poem, as it reflects Herbert's earlier manner. *Pascha*, though later used for Easter, was in early Christian use applied to the commemoration of the day of the Crucifixion (J. Dowden, *The Church Year and Kalendar*, p. 104), and the contents of the poem show that Herbert has Good Friday in mind. Easter Day did not fall on 3 Apr. in his lifetime.

ll. 9–10. As in ll. 7–8, a present subjunctive is followed by a future indicative; the emendation *vbi* will make l. 9 subordinate to l. 10, as l. 7 is to l. 8. Herbert is very free with his use of the subjunctive in subordinate clauses.

In Obitum Reginae Annae (Page 435)

Anne of Denmark, James I's consort, died on 2 Mar. 1618/19.

Ad Autorem Instaurationis Magnae (Page 435)

This and the next two poems are addressed to Bacon. On Herbert's close association with Bacon see Introduction, p. xl. *Novum Organum*, the second part of *Instauratio Magna*, was published on 12 Oct. 1620.

Comparatio inter Munus et Librum (Page 435)

Herbert, as Orator, acknowledged Bacon's gift of his book to the University in a letter dated 4 Nov. 1620 (see pp. 463, 606). Bacon had used his office (*munus*) of lord chancellor in the interest of Cambridge (*Epistolae* v and XIV).

In Honorem D.D. Verulamii, &c. (Page 436)

This, the most famous of Herbert's Latin poems, besides appearing in several manuscript collections, was printed in four books with different editors in twenty-five years. Its first appearance in print, so far as can be discovered, is in an unexpected quarter; it stands, with his name and his style as Public Orator, next after the title-page of *Caesares*, a collection of Latin verse by an Italian Jesuit, Emanuele Tesauro (Thesaurus), printed at Oxford by Leonard Lichfield in 1637, the only other poem not by the author being one by the Dutch scholar Heinsius. The book is called the second edition; Herbert's poem is not in the first edition, printed at Lyons in 1635. The explanation of Tesauro's book being accepted by an Oxford printer may be that he had left the Society in 1634 (Somervogel, *Bibliothèque de la Compagnie de Jésus*, vol. vii, p. 1943); but he is still described as 'e societate Iesu' on the title-page of the Oxford volume. It may have occurred to the author or the printer to help the sale of a foreigner's book by placing in a prominent position Herbert's much-talked-of poem. The Duke of Devonshire's MS. is nearer to the text found in *Caesares* than to the versions in other seventeenth-century books; the author is there described as 'Gulielmus Herbert, Orator publicus in Acad: Cantabr.'

The title of the poem suggests that the date of composition must lie between 27 Jan. 1620/1, when Bacon was created Viscount St. Alban, and the following 1 May, when he was deprived of the Great Seal.

l. 4. *Inductionis Dominus*. A principal theme of Book II of *Novum Organum* is the improvement in the method of inductive reasoning.

l. 5. *magister . . . Artium*. Bacon received his M.A. on 27 July 1594; he proceeded to no higher degree.

l. 12. *Promus*: a steward, one in charge of a storehouse. There is probably an allusion to Bacon's having compiled for his own use a collection of adages and proverbs, English and foreign, in a MS. volume, now in the British Museum, entitled *A Promus of Formularies and Elegancies*; it was not fully printed till 1882.

Fugator Idolûm. An allusion to the refutation of the idols of the tribe, the cave, the market-place, and the theatre, in Book I of *Novum Organum*.

l. 21. *matris*, sc. *Veritatis* (cf. l. 23).

PAGE 437, l. 27. *probè*, the reading in *Caesares* and the Devonshire MS., is altered to the more familiar word *prope* in all other MSS. and reprints, although 'thoroughly' makes better sense here than 'almost', and with *prope* the line is a syllable short.

Aethiopissa ambit Cestum (Page 437)

For the English poem addressed to Bacon, which the author of this 'Blackamoor' Latin poem sent with it, see above, p. 209. *Aethiopissa* is as secular as anything attributed to Herbert. Included in the *Poems* (1657) of Henry King, Herbert's contemporary at Westminster, is a free translation of 'Aethiopissa' (without Herbert's name) headed 'A Blackmoor Mayd wooing a fair Boy: sent to the Author by Mr. Hen. Rainolds', and King's rejoinder, 'The Boyes Answer to the Blackmoor'. The two poems are also found in a MS. dated 1647. Reynolds, a friend of Drayton, translated Tasso's *Aminta* (1628). John Cleveland included in *The Character of a London Diurnal, with Severall Select Poems* (1647) an inversion of the same theme, 'A Faire Nymph scorning a Black Boy courting her'; he exactly reproduces Herbert's ll. 9–10:

My face is smoak, thence may be guest
What flames within have scortch'd my brest.

T. Browne (*Pseudodoxia*, v. xxii. 8) discusses the saying 'That smoake doth follow the fairest', and quotes a parasite's description of himself in Athenaeus: 'Like smoake unto the Fair I fly.'

Dum petit Infantem (Page 437)

True Copies of all the Latine Orations (1623) prints the speeches, including Herbert's (see p. 440), on the occasion of degrees being conferred on the Spanish and Flemish ambassadors on 27 Feb. 1622/3, and also the Vice-Chancellor's Oration at the visit of James I on 12 Mar. following (wrongly given there as 19 Mar.). The Vice-Chancellor ends with the customary *Dixi*, which is immediately followed by this epigram, without explanation or author's name. In the English translations at the end of the book a version of the epigram is given, again without author's name.

Joseph Mede (Meade), writing from Christ's College to his cousin Sir Martin Stutevile on 15 Mar. (B.M. MS. Harl. 389, f. 298), states that on the previous Wednesday (12 Mar.) King James witnessed the Latin comedy *Loiola*. 'At dinner before the comedy there talke in the presence (as I heare) was most of the Prince', that is, of Charles's visit to Spain to negotiate a marriage with the Infanta. Mede adds that Dr. Richardson, Master of Trinity, 'brought before the King a paper of verses in manner of a Epigram which B[ishop] Neale & others read. A friend of mine over the Bishops shoulder gott two of them by heart', which he proceeds to quote. A week later (ibid. f. 300) he writes: 'I will give you the Epigram whole which our orator made.' Though Mede's account of the circumstances is worth having, his version of the epigram has not the authority of the official *True Copies*, but, as it is found in books which are still consulted (e.g. Nichols, *The Progresses of King James I*, iv. 838, and C. H. Cooper, *Annals of Cambridge*, iii. 158) it is worth recording. For Herbert's 'Farewell Speech' on the king's leaving Cambridge, see above, p. 443.

l. 1. *Infantem*. Currency has been given in many books to a mistaken reading *Infantam*, and its origin can be explained. Mede wrote *a* above the letter *e* of *Infantem*, and in the margin '*a* The Infanta'. Baker, in his transcript of Mede's letter (B.M. MS. Harl. 7041), took this to be a correction to *Infantam*, and so wrote the word. There can be no doubt that Herbert used *Infantem*, a noun of common gender, there being no recognized Latin form *Infanta*.

The copy of these lines, pasted in a copy of Walton's *Life of Herbert* (1670), once owned by Pickering and now at Harvard, is not in Herbert's hand, and there is no example of his signing his first name 'Geor.', as in this copy.

In Obitum Francisci Vicecomitis Sancti Albani (Page 438)

Memoriae Francisci Baronis de Verulamio Sacrum (London, 1626), in which this poem first appears, is a Cambridge tribute to her famous son, who died on 9 Apr. 1626. The Latin preface is by William Rawley, Bacon's chaplain, but it may be surmised that Herbert had a considerable part in collecting the contributors (see Introduction, p. xxx). *Memoriae* was reprinted in *Harleian Miscellanies*, vol. x, 1813; a note on p. 301 states that in Herbert's copy of *Memoriae* (which cannot now be traced) he has transcribed a Dedication to Prince Charles and a poem to Bacon, both of them taken from Thomas Peyton's *The Glasse of Time* (1620 and 1623). E. K. Rand caused to be privately printed *A Translation of 32 Latin poems in honor of Francis Bacon* (Boston, 1904). G. Cantor edited, with a German translation, *Die Rawley'sche Sammlung von 32 Trauergedichten auf F. Bacon* (Halle, 1897).

In Sacram Anchoram (Page 438)

Donne's Latin verses, 'To Mr. *George Herbert*, with one of my Seal[s], of the Anchor and Christ', with an English version, appeared in *Poems. By J. D.* (1650), and in the editions of his *Poems* in 1654 and 1669. Herbert's Latin lines in answer, with an English version, followed in these three editions. Herbert's Latin verses, without a translation, appeared in *Herbert's Remains* (1652). In all these editions the couplet beginning 'Munde, fluas' ended the poem, and the corresponding English couplet was at the end in the Donne editions. In this form the Latin poem consisted of a set of seven lines, followed by two disconnected triplets and a final couplet; and this was represented in the English version by a set of eight lines, followed by two quatrains and a couplet. But in Walton's *Life of Donne* (1658), where Herbert's English lines appear, with the first two lines and a half only of the Latin, the couplet is attached to the first set, and is followed by the first quatrain only. This appears to be the right place for the couplet both in the Latin and the English, and I follow Sir Herbert Grierson in adopting this order (*The Poems of John Donne*, ii. 261–2); as he says, the two disconnected stanzas 'may or may not be by Herbert'. The opening lines are addressed to Donne, but the additional stanzas seem to be written after his death on 31 Mar. 1631.

In his *Life of Herbert* (1670) and the collected *Lives* (1670) Walton desired 'to add one testimony' to what he had already written in his *Life of Donne* (1658) about Donne's friendship with Herbert, 'namely, that a little before his death, he caused many *Seals* to be made, and in them to be ingraven the figure of *Christ crucified* on an *Anchor*, which is the emblem of hope, and of which Dr. *Donne* would often say, *Crux mihi Anchora*'. Herbert and Walton himself were among the friends who received seals, and 'at Mr. *Herberts* death, these Verses were found wrap't up with that Seal which was by the

Doctor given to him'. Here follows the set of four lines beginning 'When my dear Friend', which seems to be a *pastiche* of the first quatrain and of the couplet beginning 'Let the world reel', or perhaps, in Walton's manner, he has trusted to his memory. The fact that he omitted the second quatrain from his *Life of Donne* (1658) and both quatrains from his revision of that life in the collected *Lives* (1670) may indicate that he doubted their authenticity, and preferred the version which he gave for the first time in his *Life of Herbert* (1670).

ORATIONES

I. *Oratio coram Legatis* (Page 440)

In view of the projected marriage of Prince Charles with the Infanta of Spain it was politic of the university of Cambridge to pay honour to the representatives of the Habsburg thrones. Charles and Buckingham had left England on 17 Feb. 1622/3, travelling incognito to Madrid. Ten days later Don Carlos de Coloma, the Spanish ambassador, and Ferdinand, Baron de Boyschot, ambassador of Isabella, archduchess of Austria and sovereign ruler of Flanders, were admitted Masters of Arts at a special Congregation. The orations of the Vice-Chancellor, the Orator, and others were 'published by command', with English translations. There is nothing to determine whether Herbert was himself responsible for the translation of his oration.

l. 18. *Herculeas columnas*: the Straits of Gibraltar.

l. 23. *Iacobus tutelaris Diuus*. The shrine of St. James, patron saint of Spain, at Compostella was a famous place of pilgrimage.

II. *Oratio in Discessum Regis ab Academia* (Page 443)

James I paid his third visit to Cambridge on Wednesday 12 Mar. 1622/3, when he attended a performance of the Latin play *Loiola* by John Hacket. Mede, writing to Stutevile on the Saturday following, remarks that the king 'expressed no remarkable mirth thereat. He laughed once or twice toward the end.' Baker, in his Cambridge Collections (B.M. Harl. MS. 7041, f. 38v), cites a contemporary account of what followed the comedy. After refreshments they brought the king 'to the door, entring into ye Court, where his Coach did wait for him: but his Majesty was pleased to stay there, while the Orator Mr. Herbert did make a short Farewell Speech unto him. Then he called for a copy of the Vice-Chancellor's Speech, & likewise for an Epigram the Orator made.' (For the epigram, see above, p. 437.) The Orator's speech, from a copy in the Record Office, is here printed for the first time.

l. 15. *latera*: the Orator's lungs. Cf. Cic. Verr. ii. 4. 30, § 67: 'quae vox, quae latera, quae vires!'

l. 17. *omnia disponit suauiter*. Quoted from Wisdom viii. 1.

l. 19. *vapulant Iesuitae*. An allusion to the play *Loiola*. James I in many of his writings, notably in *A premonition to All Monarches and States of*

Christendom (1609), attacked the Jesuits. 'He stood in the lists as champion against the most redoubtable controversialist of the time, Cardinal Bellarmine' (C. J. Sisson in *Seventeenth Century Studies*, p. 57).

Page 444, ll. 2–3. 'We can only emulate your Majesty's remarkable qualities by being ourselves remarkable for the brevity of our oration; our eloquence is our dumbfoundedness.'

III. *Oratio Caroli Reditum celebrans* (Page 444)

After nearly six months in Spain Charles and Buckingham were obliged to recognize the failure of their expedition, and they landed in England on 5 Oct. 1623. The Spanish match was very unpopular in England, and the news of the prince's return with his marriage ring now free to bestow elsewhere (p. 444, ll. 19–22) was received with great rejoicings at Cambridge, as generally throughout the country. On 8 Oct. 'the University assembled; in the forenoone to a gratulatorie Sermon at St. Marie's, in the afternoone to a publick Oration' (letter of Mede to Stutevile, 11 Oct.). Apart from the extravagant adulation of Charles, the most striking feature of Herbert's oration is the vehement indictment of war (447.26–449.11). S. R. Gardiner (*Hist. of Engl. 1603–42*, vii. 266–7) credits Herbert with courage and sincerity, since 'it was no secret that the Prince had come back bent on war. . . . From Charles, rushing headlong into war, the lover of peace had no favour to expect.'

l. 14. *Polycrates.* Hdt. iii. 40–3.

Page 445, l. 27. *purpurâ.* As Grosart noted, doctors would be wearing scarlet.

Page 446, l. 12. *si cochleas colligeret.* Caligula, having brought an army to the north coast of Gaul A.D. 40, as if to invade Britain, gave orders to collect shells, which he called the spoils of conquered Ocean.

l. 14. *si muscas captaret.* Suetonius says of Domitian that he was wont 'muscas captare ac stilo praeacuto configere' (Domit. 3).

l. 15. *Austriacam familiam.* Philip IV, who ascended the Spanish throne in 1621, was a great-grandson of Charles V, of the House of Austria.

l. 16. 'Aquila non captat muscas' (*Erasmi Adagiorum Chiliades Tres*, 1508, III. clxxvii). Erasmus comments on it: 'Summi uiri negligunt minutula quaepiam. Animus excelsus res humiles despicit.'

l. 19. *Medicorum Alpha*: Hippocrates. Galen, De constitutione artis medicae ad Patrophilum, § 7 (Kühn, i. 247). Galen has οὐδέποτ' for οὐκ. I owe this reference to Dr. Charles Singer.

l. 19. *Thraces dicti sunt ἄβιοι.* Strabo (vii, p. 296) reports that Posidonius speaks of Mysians who lived on milk foods and of Thracians οἳ χωρὶς γυναικὸς ζῶσι, quoting Hom. Il. xiii. 4–6 in support.

l. 20. ἀτιμίαν προσέθηκε τοῖς ἀγάμοις. Plut. Lycurg. xv.

Page 447, ll. 5–8. An edition of the Germania of Tacitus, published at Augsburg in 1580, has a section 'Etymologiae Quaedam Cimbriacae, è Ioannis Geropij opere historico' with this sentence on p. 267: 'Coning: Regis à scientia, potentia, audacia: à quibus populus pendeat, können, kün.'

Etymologists no longer allow this derivation, but Carlyle still made use of it in his lecture 'The Hero as King' (*On Heroes*, 1841).

ll. 14–15. *Ὅταν δὲ κρηπὶς κ.τ.λ.* Eur. Herc. Fur. 1261–2. The first line, as printed in 1623, has two errors and does not scan; it is probable that Herbert did not see the proof.

ll. 31–2. *Ὅταν νομεὺς κ.τ.λ.* Xen. Mem. II. ix. 7.

ll. 34–5. *fraena ferox spumantia mandit.* From Virg. Aen. iv. 135.

PAGE 448, ll. 1–4. *Iam nunc minaci* &c. Hor. C. II. i. 17–20, Herbert substituting *Stringuntur* for *Perstringis.*

ll. 14–15. *Εἰρήνη γεωργὸν κ.τ.λ.* The lines are attributed to Menander and should read

εἰρήνη τὸν γεωργὸν κἂν πέτραις
τρέφει καλῶς, πόλεμος δὲ κἂν πεδίῳ κακῶς.

ll. 31–2. When Syracuse was taken by Marcellus in 212 B.C., Archimedes was killed by Roman soldiers while he was engaged upon a mathematical problem. See note on *Lucus* XXXII. 41 (p. 593).

l. 36. *perdiae, pernoctes.* Willmott's emendation *perdies* is clearly wrong, as Herbert had precedent for his phrase in Aulus Gellius 2. 1. 1: 'stare solitus Socrates dicitur, pertinaci statu perdius atque pernox.'

PAGE 449, ll. 14–15. *Σωφρόνων ἐστὶ κ.τ.λ.* Plut. Apoph. Reg.

ll. 17–18. *Leones mansueti.* Cf. 'Humilitie', p. 70, ll. 9–10.

l. 21. *lacum, cuius altitudo ignota erat.* Dionysius of Halicarnassus (Ant. Rom. I. xv) describes a lake in the Sabine country as bottomless and as consecrated to Victory. It was called the *umbilicus* of Italy and was regarded as so sacred that its banks might only be approached at certain festivals.

l. 24. *nullis perspicillis, ne Belgicis quidem.* Kepler in 1610 and Galileo in 1610/11 used *perspicillum* of the telescope recently invented in the Low Countries. Cf. *Musae Resp.* viii. 11: 'Quisquis tuetur perspicillis Belgicis', and 'that Dutch optick' in 'To the Queene of Bohemia', l. 13.

PAGE 450, ll. 8–9. *Τυφλοὺς εἶναι κ.τ.λ.* Philo Judaeus, II. ii (De Abrahamo).

l. 16. *Vicini quo pacto &c.* Cato, de Re Rustica, i. 2. Seneca used the phrase *Catoniana praecepta*, e.g. in Ep. xciv. 27.

l. 28. *ligna obliqua*: beams leaning towards and upon each other, like the two sides of the letter A.

PAGE 451, l. 4. *de Tago, Pactolo.* The Spanish river Tagus, like the Lydian river Pactolus, was famous for its golden sands: cf. Virg. Aen. x. 142 'Pactolusque irrigat auro', and Ovid Am. I. xv. 34 'auriferi ripa beata Tagi'. There is probably a playful allusion in *mala aurea* (l. 3) to the orange groves of Spain.

l. 20. Juv. Sat. ii. 161.

PAGE 452, l. 18. *magnum tonitru.* For a parallel see note on 'Content', p. 500, ll. 22–4. There is only the grammarians' authority for the neuter nominative *tonitru*, but Herbert allows himself such licences, e.g. 454. 24, *tenebriones.*

l. 27. *solebant ventres eximere.* The Egyptian practice of removing the entrails to appease the sun is remarked by Plutarch in 'Sapientum Convivium' and in 'De Carnium Esu oratio posterior'.

PAGE 453, l. 3. *Ὥσπερ τοῖς πτεροῖς κ.τ.λ.* Not an exact quotation from Lucian Salt. 2.

l. 7. *Codri amor.* The last Athenian king sacrificed his life to save his country from invasion.

PAGE 454, l. 18. *in Geoponicis. Τὰ Γεωπονικά*, a treatise on agriculture by Cassianus Bassus.

l. 36. *anus subsultans* &c. A Spanish proverb: 'Vieja che bayla mucho polvo levanta.'

PAGE 455, l. 10. Daphne, pursued by Apollo, was at her prayer changed into a laurel (δάφνη), which later became an emblem of triumph.

l. 18. Virg. Ecl. viii. 13.

EPISTOLAE (Page 456)

Herbert's letters as Orator, I–XVI, are taken from the manuscript official collection, 'Epistolae Academicae', otherwise known as the Orator's Book, now in the University Registry. It was formerly in the keeping of the Orator or his deputy: Herbert (XVII. 9) bids Creighton, on becoming his deputy, obtain the Orator's Book and lamp from Thorndike, who has been acting as deputy. On the blank page 532 of volume ii, following Nethersole's letters, is the entry: 'Franciscus Nethersole Oratorio munere cessit 19 Jan 1619 Procancellario Rev:o Dno Dre Scott, Procuratoribus Mro Roberts & Mro Mason. eidem successit Georgius Herbert.' In fact, Sir Francis Nethersole signed his resignation on 18 Jan. 1619/20, the resignation was declared on 20 Jan., and his successor was elected on Friday 21 Jan. (cf. Herbert's *Letter* IX, to his step-father, on 19 Jan.: 'Concerning the Orator's place all goes well yet, the next *Friday* it is tryed'). Herbert continued to be Orator until he was succeeded by Creighton on 28 Jan. 1627/8; but the latest letter in the Orator's Book before his resignation is dated 8 Oct. 1621. By Grace of 11 June 1624 Herbert was granted leave of absence for six months, and during the next three years he employed in succession as his deputies Herbert Thorndike (470. 9) and Creighton, but no letters of theirs for these years are entered in the Orator's Book. *Scrinia Sacra* (1654, ii. 215–16) prints two letters of 8 June 1626 from the university to Charles I and Buckingham on the duke's election as chancellor of the university; it is not known whether they are Herbert's. 'The orator' made a Latin speech at the duke's installation at York House on 13 July, but it has not survived (see Introduction, p. xxx).

It is evident from the dates either given in the letters or to be inferred from their contents that the first twelve letters following the entry of Herbert's appointment as Orator in the Orator's Book are out of order and cannot, therefore, have been entered at the time of their composition but collectively; the remaining four (XIII–XVI) are in chronological order. William Cole in his Cambridge collections dated 1777 (B.M. Add. MS. 5873) has copies of ten of these letters from a transcript in the hand of Archbishop Sancroft; his order, presumably following Sancroft's, is nearer to that adopted in this edition than to that of the Orator's Book. The first twelve of Herbert's letters in the Orator's Book are those numbered in the present edition VI, VII, II, I, VIII, XI, X, IX, XII, III, IV, V.

I (p. 456). The earl (*C.* in the title stands for *Comitem*) was created marquis of Buckingham on 1 Jan. 1617/18 (*State Papers Domestic*, xcv. 3), a year earlier than the date given in the D.N.B. and in the Orator's Book. As this letter is included among others of Herbert's in the Orator's Book it is presumably his, but composed by him when he was acting for Nethersole.

l. 4. Cf. Hor. C. I. xxxvi. 20: 'lascivis hederis ambitiosior.'

II (p. 457). Sir Robert Naunton, a former Orator (1594–1611), was secretary of state (*Secret.* in title of VI) for five years from 8 Jan. 1617/18. We may infer from VI that he had replied to the university's congratulations on his appointment by asking what return of service he might make, and that he had quickly (cf. VI. 14, *festinasti*) sought to protect the interests of Cambridge in the proposed scheme of draining the Bedford levels (see IV). From 1618 until its abandonment in May 1620 the scheme continued to agitate the university. This letter, however, can be more exactly dated by the reference in it to protection against fire. On 6 May 1619 'a fearful fire seized upon Cambridge and burnt up three score dwelling-houses together, situated between Jesus and Sidney Colleges, which were endangered by them likewise' (letter of Lorkin to Sir T. Puckering, 11 May, cit. ap. *Court and Times of James I*, ii. 161). The Privy Council on 2 June following, with 'Mr. Secretary Naunton' present, passed an ordinance authorizing the Vice-Chancellor to forbid the erection or rebuilding of thatched houses and sheds (C. H. Cooper, *Annals of Cambridge*, iii. 126–8). Cole's transcript has 'Datae 1619' at the end, and it places II earlier than VI, although in the Orator's Book both are undated and VI precedes II.

III (p. 458). The date at the head, 18 May, differs from the Latin date at the end, 20 May, which is probably correct, the heading being added carelessly. James I presented his *Opera Latina* (London, 1619) with an accompanying letter. The king's greater interest in Cambridge has sometimes been supposed from the fact that a similar copy was not sent to Oxford till 29 May (*State Papers Domestic*, cxv. 56); but a copy of an earlier issue, also dated 1619, had been previously sent there (J. P. R. Lyell, 'James I and the Bodleian Catalogue', in *The Bodleian Quarterly Record*, vii, No. 79, 1934). That the contemporary estimate of James as writer and thinker was not altogether unjustified is the contention of Professor C. J. Sisson in his chapter 'King James the First as Poet and Political Writer' in *Seventeenth Century Studies* (1938).

l. 15. *gloriam absque crudelitate* &c. Herbert's love of peace was in sincere accord with James's pacific policy at a time when most of Europe (*inter tantas mundi trepidationes*, l. 2) was being drawn into the Thirty Years' War.

PAGE 459, l. 16. *lignum contra omnia venena validum*. Bede says of Ireland (*Eccl. Hist.* I. i, tr. A. M. Sellar): 'Almost all things in the island are efficacious against poison. In truth, we have known that, when men have been bitten by serpents, the scrapings of leaves of books that were brought out of Ireland, being put into water, and given them to drink, have immediately absorbed the spreading poison, and assuaged the swelling.'

l. 30. *Quid Vaticanam Bodleiumque* &c. James I had shown singular favour to Sir Thomas Bodley's refounding of the university library at Oxford, and Herbert in his letter to Bacon (VIII. 28), more honestly than here, admits the need of a better library at Cambridge. Currency has been given to the reading *Bodleianamque* through Walton having quoted the epigram so in his *Lives*; Duport, one of the best scholars of the day, also has it; perhaps *Bodleianam* was regarded as a trisyllable. The first three syllables of *Vaticanam* are long here, as in Juvenal and Martial, though Horace (C. I. xx. 7) and Herbert elsewhere (*Musae Resp.* xxx. 2) have the second syllable short. Cole has *Vaticanum Bodleiumque*.

IV (p. 460). Nothing agitated Cambridge more in these years than the project of the Commissioners of Sewers to authorize contractors or undertakers (*redemptores*) to drain the Bedford fens. It was feared that the navigation of the Ouse and the Cam, the principal means of supply and trade, would be impaired. The matter was discussed by the Privy Council, the king presiding, on 11 Apr. 1620. The lord chancellor, the chancellor of the exchequer (Grevile), and Naunton were present, and representatives of the town and university of Cambridge attended. The king showed 'his ever watchful care for the publick good' and required that the undertakers should put their guarantees in writing. Their written proposals were submitted to the lord chancellor at York House on 11 May, and, as a result of further disagreement between the Commissioners and the undertakers, the contract was not made (T. Badeslade, *The History of the Navigation of King's Lynn and Cambridge*, 1725: H. C. Darby, *The Draining of the Fens*, 1940). This temporary reprieve was the occasion of four grateful letters (IV–VII) to those who had been chiefly instrumental in effecting it.

l. 11. *paulum aquae à Sinaetâ*. Plutarch tells the story twice, in *Vitae* and *Apoph.*, without giving the man's name, but Aelian (Var. Hist. I. xxxii) gives it as Σιναίτης.

V, l. 20. *obscurus ille philosophus*. Bacon, *Apophthegmes* (1625), No. 258: 'Heraclitus the Obscure sayd; *The drie Light was the best Soule*. Meaning, when the Faculties Intellectuall are in vigour, not wet, nor, as it were, blouded by the Affections.'

PAGE 461, ll. 2–5. Alludes to a saying of Ennius quoted in Cic. Off. I. 16. 51.

ll. 26–7. *quasi mixtam personam*. The chancellor as the keeper of the king's conscience, and as holding an office usually assigned in the Middle Ages to a churchman, might be said to have a quasi-clerical status. Mede, writing to Stutevile 3 Feb. 1625/6, about a prayer used at the coronation of Charles I, says: 'It understands the King not to be merely laic, but a mixed person.'

VI. It is possible that this and the following letter, which stand first and second of Herbert's letters in the Orator's Book, should be assigned to the previous year, but, whereas II refers in quite general terms to Naunton's care for the river, the description in VI and VII of the undertakers being completely routed seems to fit the situation only after their scheme had foundered in the summer of 1620. Cole has 'Datae 1619' at the end of this letter, but gives it after II.

PAGE 462, ll. 8–9. *maris quasi Flagellatores*. Xerxes had the Hellespont flogged for breaking down his bridge of boats (Hdt. vii. 35).

VII, l. 26. *fouisti literatos*. Sir Fulke Grevile, who directed that 'friend to Sir Philip Sidney' should be placed on his monument, was a generous patron of Daniel, D'Avenant, and other poets.

l. 28. *quod expectamus indies futurum*. In fact Grevile was created Baron Brooke on 29 Jan. 1620/1.

VIII (p. 463). Bacon sent to Cambridge a copy of his *Instauratio Magna*, having for its second title *Novum Organum*, with a letter dated 31 Oct. 1620.

ll. 6–7. *non gremio solùm* (*quod innuis*). Bacon in his letter had said that it was his pleasure 'partum meum nuper editum vobis in gremium dare'. Herbert (ll. 24–7) plays on Bacon's description of his book as his offspring.

ll. 8–9. *more nostro*. Noblemen's sons had the privilege of proceeding at once to the Master's degree as soon as they had qualified for the Bachelor's.

l. 30. *ab Archiepiscopo Eboracensi extructa*. Thomas Rotheram, chancellor of England and archbishop of York, and several times chancellor of Cambridge, built a library, which long before Herbert's day had become inadequate for the university. The earl of Suffolk, on becoming chancellor in 1614, was urged to promote the building of a university library, but nothing had come of it.

PAGE 464, l. 1. *ex aedibus Eboracensibus*. Bacon addressed his letter from York House in the Strand, which both his father and he leased as lord keeper from the archbishop of York.

IX. Sir Henry Montagu, of Christ's College, chief justice from 1616, was appointed lord high treasurer on 3 Dec. 1620. Since the deprivation of the previous holder, the earl of Suffolk, on 19 July, the office had been in commission (cf. *Pendulam hanc dignitatem*, l. 11). Montagu, who was created earl of Manchester in 1626, is remembered as the author of *Contemplatio Mortis* (1631), better known by the title which it bore in later editions, *Manchester al Mondo*.

X (p. 465). Naunton was elected burgess or member of parliament for the university in Jan. 1620/1, and was re-elected in 1624 and 1625.

XI. Sir Thomas Coventry had already been congratulated by Cambridge on becoming solicitor-general on 19 Mar. 1616/17. He was promoted attorney-general (*Cognitor Regis*) on 11 Jan. 1620/1. He was to give 'third and fourth occasions' (l. 25) of being congratulated, as he became lord keeper in 1625 and was created Baron Coventry in 1628.

XII (p. 466). Robert Heath was nominated solicitor-general in succession to Coventry on 22 Jan. 1620/1 and was knighted on 28 January. In 1625 he became attorney-general and in 1631 chief justice.

XIII. Cambridge relied upon a charter (cf. XIV. 21) of Henry VIII, granted on 20 July 1534 (Rymer, *Foedera*, xiv. 543), allowing the university to elect three stationers and printers to print all books (*omnimodos Libros*) approved by the chancellor or his vicegerent and three doctors. The same charter allowed the stationers to sell all books, printed at home or abroad, that were approved by the same authorities. The Stationers' Company, incorporated in 1557, sought a virtual monopoly, and from 1583 constantly contested the rights of Cambridge. George Abbot, archbishop of Canterbury 1611–33, was in virtue of his office associated with the Stationers' Company.

PAGE 467, ll. 1–2. *humanitas tua*. The marginal note *ferina missa* probably refers to a present of a buck; if so, it is a strange reflection that on 24 July of the next summer Abbot, in shooting at a buck with a cross-bow, shot a gamekeeper dead, and was for a time debarred *a sacris*.

XV (p. 468). Sir James Ley (*Leigh* in the Orator's Book) succeeded Montagu as chief justice on 29 Jan. 1620/1. He became lord treasurer in 1624, earl of Marlborough in 1625, and president of the council in 1628; he died on 14 Mar. 1628/9. Milton, in his sonnet to the Lady Margaret Ley, addresses her as

> Daughter to that good Earl, once President
> Of *Englands* Counsel, and her Treasury,
> Who liv'd in both, unstain'd with gold or fee.

The bracketed word *Camden* at the head of the letter is not readily explained, unless it means that Herbert had intended alluding to Ley's antiquarian interests, which would have linked him with William Camden, whom Herbert reverenced as a former head master of Westminster.

PAGE 469, ll. 1–2. *Demosthenes doluit* &c. Cic. Tusc. Disp. IV. xix. 44: 'Cui non sunt auditae Demosthenis vigiliae? qui dolere se aiebat, si quando opificum antelucana victus esset industria.'

XVI. Sir Lionel Cranfield took a prominent part in the attack on Bacon in the parliament of 1621, and hoped to succeed him as chancellor. When James appointed Bishop Williams as lord keeper, suspending the office of chancellor, he sought to console Cranfield by making him Baron Cranfield on 9 July 1621 and by appointing him to succeed Montagu (viscount Mandeville) as treasurer on 30 September. A year later Cranfield was made earl of Middlesex. Nicholas Ferrar was one of the three members of parliament appointed by the house in 1624 to draw up articles for the impeachment of Middlesex for bribery; Middlesex was heavily sentenced and disgraced.

XVII (p. 470). Robert Creighton (1593–1672), born in the same year as Herbert, and like him educated at Westminster and Trinity, was regius professor of Greek 1625–39, succeeded Herbert as Orator, and for the last two years of his life was bishop of Bath and Wells.

l. 9. *Thorndick nostrum*. Herbert Thorndike, fellow of Trinity, a considerable theologian, succeeded Herbert as prebendary of Leighton Ecclesia in Lincoln Cathedral, and was a prebendary of Westminster at the time of his death in 1672.

l. 17. κομμώτρια is used in Ar. Eccl. 737 of a tirewoman.

l. 19. ὀφθαλμῶν ὑπογραφὰς κ.τ.λ. Quoted from St. John Chrysostom, De Sacerdotio b. 2 (507).

l. 31. *Ixionis congressus*: i.e. as futile as Ixion's mating with a cloud. When he sought to win Hera, Zeus foiled him by providing a cloud in her semblance.

PAGE 471, l. 4. τετράγωνος. Cf. Ar. Eth. N. I. x. 11.

l. 7. *apicem*. Like a *flamen* wearing the heavy conical *apex*, Herbert had borne the office of Orator for about eight years.

l. 9. *audi Platonem*. Rep. 328 E.

XVIII. The date of this letter can be approximately determined by the reference (472. 26) to Herbert being engaged both in Rhetoric and in Orator's business, though expecting shortly to be free from the former. He was appointed Praelector in Rhetoric on 11 June 1618, the duties probably to begin from the Michaelmas term and to continue for one year. He was appointed deputy Orator on 21 Oct. 1619, and already in September he was preparing a Latin oration (*Letter* VII); the Rhetoric lectures were prescribed to be in English. Andrewes was translated from Ely to Winchester in Feb. 1618/19.

Walton (*Lives*, p. 26) tells of 'a long Letter written in Greek', containing aphorisms on predestination and sanctity of life, which Herbert sent to Andrewes, and which the bishop often showed to scholars; the letter cannot now be traced.

PAGE 472, l. 8. *lacteam aliquam viam*. Cf. Ov. Met. i. 168–71.

ll. 17–18. Martial x. iii. 11–12. The received text of the second line is 'Constare gratis cum silentium possit?', but the line as Herbert gives it is recorded in the App. Crit. of Valpy's Delphin edition.

l. 29. *Rhetorici*, sc. *agri*; cf. *praediola*, l. 30. He would not exchange the bishop's favour for any number of such holdings.

l. 36. *Philosophus de Tactu & Visu*. The reference may be to Ar. Eth. N. III. x and De Sensu i. 436 b 10, or, from a rather different angle, to Plat. Meno 76 c.

PAGE 473, l. 9. *Crescent illae, crescetis amores*. Virg. Ecl. x. 54.

APPENDIX

PRO SVPPLICI EVANGELICORUM MINISTRORUM IN ANGLIA

Ad Serenissimum Regem
contra Larvatam geminae Academiae Gorgonem Apologia,
sive Anti-tami-cami-categoria,
Authore *A.M.*

Responsum non dictum.

INsolens, audax, facinus nefandum,
Scilicet, poscit ratio ut decori,
Poscit ex omni officio ut sibi mens
Conscia recti
Anxiam Christi vigilemque curam,
Quae pias terris animas relictis
Sublevans deducit in astra, nigroque
Invidet Orco,
De sacri castâ ratione cultus,
De sacrosancti officij decoro
Supplicem ritu veteri libellum
Porgere Regi,
Simplici mente atque animo integello,
Spiritu recto, et studijs modestis,
Numinis sancti veniam, et benigni
Regis honorem
Rite praefantem: Scelus expiandum
Scilicet taurorum, ovium, suumque
Millibus centum, voluisse nudo
Tangere verbo
Praesulum fastus: monuisse ritus
Impios, deridiculos, ineptos,
Lege, ceu labes maculasque, lectâ ex
Gente fugandos.
Iusque-jurandum ingemuisse jura
Exigi contra omnia; tum misellis
Mentibus tristem laqueum inijci per
Fasque nefasque.

From David Calderwood's Parasynagma Perthense. Anno *M.DC.XX* (*no printer's name or place: the poem is described in a note as the work* A. Meluini). *Also appended to Calderwood's* Altare Damascenum (1623), *and included in Duport's* Ecclesiastes Solomonis (1662). *Heading*: *A.M.*] A. Melvino. 1604. *1623*: Andrea Melvino. *1662*   5–8 *om. 1623*   18 taurorum, ovium *1662*: tauro, & ovium *1620 1623*

Turbida illimi crucis in lavacro
Signa consignem? magico rotatu
Verba devolvam? sacra vox sacratâ im-
murmuret undâ
Strigis in morem? Rationis usu ad-
fabor infantem vacuum? canoras
Ingeram nugas minus audienti
Dicta puello?
Parvulo impostis manibus sacrabo
Gratiae foedus? Digitone sponsae
Annulus sponsi impositus sacrabit
Connubiale
Foedus aeternae bonitatis? Vndâ
Num salutari mulier sacerdos
Tinget in vitam, Sephoramque reddet*
Lustrica mater?
Pilei quadrum capiti rotundo
Rite quadrabit? Pharium Camillo
Supparum Christi, et decus Antichristi
Pontificale?
Pastor examen gregis exigendum
Curet invitus, celebrare coenam
Promptus arcanam, memorando Iesu
Vulnera dira?
Cantibus certent Berecinthia aera
Musicum fractis, reboentve rauco
Templa mugitu? Illecebris supremi ah
Rector Olympi
Captus humanis? libitumque nobis,
Scilicet, Regi id Superûm adlubescet?
Somniumque aegri cerebri profanum est
Dictio sacra?
Haud secus lustri lupa Vaticani
Romuli faecem bibit, et bibendam
Porrigit poc'lo populisque et ipsis
Regibus aureo.
Non ita aeterni Wittakerus acer
Luminis vindex patriaeque lumen
Dixit aut sensit: neque celsa summi
Penna Renoldi,

* Exod. iv. 25

55 ah] an *conj. Ed* 57–60 *Interrogation-marks from 1662* 62 bibendam *1662* : bibendum *1620 1623* 65 Wittakerus *1620 1623* : *Witakerus 1662*

Certa sublimes aperire calles,
Sueta coelestes iterare cursus,
Laeta misceri niveis beatae
Civibus aulae:
Nec Tami aut Cami accola saniore
Mente, qui coelum sapit in frequenti
Hermathenaeo et celebri Lycaeo
Culta juventus;
Cujus affulget Genio Iovae lux:
Cui nitens Sol justitiae renidet:
Quem jubar Christi radiantis alto
Spectat Olympo.
Bucerum laudem, an memorabo magnum
Martyrem? Gemmas geminas renati
Aurei saecli, duo dura sacri
Fulmina belli.
Alterum Camus liquido recursu,
Alterum Tamus trepidante lymphâ
Audijt, multum stupuitque magno
Ore sonantem.
Anne mulcentem Rhodanum et Lemannum
Praedicem Bezam, viridi in senectâ?
Octies cujus trepidavit aetas
Claudere denos
Solis anfractus reditusque, et ultra
Quinque percurrens spatiosa in annos
Longius florem viridantis aevi
Prorogat et ver.
Oris erumpit scatebrâ perenni
Amnis exundans, gravidique rores
Gratiâ foecundâ animos apertis
Auribus implent.
Major hic omni invidiâ, et superstes
Millibus mille, et Sadeele, et omnium
Maximo Calvino, alijsque veri
Testibus aequis;
Voce olorinâ liquidas ad undas
Nunc canit laudes Genitoris almi,
Carmen et Nato canit eliquante
Numinis aurâ,

81 laudem, an memorabo] laudem? memorémque *1662* 94 procurrens 1623

Sensa de castu sacra puriore,
Dicta de cultu potiore sancta,
Arma quae in castris jugulent severi
Tramitis hostes.
Cana cantanti juga ninguidarum
Alpium applaudunt, resonantque valles:
IVRA concentu nemorum sonoro
Et pater Ister
Consonant longe: pater et bicornis
Rhenus assensum ingeminat: Garumna,
Sequana, atque Arar, Liger: insularum et
Vndipotentum
Magna pars intenta Britannicarum
Voce conspirat liquidâ: solumque,
Et salum, et coelum, aemula praecinentis
More modoque
Concinunt Bezae numeris modisque
Et polo plaudunt: referuntque leges
Lege quas sanxit pius ardor et Rex
Scotobritannus.
Sicut edictum in tabulis ahenis
Servat aeternum pia cura Regis,
Qui mare et terras varijsque mundum
Temperat horis:
Cujus aequalis Soboles Parenti
Gentis electae Pater atque Custos:
Par et ambobus veniens utrinque
Spiritus almus.
Quippe Tres-unus Deus; unus Actus,
Vna natura est tribus; una virtus,
Vna majestas, Deitas et una,
Gloria et una.
Vna vis immensa, perennis una
Vita, lux una, et sapientia una,
Vna mens, una et ratio, una vox et
Vna voluntas,
Lenis, indulgens, facilis, benigna;
Dura et inclemens, rigida et severa;
Semper aeterna, omnipotens et aequa,
Semper et alma:

118 assensum] ascensum *1662* 124 salum, & coelum, *1662*: salum coeli *1620 1623*

Lucidum cujus speculum est, reflectens
Aureum vultus jubar et verendum,
Virginis proles sata coelo, et alti in-
terpres Olympi:
Qui Patris mentemque animumque sancti
Filius pandit face noctilucâ,
Sive doctrinae documenta, seu com-
pendia vitae,
Publicae, privae, sacra scita Regni
Regis ad nutum referens, domusque
Ad voluntatem Domini instituta
Singula librans,
Luce quam Phoebus melior refundit,
Lege quam legum tulit ipse lator,
Cujus exacti officij suprema est
Norma voluntas.
Caeca mens humana, hominum voluntas
Prava, et affectus rabidi: indigetque
Luce mens, normâ officij voluntas,
Lege libido.
Quisquis hanc surdâ negat aure, et orbâ
Mente dat ferri rapidis procellis,
Ter quater caudex, stolidusque et omni ex
Parte misellus.
Quisquis hanc pronâ bibit aure, quâ se
Fundit ubertim liquidas sub auras,
Ille ter prudens, sapiensque et omni ex
Parte beatus.
Ergo vos Cami proceres, Tamique,
Quos viâ flexit malesuadus error,
Denuo rectum, duce Rege Regum, in-
sistite callem.
Vos metus tangit si hominum nec ullus,
At Deum fandi memorem et nefandi
Vindicem sperate, et amoena solis
Tartara Diris:
Quae manent sontes animas, trucesque
Praesulum fastus; male quos perurit
Pervigil zelus vigilum, et gregis cus-
todia pernox,

169 Quisquis hanc surdâ negat aure, quà se *followed by ll.* 174–6 *as given above 1662*: *evidently the copyist or printer was misled by* aure *occurring in l.* 173 170–3 *om. 1662, Pickering, Willmott* 173 pronâ] prava *Grosart*

Veste bis tinctâ Tyrio superbos
Murice, et pastos dape pinguiore
Regiâ quondam aut Saliari inunctâ ab-
domine coenâ.
Qualis Vrsini Damasique fastus* *Ammianus Marcell. (lib. 27
Turgidus, luxuque ferox, feroque
Ambitu pugnax, sacram et aedem et urbem
Caede nefandâ
Civium incestavit, et ominosum
Traxit exemplum veniens in aevum
Praesulum quod nobilium indecorus
Provocat ordo.
Quid fames auri sacra? quid cupido
Ambitus diri fera non propagat
Posteris culpae? mala damna quanta
Plurima fundit?

193 *Marginal reference 1620* 202 Ambitus diri] Ambitu diro *1662*

INDEX OF FIRST LINES

An asterisk is placed against poems doubtfully ascribed to Herbert